**Footprint** Handbook

# Patagonia

BEN BOX & CHRIS WALLACE

# This is
## Patagonia

Squeezed between two oceans and split by the tail of the Andes, Patagonia is a land of vast horizons and limitless possibilities. The region has earned an almost mythic status as a travel destination, and for good reason. Its windswept landscapes are cinematic in their beauty, and its immensity and sprawling emptiness are at once liberating and lonely. No wonder it has attracted pioneers and runaways from the modern world. From Welsh settlers to Butch and Sundance; from Bruce Chatwin to Ernesto 'Che' Guevara riding the Ruta 40, Patagonia invites adventure.

East of the Andes, Patagonia makes up the whole southernmost cone of the Americas: a vast expanse of treeless steppe, dotted with the occasional sheep estancia. But at its edges are extraordinary extremes: whales bask and thousands of sea lions cavort at Península Valdés, and descendants of the Welsh still hold Eisteddfods (Welsh Festival of Arts) at Gaiman. Thousands of handprints are testimony to Stone Age life at Cueva de las Manos, and there are two petrified forests of mighty fallen monkey puzzle trees.

Head south on the ultimate road trip, along the Ruta 40, and you'll travel hundreds of kilometres without seeing a soul, until the magnificent granite towers of Mount Fitz Roy rise up from the flat plains: this trekking mecca is far less crowded than Torres del Paine. El Calafate is the base for boat trips to the Perito Moreno Glacier: put on your crampons to walk its sculpted turquoise curves. Once you've seen Upsala Glacier stretching out into a milky Prussian-blue lake, silent and pristine, you'll be addicted. Allow plenty of time, bring walking boots and don't forget your camera.

Seals and migrating whales animate the deserted beaches of the Atlantic, while on the Pacific coast, the land splinters into a labyrinth of islets, fjords and looming icebergs. The oceans meet at the tip of Patagonia where the 'Land of Fire' is a final frontier at the end of the world.

*Chris Wallace*

# Best of
## Patagonia

### ❷ Parque Nacional Los Alerces

There are few better vantage points from which to enjoy the Patagonian Andes in all their splendour than Los Alerces. Christened after the superlatively thick tree of the same name, this national park has virgin forest, hanging glaciers and perfect hikes. It's also just a short jaunt from the Patagonian town of Esquel. Page 148.

### ❸ Península Valdés

This promontory jutting into the Atlantic Ocean enjoys some of the best wildlife spotting on the coast of Patagonia. A conservation site for marine mammals, the peninsula is a natural habitat for several threatened species, including the southern right whale. A few of the highlights include ravenous orcas, penguin colonies, elephant seals and glorious beaches. Page 167.

### ❶ Lake District around Bariloche

The pristine lakes and beautiful peaks of this region are favoured with great tourist infrastructure. Many of the lakes and their surroundings are protected by national parks and there are countless opportunities for hiking, riding, boat trips and fishing, while in winter there is skiing on the slopes. Page 108.

## ❹ Cueva de las Manos

In a beautiful volcanic canyon, a series of rock galleries contain an exceptional collection of cave art, executed between 9500 and 13,000 years ago: stencils of human hands and animals in red, orange, black, white and green. It was declared a World Heritage Site in 1999. Page 197.

## ❺ Glaciar Perito Moreno

Tourists from around the globe are overawed by the immensity of this glacier. An expanse of white stretches apparently without end until a wall of jagged blue ice, millions of years old, rumbles and fractures, crashing into the turquoise waters below. Perito Moreno is the world's only advancing and retreating glacier. Page 215.

## ❻ Pucón

Gateway to the Chilean Lake District, Pucón has volcanoes, fishing and whitewater rafting nearby. Marvel at the sapphire waters of the legendary Ojos de Caburga, or unwind in one of the area's many thermal baths. The more adventurous can climb Volcán Villarrica or simply sit back and wait; you may get lucky and catch an eruption. Page 270.

## ❼ Chiloé

This is a magical island of fishing, forests and mythical creatures. It could even be considered an island nation unto itself. From the unspoilt forests to the vast Pacific beaches and the little towns on quiet bays, Chiloé is at once fundamentally Chilean and yet wholly different. Page 334.

## ❽ Carretera Austral

Cycle, hike or hitch your way through spectacular scenery between Puerto Montt and Villa O'Higgins. Some of the last untamed wild in the world can be found along this highway's 1240 km. Waterfalls cut through mammoth forested Andean peaks feeding rivers that shine every imaginable shade of blue and green. Page 358.

## ❾ Parque Pumalín

Native temperate rainforests are preserved here for posterity, along with ancient glaciers and mist-enshrouded fjords that seem lost in time. The late billionaire conservationist, Douglas Tompkins, created this park in 1991, not without some initial controversy, but it has outgrown its private status to become a Chilean nature sanctuary. Page 365.

6

## ⑩ Futaleufú

Here is the best whitewater in the southern hemisphere on a deep blue river with everything from easy Grade II-III sections to the extremely challenging Hell Canyon. Although the town is only at 350 m, the spectacular mountain scenery makes you feel as if you are high up in the Andes. Page 370.

## ⑪ Torres del Paine

Quite simply one of the world's greatest national parks. When trekkers dream, they dream of Torres del Paine. Those with iron wills can put themselves to the ultimate test and attempt the full circuit, a seven- to eight-day trek that showcases all the splendour the park has to offer. Page 427.

## ⑫ Tierra del Fuego

The island at South America's southernmost tip is divided between Argentina and Chile and to get to either side you have to go through Chile. Here you will find the last vestiges of pioneer life, boat trips along the Beagle Channel, demanding treks, winter snows for skiing and spectacular views at the end of the world. Page 436.

9

# Route
## planner

Patagonia is vast and it's no surprise that getting around takes some organization. The region offers incredibly diverse geography: snow, mountains, lakes and an endless coastline, but possibly its most impressive characteristic is the sense of limitless space and freedom. It takes time to drink in the sheer size of it, the immense skies and the silence, so whatever you do, allow more time than you think you'll need and accept from the start that you can't see it all.

Patagonia is the whole southern cone of South America, combining all parts of Argentina and Chile, south of the Río Colorado. The following provinces are generally considered part of Patagonia: Neuquén, Río Negro, Chubut and Santa Cruz in Argentina; Aysén, Magallanes and the southern part of Los Lagos in Chile. Our coverage includes the Lake Districts in both countries, the Argentine Atlantic coast south of Viedma, the Chilean southwest coast, the far south and the islands of Chiloé and Tierra del Fuego.

## One week in Argentina

*from Alpine style to the ends of the Earth*

The Argentine Lake District is the most easily accessible region for a short visit. Base yourself in picturesque Bariloche with its chalet-style hotels, chocolate shops and a backdrop of peaks. You could hike here for days without getting bored, but to catch a flavour of a different part of the lakes, either go south to the trekking capital, El Bolsón and Parque Nacional Los Alerces, or north to San Martín de los Andes and Pehuenia. Alternatively, fly direct from Buenos Aires to El Calafate for access to Parque Nacional Los Glaciares. Cross an iceberg-strewn lake for breathtaking views of the Southern Ice Field and attempt an ice trek on the Perito Moreno glacier. From here you could either take a bus to the small town of El Chaltén (three hours)

Right: San Carlos de Bariloche
Opposite page:
La Trochita, the Old Patagonian Express

11

to hike around Cerro Fitz Roy and to breathe in the mountain air, or fly on to Ushuaia for the Parque Nacional Tierra del Fuego and the famous Estancia Harberton. Allow time for long bus journeys between each place.

## One week in Chile

*forests, fjords, volcanoes and adventure*

Chilean Patagonia does not have the limitless *pampa* of its Transandean neighbour. The Pacific side of the Andes is dominated by green forests rising up from fjords, rivers and lakes, and overlooked by snow-capped peaks. Take an overnight bus or a direct flight in summer from Santiago to the adventure tourism hub of Pucón to explore the forests and hills around Lago Villarrica and to climb the famous volcano nearby. Do a day trek in the araucaria forests of Huerquehue or Cañi, go whitewater rafting and relax in natural thermal springs, before flying from Puerto Montt to Puerto Natales and spending three or four days in Torres del Paine, one of the world's great national parks. You can go trekking here with a backdrop of dark granite peaks and eerie blue glaciers, either camping or staying at the huts along the way.

## Two weeks: the best of both

*wildlife watching and border-hopping by boat and mountain pass*

In two weeks you could just about fit in both of the above itineraries. Alternatively, use the time to see the extraordinary wildlife at Península Valdés on the Atlantic Coast, including whales in spring. Visit the nearby Welsh village of Gaiman and enjoy an afternoon tea. Then fly from Trelew to either Bariloche for the lakes or El Calafate for the glaciers.

Two weeks in summer is perfect for exploring the Lake District at length, with time for a longer trek, or for visiting two or three different areas. Consider hiring a *cabaña* and hanging out in Butch and Sundance country, or staying at an estancia to try your hand at horse riding. Or you could cross the border by bus and ferry via Lago Todos Los Santos to explore the area around Lago Llanquihue, where the Osorno volcano provides a spectacular backdrop to the lake. The impressive Petrohué waterfalls are an hour to the east. Activities include horse riding, trekking and sea kayaking. Another possibility is to head over the Andes via Los Alerces to Futaleufú for a spot of fly-fishing or whitewater rafting and on to the main spine of the Carretera Austral. Parque Pumalín is an incredible conservation project with a diverse ecosystem and excellent trails to explore.

Below: National Gaucho Day
Opposite page top: Tierra del Fuego
Opposite page middle: Ushuaia
Opposite page bottom: Beagle Channel

If you fly in to Santiago, you could catch a plane south to Puerto Montt or even all the way down to Punta Arenas, in order to hike at Torres del Paine or for access to Tierra del Fuego. For a complete contrast, city lovers should spend 24 hours in Buenos Aires at the end of their trip to enjoy the urban bustle after the wide open spaces.

## A month of adventure

remote roads, secluded lakes and mythical islands

A month allows you to get a real feel for Patagonia's scale and extraordinary contrasts. You could get off the not-very-beaten track to some remote estancias in Santa Cruz, drive along the isolated Ruta 40 from Los Antiguos to El Calafate or cycle a stretch of the wild Carretera Austral past hanging glaciers, a thousand waterfalls, enchanted forests and fairy-tale mountains.

From Puerto Montt, head north into the lakes, visit the magical island of Chiloé or take the long ferry south to Puerto Natales. Combine short trips to Península Valdés, the glaciers, Ushuaia and Torres del Paine, ending up in the Argentine and Chilean Lake Districts to relax, before a short stay in Buenos Aires to finish off the trip.

# Best
## treks

### Volcán Villarrica

If you have ever wanted to climb an active volcano, the Volcán Villarrica hike is probably the most popular trek in Chile and for good reason. This snow-covered perfect cone of a mountain is a stiff half-day trek with ice axe and crampons to the fore. No previous experience is required but you do need to be reasonably fit. On still days you can peer from the summit into the crater and see molten lava bubbling away, while in the distance half a dozen other volcanoes loom up from lakes and forests. The best part is still to come. Forget walking back down – lie back and slide, toboggan style. Pages 84 and 88.

### El Chaltén

Cornered between jagged peaks, and snow-laden valleys, El Chaltén (known as the capital of trekking) is the perfect base for one- and two-day treks in the area. Follow the signs from the edge of town and in less than 30 minutes you'll be completely alone on a mountain pass overlooking deep blue lakes and fertile valleys. Return to your hostel and relax in one of the lively restaurants in town. The treks range from easy to challenging. Page 217.

### Volcán Lanín

One of the world's most beautiful mountains, Lanín (3776 m) is geologically one of the youngest volcanoes (though now extinct) of the Andes. To reach the summit is a challenging three-day climb, with two *refugios* at 2400 m. The

Right: Hiking around El Chaltén
Above: Volcán Villarrica
Opposite page
Top left: Volcán Lanín
Top right: Dientes de Navarino
Bottom left: Torres del Paine

views are spectacular but the climb will keep you out of breath. Because of its relative accessibility, the risks are often underestimated: crampons and ice axe are essential. Page 280.

## The W

Trek for days through some of the most spectacular scenery in Patagonia among iceberg-filled lakes, valleys, waterfalls, glaciers, all the time dominated by the imposing giant granite plugs of the Paine Massif. Experience four seasons in a few hours and have a warm bed and a cooked meal at the end of an arduous day's trekking. If you want to get away from the crowds for a real Patagonian wilderness experience pack up your tent and head off around the north side of the mountains on the week-long circuit trek. Page 431.

## Dientes de Navarino

Named after the teeth-like chain of mountains around which the trail leads, this three- to five-day fully self-contained route is only for hardy, dedicated trekkers. The southernmost trekking route on Earth passes through the Patagonian wilds where trees grow at a 45° angle, sculpted by the shattering westerly winds and where the paths often have a gradient to match. The route will take you past semi-frozen lakes and fast-flowing rivers replete with beaver dams. Views from the passes will leave you speechless with their beauty: the thick forests below and the Beagle Channel to the north with the outline of Tierra del Fuego in the distance, while a solitary condor circles overhead. This really is trekking at the end of the world. Page 445.

Torres del Paine, Chile

# When
## to go

… and when not to

## Climate

The southern hemisphere summer lasts from December to March. The weather can be positively warm in the Lake District and along the Carretera Austral but the far south suffers from very strong winds at this time. January and February are when Argentine and Chilean schools have their holidays, so the main tourist centres (Bariloche, San Martín, El Calafate, Pucón, Puerto Varas, Puerto Natales and Ushuaia) can get impossibly busy and prices rise significantly. You should book flights, buses and accommodation as far ahead as possible. However, you'll still find plenty of less popular centres offering a good range of accommodation, close to the national parks. December and March are good months for trekking but be aware that transport services may not be running as frequently in rural areas and that the weather will be more unpredictable.

April is a spectacular time to visit both the Lake District and further south, as the leaves turn golden and scarlet and days can be clear and windless. Rainfall tends to be higher in these months, but the tourist areas are quieter. Easter week is a major holiday in Argentina, however, so book well ahead.

Much of southern Patagonia closes down entirely for winter; accommodation is often shut from May to October, transport services run a reduced schedule and many passes across the Andes are closed by snowfall. However, if you like skiing, then this is the season to visit. The best months are July and August,

## Weather Temuco (northern Patagonia)

| January | February | March | April | May | June |
|---------|----------|-------|-------|-----|------|
| 22°C | 22°C | 20°C | 17°C | 13°C | 11°C |
| 10°C | 10°C | 8°C | 6°C | 6°C | 5°C |
| 40mm | 40mm | 40mm | 70mm | 170mm | 180mm |

| July | August | September | October | November | December |
|------|--------|-----------|---------|----------|----------|
| 11°C | 12°C | 14°C | 16°C | 18°C | 21°C |
| 4°C | 4°C | 5°C | 6°C | 7°C | 9°C |
| 180mm | 130mm | 90mm | 80mm | 50mm | 50mm |

although many resorts have snow from late June and until September. Ski resort accommodation and transport are generally well organized but bear in mind that July is a school holiday.

The rich marine life on the Atlantic Coast is most exciting in the spring, with whale spotting possible from Península Valdés at its best in September and October. Elsewhere, there are fewer tourists and cheaper accommodation than during the summer but still enough daylight hours for trekking. Winds in the far south are less fierce at this time of year.

## Festivals

The main holiday period is January and February when school children are on holiday and many families go away for a few weeks. All popular tourist destinations become extremely busy at this time, with foreign visitors adding to the crowds, particularly in Bariloche, El Calafate and Ushuaia. You should book transport and accommodation ahead. During Easter week and the winter school holidays throughout July hotels may also fill up fast, particularly in the ski resorts. No one works on the national holidays, and these are often long weekends, with a resulting surge of people to popular holiday places. See also Public holidays, page 493.

**January Fiesta Nacional de la Cereza** (Argentina). Los Antiguos comes alive as people from all over the country flock here to enjoy the local produce.

**20 January Fiesta de la Piedra Santa** (Chile). Mapuche festival of the Holy Stone in the Lake District.

**10 June Malvinas Day** (Argentina). When Argentina affirms its sovereignty over the Islas Malvinas/Falkland Islands.

**29 June Fiesta de San Pedro** (Chile). Processions, dancing and lots of fish eating in all coastal towns and villages in celebration of the patron saint of fishermen.

| **Weather** Punta Arenas (southern Patagonia) | | | | | |
| --- | --- | --- | --- | --- | --- |
| January | February | March | April | May | June |
| 13°C | 13°C | 12°C | 9°C | 6°C | 3°C |
| 7°C | 7°C | 5°C | 3°C | 1°C | -1°C |
| 30mm | 20mm | 40mm | 40mm | 40mm | 30mm |
| July | August | September | October | November | December |
| 3°C | 5°C | 7°C | 10°C | 11°C | 13°C |
| -1°C | 0°C | 1°C | 3°C | 4°C | 6°C |
| 30mm | 30mm | 20mm | 20mm | 20mm | 30mm |

# What to do

Patagonia might have been designed for adventure tourism. The spectacular geography offers a huge range of outdoor activities, from rafting and skiing to some of the finest trekking and fishing in the world. The infrastructure for 'soft' adventure tourism, such as half-day rafting on a Grade III river or a day spent climbing a volcano, is particularly good in the lake districts of Argentina and Chile. Remote estancias in Argentina are appealing bases for horse riding and wildlife spotting, while further south the terrain promises hardcore self-contained trekking and mountain biking. It is important to check the experience and qualifications of any agency offering trips to remote areas.

The national park authorities in both countries are useful sources of information: **Administración de Parques Nacionales** ① *www.parquesnacionales. gob.ar*; and **CONAF** ① *T2-2663 0000, www.conaf.cl*. Details of companies offering adventure activities are given in the What to do sections throughout this guide.

## Canopy tours

This activity consists of gliding down zip-lines from tree to tree through native forests. Runs are of different lengths and range from easy, child-friendly lines to vertigo-inducing descents from 60 m high. Check your equipment carefully as some operators are more responsible than others. Head for **Pucón**, **Puerto Varas**, **Ensenada**, **Volcán Osorno** and **Cruce Maitén** (on the Carretera Austral).

## Climbing

In Argentina, contact **Club Andino** (www.caba.org.ar) which have offices in all mountain areas selling maps, advising on routes and providing guides. In Chile, permits, expeditions and equipment

hire are available from **Federación de Andinismo de Chile**, Almte Simpson 77, Santiago, T2-2222 0888, www.feach.cl. At the same address is **ENAM (Escuela Nacional de Montaña de Santiago)**, www.enam.cl, which runs rock- and ice-climbing courses and administers the *Carnet de La Federación de Chile*, which is often required to climb mountains where **CONAF** controls access. To climb many mountains in border areas, permission must be obtained from the **Dirección Nacional de Fronteras y Límites del Estado**, 7th floor, Teatinos 180, Santiago, T2-2827 5900, www. difrol.cl. Apply well in advance.

The Andes offer great climbing opportunities. Popular climbs include

Volcán Lanín and Cerro Tronador in the Argentine Lake District, as well as Cerro Fitz Roy and the northern part of Parque Nacional Los Glaciares around El Chaltén, where you can also go ice trekking. One of Argentina's most popular ski resorts, Cerro Catedral, is an excellent base for climbing in summer. In Chile, the sheer walls of the Torres del Paine attract climbers year round. In the northern Chilean Lake District near Pucón is Volcán Villarrica, while in the southern section is Volcán Osorno and Cerro Picada. For the inexperienced, Vía Ferrata, near Pucón, is an easy introduction to climbing a sheer rock face with the aid of metal hand-holds embedded in the mountainside.

## Cycling and mountain biking

Mountain biking is extremely popular in both Argentine and Chilean Patagonia, particularly on descents from peaks around Bariloche. Not only is the area surrounding Bariloche spectacular but the Parque Nacional Los Alerces offers lush, picturesque trails. Longer routes include the Siete Lagos in the Lake District and south along the iconic Carretera Austral, through the Parque Nacional Los Glaciares and on to Tierra del Fuego. Other notable areas include Parque Nacional Villarrica and Puerto Varas. Most towns will have a bicycle repair shop but don't count on these for more than basic repairs. Take a tool kit and as many spare parts as you can carry.

## Fishing

Contact the Fly Fishing Association of Argentina, T011-4773 0821, www.aapm. org.ar, for fishing licences; in Patagonia, there's assistance from the National Parks Administration, T011-4311 8853/ 0303. In Chile, contact Servicio Nacional de Pesca y Acuicultura, Victoria 2832, Valparaíso, T32-281 9100, http://pescarecreativa.sernapesca.cl.

Patagonia has arguably the finest fly-fishing (*pesca con mosca*) in the world, set in unbelievably beautiful surroundings. In the Argentine Lake District watch out for world-class trout (rainbow, brown and brook) from November to April, particularly in Junín de los Andes, called the trout capital of Argentina and with some of the country's best fly-fishing. In Chile, Pucón, in the northern Lake District, is also good. Fishing near the Carretera Austral is excellent; including Futaleufú, Coyhaique with the best fishing in Chile and, further south, Río Baker. Look for huge brown trout on both sides of Tierra del Fuego, such as Río Grande in Argentina and Lago Blanco in Chile. Along the Atlantic coast try your hand at shark fishing (bacota and bull shark). All rivers in Argentina are 'catch and release' and to fish anywhere in Argentina you need a permit. In Chile, a licence is needed and is usually available at the local Municipalidad or some tourist offices.

## Horse riding

This is a great way to get to the heart of Patagonia's rural tradition and to see some varied and spectacular scenery. Many estancias throughout Argentina offer opportunities for riding. In Chile the scenery is more rugged, such as in Torres del Paine, and options range from gallops across the windswept plains of the south to breathtaking thick-forested valleys or high up in the Andes around **Cochamó**. Day rides are offered in all the major tourist centres but a multi-day trip is one of the best ways of getting off the beaten track. **Pucón** and **Puerto Varas** in the Lake District, around the Carretera Austral, **Puerto Natales** in the far south, and the west coast of **Chiloé** are some of the main riding areas in Chile.

## Skiing

The season runs from mid-June to mid-October, but dates vary between resorts. Argentine Lake District resorts such as **Cerro Catedral** near Bariloche and **Cerro Bayo** (Villa la Angostura), **La Hoya** (Esquel) and **Cerro Chapelco** (San Martín de los Andes) are very well run. Facilities in the far south of Chile are basic. However, skiing on an active volcano looking down on three huge lakes (Villarrica/Pucón) or skiing within sight of the sea at the end of the world (**Cerro Castor** near Ushuaia) or just with a sea view (**Cerro Mirador** near Punta Arenas) are memories that will truly last a lifetime. Other resorts include **Antillanca** and **Volcán Osorno** in the Chilean Lake District and **El Fraile** (Coyhaique) on the Carretera Austral.

## Trekking

Contact the national park authorities and specialist tour operators.

The whole of the Andes region offers superb opportunities for both short and long treks in varied landscapes. The best season for walking is December-April. National parks in both the Argentine and Chilean lake districts offer spectacular hikes on well-marked routes with maps,

guides and plenty of information, such as the **Parque Nacional Lanín** and **Parque Nacional Nahuel Huapi** in Argentina and the **Parque Nacional Huerquehue** (Pucón) and **Reserva Forestal Cañi** in Chile. It's also worth exploring the lesser known lake regions, such as **Pehuenia** in the north, **Parque Nacional Los Alerces** and the **Seven Lakes** in Argentina. The most dramatic trekking is around Cerro Fitz Roy near El Chaltén in the **Parque Nacional Los Glaciares** where you can walk on the Southern Ice Cap and climb glaciers, as well as in **Parque Nacional Torres del Paine** and **Parque Nacional Tierra del Fuego**.

In Chile, over 1000 km of hiking opportunities have been opened up by the building of the Carretera Austral, including the **Parque Pumalín** and its millennial alerce forests and the four- and five-day circuits around the fairytale castle of **Cerro Castillo**, though heavy rainfall can be a drawback here outside summer. The **Sendero de Chile** (www.senderodechile.cl) is a series of walking routes dotted all the way from the Peruvian border to Tierra del Fuego, a long-term project with new stretches opening regularly. Further south still is Isla Navarino with the **Dientes de Navarino** and the southernmost trekking route on Earth.

You should be reasonably fit before attempting any hikes in Patagonia, especially overnight treks in the far south. Remember that conditions can be harsh at these latitudes and never overestimate your own abilities. Take account of the season, weather and terrain and make sure you are properly equipped. If trekking

## National parks and natural phenomena

The snow-capped mountains, sheer cliffs and deep valleys of Patagonia are home to stunning national parks and incredible natural wonders. There is an extensive network of reserves and protected areas, the most important of which are designated national parks (additional areas are designated as natural monuments and natural reserves). From glaciers and waterfalls to fjords and ancient land marks, Patagonia is a great place to enjoy nature in all its fabulous forms.

National parks in Argentina are managed by **Administración de Parques Nacionales** ① *Santa Fe 690, opposite Plaza San Martín, Buenos Aires, T011-4311 0303, www.parques nacionales.gob.ar, Mon-Fri 1000-1700*. Most parks have *guardaparque* (ranger) stations at the main entrance where you can get advice and basic maps. *Guardaparques* are usually knowledgeable about wildlife and walks. Parks in the Lake District are particularly well set up for trekking, with signed trails, *refugios* and campsites.

All reserves and national parks in Chile are managed by **CONAF (Corporación Nacional Forestal)** ① *Paseo Bulnes 285, Santiago, T2-2663 0000, www.conaf.cl*. CONAF's staff are dedicated and knowledgeable, though those in the parks themselves are usually much more helpful than the regional head offices. CONAF publishes a number of leaflets and has documents and maps, but these are not very useful for walking. Most parks have public access and camping areas are usually clearly designated; wild camping is discouraged and frequently banned. **CODEFF (Comité Nacional Pro-Defensa de la Fauna y Flora)** ① *Ernesto Reyes 35, Providencia, Santiago, T2-2777 2534, www.codeff.cl*, can also provide information on environmental questions.

### Petrified forests

Some 130 million years ago during the Jurassic period, parts of southern Patagonia were covered in forests of giant araucarias (a version of today's monkey puzzle trees), and the climate was moist and stable. Then, at the beginning of the Cretaceous period, intense volcanic activity resulted in these forests being buried in ash – a natural preservative. The remains of these petrified forests can be seen today in two areas of Argentine Patagonia: **Monumento Natural Bosques Petrificados** (halfway between Caleta Olivia in the north and San Julián in the south, see page 181) and **Bosque Petrificado José Ormachea** (near Sarmiento, see page 179). Lying, strewn along the ground are large tree trunks which look like wood, but are actually stone.

### Southern Patagonian Ice Field

With an area of over 16,800 km (of which 14,200 km belongs to Chile and 2600 km to Argentina) and extending 350 km, the Southern Patagonian Ice Field is the third biggest extension of continental ice after Antarctica and Greenland. The ice field feeds many of Patagonia's glaciers such as Upsala, Viedma, Bruggen, Grey and the famous Perito Moreno, and is home to several volcanoes that lie undisturbed under the ice. Spread over three national parks – **Los Glaciares** (see page 205), **Bernardo O'Higgins** (see page 426) and **Torres del Paine** (see page 427) – this enormous ice field is one of two remnants of the Patagonian Ice Sheet, which was a narrow sheet of ice that covered southern Chile during the last ice age. The other remnant is the much smaller

Northern Patagonian Ice Field found within the borders of **Laguna San Rafael National Park** (see box, page 375).

### 3000-year-old living trees

Just south of Bariloche are the clear blue mountain streams and lush forests of **Parque Nacional Los Alerces** (see page 148). Named after a species of slow-growing trees that are found in the area, the park is a great place to enjoy fly-fishing and trekking and it is easily accessible from nearby Esquel. Deep inside the park is an alerce tree that has been growing in the same place for more than 3000 years, and several others which are slightly younger. Growing only 1 mm per year, the alerce trees in this region attract so much attention that scientists have kept the location of one of the oldest trees a secret from prying eyes. So for now you'll have to be happy with visiting a 2000-year-old alerce tree.

### Volcanoes and hot springs

Patagonia marks the end of the so-called Pacific ring of fire and is home to over two dozen active volcanoes running in a chain along the west of the Andes. The perfect cones of **Villarrica** (in the national park of the same name; see page 277), Osorno (on the edge of **Parque Nacional Pérez Rosales**; see page 319) and Choshuenco have a history of relatively gentle eruption with lava rising and spilling over the crater's edge. In Volcán Villarrica, for example, lava rises and falls cyclically, and when particularly active the crater rim can be seen from afar glowing red in the night. When in a benign state, though, these volcanoes are perfect for hiking up and skiing down.

What's more, the same tectonic forces that gave Chile so many volcanoes and the occasional destructive earthquake are also responsible for the abundance of hot springs, especially Termas de Quimey-co, de Huife and los Pozones, east of **Pucón** (see page 278).

Many people swear by the medicinal properties of the springs due to their temperature and high mineral content and every year Chileans flock from the capital to 'take the waters'. They may or may not be a cure for rheumatism, but what is certain is that there is nothing better after an arduous day's Patagonian trekking than a long soak in a thermal bath.

### Parque Pumalín

The Parque Pumalín (see page 365) is quite simply one of the world's great conservation projects. Stretching from the Gulf of Ancud in the west to the Argentine border in the east, the park began as the private initiative of the late US multi-millionaire Douglas Tompkins who bought up some three-quarters of a million acres of private land covered in temperate rainforest to save it from exploitation by the timber industry. The result is a park run along a strict policy of conservation, with sustainable small organic farms within the park that double as information centres. The park is home to a vibrant ecosystem, with a wide variety of trees and plants, including coigue, lenga, ulmo and ancient alerces, all easily accessible from the main road. The park is also home to the endangered pudu and huemul as well as the Andean puma and a rich variety of birdlife. For hikers there are a dozen well-marked and well-maintained trails and a series of neat campsites. The Parque Pumalín seems to have set an example, as land has been bought privately in both Chiloé and Argentina for similar conservation projects.

with a tour operator or guide, check their credentials, equipment and experience. Avoid hiking alone, even in tourist areas, and always register with *guardaparques* or other authorities before you set out. Hikers have little to fear from the animal kingdom – in fact, you are much more of a threat to the environment than vice versa.

## Watersports

Water-based activities include canoeing, scuba diving, waterskiing, windsurfing, jet-skiing and sailing. The tourist resorts in both lake districts, such as **Bariloche** and **Río Aluminé** in Argentina and **Lago Villarrica** and **Lago Llanquihue** in Chile, offer a wide range of watersports. Sea-kayaking has become a popular activity in the **Golfo de Ancud** between Chiloé and Hornopirén on the Chilean mainland. Several companies offer day tours but for an unforgettable experience go for a week navigating between fjords and islands and visiting isolated hot springs.

## Whitewater rafting

Rafting is generally well organized and equipment is usually of high quality. Access to the headwaters of most rivers is easy. In Chile, beginners might be more comfortable in the calmer waters of the **Río Petrohué** or **Río Baker**, while adrenalin junkies will want to head for **Futaleufú** with long stretches of Grade V rapids including the infamous **Cañón del Infierno** (Hell Canyon). Also check out **Río Aluminé** and **Río Manso** (Bariloche) in the Argentine Lake District and **Río Trancura**

(Pucón) in Chile. Tours are operated by several agencies. Choose with care as some of the cut-price operators also cut corners on safety. Rafts should carry no more than six people plus guide.

## Wildlife watching

The Atlantic Coast provides the best opportunities for getting close to wildlife. Near Puerto Madryn, **Península Valdés** is a UNESCO World Heritage Site, home to sea birds, elephant seals, penguins, sea lions and southern right whales. Further south over half a million Magellanic penguins come to breed and raise their young at the **Reserva Provincial Punta Tumbo**. **Tierra del Fuego** is a birdwatcher's paradise: take a boat trip to **Isla Martillo/Yécapasela** to see the resident colony of Magellanic penguins as well as black-browed albatross, cormorants and petrels. Visit the Tierra del Fuego national park to see forest-dwelling birds as well.

Inland, **Torres del Paine** national park has a plethora of interesting wildlife away from the well-trodden trekking paths: guanacos, the ostrich-like ñandú, chilla and culpeo foxes and the elusive puma. Birdlife includes upland geese, pygmy owls, southern lapwings, flamingos and the majestic Andean condor. Specialized wildlife tours are available. If you're lucky, the shy and beautiful heumul can be found in the **Reserva Nacional Río Claro**, just to the west of Coyhaique, or in the **Reserva Nacional Tamango**, a short distance from Cochrane.

# Where to stay

remote estancias, summer albergues and wild camping

Tourist destinations in Patagonia and, especially in the Lake District, have a good range of **hotels** and *hosterías*, although on the Chilean side, there is good-value budget accommodation and some relatively high-end hotels, but not much choice in between. *Hosterías* have less than 20 rooms; rather than being lower quality than hotels, they are often family-run and can be very good value in more remote areas. *Residenciales* and *hospedajes* tend to provide simpler accommodation, often with full board offered. *Hostales* traditionally offer dorm beds but most also have double rooms for couples and may also offer services geared specifically towards foreign backpackers, such as tours, bicycle hire, etc. In Chile, some places advertised as *hostales* do not have dorms and only offer private rooms. *Cabañas* are well-equipped self-catering cottages, cabins or apartments, often in superb locations. They're a great option if you have your own transport and are travelling in a small group. Throughout the Argentine Lake District, *cabañas* are plentiful and competitively priced.

**Camping** is popular and there are many superbly situated sites with good facilities, although official Chilean campsites can be expensive, with no reductions for single travellers or couples. In Chile, however, more and more hostels allow camping in their garden and offer very good value rates. There are also *refugios* (refuges) for walkers in national parks and reserves; facilities vary hugely. Camping wild is generally safe, even in remote areas, but always consult *guardaparques* (park rangers) before pitching your tent in a national park.

## Price codes

| Where to stay | Restaurants |
|---|---|
| $$$$ over US$150 | $$$ over US$12 |
| $$$ US$66-150 | $$ US$7-12 |
| $$ US$30-65 | $ US$6 and under |
| $ under US$30 | |
| Price of a double room in high season, including taxes. | Price for a two-course meal for one person, excluding drinks or service charge. |

When camping, don't bathe in rivers and lakes, and take water away from its source to wash. Don't go to the toilet near water sources, and take all rubbish away with you. A gas/alcohol stove is essential for camping in some regions as fires can be prohibited in protected areas, such as Cerro Fitz Roy.

## Youth hostels

For hostels, see **Hostelling International Argentina** ⓘ *Florida 835 of 107, T011-4511-8723, www.hostels.org.ar, Mon-Fri 0900-1900.* HI no longer has a major presence in Argentina, but their website does provide a list of hostels, and a few of them still offer a discount to cardholders. *Albergues* spring up in summer all over the south of Chile. These are usually schools earning extra money by renting out floor space. They are very cheap (rarely more than US$7 per person) and are excellent places to meet young Chileans. Do not go to them if you want a good night's sleep, though; guitars often play on into the small hours. There is no need for a HI card to stay in *albergues*, but there is rarely much security either.

HI youth hostels throughout Chile cost about US$10-24 per person. The HI card (US$20) is usually readily accepted; buy it from **Asociación Chilena de Albergues Turísticos Juveniles** ⓘ *Hernando de Aguirre 201, of 401, Providencia, Santiago, T2-2577 1200.* HI hostels in Chile, while generally decent, are not necessarily better than any other hostel. You can often find other better value places.

## Prices

Prices may have risen in recent years, but accommodation in Argentina is still good value. Having said that, some hotels in tourist destinations, including Buenos Aires, Puerto Madryn, Bariloche and El Calafate, charge higher prices for *extranjeros* (non-Argentines) in US dollars, which is unavoidable since a passport is required as proof of residency. If you pay in cash you may get a reduction. Room tax (VAT) is 21% and is not always included in the price, so ask when you check in. Prices often rise in high summer (January to February), at Easter and in July. The ski resorts are more expensive during the winter school holidays.

Accommodation in Chile is just a little more expensive, and prices tend to be higher in Santiago and the further south you go from Puerto Montt. However, single travellers do not come off too badly in southern Chile, as many *hospedajes* charge per person (although you may have to share your room). The Chilean government waives the VAT charge (IVA 19%) for bills paid in dollars at designated high-end hotels, but some establishments may get round this apparent discount by offering you a low dollar exchange rate. Prices often rise in high season (*temporada alta*), especially during January and February, at Easter and around the Independence Day holidays in mid-September, but off-season you can often bargain for a discount (*descuento*) if you are staying for two or more days.

In both countries you should always book ahead during high season and for public holidays and establish clearly in advance what is included in the price before booking. Sometimes hotels offer cheaper deals through their websites. For further information on hotels, see **www.welcomeargentina.com**; for hostels, consult **www.hostels.com**, **www.hihostels.com** and **www.backpackerschile.com**.

## Estancias

Estancias are huge sheep and cattle ranches found all over Argentine Patagonia, and many of them now welcome paying guests. They offer a marvellous way to see remote landscapes and enjoy horse riding and other activities, as well as providing an authentic experience of rural Argentine life. There are two types of estancia: rural hotels and those where you're welcomed as a guest of the family. The latter are particularly recommended as a great way to meet Argentine people.

Some estancias offer a *día de campo* (day on the farm), which will include horse riding, a ride in a horse-drawn carriage, an *asado* lunch, other farm activities, or time for relaxation. While this is a great way to get a taste of estancia life, especially for those on a budget, try to stay at least two nights. Most are well off the beaten track, so you'll need to hire a car, or arrange to be picked up in the nearest town. Estancias can be more expensive than hotels, but they offer a unique experience and, once you add the activities, meals and wine, are often good value.

Estancias vary enormously. In Patagonia there are giant sheep estancias overlooking glaciers, mountains and lakes, such as **Helsingfors** and **Cristina**. There are estancias on Tierra del Fuego that are full of early pioneer history (Harberton), while on the Atlantic coast **Estancia Monte Dinero** has a colony of Magellanic penguins on its doorstep. Also see **www.turismo.gob.ar** (in English; look for *alojamiento rural* under each province), and www.estanciasdesantacruz.com.

# Food
## & drink

Buffet-style 'American breakfasts' are served in international hotels but elsewhere, breakfast (*desayuno*) is a very simple affair. Lunch (*almuerzo*) is eaten any time from 1300 to 1530 and is followed, in Argentina (but not Buenos Aires), by a siesta. At around 1700, many Argentines go to a *confitería* for *merienda* (tea, sandwiches and cakes), while Chileans have a snack meal known as *onces* (literally elevenses). Restaurants open for *cena* (dinner) at about 2000 in Chile but rarely before 2100 in Argentina, where most people don't eat until 2230 or later. Many restaurants in Chile serve a cheaper fixed-price meal at lunch time, called *la colación* or *el menú*. In Argentina this is known as *el menú fijo*. Those on a tight budget should also try *tenedor libre* (free fork) restaurants, where you can eat all you want for a fixed price. Some hotels, particularly in the Lake District, will offer a packed lunch to take on hikes and to see the glaciers; ask the night before.

## Food

Argentina has become known for its fresh and sophisticated cuisine; especially salmon and wild game from Patagonia. In general, the meat is legendary. The classic meal is the *asado* – beef or lamb (in Patagonia) cooked over an open fire. In rural areas, a whole lamb is splayed out on a cross-shaped stick at an angle over the fire. *Parrilla* restaurants, found all over Argentina, grill cuts of meat in much the same way; they can be ordered as individual dishes or as *parrillada* (basically a mixed grill). Other meat or fish to try includes salmon in Patagonia, wild boar in Bariloche and even guanaco. The *trucha* (trout) is very good in the Lake District and is best served grilled. Also sample the local raspberries and strawberries, particularly around El Bolsón. And in Pehuenia, you must try the pine nuts of the monkey puzzle trees: sacred food to the Mapuche people. Italian immigration has left a legacy of pizza, *pasta casera* (home-made pasta) and *ñoquis* (gnocchi) throughout the country.

Perhaps the most outstanding ingredient in Chilean cuisine is the seafood. Some of the best is to be had found in Angelmó (Puerto Montt). The most popular fish are *merluza* (a species of hake, better the further south it is fished), *congrio* (ling), *corvina* (bass – often served marinated in lemon juice as ceviche),

## Chilean shellfish

Look out for *choritos*, *cholgas* and *choros maltón* (all varieties of mussel), *ostiones* (queen scallops), *ostras* (oysters) and *erizos* (sea urchins). Prawns are known as *camarones*, but these are often imported from Ecuador and can be tasteless and expensive. Chile's most characteristic products are the delicious *erizos*, *machas*, *picorocos* and *locos*, which are only found in these seas. *Machas a la parmesana* are a kind of razor clam prepared in their shells with a parmesan cheese sauce, grilled and served as a starter. *Picorocos* (giant barnacles), which are normally boiled or steamed in white wine, are grotesque to look at but have a very intense, smoky yet sweet taste: it may be very disconcerting to be presented with a plate containing a rock with feathery fins but it is well worth taking up the challenge of eating it, although only the white fleshy part is edible. *Locos*, a kind of abalone, are the most popular Chilean mollusc, but because of overexploitation their fishing is frequently banned. The main crustaceans are *jaiba* (purple crab), *langosta* (lobster) and *centolla*, an exquisite king crab from the south.

*reineta* (a type of bream), *lenguado* (sole), *salmón* and *albacora* (sword fish). There is an almost bewildering array of unique shellfish; see box, above. On Chiloé you should try the famous *curanto*, a stew of shellfish, pork, chicken and other ingredients. Beware of eating seafood in the far south when there is an infestation of the poisonous *marea roja* (toxic algae blooms).

### Drink
Both Argentine and Chilean wines are excellent and even the cheapest varieties are very drinkable. In Argentina, the local **beers**, mainly lager-type, are passable: **Quilmes** is the best seller, but microbreweries producing good-quality beer are popping up more and more throughout the country. **Antares** is one such chain, offering tasty brews and good food. The emergence in recent years of several small independent breweries means that Chilean beer is no longer as bland as it used to be. **Austral**, brewed in Patagonia, is a real gem. **Kunstmann** is the best of the nationwide beers. Also recommended are **Los Colonos** (Llanquihue) and **Imperial** (Punta Arenas).

Cider (*chicha de manzana*) is popular in southern Chile. The most famous spirit in Chile is *pisco*, made with grapes and usually drunk with lemon or lime juice as pisco sour, or mixed with Coca Cola or Sprite. The great Argentine drink (also widely drunk in Chilean Patagonia) is *mate* (pronounced mattay), an important social convention. The experience of sharing a *mate* is a great way to make friends and transcends social boundaries (see box, page 30). For coffee, a **cortado** is an espresso coffee with hot frothed milk served in a glass.

## The mate ritual

*Mate* (pronounced mattay) is the essential Argentine drink. All over the country, whenever groups of Argentines get together, they share a *mate*. It's an essential part of your trip to Argentina that you give it a go, at least once. It's a bitter green tea made from the leaves of the *yerba mate* plant, *Ilex paraguaiensis*, and is mildly stimulating, less so than caffeine, and effective at ridding the body of toxins as well as being mildly laxative and diuretic. It was encouraged by the Jesuits as an alternative to alcohol and grown in their plantations in the northeast of Argentina.

The *mate* container is traditionally made from a hollowed gourd, but can be made of wood or tin. There are also ornate varieties made to traditional gaucho patterns by the best silversmiths.

Dried yerba leaves are placed in the *mate* to just over half full and then the whole container is shaken upside down using a hand to prevent spillage. This makes sure that any excess powder is removed from the leaves before drinking. Hot water is added to create the infusion, which is then sipped through the *bombilla*, a perforated metal straw. One person in the group acts as *cebador*, trickling fresh hot water into the *mate*, having the first sip (which is the most bitter) and passing it to each person in turn to sip. The water must be at 80-82°C (just as the kettle starts to 'sing') and generally *mate* is drunk *amargo* (bitter) – without sugar. But add a little if it's your first time, as the drink is slightly bitter. When you've had enough, simply say *gracias* as you hand the *mate* back to the *cebador*, and you'll be missed out on the next round.

If you're invited to drink *mate* on your visit to Argentina, always accept, as it's rude not to, and then keep trying: it might take a few attempts before you actually like the stuff. To share a *mate* is to be part of a very special Argentine custom and you'll delight your hosts by giving it a go.

# Menu reader

## Argentine parrilla and asado

The most important vocabulary is for the various cuts of meat in the *asado*, or barbecue, which you can eat at any *parrilla* or steakhouse.

**achuras** offal
**bife a caballo** steak with a fried egg on top
**bife ancho entrecôte** steak
**bife angosto** sirloin
**bife de chorizo or cuadril** rump steak
**cerdo** pork
**chinchulines** entrails
**chivito** kid
**choripán** hot dog, made with meat sausage
**chorizos** beef sausages
**ciervo** venison
**cocina criolla** typical Argentine food
**cordero** lamb
**costilla** pork chop
**empanadas** small pasties, traditionally meat, but often made with cheese or other fillings
**fiambre** cold meats, hams, salami
**guiso** meat and vegetable stew
**humitas** a puree of sweetcorn, onions and cheese, wrapped in corn cob husks, steamed
**jabalí** wild boar
**locro** stew made with corn, onions, beans, and various cuts of meat, chicken or sausage
**lomito** sandwich of thin slice of steak in a bread roll, *lomito completo* comes with tomato, cheese, ham and egg
**lomo** fillet steak
**matambre** stuffed flank steak with vegetables and hard-boiled eggs
**molleja** sweetbread
**morcilla** blood sausage
**picada** a selection of *fiambre*, cheeses and olives to accompany a drink
**pollo** chicken
**riñón** kidney
**tamales** cornflour balls with meat and onion, wrapped in corn cob husks and steamed
**tira de asado** ribs

## Chilean specialities

**agüita** a herbal infusion
**barros jarpa** sandwich with grilled cheese and ham
**barros luco** sandwich with steak and grilled cheese
**bife or lomo a lo pobre** (a poor man's steak) steak topped by two fried eggs, chips and onions
**cazuela de mariscos** seafood stew
**chacarero** sandwich containing thinly sliced steak and salad
**chorillana** chips covered with sliced steak, fried onions and scrambled eggs
**churrasco** a minute steak in a bun; can be ordered with any variety of fillings
**cochayuyo** dried seaweed
**completo** hotdog with plenty of extras. *Completo italiano* has avocado, but no sauerkraut
**empanada** pastry turnovers made *de pino* (with meat, onions, egg and an olive), *queso* (cheese) or *mariscos* (shellfish)
**hallulla** a crisp, slim bread roll
**humitas** mashed sweetcorn mixed with butter and spices and baked in sweetcorn leaves
**marraquetas** a pair of fluffy bread rolls
**mote con huesillo** made from wheat hominy and dried peaches, a very refreshing summer drink
**paila** literally a serving dish, usually a light stew or soup, eg *paila marina*, but also made with eggs
**pastel de choclo** casserole of chicken, minced beef and onions with olives, topped with polenta, baked in an earthenware bowl
**pastel de papas** meat pie covered with mashed potatoes
**porotos** beans
**prieta** blood sausage stuffed with cabbage leaves
**schop** draught lager

# Improve your travel photography

Taking pictures is a highlight for many travellers, yet too often the results turn out to be disappointing. Steve Davey, author of Footprint's *Travel Photography*, sets out his top rules for coming home with pictures you can be proud of.

## Before you go

Don't waste precious travelling time and do your research before you leave. Find out what festivals or events might be happening or which day the weekly market takes place, and search online image sites such as Flickr to see whether places are best shot at the beginning or end of the day, and what vantage points you should consider.

## Get up early

The quality of the light will be better in the few hours after sunrise and again before sunset – especially in the tropics when the sun will be harsh and unforgiving in the middle of the day. Sometimes seeing the sunrise is a part of the whole travel experience: sleep in and you will miss more than just photographs.

## Stop and think

Don't just click away without any thought. Pause for a few seconds before raising the camera and ask yourself what you are trying to show with your photograph. Think about what things you need to include in the frame to convey this meaning. Be prepared to move around your subject to get the best angle. Knowing the point of your picture is the first step to making sure that the person looking at the picture will know it too.

## Compose your picture

Avoid simply dumping your subject in the centre of the frame every time you take a picture. If you compose with it to one side, then your picture can look more balanced. This will also allow you to show a significant background and make the picture more meaningful. A good rule of thumb is to place your subject or any significant detail a third of the way into the frame; facing into the frame not out of it.

This rule also works for landscapes. Compose with the horizon two-thirds of the way up the frame if the foreground is the most interesting part of the picture; one-third of the way up if the sky is more striking.

Don't get hung up with this so-called Rule of Thirds, though. Exaggerate it by pushing your subject out to the edge of the frame if it makes a more interesting picture; or if the sky is dull in a landscape, try cropping with the horizon near the very top of the frame.

## Fill the frame

If you are going to focus on a detail or even a person's face in a close-up portrait, then be bold and make sure that you fill the frame. This is often a case of physically getting in close. You can use a telephoto setting on a zoom lens but this can lead to pictures looking quite flat; moving in close is a lot more fun!

## Interact with people

If you want to shoot evocative portraits then it is vital to approach people and seek permission in some way, even if it is just by smiling at someone. Spend a little time with them and they are likely to relax and look less stiff and formal. Action portraits where people are doing something, or environmental portraits, where they are set against a significant background, are a good way to achieve relaxed portraits. Interacting is a good way to find out more about people and their lives, creating memories as well as photographs.

## Focus carefully

Your camera can focus quicker than you, but it doesn't know which part of the picture you want to be in focus. If your camera is using the centre focus sensor then move the camera so it is over the subject and half press the button, then, holding it down, recompose the picture. This will lock the focus. Take the now correctly focused picture when you are ready.

Another technique for accurate focusing is to move the active sensor over your subject. Some cameras with touch-sensitive screens allow you to do this by simply clicking on the subject.

## Leave light in the sky

Most good night photography is actually taken at dusk when there is some light and colour left in the sky; any lit portions of the picture will balance with the sky and any ambient lighting. There is only a very small window when this will happen, so get into position early, be prepared and keep shooting and reviewing the results. You can take pictures after this time, but avoid shots of tall towers in an inky black sky; crop in close on lit areas to fill the frame.

## Bring it home safely

Digital images are inherently ephemeral: they can be deleted or corrupted in a heartbeat. The good news though is they can be copied just as easily. Wherever you travel, you should have a backup strategy. Cloud backups are popular, but make sure that you will have access to fast enough Wi-Fi. If you use RAW format, then you will need some sort of physical back-up. If you don't travel with a laptop or tablet, then you can buy a backup drive that will copy directly from memory cards.

*Recently updated and available in both digital and print formats, Footprint's Travel Photography by Steve Davey covers everything you need to know about travelling with a camera, including simple post-processing. More information is available at www.footprinttravelguides.com*

# Buenos Aires

birthplace of the tango, people of the port

Often viewed by visitors as 'Paris of the south' due to its baroque architecture and fashion-conscious inhabitants, Buenos Aires exists in two worlds.

Those looking for a prototypical metropolitan experience will find it in the expansive boulevards, neat plazas, leafy parks and ornate theatres. It can be touched and tasted in the city's chic shops, convivial restaurants and breezy cafés. However, it's in the enormous steaks, passionate tango and 24/7 *boliches* where you'll discover the distinctly Argentine voice of the city, one which echoes throughout the entire country.

Buenos Aires has been virtually rebuilt since the beginning of the 20th century and its oldest buildings mostly date from the early 1900s, with some elegant examples from the 1920s and 1930s. The centre has maintained the original layout since its foundation and so the streets are often narrow and mostly one way.

Its original name, 'Santa María del Buen Ayre' referred to the favourable winds which brought sailors across the ocean.

**Best** for
Culture ▪ Nightlife ▪ Shopping

# Footprint
## picks

### ★ Café Tortoni, page 39
Stop in at the city's oldest café and enjoy a coffee amid opulent surroundings, a throwback to another era.

### ★ Cementerio Recoleta, page 43
See Evita's final resting place among the rows of ornate tombs in this famous cemetery.

### ★ Palermo Viejo, page 45
Shop and dine in the trendiest enclave in the city.

### ★ San Telmo, page 46
Cobbled streets, corner cafés and outdoor markets make this neighbourhood a must-see.

Footprint
picks

1 Café Tortoni, page 39
2 Cementerio Recoleta, page 43
3 Palermo Viejo, page 45
4 San Telmo, page 46

To Route 9, Route 8, Tigre & San Antonio De Areco

VICENTE LOPEZ

GENERAL SAN MARTIN

SAAVEDRA

BELGRANO

Río de la Plata

Aeroparque

Parque 3 de Febrero

CHACARITA

PALERMO

RECOLETA

Retiro Bus Terminal

Plaza San Martín

PATERNAL

VILLA DEL PARQUE

CABALLITO

9 De Julio

Plaza de Mayo

SAN TELMO

Reserva Ecológica Costanera Sur

Puerto Madero

To Route 5 to Luján

Autopista 25 De Mayo

FLORES

LINIERS

MATADEROS

BARRACAS

LA BOCA

General Paz

Río Riachuelo

AVELLANEDA

LANUS

LOMAS DE ZAMORA

To Route 2

To Ezeiza Airport

To Route 2, La Plata & Mar del Plata

N

1 km
1 miles

Buenos Aires maps

1  Buenos Aires orientation, page 36
2  Buenos Aires centre, page 40
3  Recoleta & Palermo, page 44
4  San Telmo, page 47

General Paz

Libertador

Córdoba

Santa Fe

Callao

36 • Buenos Aires

## Around Plaza de Mayo

The heart of the city is the **Plaza de Mayo**. On the east side is the **Casa de Gobierno**. Called the Casa Rosada because it is pink, it contains the presidential offices. It is notable for its statuary and the rich furnishing of its halls. The **Museo Casa Rosada** ⓘ *Paseo Colón 100, T011-4344 3802, www.casarosada.gob.ar, Wed-Sun and holidays 1000-1800, free*, in the Fuerte de Buenos Aires and Aduana Taylor, covers the period 1810-2010 with historical exhibits and art exhibitions, permanent and temporary. The **Antiguo Congreso Nacional** (Old Congress Hall, 1864-1905) ⓘ *Balcarce 139, guided tours every Mon, Tue, Thu and Fri at 1230 and 1700, closed Jan, free*, on the south of the Plaza, is a national monument. The **Cathedral** ⓘ *San Martín 27, T011-4331 2845, www.catedralbuenosaires.org.ar, Mon-Fri 0800-1900, Sat-Sun 0900-1930; guided visits to San Martín's Mausoleum and Crypt, religious artefacts, and Temple and Crypt; Mass is held daily, check times*, on the north of Plaza, stands on the site of the first **church** in Buenos Aires. The current structure dates from 1753-1822 (its portico built in 1827), but the 18th-century towers were never rebuilt.

The imposing **tomb** (1880)ⓘ *Mon-Fri 0900-1900*, of the Liberator, General José de San Martín, is guarded by soldiers in fancy uniforms. A small exhibition to the left of the main nave displays items related to Pope Francis, former archbishop of Buenos Aires. The **Museo del Cabildo y la Revolución de Mayo** ⓘ *Bolívar 65, T011-4334 1782, www.cabildonacional.cultura.gob.ar, Tue, Wed, Fri 1030-1700, Thu 1030-2000, Sat-Sun and holidays 1030-1800, guided visits in English Oct-Mar, free*, is in the old Cabildo where the movement for Independence from Spain was first planned. It's worth a visit for the paintings of old Buenos Aires, the documents and maps recording the May 1810 Revolution, and memorabilia of the 1806 British attack; also Jesuit art. There are booklets in English in each of the rooms. In the patio is a café and restaurant and stalls selling handicrafts (Thursday-Friday 1100-1800). Also on the Plaza is the Palacio de Gobierno de la Ciudad (City Hall). Within a few blocks north of the Plaza are the main banks and business houses, such as the **Banco de la Nación**, opposite the Casa Rosada (see above), with an impressively huge main hall and topped by a massive marble dome 50 m in diameter.

On the Plaza de Mayo, the **Mothers of the Plaza de Mayo** ⓘ *H Yrigoyen 1584, T011-4383 0377, www.madres.org, and Piedras 153, T011-4343 1926, www.madresfundadoras.blogspot.com.ar*, march in remembrance of their children who disappeared during the 'dirty war' of the 1970s. The Mothers march anti-clockwise round the central monument every Thursday at 1530, with photos of their disappeared loved ones pinned to their chests.

| **Weather** Buenos Aires | | | | | |
|---|---|---|---|---|---|
| **January** | **February** | **March** | **April** | **May** | **June** |
| 30°C | 29°C | 26°C | 23°C | 19°C | 16°C |
| 20°C | 19°C | 17°C | 14°C | 10°C | 8°C |
| 100mm | 100mm | 100mm | 80mm | 70mm | 50mm |
| **July** | **August** | **September** | **October** | **November** | **December** |
| 15°C | 17°C | 19°C | 23°C | 25°C | 28°C |
| 7°C | 9°C | 10°C | 13°C | 16°C | 18°C |
| 50mm | 50mm | 60mm | 100mm | 90mm | 80mm |

# Essential Buenos Aires

## Finding your feet

Buenos Aires has two **airports**, Ezeiza, for international and few domestic flights, and **Aeroparque**, for domestic flights, most services to Uruguay and some to Brazil and Chile. Ezeiza is 35 km southwest of the centre, while Aeroparque is 4 km north of the city centre on the riverside.

A display in immigration in **Ezeiza** airport details transport options. The safest way between the airport and the city is by an airport bus service (every 30 minutes 0500-2100, one way US$13 to Puerto Madero, US$13.50 to Aeroparque airport; pay in pesos, dollars, euros or credit card) operated by **Manuel Tienda León** (T0818-888-5366, www.tiendaleon.com); the office is in front of you as you arrive. *Remise* taxis for up to four (**Manuel Tienda León**, **Taxi Ezeiza**, www.taxiezeiza.com.ar, and other counters at Ezeiza) charge between US$30-40 but less from city to airport. Radio taxis charge a minimum US$40 (make sure you pay for your taxi at the booth and then wait in the queue), see Taxi, page 63. **Manuel Tienda León** operates buses between Ezeiza and Aeroparque airports, US$14. On no account take an unmarked car at Ezeiza, no matter how low the fare. Always ask to see the taxi driver's licence. If you take an ordinary taxi the Policía de Seguridad Aeroportuaria on duty notes down the car's licence and time of departure.

Local bus No 45 runs from outside **Aeroparque** airport to the Retiro railway station. No 37 goes to Palermo and Recoleta and No 160 to Palermo and Almagro. *Remise* taxis to Ezeiza, operated by **Manuel Tienda León**, cost around US$50; to the city centre US$18. Taxi to centre US$10.

All international and interprovincial buses use the Retiro **bus terminal** at Ramos Mejía y Antártida Argentina, next to the Retiro **railway station**. See Transport, page 61.

## Orientation

The commercial heart of the city runs from Retiro station and Plaza San Martín through Plaza de Mayo to San Telmo, east of Avenida 9 de Julio. Street numbers start from the dock side rising from east to west, but north/south streets are numbered from Avenida Rivadavia, one block north of Avenida de Mayo rising in both directions. Avenida Roque Sáenz Peña and Avenida Julio A Roca are commonly referred to as Diagonal Norte and Diagonal Sur respectively.

## Getting around

The commercial centre can be explored on foot, but you'll probably want to take a couple of days to explore its museums, shops and markets. Many places of interest lie outside this zone, so you will need to use public transport. City **buses** (*colectivos*) are plentiful. See What to do, page 60, for city guides. The **metro**, or Subte, is fast and clean; see Transport, page 62, for fares. Yellow and black **taxis** can be hailed on the street, but if possible, book a radio or a *remise* taxi by phone. Again, see Transport for details.

## Useful addresses

**Central Police Station**, Moreno 1550, Virrey Cevallos 362, T011-4346 5700 (emergency, T101 or 911 from any phone, free). **Immigration (Migración)**, Antártida Argentina 1355, edif 4, T011-4317 0234, www.migraciones.gov.ar. Monday-Friday 0830-1330.

## Best parrillas

**Don Julio**, page 56
**La Brigada**, page 57
**Cabaña Las Lilas**, page 57

## West of Plaza de Mayo

Running west from the Plaza, the Avenida de Mayo leads 1.5 km to the **Palacio del Congreso** (Congress Hall) ① *Plaza del Congreso, Av Rivadavia 1864, T011-6310 7222 for 1-hr guided visits, Sat at 1600 and 1700, Sun at 1100 and 1600, www.congreso.gob.ar; passport essential.* This huge Greco-Roman building houses the seat of the legislature. Avenida de Mayo has several examples of fine architecture of the early 20th century, such as the sumptuous La Prensa building (No 575, free guided visits at weekends), the traditional ★ **Café Tortoni** ① *No 825, www.cafetortoni.com.ar,* or the eclectic **Palacio Barolo** ① *No 1370, www.pbarolo.com.ar,* and many others of faded grandeur. Avenida de Mayo crosses **Avenida 9 de Julio**, one of the widest avenues in the world, which consists of three major carriageways with heavy traffic over 140 m wide, separated in some parts by wide grass borders.

Five blocks north of Avenida de Mayo the great **Plaza de la República**, with a 67-m obelisk commemorating the 400th anniversary of the city's founding, is at the junction of Avenida 9 de Julio with Avenidas Roque Sáenz Peña and Corrientes.

**Teatro Colón** ① *Cerrito 628, entrance for guided visits Tucumán 1171, T011-4378 7109, www.teatrocolon.org.ar,* is one of the world's great opera houses. The interior is resplendent with red plush and gilt; the stage is huge and salons, dressing rooms and banquet halls are equally sumptuous. Consult the website for details of performances, tickets and guided visits. Close by is the **Museo Judío** ① *Libertad 769, T011-4123 0832, www.judaica.org.ar; for visits make an appointment with the rabbi (take identification),* which has religious objects relating to Jewish presence in Argentina in a 19th-century synagogue. Not far away is the **Museo del Holocausto (Shoah Museum)** ① *Montevideo 919, T011-4811 3588, www.museodelholocausto.org.ar, Mon-Thu 1000-1900, Fri 1000-1600, US$4.50 (ID required),* a permanent exhibition of pictures, personal and religious items with texts in Spanish on the Holocaust, antisemitism in Argentina and the lives of many Argentine Jews in the pre- and post-war periods.

**La Chacarita** ① *Guzmán 670, daily 0730-1700, take Subte Line B to the Federico Lacroze station,* is a well-known cemetery with the lovingly tended tomb of **Carlos Gardel**, the tango singer. See box, page 42, and the unofficial website: www.cementeriochacarita.com.ar.

## North of Plaza de Mayo

The city's traditional shopping centre, Calle Florida, is reserved for pedestrians, with clothes and souvenir shops, restaurants and the elegant **Galerías Pacífico** ① *Florida entre Córdoba y Viamonte, www.galeriaspacifico.com.ar, guided visits from the fountain on lower ground floor on Mon-Fri at 1130 and 1630,* a beautiful mall with fine murals and architecture, many exclusive shops and good food outlets. More shops are to be found on Avenida Santa Fe, which crosses Florida at Plaza San Martín. Avenida Corrientes, a street of theatres, bookshops, restaurants and cafés, and nearby Calle Lavalle (partly reserved for pedestrians), used to be the entertainment centre, but both are now regarded as faded. Recoleta, Palermo and Puerto Madero have become much more fashionable (see below).

The **Basílica Nuestra Señora de La Merced** ① *J D Perón y Reconquista 207, mass times, Wed 1730, Sun 11300,* founded 1604, rebuilt for the third time in the 18th century, has a beautiful interior with baroque and rococo features. In 1807 it was a command post against the invading British. **Museo y Biblioteca Mitre** ① *San Martín 336, T011-4394 8240, www.museomitre.gob.ar, Mon-Fri 1300-1730 (library archives Wed 1400-1730), US$1.30,* preserves intact the household of President Bartolomé Mitre and has a coin and map collection and historical archives.

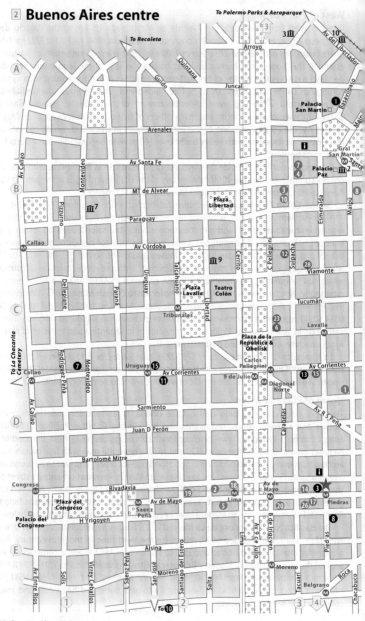

➡ **Buenos Aires maps**

1 Buenos Aires orientation, page 36
2 **Buenos Aires centre, page 40**
3 Recoleta & Palermo, page 44
4 San Telmo, page 47

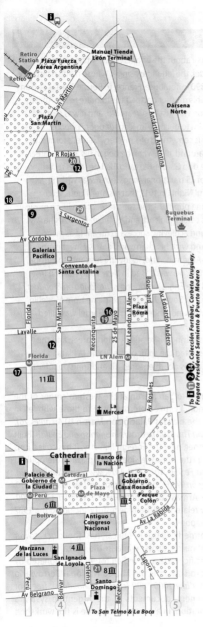

200 metres
200 yards

**Where to stay** 🛏

1 06 Central *D3*
2 BA Stop *D2*
3 Bisonte Palace *B3*
4 Casa Calma *B3*
5 Castelar *E2*
6 Colón *C3*
7 Dolmen *B3*
8 Dorá *B3*
10 El Conquistador *B3*
11 Faena *C5*
12 Goya *C3*
13 Hispano *D3*
15 Hostel Suites Obelisco *D3*
17 La Argentina *E3*
18 Limehouse Hostel *D2*
19 Marbella *E2*
20 Milhouse Hostel *E3*
21 Moreno *E4*
23 Panamericano & Tomo 1 restaurant *C3*
26 Portal del Sur *E3*
28 V&S *C3*
29 Waldorf *B4*

**Restaurants** 🍴

1 Basa
2 Cabaña Las Lilas *D5*
3 Café Tortoni *D3*
6 Dadá *B4*
7 El Gato Negro *C1*
8 Fikä *E3*
9 Florida Garden *B4*
12 Gianni's *B4/C4*
10 Gijón *E2*
11 Güerrín *D2*
13 Las Cuartetas *D3*
14 Le Grill *D5*
15 Los Inmortales *C2*
16 Sam Bucherie *C4*
17 Sorrento *C4*
18 Tancat *B3*

**Bars & clubs** 🍸

19 Bahrein *C4*
20 Druid In *B4*

**Museums** 🏛

2 Museo de Armas *B3*
3 Museo de Arte Hispanoamericano Isaac Fernández Blanco *A3*
4 Museo de la Ciudad *E4*
5 Museo Casa Rosada *E5*
6 Museo del Cabildo y la Revolución de Mayo *E4*
7 Museo del Holocausto *B1*
8 Museo Etnográfico JB Ambrosetti *E4*
9 Museo Judío *C2*
10 Museo Nacional Ferroviario *A3*
11 Museo y Biblioteca Mitre *D4*

## ON THE ROAD

## Carlos Gardel

To this day there is still a lot of controversy about the origins of Argentina's favourite performer. Most people argue that Gardel, the legendary singer whose name is virtually synonymous with tango, was born in 1890 in Toulouse, France, to Berthe Gardès and an unknown father. To avoid social stigma, his mother decided to emigrate to the Abasto market area of Buenos Aires when her son was just two years old, and it was partly these humble beginnings that helped him to become an icon for poor *Porteños*.

Just as the exact origin of tango itself is something of a mystery, Gardel's formative years around the city are obscure, until around 1912 when he began his artistic career in earnest, performing as one half of the duo Gardel-Razzano. He began his recording career with Columbia with a recording of 15 traditional songs, but it was with his rendition of *Mi Noche Triste* (My Sorrowful Night) in 1917, that his mellifluous voice became known. As *tango-canción* became popular – the song rather than just a musical accompaniment to the dance – Gardel's career took off, and by the early 1920s he was singing entirely within this new genre, and achieving success as far afield as Madrid.

Gardel became a solo artist in 1925 and with his charm and natural machismo was the very epitome of tango both in Argentina and, following his tours to Europe, around the world. Between 1933 and 1935, he was based in New York, starring in numerous Spanish-speaking films, and the English-language *The Tango on Broadway* in 1934. On 24 June 1935, while on a tour of South America, his plane from Medellin, Colombia, crashed into another on the ground while taking off. Gardel was killed instantly; he was only 45 years old.

Gardel had recorded some 900 songs during his relatively short career, and the brilliance of his voice, the way he represented the spirit of the Río de la Plata to his fans at home, and the untimely nature of his death ensured his enduring popularity.

The **Plaza San Martín** has a monument to San Martín at the western corner of the main park and, at the north end, a memorial with an eternal flame to those who fell in the Falklands/Malvinas War of 1982. On the plaza is **Palacio San Martín** ① *Arenales 761, T011-4819 7297, www.mrecic.gov.ar, Tue and Thu 1500 free tours in Spanish and English*. Built 1905-1909, it is three houses linked together, now the Foreign Ministry. It has collections of pre-Hispanic and 20th-century art. On the opposite side of the plaza is the opulent **Palacio Paz (Círculo Militar)** ① *Av Santa Fe 750, T011-4311 1071, www.circulomilitar.org, guided tours Tue-Fri 1100, 1500 (1100 only on Wed), tours in English on Thu at 1530, US$10*. The Círculo Militar includes **Museo de Armas** ① *Av Santa Fe 702, Mon-Fri 1300-1900, US$2.60*, which has all kinds of weaponry related to Argentine history, including the 1982 Falklands/Malvinas War, plus Oriental weapons.

**Plaza Fuerza Aérea Argentina** (formerly Plaza Británica) has the clock tower presented by British and Anglo-Argentine residents, while in the **Plaza Canadá** (in front of the Retiro Station) there is a Pacific Northwest Indian totem pole, donated by the Canadian government. Behind Retiro station is the **Museo Nacional Ferroviario** ① *Av del Libertador 405, T011-4318 3343, daily 1000-1800 (closed on holidays), free*. For railway fans, it has locomotives, machinery, documents of the Argentine system's history; the building is in very poor condition. In a warehouse beside is the workshop of the sculptor Carlos Regazzoni (**Regazzoni Arts**, see Facebook) who recycles refuse material from railways.

The **Museo de Arte Hispanoamericano Isaac Fernández Blanco** ① *Suipacha 1422 (3 blocks west of Retiro), T011-4327 0228, www.museos.buenosaires.gob.ar/mifb.htm, Tue-Fri, 1300-1900, Sat, Sun and holidays 1100-1900, Wed free, US$0.65*, is one of the city's best museums. It contains a fascinating collection of colonial art, especially paintings and silver, as well as temporary exhibitions of Latin American art, in a beautiful neocolonial mansion, the **Palacio Noel**, dating from the 1920s, with Spanish gardens. Weekend concerts are also held here.

## Recoleta

**Nuestra Señora del Pilar** ① *Junín 1898*, is a jewel of colonial architecture dating from 1732 (renovated in later centuries), facing onto the public gardens of Recoleta. A fine wooden image of San Pedro de Alcántara, attributed to the famous 17th-century Spanish sculptor Alonso Cano, is preserved in a side chapel on the left, and there are stunning gold altars. Upstairs is an interesting museum of religious art.

Next to it, the ★ **Cementerio Recoleta** ① *entrance at Junín 1760, near Museo de Bellas Artes (see below), www.cementeriorecoleta.com.ar, 0700-1745, tours in Spanish and English are available Tue-Fri at 1100, Sat-Sun at 1100 and 1500 (visitasguiadasrecoleta@buenosaires. gob.ar)*, is one of the must-see sights of Buenos Aires. With its streets and alleys separating family mausoleums built in every imaginable architectural style, La Recoleta cemetery is often compared to a miniature city. Among the famous names from Argentine history is Evita Perón who lies in the Duarte family mausoleum: to find it from the entrance go to the first tree-filled plaza; turn left and where this avenue meets a main avenue (go just beyond the Turriaca tomb), turn right; then take the third passage on the left. On Saturday and Sunday there is a good craft market in the park on Plaza Francia outside the cemetery (1000-1800/1900), with street artists and performers. Next to the cemetery, the **Centro Cultural Recoleta** ① *Junín 1930, T011-4803 1040, www.centroculturalrecoleta.org, Tue-Fri 1330-2030, Sat, Sun, holidays 1130-2030*, specializes in contemporary local art.

The excellent **Museo de Bellas Artes** (National Gallery) ① *Av del Libertador 1473, T011-5288 9900, www.mnba.gob.ar, Tue-Fri 1130-1930, Sat-Sun 0930-1930, free*, gives a taste of Argentine art, as well as having a fine collection of European works, particularly post-Impressionist. It has superb Argentine 19th- and 20th-century paintings, sculpture and wooden carvings; it also hosts films, classical music concerts and art courses. The **Biblioteca Nacional** (National Library) ① *Av del Libertador 1600 y Agüero 2502, T011-4808 6000, www.bn.gov.ar, Mon-Fri 0900-2100, Sat and Sun 1200-1900, closed Jan*, is housed in a modern building and contains an art gallery and periodical archives (only a fraction of the extensive stock can be seen); cultural events are held here too. Next to it is the **Museo del Libro y de la Lengua** ① *Av Las Heras 2555, T011-4808 0090, Tue-Sun 1400-1900, free*, whose exhibitions illustrate singularities of the Spanish (Castellano) spoken in Argentina and the local publishing industry. The **Museo Nacional de Arte Decorativo** ① *Av del Libertador 1902, T011-4802 6606, www.mnad.org, Tue-Sun 1400-1900 (closed Sun in Jan), US$1.30, Tue free, guided visits in English Tue-Fri at 1430, US$4*, contains collections of painting, furniture, porcelain, crystal and sculpture exhibited in sumptuous halls, once a family residence.

## Palermo

**Palermo Chico** is a delightful residential area with several houses of once-wealthy families, dating from the early 20th century. The predominant French style of the district was broken in 1929 by the rationalist lines of the **Casa de la Cultura** ① *Rufino de Elizalde 2831,*

# 3 Recoleta & Palermo

**Where to stay**
1 Alvear Palace
2 Art
3 Back in BA
5 Bo Bo
8 Hostel Suites Palermo
9 Krista
10 Legado Mítico
11 Magnolia
12 Querido
13 Solar Soler

**Restaurants**
1 Al Paso y Algo Más
2 Arkakao
3 Basa
4 Bröet
5 Clásico y Moderna
6 Como en Casa
7 El Mirasol de la Recova
8 Juana M
9 La Madeleine
10 María de Bambi
11 Persicco
12 Rodi Bar

**Bars & clubs**
13 Buller Brewing Company
14 Casa Bar
15 Gran Bar Danzón
16 Milion
17 Notorious
18 The Shamrock

➡ **Buenos Aires maps**
1 Buenos Aires orientation, page 36
2 Buenos Aires centre, page 40
3 Recoleta & Palermo, page 44
4 San Telmo, page 47

*T011-4808 0553, www.fnartes.gov.ar, Tue-Sun 1500-2000 (Jan closed).* The original residence of the writer Victoria Ocampo, this was a gathering place for artists and intellectuals and is now an attractive cultural centre with art exhibitions and occasional concerts.

The **Museo de Arte Popular José Hernández** ① *Av del Libertador 2373, T011-4803 2384, www.buenosaires.gob.ar/museojosehernandez, Tue-Fri 1300-1900, Sat-Sun and holidays 1000-1800, US$0.65, free Wed; see website for exhibitions, events and workshops*, has a wide collection of Argentine folkloric art, with rooms dedicated to indigenous, colonial and gaucho artefacts; there's a handicraft shop and library. The **Museo de Arte Latinoamericano (MALBA)** ① *Av Figueroa Alcorta 3415, T011-4808 6500, www.malba. org.ar, Thu-Mon and holidays 1200-2000, US$5.50, students and seniors US$3 (Wed half price, students free, open till 2100); Tue closed*, one of the most important museums in the city, houses renowned Latin American artists' works: powerful, moving and highly recommended. It's not a vast collection, but representative of the best from the continent. It also has a good library, cinema (showing art house films as well as Argentine classics), seminars and a shop, as well as an elegant café, serving delicious food and cakes.

Of the fine Palermo parks, the largest is **Parque Tres de Febrero**, famous for its extensive rose garden, Andalusian Patio, and the delightful **Jardín Japonés** (with café) ① *T011-4804 4922, www.jardinjapones.org.ar, daily 1000-1800, US$4.50, seniors free*. It is a charming place for a walk, delightful for children, and with a good café serving some Japanese dishes. Close by is the **Hipódromo Argentino** (Palermo racecourse) ① *T011-4778 2800, www.palermo.com.ar, races 10 days per month, free*. Opposite the parks are the Botanical and Zoological Gardens. At the entrance to the **Planetarium** ① *just off Belisario Roldán, in Palermo Park, T011-4771 6629, www.planetario.gob.ar, 2 presentations Tue-Fri, 6 at weekends, US$4; small museum*, are several large meteorites from Campo del Cielo. The **Museo de Artes Plásticas Eduardo Sívori** ① *Av Infanta Isabel 555 (Parque Tres de Febrero), T011-4774 9452, www.buenosaires.gob.ar/museosivori, Tue-Fri 1200-1900, Sat-Sun and holidays 1000-1900 (1800 in winter), US$1.60, Wed and Fri free*, emphasizes 19th- and 20th-century Argentine art, sculpture and tapestry.

The **Botanical Gardens** ① *Santa Fe 3951, T011-4831 4527, entrance from Plaza Italia (take Subte, line D) or from C República Arabe Siria, Tue-Fri 0800-17450, Sat-Sun 0930-1745 (closes at 1845 in summer), free guided visits Sat-Sun and holidays 1030, 1500*, contain characteristic specimens of the world's vegetation. The trees native to the different provinces of Argentina are brought together in one section; see also the *yerba mate* section. One block beyond is **Museo Evita** ① *Lafinur 2988, T011-4807 0306, www.museoevita.org, Tue-Sun 1100-1900, US$5*. In a former women's shelter run by Fundación Eva Perón, the exhibition of dresses, paintings and other items is quite interesting though lacks the expected passion; there's also a library and a café-restaurant.

Southwest of here, around Plaza Cortázar, is ★ **Palermo Viejo**, the most atmospheric part of Palermo. It's a very seductive place, characterized by leafy, cobbled streets, bohemian houses and chic eateries and shops.

## Belgrano

In Belgrano is the **Museo de Arte Español Enrique Larreta** ① *Juramento 2291, T011-4784 4040, www.buenosaires.gob.ar/museolarreta Mon-Fri, 1200-1900, Sat-Sun 1000-2000, guided visits Mon-Fri 1430, Sat-Sun 1600, 1800, US$0.65, Thu free*. The home of the writer Larreta, with paintings and religious art from the 14th to the 20th century, it also has a beautiful garden. Also in Belgrano is the **Museo Histórico Sarmiento** ① *Juramento 2180, T011-4782 2354, www.museosarmiento.cultura.gob.ar, Mon-Fri 1300-1800, Sat-Sun 1400-1900,* and **Museo Casa de Yrurtia** ⓘ *O'Higgins 2390, T011-4781 0385, www.museoyrurtia.cultura. gob.ar, closed for restoration in 2016.*

## South of Plaza de Mayo

The church of **San Ignacio de Loyola**, begun in 1664, is the oldest colonial building in Buenos Aires (renovated in the 18th and 19th centuries). It stands in a block of Jesuit origin, called the **Manzana de las Luces** (Block of Enlightenment – Moreno, Alsina, Perú and Bolívar). Also in this block are the **Colegio Nacional de Buenos Aires** ⓘ *Bolívar 263, T011-4331 0734 www.cnba.uba.ar,* formerly the site of the Jesuits' Colegio Máximo, the Procuraduría de las Misiones (today the **Mercado de las Luces**, a crafts market) and 18th-century **tunnels**. For centuries the whole block was the centre of intellectual activity, though little remains today but a small **cultural centre** ⓘ *T011-4343 3260, www.manzanadelasluces.gov.ar, guided tours from Perú 272, Mon-Fri 1500, Sat and Sun 1500, 1630, 1800 in Spanish (in English by prior arrangement), arrive 15 mins before tour, US$3.25; the tours explore the tunnels and visit the buildings on C Perú,* with art courses, concerts, plays and film shows. The **Museo de la Ciudad** ⓘ *Alsina 412, T011-4343 2123, www.buenosaires.gob.ar/museodelaciudad, daily 1100-1800, US$0.30, free on Mon and Wed,* has a permanent exhibition covering social history and popular culture, and special exhibitions on daily life in Buenos Aires that are changed every two months. There's also a reference library open to the public.

**Santo Domingo** ⓘ *Defensa y Belgrano, T011-4331 1668, www.op.org.armass, Mon-Fri 0700-1800, Sat afternoon only, Sun 1000-1300, mass held Mon-Fri at 1230, Sat 1830, Sun 1100,* was founded in 1751. During the British attack on Buenos Aires in 1806 some of Whitelocke's soldiers took refuge in the church. The local forces bombarded it, the British capitulated and their regimental colours were preserved in the church. General Belgrano is buried here. The church holds occasional concerts.

**Museo Etnográfico JB Ambrosetti** ⓘ *Moreno 350, T011-4345 8196, see Facebook, Tue-Fri 1300-1900, Sat-Sun 1500-1900 (closed Jan), US$2, guided visits Sat-Sun 1600,* contains anthropological and ethnographic collections from Patagonian and Argentina's northwest cultures (the latter a rich collection displayed on the first floor). There's also a small international room with a magnificent Japanese Buddhist altar.

## ★ San Telmo

One of the few places which still has late colonial and Rosista buildings (mostly renovated in the 20th century) is the barrio of San Telmo, south of Plaza de Mayo. It's a place rich in culture, with lots of cafés, antique shops and little art galleries. On Sundays, it has a great atmosphere, with an antiques market at the Plaza Dorrego (see page 60), with the occasional free tango show and live music. The **Museo de Arte Moderno de Buenos Aires (MAMBA)** ⓘ *Av San Juan 350, T011-4361 6919, Tue-Fri 1100-1900, Sat, Sun and holidays 1100-2000, US$1.31, Tue free,* has temporary art exhibitions from local and foreign artists. Next door is the **Museo de Arte Contemporáneo de Buenos Aires (MACBA)** ⓘ *T011-5299 2010, www.macba.com.ar, Mon-Fri (closed Tue) 1100-1900, Sat, Sun 1100-1930, US$3.90 (Wed US$2.60),* focusing on geometric abstraction.

## La Boca

East of the Plaza de Mayo, behind the Casa Rosada, a broad avenue, Paseo Colón, runs south towards San Telmo and, as Avenida Almirante Brown, on to the old port district of La Boca, where the Riachuelo flows into the Plata. The much-photographed, brightly painted tin and wooden houses cover one block of the pedestrianized Caminito. As

La Boca is the poorest and roughest area within central Buenos Aires, tourists are limited to this little street running from the Plaza La Vuelta de Rocha.

You can also visit **Fundación Proa** ① *Av Pedro de Mendoza 1929, T011-4104 1000, www.proa.org, Tue-Sun 1100-1900*, for varied art exhibitions, cultural events and for its café-restaurant with a view, and the **Museo de Bellas Artes Benito Quinquela Martín** ① *Av Pedro de Mendoza 1835, T011-4301 1080, www.buenosaires.gob.ar/museo quinquelamartin, Tue-Fri 1000-1800, Sat, Sun and holidays 1115-1800, US$2*, with over 1000 works by Argentine artists, particularly Benito Quinquela Martín (1890-1977), who painted La Boca port life. It also houses sculptures and figureheads rescued from ships. Do

**Tip...**
La Boca is reportedly up-and-coming and less dangerous than in recent years, but always ask about safety, especially if you're thinking of going at night. Travel by radio taxi (US$5 one way from the centre or San Telmo); to return, call a taxi from any café.

⬛4 **San Telmo**

➡ **Buenos Aires maps**
1 Buenos Aires orientation, page 36
2 Buenos Aires centre, page 40
3 Recoleta & Palermo, page 44
4 San Telmo, page 47

200 metres
200 yards

**Where to stay** 🛏
1 Art Factory
3 Circus
4 Garden House
5 Hostal de Granados
6 Hostel-Inn Buenos Aires
7 Imagine Hotel Boutique
8 Kilca Hostel & Backpacker
9 La Casita de San Telmo
11 Lugar Gay de Buenos Aires
12 Mansión Dandi Royal
13 Ostinatto
14 Sabatico Travelers Hostel
16 Telmho

**Restaurants** 🍴
1 Brasserie Petanque
2 Británico
3 Dorrego
4 Dylan
5 Gran Parilla del Plata
6 La Brigada
7 La Poesía
8 Naturaleza Sabia
9 Nonna Bianca
10 Pride Café

**Bars & clubs** 🍸
11 Bar Seddon
12 Gibralter Pub
13 La Puerta Roja

not go anywhere else in La Boca and avoid it at night. The area is especially rowdy when the Boca Juniors football club is playing at home. At Boca Juniors stadium is **Museo de la Pasión Boquense** ① *Brandsen 805, T011-4362 1100, www.museoboquense.com, daily 1000-1800, US$9, guided tour of the stadium in Spanish or English, daily 1000-1800, plus ticket to the museum, US$12.*

## Puerto Madero

The Puerto Madero dock area has been renovated; the 19th-century warehouses are restaurants and bars, an attractive place for a stroll and popular nightspot. **Fragata Presidente Sarmiento** ① *dock 3, Av Alicia Moreau de Justo 980, Puerto Madero, T011-4334 9386, daily 1000-1900, entry by donation,* was a naval training ship until 1961; now it's a museum. Nearby, in dock 4, is the **Corbeta Uruguay** ① *T011-4314 1090, for both ships see www.ara.mil.ar, daily 1000-1900, entry by donation,* the ship that rescued Otto Nordenskjold's Antarctic expedition in 1903. In dock 4 there is also **Colección Fortabat** ① *Olga Cossettini 141, T011-4310 6600, www.coleccionfortabat.org.ar, Tue-Sun 1200-2000, US$4.50,* which houses a great art collection.

## Costanera Sur

East of San Telmo on the far side of the docks, the Avenida Costanera runs as a long, spacious boulevard. A stretch of marshland reclaimed from the river forms the interesting **Costanera Sur Wildlife Reserve** ① *entrances at Av Tristán Achával Rodríguez 1550 (take Estados Unidos east from San Telmo) or next to the Buquebús ferry terminal (take Av Córdoba east), T0800 444 5343; for pedestrians and bikers only, Tue-Sun 0800-1800 (in summer, closes at 1900), free,* where over 150 bird species have been spotted over the past few years.

There are free guided tours at weekends and holidays 0930, 1600 (1030-1530 in winter), from the administration next to the southern entrance, but much can be seen from the road before then (binoculars useful). Also free nocturnal visits operate every month on the Friday closest to the full moon (book Monday before, visitasguiadas_recs@ buenosaires.gob.ar). To get there take *colectivos* 4, 130 or 152. It's a 30-minute walk from the entrance to the river shore and it takes about three hours to walk the whole perimeter. In summer it's very hot with little shade. For details (particularly birdwatching) contact **Aves Argentinas/AOP** (see Birdwatching, page 60), or see www.reservacostanera.com.ar (English version).

## Tourist information

A good guide to bus and subway routes is *Guía T*, available at newsstands. There is also the interactive map at www.mapa. buenosaires.gob.ar. Other useful maps found at newsstands include Mapa-Guia's pocket map of Buenos Aires (US$3.50), the more detailed city map (US$6.75) and the robust GBA Gran Buenos Aires map, which includes outlying neighbourhoods. Otherwise it is easy to get free maps of the centre from tourist kiosks and most hotels. The daily press has useful supplements, such as the Sunday tourism section in *La Nación* (www.lanacion.com.ar), *Sí* in *Clarín* (www.si.clarin.com) and the equivalent *No* of *Página 12* (www.pagina12. com.ar). The *Buenos Aires Herald* also has information on what's on at www. buenosairesherald.com, or see www. agendacultural.buenosaires.gob.ar, www.vuenosairez.com and www.wipe. com.ar. Also very useful are www.gringo inbuenosaires.com and www.discover buenosaires.com. Blogs worth exploring include www.baexpats.com and www. goodmorningba.com.

### City information
*www.turismo.buenosaires.gob.ar, in Spanish only.*
There are tourist kiosks open daily (0900-1800) downtown at Florida 50, in Recoleta (Av Quintana 596, junction with Ortiz), in Puerto Madero (JM Gorriti 200), and at Retiro bus station (ground floor, daily 0730-1630).

### Defensoría del Turista
*Defensa 1302 (San Telmo), T011-4307 5102, turistasantelmo@defensoria.org.ar. Mon-Fri 1000-1800, Sat-Sun and holidays 1100-1800.*
To report being overcharged or cheated.

### National office
*Av Santa Fe 883, T011-4312 2232 or T0800-555 0016, info@turismo.gov.ar. Mon-Fri 0900-1900.*

Has maps and literature covering the whole country. There are kiosks at Aeroparque and Ezeiza airports (Mon-Fri 0900-1700, Sat-Sun 0900-1800).

## Where to stay

Shop around for hotels offering discounts on multi-night stays. The tourist offices at Ezeiza and Aeroparque airports book rooms. A/c is a must in high summer. Finding hotels for Fri, Sat, Sun nights can be difficult and hostels can get very busy, resulting in pressure on staff. A bed in a hostel dorm costs US$11-21. The range of 'boutique' hotels and hostels is impressive, especially in Palermo and San Telmo. The same applies to restaurants, bars and clubs. There are far more than we can list here. There are fine examples of the **Four Seasons** (www.fourseasons.com/ buenosaires), **Hilton** (www.hilton.com), **Hyatt** (www.buenosaires.park.hyatt.com), **Marriott** (www.marriott.com), **NH** (www. nh-hoteles.com), **Pestana** (www.pestana. com/en), **Sofitel** (www.sofitel.com) and **Unique Hotels** (www.uniquehotels.com.ar). Hotels will store luggage, and most have English-speaking staff.

**Centre** *maps pages 40 and 44.*

### $$$$ Alvear Palace
*Av Alvear 1891, T011-4808 2100, www.alvearpalace.com.*
The height of elegance, an impeccably preserved 1920s Recoleta palace, sumptuous marble foyer, with Louis XV-style chairs, and a charming orangery where you can take tea with superb patisseries. Antique-filled bedrooms. Recommended.

### $$$$ Casa Calma
*Suipacha 1015, T011-4312 5000, www.casacalmahotel.com.*
A relaxing haven in a downtown setting, homely yet luxurious, with a wellness centre and honesty bar.

### $$$$ Faena
*Martha Salotti 445 (Puerto Madero),*
*T011-4010 9000, www.faena.com.*
Set in a 100-year-old silo, renovated by
Philippe Starck, this is not for all budgets
or tastes. Eclectic decoration, staff trained
to be perfect.

### $$$$-$$$ Castelar
*Av de Mayo 1152, T011-4383 5000,*
*www.castelarhotel.com.ar.*
A wonderfully elegant 1920s hotel which
retains all the original features in the
grand entrance and bar. Cosy bedrooms,
charming staff, and excellent value. Also
a spa with Turkish baths and massage.
Highly recommended.

### $$$$-$$$ Dolmen
*Suipacha 1079, T011-4315 7117,*
*www.hoteldolmen.com.ar.*
Good location, smart spacious entrance
lobby, with a calm relaxing atmosphere, good
professional service, modern, comfortable
well-designed rooms, small pool.

### $$$$-$$$ El Conquistador
*Suipacha 948, T011-4328 3012,*
*www.elconquistador.com.ar.*
Stylish 1970s hotel, which retains the wood
and chrome foyer, but has bright modern
rooms, and a lovely light restaurant on the
10th floor with great views. Well situated,
good value.

### $$$$-$$$ Panamericano
*Carlos Pellegrini 551, T011-4348 5000,*
*www.panamericano.us.*
Very smart and modern hotel, with luxurious
and tasteful rooms, covered rooftop pool,
**Celtic Bar** pub with a cigar club, and the
superb restaurant, **Tomo 1**. Excellent service
too. Also has properties in Bariloche (www.
panamericanobariloche.com) and El Calafate
(www.casalossauces.com).

### $$$ Art
*Azcuénaga 1268, T011-4821 6248,*
*www.ahotel.com.ar.*

Charming boutique hotel on a quiet
residential street, only a few blocks from
Recoleta or Av Santa Fe, simple but warmly
decorated, good service, solarium, compact
standard rooms.

### $$$ Bisonte Palace
*MT de Alvear 902, T011-4390 7830,*
*www.bisontepalace.com.*
Charming, with calm entrance foyer, which
remains gracious thanks to courteous staff.
Plain but spacious rooms, ample breakfast,
good location. Very good value.

### $$$ Colón
*Carlos Pellegrini 507, T011-4320 3500,*
*www.exehotelcolon.com.*
Splendid location overlooking Av 9 de
Julio and Teatro Colón, extremely good
value. Charming bedrooms, comfortable,
gym, great breakfasts, and perfect service.
Highly recommended.

### $$$ Dorá
*Maipú 963, T011-4312 7391,*
*www.dorahotel.com.ar.*
Charming and old-fashioned with
comfortable rooms, good service,
attractive lounge with paintings.
Warmly recommended.

### $$$ Goya
*Suipacha 748, T011-4322 9269,*
*www.goyahotel.com.ar.*
Welcoming and central, worth paying
more for superior rooms, though all are
comfortable. Good breakfast, English spoken.

### $$$ Hispano
*Av de Mayo 861, T011-4345 2020,*
*www.hhispano.com.ar.*
Plain but comfortable rooms in this hotel
which has been welcoming travellers since
the 1950s, courtyard and small garden, central.

### $$$ Marbella
*Av de Mayo 1261, T011-4383 3573,*
*www.hotelmarbella.com.ar.*
Modernized, and central, though quiet,
multilingual. Recommended.

### $$$ Moreno
*Moreno 376, T011-4831 6831,*
*www.morenobuenosaires.com.*
150 m from the Plaza de Mayo, decorated
in dark, rich tones, large rooms, good
value, jacuzzi, gym and chic bar, winery
and restaurant.

### $$$ Waldorf
*Paraguay 450, T011-4312 2071,*
*www.waldorf-hotel.com.ar.*
Welcoming staff and a comfortable mixture
of traditional and modern in this centrally
located hotel. Good value, with safe boxes
in all rooms and a buffet breakfast, English
spoken. Recommended.

### $ La Argentina
*Av de Mayo 860, T011-4342 0078.*
Cheap, central and rickety, but it stands the
test of time. Amazing old building, bringing
new meaning to the term 'high-ceilinged';
can be noisy if your room is near the 'slam-
the-door-shut' elevator. Good, cheap and
cheerful restaurant attached, doing very
affordable *menú del día*. Recommended.

## Youth hostels

### $ pp 06 Central
*Maipú 306, T011-5219 0052,*
*www.06centralhostel.com.*
A few metres from the Obelisco and
Av Corrientes, simple, spacious dorms,
attractively decorated doubles ($$), cosy
communal area.

### $ pp BA Stop
*Rivadavia 1194, T011-6091 2156,*
*www.bastop.com.*
In a lovely converted 1900s corner block,
dorms for 4-8 people, 11 private rooms ($$
double), TV, table tennis, English spoken,
safe, very helpful staff can organize tours,
Spanish classes. Repeatedly recommended;
the best hostel in the centre.

### $ pp Hostel Suites Obelisco
*Av Corrientes 830, T011-4328 4040,*
*www.hostelsuites.com.*

Elegant hostel built in a completely restored
old building in the heart of the city. Dorms,
doubles and private apartments ($$), DVD
room, laundry service. Free transfer from
Ezeiza airport.

### $ pp Limehouse Hostel
*Lima 11, T011-4383 4561,*
*www.limehouse.com.ar.*
Dorms for up to 8 and doubles with and
without bath ($$), popular, typical city hostel
with bar, roof terrace, 'chilled', great if you
like the party atmosphere, efficient staff.
Recommended.

### $ pp Milhouse Hostel
*Hipólito Yrigoyen 959, T011-4345 9604,*
*www.milhousehostel.com.*
In an 1890 house, lovely rooms ($$$ in double)
and dorms, comfortable, laundry, tango
lessons, very popular so reconfirm bookings
at all times. Also at Av De Mayo 1245.

### $ pp Portal del Sur
*Hipólito Yrigoyen 855, T011-4342 8788,*
*www.portaldelsurba.com.ar.*
Good dorms and especially lovely doubles
($$) and singles in a converted 19th-century
building. Recommended for single travellers.

### $ pp V&S
*Viamonte 887, T011-4322 0994,*
*www.hostelclub.com.*
Central popular hostel ($$ in attractive
double room, bath), café, tango classes,
tours, warm atmosphere, welcoming.
Recommended.

---

## Palermo *map page 44.*

### $$$$ Legado Mítico
*Gurruchaga 1848, T011-4833 1300,*
*www.legadomitico.com.*
Stylish small hotel with 11 rooms named
after Argentine cultural legends. They
use local designs and products. Luxurious
and recommended.

### $$$$ Magnolia
*Julián Alvarez 1746, T011-4867 4900,*
*www.magnoliahotelboutique.com.*

Lovely boutique hotel in a quiet area. This refurbished early 20th-century house has attractively designed rooms opening onto the street or to inner courtyards and a perfect retreat on its rooftop terrace.

### $$$$ Querido
*Juan Ramírez de Velazco 934, T011-4854 6297, www.queridobuenosaires.com.*
Purpose-built, designed and cared for by a Brazilian-English couple. 7 rooms, 4 of which have balconies, for a comfortable stay in Villa Crespo area, a few blocks from Palermo Soho and from the subway.

### $$$$-$$$ Bo Bo
*Guatemala 4870, T011-4774 0505, www.bobohotel.com.*
On a leafy street, 15 rooms decorated in contemporary style, some with private balconies, excellent restaurant.

### $$$$-$$$ Krista
*Bonpland 1665, T011-4771 4697, www.kristahotel.com.ar.*
Intimate, hidden behind the plain façade of an elegant townhouse, well placed for restaurants. Good value, comfortable, individually designed spacious rooms, wheelchair access.

### $$$ Solar Soler
*Soler 5676, T011-4776 7494, www.solarsoler.com.ar.*
Welcoming B&B in Palermo Hollywood, excellent service. Recommended.

## Youth hostels

### $ pp Back in BA
*El Salvador 5115, T011-4774 2859, www.backinba.com.*
Small hostel with dorms for up to 6 and private rooms ($$), lockers with charging points, patio, bar, Netflix, information, tours, apartment rentals, and classes can be arranged, good Palermo Soho location.

### $ pp Hostel Suites Palermo
*Charcas 4752, T011-4773 0806, www.palermo.hostelsuites.com.*

A beautiful century-old residence with the original grandeur partially preserved and a quiet atmosphere. Comfortable renovated dorms and private rooms with bath ($$ doubles), good service, small travel agency, Wi-Fi, cooking and laundry facilities, DVD room and breakfast included. Free transfer from Ezeiza airport.

### $ Play Hostel
*Guatemala 3646, T011-4832 4257, www.playhostel.com.*
Popular option with dorms for 4-10 people. Wi-Fi, laundry service, bike hire, tourist info and tango classes.

---

**San Telmo and around** *map page 47.*

### $$$$ Mansión Dandi Royal
*Piedras 922, T011-4361 3537, www.hotelmansiondandiroyal.com.*
A wonderfully restored 1903 residence, small upmarket hotel with an elegant tango atmosphere, small pool, good value. Daily tango lessons and *milonga* every Fri at 2130.

### $$$$-$$$ Imagine Hotel Boutique
*México 1330, T011-4383 2230, www.imaginehotelboutique.com.*
9 suites in a beautifully restored 1820s house, each room individually designed, quiet, buffet breakfast, parking. Recommended.

### $$$ La Casita de San Telmo
*Cochabamba 286, T011-4307 5073, www.lacasitadesantelmo.com.*
7 rooms in restored 1840s house, most open onto a garden with a beautiful fig tree, owners are tango fans; rooms rented by day, week or month.

### $$$ Lugar Gay de Buenos Aires
*Defensa 1120 (no sign), T011-4300 4747, www.lugargay.com.ar.*
A men-only gay B&B with 8 comfortable rooms, video room and jacuzzi. A stone's throw from Plaza Dorrego.

### $$$ Telmho
*Defensa 1086, T011-4307 9898, www.telmho-hotel.com.ar.*

Smart rooms overlooking Plaza Dorrego, huge beds, modern bathrooms, lovely roof garden, helpful staff.

## Youth hostels

### $ pp Art Factory
*Piedras 545, T011-4343 1463,*
*www.artfactoryba.com.ar.*
Large, early 1900s house converted into a hostel, informal atmosphere with individually designed and brightly painted private rooms (some with bath, **$$**), dorms, halfway between the centre and San Telmo.

### $ pp Circus
*Chacabuco 1020, T011-4300 4983,*
*www.hostelcircus.com.*
Stylish rooms for 2 (**$$**) to 4 people, tastefully renovated building, small heated swimming pool.

### $ pp Garden House
*Av San Juan 1271, T011-4304 1824,*
*www.gardenhouseba.com.ar.*
Small, welcoming independent hostel for those who don't want a party atmosphere; good barbecues on the terrace. Dorms and some doubles (**$$**). Recommended.

### $ pp Hostal de Granados
*Chile 374, T011-4362 5600,*
*www.hostaldegranados.com.ar.*
Small, light, well-equipped rooms in an interesting building on a popular street, rooms for 2 (**$$**), dorms for 4 to 8, laundry.

### $ pp Hostel-Inn Buenos Aires
*Humberto Primo 820, T011-4300 7992,*
*www.hibuenosaires.com.*
An old 2-storey mansion with dorms for up to 8 people and also private rooms (**$$**), activities, loud parties and individual lockers in every room.

### $ pp Kilca Hostel & Backpacker
*México 1545, between Sáenz Peña and Virrey Cevallos, T011-4381 1166,*
*www.kilcabackpacker.com.*
In a restored 19th-century house with attractive landscaped patios. A variety of

rooms from dorms to doubles; all bathrooms shared, but 1 double with bath (**$$**). Offers a host of guest services including bike rental, pub crawl, tango classes, Spanish lessons, football tickets and more.

### $ pp Ostinatto
*Chile 680, T011-4362 9639,*
*www.ostinatto.com.*
Minimalist contemporary design in a 1920s building, promotes the arts, music, piano bar, movie room, tango lessons, arranges events, rooftop terrace. Shared rooms, also has double rooms with and without bath (**$$**), and apartments for rent.

### $ pp Sabatico Travelers Hostel
*México 1410, T011-4381 1138,*
*www.sabaticohostel.com.ar.*
Hostel in a good location, with dorms and double rooms with and without bath (**$$**). It offers a full range of services and information, a rooftop barbecue, mini pool and bar.

## Apartments/self-catering/homestays

### Argenhomes
*T011-4044 5978, www.argenhomes.com.*
For those who like attentive, personalized service, this is the best apartment-rental option. A limited selection of charming flats in San Telmo, Recoleta, Belgrano, Palermo and even Tigre. Accepts dollars, euros, pounds and pesos; no credit cards.

### B&T Argentina
*T011-4876 5000, www.bytargentina.com.*
Accommodation in student residences and host families; also furnished flats. Reputable.

### Bahouse
*T011 5811 3832, www.bahouse.com.ar.*
Very good flats, by the week or month, all furnished and well located in San Telmo, Retiro, Recoleta, Belgrano, Palermo and the centre.

### Casa 34
*Nicaragua 6045, T011-4775 0207,*
*www.casa34.com.*
Helpful, with a big range of options.

## Restaurants

Eating out in Buenos Aires is one of the city's great pleasures, with a huge variety of restaurants from the chic to the cheap. To try some of Argentina's excellent steaks, choose from one of the many *parrillas*, where your huge slab of lean meat will be expertly cooked over fiery *carbón* (charcoal).

If in doubt about where to eat, head for Puerto Madero, the revamped docks area, an attractive place to stroll along the waterfront before dinner. There are good places here, generally in stylish interiors, serving international as well as local cuisine, with good service if a little overpriced. Less expensive yet just as delicious and longer-standing parrillas can be found in San Telmo. Take a radio taxi to Palermo or Las Cañitas for a wide range of excellent restaurants all within strolling distance. For more information on the gastronomy of Buenos Aires see: www.guiaoleo.com.ar, a restaurant guide in Spanish.

There is a growing interest in less conventional eating out, from secret, or *puerta cerrada*, restaurants, to local eateries off the normal restaurant circuit, exploring local markets and so on. 3 solid food-oriented blogs in English are: www.salt shaker.net, by chef Dan Perlman who also runs a highly recommended private restaurant in his house, see website for details; www.buenosairesfoodies.com; and the *Yanqui* expat-penned www.pickupthe fork.com. Another highly regarded closed-door option can be found at **The Argentine Experience** (www.theargentineexperience. com), while tours are run by **Parrilla Tour Buenos Aires** (www.parrillatour.com).

Some restaurants are *tenedor libre*: eat as much as you like for a fixed price. Most cafés serve tea or coffee plus *facturas* (pastries) for breakfast.

**Centre** *map page 40.*

### $$$ Dadá
*San Martín 941.*
A restaurant and bar with eclectic decoration. Good for gourmet lunches.

### $$$ Sorrento
*Av Corrientes 668 (just off Florida), www.sorrentorestaurant.com.ar.*
Intimate, elegant atmosphere, one of the most traditional places in the centre for very good pastas and seafood.

### $$$ Tancat
*Paraguay 645, www.tancatrestaurante.com.*
Delicious Spanish food, very popular at lunchtime.

### $$$-$$ Gijón
*Chile y San José.*
Very good-value *parrilla* at this popular *bodegón*, south of Congreso district.

### $$ Fikä
*Hipólito Yrigoyen 782, see Facebook. Mon-Fri open till 1700.*
Popular at lunchtime with a varied menu, this place is also attractive for a coffee break or a drink.

### $$ Gianni's
*Reconquista 1028, www.giannisonline.com.ar. Open till 1700.*
The set menu with the meal-of-the-day makes an ideal lunch. Good risottos and salads. Slow service.

### $$ Güerrín
*Av Corrientes 1368, www.pizzeriaguerrin.com.*
A Buenos Aires institution. Serves filling pizza and *faina* (chickpea polenta) which you eat standing up at a bar, or at tables, though you miss out on the colourful local life that way. For an extra service fee, upstairs room is less crowded or noisy. Try the chicken *empanadas al horno* (baked pies).

## $$ Las Cuartetas
*Av Corrientes 838, www.lascuartetas.com.*
Another local institution open early to very late for fantastic pizza, can be busy and noisy as it's so popular.

## $$ Los Inmortales
*Corrientes 1369, www.losinmortales.com.*
Opposite **Güerrín**, this does some of the city's other best pizza (with a thinner crust). It's also a *parrilla*.

## $$ Sam Bucherie
*25 de Mayo 562. Open till 1800.*
The most imaginative sandwiches and salads downtown.

## Cafés

### Café Tortoni
*Av de Mayo 825-9.*
This most famous Buenos Aires café has been the elegant haunt of artists and writers for over 100 years, with marble columns, stained-glass ceilings, old leather chairs, and photographs of its famous clientele on the walls. Live tango. Packed with tourists, pricey, but still worth a visit.

### El Gato Negro
*Av Corrientes 1669, see Facebook.*
A beautiful tearoom, serving a choice of coffees and teas, and good cakes. Delightfully scented from the wide range of spices on sale.

### Florida Garden
*Florida y Paraguay,*
*www.floridagarden.com.ar.*
Another well-known café, popular for lunch, and tea.

### Ice cream
The Italian ice cream tradition has been marked for decades by '*heladerías*' such as **Cadore** (Av Corrientes 1695, www. heladeriacadore.com.ar), or **El Vesuvio** (Av Corrientes 1181), the oldest of all.

---

**North of Plaza de Mayo** *map page 44.*
3 blocks west of Plaza San Martín, under the flyover at the northern end of Av 9 de Julio, between Arroyo and Av del Libertador in La Recova, are several recommended restaurants.

## $$$ BASA
*Basavilbaso 1328, www.basabar.com.ar.*
Great food and smart cocktails in ultra-chic surroundings. Same owners as other upscale hangout **Gran Bar Danzón**, see Bars and clubs, page 58.

## $$$ El Mirasol de la Recova
*Posadas 1032, elmirasol.com.ar.*
Serves top-quality *parrilla* in an elegant atmosphere.

## $$$ Juana M
*Carlos Pellegrini 1535 (downstairs),*
*www.juanam.com.*
Excellent choice, popular with locals for its good range of dishes, and its excellent salad bar.

---

**Recoleta and Palermo** *map page 44.*

## $$$ Rodi Bar
*Vicente López 1900.*
Excellent *bife* and other dishes in this typical *bodegón*, welcoming and unpretentious.

## $$$-$$ La Madeleine
*Av Santa Fe 1726.*
Bright and cheerful choice, quite good pastas.

## $$$-$$ María de Bambi
*Ayacucho 1821 (with a small branch at Arenales 920). Open till 2200 (2300 Fri and Sat), closed on Sun.*
This small, quiet place is probably the best value in the area, serving very good and simple meals, also *salón de té* and patisserie.

## $$ Al Paso y Algo Más
*Juncal 2684, www.alpasoyalgomas.com.*
Recommended choice for *choripán* and *churrasquito* sandwiches plus other meat dishes.

## Tea rooms, café/bars and ice cream

### Arkakao
*Av Quintana 188, www.arkakao.com.ar.*
Great ice creams at this elegant tea room.

### Bröet
*Azcuénaga 1144, see Facebook.*
Austrian-owned artisanal bakery with traditionally made bread from around the world.

### Clásica y Moderna
*Av Callao 892, T011-4812 8707, www.clasicaymoderna.com.*
One of the city's most welcoming cafés, with a bookshop, great atmosphere, good breakfast through to drinks at night, daily live music and varied shows.

### Como en Casa
*Av Quintana 2, Riobamba 1239, Laprida 1782 and at Céspedes 2647 (Belgrano), www.tortascomoencasa.com.*
In the former convent of Santa Catalina, this place is very popular in the afternoon for its varied and delicious cakes and fruit pies.

### Freddo and Un'Altra Volta
Ice cream parlours, both with several branches in the city.

---

## Palermo
This area of Buenos Aires is very popular with tourists and expats (on the streets you're more likely to hear English spoken than Spanish). There are many chic restaurants and bars in Palermo Viejo (referred to as 'Palermo Soho' for the area next to Plaza Cortázar and 'Palermo Hollywood' for the area beyond the railways and Av Juan B Justo) and the Las Cañitas district. It's a sprawling district, so you could take a taxi to one of these restaurants, and walk around before deciding where to eat. It's also a great place to stop for lunch, with cobbled streets, and 1900s buildings, now housing chic clothes shops. The Las Cañitas area is fashionable, with a wide range of interesting restaurants mostly along Báez.

### $$$ Bio
*Humboldt 2192, T011-4774 3880, www.biorestaurant.com.ar. Daily.*
Delicious gourmet organic food, on a sunny corner.

### $$$ Campobravo
*Báez y Arévalo and Honduras y Fitz Roy, www.campobravo.com.ar.*
Stylish, minimalist, superb steaks and vegetables on the *parrilla*. Popular, can be noisy. Recommended.

### $$$ Don Julio
*Guatemala 4691, www.parrilladonjulio.com.ar.*
Regarded, along with **La Brigada** in San Telmo, as one of the best *parrillas* in the city. The *entraña* (skirt steak) has a sterling reputation.

### $$$ El Manto
*Costa Rica 5801, T011-4774 2409, www.elmanto.com.*
Genuine Armenian dishes, relaxed, good for a quiet evening.

### $$$ El Preferido de Palermo
*Borges y Guatemala, T011-4774 6585.*
Very popular *bodegón* serving both Argentine and Spanish-style dishes.

### $$$ Janio
*Malabia 1805, T011-4833 6540. Open for breakfast through to the early hours.*
One of Palermo's first restaurants, sophisticated Argentine cuisine in the evening.

### $$$ Morelia
*Baez 260 and Humboldt 2005, http://morelia.com.ar.*
Cooks superb pizzas on the *parrilla*, and has a lovely roof terrace for summer.

### $$$ Siamo nel forno
*Costa Rica 5886, see Facebook.*
Excellent true Italian pizzas. The tiramisu is recommended.

### $$$ Social Paraíso
*Honduras 5182, see Facebook.*
*Closed Sun evening and Mon.*

Simple delicious dishes in a relaxed chic atmosphere, with a lovely patio at the back. Good fish and tasty salads.

### $$$-$$ El Tejano
*Honduras 4416, T011-4833 3545,*
*www.eltejanoba.com.ar.*
A delight for those who like to compare and contrast traditional Argentine *asado* with authentic US barbecue. This small eatery showcases expat owner Larry's hot sauces and smoked meats, a model of Texas hospitality.

### $$$-$$ La Fábrica del Taco
*Gorriti 5062, www.lafabricadeltaco.com.*
While not on par with the Real McCoy, it's some of the most authentic Mexican food in South America.

### $$ Krishna
*Malabia 1833, www.krishnaveggie.com.*
A small, intimate place serving Indian-flavoured vegetarian dishes.

### Tea rooms, café/bars and ice cream
Palermo has good cafés opposite the park on Av del Libertador.

### Persicco
*Honduras 4900 and multiple other locations,*
*www.persicco.com.*
The grandsons of **Freddo**'s founders also offer excellent ice cream.

### San Telmo *map page 47.*

### $$$ Brasserie Petanque
*Defensa y México,*
*www.brasseriepetanque.com.*
Very attractive, informal French restaurant offering a varied menu with very good, creative dishes. Excellent value for their set lunch menus.

### $$$ Gran Parrilla del Plata
*Chile 594, T011-4300 8858,*
*www.parrilladelplata.com.*
Popular, good value *parrilla* on a historic corner.

### $$$ La Brigada
*Estados Unidos 465, T011-4361 5557,*
*www.parrillalabrigada.com.ar.*
Excellent *parrilla*, serving Argentine cuisine and wines. The *asado de tira* (grilled short rib, order it *jugoso*) is consistently ranked one of the best cuts of meat in the city. Very popular, always reserve.

### $$$-$$ Naturaleza Sabia
*Balcarce 958, www.naturalezasabia.com.ar.*
Tasty vegetarian and vegan dishes in an attractive ambience.

### Tea rooms, café/bars and ice cream

### Británico
*Brasil y Defensa 399.*
Historic 24-hr place with a good atmosphere at lunchtime.

### Dorrego
*Humberto Primo y Defensa.*
Bar/café with great atmosphere, seating outside on plaza, good for late-night coffee or drinks.

### Dylan
*Perú 1086, see Facebook.*
Very good ice cream.

### La Poesía
*Chile y Bolívar, www.cafelapoesia.com.ar.*
More character than you can shake a stick at. Ideal for a coffee break on the sunny sidewalk.

### Nonna Bianca
*Estados Unidos 425.*
For ice cream in an internet café.

### Pride Café
*Balcarce y Giuffra, see Facebook.*
Wonderful sandwiches, juices, salads and brownies, with lots of magazines to read.

### Puerto Madero *map page 40.*

### $$$ Cabaña Las Lilas
*Av Moreau de Justo 516, T011-4313 1336,*
*www.restaurantlaslilas.com.ar.*
A solid upscale *parrilla* with a good reputation, pricey and popular with foreigners and business people.

### $$$ Le Grill
*Av Moreau de Justo 876, T011-4331 0454,*
*www.legrill.com.ar/esp.*
A gourmet touch at a sophisticated *parrilla*
which includes dry-aged beef, pork and lamb
on its menu.

## Bars and clubs

Generally it is not worth going to clubs
before 0230 at weekends. Dress is usually
smart. Entry can be from US$10-15,
sometimes including a drink. A good way
to visit some of the best bars is to join a
pub crawl, eg **The Buenos Aires Pub Crawl**,
www.buenosairespubcrawl.com, whose
daily crawls are a safe night out.

### Bars
The corner of Reconquista and Marcelo T de
Alvear in Retiro is the centre of the small 'Irish'
pub district, overcrowded on St Patrick's Day,
17 Mar. **Druid In** (Reconquista 1040, Centre), is
by far the most attractive choice there, open
for lunch and with live music weekly. **The
Shamrock** (Rodríguez Peña 1220, in Recoleta,
www.theshamrock.com.ar), is another Irish-
run, popular bar, happy hour until 0000.

### Buller Brewing Company
*Roberto M Ortiz 1827, Recoleta,*
*www.bullerpub.com.*
Brew pub which also serves international food.

### Chez Juanito
*Cabrera 5083, Palermo Soho, next to La Cabrera.*
Cheerful, popular bar serving drinks, snacks
and pizzas. Good for a relaxed evening.

### Gibraltar
*Peru 895, www.thegibraltarbar.com.*
An inauthentic British pub that somehow
does everything right. Popular San Telmo
option and a great place to shoot pool.

### Gran Bar Danzón
*Libertad 1161, www.granbardanzon.com.ar.*
Original BA swank and a good dark ambience
for a cocktail and romance. Same owners as
**BASA** (see Restaurants, page 55).

### La Puerta Roja
*Chacabuco 733 (upstairs).*
The 'Red Door' is San Telmo's best dive.

### Milion
*Paraná 1048.*
In a beautifully restored mansion with
unique (almost unsettling) art on the walls,
supposedly once a favourite haunt of Borges'
widow. Great bartenders, also serves tapas.
Recommended Fri after midnight.

### Mundo Bizarro
*Serrano 1222, Palermo Viejo, see Facebook.*
Famous for its weird films, cocktails,
American-style food, electronic and pop
music. A solid dive bar.

### Seddon
*Defensa y Chile, hbarseddon.blogspot.com.ar.*
Traditional bar open till late with live music
on Fri.

### Sugar
*Costa Rica 4619, Palermo Viejo,*
*www.sugarbuenosaires.com.*
Welcoming bar with cheap beer and drinks,
happy hour nightly, shows international sports.

### Clubs

### Bahrein
*Lavalle 345, Centre, www.bahreinba.com.*
Funky and electronic.

### El Living
*Marcelo T de Alvear 1540 (upstairs).*
Smaller intimate club good for dancing to
80s and Britpop.

### L'Arc
*Niceto Vega 5452, Palermo Viejo.*
Hosts **The X Club** weekly, with a cocktail bar
and live bands.

### Niceto Club
*Niceto Vega 5510, Palermo Viejo, T011-4779
9396, www.nicetoclub.com.*
Early live shows and dancing afterwards.
Club 69 weekly parties for house, electronic,
hip hop and funk music.

**Gay clubs** Most gay clubs charge from US$10 entry. **Amerika** (Gascón 1040, Almagro, www.ameri-k.com.ar, Fri-Sun), attracting more than 2000 party-goers over 3 floors; **Bach Bar** (Cabrera 4390, www.bach-bar.com.ar, Fri-Sun), a friendly lesbian bar in Palermo Viejo; **Sitges** (Av Córdoba 4119, Palermo Viejo, T011-4861 3763, see Facebook, Thu-Sun), a gay and lesbian bar.

**Jazz clubs** **Notorious** (Av Callao 966, T011-4813 6888, www.notorious.com.ar). Live jazz at a music shop with bar and restaurant. **Thelonious** (Salguero 1884, T011-4829 1562, www.thelonious.com.ar), for live jazz and DJs; **Virasoro Bar** (Guatemala 4328, T011-4831 8918, www.virasorobar.com.ar), for live jazz in a 1920s art deco house.

**Salsa clubs** **La Salsera** (Yatay 961, Palermo Viejo, T011-4866 1829, www.lasalsera.com), is highly regarded.

**Entertainment**

**Tango shows**
There are 2 ways to enjoy tango: you can watch the dancing at a tango show. Most pride themselves on very high standards and, although they are not cheap (show only US$50-90, show and dinner US$75-150), this is tango at its best. Most places include drinks and hotel transfers. Or you can learn to dance at a class and try your steps at a *milonga* (tango club). The Tango page on www. turismo.buenosaires.gob.ar lists *tanguerías* for tango shows, classes and *milongas*.

See also the websites www.tangocity.com and www.todotango.com.

Every Aug there is a tango dancing competition, **Festival y Mundial de Baile**, open to both locals and foreigners. **Bar Sur**, *Estados Unidos 299, T011-4362 6086, www.bar-sur.com.ar. Open 2000-0200*. Price with or without dinner. Good fun, the public sometimes join the professional dancers.

**El Querandí**, *Perú 302, T011-5199 1770, www. querandi.com.ar. Daily shows, with or without dinner, also open for lunch*. Tango show restaurant, dating back to 1920s.
**El Viejo Almacén**, *Independencia y Balcarce, T011-4307 7388, www.viejoalmacen.com.ar. Daily, dinner from 2000, show 2200*. Impressive dancing and singing. Recommended.
**Esquina Carlos Gardel**, *Carlos Gardel 3200 y Anchorena, T011-4867 6363, www. esquinacarlosgardel.com.ar*. Opposite the former Mercado del Abasto, this is the most popular venue in Gardel's own neighbourhood; dinner at 2100, show at 2200. Recommended.
**Esquina Homero Manzi**, *Av San Juan 3601 (Subte Boedo), T011-4957 8488, www. esquinahomeromanzi.com.ar*. Traditional show at 2200 with excellent musicians and dancers, dinner (2100) and show available, tango school. Recommended.
**Piazzolla Tango**, *Florida 165 (basement), Galería Güemes, T011-4344 8201, www. piazzollatango.com*. A beautifully restored belle époque hall hosts a smart tango show; dinner at 2045, show at 2215.

**Milongas** These are very popular with younger *Porteños*. You can take a class and get a feel for the music before the dancing starts a couple of hours later. Both tango and *milonga* (the music that contributed to the origins of tango and is more cheerful) are played. It costs from around US$8; even beginners are welcome.
**Centro Cultural Torquato Tasso**, *Defensa 1575, T011-4307 6506, www.torquatotasso. com.ar*. See web for programme and prices (daily lessons), English spoken.
**La Viruta (at Centro Armenio)**, *Armenia 1366, Palermo Viejo, T011-4774 6357, www. lavirutatango.com*. Very popular, classes every day except Mon, entry US$5.50 Mon and Tue, US$6.50 Wed and Sun (check website for times), also salsa, zumba, and rock dancing classes, with restaurant.

## Shopping

The main, fashionable shopping streets are Florida and Santa Fe (from Av 9 de Julio to Av Pueyrredón). Palermo is the best area for chic boutiques, and well-known international fashion labels; head for C Honduras and C El Salvador, between Malabia and Serrano. C Defensa in San Telmo is known for its antique shops. It also has a few craft stalls around C Alsina, Fri 1000-1700. **Pasaje de la Defensa** (Defensa 1179) is a beautifully restored 1880s house containing small shops.

Markets can be found in many of the city's parks and plazas, which hold weekend fairs. You will find they all sell pretty much the same sort of handicrafts.

The city has many fine shopping malls, including **Alto Palermo** (Santa Fe 3253, www. altopalermo.com.ar, Subte line D at Bulnes), the most popular and fashionable mall in the city. There's also **Abasto de Buenos Aires** (Av Corrientes 3247, www.abasto-shopping. com.ar, nearest Subte: Carlos Gardel, line B), in the city's impressive, art deco former fruit and vegetable market building.

## What to do

### Birdwatching
**Aves Argentinas/AOP**, *Matheu 1246, T011-4943 7216, www.avesargentinas.org.ar.* For information on birdwatching and specialist tours. Also has a good library Mon-Fri 1030-1330 and 1430-2030 (closed Jan). A BirdLife International partner.

### Language schools
**Amauta Spanish School**, *Av de Mayo 1370, T011-4383 7706, www.amautaspanish.com.* Spanish classes, one-to-one or small groups, centres in Buenos Aires and Bariloche.
**Argentina ILEE**, *T011-4782 7173, www. argentinailee.com.* Recommended by individuals and organizations alike, with a school in Bariloche.

## Tour operators and travel agents
Guided tours are organized by the city authorities, including a Pope Francis tour (0900 and 1500) throughout the city and bike tours in Palermo parks, both on weekends and holidays only: free leaflet from city-run offices and other suggested circuits on city website.
**Buenos Aires Bus (Bus Turístico)**, *www. buenosairesbus.com.* Open yellow double-decker buses follow 2 routes every 20 mins, 3½ hrs covering main sights from La Boca to Núñez with multilingual recorded tours. 1-day pass (US$24) and 2-day pass (US$32) hop-on/ hop-off tickets can be purchased online or on board. Find bus stops on website or on map provided at city's tourist offices.
**Buenos Aires Vision**, *Esmeralda 356, p 8, T011-4394 4682, www.buenosaires-vision. com.ar.* City tours and tango (cheaper without dinner).
**Cultour**, *T011-5624 7368 (mob), www.cultour. com.ar.* A highly recommended walking tour of the city, 3-4 hrs led by a group of Argentine history/tourism graduates. In English and Spanish.
**Eternautas**, *Av Julio A Roca 584 p 7, T011-5031 9916, www.eternautas.com.* Historical, cultural and artistic tours of the city guided in English, French or Spanish by academics from the University of Buenos Aires, flexible.
**Kallpa**, *Tucumán 861, p 2, T011-5278 8010, www.kallpatour.com.* Tailor-made tours to natural and cultural destinations including Patagonia.
**Mai10**, *Av Córdoba 657, p 3, T011-4314 3390, www.mai10.com.ar.* High-end, personalized tours for groups and individuals, covers the whole country, special interests include art, cuisine, estancias, photo safaris, fishing and many more.
**Say Hueque**, *branches in Palermo at Thames 2062, T011-5258 8740, and in San Telmo at Chile 557, T011-4307 3451, www.sayhueque.com.* Recommended travel agency offering good-value tours aimed at independent travellers, friendly English-speaking staff.

**Tangol**, *Florida 971, PB local 31, Centro, and Defensa 831, San Telmo, T011-4363 6000, www.tangol.com*. Friendly, independent agency specializing in football and tango, plus various other sports, such as polo and paragliding. Can arrange tours, plane and bus tickets, accommodation. English spoken. Discounts for students. Overland tours in Patagonia Oct-Apr.

## Transport

### Air

**Ezeiza** (officially Ministro Pistarini, T011-5480 6111, www.aa2000.com.ar), the international airport, is 35 km southwest of the centre (also handles some domestic flights). The airport has 3 terminals: 'A', 'B' and 'C'. There are duty free shops (expensive), ATM and exchange facilities at **Banco Nación** (terminal 'A') (only change the very minimum to get you into the city), a **Ministerio de Turismo** desk, and a post office (Mon-Fri 1000-1800, Sat 1000-1300). No hotels nearby, but there is an attractive B&B 5 mins away with transfer included: **$$$ Bernie's**, Estrada 186, Barrio Uno, T011-4480 0420, www.posadabernies.com, book in advance.

There is a **Devolución IVA/Tax Free** desk (return of VAT) for purchases over the value of AR$70 (ask for a Global Refund check plus the invoice from the shop when you buy). A hotel booking service is at the Tourist Information desk; staff are helpful, but prices are higher if booked in this way.

For Transport from **Ezeiza** and **Aeroparque** airports, see Finding your feet, page 38. For transport to Ezeiza airport, take a **Manuel Tienda León** bus (office and terminal at Av Madero 1299 y San Martín, behind the **Sheraton Hotel** in Retiro; take a taxi from the terminal; do not walk outside, T0818-888-5366, www.tiendaleon.com). **Manuel Tienda León** will also collect passengers from addresses in centre for a small extra fee, book the previous day.

**Aeroparque** (officially Jorge Newbery Airport, T011-5480 6111, www.aa2000.com.ar) handles all internal flights, and some flights to neighbouring countries. On the 1st floor there is a *patio de comidas* (food hall) and many shops. At the airport there is also tourist information, car rental, bus companies, ATM, public phones and luggage deposit (ask at information desk in sector B). **Manuel Tienda León** buses run to Aeroparque (see above for address) from Puerto Madero, more or less hourly, 24 hrs a day, a 20-min journey, US$6. If going to the airport, make sure it goes to Aeroparque by asking the driver.

The helpful **Argentine Youth and Student Travel Organization** runs a Student Flight Centre, Florida 835, p 3, oficina 320, T0810-4328 7907, www.almundo.com.ar, Mon-Fri 0900-2000, Sat 0900-1500 (with many branches in BA and around the country). Booking for flights, hotels and travel; information for all South America, noticeboard for travellers, English and French spoken. Cheap fares also at **TIJE**, San Martín 601, T011-5272 8453 or branches at Av Santa Fe 898, T011-5272 8450, and elsewhere in the city, Argentina, Uruguay and Chile, www.tije.com.

## Bus
**Local** City buses are called *colectivos* and cover a very wide radius. They are clean, frequent, efficient and very fast. *Colectivo* fares are calculated in 3-km sections, US$0.50, but fares are cheaper if you have a pre-paid smart card called *Sube* (see www.xcolectivo.com.ar for details). If not using a smart card, have coins ready for ticket machine as drivers do not sell tickets, but may give change. The bus number is not always sufficient indication of destination, as each number may have a variety of routes, but bus stops display routes of buses stopping there and little plaques are displayed in the driver's window. A rapid transit system, **Metrobús**, incorporating existing bus routes, runs along Av 9 de Julio.

See www.omnilineas.com.ar for city guides listing bus routes.

**Long distance** The bus terminal for all international and interprovincial buses is at Ramos Mejía y Antártida Argentina (Subte Line C), behind Retiro station, T011-4310 0700, www.tebasa.com.ar. The terminal is on 3 floors.

Bus information is at the Ramos Mejía entrance on the middle floor. Ticket offices are on the upper floor, but there are hundreds of them so you'll need to consult the list of companies and their office numbers at the top of the escalator. They are organized by region and are colour coded. The Buenos Aires city information desk is on the upper floor. It is advisable to go to the bus station the day before you travel to get to know where the platforms are so that when you are fully laden you know exactly where to go. At the basement and ground levels there are left-luggage lockers; tokens are sold in kiosks; for large baggage, there's a *guarda equipaje* on the lower floor. For further details of bus services and fares, look under proposed destinations. There are no direct buses to either of the airports.

## Car
Driving in Buenos Aires is no problem, provided you have eyes in the back of your head and good nerves. Traffic fines are high and police look out for drivers without the correct papers. Car hire is cheaper if you arrange it when you arrive rather than from home. Companies include **Localiza**, Cerrito 1575, T0800-999 2999, www.localiza.com/argentina/es-ar; **Ruta Sur**, T011-5238 4071, www.rutasur.eu, rents 4WDs and motorhomes; and **Sixt**, Cerrito 1314, www.sixt.com.ar.

## Metro (Subte)
7 lines link the outer parts of the city to the centre. **Line 'A'** runs under Av Rivadavia, from Plaza de Mayo to San Pedrito (Flores). **Line 'B'** from central Post Office, on Av L N Alem,

under Av Corrientes to Federico Lacroze railway station at Chacarita, ending at Juan Manuel de Rosas (Villa Urquiza). **Line 'C'** links Plaza Constitución with the Retiro railway station, and provides connections with all the other lines but 'H'. **Line 'D'** runs from Plaza de Mayo (Catedral), under Av Roque Sáenz Peña (Diagonal Norte), Córdoba, Santa Fe and Palermo to Congreso de Tucumán (Belgrano). **Line 'E'** runs from Plaza de Mayo (Cabildo, on C Bolívar) through San Juan to Plaza de los Virreyes (connection to Line 'P' or Premetro train service to the southwest end of the city). **Line 'H'** runs from Corrientes, via Once to Hospitales (Parque Patricios), under Av Jujuy and Av Almafuerte. Note that 3 stations, 9 de Julio (Line 'D'), Diagonal Norte (Line 'C') and Carlos Pellegrini (Line 'B') are linked by pedestrian tunnels. The fare is US$0.30, the same for any direct trip or combination between lines; magnetic cards (for 1, 2, 5, 10, or 30 journeys) must be bought at the station before boarding; only pesos accepted. Trains are operated by **Metrovías**, T0800-555 1616, www.metrovias. com.ar, and run Mon-Sat 0500-2200/2300 (Sun 0800-2230). Line A, the oldest was built in 1913, the earliest in South America. Backpacks and luggage allowed. Free map (if available) from stations and tourist office.

## Taxi

Taxis are painted yellow and black, and carry Taxi flags. Fares are shown in pesos. The meter starts at US$1.40 when the flag goes down; make sure it isn't running when you get in. A fixed rate of US$0.15 for every 200 m or 1-min wait is charged thereafter. The fare from 2200 to 0600 starts at US$1.70, plus US$0.18 for every 200 m or 1-min wait. A charge is sometimes made for each piece of hand baggage (ask first). Tipping isn't mandatory, but rounding the change up is appreciated. For security, take a *remise* or radio taxi booked by phone or at the company's office. Check that the driver's licence is displayed. Lock doors on the inside. The 2 airports and Retiro bus station are notorious for unlicensed taxi crime; use the airport buses and *remises* listed on page 38, and taxis from the official rank in the bus terminal which are registered with police and safe.

**Radio taxis** are managed by several different companies. Phone a radio taxi from your hotel (they can make recommendations), a phone box or *locutorio*, giving the address where you are, and you'll usually be collected within 10 mins. **City**, T011-4585 5544; **Porteño**, T011-4566 5777, www.radiotaxiportenio.com; **Premium**, T011-5238 0000, www.taxipremium.com; **Tiempo**, T011-4854 3838, www.radiotaxi tiemposrl.com.ar.

*Remise* taxis operate all over the city, run from an office and have no meter. The companies are identified by signs on the pavement. Fares are fixed and can be cheaper than regular taxis, verifiable by phoning the office, and items left in the car can easily be reclaimed. **Universal**, T011-4105 5555, www.remisesuniversal.com.

## Tram

Old-fashioned trams operate Mar-Nov on Sat and holidays 1600-1930 and Sun 1000-1300, 1600-1930 and Dec-Feb on Sat and holidays 1700-2030, Sun 1000-1300, 1700-2030, free, and depart every 20 mins on a circular route along the streets of Caballito district, from C Emilio Mitre 500, Subte Primera Junta (Line A) or Emilio Mitre (Line E), no stops en route. Operated by **Asociación Amigos del Tranvía**, T011-4431 1073, www.tranvia.org.ar.

# Argentine
# Lake District

Trek amongst craggy snow-capped peaks flanked by glaciers and crystalline rivers running through virgin Valdivian rainforest to lakes of peppermint green and Prussian blue.

Ski down long pistes with panoramic views of lagoons below, or hike for days among remote mountain tops. Take a slow boat across fjords or a hair-raising whitewater rafting trip. Whatever you choose to do, Argentina's Lake District is spectacular and unforgettable.

Bariloche is the main tourist centre, a friendly but large town in alpine style with chocolate shops, lakeside hotels and chalet-style restaurants. Towering above is a range of peaks where you can hike, ski or cycle.

A magical road winds north from here through seven lakes and three national parks to the pretty tourist towns of Villa La Angostura and San Martín de los Andes. Retreat to Lago Huechulafquen, where perfectly conical Volcán Lanín is reflected in cobalt blue waters. North of here, it's wilder and less visited. Pehuenia is a quiet haven with forests of prehistoric monkey puzzle trees, broad lagoons and the rich culture of the native Mapuche people.

At the southern end of the lakes, El Bolsón and Esquel are wonderfully relaxed places for a few days' hiking. Take the *Old Patagonian Express*, try a Welsh tea in quaint Trevelin, and then explore the region's most unspoilt national park, Los Alerces.

**Best** for
Camping ▪ Skiing ▪ Trekking

# Footprint
## picks

★ **Villa Pehuenia**, page 76

Monkey puzzle trees are in
abundance at this remote lakeside retreat.

★ **Bariloche**, page 108

Ski, trek or camp in the untouched wilderness just outside this most
famous of towns in the Lake District.

★ **Estancia Peuma Hue**, pages 120 and 122

A true Argentine estancia experience offering horse riding, kayaking
and world-class fly-fishing.

★ **Mount Tronador**, page 127

Mountaineering at its finest, with glaciers, coihue forests and panoramic
views of Lago Nahuel Huapi.

★ **Parque Nacional Los Alerces**, page 148

Patagonian steppe meets Andean forest in an area known for glassy
lakes, snow-capped peaks and the famed alerce tree.

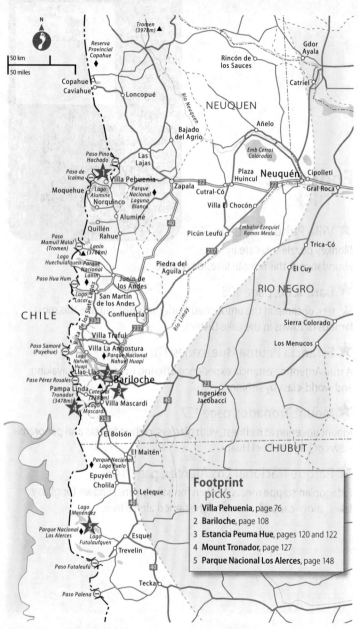

**Footprint**
picks

1 **Villa Pehuenia**, page 76
2 **Bariloche**, page 108
3 **Estancia Peuma Hue**, pages 120 and 122
4 **Mount Tronador**, page 127
5 **Parque Nacional Los Alerces**, page 148

# Eastern &
## central Neuquén

The northern half of the Lake District falls into the province of Neuquén, encompassing an enormous region that stretches from the border with Mendoza, beyond Copahue and Caviahue in the north, to just north of Bariloche in the south.

The provincial capital is the pleasant modern city of Neuquén, centre of an important fruit-growing area, providing most of Argentina's apples, pears and grapes.

You're likely to stop off only briefly here on the way to greater adventures in the mountains further west, but it's worth making time for a brief encounter with dinosaurs at several sites easily reached from Neuquén city. There are incredibly huge dinosaur footprints and a good museum at Villa El Chocón, where you can see proof that the largest carnivores ever known actually stomped around these lands 100 million years ago. You could try a spot of excavation yourself at Valle Cretacico or see the skeleton of the largest herbivorous dinosaur on earth in Plaza Huincul. For more information, see www.neuquen.com.

# **Essential** Lake District

## Finding your feet

### Air

There are several flights daily from Buenos Aires to Neuquén, Chapelco (for Junín and San Martín de los Andes), Bariloche and Esquel (for the southern lakes), as well as flights from Santiago in Chile to Bariloche. The army airline **LADE** runs weekly flights connecting Bariloche with other Patagonian towns. If you're short on time, flying is preferable to long bus journeys, and it's inexpensive. Consider buying two singles (same price as a return), flying to San Martín de los Andes in the north and leaving from Esquel in the south, allowing you to see the whole area by hired car or bus. Book well in advance from December to March.

### Bus

Long-distance buses connect Neuquén and Bariloche with Buenos Aires, other major cities in Argentina and the Chilean border. But distances are huge so it's better to fly.

### Train

One of the country's few long-distance railways, the *Tren Patagónico*, runs to Bariloche from Viedma, a comfortable overnight service that also carries cars. See www.trenpatagonico-sa.com.ar.

## Getting around

### Bicycle

The area is fabulous for cycling. Avoid cycling in January and early February when it's busy with traffic. There are good bike shops in Bariloche and San Martín. You can also rent bikes, although they're not of the highest standard. Carry plenty of food and water.

### Boat

There are lots of boat trips around Lago Nahuel Huapi. The Three Lakes Crossing to Chile from Bariloche is a good way of getting to Puerto Montt in Chile, but the bus is cheaper. For more on the Three Lakes Crossing, see box, page 124.

### Bus and car

Hiring a car is the most flexible option but distances are huge. There are excellent bus services around Bariloche and regular bus services running between Junín de los Andes, San Martín de los Andes, Bariloche and El Bolsón, and on to Esquel, with less frequent services via Cholila, Lagos Puelo and Epuyen. Many big buses will take bicycles; book beforehand. The national parks are less easy to access by bus, although there is a daily bus linking Los Alerces and Esquel. Reaching Pehuenia and the dinosaur region near Neuquén is almost impossible by bus.

It's best to visit the northern lakes by car or on a tour. Car hire is easiest in Bariloche, but is also possible in San Martín de los Andes, El Bolsón, and Esquel. Tell the car rental company if you're taking a hire car into Chile.

### Walking

There are plenty of *refugios* in the mountains behind Bariloche, near Pampa Linda, around El Bolsón, and in Los Alerces and Lanín national parks. Get advice from park offices or **Club Andino offices** (see page 19).

## When to go

Summer (December to February) is the obvious time to come, but January is impossibly busy. In summer, *tábanos* (horseflies) are common on lakes and at lower altitudes. In March and early April there are far fewer visitors. Late spring and early summer (October to November) can be lovely, though cool, and also busy. Autumn has brilliant displays of autumn leaves in late April and early May. The ski season runs from late June to September and is busiest in July, when prices rise and Bariloche is inundated. Hotels are all more expensive in peak periods, with the highest prices in January and July.

**dinosaur fossils offer a prehistoric welcome**

The provincial capital is at the eastern tip of the province and is an attractive industrial town, founded in 1904, just after the arrival of the railway. It's on the opposite side of the Río Neuquén from Cipolletti, a prosperous centre of the Río Negro fruit-growing region. While it has no major tourist attractions, it's a useful stopping point for the lakes and also a good base for exploring the dinosaur finds in the area to the immediate southwest.

## Sights

At the northern end of Avenida Argentina at the Parque Centenario is the **Mirador Balcón del Valle** with panoramic views over the city and the confluence of the rivers (be sure not to take the bus to Centenario industrial suburb). The city is home to the **Museo Paleontológico de la Universidad Nacional del Comahue**, but as of 2016 is closed indefinitely. Consult the tourist office (see Tourist information, below) about the possible reopening of the museum as well as exhibitions of dinosaur fossils found in the region. The **former railway station**, at Olascoaga and Pasaje Obligado, has been converted into a cultural centre and exhibition centre.

South of the centre there is a pleasant walk along the Río Limay. There's also the **Bodega del Fin del Mundo** ① *R8, Km 9, near San Patricio de Chañar, T0299-15-580 9085, www.bodegadelfindelmundo.com, Tue-Sun 1000-1630.* Free tours take an hour and include a tasting.

## Routes to the lakes

From Neuquén, there are various ways to approach the lakes. An attractive route involves continuing due west to Zapala on Ruta 22, and then south to Junín de los Andes on Ruta 40. Or from Zapala, you could continue west to Villa Pehuenia, or north to Caviahue and Copahue. For the direct route to Bariloche, take Ruta 237, via **Piedra del Aguila** and Confluencia and the astounding scenery of the **Valle Encantado**, with mountains whipped into jagged peaks. The road continues to Lago Nahuel Huapi where there are fine views over Cerros Catedral and Tronador.

## Essential Neuquén city

### Finding your feet

The **airport is** 7 km west of town. A taxi costs US$8-10 or take city buses No 10 or 11. The **bus terminal** is at Ruta 22 y Solalique, 4 km west of town. A taxi to the centre costs US$4-5.

### Getting around

The town can easily be explored on foot in a few hours, with most hotels and restaurants around the main street Avenida Argentina, which runs north from the disused railway track running east–west across the town, just south of General San Martín. Don't get confused with the street Félix San Martín, three blocks further south. Note that city buses, **Indalo**, take rechargeable magnetic cards, sold at the bus terminal and elsewhere, from US$1.75.

### Useful addresses

**Chilean consulate**, La Rioja 241, T0299-442 2447.

## Useful websites

To plan your trip and for more information before you come, check out these sites: www.neuquentur.gob.ar (in English); www.trekbariloche.com (trekking information, in English); www.interpatagonia.com (excellent site for general information on the area in English); www.clubandino.org (for walks and mountain climbing); www.activepatagonia.com.ar (hiking and trekking expeditions); and www.revistapatagonia.com.ar (a useful magazine).

## Listings Neuquén city

### Tourist information

**Municipal tourist office**
*Av Argentina y Roca 8300, T0299-15-576 4264. Mon-Fri 0700-1400 (summer), 0800-1500 (winter).*
There's another tourist office at the bus terminal, T0299-449 1200 ext 4354.

**Tourist office**
*Félix San Martín 182, T0299-442 4089, and El Ceibo 438, Barrio Alta Barda, T0299-449 1200, www.neuquentur.gob.ar, www.neuquen.com. Daily 0800-2100.*
Provides helpful lists of accommodation and a map.

### Where to stay

**$$$$ Del Comahue**
*Av Argentina 377, T0299-443 2040, www.hoteldelcomahue.com.*
4-star, extremely comfortable, spa, pool, good service, wine bar and excellent restaurant, **1900 Cuatro**, specializing in Patagonian fare.

**$$$ Hostal del Caminante**
*JJ Lastra (Ruta 22, Km 1227), 13 km west of Neuquén, towards Zapala, T0299-444 0118, www.hostaldelcaminante.com.*
A comfortable suburban place set among fruit plantations with garden, swimming pool and restaurant.

**$$$ Royal**
*Av Argentina 143, T0299-448 8902, www.hotelroyal.com.ar.*
Central hotel with all services, free continental breakfast, parking.

**$ Hostel Punto Patagónico**
*Periodistas Neuquinos 94, T0299-447 9940, www.puntopatagonico.com.*
A bit out of the centre, good hostel, breakfast, rustic furniture. Recommended.

### Restaurants

**$$$-$$ La Toscana**
*Lastra 176, T0299-447 3322, www.latoscanarestaurante.com.*
Rustic cuisine in chic surroundings. Extensive wine list.

**$$ El Ciervo**
*Argentina 219.*
Good central option featuring an abundance of fresh seafood dishes.

### What to do

**Arauquen**, *H Yrigoyen 720, T0299-442 5101, www.arauquen.com.* Great local agency that can organize day tours and trips further afield.

### Transport

**Air**
Flights to **Buenos Aires** (daily) and **Comodoro Rivadavia**; LADE also flies

to **Bariloche**. Schedules change frequently.
**Airport**, T0299-440 0245, www.anqn.com.ar.

**Bus**
The bus terminal (T0299-445 2300) is
huge and modern, with lots of services
and clean toilets.

Many companies to **Buenos Aires**, daily,
15-19 hrs, US$88-100. To **Zapala**, daily, 3 hrs,
US$12-16. To **Junín de los Andes**, 5-6 hrs,
US$23-36, with **Albus**, T0810-333 7575, www.
albus.com.ar. To **San Martín de los Andes**,

7 hrs, US$25-40, **Albus**. Also **Albus** daily to
**Villa Pehuenia**, 7 hrs, US$33, and **Aluminé**,
6 hrs, US$25 (less predictable in winter,
when the roads are covered in snow.
To **Bariloche**, many companies, 5-6 hrs,
US$25-39, sit on left. To **Mendoza**, with
**Andesmar**, **Cata**, and others, daily, 12-13 hrs,
US$52-75. To **Chile**: several companies,
eg **Albus**, run to **Temuco**, 12-14 hrs, US$28,
also from Zapala. Buy Chilean pesos before
leaving. See box, page 78.

See box, page 78.

## South and west of Neuquén

*follow the rivers that feed the lakes*

To the southwest of Neuquén lies the huge lake Embalse Ezequiel Ramos Mexía in
an area that has become famous in recent years for the wealth of dinosaur fossils
found here from the Cretaceous period (100 million years ago). There are a number of
places where you can see the finds and even walk close to the footsteps of dinosaurs.
The towns themselves are not appealing, but they make convenient stopping points
along the road from Neuquén to the lakes, with a good museum at Villa El Chocón.

### Villa El Chocón *Colour map 1, A5.*
*For information on reaching the footprints and how they were formed, see www.
interpatagonia.com/paseos/huellas (in English).*
.............................................................................................................................

Your only reason to visit Villa El Chocón at the northern end of Lago Ezequiel Ramos Mexía,
72 km from Neuquén, is to see the remains of dinosaurs. It's a neat, rather uninspiring
town, a strictly functional place built for workers on the hydroelectric dam. To see the
amazing evidence of **dinosaurs**, take Route 237 towards Piedra del Aguila and turn
left at Barrio Llanquén, where indicated, to the lake shore. Red sedimentary rocks have
preserved, in relatively good condition, bones and even footprints of the creatures that
lived in this region during the Cretaceous period about 100 million years ago. Some of
the fossils can be seen in the **Museo Paleontológico Ernesto Bachmann** ① *Civic Centre,
El Chocón, T0299-490 1223, www.interpatagonia.com/paseos/ernestobachmann, daily
0800-1830, US$1.50*, where there's a well laid out and informative display and guides give
very good tours. Exhibits include fossils of the mighty 10-ton, 15-m-long *Gigantosaurus
carolinii*, a carnivorous dinosaur larger than the famous *Tyrannosaurus rex*.

### Excavation at Valle Cretácico
*www.interpatagonia.com/paseos/valle_cretacico2, has information in English.*
.............................................................................................................................

The lunar landscape around Villa El Chocón is rather amazing and contains a surprising
number of dinosaur remains. So much so that an area has been named 'Cretaceous Valley'.
The valley lies 18 km south of Villa El Chocón, near the Dique, and has improbably shaped
pedestals of eroded pink rock coming out of the blue water. There are two walks beside
the lake to see the dinosaur footprints, which are incredibly well preserved.

## ON THE ROAD

## Walking with dinosaurs

Few countries are as important as Argentina for palaeontologists. The relative abundance of fossils near the surface has made the country a centre for the study of dinosaur evolution. The Ischigualasto and Talampaya parks (in San Juan and La Rioja respectively) have yielded rich evidence of dinosaurs from the Triassic period (225-180 million years ago), among them, the small *Eoraptor lunensis*, 220 million years old.

Patagonia was home to Jurassic dinosaurs (180-135 million years old), with some outstanding examples found here: Cerro Cóndor in Chubut is the only site of Middle Jurassic period dinosaurs found in the Americas, and has given palaeontologists an important breakthrough in understanding the evolutionary stages of the period. The five examples of *patagosaurus* found here indicated that these dinosaurs were social creatures, perhaps uniting for mutual defence. In Santa Cruz, traces of dinosaurs from the Upper Jurassic period have been found in rocks, surprising palaeontologists with the news that dinosaurs could live and breed in arid and desert-like conditions.

The most important discoveries of dinosaurs from the Cretaceous period (135-70 million years ago) have been made in Neuquén and Chubut. Dating from the period of separation of the continents of South America and Africa, these provide evidence of the way dinosaurs began to evolve differently due to geographic isolation. The *Carnotaurus sastrei* found in Chubut has horns and small hands, for example, whereas the Patagonian dinosaurs are huge. The carnivorous *Gigantosaurus carolinii*, found near Neuquén city, was larger even than the better known *Tyrannosaurus rex*, discovered in North America. You'll find dinosaur footprints, eerily well preserved, near Villa Chocón, southwest of Neuquén city. You can even take part in excavation at a site in Cretaceous Valley, and there are remains of the largest herbivorous dinosaur on earth at Plaza Huincul's famous museum.

Trelew on the Atlantic coast has the country's finest dinosaur museum, the Museo Paleontológico Egidio Feruglio (www.mef.org.ar). There's an associated site with 40 million years of history near the Welsh village of Gaiman (see page 174). In 2013, scientists led by MEF researchers discovered the remains of the largest dinosaur found to date: a 40-m-long, 80,000-kg herbivorous Titanosaur found near Trelew.

### Plaza Huincul *Colour map 1, A5.*

There are more dinosaur remains at a quite impressive little museum in the otherwise rather dull town of Plaza Huincul (population 13,000). The road to Zapala, Route 22, leaves Neuquén and passes through the fruit-growing region of the Río Limay and the much duller oil-producing zone. Situated 107 km west of Neuquén, Plaza Huincul was the site of the country's first oil find in 1918. The **Museo Municipal Carmen Funes** ① *on the way into Plaza Huincul, at the crossing of R22 and RP17, T0299-496 5486, Mon-Fri 0900-1900, Sat-Sun 1030-2030, US$0.75*, includes the vertebrae of *Argentinosaurus huinclulensis*, believed to have weighed over 100 tons and to have been one of the largest herbivorous dinosaurs ever to have lived, as well as a nest of fossilized dinosaur eggs. It's mainly a centre for research, and you can see the results of the fieldwork in fossils, photographs and videos, as well as the skeletons themselves. For more information, see www.plazahuincul.com.ar and www.plazahuincul.gov.ar (in Spanish).

## Zapala *Colour map 1, A4.*

Zapala (population 43,000, altitude 1012 m) lies in a vast dry plain with views of snow-capped mountains to the west. It's a modern and rather unappealing place, but you'll need to stop here at the **bus terminal** ⓘ *Etcheluz y Uriburu, T02942-423191,* if you want to take buses to Pehuenia, Copahue and Caviahue, or to cross the border into Chile at the Icalma Pass; see box, page 78.

The **Museo Mineralógico Dr Juan Olsacher** ⓘ *Etcheluz 52 (by bus terminal), T02942-422928, Mon-Fri 0900-1930, free,* is one of the best fossil museums in South America; it contains over 2000 types of mineral and has the finest collection of fossils of marine reptiles and marine fauna in the country. On display is the largest turtle shell from the Jurassic period ever found and an ophthalmosaur, as well as photos of an extensive cave system being excavated nearby.

## Parque Nacional Laguna Blanca
*Colour map 1, A4.*

Covering 11,250 ha at altitudes of between 1200 m and 1800 m, this park is one of only two reserves in the Americas created to protect swans and lies 35 km southwest of Zapala. This is a rare example of high arid steppe, and its 1700-ha lagoon is one of the most important nesting areas of the black-necked swan in Argentina. Other birdlife includes several duck species, plovers, sandpipers, grebes and Chilean flamingos, with birds of prey such as the red-backed hawk and the peregrine falcon nesting on the steep slopes of the *laguna*. The landscape is very dry, and rather bleak, with fierce winds, encouraging only the lowest and most tenacious plant life. A rough track runs round the lake, suitable for 4WD vehicles only. There's a hiking trail which takes in 10 lagoons in all.

Nearby, the **Arroyo Ñireco** has eroded the volcanic rock to form a deep gorge, and it's worth seeking out a small cave, inhabited in prehistoric times and decorated with cave paintings. Southwest of the park Route 46 continues through the spectacular Bajada de Rahue, dropping 800 m in under 20 km before reaching the town of Rahue, 120 km southwest of Zapala.

## Essential Parque Nacional Laguna Blanca

### Access

The park entrance is 10 km from the junction of Route 46 (which runs across the park) with Ruta 40. The *laguna* itself lies 5 km beyond this. There's no public transport, so without your own vehicle the only option is a tour from Zapala. There's a *guardería* post near the southeast corner of the *laguna*, with a **visitor centre** (daily 0900-1600, free).

### When to go

The park is best visited in spring, when young can be watched at many sites around the *laguna*.

### Where to stay

There's free camping by the *guardaparque*; otherwise Zapala has the nearest accommodation; see www.pnlagunablanca.com.ar or www.parquesnacionales.gov.ar.

### What to take

Take drinking water and a hat for the heat.

## Tourist information

### Villa El Chocón

Tourist office
*Ruta 237, T0299-552 0760. Mon-Fri 0800-1500.*

### Zapala

Tourist office
*RN 22, Km 1392, T02942-424296. Daily 0700-2100 in summer, closes earlier off season.*

## Where to stay

### Villa El Chocón

**$$$ La Posada del Dinosaurio**
*Costa del Lago, Barrio 1, Villa El Chocón, T0299-490 1201,www.posadadeldinosaurio. com.ar.*
Comfortable, modern, all rooms have lake view.

### Plaza Huincul

**$$ Hotel Tortorici**
*Av Olascoaga and Di Paolo, Cutral-Co, 3 km west, T0299-496 3730, www.hoteltortorici.com.ar.*
The most comfortable option is this basic but slightly run-down hotel with neat rooms and a restaurant. Can arrange golf on a nearby course.

### Zapala

**$$$ Hue Melén**
*Brown 929, T02942-422407, www.hotelhuemelen.com.ar.*
Good value, decent rooms and restaurant with the best food in town. Try your luck in the downstairs casino.

**$$ Coliqueo**
*Etcheluz 159, opposite bus terminal, T02942-421308.*
Convenient and a reasonable place to stay.

**$$ Pehuén**
*Elena de la Vega y Etcheluz, 1 block from bus terminal, T02942-423135.*
Comfortable and recommended.

## Restaurants

### Zapala

See also Where to stay, above, for hotel restaurants.

**$$ Del Hotel Hue Melen**
*Brown 929.*
Great value for money and has a varied menu.

**$ El Chancho Rengo**
*Av San Martín and Etcheluz, T02942-430956.*
Where all the locals hang out.

## Festivals

All the towns in the valley celebrate the **Fiesta Nacional de la Manzana** (apples are the main local crop) in early Feb.

## What to do

### Zapala

**Mali Viajes**, *Alte Brown 760, T02942-432251.*
**Monserrat Viajes y Turismo**, *Etcheluz 101, T02942-422497.* Both offer traditional day tours to the surrounding area. Can help with bus and plane tickets.

## Transport

### Zapala
**Bus**
To **San Martín de los Andes**, 4 hrs, US$20-25, via Junín de los Andes.
To **Bariloche**, change at San Martín.

# Pehuenia &
## northwest Neuquén

Pehuenia is the area due west of Zapala, running along the border with Chile. It is a wonderful expanse of unspoilt wilderness, which is only now opening up to visitors, around the picturesque villages of Villa Pehuenia and Moquehue. Pehuenia is quite different from the southern lakes, thanks to its large forests of ancient *pehuén* or araucaria – monkey puzzle trees. These magnificent silent forests exert a mysterious force and give a prehistoric feel to the landscape, while the sleepy backwater feel of the villages makes them appealing for a few days' rest or gentle walking.

Further north there are two little-visited tourist centres, useful stopping points if you're heading to Mendoza: Caviahue is good for walking in rugged and unspoilt landscapes or skiing in winter, while bleaker Copahue is known for its high-quality thermal waters.

### a quiet escape nestled amid monkey puzzle trees

The magical and unspoilt region of Pehuenia is named after the unique forests of *pehuén* trees, which grow here in vast numbers. Covering a marvellous open mountainous landscape, these ancient, silent trees create a mystical atmosphere, especially around the lakes of Aluminé and Moquehue, where a pair of small villages provides good accommodation.

Villa Pehuenia is the best set up for tourism, with its picturesque setting on the lakeside, a cluster of upmarket *cabañas* and one exceptionally lovely boutique hotel, **La Escondida** ① *www.posadalaescondida.com.ar*. Moquehue is quite different in style: more sprawling and relaxed. There are more *cabañas* here, excellent hiking up La Bella Durmiente and good fly-fishing. You can approach Pehuenia from Neuquén city or, even closer, from Temuco over the border in Chile.

## ★ Villa Pehuenia

This pretty village on sprawling Lago Aluminé's northern shore is beautifully set amongst steep wooded hills, and makes a lovely base for a few days' relaxation or gentle walks in the hills and forests around.

This is Mapuche land and was chosen for a settlement when the Mapuche were forcefully flushed out of Buenos Aires province in the late 19th century. It has special significance because seven volcanoes in a chain are visible from here, and because the area abounds with *pehuén* (monkey puzzle) trees, which are sacred to the Mapuche (see box, opposite).

With the rapid building of *cabaña* complexes, tourism is slowly taking off here, and at the moment you have the best of both worlds: an unspoilt feel but enough tourist infrastructure to stay in comfort, with good restaurants.

The centre of the village is just off the main road, Route 13, where you'll find a service station, *locutorios*, food and handicrafts shops, and a pharmacy. There are tour operators who can arrange trekking, boat trips on the lake and bike hire, and there is another area of restaurants and tea rooms by the lake side.

## Parque de Nieve Batea Mahuida
*www.cerrobateamahuida.com.*

Just off the main road, a few kilometres west of town, this reserve was created to protect an area of *pehuén* trees and the majestic Volcán Mahuida (1900 m), which is regarded as sacred by the Mapuche people. The skiing and winter sports area here is one of the few businesses in the area run by Mapuche people, and is good for limited skiing in winter, with snowmobile and snowshoe walking. It's also a lovely place for walking in summer, with tremendous views of all seven volcanoes around. Delicious home-cooked food is served; contact the Mapuche Puel community at the entrance. It takes three hours to walk up here or one hour by bike.

## Walk to Lago Moquehue

For walks through the araucaria forests, drive west from Villa Pehuenia towards Chile for 4 km, until you reach the end of

**Tip...**
Walk onto the peninsula stretching out into the lake from Villa Pehuenia for wonderful walks along the araucaria-fringed shore, and up to the Mirador del Ciprés with fabulous views.

## ON THE ROAD
## Monkey puzzle trees and the Mapuche

The stunningly beautiful area of Pehuenia is remarkable for its forests of araucaria, or monkey puzzle trees (*Araucaria araucana*). Growing slowly to a mighty 40 m high and living for 1200 years, the trees exert a powerful presence when seen en masse, perhaps because their forests are silent, moving little in the breeze. A true conifer, the araucaria is a descendent of the petrified pines found in Argentina's *bosques petrificados*.

For centuries the *pehuén* or araucaria have been revered by indigenous peoples, and the local Mapuche still eat its pine nuts. The custom of collecting their nuts, around which a whole array of foods and a celebratory harvest festival are based, has been the source of a bitter territory dispute in parts of the northern Lake District. The Mapuche feel that they have a natural right to harvest the fruits of their trees, and local landowners, backed by local government, clearly don't agree.

There's a growing respect for the Mapuche in the area, and they are beginning to get involved in the provision of basic tourist services. You'll see *pan casero* (home-made bread), *tortas fritas* (fried pastries) and handicrafts for sale on roadsides, as well as the winter sport centre near Villa Pehuenia, all run by the local Mapuche. These small enterprises enable them to survive financially, while retaining their traditions and customs and, with luck, access to the magnificent araucarias which they hold so sacred.

the lake, where you turn left at the *gendarmería*, following a dirt road across the bridge over a narrow strip of water, La Angostura. Follow the arrow to a campsite 50 m further on, **El Puente** (a delightful place, recommended). Continue past it and, when you come to a little hut and a sign to Lago Redonda, take the right fork and follow the track. Park or leave your bike at the largest of the three small *lagunas*, and take the path due south when the track comes to an end at a farmstead by a large lagoon. Climb from here to a ridge with great views, and then take the path which drops and skirts around **Lago Moquehue** – the view is awe-inspiring. You could walk to Moquehue from here, but you need a map; ask for the *Sendas y Bosques* map of Norte Neuquino, which shows the Pehuenia-Moquehue area, and some paths.

This whole area is the heart of the Mapuche community: many houses offer *pan casero* (home-made bread), horse riding or walking guides.

### Moquehue
Another 10 km on Route 13 brings you to the sprawling village of Moquehue (population 600). It's a wilder, more remote place than Villa Pehuenia, spreading out on the shores of its lake, with a lovely wide river. Famous for fishing, this is a beautiful and utterly peaceful place to relax and walk, and it has a less cultivated feel, inspiring adventurous treks. A short stroll through araucaria forests brings you to a lovely waterfall; a longer hike to the top of Cerro Bandera (four hours return) gives wonderful views over the area, and to Volcán Llaima. There are fine camping spots and a couple of comfortable places to stay. For more information, see www.villapehuenia.org (in English).

### Aluminé *Colour map 1, A3.*
In the splendid Aluminé Valley, on Route 23 between Pehuenia and Junín de los Andes, lies the area's self-proclaimed rafting capital, the small town of Aluminé (population 5000).

**Paso Pino Hachado**

Paso Pino Hachado (1864 m) lies 115 km west of Zapala via Route 22, which is almost completely paved. Buses from Zapala and Neuquén to Temuco in Chile use this crossing. For the Chilean side, including details of immigration and customs, see box, page 264.

**Argentine immigration and customs** 9 km east of the border, daily 0800-2000.
See www.gendarmeria.gob.ar/pasos-chile/pino-hachado.html.

**Paso de Icalma**

Paso de Icalma (1303 m) lies 132 km west of Zapala and is reached by Route 13 (*ripio*). It is used as an alternative border crossing when other crossings at higher altitude are closed due to snow. For the Chilean side, including details of immigration and customs, see box, page 264.

**Argentine immigration and customs** 9 km east of the border, daily 0900-2000.
All paperwork is carried out at the customs office, clearly signposted.

There is indeed superb rafting (Grades II or IV to VI, depending on rainfall) nearby on Río Aluminé. There are places to stay, but despite the lovely setting, it's a drab place. There's a service station, the last between Villa Pehuenia and Junín de los Andes. See also What to do, page 81.

## Rucachoroi

From Aluminé there is access to Lago Rucachoroi, 23 km west, inside Lanín national park. The biggest Mapuche community in the park live here, in gentle farmland surrounded by ancient *pehuén* forests. Access is by a rough *ripio* road, best in a 4WD in winter, and spectacular in autumn when the deciduous trees are a splash of orange against the bottle-green araucarias. The only accommodation is in two campsites, both offering Mapuche food and horse riding. Here too, there's a *guardería* where you can ask about a possible trek to Lago Quillén. The landscape is very beautiful and you will want to linger, but bring provisions and camping gear. Private transport is essential.

## Lago Quillén

At the junction by the small town of Rahue, 16 km south of Aluminé, a road leads west to the valley of the Río Quillén and the exquisite Lago Quillén, from where there are fine views of Volcán Lanín peeping above the mountains. The lake itself is one of the region's most lovely, jade green in colour, with beaches along its low-lying northern coast. Further west, where annual rainfall is among the heaviest in the country, the slopes are thickly covered with superb Andean Patagonian forest. There's no transport, and the only accommodation (with food shop and hot showers) is at **Camping Quillén** ① *T02942-496599, camping.ruka@gmail.com*, on the lake shore. Here you can get advice about walks, and register with *guardaparques* if you plan to hike to Rucachoroi. There's another walk to the remote **Lago Hui Hui**, 6 km north from the second campsite (3½ hours return). For fishing, contact **Estancia Quillén** (see Where to stay, page 80).

## Tourist information

### Villa Pehuenia

**Tourist kiosk**
*Off the main road, by the turning
for Villa Pehuenia, T02942-498044,
www.villapehuenia.gov.ar.*
Along with most hotels, this kiosk has the
excellent free leaflet showing a detailed
map of Villa Pehuenia with all the hotels
and restaurants marked.

### Aluminé

**Tourist office**
*C Christian Joubert 321, T02942-496001,
www.alumine.gov.ar. Daily 0800-2000.*
Very friendly.

## Where to stay

### Villa Pehuenia

You'll find a superb boutique hotel, and plenty
of *cabañas*, many with good views over the
lake and set in idyllic woodland. Email or ring
first for directions, since there are no road
names or numbers here. For more listings,
see www.villapehuenia.org (in English).

**$$$$-$$$ La Escondida**
*Western shore of the peninsula, T02942-15-
691166, www.posadalaescondida.com.ar.*
By far the best place to stay in the whole
area, this is a really special boutique hotel
with just 6 rooms in an imaginatively
designed building on the rocky lakeside.
Each room is spacious and beautifully
considered, with smart bathrooms (all with
jacuzzi), and private decks, all with gorgeous
views over the lake. The restaurant is superb
and non-residents can dine here with a
reservation. The whole place is relaxing
and welcoming. Highly recommended.

**$$$ Altos de Pehuén**
*T02942-15-5383 6300,
www.altosdelpehuen.com.ar.*

Comfortable *cabañas* with lovely views, and
a *hostería*.

**$$$ Cabañas Caren**
*T02942-15-400615, www.cabanascaren.
com.ar.*
Simple A-frame *cabañas*, but with
open views and balconies, and made
especially welcoming by the warm
friendly owner Walter.

**$$$ Complejo Patagonia**
*T02942-15-548787 (T011-15-5011 4470 in
Buenos Aires), www.complejopatagonia.
com.ar.*
Very comfortable indeed, these lovely
*cabañas* are traditionally designed and the
service is excellent. Recommended.

**$$$ Complejos del Lago Aluminé**
*T02942-15-665068, www.villa-pehuenia.
com.ar.*
Complejo La Serena has beautifully equipped
and designed *cabañas* for 2-6 people with
lovely uninterrupted views, gardens going
down to beach, sheltered from the wind
and furnished with rustic-style, handmade
cypress furniture, and wood stoves, all very
attractive. Also has Complejo Culle Lafquen.

**$$$-$$ Cabañas Bahía Radal**
*T02942-498057, www.bahiaradal.com.ar,
on the peninsula (ask the tourist office
for directions).*
Luxurious *cabañas*, with clear lake views
from its elevated position.

**$$$-$$ Las Terrazas**
*T02942-498036, www.lasterrazaspehuenia.
com.ar.*
The owner is an architect, who has retained
Mapuche style in his beautiful design of
these comfortable *cabañas*, which are
tasteful, warm and with perfect views over
the lake. Also with bed and breakfast. He
can direct you to magical places for walking,
and to Mapuche communities to visit.
Recommended.

**\$\$ Puerto Malén Club de Montaña**
*T02942-498007 (T011-4226 8190 in Buenos Aires), www.puertomalen.com.*
Well-built wooden *cabañas* with lake views from their balconies, and the highest-quality interiors. Also a luxurious *hostería* (\$\$\$). Recommended.

## Moquehue

**\$\$ La Bella Durmiente**
*T02942-660993, www.bdurmientemoquehue. com.ar.*
In a rustic building, rooms heated by wood fires, also camping, summer only, the welcoming owner offers good food and also trekking, horse riding, diving in the lake and mountain biking. Call for directions.

### Cabañas

**\$\$\$ Cabañas Los Maitenes**
*T02942-15-665621, www. complejolosmaitenes.com.ar.*
Right on the lake, well-equipped *cabañas*, with breakfast included and friendly owners. Recommended.

**\$\$\$ La Busqueda**
*T02942-15-660377, www. labusquedamoquehue.com.ar.*
Just north of the lake, before you reach the head of Lago Moquehue. Interesting design in these well-equipped *cabañas* with TV, including breakfast. Recommended

### Camping

Along R13, 11 km to Lago Ñorquinco, past mighty basalt cliffs with *pehuenes* all around, there's idyllic camping.

### Camping Trenel
*T02942 487202.*
In a fabulous site elevated on the southern shore of Lago Moquehue, just beyond the **Hostería Moquehue**. Beautiful, well-kept sites in the thick of little *nirre* trees, with seats and *parrillas* overlooking the lake. Smart, hot showers, good restaurant, food shop, information and trips. Recommended.

**Ecocamping Ñorquinco**
*T02942-496155, www.ecocamping.com.ar. Dec or Mar, Apr to Easter.*
There is an amazing rustic *cabaña* right on the lake, with a café by the roadside. Great fishing, hot showers and a *proveduría*. Lovely place to eat if it rains.

**Los Caprichosos**
*On Lago Ñorquinco. Nov-Apr only.*
With water and food shop.

## Aluminé

**\$\$\$ Piedra Pintada**
*T11-4328 0145, www.piedrapintada.com.*
Only 35 km from town, this is the best option. 12 rooms, stylishly fitted out, with a sauna, fantastic views over the lake and impressive restaurant.

**\$\$ Aluminé**
*C Joubert 312, T02942-496174, www.hosteriaalumine.com.ar.*
In the middle of town, opposite tourist information, this is a drab 1960s place, with clean, functional rooms. There's an excellent little restaurant next door, **La Posta del Rey**.

## Rucachoroi
### Camping

There are 2 sites, **Rucachoroi 1** and **Rucachoroi 2**, located before and after the lake (www.campingruka.blogspot.com). Open all year, but ideal only Dec-Feb. The first has more facilities, with toilets, but no hot water, some food supplies, including Mapuche home-made bread and sausages, and horse riding.

## Lago Quillén

**\$\$\$ Estancia Quillén**
*R46 near Rahue, near the bridge crossing Río Aluminé, T02942-496196, www. interpatagonia.com/quillen. Dec-Apr.*
A comfortable, traditionally furnished house, with spacious rooms and a restaurant, where you'll be welcomed by the estancia owners. Great for fishing and hunting.

## Restaurants

### Villa Pehuenia

**$$$ La Escondida**
*On the western shore of the peninsula, T02942-15-691166, www.posadalaescondida.com.ar.*
By far the best in town. Only open to non-residents with a reservation, this is really special cuisine. All local ingredients, imaginatively prepared and served. Highly recommended.

**$$ Anhedonia**
*On the lakeside, T02942-15-469454.*
Fondue, beef and pasta.

**$$ Gnaien Chocolatería and tea room**
*On the lakeside, T02942-498082.*
Good for tea, lovely views of the lake, chocolate delicacies, *picadas* and range of wines.

**$$ La Cantina del Pescador**
*On the lakeside, T02942-498086.*
Fresh trout.

**$ Costa Azul**
*On the lakeside, T02942-498 035.*
Tasty local dishes and pasta; *chivito al asado* (roast kid) is the speciality of the house.

### Aluminé

**$ La Posta del Rey**
*Next to the service station, opposite the plaza, Cristian Joubert, T02942-496174, www.lapostadelrey.7p.com.*
The best place by far, with friendly service, great trout, local kid, delicious pastas and sandwiches. Recommended.

## Festivals

### Villa Pehuenia

Mar **Fiesta del Pehuén**, www.villapehuenia.org (in Spanish). The harvest of the *piñones*, celebrated with riding displays and live music.

## What to do

### Villa Pehuenia

**Los Pehuenes**, *T02942-15-566 4827, www.pehuenes.com.ar.* Excellent company offering wide range of trips and adventures: trekking in the mountains; rafting (Grade IV); horse riding; visits to the local Mapuche communities, with roast kid, and local history and culture; and fishing and boat trips. Professional, helpful and friendly. Ask for Fernando. Can also arrange transfers to Pehuenia from San Martín and Neuquén.

### Aluminé

**Aluminé Rafting**, *Villegas 610, T02942-496322, www.interpatagonia.com/alumine rafting.* Price for 3 hrs' rafting depends on difficulty, Grades II-VI, all equipment included. Options are: Circuito Abra Ancha, 2½ hrs, Grade II, 6 km, very entertaining, suitable for everyone; Circuito Aluminé Superior, 12 or 15 km run, 5-6 hrs, Grade III-IV, very technical river leaving Lago Alumine, for those who like a thrill, passing little woods of araucarias and *ñirres*; family trips Grades I and II. Also offers trekking, kayaking and biking.

## Transport

### Villa Pehuenia

To reach Villa Pehuenia, you could take one of the daily buses from Neuquén city, but these take a long time, and once you're here you may want to explore the area in your own transport so car rental is the best option. Hire a car in Neuquén (3½-hr drive) and drop it off in San Martín de los Andes or Bariloche afterwards. Route 13 continues to the Paso de Icalma crossing to Chile, just a few kilometres from Villa Pehuenia, with easy access to Temuco, 130 km further, on the other side. See box, page 78.

**Albus** (www.albus.com.ar) has daily buses to **Neuquén** via Zapala (less predictable in winter, when the roads are covered in snow), 7 hrs, US$33. Also to **Aluminé**, 1 hr, US$8.

### Aluminé

Buses daily to **Neuquén** via **Zapala**, 3 hrs, with **Albus** (T02942-496672) and **Campana Dos** (T02942-496666). **Albus** also daily to **Villa Pehuenia**, 1 hr.

**a lost world in the Lake District**

About 150 km north of Zapala, the Reserva Provincial Copahue covers an arid, dramatic and otherworldly landscape at whose heart is a giant volcanic crater surrounded by mountains. The park was created to protect the araucaria trees and there are some wonderful walks in unexpectedly stunning landscapes.

There's an ATM at the *municipalidad*, several restaurants and a tea room, as well as some decent accommodation.

## Caviahue and around

**Caviahue** is by far the most attractive of the two towns in this area, with an appealing lakeside setting and opportunities for walking and horse riding; it converts into a skiing and winter sports centre from July to September and swells to a winter population of over 10,000. There are three 22 *pistas*, excellent areas for cross-country skiing, snow-shoeing and snowmobiling, all with tremendous views, and it's one of the region's cheaper resorts.

Volcán Copahue on the Chilean–Argentine border is an active volcano, with recent eruptions in 2013. In 2000 an eruption destroyed the bright blue lake in its crater, but it's still popular for horse riding, and the views of the prehistoric landscape are astounding. The most highly recommended excursion, however, is to **El Salto del Agrio**, 15 km northeast of Caviahue along Route 27. This is the climax in a series of delightful falls, approached by a road passing between tall, ancient araucaria trees poised on basalt cliffs.

## Copahue and around

**Copahue** (1980 m) is a thermal spa resort enclosed in a gigantic amphitheatre formed by mountain walls with the best thermal waters in South America, though it's decidedly the bleaker of the two towns. A fantastic walk is to the extraordinary **Las Máquinas**, 4 km south, where sulphurous steam puffs through air holes against a panoramic backdrop, making the weirdest noises. At **El Anfiteatro**, thermal waters reach 150°C, in a semicircle of rock edged with araucaria trees. Just above Copahue, a steep climb takes you to **Cascada Escondida**, a 15-m-high waterfall surrounded by an araucaria forest; above it Lago Escondida is a magical spot.

## Listings Caviahue and Copahue

### Tourist information

**Caviahue**

Tourist office
*8 de Abril, bungalows 5 and 6, T02948-495408, www.caviahue-copahue.gov.ar.*

**Copahue**

Tourist office
*On the approach road into town, Route 26.*

### Where to stay

**Caviahue**

**$$$ Lago Caviahue**
*Costanera Quimey-Co, T02948-495110, www.hotellagocaviahue.com.*
Better value than the Nevado; comfortable but dated lakeside apartments with kitchen, also a good restaurant and great views. 2 km from the ski centre.

**$$$ Nevado Caviahue**
*8 de Abril s/n, T02948-495053, T011-4313 7639
(Buenos Aires) www.hotelnevado.com.ar.*
Plain, modern rooms, and there's a restaurant
and cosy lounge with wood fire. Also
13 *cabañas*, well-equipped but not luxurious.

**$$ Farallón**
*Caviahue Base, T02948-495085,
www.hotelfarallon.com.ar.*
Neat apartments, some with kitchens.

**$$ La Casona de Tito**
*Puesta del Sol s/n, T02948-495093.*
*Cabañas*, excellent meals.

### Hostels

**$ pp Hebe's House**
*Mapuche y Puesta del Sol, T02948-495138,
www.hebeshouse.com.ar.*
Lovely chalet-style building with great
communal areas and only 2 blocks from the
centre of town. Doubles (**$$**) available.

### Camping

**Copahue**
*T02948-495111, Hueney Municipal.
Summer only.*
Basic but well maintained.

### Copahue

**$$$ Aldea Termal**
*T0299-15 504 7694, www.aldeatermal.com.*
Attractively decorated chalet-style
apartments. Recommended.

**$$$ Hotel Copahue**
*Olascoaga y Bercovich, T0236-442 3390,
www.copahuejunin.com.ar.*
This lovely old place, where you'll be warmly
welcomed by Pocho and Moriconi, is the
most recommended place in Copahue. There
are well-built wood and stone *cabañas*.

## Restaurants

### Caviahue

**$ Hotel Lago Caviahue**
*See Where to stay, above.*
The most stylish place to eat with an inspired
*chivo a la cerveza* (kid cooked in beer),
traditional favourites and local specialities.

### Copahue

**$ Copahue Club Hotel**
*Valle del Volcán T02948 495020.*
Serves good *chivito al asado* and local trout.

## What to do

### Caviahue
To find out about the ski centre, contact
**Caviahue Base** (www.caviahue.com).
**Caviahue Tours**, *Maipu 42, Buenos Aires,
T011-4343 1932, www.caviahuetours.com.*
Good information, including details of
thermal waters.

## Transport

### Caviahue
**Bus**
To **Neuquén**, 6 hrs via Zapala, 4 daily, with
**Conosur**, US$27; tickets can be booked
through **Caviahue Tours**, see above.

# Parque Nacional
## Lanín

Some of the most beautiful sights in the Lake District are to be found in one of the country's largest national parks, Lanín. The park's centrepiece, and its most climbed peak, is the magnificent, extinct, snow-capped Volcán Lanín. Lanín is especially superb seen from the two connected lakes in the centre of the park: Lago Huechulafquen and Lago Paimún. These lakes are the easiest part of the park to visit.

Quiet Lago Lolog further south also offers good fishing, and it's worth the drive to find two more tranquil and very pretty lakes hidden away in the mountains: Lago Curruhué Grande and Lago Chico. Further along the same road, there are thermal waters at Lahuen-Co.

The southern park can be visited easily from San Martín de los Andes, which sits at the head of picturesque Lago Lacar. Northernmost areas of the park are harder to access. But there are several Mapuche communities living in the park who organize campsites and horse riding, making this area interesting to visit.

The whole park is definitely more rewarding if you visit in your own transport, as bus services are sporadic at best, and there is a great deal of unspoilt landscape to explore, varying from lowland hills in the east to steep craggy mountains in the west, all heavily clad in native beech trees, *coihue*, *lenga* and *ñire*.

# Essential Parque Nacional Lanín

## Access

Bus transport into the park is tricky. There are some high season services from Junín de los Andes to Lago Paimún, and **KoKo Bus** (www.empresakoko.com.ar) usually runs a service to Lago Huechulafquen from San Martín de los Andes, although the timetable varies from year to year. To explore the park, you will need to join a tour or have your own transport.

The park has two official entrances. **Lago Huechulafquen** provides the easiest access to the beautifully situated lakes in the centre of the park. To get there, travel west on Route 61 from Junín de los Andes, a good dirt road, as far as the *guardaparque* office at the eastern end of the lake, where you can get free maps and information on hikes. The other entrance to the park is at **San Martín de los Andes**, which is the main tourist centre and gives easy access to Lago Lacar and the River Hua Hum on its western end. It is also the access point for Lago Lolog further north.

The very north of the park is hard to access, since the roads are poor, but it's possible to reach Quillén from Rahue by heading west along Route 46, which is signposted off Route 23. There's little infrastructure when you reach Quillén, but there are Mapuche communities to visit and some rural campsites. For details of this area, see page 78.

## Park information

Park entry is US$10 (paid at the entry point). You're supposed to register at the **park administration**, Perito Moreno 749 y Elordi, San Martín de los Andes, T02972-427233, informeslanin@apn.gov.ar, Monday-Friday 0800-1300, before setting out on any major treks. If you don't manage this, then be sure to notify the *guardaparque* office at the Huechulafquen entrance to the park instead. Ask them about your route and if paths are open. They have two really good free leaflets: one on the park itself and another on climbing Lanín, both with sections in English. You should also check out www.parquesnacionales.gob.ar (Areas Protegidas section) or www.tresparques.com.ar/lanin.

Having a good map is essential: look out for the *Sendas y Bosques* (Walks and Forests) map for Parque Nacional Lanín, 1:200,000, which is laminated and easy to read, with a book containing English summaries of the walks, www.guiasendasybosques.com.ar.

### Tip...

Always put out campfires with lots of water, not just earth because wherever you are in the park, fires are a serious hazard. Make sure you take all your rubbish away with you.

epic hikes in a sprawling national park

## Lago Huechulafquen and around

From Lago Huechulafquen there are fabulous walks up into the hills and along the shore, and along beautiful Lago Paimún further west. Three *hosterías* and great campsites offer accommodation, and there are simple food shops and places to eat. Trips on the comfortable catamaran **José Julián** ① *T02972-428029, www.catamaranjosejulian.com.ar, US$32,* start at Puerto Canoa, on the northern shore of Lago Huechulafquen. This is a fantastic boat trip, offering the chance to see Lanín and the beautiful surrounding mountains from the water, and to reach the relatively inaccessible Lago Epulafquen with its impressive 6-km lava deposit.

## Termas de Lahuen-Co

It's well worth getting to beautiful Lago Curruhué and the thermal pools at **Lahuen-Co** in the far west of the park. You can hike there in two days from Lago Paimún (see below), but if that's too much, they can also be accessed on Route 62, a good dirt road, starting either south of Junín, or from Lago Lolog. Route 62 heads west past Lago Curruhué Chico and Lago Grande, through ancient *pehuén* forests along the southern shores, and then passes the impressive lava field at Laguna Escorial. At the thermal baths there is a fantastic spa and eco lodge (www.lahuenco.com), which organizes tours in the area.

## Trekking routes

There are some delightful walks near Lago Huechulafquen, indicated by yellow arrows; allow plenty of time to return before dark. Guides are only needed for the longer treks where paths are not marked. (For these, ask in the Junín park office or at San Martín de los Andes.) Ask the *guardaparques* for advice on routes before setting off.

**El Saltillo Falls** ① *2 hrs return, fabulous views.* Start from campsite **Piedra Mala** (where you can stock up on provisions) at Lago Paimún, and head west towards the Paimún *guardaparque* office. From here you can also walk on to Río Paimún, three to four hours one way, from Piedra Mala campsite.

**Termas de Lahuen-Co** ① *Best done over 2 days.* Start from beautiful **La Unión**, where Lago Huechulafquen meets Lago Paimún. (To cross to the other side of Lago Paimún at La Unión, there's a boat operated by the local **Mapuche** community, US$5; just ring the bell.) From here, it is an eight-hour walk along the northern shore to reach the western end of Lago Paimún, then four more to reach the Termas. You must consult the book of walks *Sendas y Bosques* for Parque Nacional Lanín, and notify *guardaparques* and the San Martín administration office before setting off. It's a beautiful walk, and you'll be rewarded by a soak in the pools at the end.

**Base of Volcán Lanín** ① *8 hrs return.* A satisfying walk. Start from Puerto Canoa. For other walks and the ascent of Lanín, see box, page 88.

**Cerro El Chivo** ① *2064 m, 8-9 hrs return.* Set off early, and register in campsite at Bahía Cañicul. This is a more challenging walk through forest. Note that heavy snow can lie till January. Potentially dangerous without a guide. See the *Sendas y Bosques* book for Parque Nacional Lanín (see Park information in the box, page 85), and notify the *guardaparques*.

# Parque Nacional Lanín

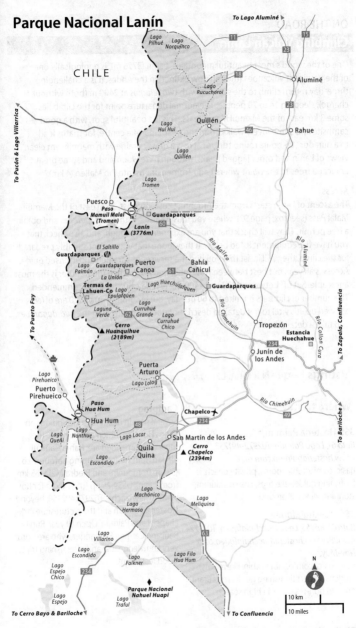

CHILE

To Pucón & Lago Villarrica

To Lago Aluminé ▶

Lago Pilhué
Lago Norquinco

11
15
23
18
Lago Rucuchoroi

● Aluminé

Lago Hui Hui

Quillén ○
46

23
● Rahue

Lago Quillén

Lago Tromen

Puesco ○
Paso Mamuil Malal (Tromen)
□ Guardaparques
▲ Lanín (3776m)
60

El Saltillo

Guardaparques ■
Lago Paimún
Guardaparques □
Puerto Canoa ○
61
Bahía Cañicul

La Unión

Termas de Lahuen-Co □
Lago Epulafquén
Lago Huechulafquen
Guardaparques ■

Laguna Verde
62
Lago Currehué Grande
Lago Currehué Chico

▲ Cerro Huanquihue (2189m)

To Puerto Fuy

Río Malleo

Río Curruhué

Río Chimehuín

Río Aluminé

● Tropezón

Estancia Huechahue

○ Junín de los Andes

To Zapala, Confluencia

Puerta Arturo ○
Lago Lolog

Lago Pirehueico

Puerto Pirehueico ○
Paso Hua Hum
● Hua Hum
48
Lago Nonthué
Lago Lacar
Lago Queñi

✈ Chapelco
234

○ San Martín de los Andes

Río Chimehuín
49

To Bariloche

Quila Quina ○
▲ Cerro Chapelco (2394m)

Lago Escondido

Lago Machónico
Lago Meliquina

Lago Hermoso

Lago Villarino
63
Lago Filo Hua Hum

Lago Escondido
Lago Falkner

Lago Espejo Chico

Parque Nacional Nahuel Huapi ◆

Lago Espejo
234
Lago Traful

To Cerro Bayo & Bariloche ▼

To Confluencia ▼

N

10 km
10 miles

## ON THE ROAD

## Climbing Volcán Lanín

One of the world's most beautiful mountains, Lanín (3776 m), is geologically one of the youngest volcanoes (though now extinct) in the Andes. It is a challenging three-day return climb to the summit, with two *refugios* at 2400 m (both without charge), sleeping 14 to 20 people. The normal departure point for the climb lies some 3 km east of the Mamuil Mamal pass. This is a beautiful spot, with a good campsite and some lovely walks: from the guardaparque centre, footpaths lead to a mirador (1½ hours round trip), or across a grassy prairie with magnificent clear views of Lanín and other jagged peaks, through ñirre woodland and some great araucaria trees to the point where Lago Tromen drains into Río Malleo (4 km).

### Access

The ascent of Lanín starts from the Argentine customs post, 3 km east of the Mamuil Malal Pass (see box, page 93), where you must register with *guardaparques* and obtain a free permit. They will check that you are experienced enough, and also check that you have the equipment listed below. If they judge that you are not suitably prepared for the climb, they will insist that you hire the services of a trained and licensed guide. Access is all year, but best between November and April, when the weather is the most agreeable. Set off between 0800 and 1400 the first day, but 1000 is recommended. The number of climbers is limited to 60 per day, but in summer up to 120 are often allowed up. It's vital to get detailed descriptions of the ascent from the *guardaparques*, and take a detailed map.

---

**Listings** Parque Nacional Lanín *map page 87.*

### Where to stay

**$$$ Hostería Paimún**
*Ruta 61, Lago Paimún, T02972-491758,*
*www.hosteriapaimun.com.ar.*
Basic, comfortable rooms, private beach, fly-fishing guide, lake trips, cosy restaurant, stunning views all around.

**$$$ Huechulafquen**
*Ruta 61, Km 55, Lago Huechulafquen, T02972-427598, www.hosteriahuechulafquen.com. Nov-May.*
Half board, comfortable cabin-like rooms, gardens, expert fly-fishing guide, restaurant open to non-residents in high season.

### Camping

Several sites in beautiful surroundings on Lagos Huechulafquen and Paimún. The most recommended are: **Bahía Cañicul** (48 km from Junín), **Camping Lafquen-co** (53 km from Junín) and **Piedra Mala** (65 km from Junín); US$4.25 pp (US$1 extra for hot water). **Mawizache**, T02972 492150, beyond **Hostería Paimún** and the picturesque little chapel, Lago Paimún. Open all year. Run by Raúl and Carmen Hernández, who are both very knowledgeable and offer fishing trips. Good restaurant.

## Preparation and cautions

Because of its relative accessibility, the risks of climbing Lanín are often underestimated. An authorized guide is absolutely necessary for anyone other than the very experienced, and crampons and ice-axe are essential. Other equipment you will be required to show includes: good walking boots, an all-season sleeping bag, stove and fuel, sunglasses, torch, first-aid kit, walking sticks, helmet and VHF radio (frequency is VHF 155675). Start hydrating 24 hours before setting off and continue doing so as you climb. Take at least two litres of water with you. Eat light and frequent snacks, including bananas, raisins, cereal bars and chocolate. Bring all rubbish down with you. You will be given numbered waste bags for this purpose. On your return, it is essential to check in with the *guardaparques*, so that they can log your safe return.

## Route

To climb the north face, follow the path through *lenga* forest to the base of the volcano, over Arroyo Turbio and up the Espina de Pescado (fish bone), following red and yellow marks. From here the path becomes steeper. Follow the signs to the Camino de Mulas (mule track), and then follow the red markers to reach the Nuevo Refugio Militar (new military shelter). From here keep right to the Viejo Refugio Militar (old military shelter) and the CAJA Refugio. From then on, the ascent is steep and requires ice-climbing techniques. The section to the *refugios* may be done in one day if you set out early and are mentally and physically prepared. See the excellent free leaflet produced by the Parque Nacional Lanín on the ascent, with all GPS references provided and English translation.

## Mountain guiding agency

Alquimia Viajes, O'Higgins 603, Junín de los Andes, T02972-491355, www.alquimiaturismo.com.ar.

## Restaurants

There are lots of places to eat on Lago Huechulafquen, with *provedurías* selling good *pan casero* at Bahía and Piedra Mala. **Mawizache** campsite (see Camping, above) has a great restaurant serving fabulous local dishes very inexpensively, plus hot chocolate and cakes.

## What to do

### Horse riding

You can explore much of the area on horseback, including the trek to the base of Volcán Lanín. 5 places along the lake hire horses: ask *guardaparques* for advice, or ask at the local Mapuche community where you see the signs, *cabalgatas* (horse rides).

### Spas

**Lahuen Co**, *T02972-424709, www.lahuenco. com*. This thermal spa resort can organize trekking, kayaking, biking and fishing trips in the area, and afterwards you can relax in their thermal water pool.

**a haven for anglers**

Situated on the Río Chimehuin, the quiet town of Junín de los Andes (population 10,300, altitude 773 m) is justifiably known as the trout-fishing capital of Argentina. It offers some of the best fly-fishing in the country during the season from mid-November to May. Junín is also an excellent base for exploring the wonderful Parque Nacional Lanín to the west and for climbing its extinct volcano, as well as for rafting on Río Aluminé further north.

Founded in 1883, Junín is a real town, not as picturesque or tourist-orientated as its neighbour, San Martín: there are far fewer chalet-style buildings and few chocolate shops here. But it's a quiet, neat place with genuinely friendly people. The hotels are not as upmarket as San Martín, but **Estancia Huechahue** nearby (see Where to stay, page 92) is superb, and there are some decent family-run hotels here, plus a couple decent

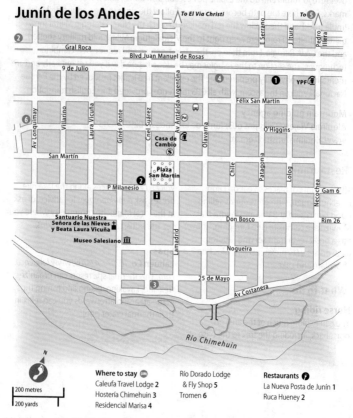

# Junín de los Andes

**Where to stay**
Caleufa Travel Lodge **2**
Hostería Chimehuin **3**
Residencial Marisa **4**

Río Dorado Lodge
& Fly Shop **5**
Tromen **6**

**Restaurants**
La Nueva Posta de Junín **1**
Ruca Hueney **2**

restaurants and *parrillas*, making it worth an overnight stop. Don't forget to try the celebrated local trout.

## Sights

Most of what you need can be found within a couple of blocks of the central Plaza San Martín with its fine araucaria trees among mature *alerces* and cedars. The small **Museo Salesiano** ① *Ginés Ponte and Nogueira, Mon-Fri 0900-1200, 1500-2000*, has a fine collection of Mapuche weavings, instruments and arrowheads, and you can buy a whole range of excellent Mapuche handicrafts in the **Feria Artesanal** behind the tourist office.

There's an impressive religious sculpture park, **El Vía Christi**, situated among pine forest on a hillside just west of town. To get there from the plaza, walk up Avenida Antárida Argentina across the main road, Route 234, to the end. The Stations of the Cross are illustrated with touching and beautifully executed sculptures of Mapuche figures, ingeniously depicting scenes from Jesus's life together with a history of the town and the Mapuche community. It's a lovely place to walk and highly recommended. The church, **Santuario Nuestra Señora de las Nieves y Beata Laura Vicuña**, also has fine Mapuche weavings, and is a pleasing calm space.

Some 7 km away, clearly signposted, at Km 7 on Route 61 towards Lago Huechulafquen, is the **Centro Ecológico Aplicado de Neuquén** (CEAN) ① *Mon-Fri 0900-1400, free*, where trout are farmed, and ñandus and llamas can be seen; it's a good place for kids.

**Fishing** is undoubtedly one of the great attractions of Junín, and the best fishing is at the mouth of the Río Chimehuin, 22 km from town on the road to Lago Huechulafquen. On your way to the national park, stop off here for a moment to appreciate the heavenly turquoise water edged by a black sandy shore. In the town itself, there are pleasant places to fish and picnic along the river, and there are several fishing lodges in the area that cater for experts, with guides whose services you can hire. See also What to do, below.

## Listings Junín de los Andes *map page 90.*

### Tourist information

#### Tourist office
*On the main plaza, Domingo/Padre Milanesio and C Suárez, T02972-491160. Daily 0800-2100 in summer, 0800-2000 in winter.*
Fantastic office with friendly staff who can advise on accommodation and hand out maps. The **Parque Nacional Lanín office** (T02972-492748), is in the same building and is very helpful. See also www.junindelosandes.com.

### Where to stay

**$$$$ Río Dorado Lodge & Fly shop**
*Pedro Illera 378, T02972-492451,*
*www.riodoradolodge.com.*

Comfortable rooms in log cabin-style fishing lodge, big American breakfast, good fly shop, fishing excursions to many rivers and lakes, lovely gardens, attentive service.

**$$$ Caleufu Travel Lodge**
*JA Roca 1323 (on Ruta 234), T02972-492757,*
*www.caleufutravellodge.com.ar.*
Excellent value, welcoming, very good, homely rooms, neat garden, also comfortable apartments for up to 5 people, 3- to 6-night packages and fly-fishing. Owner Jorge speaks English. Recommended.

**$$ Hostería Chimehuin**
*Col Suárez y 25 de Mayo, T02972-491132,*
*www.hosteriachimehuin.com.ar. Closed May.*
Cosy, quaint fishing lodge by the river, fishing and mountain guides. Recommended.

## $$ Residencial Marisa
*JM de Rosas 360 (on Ruta 234), T02972-491175, residencialmarisa@hotmail.com.*
A simple place with helpful owners, breakfast extra, very good value.

## $ pp Tromen
*Lonquimay 195, T02972-491498, see Facebook.*
Small house with dorms and private rooms for up to 4 people. At night take a taxi from the bus station as the streets in the area have no signs or lights.

### Estancias

## $$$$ Estancia Huechahue
*30 km east of town off R234, near Río Collon Curá and junction with Ruta 40, www.huechahue.com.*
The best riding in the Lake District is at this marvellous self-sufficient, traditional Patagonian estancia, where they breed horses and cattle and welcome guests to stay in very comfortable rooms in the main house and in cabins. Other activities on offer include fishing, rafting and walking. Sauna and jacuzzi, great *asados* in the open air. Highly recommended.

## Restaurants

## $$$ Ruca Hueney
*Col Suárez y Milanesio, T02972-491113, www.ruca-hueney.com.ar.*
Good steak, trout and pasta dishes, popular, great atmosphere. The roast lamb might be the best in the country.

## $ La Nueva Posta de Junín
*JM de Rosas 160 (on Ruta 234), T02972-492080.*
*Parrilla* with good service and wine list; also trout, pizza and pastas.

## Festivals

**Jan Agricultural show** and **exhibition of flowers** and **local crafts**, at the end of the month.

**Feb Fiesta Provincial de Puestero**, www.fiestadelpuestero.org.ar. Mid-Feb sees the election of the queen, handicrafts, *asados* with local foods and fabulous gaucho riding. This is the most important country fiesta in the south of Argentina.
**Mar Carnival**.
**Jul Festival of Aboriginal Arts**, mid-month.
**Nov** Opening of the fishing season, 2nd Sat.
**Dec** Inauguration of the church of **Laura Vicuña**, with a special Mass on the 8th and singing to celebrate the life of Laura Vicuña.

## Shopping

**Patagonia Rodeo**, *Padre Milanesio 562, 1st floor, T01972-492839, see Facebook.*
A traditional shop selling what real gauchos wear in the field, plus quality leather work: belts, wallets, saddlery. Look like the real thing before you turn up at the estancias.

## What to do

### Fishing
The season runs from 8 Nov to 1 May. For fly casting and trolling the best places are lakes Huechulafquen, Paimún, Epulaufken, Tromen and Currehue, and the rivers Chuimehuin, Malleo, Alumine and Quilquihué. Ask the helpful tourist office for more information and also see Tour operators, below.
**Río Dorado Lodge**, *Pedro Illera 448, T02972-492451, www.riodoradolodge.com.* The luxury fishing lodge at the end of town has a good fly shop, and organizes trips, run by experts and fishermen.

### Horse riding
**Estancia Huechahue**, *www.huechahue.com.* Located northeast of Junín, this estancia offers unbeatable riding and hospitality. Rides into the national park enable you to reach areas that are otherwise completely inaccessible. Recommended.

## BORDER CROSSING
## Argentina–Chile

### Paso Mamuil Malal (formerly Tromen)

Paso Mamuil Malal is 64 km northwest of Junín de los Andes and reached by *ripio* Route 60 which runs from Tropezón on Route 23, through Parque Nacional Lanín. Parts of the road are narrow and steep, so it is unsuitable for bicycles. On the Chilean side the road continues through glorious scenery, with views of the volcanoes of Villarrica and Quetrupillán to the south, to Pucón, 76 km west of the pass, on Lago Villarrica.

The border is open all year, but is closed during heavy rain or snow (phone the gendarmerie to check, T02972-427339). See www.gendarmeria.gob.ar/pasos-chile/mamuil-mamal.html.

**Argentine immigration and customs**  Puesto Tromen, 3 km east of the pass, daily 0900-2000, co-ordinated with the Chilean side.

**Chilean immigration and customs**  Puesco, 8 km west of the pass, daily 0800-1900.

**Transport**  Buses San Martín run from Junín de Los Andes and San Martín de Los Andes, four to five hours, US$23.

### Tour operators

**Alquimia Viajes and Turismo**, *O'Higgins 603, T02972-491355, www.alquimiaturismo.com.ar.* Offers fishing excursions with expert local guides among a range of adventure tourism options, including climbing Lanín, climbing in rock and ice, rafting, and transfers.

**Tromen**, *Lonquimay 195, T02972-491498, see Facebook.* Trips up Volcano Lanín, horse riding, mountain biking, car rental and bicycle rental.

### Transport

#### Air

Chapelco airport is served by **Aerolíneas Argentinas** from Buenos Aires. The airport is 19 km southwest of town on the road to San Martín de los Andes, with buses to the centre. A taxi will cost around US$20.

#### Bus

The bus terminal is on Olavarría and Félix San Martín (don't confuse it with Gen San Martín), information T02972-492038. There's a public phone but no other facilities. To **San Martín**, with **Albus**, **Ko Ko** and others, 50 mins, US$3-4. To **Buenos Aires**, 20-21 hrs, US$130. To **Chile** (via Paso Mamuil Malal), see box, above.

San Martín de los Andes (population 30,000) is a charming upmarket tourist town in a beautiful setting on the edge of Lago Lacar, with attractive chalet-style architecture and lots of good accommodation. It's an excellent centre for exploring southern parts of the Parque Nacional Lanín including the nearby lakes Lolog and Lacar, where there are beaches for relaxing and good opportunities for rafting, canoeing, mountain biking, trekking and even diving. There is also excellent skiing at the Chapelco resort.

## Sights

The main street, San Martín, runs perpendicular to the *costanera*, and here you'll find most shops and plenty of places to eat. Of the two plazas, the more interesting is Plaza San Martín, which has a sporadic crafts market. It's a pleasant 1½-hour walk north and west up the hill to **Mirador Bandurrias**, with great views. Start at the far northernmost end of the *costanera*, passing the fish trap and walk along the shore before ascending the path, 40 minutes up. Even lovelier, set off from the *costanera* up to **Mirador Arrayán**, where there's a gorgeous tea room, La Casa de Té Arrayán, and *hostería* with spectacular views over the lake.

The town is surrounded by lakes and mountains that are ripe for exploration. In addition to trips around Lago Lacar, the most popular trips are south along the **Seven Lakes Drive** to Lagos Traful, Meliquina, Filo Hua Hum, Hermoso, Falkner and Villarino (see page 100) and north to the thermal baths at **Termas de Lahuen-Co** (see above). Trips to the *termas* via **Lago Curruhué** are offered by tour operators, but you could also cycle or drive there along *ripio* roads from Lago Lolog. There's no public transport to these places at present.

## Lago Lacar

The north shore of Lago Lacar can be explored by car along much of its length, following *ripio* Route 48 towards the Chilean border at **Paso Hua Hum**, 41 km; see box, opposite. **Río Hua Hum** has become a popular place for rafting, with some good stretches of rapids, as the river flows west towards the Pacific; take a tour from an agency in town. You can cycle or walk all the way around the lake on a rough track along to **Lago Escondido** to the south. There are beaches at **Catrite**, 4 km south of San Martín, at **Hua Hum** and at **Quila Quina** on the southern shore, 18 km from San Martín. This is a quieter beach, with a walk to a lovely waterfall along a guided nature trail. There's also a two-hour walk from here that takes you to a tranquil Mapuche community in the hills above the lake. Both Quila Quina and Hua Hum can be reached by boat from the pier in San Martín, T02972-428427: to Quila Quina hourly, 30 minutes each way, US$21 return; to Hua Hum, US$64 return, three daily in season.

## Chapelco ski and summer resort

*19 km south of San Martín, www.chapelco.com.*

**Cerro Chapelco** (2394 m) offers superb views over Lanín and many Chilean peaks. The ski resort is well organized, with 29 km of pistes for skiing and snowboarding, many of them challenging, including several black runs and a lovely long easy piste for beginners. With an overall drop of 730 m and very good slopes and snow conditions, this is a popular resort for wealthier Argentines and, increasingly, foreigners. There's also a ski school and snowboards for hire.

**Essential** San Martín de los Andes

### Finding your feet

The nearest **airport** is Chapelco, northeast of town on Route 234 towards Junín de los Andes (see Transport, above); a transfer costs US$8.50. The **bus terminal** on Villegas y Juez del Valle is reasonably central.

### Getting around

It's easy to orient yourself here as the town nestles in a valley surrounded by steep mountains at the eastern end of Lago Lacar. Beware of confusing street names: Perito Moreno runs east–west, crossing Mariano Moreno, which runs north–south, and Rudecindo Roca which is two blocks north of General Roca.

## Argentina–Chile

### Paso Hua Hum

Paso Hua Hum (659 m) lies 47 km west of San Martín de los Andes along Route 48 (*ripio*), which runs along the north shore of Lago Lacar and crosses the border to Puerto Pirehueico (very tough going for cyclists) 11 km from the crossing. From here, a boat crosses Lago Pirihueico, a long, narrow and deep lake, to Puerto Fuy at its northern end. The border is usually open all year 0800-2000 (Chile open till 1900) and is an alternative to the route via the Paso Mamuil Malal (Tromen); see page 93. See www.gendarmeria.gob.ar/pasos-chile/hua-hum.html.

**Transport** Ko Ko/Lafit (T02972-427422) run buses from San Martín to Puerto Pirehueico, two hours, leaving San Martín early in the morning; check with the terminal for the schedule. They connect with **Somarco** ferries across the lake to Puerto Fuy (T+56 63-228 2742/T+56 2-2322 3900, www.barcazas.cl). These run three times a day in January to February, but at 1300 only the rest of the year. Fares are US$1.30 for foot passengers, US$7.50 for motorbikes and US$25 for cars; bicycles are also taken. Buses connect Puerto Pirehueico with Panguipulli, from where transport is available to other destinations in the Chilean Lake District. For further information, contact the tourist office in Panguipulli, T+56 63-231 0436, or see www.sietelagos.cl and www.municipalidadpanguipulli.cl.

The price of a day pass varies from US$75 in high season (10-30 July). There is a daily bus in high season from San Martín to the slopes, US$8 return, with **Siete Lagos Turismo** ⓘ *T02972-427877*. Details of the resort, passes and equipment hire are available in season from the **Chapelco office** ⓘ *Moreno 859, T02972-427845, www.sanmartindelosandes.gov.ar*. At the foot of the mountain is a restaurant and base lodge, with three more restaurants on the mountain and a small café at the top.

In summer this is a good place for cycling (take your bike up on the cable car then cycle down), trekking, archery or horse riding.

## Listings San Martín de los Andes and around

## Tourist information

### Tourist office
*San Martín y J M de Rosas 790, on the main plaza, T02972-427347, www.sanmartinde losandes.gov.ar/turismo, www.sanmartinde losandes.com (in English). Daily 0800-2100.*
This large and helpful tourist office hands out maps and has lists of accommodation, with prices up on a big board. The staff speak English and Portuguese, but are very busy in summer, when it's advisable to go early in the day before they get stressed. Also check out www.chapelco.com.

## Where to stay

There are 2 high seasons, when rates are much higher: Jan/Feb and Jul/Aug. Single rooms are expensive all year. *Cabañas* are available in 2 main areas: up Perito Moreno on the hill to the north of town, and down by the lakeside; prices for these increase in high season but they are good value for families or groups. When everywhere else is full, the tourist office will provide a list of private addresses in high season. See www.sanmartindelosandes. gov.ar for a full list of places to stay. All those listed here are recommended.

#### $$$$ La Casa de Eugenia
*Coronel Díaz 1186, T02972-427206,*
*www.lacasadeeugenia.com.ar.*
B&B in a beautifully renovated 1900s house,
very welcoming and relaxing, cosy rooms,
huge breakfast, charming hosts.

#### $$$$ Le Châtelet
*Villegas 650, T02972-428294,*
*www.lechatelethotel.com.*
Chic and luxurious, beautiful chalet-style
hotel with excellent service to pamper you.
Wood-panelled living room, gorgeous
bedrooms and suites, buffet breakfast,
spa and pool with massage and facial
treatments. Also, a welcome glass of wine
is offered on arrival.

#### $$$ Arco Iris
*Los Cipreses 1850, T02972-428450,*
*www.arcoirisar.com.*
Comfortable, well-equipped *cabañas* with
Wi-Fi and cable TV in a quiet area of town,
each has a cosy living room and spacious
kitchen. Own access to the river, so you can
fish before breakfast or enjoy a drink on the
water side in the evening.

#### $$$ Hostería Bärenhaus
*Los Alamos 156, Barrio Chapelco (8370),*
*T02972-422775, www.barenhaus.com.ar.*
5 km outside town, pick-up from bus
terminal and airport arranged. Welcoming
young owners, very comfortable rooms
with heating, English and German spoken.

#### $$$ Hostería Walkirias
*Villegas 815, T02972-428307, www.*
*laswalkirias.com. Open all year.*
A lovely place, smart, tasteful rooms with
big bathrooms. Sauna and pool room.
Buffet breakfast. Great value off season
and for longer stays.

#### $$$ Plaza Mayor
*Coronel Pérez 1199, T02972-427302,*
*www.hosteriaplazamayor.com.ar.*
A chic and homey *hostería* in a quiet
residential area, with traditional touches in
the simple elegant rooms, excellent home-

made breakfast, heated pool with solarium,
barbecue and parking.

#### $$ Crismalú
*Rudecindo Roca 975, T02972-427283,*
*www.interpatagonia.com/crismalu.*
Simple rooms in attractive chalet-style
converted home, good value.

#### $$ Hostería Las Lucarnas
*Cnel Pérez 632, T02972-427085, www.*
*hosterialaslucarnas.com. Open all year.*
Great value, centrally located, pretty place
with simple comfortable rooms, English-
speaking owner, breakfast included.
Discounts for more than 5 nights.

#### $ pp Puma
*A Fosbery 535 (north along Rivadavia,*
*2 blocks beyond bridge), T02972-422443,*
*www.pumahostel.com.ar.*
Discount for ISIC members, small dorms with
bath and a double room with view, laundry,
bikes for hire, very well run by mountain
guide owner, good value.

#### $ pp Rukalhue
*Juez del Valle 682 (3 blocks from terminal),*
*T02972-427431, www.rukalhue.com.ar.*
Large camp-style accommodation with
1 section full of dorm rooms (US$15-21)
and 1 section with doubles, triples and
apartments ($$$-$$). Also has apartments
with private bath and kitchenette.

### Camping

#### ACA Camping
*Av Koessler 2175, T02972-429430,*
*www.interpatagonia.com/aca.*
With hot water and laundry facilities, also
*cabañas*.

#### Camping Quila Quina
*T02972-411919, www.campingquilaquina.*
*com.ar. Summer to Easter.*
Lovely site on a stream near Lago Lácar,
18 km from San Martín, with beaches,
immaculate toilet blocks, restaurant and
shop, access to boats and treks.

## Restaurants

**$$ El Regional**
*San Martín and Mascardi, T02972-414600,*
*www.elregionalpatagonia.com.ar.*
Popular for regional specialities – smoked
trout, venison, wild boar, pâtés and hams,
and El Bolsón's home-made beer. Cheerful
German-style decor.

**$$ La Costa del Pueblo**
*Costanera opposite pier, T02972-429289,*
*www.lacostadelpueblo.com.ar.*
Overlooking the lake, huge range of pastas,
chicken and trout dishes, generous portions,
good service, cheerful.

**$$ La Tasca**
*Mariano Moreno 866, T02972-428663.*
Good for venison, trout and home-made
pastas, varied wine list.

## Cafés

**Beigier**
*Av Costanera 815.*
Hidden cottage with views of the bay
serving a fantastic afternoon tea with
home-made goodies.

**Vieja Deli**
*Villegas y Juez del Valle, T02972-428631.*
Affordable place with views of the bay and
nice salads, pastas and pizzas.

## Bars and clubs

**Down Town Matias**
*San Martín 598, T02972-413386,*
*www.downtownmatias.com/andes.*
Fantastic, welcoming building, good for a
late night drink with snacks.

**Dublin South Bar**
*Av San Martín 599, T02972-410141.*
Huge pub (with no reference to Ireland at all)
with comfy seats, great food – try the home-
made pasta – and a good atmosphere.

## Shopping

A great place for shopping, with chic
little shops selling clothes and handmade
jumpers; try **La Oveja Negra** (San Martín
1025, T02972-428039, see Facebook), for
wonderful handmade scarves and jumpers,
plus esoteric crafts and interesting souvenirs.
There's also a handicraft market in summer in
Plaza San Martín. There are 2 recommended
places for chocolates: **Abuela Goye** (San
Martín 807, T02972-429409, www.abuela
goye.com), which serves excellent ice
creams and a killer hot chocolate, and
**Mamusia** (San Martín 601, T02972-427560,
see Facebook), which also sells home-made
jams. Lots of outdoor shops on San Martín
sell clothes for walking and skiing, including
**Nomade** (San Martín 881).

## What to do

### Canopying

**Canopy**, *8 km from town, T0294-15-459 6215,*
*see Facebook.* 1400 m of course, spread over
10 different resting stations with a height
that varies from 8 to 20 m off the ground.
Recommended.

### Cycling

Many places in the centre rent mountain
and normal bikes, US$10-20 per day,
maps provided.
**HG Rodados**, *San Martín 1061, T02972-*
*427345, hgrodados@smandes.com.ar (also*
*see Facebook).* Arranges trips, rents mountain
bikes, also spare parts and expertise.

### Fishing

For guides contact the tourist office or the
park office. A licence costs US$26 for a day,
US$78 for a week, and US$104 for a season,
with extra charges for trolling.
**Hernan Zorzit**, *T02972-414538, www.patagon*
*fly.com.* Also runs tours to Junín de los Andes.
**Jorge Cardillo Pesca**, *Villegas 1061,*
*T02972-428372, www.jorgecardillo.com.*
Sells equipment and fishing licences and
offers excursions.

**Jorge Trucco**, *based in Patagonia Outfitters, Pérez 662, T02972-429561, www.jorgetrucco. com*. Expert and professional trips, good advice and many years of experience.

## Skiing
For details of the Chapelco resort, see page 94.

## Tour operators
Prices for conventional tours, such as the Seven Lakes Drive, are similar with most agencies. Most tours operate from 2 Jan. 1 day's rafting at Hua Hum costs US$60-70.
**El Claro**, *Coronel Díaz 751, T02972-428876, www.elclaroturismo.com.ar*. For conventional tours, horse riding, mountain biking and trekking.
**El Refugio**, *Villegas 698, corner of Coronel Pérez, upstairs, T02972-425140, www.elrefugio turismo.com.ar*. Bilingual guides, conventional tours, boat trips, also mountain bike hire, rafting, horse riding and trekking. Recommended.
**Lanín Turismo**, *San Martín 437, oficina 3, T02972-425808, www.laninturismo.com*.

Adventure tourism and trekking in Lanín area, ascents of the volcano, Chapelco skiing packages and more.

## Transport

### Air
See Transport, under Junín de los Andes above. **LADE** office in bus terminal, T02972-427672.

### Bus
The bus terminal, T02972-427044, has all the usual services, including a luggage store, toilets and a *locutorio*.

To **Buenos Aires**, 21-22 hrs, US$135, daily. To **Villa La Angostura**, **Albus** 2 a day, US$9. To **Bariloche** (not via 7 Lagos), 3½-4 hrs, US$14, **Vía Bariloche** and **Ko Ko**. To **Chile**: **Pucón**, **Villarrica** and **Valdivia** via **Junín de los Andes** and **Paso Mamuil Malal**, US$23, 5 hrs to Pucón with **San Martín**, heavily booked in summer (see also box, page 93). Alternatively, **Ko Ko/Lafit** (T02972-427422) run buses to **Puerto Pirehueico**, via **Paso Hua Hum**, 2 hrs; check terminal for schedule (see also box, page 95).

# San Martín
## to Bariloche

The journey south to Bariloche along the celebrated Seven Lakes Drive is the most famous tourist route in the Argentine Lake District. It follows Route 234 through the Lanín and Nahuel Huapi national parks and passes seven magnificent lakes, all flanked by mixed natural forest; it is particularly attractive in autumn (April to May).

The seven lakes are (from north to south): Lácar, Machónico, Falkner, Villarino, Espejo, Correntoso and Nahuel Huapi. The road is paved.

On the way from picturesque San Martín de los Andes, there are two good bases. Remote Villa Traful is tucked into a deep fold between dramatic, spired mountains, on the side of a navy blue sliver of lake. It's a peaceful place for a few days' rest, with good walks and some appealing places to stay.

Further south, on the northern side of Lake Nahuel Huapi, is the pretty, upmarket town of Villa la Angostura. Much loved by wealthier Argentines, there's no shortage of smart places to stay and eat here, such as the famous and blissful boutique hotel, Las Balsas. From Villa la Angostura you can visit the tiny national park, Los Arrayanes, which protects a rare forest of *arrayán* trees with their cinnamon-coloured bark and twisting trunks.

Leaving San Martín, the first lake you reach in the Nahuel Huapi national park is Lago Falkner, which is popular with fishermen. It's a wide and open lake, with thickly forested fjord-like mountains descending steeply into it. There's a long narrow sandy beach on the roadside, a good place for a picnic stop, and wild camping; Camping Lago Falkner nearby has facilities. To the south, there's another pretty, if exposed, free campsite (with no facilities) by the deep green Río Villarino, near Lago Villarino, and a campsite and picnic ground amidst little beech trees at Pichi Traful, at the northern tip of Lago Traful. This is a beautiful spot by the wide green banks of a river, with steeply rising mountains on all sides.

At Km 77, Route 65 branches off to the east, running along the south shore of Lago Traful through Villa Traful to meet the main Neuquén–Bariloche highway (Route 237) at Confluencia. If you have a couple of days to spare, this makes a lovely detour (see below). Continuing south, however, the drive passes gorgeous, secluded Lago Espejo ('lake mirror'), which has lovely beaches on its shore. Opposite, you'll be treated to a superb view of Lago Correntoso on the final stretch towards Villa la Angostura on Lago Nahuel Huapi.

You can see the route from the windows of a bus on a round trip from Bariloche, Villa la Angostura or San Martín, which will take about five hours, but you may prefer your own transport, so you can stop and explore. Buses will stop at campsites on the route. It's a good route for cycling, as you can really appreciate the beauty of the ever-changing landscape, though note that there's more traffic in January and February.

### The alternative route to Bariloche

There's a quicker route from San Martín to Bariloche, via **Confluencia**, further east. Head south from San Martín on Route 234, but at Lago Machónico, instead of continuing southwest, take Route 63 along the tranquil shore of Lago Meliquina. Further south, you could turn off to the isolated Lago Filo-Hua-Hum at Km 54 (unpaved track). A little further on the road climbs to the **Paso de Córdoba**, Km 77 (1300 m), with fabulous views, from where it descends to the valley of the Río Traful, following it east to Confluencia. From Confluencia, you can head west along Route 65 to Villa Traful and rejoin the Seven Lakes Drive, or continue south to Bariloche on Route 237 through the astounding **Valle Encantado**, where there are bizarre rock formations including El Dedo de Dios (The Finger of God) and El Centinela del Valle (The Sentinel of the Valley).

### Villa Traful

If you want to get off the beaten track, Villa Traful (population 503) is ideal. It was created after the Nahuel Huapi National Park was set up, with the aim of giving visitors the greatest possible contact with nature. Approaching from the west, along the southern shore of Lago Traful, the winding road passes through forests of lenga and tall *coihue* trees, their elegant trunks creating a woody cathedral, with idyllic spots to camp all along the shore.

The quiet pretty village sprawls alongside the narrow deep-blue sliver of

**Tip...**
The best time to visit Villa Traful is December or late February to March when the few restaurants aren't full of tourists.

Lago Traful, enclosed on both sides by stunning sharp-peaked mountains. There's not much to do here, but it's popular with fishermen, and there are a couple of wonderful walks and waterfalls to see, it's a pleasant place to unwind. At the heart of the village opposite the main pier is a kiosk selling basic supplies and bus tickets, and the best restaurant. Traful is prone to mercurial winds, so check the forecast if you're coming for a few days as it's miserable being stuck here in bad weather and the buses are infrequent.

## Walks around Villa Traful

A 1½-hour walk from the village centre takes you to the lovely **Cascadas del Arroyo Coa Có y Blanco** waterfalls thundering down through beech forest and *cañas colihues* bamboo. Walk up the hill from the Ñancu Lahuen restaurant and take the left-hand path to the mirador over Cascada Coa Có, and from here take the right-hand path through *coihue* forest. Better still, there's a satisfying hike up to **Cerro Negro** (2000 m) five hours up, following uncertain yellow markers. Ask at the national park office to get the best advice on the route. It's a stiff climb to start with, through gorgeous *coihue* and *lenga* forest, and the views as you clear the tree line are unbelievable, with the dramatic spired peaks visible on the northern side of Lago Traful. There's a lot of scree near the summit, but the views of Lanín, Tronador and the others make it all worthwhile. Alternatively, cross the lake (15 minutes) by boat, leaving from the main pier, to reach a sand beach from where you can walk up a steep path to twin lagoons and some superbly well conserved prehistoric cave paintings nearby. Ask in the tourist office (see Tourist information, below) to see which companies are currently running trips.

## Listings La Ruta de los Siete Lagos

### Tourist information

#### Villa Traful
The national park *guardería* is opposite the pier, open only in high season, with advice on walks.

#### Tourist office
*Ruta Provincial 65, T0294-447 9099, see www.villatraful.gov.ar or www. interpatagonia.com/villatraful.*
Small but very helpful, this tourist office has information on walks, riding and fishing.

### Where to stay

#### The alternative route to Bariloche

**$$$-$$ Hostería La Gruta de las Vírgenes**
*Confluencia, T0294-442 6138.*
On a hill with views over the 2 rivers, very hospitable.

#### Villa Traful

**$$$ Hostería Villa Traful**
*T0294-447 9005, www.hosteriavillatraful.com.*
A cosy house with a tea room by the lake, also *cabañas* for 4-6 people, pretty gardens, good value. The owner's son, Andrés, organizes fishing and boat trips.

**$$ Cabañas Aiken**
*T0294-447 9048, www.aiken.com.ar.*
Well-decorated *cabañas* in beautiful surroundings near the lake (close to the tourist office), each with its own *parrillada*, also has a restaurant. Recommended.

**$ pp Vulcanche Hostel**
*Ruta Provincial 61, T0294-15-469 2314, www.vulcanche.com.*
Chalet-style hostel in gardens with good views, with good dorms and $$ doubles, breakfast extra, large park for camping.

## Restaurants

**Villa Traful**

**$$ Ñancu Lahuen**
*T0294-447 9017.*
A chocolate shop, tea room and restaurant serving local trout. Delightful and cosy, with big open fire, delicious food and reasonably priced.

## Transport

**Villa Traful**
**Bus**
In high summer, a **La Araucana** bus (info@araucana.com.ar) between **Villa la Angostura** and **San Martín** stops here daily; otherwise there are buses to **Bariloche** with **Via Bariloche**, US$4.50. **Kiosko El Ciervo**, by the YPF service station, sells tickets and has the timetable.

## Villa La Angostura and around *Colour map 1, B3.*

a tiny star in the Lake District

Villa La Angostura (population 13,285) is a delightful little town which, apart from in January when it is packed out, is an appealing place to stay, especially for those who like their nature seen from the comfort of a luxurious hotel. There are some superb restaurants here and some seriously chic hotels. *Cabaña* complexes and great hostels have mushroomed up everywhere, so there's no shortage of places to stay. And there are some good walks nearby, excellent fly-fishing, and a golf course, as well as skiing in winter.

### Sights

The town is divided into several different *barrios*: around the sprawling centre, **El Cruce**; around the lakeside area of **Puerto Manzano**, and around the picturesque port, known as **La Villa**, 3 km away at the neck of the Quetrihué Peninsula, which dips into the northern end of Lago Nahuel Huapi. From La Villa it's a short trip on foot or by boat to Villa La Angostura's great attraction, the **Parque Nacional Los Arrayanes** (see box, opposite), at the end of the peninsula. Also from La Villa, a short walk leads to lovely **Laguna Verde**, an intense emerald-green lagoon surrounded by mixed *coihue* cypress and *arrayán* forests, where there's a 1-km self-guided trail, taking about an hour. There are no services in La Villa apart from a *kiosko*, a tea room in high season, and the restaurant at Hotel Angostura. A bus runs from the centre at El Cruce to La Villa every couple of hours, taking 15 minutes, but it's a pleasant walk.

About halfway between the two centres is a chapel (1936), designed by Bustillo, the famous architect who gave this region's buildings their distinctive style, and nearby is **El Messidor** (1942), the summer resort of Argentine presidents, where you can visit the beautiful gardens with lake views. There's also a tiny museum, **Museo Regional** ⓘ *Blvd Nahuel Huapi 2177, on the road to La Villa, museo.vla@gmail.com, Tue-Sat 1030-1700, donation,* with interesting photos of the original indigenous inhabitants.

In winter, there's good skiing at Villa La Angostura's popular ski resort **Cerro Bayo** ⓘ *9 km north of town, T0294-449 4189, www.cerrobayoweb.com,* with 24 pistes, 20 km in total, many of them fabulously long, and all with excellent views over the lakes below. It's a great area for snowboarding. This is one of Argentina's pricier resorts: a one-day ski pass costs US$68 for adults in high season.

This park covers the Quetrihué Peninsula, which dips south from Villa La Angostura into the Lago Nahuel Huapi and lies within the Parque Nacional Nahuel Huapi. It was created to protect a rare forest of *arrayán* trees, since it's one of the few places in the world where the *arrayán* grows to full size, and some of the specimens are 300 years old. This myrtle-like tree grows near water in groves and likes to have its roots wet, since it really has no bark. The trunks are extraordinary: a smooth powdery or peeling surface, bright cinnamon in colour and cold to the touch. They have no outer bark to protect them, but the surface layer is rich in tannins that keep the tree free from disease. They have creamy white flowers in January and February, and produce blue-black fruit in March. The sight of so many of these trees together, with their twisting trunks, creates a wonderful fairy-tale scene. The most rewarding way to see the wood is to take the boat trip across the deep-blue lake, fringed with spectacular peaks, to the tip of the peninsula, and then take a leisurely walk along the wheelchair-friendly wooden walkways through the trees, waiting until the guided tour has left. Halfway along you'll see a small wooden café which serves tea and coffee and has great views of the forest. Stroll back to the port through the mixed forest, passing two pretty and secluded lakes, Laguna Patagua, and Laguna Hua Huan.

### Access
The entrance to the park is a walkable 2 km south of the port area of Villa la Angostura, known as La Villa. Bus company **15 de Mayo** runs buses from El Cruce to La Villa every few hours (15 minutes) from 0830-1900 US$1. A taxi to Villa costs US$6. For information contact the Nahuel Huapi **park office** in Bariloche, San Martín 24, T0294-442 3121, www.parquesnacionales.gob.ar. You may enter the park 0900-1400 in summer, 0900-1200 in winter, US$10. You must leave the park by 1700 and 1500 respectively.

### Walking and cycling
There's a clear path all the way from the tip of the Quetrihué Peninsula where the boat arrives, through the prettiest part of the *arrayán* forest, and then running the length of the peninsula back to La Villa. You can walk or cycle the whole length: three hours one-way walking; two hours cycling (for cycle hire, see page 106).

### Boat trips
Two companies run catamarans from the pier in La Villa to the end of the peninsula, and take passengers on a short guided tour through the forest. **Catamarán Patagonia Argentina**, T0294-449 4463, www.catamaranpatagonia.com.ar, and **Greenleaf Turismo**, Avenida Siete Lagos 118 Piso 1 Of C, Villa La Angostura, T0294-449 4004, www.bosquelosarrayanes.com.ar; tickets, US$32 return. Boats also run from Bariloche, via Isla Victoria, with **Turisur**, T0294-442 6109, www.turisur.com.ar.

## Walks around Villa La Angostura
**Parque Nacional Los Arrayanes** For an easy flat walk, take the boat to the head of the Quitrihué Peninsula and walk the 13 km back. See box, above.

## ON THE ROAD
## National parks in the Lake District

There are five national parks covering enormous swathes of the Lake District, and these areas are generally where you'll find the best hiking, rafting and horse riding, in the most unspoilt forests and mountain landscapes you can imagine. The area's main centre, **Bariloche**, is inside **Parque Nacional Nahuel Huapi** (see box, page 112) and has a well-developed infrastructure for activities in the park. Inside this park is another tiny park, **Parque Nacional Los Arrayanes**, accessed from **Villa La Angostura**; see box, page 103.

Immediately to the north of Nahuel Huapi is **Parque Nacional Lanín**, which contains the town of **San Martín de los Andes**, and also has superb hiking, especially around **Volcán Lanín** (see box, page 88). South of Bariloche there is the tiny but beautiful **Parque Nacional Lago Puelo**, just south of **El Bolsón**. Finally, **Los Alerces** is the most pristine of all the parks, with just one road running through it, and most areas accessible only on foot. The nearest towns are **Esquel** and **Trevelin**, see pages 142 and 146.

Each park has a ranger's station, where *guardaparques* will give you a map and advise on walks in the park, as well as on accommodation and the state of the paths.

**Mirador Belvedere** Offers fine views of Lagos Correntoso and Nahuel Huapi. It's a 3-km drive or walk up the old road, northwest of El Cruce; and from the mirador a path to your right goes to **Cascada Inacayal**, a waterfall 50 m high, situated in an area rich in native flora and forest.

**Cascada Río Bonito** A delightful walk leading to a beautiful waterfall, lying 8 km east of El Cruce off Route 66. The steep path gives tremendous views, and the falls themselves are impressive, falling 35 m from a chasm in basalt cliffs to an emerald-green pool. Further along the same path, you can reach the summit of Cerro Bayo (1782 m). Alternatively, 1 km further along the road, a ski lift takes you to the platform at 1500 m, where there's a restaurant with great views, and from here, it's a short trek to the summit. The ski lift runs all year; cyclists can take bikes up in the lift and cycle down.

## Listings Villa La Angostura and around

### Tourist information

**Tourist office**
*Av Arrayanes 9, T0294-449 4124, www.villalaangostura.gov.ar, near the bus terminal, Av Siete Lagos 93. High season 0800-2200, low season 0800-2000.*
Helpful, with lots of information, but a madhouse in summer. English spoken.

### Where to stay

**$$$$ La Escondida**
*Av Arrayanes 7014, T0294-482 6110, www.hosterialaescondida.com.ar.*
Wonderful setting, right on the lake, 14 rooms, heated pool, offers mid-week, weekend and long-stay specials. Recommended.

### $$$$ La Posada
*R 231, Km 64.5, Las Balsas (no number), T0294-449 4450, www.hosterialaposada.com.*
In a splendid elevated position off the road with clear views over the lake, welcoming, beautifully maintained hotel in lovely gardens, with pool, spa, fine restaurant; a perfect place to relax.

### $$$$ Las Balsas
*on Bahía Las Balsas (signposted from Av Arrayanes), T0294-449 4308, www.lasbalsas.com.*
One of the best small hotels in Argentina, with fabulous cosy rooms, warm relaxed public areas, fine cuisine, impeccable service, and a wonderfully intimate atmosphere in a great lakeside location with its own secluded beach. Lakeside heated swimming pools, spa, and trips arranged. Highly recommended.

### $$$ Hostería ACA al Sur
*Av Arrayanes 8 (behind the petrol station), T0294-448 8412, www.aca.tur.ar/hoteles.*
Modern, attractive single-storey hotel with well-designed rooms in the centre of town. Recommended.

### $$$ Hostería Le Lac
*Av de los 7 Lagos 2350, T0294-448 8029, www.hosterialelac.com.ar.*
3-star, 8 rooms, some with jacuzzi and DVD, gardens, lake view, can arrange lots of activities, several languages spoken by owner.

### $$$ Hotel Angostura
*Nahuel Huapi 1911, at La Villa, T0294-449 4224, www.hotelangostura.com.*
Built in 1938, this traditional hotel has a lovely lakeside setting and a good restaurant and tea room, **Viejo Coihue**. Also has 3 cabins for 6 ($$$$). Boat excursions along the nearby shore are arranged.

### $$ Bajo Cero
*Av 7 Lagos al 1200, T0294-449 5454, www.bajocerohostel.com.*
Well-situated, rooms for 2-6, can arrange trekking, cycling and other trips.

### $ pp Hostel La Angostura
*Barbagelata 157, 150 m up road behind tourist office, T0294-449 4834, www.hostellaangostura.com.ar.*
A warm, luxurious hostel, all small dorms have bathrooms (US$21), good doubles (US$60), HI discounts, welcoming owners organize trips and rent bikes. Recommended.

### $ pp Italian Hostel
*Los Maquis 215 (5 blocks from terminal), T0294-449 4376. Closed Apr-Oct.*
Welcoming, small, with dorms and doubles. Rustic, functional and pleasant, run by a biker. Fireplace and orchard from where you can pick berries and herbs for your meals. Recommended.

## Camping

### Osa Mayor
*Signposted off main road, close to town, T0294-449 4304, www.campingosamayor.com.ar.*
Well-designed leafy and level site, US$8-10, all facilities, also rustic *cabañas* US$140 for up to 4 people, and dorms US$140 for up to 6 people, helpful owner.

## Restaurants

Plenty of places are to be found on the main Av Arrayanes, lots of them chalet-style and open all day from breakfast onwards. Prices reflect the fact that this is a popular tourist town. Don't miss out on some of the really excellent places for fine cuisine here.

### $$$ Cocina Waldhaus
*Av Arrayanes 6431, T0294-447 5323, see Facebook.*
Highly recommended, this is 'auteur cuisine' with gorgeous local delicacies created by Chef Leo Morsea, served in a charming chalet-style building.

### $$ El Esquiador
*Las Retamas 146 (behind the bus terminal), T0294-449 4331, see Facebook.*

Good, popular *parrilla* has an all-you-can-eat choice of cold starters, a main meal and a dessert.

**$$ Los Pioneros**
*Av Arrayanes 267, T0294-449 5525.*
Famous for fine local dishes in a chalet-style building and great Argentine steaks. Great pizza place next door run by the same owners. They also serve locally brewed beers.

**$ Jardín Patagonia**
*Av Arrayanes 4.*
Popular pizzeria and *parrilla*.

**$ TemaTyCo**
*Ruta 231 y Mirlo, T0294-447 5211.*
Chic tearoom with a wide range of teas and delicious cakes.

## What to do

**Boat trips**
There are a few companies running catamaran trips, including the following:
**Catamarán Patagonia Argentina**, *Huapi 2159, T0294-449 4463, www.catamaran patagonia.com.ar.* Runs trips on a 60-passenger catamaran.
**Greenleaf Turismo**, *Av Siete Lagos 118, Piso 1 Of C, T0294-449 4004, www.bosquelos arrayanes.com.ar.* Runs the 105-passenger *Catamarán Futuleufu*.
**Turisur**, *Mitre 219 T0294-442 6109, www.turisur.com.ar.* Runs boats from Bariloche, via Isla Victoria.
**Velero Luz de Luna**, *T0294-449 4834.* Offers trips on sailing boats with a special meal on board, or a drink with *picadas* of smoked meat and fish.

**Canopying**
**Canopy Villa la Angostura**, *Curruhué and Melinquina, T02944 15 579071, www.canopy bariloche.com.* Runs a great trail in the forest nearby, with over 1400 m of cable to zoom along.

**Climbing**
**Club Andino Villa La Angostura**, *Cerro Bayo 295, T0294-449 4954, www.cavla.com.ar.* Excursions, maps and information.

**Cycling**
Expect to pay around US$15-20 per day for bike hire.
**Bayo Abajo**, *Av Siete Lagos 94, T0294-448 8383, bayoabajo@argentina.com.* Bike hire starting at around US$15 per day.
**Taquari Bici Shop**, *Av Arrayanes 259, T0294-448 8415, see Facebook.* New bikes, knowledgeable.

**Fishing**
The season runs from mid-Nov to May. For permits and a list of fishing guides, ask at the tourist office.
**Anglers Home Fly Shop**, *Belvedere 22, T0294-449 5222.* Arranges fishing trips.
**Banana Fly Shop**, *Av Arrayanes 282, T0294-449 4634.* Fly shop.
**PatagonFly**, *www.patagonfly.com.* A fly shop and association of local fishing guides, also runs trips.

**Horse riding**
**Cabalgatas Correntoso**, *Cacique Antrao 1850, T02944-15-451 0559, see Facebook.* Offers horseback excursions in the surrounding area and to Villa Traful.

**Skiing**
**Cerro Bayo**, *www.cerrobayoweb.com.* Although smaller, this is more popular with families than the famous Cerro Catedral in Bariloche. See description, page 120.

**Tour operators**
**Nómades de la Montaña**, *Ruca Choroy 38 y Cerro Inacayal 35, T0294-15-455 1385.* Offering everything from trekking and mountain biking to rappelling, diving and fly-fishing.
**Rucán Turismo**, *Av 7 Lagos 239, T0294-447 5263, www.rucanturismo.com.* Offers skiing, riding, mountain biking and conventional tours.

## BORDER CROSSING
### Argentina–Chile

#### Paso Samoré
Paso Samoré, formerly **Paso Puyehue** (1280 m), lies 125 km northwest of Bariloche on Route 231 at Km 122. It's a spectacular six-hour journey, with plenty of buses from Bariloche, making it a cheaper alternative to the expensive Three Lakes Crossing (see box, page 124). Cyclists should note that there are no supplies between Villa La Angostura and Entre Lagos. For more information, contact the *gendarmería* in Bariloche, T0294-442 2711 or see www.gendarmeria.gob.ar/pasos-chile/cardenal-antonio-samore.html.

**Argentine customs and immigration** El Rincón, Route 231, Km 105. Open daily 0900-1900 but liable to be closed after snowfalls.

**Chilean immigration** It's 22 km from the pass to Chilean customs at Pajarito (Km 145) in the middle of a forest, over a wonderful mountain pass. Immigration is open daily 0800-1800.

**Accommodation** Termas Puyehue, Route 215, Km 76, T+56-600-293 6000, www.puyehue.cl. Luxurious accommodation and excellent thermal baths at a huge complex set in beautiful open parkland, framed by mountains, with an impressive spa. There are humbler places to stay in the town of Entre Lagos at the southwestern end of Lago Puyehue.

**Transport** For bus services from Bariloche to Osorno, Puerto Montt and Valdivia, see page 117.

### Trekking
**Alma Sur**, *T0294-456 4724/T0294-15-456 4724, www.almasur.com*. Great trips in the local area and further afield, with bilingual, knowledgeable Anthony Hawes. A trained guide of Nahuel Huapi National Park, he creates really imaginative walks, which can include boats, climbing and hiking way off the beaten track. Recommended.

### Transport

#### Bus
The small bus terminal at the junction of Av 7 Lagos and Av Arrayanes is opposite the ACA service station and offers a left-luggage service. Urban buses, run by **15 de Mayo**, US$1, link El Cruce (main bus stop on main road, 50 m from tourist office), La Villa, Correntoso and Puerto Manzano, and go up to Lago Espejo and Cerro Bayo in high season.

To **Bariloche**, 1 hr 15 mins, US$5, several companies. Buses from Bariloche to **Osorno** in Chile will pick you up in La Angostura by arrangement. For transport to Chile from Bariloche, see page 117.

# Bariloche
## & around

★ Beautifully situated on the steep and wooded southern shore of Lago Nahuel Huapi, surrounded by high peaks, San Carlos de Bariloche (its official name) is an ideal base for exploring the Lake District. It's right in the middle of Nahuel Huapi National Park.

The town was founded in 1902 but really took off in the 1930s when the national park was created. The chalet-style architecture was established at this time by early German and Swiss settlers.

Bariloche is well set up for tourism with the main street, Mitre, bustling with tour operators, outdoor clothing shops and chocolate makers. There are plenty of hotels and restaurants in the town centre, but the best places are sprinkled along the shore of Lake Nahuel Huapi, towards Llao Llao, where Argentina's most famous hotel enjoys a spectacularly beautiful setting.

To the immediate south of Bariloche there are fabulous walks in the mountains, and up giant Mount Tronador, reached from Pampa Linda further west. On the way are two gorgeous lakes: Gutiérrez and Mascardi. Ski resort Cerro Catedral is arguably the best in South America and makes a great base for trekking in summer.

# Essential Bariloche and around

## Finding your feet

The **airport** is 15 km east of town; bus service 72 runs to the town centre, as do *colectivos* and taxis (US$18-20). If you're staying on the road to Llao Llao, west of town, expect to pay more for transport to your hotel.

The **bus station** and the **train station** are both 3 km east of the centre. A taxi into town costs US$15-18. Otherwise, there are urban bus companies that run *colectivos*: **Santa De** and **Grottoes**. These lines travel between the bus station and the centre: 20, 21, 22 and 10. Buy a rechargeable card, US$2.50, before travelling; *colectivos* don't accept cash. See also Transport, page 117.

## Best hotels

**Premier**, page 114
**Tres Reyes**, page 114
**Hotel Llao Llao**, page 121
**Tunquelén**, page 121

## Getting around

Bariloche is an easy city to walk around. Avenida Bustillo (see Orientation, below) is a viable place to stay even if you haven't got a car since frequent local buses, run by **3 de Mayo**, run along its length. Take No 20 to Llao Llao, for lakeside hotels and restaurants and Puerto Pañuelo; No 10 to Colonia Suiza and Bahía López for trekking; No 50 to Lago Gutiérrez, via the base for the cable car to Cerro Otto; and the bus labelled 'Catedral' for Cerro Cathedral.

## Orientation

It's straightforward to orient yourself in the city, since the lake lies to the north and the mountains to the south. The main street is Mitre, running east to west, and unmistakable with its souvenir and chocolate shops. Here you'll find all the tour operators, *locutorios* and internet cafés, as well as banks and some food shops. The tourist information office (see Listings, below) is in the distinctive chalet-style Centro Cívico, with an open space giving good views onto the lake, and most hotels and restaurants are gathered within three or four blocks from here, with cheaper accommodation and hostels tending to be a few blocks further south on the upper slopes of town. More upmarket hotels and many restaurants are spread out along Avenida Bustillo, the road running beside the southern shore of Lago Nahuel Huapi for some 25 km, as far as the famous **Hotel Llao Llao**, and in an area known as Colonial Suiza.

## When to go

Bariloche is busiest in the school holidays (January and July), but it's also the destination for all graduating secondary school students in August, September and January, though these groups are now confined to special hotels (not listed here), and rarely stray beyond the city's bars and nightclubs for their inevitable rites of passage. Accommodation is cheaper outside the peak periods, but the weather becomes unpredictable at the end of April. For skiing, July and August are best, though hotels are packed with mass tourism from Chile and Brazil. Try June or September instead, and always book well ahead.

## Useful addresses

**Chilean Consulate**, España 275, T0294-442 3050. Monday-Friday 0900-1300 (office), 1400-1700 (phone and email). Helpful.
**Immigration office**, Libertad 191, T0294-442 3043. Monday-Friday 0800-1600.
**Police**, T0294-442 2772, or 101.

## Best camping

**El Yeti**, page 121
**Petunia**, page 121
**Selva Negra**, page 121

# Parque Nacional Nahuel Huapi

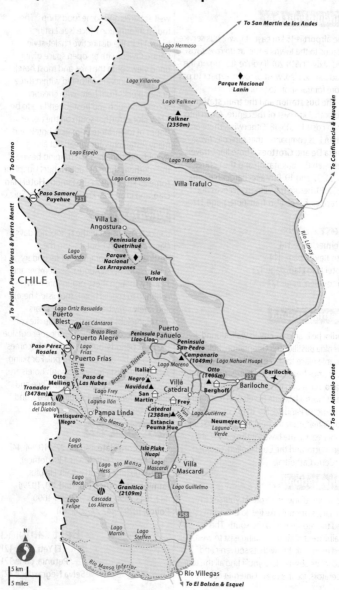

To San Martín de los Andes

Lago Hermoso

Lago Villarino

**Parque Nacional Lanín**

Lago Falkner

**Falkner (2350m)**

To Osorno

Lago Espejo

Lago Traful

Lago Correntoso

**Villa Traful** ○

To Confluencia & Neuquén

Paso Samore/Puyehue · 231

Río Limay

**Villa La Angostura** ○

**Península de Quetrihué**

**Parque Nacional Los Arrayanes**

**Isla Victoria**

Lago Gallardo

CHILE

To Peulla, Puerto Varas & Puerto Montt

Lago Ortiz Basualdo

**Puerto Blest**

Los Cántaros

**Brazo Blest**

**Puerto Alegre**

Lago Frías

**Paso Pérez Rosales**

**Puerto Frías**

**Puerto**

**Península Pañuelo**

**Llao-Llao** ○

**Península San Pedro**

**Campanario (1049m)**

Lago Nahuel Huapi

Lago Moreno

**Italia**

**Negro**

**Otto (1405m)**

**Berghoff**

**Bariloche**

To San Antonio Oeste

237

**Otto Meiling**

**Paso de Las Nubes**

Lago Frey

**Navidad**

**Villa Catedral**

**San Martín**

**Frey**

**Tronador (3478m)**

Laguna Ilón

**Catedral (2388m)**

**Garganta del Diablo**

**Ventisquera Negro**

**Pampa Linda**

Río Manso

Lago Gutiérrez

**Estancia Peuma Hue**

**Neumeyer**

**Laguna Verde**

Lago Fonck

**Isla Pluke Huapi**

Lago Mascardi

**Villa Mascardi**

Lago Hess

Río Manso

Lago Roca

**Granítico (2109m)**

Lago Guillelmo

81

Lago Felipe

**Cascada Los Alerces**

258

Lago Martín

Lago Steffen

N

5 km
5 miles

Río Manso Inferior

**Río Villegas** ○

To El Bolsón & Esquel

**what to do in the Alpine city**

The famous Hotel Llao Llao (www.llaollao.com) and the civic centre, at the heart of Bariloche (population 120,000), were designed by major Argentine architect Bustillo, who set the trend for 'Bariloche Alpine style', with local stone, brightly varnished wood and carved gable ends, now ubiquitous throughout the region.

The Centro Cívico is set on an attractive plaza above the lake, where there's also a small museum, **Museo de la Patagonia** ⓘ *T0294-442 2309, www.museodelapatagonia.nahuel huapi.gov.ar, Tue-Fri 1000-1230 and 1400-1900, Saturday 1000-1700, entry by donation*, with some indigenous artefacts and material from the lives of the first white settlers. Mitre is the main commercial area, and here all the chocolate shops are clustered – a sight in themselves, and not to be missed: Abuela Goye and Mamushka are most highly recommended. The cathedral, built in 1946, lies south of Mitre; opposite is a huge rock left in this spot by a glacier during the last glacial period.

On the lakeshore is the **Museo Paleontológico** ⓘ *12 de Octubre and Sarmiento, T0294-15-461 1210, Mon-Sat 1500-1800, US$2.25*, which has displays of fossils mainly from Patagonia including an ichthyosaur and replicas of a giant spider and shark's jaws.

Bariloche's real sights are the mountains themselves; don't miss a cable car trip up to either **Cerro Campanario** (page 118) or **Cerro Otto** (page 119) to see lakes and mountains stretching out in front as far as the eye can see.

> ➡ **Bariloche maps**
> 1  Bariloche, page 111
> 2  Bariloche – the road to Llao Llao, page 118

**Where to stay**
1 41 Below *A1*
2 Antiguo Solar *B2*
5 Hostel Inn Bariloche *A1*
6 Hostería Güemes *B1*
7 La Bolsa *B2*
8 Penthouse 1004 *A1*
9 Periko's *B1*
10 Premier *A2*
11 Pudu *A1*
12 Ruca Hueney *B2*
13 Tres Reyes *A2*

**Restaurants**
1 Chez Philippe *B1*
2 Covita *A3*
3 Días de Zapata *B2*
4 El Boliche de Alberto *B2*
5 El Vegetariano *B1*
6 Huang Ji Zhong *A2*
7 Jauja *B2*
8 La Alpina *A2*

**Bars & clubs**
11 Cerebro *A1*
12 Wilkenny *A1*

## Parque Nacional Nahuel Huapi

Nahuel Huapi is the national park you're most likely to visit since Bariloche is right at its heart. It stretches along the Andes for over 130 km, from south of Lago Mascardi to north of Villa Traful, and so there are no official entry points like most of the other national parks. It was Argentina's first ever national park, created in 1934 from a donation made to the country by naturalist Francisco 'Perito' Moreno of 7500 ha of land around Puerto Blest. Extending across some of Argentina's most dramatic mountains, the park contains lakes, rivers, glaciers, waterfalls, torrents, rapids, valleys, forest, bare mountains and snow-clad peaks. Among those you can climb are Tronador (3478 m), Catedral Sur (2388 m), Falkner (2350 m), Cuyín Manzano (2220 m), López (2076 m), Otto (1405 m) and Campanario (1052 m). The outstanding feature is the splendour of the lakes and the pristine nature of the virgin forests.

### Park information

To enter the park costs US$10. There are many centres within the park, at Villa la Angostura and at Villa Traful, for example, but Bariloche (see page 108) is the usual first port of call for park activities, and here you can equip yourself with information on transport, walks and maps. The National Park Intendencia, San Martín 24, Bariloche, T0294-442 3111, www.nahuelhuapi.gov.ar, daily 0800-1600, is fairly unhelpful, with little hard information. Much better information on walks, refugios and buses is available from the trained guides and mountaineers at Club Andino Bariloche (CAB), see Tourist information, below. Ask for the Sendas y Bosques (walks and forests) series, which are 1:200,000, laminated and easy to read, with good books containing English summaries of the walks, www.guiasendasybosques.com.ar. Also recommended is the Active Patagonia map, with fabulous detail, and the Carta de Refugios, Senderos y Picadas for Bariloche. CAB can also tell you about transport: services: these vary from year to year and between high and low season, so it's best to check.

### Flora and fauna

Vegetation varies with altitude and climate, but you're most likely to see large expanses of southern beech forest – the magnificent coihue trees (small-leaved evergreen

## Listings Bariloche map page 111.

### Tourist information

Nahuel Huapi National Park intendencia
San Martín 24, T0294-442 3111,
www.nahuelhuapi.gov.ar.
Daily 0800-1600, Sat 1000-1600.
Pretty unhelpful; it's far better to go straight to Club Andino Bariloche (CAB) (just above the Centro Cívico, 20 de Febrero No 30, T0294-442 2266, www.clubandino.org, Mon-Fri 0900-1330, 1500-1930) for information on walks, hikes, mountain climbs, refugios and buses to reach all the local areas for walking. They sell excellent maps and books for walks, including Carta de Refugios, Senderos y Picadas maps for Bariloche and the book Infotrekking de la Patagonia, which gives great detail on all the possible walks, times, distances and refugios where you can stay, with satellite-based maps to guide you. All Club Andino

beeches) – many over 450 years old, and near the Chilean border where rainfall is highest, there are areas of magnificent virgin rainforest. Here you will see an **alerce** tree over 1000 years old, with the ancient species of bamboo cane *caña colihue* growing.

Eastern parts of the park are more steppe-like with arid land, supporting only low shrubs and bushes. Wildlife includes the small pudu deer, the endangered huemul and river otter, as well as foxes, cougars and guanacos. Among the birds, scarlet-headed Magellan woodpeckers and green austral parakeets are easily spotted as well as large flocks of swans, geese and ducks.

## Around the park

The centrepiece of the park is its largest lake, Lago Nahuel Huapi, which measures a huge 531 sq km and is 460 m deep in places. It is particularly magnificent to explore by boat since the lake is very irregular in shape and long fjord-like arms of water, or *brazos*, stretch far into the west towards Chile, where there is superb virgin Valdivian rainforest. There are many islands, the largest of which is Isla Victoria, which has a luxurious hotel (www.islavictoria.com). On the northern shores of the lake is the Parque Nacional Los Arrayanes (see box, page 103), which contains a rare woodland of exquisite *arrayán* trees, with their bright cinnamon-coloured flaky bark. Access to this park within a park is from the small, upmarket village of Villa La Angostura at the southern end of the famous Seven Lakes Drive (see page 99). The northernmost stretch of this drive and three of its lakes are in Parque Nacional Lanín (see page 84), but Lagos Correntoso and Espejo near Villa Angostura are both within Nahuel Huapi and offer stunning scenery and tranquil places to stay and walk. Another tiny centre, Villa Traful (see page 100), lies on the shore of navy blue Lago Traful, with fishing, camping and walking.

The tourist town of Bariloche (see page 108) on the southern shore of Lago Nahuel Huapi is the main tourist centre in the national park. It has plentiful accommodation and opportunities for hiking, rafting, tours and boat trips. West of Bariloche, there are glaciers and waterfalls near Pampa Linda, the base for climbing Mount Tronador and starting point for the trek through Paso de las Nubes to Lago Frías. South of Lago Nahuel Huapi, Lagos Mascardi, Guillelmo and Gutiérrez have even grander scenery, offering horse riding, trekking and rafting along the Río Manso.

staff know the mountains well and some of them speak English, French or German.

## Tourist office

*Centro Cívico, Mitre and Reconquista, T0294-442 9850, www.barilocheturismo.gob.ar. Daily 0800-2100.*
Helpful staff speak English (all), French, German and Portuguese (some), and have maps showing the town and whole area, with bus routes marked. They can also help with accommodation and campsites in the area.

## Where to stay

Prices rise in 2 peak seasons: Jul-Aug for skiing, and mid-Dec to Mar for summer holidays. If you arrive in the high season without a reservation, consult the listing published by the tourist office (address above). This selection gives lake-view and high-season prices where applicable. In low season you pay half of these prices in most cases. All those listed are recommended.

### $$$ Premier
*Rolando 263, T0294-442 6168,*
*www.hotelpremier.com.*
Good central choice (very good value in
low season), small 'classic' rooms and larger
superior rooms, English spoken.

### $$$ Tres Reyes
*12 de Octubre 135, T0294-442 6121,*
*www.hotel3reyes.com.ar.*
Traditional lakeside hotel with spacious
rooms, splendid views, all services, gardens.

### $$ Antiguo Solar
*A Gallardo 360, T0294-440 0337,*
*www.antiguosolar.com.*
Not far from the centre, this pleasant, simple
B&B on the upper level of an attractive
residential building has parking. Breakfast
includes fresh biscuits and local jams.

### $$ Hostería Güemes
*Güemes 715, T0294-442 4785,*
*www.hosteriaguemes.com.ar.*
Lovely, quiet, lots of space in living areas,
very pleasant, big breakfast included, owner
is a fishing expert and very knowledgeable
about the area.

### $ pp 41 Below
*Pasaje Juramento 94, T0294-443 6433,*
*www.hostel41below.com.*
Central, quiet, relaxing atmosphere, good
light rooms for 4-6 (US$18-22) and a double
with lake view (US$72 in high season).

### $ pp Hostel Inn Bariloche
*Salta 308, T0294-442 6084,*
*www.hostelbariloche.com.*
Large, well-designed hostel with great
views of the lake from the communal areas
and rooms. Comfortable beds, in dorm
(from US$10 pp); also doubles (from US$35),
discount for HI members. The best feature
is the great deck with a view in the garden.
Neighbouring **Marco Polo Inn** (T0294-440
0105), is in the same group.

### $ pp La Bolsa
*Palacios 405 y Elflein, T0294-442 3529,*
*www.labolsadeldeporte.com.ar.*

Relaxed atmosphere, rustic rooms with
duvets, 1 double with bath, some rooms
with views, deck to sit out on.

### $ pp Penthouse 1004
*San Martín 127, 10th floor, T0294-443 2228,*
*www.penthouse1004.com.ar.*
Welcoming hostel at the top of a block of
apartments with amazing views. Helpful
staff, cosy rooms, dorms US$18-19, doubles
US$48-50. Big communal area for chilling
and watching the sunset.

### $ pp Periko's
*Morales 555, T0294-452 2326,*
*www.perikos.com.*
Welcoming, quiet, nice atmosphere, dorms.
US$13-15, and doubles US$38-44 (depending
on season), breakfast included, washing
machine. Arranges tours, including to Ruta
40. Reserve in advance by email.

### $ pp Pudu
*Salta 459, T0294-442 9738,*
*www.hostelpudu.com.*
"A gem". Irish/Argentine-run, dorms US$21-
25 and doubles US$65 with spectacular lake
views, downstairs is a small garden and a bar.
Long-term rates available.

### $ pp Ruca Hueney
*Elflein 396, T0294-443 3986,*
*www.rucahueney.com.*
Lovely and calm, comfortable beds with
duvets, rooms for 2 to 6 people, great view,
very kind owners.

## Restaurants

Bariloche is blessed with superb food, much
of it locally produced, including smoked trout
and salmon, wild boar and other delicacies,
not least fine chocolate and, in season,
delicious berries. There are many good delis.

### $$$ Chez Philippe
*Primera Junta 1080, T0294-442 7291,*
*see Facebook.*
Delicious local delicacies and fondue, fine
French-influenced cuisine. Intimate and
secluded, away from the centre.

### $$$ Jauja
*Elflein 148, T0294-442 2952,*
*www.restaurantejauja.com.ar.*
Recommended for delicious local dishes,
quiet and welcoming, good value.

### $$$-$$ Días de Zapata
*T0294-442 3128.*
Mediocre Mexican, but a welcome change
from all the grilled meat.

### $$ Covita
*Rolando 172, T0294-442 1708.*
*Mon-Sat for lunch, Thu-Sat for dinner.*
Vegetarian restaurant (also serves fish),
offering curries, masalas and pastas.

### $$ El Boliche de Alberto
*Villegas 347, T0294-443 1433,*
*www.elbolichedealberto.com.*
Very good pasta, huge portions, popular
after 2000 (queues in summer). There is a
second location at Bustillo Km 8800 that
specializes in grilled meats.

### $$ El Vegetariano
*20 de Febrero 730, T0294-442 1820.*
Also fish, excellent food, beautifully served,
warm atmosphere, takeaway available.
Highly recommended.

### $ Huang Ji Zhong
*Rolando 268, T0294-442 8168.*
Good Chinese, next to a bowling alley.

## Cafés

### La Alpina
*Moreno 98.*
Old-fashioned café serving delicious cakes,
good for tea, Wi-Fi, charming.

## Bars and clubs

### Cerebro
*JM de Rosas 406, www.cerebro.com.ar.*
*Jun-Dec.*
The party starts at 0130, Fri is the best night.

### Wilkenny
*San Martín 435, T0294-442 4444.*
Lively Irish pub with expensive food but it
really gets busy around 2400. Great place to
watch sports on TV.

## Shopping

The main shopping area is on Mitre between
the Centro Cívico and Beschtedt, also on San
Martín. Local chocolate is excellent, and wines
from the Alto Río Negro are also good buys.

### Chocolate
Several shops on Mitre.
**Abuela Goye**, *Mitre 252, www.abuelagoye.*
*com.* First-rate chocolatier and café (5 other
branches and outlets nationwide).
**Fenoglio**, *Av Bustillo 1200, www.museo*
*chocolate.com.ar.* Chocolate museum
and production facility with tastings and
a good shop.
**Mamuschka**, *Mitre y Rolando, www.*
*mamuschka.com.* Considered the best
chocolate here, also with café.

### Handicrafts
**Feria Artesanal Municipal**, *Moreno y Villegas.*

## What to do

### Adventure tours
**Canopy**, *Colonia Suiza, Cerro López, T0294-*
*445 8585, www.canopybariloche.com.* Zip line
adventure in the forest, including 4WD ride
to get there and night descents.
**Eco Family**, *20 de Junio 728, T0294-442 8995,*
*www.eco-family.com.* Riding, walking,
skiing, other adventures, bilingual guides.
Highly recommended.
**Senza Limiti Adventures**, *J Cortázar 5050,*
*T0294-452 0597, www.slimiti.com.*
Adventure travel company, including
kayaking, mountain-biking, hut-to-hut
treks and much more, licensed by National
Parks Administration.
**Tronador Turismo**, *Quaglia 283, T0294-*
*442 5644, www.tronadorturismo.com.ar.*
Conventional tours, trekking and rafting. Also

to Refugio Neumeyer, and to Chilean border. Great adventurous wintersports options.

## Climbing

Note that at higher levels, winter snow storms can begin as early as Apr, making climbing dangerous. Contact **Club Andino Bariloche** (see page 112) for mountain guides and information.

## Cycling

Bikes can be hired at many places in high season.

**Circuito Chico**, *Av Bustillo 18300, T0294-459 5608, www.circuitochicobikes.com*. Rents mountain bikes, with road assistance service, and kayaks.

**Dirty Bikes**, *Lonquimay 3908, T0294-444 2743, www.dirtybikes.com.ar*. Very helpful for repairs, tours and bike rentals (US$20-45 per day).

## Fishing

**Martín Pescador**, *Rolando 257, T0294-442 2275, see Facebook*. Fishing, camping and skiing equipment.

## Horse riding

**Ariane Patagonia**, *T0294-441 3468, www.arianepatagonia.com.ar*. Horse-riding trips, visits to farms and estancias, personalized service.

**Bastión del Manso**, *Av Bustillo 13491, T0294-445 6111, www.bastiondelmanso.com*. Relaxed place with tuition and full-day's riding offered, including rafting and longer treks. See also **Estancia Peuma Hue**, page 122.

## Kayaking and rafting

**Aguas Blancas**, *Morales 564, T0294-443 2799, www.aguasblancas.com.ar*. Rafting on the Río Manso, all grades, with expert guides, and all equipment provided, also 'duckies' – inflatable kayaks for beginners.

**Patagonia Infinita**, *T0294-15-455 3954, www.patagoniainfinita.com.ar*. Kayaking and trekking trips in Parque Nacional Nahuel Huapi.

**Pura Vida Patagonia**, *T0294-15-441 4053, www.puravidapatagonia.com*. Informative, attentive guides, good-value trips from 1-9 days in Nahuel Huapi.

## Language schools

**ILEE**, *www.argentinailee.com*. Arranges classes and home stays.

**La Montaña**, *Elflein 251, T0294-452 4212, www.lamontana.com*. Spanish courses, family lodging, activities and volunteering.

## Paragliding

There are several paragliding schools. Take-offs are usually from Cerro Otto, but there are other starting points, 10- to 40-min tandem flights.

## Skiing

**Cerros Otto** and **Catedral**, *see pages 119 and 120*.

## Tours

Check what your tour includes; cable cars and chair lifts are usually extra. Tours get booked up in season. Most travel agencies will pick you up from your hotel, and charge roughly the same prices: Circuito Chico half day, US$17; Isla Victoria and Bosque de Arrayanes, full-day boat trip from Puerto Pañuelo, US$50, or US$30 from other departure points (park entry, US$10, not included); Tronador, Ventisquero Negro and Pampa Linda, US$45 plus National Park entry via Lago Mascardi by boat; El Bolsón US$45, full-day, including Lago Puelo; several other tours.

**Turisur**, *Mitre 219, T0294-442 6109, www.turisur.com.ar*. Boat trips to Bosque de Arrayanes, Isla Victoria on a 1937 ship and to Tronador via Lago Mascardi. Licensee for the Cruce Andino trip to Puerto Montt. Always reserve 1 day ahead.

## Trekking

For further information, contact **Club Andino Bariloche** (see page 112).

**Active Patagonia**, *20 de Febrero 30, T0294-452 9875, www.activepatagonia.com.ar*.

As well as trekking to Tronador and Refugio Frey, also offers kayaking, rafting, horse riding, mountain biking and climbing. **Andescross**, *T0294-15-463 3581, www. andescross.com*. Expert guides, all included. Trekking to Chile across the Andes, via Pampa Linda, Lago Frías, Peulla.

## Transport

### Air
The airport (T0294-440 5016) has car rental agencies, internet, exchange, ATM and a café. Many flights a day to **Buenos Aires**. AR also flies to **El Calafate** in summer only. **LADE** flies to **Buenos Aires**, **Comodoro Rivadavia** (with connections to **El Calafate**) and several other destinations in Patagonia.

### Boat
For boat trips, see page 123. For the route by boat and bus to Chile, see box, page 124.

### Bus
The bus terminal (T0294-443 2860) has toilets, small *confitería*, *kiosko*, *locutorio* with internet, left luggage and a tourist information desk.

Tickets can be bought at the bus company offices in town or at terminal: **Vía Bariloche**, Mitre 321, T0810-333 7575 and at the terminal; **Chevallier/Flechabus**, Moreno 107, T0294-442 3090. **Andesmar**, at terminal, T0294-443 0211; **Ko Ko**, at terminal, T0294-443 1135.

**Local** To **Llao Llao**, bus No 20 from Moreno y Rolando, US$1.50, 45 mins. To **Villa Catedral**, bus 'Catedral' from the bus terminal or Moreno y Palacios, every 90 mins, US$1.50, 35 mins.

**Long distance** To **Buenos Aires**, 7 companies daily, 19-22 hrs, US$120-140. To **Bahía Blanca**, with **Andesmar**, 14 hrs,

US$75-85. To **Mendoza**, US$80-113, with **Andesmar** and **Cata**, 17-19 hrs. **Marga** to **El Bolsón**, US$8, 2 hrs, and on to **Esquel**, 4-5 hrs, US$21, heavily, even over, booked in high season. To **San Martín de los Andes** (not via 7 Lagos), 3½-4 hrs, US$15-19, with **Vía Bariloche**. To **Villa La Angostura**, 1 hr, US$5, several companies. To **Comodoro Rivadavia**, US$64-73, **Andesmar**, 14 hrs, **Marga/TAQSA** (T0800-333 1188, www.taqsa.com.ar). **To El Bolsón** with **Vía Bariloche**, US$6.50, 2 hrs. It's also possible to take **Chaltén Travel**'s (www.chaltentravel.com) 3-day trip on Ruta 40 down to **El Chaltén**, **El Calafate** and **Ushuaia**, depart 0745 on odd-numbered days from 20 de Febrero 30, at Club Andino Bariloche. Operates from Nov-Apr only.

**To Chile**: **Vía Bariloche** runs daily services via Samoré pass to **Osorno**, 5 hrs, US$36, and **Puerto Montt**, 6-7½ hrs, same fare; **Andesmar** goes to **Valdivia** via Osorno, US$43-52, not daily. Take your passport when booking. Sit on the left side for the best views.

### Car hire
Rates are from US$40, up to US$120 per day, depending on the size of the vehicle. Larger companies may permit hiring in one town and returning to another for an extra charge (price depends on distance and type of vehicle). **Lagos**, Mitre 83, T0294-442 8880, www.lagosrentacar.com.ar, among many others. To enter Chile, a permit is necessary; it's generally included in the price but you should state your intention of driving to Chile when booking the car, allow 24 hrs.

### Train
Train station, T0294-442 2450. See Essential box, page 68, for **Tren Patagónico** service to **Viedma**, www.trenpatagonico-sa.com.ar.

### Llao Llao and the Circuito Chico

To really appreciate the splendid setting of Bariloche, you need to get out of town and head 25 km west towards the area known as **Llao Llao**. Named after one of Argentina's most famous hotels, this is a charming area that offers lovely walking and gorgeous views. It's at the end of Avenida Bustillo, which runs along Lago Nahuel Huapi to the port (Puerto Pañuelo), from where boat trips depart. Frequent buses run along this road, so it's easy to explore even without your own transport. (Bus No 20 departs from the big bus stop at Moreno y Rolando for a lovely 45-minute ride, US$1.50.) There's easy access to the mountains above Avenida Bustillo and parallel **Avenida de los Pioneros**: just get off the bus at the kilometre stop you want. The free tourist office map *Circuito Chico* shows the stops clearly.

The Circuito Chico is a classic old Argentine tour: you sit in the car and gaze at the view. These days, you're more likely to want to stop, hike, take photos and find somewhere to eat, so the tour as offered by tour operators can be a frustrating experience. To really enjoy this great introduction to the area, drive or cycle instead. This is a satisfying all-day cycle ride, but beware that Avenida Bustillo is a busy road, and drivers will show you no mercy, expecting you to pull over onto the gravel verges as they pass.

Start by travelling along Avenida Bustillo. At Km 17.5, a **chairlift** ① *T0294-442 7274, www. cerrocampanario.com.ar, daily 0900-1730, 7 mins, US$11 return, extended opening in summer;* bus No 10, 20 or 22, goes up to **Cerro Campanario** (1049 m). There is a restaurant and bar at

### ② Bariloche – the road to Llao Llao

| 1 km | | |
| 1 miles | | |

| **Where to stay** 🛏 | 5 El Yeti | 9 Llao-Llao |
| 1 Alaska | 6 Gringos Patagonia | 10 Petunia |
| 2 Aldebaran | 7 Hostería Santa Rita | 11 Selva Negra |
| 3 Departamentos Bellevue | 8 La Caleta | 12 Tunquelén |

the top with fabulous views of the lake, edged with mountains, as well as of the San Pedro peninsula below and Lago Moreno.

**Tip...**
Hotel Llao Llao is a good place for tea on the terrace, with stunning views.

Back on Avenida Bustillo, turn off at Km 18.3 to go around Lago Moreno Oeste, past Punto Panorámico (with really great views) and continue around **Bahía López**, through the Parque Municipal Llao Llao. Covering a small peninsula that juts into the lake, the park offers superb walks in beautiful virgin forest that is rich in wildlife. There's a small hill to climb and a little beach, **Villa Tacul**, both offering good views. **Hotel Llao Llao** and **Puerto Pañuelo** are located just east of the park.

Hotel Llao Llao (see Where to stay, page 121) is one of Argentina's finest hotels and worth the extortionate rates for its view, spa and restaurant. Superbly situated on a hill, it has incredible views over the lake. The hotel was designed by Bustillo and opened in 1937. Originally almost entirely a wooden construction, it burned down within a few months of opening and was rebuilt using local stone.

You could extend the circuit by returning via **Colonia Suiza** and the ski resort of **Cerro Catedral** (2388 m), both of which are possible starting points for longer treks (see Trekking, page 116).

### Cerro Otto

A free bus service runs from Mitre y Villegas or Pagano y San Martín, daily from 1000 in high season, to Km 5 on Avenida de los Pioneros, from where a **cable car** (teleférico) ① T0294-444 1035, www.telefericobariloche.com.ar, daily 1000-1730 (last descent at 1900),

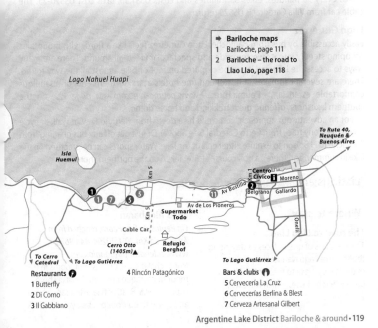

→ **Bariloche maps**
1  Bariloche, page 111
2  Bariloche – the road to
   Llao Llao, page 118

*Lago Nahuel Huapi*

*Isla Huemul*

*To Ruta 40, Neuquén & Buenos Aires*

**Centro Cívico** ℹ Moreno

Belgrano  Gallardo

Av Bustillo

**Av de Los Pioneros**

**Supermarket Todo**

Cable Car

**Cerro Otto** (1405m)▲

**Refugio Berghof**

*To Cerro Catedral*  *To Lago Gutiérrez*

*To Lago Gutiérrez*

Onelli

**Restaurants**
1 Butterfly
2 Di Como
3 Il Gabbiano
4 Rincón Patagónico

**Bars & clubs**
5 Cervecería La Cruz
6 Cervecerías Berlina & Blest
7 Cerveza Artesanal Gilbert

*US$22 return*, goes up to Cerro Otto (1405 m) with its revolving restaurant and really wonderful views over the lakes and mountains all around. Alternatively, 20 minutes' walk away on the summit at **Refugio Berghof** is a *confitería* belonging to Club Andino Bariloche. Highly recommended. Urban buses 50 and 51 also go to the cable car station, or by car, take Avenida de los Pioneros, then the signposted dirt track 1 km out of town.

To climb Cerro Otto on foot (two to three hours), turn off Avenida de los Pioneros at Km 4.6, then follow the trail past **Refugio Berghof**, with splendid views. This is not recommended alone, as paths can be confusing.

### Cerro Catedral

*T0294-440 9000, www.catedralaltapatagonia.com. Slopes are open from mid-Jun to end of Sep and are busiest 15 Jun-15 Aug (school holidays). Ski lifts daily 0900-1700 (last ascent 1615); adult passes US$55-77 per day depending on season.*

Cerro Catedral (2338 m), 21 km southwest of Bariloche, is one of the major ski resorts in Argentina and is extremely well organized with a great range of slopes for all abilities. There are 120 km of slopes of all grades, allowing a total drop of 1010 m, starting at 2000 m, and 52 km of cross-country skiing routes, all with utterly spectacular views. There are also snowboarding areas and a well-equipped base with hotels, restaurants, equipment hire, ski schools and nursery care for children. As a summer resort, there's a cable car to take you further into the hills, useful for starting walks to **Refugio Lynch** (from where you can walk on to Laguna Jakob) and **Refugio Frey**, or for cycling down to Lago Gutiérrez.

To get to Cerro Catedral, take the bus marked 'Catedral' from the bus terminal or the bus stop on Moreno y Palacios to the ski station base (known as Villa Catedral). The bus leaves every 90 minutes, takes 35 minutes and costs US$1.50; taxis cost US$20-25. The **cable car** from Villa Catedral is US$20 return.

### Lago Gutiérrez

Easily accessible by bus from Bariloche, Lago Gutiérrez feels like a fjord, with mountains dropping steeply into its western side and spectacular views all around. There are many ways to access the lake and it can be explored on foot or bike almost all the way round. There are several campsites, a hostel and fine hotels at its northern end, or a fabulous comfortable estancia, ★ **Peuma Hue** ⓘ *www.peuma-hue.com, see page 122*, on the southern lakeshore, offering great trekking and horse riding.

For an adventurous approach, you could hike down from **Refugio Frey** or walk or cycle down the stony track from Cerro Catedral (see above). Or just get off any bus heading from Bariloche to El Bolsón to explore either end of the lake. Water sports can be practised on the lake in summer, and there's a golf course at Arelauken on the northern shore.

## Listings Around Bariloche *map page 118.*

### Where to stay

#### The road to Llao Llao

There are lots of great places to stay along the shore of Lago Nahuel Huapi, many of them very close to the centre. All can be reached by buses which run every 20-30 mins.

#### $$$$ Aldebaran

*On Península San Pedro, reached from Av Bustillo Km 20.4, T0294-444 8678, www.aldebaranpatagonia.com.*
Not in chalet style, but tasteful rooms in this modern boutique hotel on the lake shore, superb views. Rustic-style restaurant, sauna and spa with outdoor pool, so you can bask

under the stars. Great service from helpful bilingual staff.

## $$$$ Llao Llao
*Av Bustillo Km 25, T0294-444 5700/8530, www.llaollao.com.*
Deservedly famous, superb location, complete luxury, golf course, pool, spa, water sports, restaurant.

## $$$$ Tunquelén
*Av Bustillo, Km 24.5, T0294-444 8400/8600, www.tunquelen.com.*
4-star, comfortable, splendid views, feels quite secluded, superb restaurant, attentive service.

## $$$ Departamentos Bellevue
*Av Bustillo, Km 24.6, T0294-444 8389, www.bellevue.com.ar. Open year-round.*
A famous tea room with beautiful views also offers accommodation with high-quality furnishings, very comfortable, well-equipped self-catering *cabañas*, delicious breakfast included. Access to beaches on Lake Moreno, lovely gardens.

## $$$ Gringos Patagonia
*Av Bustillo, Km 24.3, T0294-444 8023, www.gringospatagonia.com.*
Delightful, peaceful garden full of flowers, charming Slovenian family Kastelic (also half-board, $$$$). Also offers adventure tourism.

## $$$ Hostería Santa Rita
*Av Bustillo, Km 7.2, T0294-446 1028, www.santarita.com.ar.*
Bus 10, 20/21 to Km 7.5. Peaceful lakeside views, comfortable, lovely terrace, great service.

## $$$ La Caleta
*Av Bustillo, Km 1.95, T0294-444 3444, www.bungalows-bariloche.com.ar.*
*Cabañas* sleep 4, open fire, excellent value. Also owns **San Isidro** *cabañas* at Km 5.7, further west.

## $ pp Alaska
*Lilinquen 328 (buses 10, 20, 21, get off at La Florida, Av Bustillo Km 7.5), T0294-446 1564, www.alaskahostelbariloche.com.*
Well run, cosy with shared rustic rooms for 4, US$14 pp, also doubles US$43 (cheaper without bath), nice garden, washing machine, organizes horse riding and rafting, rents mountain bikes. Recommended.

## Camping
A list of sites is available from the tourist office. Shops and restaurants on most sites; these are closed outside Jan-Mar. These are recommended among the many along Bustillo:

## El Yeti
*Km 5.7, T0294-444 2073.*
All facilities, *cabañas*.

## Petunia
*Km 13.5, T0294-446 1969, www.campingpetunia.com.*
A lovely shady site going down to lakeside with all facilities.

## Selva Negra
*Km 2.95, T0294-444 1013, www.campingselvanegra.com.ar.*
Very good, discounts for long stay.

## Cerro Catedral

## $$$$ Pire-Hue
*Villa Catedral, T011-4782 0322 (Buenos Aires), www.pire-hue.com.ar. Prices rise in Jul/Aug and fall in Jun/Sep.*
Exclusive 5-star hotel with beautifully decorated rooms and all the facilities.

## Lago Gutiérrez

## $$$$ El Retorno
*Villa Los Coihues, on the shore of Lago Gutiérrez, T0294-446 7333, www.hosteria elretorno.com (closed for major renovation until early 2017).*
Stunning lakeside position, comfortable hunting lodge style, family-run, with a beach, tennis, very comfortable rooms ($$$ in low season) and self-catering apartments (Bus 50, follow signs off the road to El Bolsón).

#### $$$$ Estancia Peuma Hue
*Ruta 40, Km 2014, T0294-15-450 1030,*
*www.peuma-hue.com.*
Best comfort in a homely environment,
on the southern shores of Lago Gutiérrez,
below Cerro Catedral Sur. Charming owner
Evelyn Hoter and dedicated staff make it
all work perfectly: tasty home-made food,
superb horse riding and other activities,
health treatments, yoga, meditation, etc,
candlelit concerts. All inclusive, varied
accommodation. Highly recommended.

### Camping

#### Villa los Coihues
*Lago Gutiérrez, T0294-446 7481,*
*www.campingloscoihues.com.ar.*
Well-equipped and beautifully situated.
Camping from US$8.50 and dorm rooms
from US$22. Take bus No 50 or take the
track down to Gutiérrez from Cerro Catedral
(4WD advisable) or the road to El Bolsón
(Ruta 258), and follow signs.

## Restaurants

### The road to Llao Llao

#### $$$ Butterfly
*Hua Huan 7831, just off Av Bustillo Km 7.9,*
*T0294-446 1441, www.butterflypatagonia.*
*com.ar.*
2 seatings: 1945 and 2130. German/
Argentine/Irish owned, an elite dining
experience, tasting menus using local
ingredients, carefully selected wines, art
exhibitions, only 8 tables. Reserve in advance
and discuss the menu with the chef.

#### $$$ Il Gabbiano
*Av Bustillo Km 24.3, T0294-444 8346. Closed Tue.*
Delicious Italian lunches and dinners.
Booking essential (no credit cards).

#### $$$ Rincón Patagónico
*Av Bustillo, Km 14, Paraje Laguna Fantasma,*
*T0294-446 3063, www.rinconpatagonico.com.*
Traditional *parrilla* with Patagonian lamb
cooked *al palo*. Huge menu but service can
be minimal at busy times.

#### $$ Di Como
*Av Bustillo, Km 0.8, T0294-452 2118.*
A 10-min walk from town. Good pizza and
pasta, terrace and great views of the lake.

## Bars and clubs

#### Cervecería Berlina
*Ruta 79 y F Goye, T0294-445 4393,*
*www.cervezaberlina.com. Open 1200*
*until around 2400.*
3 good brews. They have a diverse menu ($$)
at their restaurant at Av Bustillo Km 11.750,
with a deck for watching the sunset.

#### Cervecería Blest
*Av Bustillo Km 11.6, T0294-446 1026,*
*www.cervezablest.com.ar.*
Wonderful brewery with delicious beers,
serving imaginative local and German dishes
and steak and kidney pie ($$$-$$).

#### Cervecería La Cruz
*Nilpi 789, T0294-444 2634,*
*www.cerverialacruz.com.ar.*
Great brewpub with many local beers on tap.
Also delicious bar food such as burgers and
thin-crust pizzas. Good place to kick back
and imbibe with ski bums.

#### Cerveza Artesanal Gilbert
*Km 24, Barrio Las Cartas, Circuito Chico,*
*T0294-445 4292, www.cerveceriagilbert.*
*com.ar. Daily 1200-1900.*
Popular beers and simple meals ($$).

## What to do

### Lago Gutiérrez
### Horse riding
From **Estancia Peuma Hue** on Lago
Gutiérrez (see Where to stay, above), you
can ride into the mountains and over to
Pampa Linda. Riding is also available from
**Los Baqueanos** (signposted from R258, on
the eastern shore of Lago Gutiérrez, T0294-
423 0556, www.complejobaqueanos.com.ar).

### Isla Victoria and Bosque de Arrayanes

There are popular trips from Puerto Pañuelo (bus No 10, 11 or 20 to get there) and other departure points to Isla Victoria and on to Parque Nacional Los Arrayanes, on the Quetrihué Peninsula (see box, page 103). Park entry (US$10) is not included in the tour price.

### Puerto Blest

The other great boat trip in the area is the all-day excursion to Puerto Blest, **Cascada de los Cántaros**, at the western end of Lago Nahuel Huapi, and **Lago Frías**, visiting native forest and Valdivian rainforest – highly recommended. This is usually done as a nine-hour trip from Bariloche, leaving at 0900 from Puerto Pañuelo

**Tip...**
Visit the national park by boat or on foot from Villa La Angostura, which allows you more time in the forest and a good 13-km hike back.

(Km 25.5), and sailing down to fjord-like Puerto Blest, where there's a good *hostería* and restaurant at the end of the lake. *Coihue*-clad mountains drop steeply into Prussian blue water, and it's usually raining, but very atmospheric. The tour then continues by short bus ride to **Puerto Alegre** on Lago Frías, and you cross the still, peppermint-green lake by launch. From Puerto Blest, the walk through beautiful forest to the **Cascada de los Cántaros** (one hour) is superb. If you set off while the rest of the party stops for lunch, you'll have time for your picnic by the splendid falls before the crowd arrives by boat. Or walk beyond them up to quiet **Lago de los Cántaros**, enclosed by vertical granite cliffs.

Boat trips run by Turisur depart Puerto Pañuelo at 1000. They cost US$49, plus an extra US$11 for a bus transfer to Puerto Pañuelo; it's cheaper to take a bus before 0800 from the centre of town. Boats are comfortable but be aware that they fill up entirely in high season; they are much more pleasant in December and March. There's a good (but expensive) *cafetería* on board and set lunch is available at **Hostería Blest**; cheaper sandwiches are available from the snack bar next door or you should stock up on picnic provisions before you go. The **Hotel y Restaurant Puerto Blest ($$$)** is a small cosy hotel built in 1904, with homely rather than luxurious rooms. It's worth staying a night if you want to try any of the treks from here, or fish for trout, and the only other option is camping *libre* with no facilities. The *guardaparques* at Puerto Blest can advise on the many walks from here (and their state), but the seven-hour, 15-km trek to **Lago Ortiz Basualdo** is recommended (mid-December to March only). For information on the Three Lakes Crossing into Chile, see box, page 124.

There are many superb walks in this area. A network of paths in the mountains and several *refugios* allow for treks over several days. *Refugios* are leased by Club Andino Bariloche, who charge US$10-20 per night, plus US$8-20 for food. Take a good sleeping bag.

Below is just a small selection of walks of various grades of difficulty, recommended for the surrounding natural beauty: There's not space here to give detailed descriptions or instructions, so for all walks contact **Club Andino Bariloche** (see page 112) for advice,

## BORDER CROSSING

### Argentina–Chile

**Three Lakes Crossing**

This popular route to Puerto Varas in Chile, with ferries across Lago Nahuel Huapi, Lago Frías and Lago Todos Los Santos, is outstandingly beautiful whatever the season, though the mountains are often obscured by rain and heavy cloud. It's a long journey, however, and is not recommended in really heavy rain. Book well ahead in high season (you can reserve online), and take your passport when booking in person. No cars are carried on the boats on this route.

The route is Bariloche to Puerto Pañuelo by road (30 minutes, departure from hotel at 0830), Puerto Pañuelo to Puerto Blest by boat (one hour at 1000), Puerto Blest to Puerto Alegre on Lago Frías by bus (15 minutes), cross the lake to Puerto Frías by boat (20 minutes) for Argentine immigration, then two hours by road to Peulla (lunch is not included in the price). Leave for Petrohué at 1600 by boat (one hour 40 minutes), cross Lago Todos Los Santos, passing the Osorno volcano and other peaks, then by bus to Puerto Varas (two hours, arrive 1900). For the route from Chile, see box, page 323.

If you take two days over the journey, you spend the first afternoon and second morning in Peulla, staying overnight in either the **Hotel Peulla** (T+56-(0)65-297 2288, www.hotelpeulla.cl) or the **Hotel Natura Patagonia** (T+56-(0)65-297 2289, www. hotelnatura.cl); breakfast is included, but supper, lodging and the second day's lunch are not. Nor are the prices of any excursions you may choose to do in Peulla, such as horse riding, canopy, boat trips or kayaking.

The mid-2016 season price was US$280 one way in high season (US$230 in low season), 50% on return ticket; check the website before booking as prices alter with the season. **Cruce Andino** (www.cruceandino.com) has the monopoly on this crossing. In Bariloche bookings are handled by **Turisur** (Mitre 219, T0294-442 6109, www.turisur.com.ar), although tickets are sold by various operators. The trip runs every day except 1 May.

**Paso Pérez Rosales**

The Three Lakes Crossing enters Chile via the Paso Pérez Rosales; see www.gendarmeria.gob.ar/pasos-chile/perez-rosales.html.

**Argentine immigration and customs** At Puerto Frías, open daily.
**Chilean immigration and customs** At Peulla, open daily 0900-2000.
Chilean currency can be bought at Peulla customs at a reasonable rate.

---

maps and to check paths are open before you set off: crucial in spring when snow may not have cleared the upper slopes. You could also consider contacting a trekking company to take you on guided hikes rather than setting off alone.

**Around Llao Llao** There are several easy and very satisfying walks from Llao Llao: a delightful easy circuit in Valdivian (temperate) rainforest in the Parque Municipal Llao Llao (turn left off the road, just past the golf course, two hours); the small hill Cerrito Llao Llao (900 m) for wonderful views (turn right off the road and follow signs – one to two hours), or a 3-km trail through to Brazo de la Tristeza (turn right off the road opposite the *guardebosque*), via tiny Lago Escondido, with magical views. Bus No 20 to Llao Llao leaves from the terminal every 20 minutes from 0540.

**Refugio López** ⓘ *2076 m, 5-7 hrs return.* This is a great hike with some of the most wonderful views of the whole area. Starting from the southeastern tip of Lago Moreno, go up alongside Arroyo López, and then along a ridge to the distinctive rose-coloured **Refugio López**, with its fabulous views. Refugio López is the only *refugio* that is privately owned and not part of CAB's chain. The owners may charge you to use the paths. From Refugio López, you could do some climbing, or continue to make this a three- to four-day trek: head south to **Refugio Italia**, which is on the shores of the incredibly calm Laguna Negra at the foot of Cerro Negro. Then from here, you could hike on via Cerro Navidad to Laguna Jakob and **Refugio San Martín**. But note that this section is poorly signposted, and advisable only for very experienced walkers who are well equipped and can use a compass proficiently. Take a trekking guide if in any doubt, and always ask at CAB for the conditions of the paths. Bus No 10 or 11 to Colonia Suiza and Arroyo López (check return times).

**Refugio Frey** ⓘ *1700 m.* From the ski station at **Villa Catedral**, there are two ways up: 1) Walk up to Refugio Frey, or take the cable car to **Refugio Lynch** (check before you set off, as precise cable-car routes change each year) and from here walk along the ridge of Cerro Catedral to Refugio Frey, which occupies a beautiful setting on a small lake (two to four hours one-way, experience necessary); or 2) from Villa Catedral, walk south and up alongside the Arroyo Van Titter to **Refugio Piedritas**, a very basic emergency shelter with no services, to reach Refugio Frey (three to six hours to climb one-way). The area around **Refugio Frey** is the best area for climbing in the whole region, with innumerable options in the granite walls around. From Refugio Frey there are several possibilities: walk on to Refugio Piedritas (four hours each way), and then down the Arroyo Van Titter to reach Lago Gutiérrez. Once you reach the lake, you could either walk around its southern head to join the Route 258, which runs from Bariloche to El Bolsón, or ask **Estancia Peuma Hue** (see Where to stay, page 122) to collect you at the start of a few night's stay there. (The same is also possible in reverse.)

**Lago Gutiérrez** This grand lake southwest of Bariloche has the relaxing ★ **Estancia Peuma Hue** on its shores with excellent horse riding (see Where to stay, page 122). You can reach the lake by walking 2 km downhill from the ski base at Cerro Catedral and along the northern lake shore, reaching the El Bolsón road (Route 258) where you can take a bus back to Bariloche (six hours). Or arrange with **Estancia Peuma Hue** to collect you by boat from the shore of Lake Gutiérrez and stay a couple of nights at the estancia for more great walks.

**Refugio Neumayer** ⓘ *Has an office in town: Diversidad, 20 de Junio 728, T0294-442 8995, www.eco-family.com.* Some 12 km south of Bariloche, this makes a really charming centre for exploring the area, with eight paths to walk, information and guides on offer. Two are particularly recommended, to **Laguna Verde**, and to a mirador through Magellanic forest at **Valle de los Perdidos**. This is a cosy, friendly *refugio*, very well set up for walkers and families, and offering a wonderful range of activities. There is also superb cross-country skiing (also called Nordic skiing) around here, with bilingual guides and equipment available for hire. Great fun.

> **Tip...**
> On treks to *refugios* remember to also allow for the costs of ski lifts and buses.

# Bariloche
## to El Bolsón

Some of Argentina's most spectacular and unspoilt scenery lies south of Bariloche, where there is a wilder, more relaxed feel to the landscape. Route 258, the road south from Bariloche to El Bolsón, is breathtaking, passing the picturesque lakes of Gutiérrez and Mascardi, lying below a massive jagged range of mountains. There are some fabulous, peaceful places to stay here and wonderful hikes and horse riding. From Villa Mascardi, a road leads to glorious Pampa Linda, where there is excellent trekking, including access to climb Mount Tronador. Further south, Río Manso Medio has become famous for whitewater rafting, and at Lago Hess there is the lovely Cascadas Los Alerces.

El Bolsón is a pretty and relaxed town, sprawled out between two mountain ranges, with superb hikes nearby and beautiful rivers, waterfalls and mountains to explore. Several microbreweries here convert local hops into fine handmade beers, and craftsmen supply the local market with wood and leather work, as well as delicious jams from the abundant soft fruits in summer.

Further south, Lago Puelo is a tiny national park, offering great fishing, some good walks and a boat trip to the Chilean border. As you head south, Cholila might attract Butch Cassidy fans, but though it feels authentically like the Wild West, there's little appeal here now.

**Lago Mascardi** *Colour map 1, B3.*

At the southern end of Lago Mascardi (Km 35), **Villa Mascardi** is a small village from where the *ripio* Route 81 runs towards Lago Hess and Cascada Los Alerces. This road operates a one-way system: going west 1000-1400, east 1600-1800, two-way 1900-0900; times may vary, check with the Bariloche **tourist office** (see page 113). Along Lago Mascardi, there are several beautifully situated places to stay, all easily reached by car, or bus when the service is running in summer. Shortly after the lovely straight beach of Playa Negro, handy for launching boats and fishing, the road forks, with the left-hand branch following the crystalline Río Manso Medio to Lago Hess. The **Río Manso** is popular for rafting (arranged through tour operators in Bariloche, see page 116). The right fork of the road, meanwhile, follows a narrow arm of Lago Mascardi northwest, with a viewpoint in lovely woodland to see Isla Piuke Huapi in the centre of the lake. A few kilometres further on is the lakeside paradise of **Hotel Tronador** before reaching Pampa Linda and Mount Tronador at the end of the road. For further information, see Where to stay, page 128.

## Pampa Linda

Pampa Linda lies 40 km west of Villa Mascardi in the most blissfully isolated location, with spectacular views of Cerro Tronador towering above. There's a ranger station with very helpful *guardaparques* who can advise on walks, and whom you must consult about the state of the paths and register your name before setting out. From Pampa Linda, a lovely track (*ripio*) continues to **Ventisquero Negro** (Black Glacier), which hangs over a fantastically murky pool in which grey 'icebergs' float. The colour is due to sediment, and while not exactly attractive, the whole scene is very atmospheric. The road ends at the awesome **Garganta del Diablo**, one of the natural amphitheatres formed by the lower slopes of Mount Tronador. A beautiful walk (90 minutes' walk there and back) from the car park through beach forest takes you to a more pristine glacier, and up to the head of the gorge, where thin torrents of ice melt from the hanging glacier above and fall in columns like sifted sugar. Another pleasant walk is to tranquil **Laguna Ilon** (5½ hours each way), with bathing on the shore in summer.

A day tour to Pampa Linda from Bariloche will usually include both **Ventisquero Negro** and the falls at **Garganta del Diablo**, as well as the beautiful lakes Gutiérrez and Mascardi en route, but will not allow much time for walking. A good way to make the most of the area is to take a tour with an agency, and then stay on at Pampa Linda for trekking, returning with the minibus service run by **Transitando lo Natural** ⓘ *20 de Febrero 25, T0294-442 3250.* Alternatively, buses to Pampa Linda run daily in season (December-15 April) from outside **Club Andino Bariloche** ⓘ *transitando1@hotmail.com, US$18.* There's a great simple *hostería* at Pampa Linda, offering lunch.

## ★ Mount Tronador

The highest peak around is the mighty Mount Tronador ('The Thunderer', 3478 m). From Pampa Linda two other paths lead up **the mountain**: the first is 15 km long and leads to **Refugio Otto Meiling** (2000 m), in itself a wonderful walk (five hours each way), situated on the edge of the eastern glacier. Another hour from the *refugio*, a path takes you to a view over Tronador and the lakes and mountains of **Parque Nacional Nahuel Huapi**. The other path leads to a *refugio* on the south side of the mountain. Otto Meiling is a good base camp for the ascent, with lots of facilities and activities, including trekking and ice climbing; always ask the *guardaparques* in Pampa Linda if there's space (capacity 60); dinner is available (let them know in advance if you're vegetarian). The lower sections of these paths are great for mountain biking in the forest,

## Paso de los Nubes

Pampa Linda is the starting point for a 22-km walk over Paso de los Nubes (1335 m) to **Laguna Frías** and **Puerto Frías** on the Chilean border. Allow at least two days; start the walk at Pampa Linda, rather than the other way around, as there's a gentler rise to the pass this way. There is camping at **Campamento Alerce** (after four hours) or **Campamento Glacier Frías** (after seven hours); from here it's another five hours to Puerto Frías. You'll see a spectacular glacial landscape, formed relatively recently (11,000 years ago), and the pass lies on the continental divide, with water flowing north to the Atlantic, and south to the Pacific. Views from the Río Frías valley are tremendous, and from Glacier Frías you enter Valdivian rainforest. Boats cross Lago Frías at 1600, but check this before leaving Bariloche. From Puerto Frías a 30-km road leads to Peulla on the shore of Chilean Lago Todos Los Santos. Or you can take a boat back to Bariloche – highly recommended.

You must register with *guardaparques* at Pampa Linda before setting out, and check with them about conditions. The route is not always well marked and should only be attempted if there is no snow on the pass (it's normally passable only between December and February) or if the path is not excessively boggy. Do not cross rivers on fallen bridges or trees. Buy the map produced by Infotrekking for Mount Tronador/Paso de las Nubes before you leave Bariloche (available from **Club Andino Bariloche**, see page 112) and also see the excellent leaflet for *Paso de las Nubes* produced by Parque Nacional Nahuel Huapi, all found online at www.nahuelhuapi.gov.ar.

## Río Manso Medio and Lago Hess

Some 9 km west of Villa Mascardi, a road runs 18 km through the beautiful valley of the Río Manso Medio to Lago Hess and on to the nearby **Cascada Los Alerces**. This is the starting point for trekking trips in a more remote area of small lakes and forested mountains, including the lakes Fonck, Roca, Felipe, and Cerros Granito and Fortaleza. Check with *guardaparques* at Lago Hess about the conditions of the paths. There is also wonderful rafting here, but you have to take an organized trip from Bariloche. Note that there is also rafting on the **Río Manso Inferior**, further south (see below). For further information, see What to do, opposite.

## Lago Steffen and Lago Martín

About 20 km south of Villa Mascardi, another one-way dirt road leads to Lago Steffen, where a footpath runs along both northern and southern shores (of Lago Steffen) to Lago Martín. Both lakes are quite outstandingly lovely, fringed with beech and *álamo* trees, with far-off mountains in the distance and pretty beaches where you can sit at the water's edge. There's also great fishing here. The *guardería* is at Lago Steffen and wild camping is possible further north on the lake shore. To the south, a road leads west from Villegas along the Río Manso Inferior towards Chile. The river here is ideal for wilder rafting and for the trip to the Chilean border, run by rafting companies in Bariloche (see page 116).

---

## Listings Bariloche to El Bolsón

### Where to stay

#### Lago Mascardi

**$$$ pp Hotel Tronador**
T0294-4449 0556, www.hoteltronador.com.
Nov-Apr.

60 km from Bariloche, on the narrow road between Villa Mascardi and Pampa Linda. A lakeside paradise, offering lovely rooms with views of Lago Mascardi, beautiful gardens, charming owner, also riding, fishing and lake trips. Full board.

## Camping

### Camping La Querencia
*R81 towards Pampa Linda, Km 5, T0294-15-461 6300, www.campinglaquerencia.com.ar. Camping US$11 for adults.*
A pretty and peaceful spot on the side of the river and the banks of the lake, opposite Playa Negro.

### Camping Las Carpitas
*Lago Mascardi, at Km 33, T0294-449 0527, www.campinglascarpitas.com.ar. Camping from US$7 and dorms from US$11.*
Set in a great lakeside position, summer only, with *cabañas* and restaurant.

### Camping Los Rápidos
*R258, Km 37, T0294-15-431 7028, www.losrapidos.com.ar.*
Attractive shaded site going down to the lake, with *confitería*, food store and all facilities, US$10 per person. Also bunk beds in a basic *albergue* for US$19 per person (sleeping bag needed). Friendly owners organize trekking, kayaking, fishing and mountain biking.

## Pampa Linda

### $$$ Hostería Pampa Linda
*T0294-449 0517, www.hosteriapampalinda. com.ar.*
A comfortable, peaceful base for climbing Tronador and many other treks (plus horse riding, trekking and climbing courses), simple rooms, all with stunning views, restaurant, full board optional, packed lunches available for hikes. Charming owners, Sebastián de la Cruz is one of the area's most experienced mountaineers. Highly recommended.

## Camping

### Los Vuriloches
*Pampa Linda, T0294-446 2131, pampalindatere@hotmail.com.*
Idyllic spacious lakeside site, with a *confitería* serving good meals and food shop. Excellent service, run by the Club Andino Bariloche.

### Río Manso Medio and Lago Hess

### $$$$ Río Manso Lodge
*T0294-492 2961, www.riomansolodge.com.*
Spectacularly set on the bank of the Río Manso in beautiful mountainous scenery, this is a top-class fishing lodge, with lovely rooms with great views from their large windows, fine food and great fishing. Loved by experts. Transfers organized.

## What to do

### Río Manso Medio and Lago Hess
**Rafting**
Rafting on the Río Manso is arranged through operators in Bariloche; see page 116.

## Transport

### Lago Mascardi
**Bus**
Services from Bariloche to **El Bolsón** pass through **Villa Mascardi**. Buses to **Los Rápidos** run from the terminal in Bariloche between 0800-0930 daily in summer. Check with **Vía Bariloche/El Valle** for times.

### Pampa Linda and Mount Tronador
**Bus**
A bus from Bariloche leaves at 0830 daily and returns at 1700 in summer only; contact **Transitando lo Natural**, 20 de Febrero 25, Bariloche, T0294-442 3250, transitando1@ hotmail.com. From Pampa Linda you can also often get a lift with a trip returning to **Bariloche**, if there's room.

El Bolsón is a very seductive little place of 16,000 with a laid-back atmosphere, sprawled out in a broad fertile valley 130 km south of Bariloche. It is contained within huge mountain ranges on either side (hence its name 'the big bag'), and it makes a great base for relaxing for a few days and for hiking in the tempting peaks around. The great serrated ridge of Cerro Piltriquitrón (2284 m) dominates the town, apparently emitting healthy positive ions, which might be why you feel so relaxed while you're here. Certainly it's a magical setting, and it's not surprising that it inspired thousands of hippies to create an ideological community here in the 1970s.

What remains is a young, friendly place where the locals make lots of handicrafts. With the sparkling Río Azul running close by and a warm sunny microclimate, you're likely to want to stay for a few days to try the home-brewed beers and fruit for which the town is famous.

Nearby there are many beautiful mountain walks, a couple of waterfalls and rafting on the Río Azul. The small national park of Lago Puelo is within easy reach, 18 km south of town, and there's a small family-orientated ski centre in the winter at **Centro de Ski Perito Moreno**.

### Around El Bolsón

El Bolsón's great attraction – apart from the pleasure of being in the town itself – is the superb hiking up to the mountains west of the town (see page 132). These start from the other side of turquoise Río Azul, where there are lovely places to sunbathe, camp and picnic. East of town, a pleasant hour-long walk will take you to the top of **Cerro Amigo**, with lovely views. Follow Calle General Roca east until it becomes Islas Malvinas and continue

## Essential El Bolsón

### Finding your feet

Note there is not a central bus terminal. Different bus companies stop at different places. Buses from Bariloche and Esquel arrive off the main street at **Via Bariloche**'s offices at Sarmiento and General Roca.

### Orientation

El Bolsón sprawls out from the spine of Avenida San Martín which runs through the town, where you'll find places to eat. There are lots of places to stay dotted around the town, though the prettiest *cabañas* are in Villa Turismo up the hill.

### Getting around

There are buses to Lago Puelo, but buses to other sites are infrequent and geared to locals rather than tourists. However, El Bolsón is a lovely place to walk around; you can hire bikes, and there are plenty of cheap *remises* (taxis).

### When to go

Summer is obviously the best time to visit, when you can take full advantage of the blissful rivers and mountains, and there's a lively atmosphere on the plaza with music at nights. But it's very busy here in January, so try to come in February or March, or even in April, when autumn turns the trees brilliant yellow and orange, and there are sunny days but cold nights. Winter is very rainy and best avoided, though there is a basic ski resort at Cerro Perito Moreno.

up the hill. Better still are the panoramic views from **Cerro Piltriquitrón**, the jagged peak looming over El Bolsón to the east. Drive, join a tour or take a taxi 10 km (US$30 for up to four people) up winding earth roads. Then it's an hour's walk to the **Bosque Tallado**, where sculptures have been carved from fallen trees by local craftspeople; from the mirador there are fabulous views over the valley to the Andes beyond. It's a six- to seven-hour round trip walking all the way. Food and shelter are available at the *refugio* (1400 m),

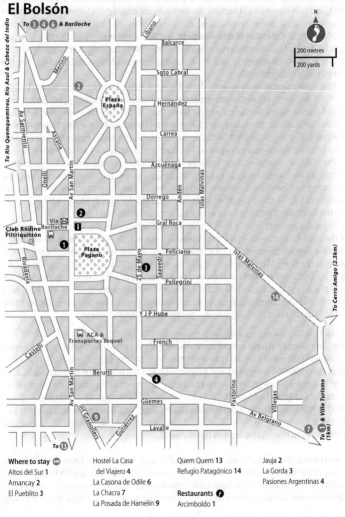

# El Bolsón

To ③ ④ ⑥ & Bariloche

To Río Quemquemtreu, Río Azul & Cabeza del Indio

Balcarce
Sgto Cabral
J Hernández
Larrea
Azcuénaga
Dorrego
Gral Roca
Feliciano
Pellegrini
Y J P Hube
French
Berutti
Güemes
Lavalle

Merino
Onelli
Av Sarmiento
Accena
Av San Martín
Rivadavia
Castelli
Av San Martín
Int Grandlles
Gutiérrez
25 de Mayo
Saavedra
Anden
Islas Malvinas
Pastorino
Villegas
Av Belgrano
Ibano

Plaza
España

②

Club Andino
Piltriquitrón

Via ✉
Bariloche ②
**i** ❶

Plaza
Pagano

🚌 ACA &
Transportes Esquel

❹

❾

To ⑬

To Cerro Amigo (2.5km)
To ⑦ & Villa Turismo
(1km)

N

200 metres
200 yards

**Where to stay** 🛏
Altos del Sur **1**
Amancay **2**
El Pueblito **3**

Hostel La Casa
del Viajero **4**
La Casona de Odile **6**
La Chacra **7**
La Posada de Hamelin **9**

Quem Quem **13**
Refugio Patagónico **14**

**Restaurants** 🍴
Arcimboldo **1**

Jauja **2**
La Gorda **3**
Pasiones Argentinas **4**

and from there it's three hours' walk to the summit. You can also do paragliding from here. See What to do, page 135.

There are also good views from **Cabeza del Indio**, so called because the rock's profile resembles a face, a good 6-km walk or bike ride from the centre. Take Calle Azcuénaga west to cross the bridge over Río Quemquemtreu and follow signs to Cabeza del Indio. From here, there's a waymarked walk north to **Cascada Escondida**. This impressive sweep of waterfalls, 10 km northwest of El Bolsón, is a good place for a picnic, with a botanical garden in woods reached from winding gravel roads. This area is also worth visiting for the good rustic *parrilla* El Quincho ① *open summer only*, which serves local lamb and other great meat dishes (vegetarians: don't even think about it). There are rather less exciting falls at **Cataratas Mallín Ahogado**, a little further north, but it's still a pleasant spot for a stop. La Golondrina runs daily buses Monday to Saturday from the plaza to the loop around Mallin Ahogado, but extra walking is required to reach both falls. See the tourist office map for details.

There are many microbreweries dotted around town; Cervecería El Bolsón ① *R258, Km 123.9, just north of town, www.cervezaselbolson.com*, is particularly worth a visit, with a brief guided tour, a restaurant and no fewer than 16 different beers on offer, including options for coeliacs. You could also ask at the tourist office for the *Agroturismo* leaflet, which details the *chacras* (fruit farms) throughout El Bolsón and El Hoyo that you can visit in summer for delicious, freshly picked soft fruits and berries, jams and other delights.

The famous narrow-gauge railway **La Trochita** ① *www.patagoniaexpress.com/el_trochita.htm*, also known as the *Old Patagonian Express*, is a novel way of seeing the landscape and catching a glimpse into Patagonia's past. As well as the better-known route from Esquel, there's another journey from El Maitén, near El Bolsón, where you can see the fascinating steam railway workshops too. See What to do, page 135.

El Bolsón benefits from a gentle microclimate which means it's warmer than much of the Lake District, even in winter. However, there is a ski centre, **Centro de Ski Perito Moreno** (www.bolsonweb.com/aventura/ski.htm), on the upper slopes of Cerro Perito Moreno (2216 m). With good snow and no wind, its 720 skiable metres are good for families, but there are three ski lifts and ski instructors too. It's a newish centre and the only place to stay at the moment is the **Refugio Perito Moreno** ① *T0294-448 3433*, with 30 beds. Ask the tourist office for more information. Leave town by Route 258, and take the left-hand turn to Río Azul. Follow signs to Refugio Perito Moreno.

## Walks *For Parque Nacional Lago Puelo, see page 136.*

There are wonderful treks in the mountains west of the town. For all walks, get the *Sendas y Bosques* (Walks and Forests) map and book for El Bolsón, Lago Puelo and Los Alerces. Maps are 1:200,000, laminated and easy to read, and the book is full of great walks, with English summaries. Register for all walks before setting off at the **Oficina de Informes de Montaña**; see Tourist information in Listings, below). There are some 14 *refugios* (shelters) which offer basic accommodation (US$22 per night, bed linen included), some meals (US$14.50), hearty breakfasts (U$S10.50), basic supplies (such as home-baked bread and home-brewed beer), camping and hot showers.

**Cerro Lindo** Due west of town, there's a great hike up Arroyo Lali to Cerro Lindo (2105 m), in one of the most beautiful mountain landscapes of the whole area, with **Refugio Cerro Lindo** halfway up, after a five-hour walk. From here, you can reach an ancient glacier and climb onwards to several viewpoints. You'll need a map, and you should check the route before setting off. The altitude difference is pretty extreme here, so you're advised to go slowly and steadily.

**Cerro Hielo Azul** This is a more serious and demanding hike up to Cerro Hielo Azul (2255 m); it's steep and takes six hours one-way. You can stay at comfortable **Refugio Cerro Azul** at 1300 m, from where you can also walk to the glacier on the slopes of Cerro Hielo Azul (three hours return), or on to Cerro Barda Negra. It's often suggested that you could walk from here via **Refugio Natación** to **Refugio Cajón de Azul**, but this is really not to be recommended without a local guide. The path can be confusing in places, the area remains marshy well into the summer months, and people have got lost, with dangerous consequences. Ask in the **Oficina de Informes de Montaña** for advice (see Tourist information, below).

**Cajón de Azul** One of the loveliest and most accessible walks can be done in a day, although once you reach the delightful *refugio* (600 m) at Cajón de Azul, you're going to wish you could stay at least a night. It's a fabulous four-hour walk up the Río Azul which flows from a deep canyon. There's a well-marked path and bridges crossing the river. It's worth it for a dip in the sparkling turquoise water on the way down. Set off early to allow for a leisurely lunch at the top, or spend the night in the *refugio* in the company of Atilio and friends, who make a fine dinner with produce from the lovely garden. To get to the start of the walk, take a *traffic* (minibus) from El Bolsón at 0900. You'll be collected by the *traffic* at 2000.

**Refugio Los Laguitos** This wonderful four-day walk takes you right into the deepest part of the Andes Cordillera, almost to the border with Chile, and through outstanding alerce forests. Allow four hours to **Refugio Cajón de Azul**, another three hours to the Mallín de los Chanchos, and another four hours on from there to reach the basic **Refugio Los Laguitos** in a beautiful spot on the shore of Lago Lahuán. A map and guidebook are absolutely essential; seek advice before setting out.

## Listings El Bolsón *map page 131.*

### Tourist information

For more information, see www.elbolson.com.

**Oficina de Informes de Montaña**
*Sarmiento and Roca, T0294-445 5810, cerroselbolson@hotmail.com. Mon-Fri 0800-2000 (until 2200 in summer).*
All walkers must register here before setting off. They have detailed advice on mountain walking.

**Tourist office**
*San Martín and Roca opposite the big post office, on the side of the semi-circular plaza, T0294-449 2604, www.turismoelbolson. gob.ar. Daily 0800-2200.*

Staff are helpful and friendly (with plenty of English speakers). They'll give you an excellent map of the town and the area, and suggest places to stay. They can also give limited advice on hikes and sell useful maps, including *Sendas y Bosques El Bolsón* and *Los Alerces*.

### Where to stay

It's difficult to find accommodation in the high season: book ahead.

**$$$ Amancay**
*Av San Martín 3207, T0294-449 2222.*
Good, comfortable and light rooms, though small and a bit old-fashioned. Breakfast included.

### $$$ La Posada de Hamelin
*Int Granollers 2179, T0294-449 2030,*
*www.posadadehamelin.com.ar.*
Charming rooms, welcoming atmosphere, huge breakfasts with home-made jams and cakes, German spoken. Highly recommended.

### $$ La Casona de Odile
*Barrio Luján, T0294-449 2753,*
*www.odile.com.ar.*
Private rooms and 3-6-bed dorms (US$12.50 pp) by stream, delicious home cooking, bicycle rental. Recommended.

### $ pp Altos del Sur
*Villa Turismo, T0294-449 8730,*
*www.altosdelsur.bolsonweb.com.*
Peaceful hostel in a lovely setting, shared rooms and private doubles, dinner available, will collect from bus station if you call ahead. Recommended.

### $ pp El Pueblito
*4 km north in Barrio Luján, 1 km off Ruta 40 (take bus "El Lujancito" from Plaza Principal), T0294-449 3560, www.elpueblitohostel. com.ar.*
Wooden building in open country, dorms from US$16 depending on season, also has cabins ($$), laundry facilities, shop, open fire. Recommended.

### $ pp Hostel La Casa del Viajero
*Libertdad y Las Flores, Barrio Usina, T0294-449 3092, www.lacasadelviajero.com.ar.*
A little out of the centre in a beautful setting, surrounded by organic gardens. Simple, comfortable rooms (dorms US$18, and private US$22). Call them for pick up from the centre of town.

### $ pp Refugio Patagónico
*Islas Malvinas y Pastorino, T0294-448 3628, www.refugiopatagonico.com.*
Basic hostel, with small dorms (US$18) and doubles (US$43), in a spacious house set in open fields, views of Piltriquitrón, 5 blocks from the plaza.

### Camping
There are many *cabañas* in picturesque settings with lovely views in the Villa Turismo, about US$60-100 for 2 people.

### Camping La Cascada
*At Mallín Ahogado, near La Cascada Escondida, north of El Bolsón, T0294-483 5304, see Facebook.*
On the edge of a botanical garden and a forest reserve. Spacious, tranquil, lovely view of the Valley of the Arroyo del Medio and the snow-capped mountains beyond. The helpful owner Pablo Panomarenko has good contacts with the *refugios* and businesses in Bolsón. Has *cabañas*, a great club house, home-grown organic vegetables available, home-made bread and beer for sale, delicious mountain spring water from the tap, swimming in the brook that feeds the waterfall. Recommended.

### La Chacra
*Av Belgrano 1128, T0294-449 2111,*
*www.lachacracamping.com.ar.*
15 mins' walk from town, well shaded, good facilities, lively atmosphere in season.

### Quem-Quem
*On Río Quemquemtreu, T0294-449 3550.*
Lovely site, hot showers, good walks, free pick-up from town.

## Restaurants

### $$$ Pasiones Argentinas
*Av Belgrano y Berutti, T0294-448 3616, see Facebook.*
Traditional Argentine food in a wonderful cosy setting.

### $$$-$$ La Gorda
*25 de Mayo 2709, T0294-472 0559.*
Hugely popular *parrilla* with portions as grandiose as its reputation.

### $$ Arcimbaldo
*Av San Martin 2790, T0294-449 2137.*
Good value *tenedor libre*, smoked fish and draft beer, open for breakfast.

## $$ Jauja
*Av San Martín 2867, T0294-449 2448, www.restaurantejauja.com.ar.*
The best restaurant in town is a great meeting place, serving delicious fish and pasta. It also makes outstanding ice cream from organic milk and local berries: there are 11 varieties of chocolate alone. English spoken.

## Cafés

### Cerveza El Bolsón
*RN 258, Km 123.9, T0294-449 2595, www.cervezaselbolson.com.*
Microbrewery where you can see how the beer is made and sample the 16 varieties. *Picadas* are served with beer, and you can sit outside in the gardens. Highly recommended.

## Festivals

**Jan Fiesta de la Fruta Fina** (Berry Festival) at nearby El Hoyo.
**Feb Fiesta del Lúpulo** (Hop Festival), at the end of the month.

## Shopping

The handicraft and food market is on Tue, Thu, Sat and Sun 1000-1600 in season around the main plaza. Some fine leather and jewellery, carved wood and delicious organic produce.

**Granja Larix**, *R40, Km 1923, T0294-449 8466, alejandra@bariloche.com.ar.* Fabulous smoked trout and home-made jams.
**La Casa de la Historia y la Cultura del Bicentenario (Cultural House)**, *Av San Martín 2219, T0294-445 5322. Mon-Fri 0800-1400 and 1600-1900.* Centre for cultural offerings such as music and locally made fabrics and textiles. Also operates occasionally as a cinema and lecture hall.

**Monte Viejo**, *San Martín y Hube, T0294-449 1735.* Excellent selection of high quality handicrafts from all over Argentina.
**Museo de Piedras Patagónicas**, *Laten K'Aike, 13 km from El Bolsón, T0294-449 1969, www.museodepiedraspatagonicas.blogspot. com.ar. Daily 1100-1800.* For exquisite semi-precious stones.
**Verde Menta Almacén Naturista**, *Av San Martín 2137, T0294-449 3576, see Facebook.* Good supplier of dried foods, fruits and cereals.

## What to do

### Tour operators
**Grado 42**, *Av Belgrano 406, on the corner with Av San Martín, T0294-449 3124, www.grado42. com.* Excellent company offering wide range of tours, including *La Trochita*'s lesser-known trip from El Maitén, where there is a superb steam railway workshop and you can learn all about how the trains work. Also rafting on the Río Manso; horse riding in glorious countryside at Cajón de Azul; wonderful fishing in Lago Puelo; paragliding from Piltriquitrón. Recommended.

## Transport

### Bus
Several daily to **Bariloche** and **Esquel**, with **Marga**, Via TAC **Andesmar**, **Don Otto** and **Vía Bariloche** (T0800-333 7575, www. viabariloche.com.ar). Very busy, even overbooked in high season; to **Bariloche**, US$7-8.50, 2 hrs; to **Esquel**, US$10-14, 2½-3 hrs. Other destinations are accessible from these towns. Buses to **Lago Puelo** with **Vía Bariloche** every couple of hours from 0915 to 1915, 30 mins, US$0.85. To **Parque Nacional Los Alerces** (a highly recommended route), with **Transportes Esquel**, departing from the information point at Lago Puelo for Parque Nacional Los Alerces every Wed, Sat and Sun at 1530, US$11.

This lovely green and wooded national park is centred around the deep turquoise-coloured Lago Puelo, 15 km south of El Bolsón on the Chilean border, surrounded by southern beech forest and framed by the spiky peaks of snow-dusted far-off mountains. It's a blissful spot out of the busy holiday season. With relatively low altitude (200 m) and high rainfall, the forest is rich in tree species, particularly the cinnamon-bark *arrayán* and the *pitra*, *coihues* (evergreen beech) and cypresses. There's lots of wildlife, including the huemul, pudu and foxes, and the lake is known for its good fishing for trout and salmon. There are gentle walks on marked paths around the northern shore area, boat trips across the lake and canoes for rent. *Guardaparques* at the park entrance can advise on these and provide a basic map.

### Walks

For all walks, get the *Sendas y Bosques* (Walks and Forests) map and book for El Bolsón, Lago Puelo and Los Alerces, www.guiasendasybosques.com.ar.

**Bosque de las Sombras** (Forest of the Shadows). An easy 400-m walk on wooden walkways, through delightful overgrown forest on the way to the shingle beach at 'La Playita', with guided trails and signs telling you what trees you're passing.

## Essential Parque Nacional Lago Puelo

### Access

The main entrance is along a pretty road south from El Bolsón, through *chacras* (small farms) growing walnuts, hops and fruit, to Villa Lago Puelo, 3 km north of the park, where there are shops, plenty of accommodation and fuel. From here the road is unpaved. Entry is also possible at El Desemboque, on the eastern side of the park: take the bus from El Bolsón to Esquel, alight at El Hoyo, then walk 14 km to El Desemboque. There are hourly buses (US$1-2) from Avenida San Martín and Dorrego in El Bolsón to the lake via Villa Lago Puelo.

### Entry fees

US$10.

### Park information

The **Intendencia** (500 m north of the lake, T0294-449 9232, lagopuelo@apn.gov.ar, Monday-Friday 0800-1500, with a booth at the pier in summer) can provide a helpful leaflet and advice on walks. Register here before embarking on long hikes, and register your return. In the town of Lago Puelo there's a **tourist office** (Avenida 2 de Abril and Los Notros, T0294-449 9591, www.lagopuelo. gob.ar, daily 0900-2100 in summer, 0900-1900 in winter) on the roundabout as you enter town. Staff are helpful, English-speaking and can advise on accommodation.

### When to go

It's best to visit between November and April, though the northern shore can get crowded in January and February. The lake is glorious in April, when trees turn yellow.

**Senda los Hitos** A 14-km (five hours each way) walk through marvellous woods to the rapids at Río Puelo on the Chilean border (passport required). There is some wild camping on the way at **Camping de Gendarmería**, after two hours.

**Cerro Motoco** There's a tremendous two-day hike up Cerro Motoco, with **Refugio Motoco** at the top of the path. Leave Lago Puelo heading north and cross the hanging bridge to access Río Motoco. It's 25 km altogether, and could be done in seven hours, one way, but you'll want to stay at the top. Take the walks book with you.

**Cerro Plataforma** From the east of the lake, you can hike to **El Turbio** and Cerro Plataforma, crossing the lake first by boat to El Desemboque (or taking the bus and walking 14 km). At Cerro Plataforma, there's a tremendous amount of marine life in evidence, as this was a beach in the ice age. It's about seven hours to Río Turbio, where there's a *guardaparque*, and then 12 hours to Cerro Plataforma; allow three days for the whole trip. There's also a three-day trek through magnificent scenery to **Glaciar y Cerro Aguaja Sur**: get advice and directions from the *guardaparques*.

## Other activities

There is wonderful **fly-fishing** in the park, thanks to the fact that this is the lowest crossing in the whole of the Andes region (at only 190 m). The lack of snow and the mild, warm summers mean that Pacific salmon come here in large numbers. Contact fishing guides through the park *guardería*. There are boat trips across Lago Puelo with **Juana de Arco** (T0294-449 8946, www.interpatagonia.com/juanadearco) and others, as well as kayaking. For further information, see What to do, page 135.

## Listings Parque Nacional Lago Puelo

### Where to stay

Apart from wild camping, there's no accommodation in the park itself, but plenty in Villa Lago Puelo, just outside, with *cabañas*, restaurants and campsites spread out along R16 through the little village.

### Cabañas

**$$$ Frontera**
*Ruta Nacional 40, 9 km from Lago Puelo, isolated in woodland, off the main road heading for Esquel, T0294-447 3092, www.frontera-patagonia.com.ar.*
*Cabañas* for 4 and *hostería*, in native forest, furnished to a very high standard, delicious breakfasts and dinner if required.

**$$$ Lodge Casa Puelo**
*R16, km 10, T0294-449 9539, www.casapuelo.com.ar.*

Beautifully designed rooms and self-catering cabins right against forested mountains where you can go walking. Good service, English-speaking owner Miguel knows the local area intimately. Very comfortable, dinner offered. *Cabañas* for up to 6. Recommended.

**$$$-$$ La Granja**
*20 m from Río Azul, T02944-499 265, www.interpatagonia.com/lagranja.*
Traditional chalet-style *cabañas* with simple furnishings, nothing out of this world, but there's a pool, and these are good value.

**$$$-$$ La Yoica**
*Just off R16, Km 5, T0294-449 9200, www.layoica.com.*
Charming Scottish/Argentine owners make you feel at home in these traditional *cabañas* set in lovely countryside with great views. Price for up to 4 people.

## $$ San Jorge
*A block from the main street, on Plaza Ilia,
Perito Moreno 2985, T02944-491313,
www.sanjorgepatagonico.com.*
Excellent value, neat but dated self-catering
apartments in a pretty garden, with friendly,
helpful owners.

## $ pp La Pasarela
*2 km from town, T02944-449 9061,
www.lpuelo.com.ar.*
Dorms (US$16 pp), cabins (us$69) and
camping US$8.50, shops, fuel.

### Camping
There are 2 free sites in the park itself, on
Lago Puelo, of which **Camping del Lago**
is most highly recommended; it offers all
facilities, plus rafting, fishing and trekking.
    Outside the park there are many
good sites with all facilities; these

are recommended: **Ailin Co** (Km 15,
T02944-499078, www.ailinco.com.ar);
**Los Quinchos** (Km 13).

## Restaurants

### $$ Familia von Fürstenberg
*R16 on the way to the national park, T0294-
449 9392, www.vonfuerstenberg.com.ar.*
In a delightful, perfectly decorated Swiss-
style chalet, try the beautifully presented
traditional waffles and home-made cakes.
Sumptuous. Also *cabañas* (**$$$**) to rent.

## Transport

**Transportes Esquel**, www.transportes
esquel.com.ar, run daily buses connecting
Lago Puelo with **Cholila**, **PN Los Alerces**
and **Esquel**.

---

## South of El Bolsón   Colour map 1, C3.

*remote outposts and outlaw havens*

### Epuyén
Some 40 km southeast of El Bolsón on Route 258, the little settlement of Epuyén (pronounced epooSHEN, population 2500) is relatively undeveloped for tourists, with nothing much to do except stroll around Lago Epuyén. Buses between El Bolsón and Esquel stop (briefly) at Lago Epuyén, though some don't enter the village itself. There's a simple *hostería*, which also has rustic *cabañas* with meals on request. Good picnic grounds with facilities (no camping) and a Centro Cultural overlook the lake. The centre sells *artesanía* and exhibits wood carving. A fire destroyed the trees on one hillside some years ago, making the area less attractive for walks, but there's a good trek around the lakeside and good fishing in the lake.

### Cholila
Cholila (population 3000) lies 76 km south of El Bolsón on Route 71, which branches off Route 258 at Km 179. It is a real Patagonian settlement that one day will make a great place to stay, thanks to its lovely setting in broad open landscape with superb views of Lago Cholila, crowned by ranges of mountains all around. For the moment, there's excellent fishing, canoeing and kayaking on rivers nearby, but very little tourist infrastructure; the accommodation is extremely limited, and there's little information.
    You might have heard that the reason to visit Cholila is to see the wooden cabins where **Butch Cassidy**, the **Sundance Kid** and **Etta Place** lived between 1901 and 1905 (see box, opposite). You can understand why they hid out here for so long: Cholila still feels remote and untouched, and the views from their land are breathtaking. The cabins themselves were rather evocative, falling to pieces, patched up with bits of wood and with a lichen-stained slatted roof, but, in 2006, the owner of the land started to 'renovate' them, by replacing the tattered timbers with brand new bright orange beams, doors and window

## ON THE ROAD
## Butch Cassidy and the Sundance Kid

Near Cholila, south of El Bolsón, is a wooden cabin which was home to infamous US bank robbers Butch Cassidy (Robert LeRoy Parker) and the Sundance Kid (Harry Longabaugh) immortalized by Paul Newman and Robert Redford in the 1969 film. In America in the late 1890s, the two were part of a loosely organized gang, known variously as the Train Robbers' Syndicate, the Hole in the Wall Gang and the Wild Bunch, which carried out hold-ups on railway payrolls and banks in the borders of Utah, Colorado and Wyoming. In 1900, the gang celebrated the wedding of one of their colleagues by having their photo taken: a big mistake. The photo was recognized by a Wells Fargo detective, and with their faces decorating Wanted posters across the land, Cassidy, Sundance and his girlfriend Etta Place escaped to Argentina in February 1901.

Using the names Santiago Ryan and Harry Place, the outlaws settled on government land near Cholila and applied to buy it, but Pinkerton detectives hot on their trail soon tracked them down and informed the Argentine authorities. The three lay low in their idyllic rural retreat until 1905, when, needing money to start up elsewhere, the gang raided banks in Villa Mercedes and a particularly audacious job in Río Gallegos. Posing as ranching company agents, they opened a bank account with US$7000, spent two weeks at the best hotels and socialized with the city's high society, and then entered the bank to close their accounts and empty the safe before escaping to Chile. Then Etta returned to the United States, and disappeared from the history books.

Butch and Sundance moved to Bolivia, and worked at the Concordia tin mine, disappearing every now and then to carry out the occasional hold-up. Lack of capital to settle as respectable ranchers was, however, their undoing. In 1908, near Tupiza in southern Bolivia, they seized an Aramayo mining company payroll, but gained only a fraction of the loot they expected. With military patrols in pursuit and the Argentine and Chilean forces alerted, they rode into the village of San Vicente and were recognized. Besieged, they did not, as in the film, run into the awaiting gunfire. Their deaths were not widely reported in the United States until the 1930s, and rumours abounded: Butch was said to have become a businessman, a rancher, a trapper and a Hollywood movie extra, while Sundance had run guns in the Mexican Revolution, migrated to Europe, fought for the Arabs against the Turks in the First World War, sold mineral water, founded a religious cult, and still found time to marry Etta.

frames. As a result, little remains of the authentic cabins where Butch and Sundance lived, and, unless you're a true fan, it might not be worth the considerable effort required to visit them. To get there make a detour from Route 258 heading south from El Bolsón, towards Los Alerces National Park's northern entrance; 13 km north of Cholila along Route 71, look out for a sign on the right; park by the little kiosk and walk 400 m to the cabins. Entry is free.

There is a good walk around **Lago Mosquito**: continue down the road from El Trébol past the lake then take a path to the left, following the river. Cross the river on the farm bridge and continue to the base of the hills to a second bridge. Follow the path to the lake and walk between the lake and the hills, crossing the river via a suspension bridge just past El Trébol – six hours.

## Leleque

Ruta 40 (paved) is a faster way to get from El Bolsón to Esquel than Route 71 via Cholila, and this is the route the bus takes. You could stop off at Leleque to see the **Museum of Patagonia (Museo Leleque)** ① *off the R40, Km 1440, 90 km from Esquel and 80 km from El Bolsón, www.benetton.com/patagonia/inglese/index-net.html, Thu-Tue 1100-1700 Mar-Dec, 1100-1900 Jan-Feb, closed May, Jun and Sep, US$3.50*, on the estate owned by Carlo and Luciano **Benetton**, of Italian knitwear fame. There's a beautifully designed exhibition on the lives of indigenous peoples, with dwellings reconstructed of animal skins, using the original techniques, a huge collection of delicate arrowheads and the *boleadoras* for catching cattle. Other moving exhibits focus on the first pioneers in Patagonia, especially the Welsh. There's an attractive café in a reconstructed *boliche* (provisions shop and bar).

## Listings South of El Bolsón

### Where to stay

#### Epuyén

**$$ El Refugio del Lago**
*T02945-499025, www.elrefugiodellago. com.ar.*
Transfers available on request. Relaxed, comfortable rooms in a lovely wooden house a short walk from the lakeshore, also cabins, dorms (US$23), with breakfast, good meals. Camping US$7 pp in high season. Recommended.

#### Camping

**Puerto Patriada**
*25 km south of El Bolsón, access through El Hoyo.*
Free and paying pitches on the shore of Lago Epuyén, also has *cabañas*.

#### Cholila

**$$$-$$ Cabañas Cerro La Momia**
*Ruta 71, Villa Lago Rivadavia, T02945-1569 6161, www.cabanascerrolamomia.com.ar.*
Very good *cabañas* for up to 6, picturesque setting among fruit orchards and wooded slopes. Restaurant, trips arranged.

### Restaurants

#### Cholila

**La Casa de Piedra**
*R71 outside village, T02945-498056.*
Welsh tea room, chocolate cake recommended.

# Southern
## Lake District

This southernmost area of the lakes is the most Patagonian in feel, with pioneer towns Esquel and Trevelin caught between the wild open steppe to the east and the dramatic mountains of the Andes to the west. Esquel retains the quiet charm of an ordinary country town but has one very famous attraction: it's the starting point for the narrow-gauge railway known as *La Trochita*, an atmospheric way to see the surrounding landscape. The town also has a family ski resort and a few places to trek and mountain bike. Far more tranquil is the village of Trevelin, which still bears signs of its origins as a Welsh colony.

Both towns make good bases for exploring the most unspoilt national park in the Lake District: Los Alerces. With just one road running through it, the park has pristine forested mountains and several stunning lakes, and is best enjoyed on foot. There are wonderful hikes, boat trips to see ancient alerce trees, and some unforgettable views, like Río Arrayanes and Lago Verde. Since this area is less developed for tourism than the rest of the lakes, it's best to hire a car to see it independently if you don't want to do a full-day tour.

One of the most authentic towns in the Lake District, Esquel (population 32,234) is a pleasant, breezy place that still feels like a pioneer outpost, set where the steppe meets the mountains. It's a typical Patagonian country town, with many buildings dating from the early 1900s and battered pickups filling the streets in the late-morning bustle when local farmers come into town. There are few tourist sights, but it's all the more appealing for that. It is the starting point for the narrow-gauge railway, *La Trochita*, made famous by Paul Theroux as the *Old Patagonian Express* and is the best base for visiting the Parque Nacional Los Alerces and for skiing at La Hoya in winter. The tranquil village of Trevelin, where the Welsh heritage is more in evidence, is just 25 km away.

### Sights

The main point of visiting Esquel is to get to Los Alerces, or Trevelin, but it's a pleasant place to walk around. There aren't any sights as such, although there is the **Museo Lituano Olgbrun** ① *Calle Los Ñires 1038, T02945-450536, see Facebook*, a few kilometres south of town, near the road to Trevelin. This is a Lithuanian museum with a well-stocked gift shop. All the food shops and services you need are contained within a few blocks east of Avenida Alvear, between Mitre and the wide Avenida Fontana.

### La Trochita

*Estación Viejo Expreso Patagónico, 6 blocks north of the town centre at the corner of Brun and Roggero, T02945-451403 in Esquel, T02945-495190 in El Maitén, www.patagoniaexpress. com/el_trochita.htm. Schedules change frequently. It's best to check the website schedules before embarking. The train runs twice daily Mon-Sat in Jan and much less frequently in winter, US$42, under 5s free; tour operators in town sell tickets.*

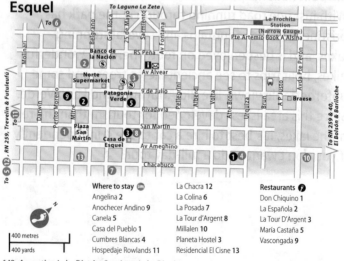

**Esquel**

Where to stay
Angelina 2
Anochecer Andino 9
Canela 5
Casa del Pueblo 1
Cumbres Blancas 4
Hospedaje Rowlands 11

La Chacra 12
La Colina 6
La Posada 7
La Tour d'Argent 8
Millalen 10
Planeta Hostel 3
Residencial El Cisne 13

Restaurants
Don Chiquino 1
La Española 2
La Tour D'Argent 3
María Castaña 5
Vascongada 9

The famous narrow-gauge railway, *La Trochita* (*Old Patagonian Express*), also known in Spanish as *El Viejo Expreso Patagónico*, chugs off into the steppe from a pretty old station north of town. While it's obviously a tourist experience, this is a thoroughly enjoyable trip, and as the steam train rumbles across the lovely valleys and mountains of the *precordillera* on tracks just 75 cm wide, you'll find yourself wanting to know how it works. There's Spanish and English commentary along the way. The quaint carriages each have little wood stoves, and there's a small tea room on board, but it's worth waiting for the home-made cakes (and handicrafts) for sale at the wild and remote Mapuche hamlet of **Nahuel Pan**, where the train stops, and where you'll hear an interesting explanation of how the engine works. Recommended.

In high season a service also runs from El Maitén at the northernmost end of the line to Desvío Thomae (55 km) three days a week in July (once or twice a week in other months), US$42.

## La Hoya
*15 km north of Esquel, information from Club Andino Esquel, Pellegrini 787, T02945-453248, see Facebook, www.skilahoya.com, www.cerrolahoya.com.*

There's good skiing on high-quality powder snow over a long season at this low-key family resort. It is popular with Argentines, since it's one of cheapest and friendliest. There are 22 km of pistes, many of them suitable for kids or beginners, with good challenging pistes too, and seven ski lifts. There are daily buses to La Hoya from Esquel leaving at 0900, 0930 and returning at 1730, US$11.50. A skipass costs US$36 per day in high season, with reductions for a week or longer. Equipment can be rented.

## Walks around Esquel
There are some challenging walks and mountain bike trails in the surrounding mountains. See the map *Sendas y Bosques* (Walks and Forests) for El Bolsón, Lago Puelo and Los Alerces, which has the trails clearly marked. It's an easy climb along a clear path to **Laguna La Zeta**, 5 km from the centre of town, with good views and a lake with birdlife. From there, head further north up the Río Percey or towards Cañadón Huemul. The path is signposted from the end of Avenida La Fontana. Another good hike, with spectacular views, is to **Cerro La Cruz**, five hours return; walk from the centre of town signposted from the end of the street 25 de Mayo. There are longer hikes to **Cerro Veinte Uno** (five to eight hours return) and the pointy cone of Cerro Nahual Pan (eight hours return).

## Listings Esquel *map page 142.*

### Tourist information

For information on Los Alerces and the whole area, see www.patagoniaexpress.com.

### Tourist office
*In a little hut on the corner of Av Alvear and Sarmiento, T02945-451927, www.esquel.tur.ar. Mon-Fri 0800-2000 Sat-Sun 0900-2000.*
Friendly enough, but doesn't seem to have much information. They do hand out a useful town map, however, and another leaflet with a yellow map of Los Alerces National Park showing all access and accommodation in the park, as well as the crossing to Chile via Paso Futaleufú. You might have to press them patiently for bus timetables.

### Where to stay

Ask at tourist office for lodgings in private houses.

### $$$ Angelina
*Av Alvear 758, T02945-452763, www.*
*hosteriaangelina.com.ar. High season only.*
Good value, welcoming, big breakfast,
English and Italian spoken.

### $$$ Canela
*Los Notros y Los Radales, Villa Ayelén,*
*on road to Trevelin, T02945-453890,*
*www.canelaesquel.com.*
Bed and breakfast and tea room in a lovely,
quiet residential area, English spoken, owner
knowledgeable about Patagonia.

### $$$ Cumbres Blancas
*Av Ameghino 1683, T02945-455100,*
*www.cumbresblancas.com.ar.*
Attractive modern building, a little out of the
centre, very comfortable, spacious rooms,
sauna, gym, airy restaurant. Recommended.

### $$$-$$ La Chacra
*Km 5 on Ruta 259 towards Trevelin, T02945-*
*452802, www.lachacrapatagonia.com.*
Relaxing, spacious rooms, huge breakfast,
Welsh and English spoken.

### $$ La Posada
*Chacabuco 905, T02945-454095,*
*www.laposadaesquel.blogspot.com.ar.*
Tasteful B&B in quiet part of town, lovely
lounge, very comfortable, excellent value.

### $$ La Tour D'Argent
*San Martín 1063, T02945-454612,*
*www.latourdargent.com.ar.*
Bright, comfortable, family-run,
very good value.

### $ pp Anochecer Andino
*Av Ameghino 482, 4 blocks from*
*the commercial centre and 2 from*
*the mountains, T02945-450498.*
Basic, helpful, can organize ski passes
and trips. They also can provide dinner
and have a bar.

### $ pp Casa del Pueblo
*San Martín 661, T02945-450581,*
*www.esquelcasadelpueblo.com.ar.*

Smallish rooms but good atmosphere
($$ double), laundry, organizes
adventure activities.

### $ pp Hospedaje Rowlands
*Behind Rivadavia 330, T02945-452578,*
*gales01@hotmail.com.*
Warm family welcome, Welsh spoken,
breakfast extra, basic rooms with shared
bath and a double with bath ($), good value.

### $ pp Planeta Hostel
*Alvear 1021, T02945-456846,*
*www.planetahostel.com.*
4- to 6-bed dorms (US$20-22), doubles $$$,
shared bath, specialize in snowboarding,
climbing and mountain biking, English spoken.

### $ Residencial El Cisne
*Chacabuco 778, T02945-452256.*
Basic small rooms, hot water, quiet,
well kept, good value, breakfast extra.

## Camping

### La Colina
*Darwin 1400, T02945-455264,*
*www.lacolinaesquel.com.ar.*
Complex a little out of the centre with
cramped dorms (US$14.50 pp), doubles
US$43 and shady camping, US$7.50 per tent
or vehicle.

### Millalen
*Av Ameghino 2063 (5 blocks from bus*
*terminal), T02945-456164.*
Good services and cabins.

## Restaurants

### $$ Don Chiquino
*Behind Av Ameghino 1641, T02945-450035,*
*see Facebook.*
Delicious pasta served in a fun atmosphere
with plenty of games brought to the tables
by magician owner Tito. Recommended.

### $$ La Española
*Rivadavia 740, T02945-451509.*
Excellent beef, salad bar and tasty pasta.
Recommended.

**$$ Vascongada**
*9 de Julio 655, T02945-452229.*
Traditional style, trout and other
local specialities.

**$ La Tour D'Argent**
*San Martín 1063, T02945-454612,*
*www.latourdargent.com.ar.*
Delicious local specialities, good-value set
meals and a warm ambience in this popular,
traditional restaurant.

## Cafés

María Castaña
*Rivadavia y 25 de Mayo, T02945 451 752,*
*see Facebook.*
Popular, good coffee.

## Shopping

**Braese**, *9 de Julio 1540, T02945-451014,*
*www.braese.com.ar.* Home-made chocolates
and other regional specialities.
**Casa de Esquel**, *25 de Mayo 415.* A range of
rare books on Patagonia, also souvenirs.

## What to do

The tourist office (see Tourist information,
above) has a list of fishing guides and
companies hiring out equipment. For details
of skiing at **La Hoya**, 15 km north, see above.

### Tour operators

**Aucan Travel**, *Alsina 1632, T02945-1552 5052,*
*www.aucantravel.com.ar.* Recommended
operator that runs trips to Los Alerces and
Lago Puelo, among others.
**Frontera Sur**, *Sarmiento 784, T02945-450505,*
*www.fronterasur.net.* Good company offering
adventure tourism of all sorts, as well as more
traditional trips, ski equipment and trekking.
**Patagonia Verde**, *9 de Julio 926, T02945-*
*454396, www.patagonia-verde.com.ar.* Boat
trips to El Alerzal on Lago Menéndez, rafting
on Río Corcovado, tickets for *La Trochita*

and for Ruta 40 to El Calafate. Also range of
adventure activities, horse riding, short local
excursions and ski passes. Ask about lodging
at **Lago Verde**. English spoken. Excellent
company, very professional.

## Transport

### Air

The airport (T02945-451676) is 20 km east
of town by paved road, US$15-18 by taxi,
US$14 by bus. There are direct flights to
**Buenos Aires** with **Aerolíneas Argentinas**.

### Bus

There's a smart modern bus terminal at
Av Alvear 1871, T02945-451584, 6 blocks
from the main commercial centre (US$2-3
by taxi). It has toilets, a *kiosko, locutorio* with
internet, café, tourist information desk and
left luggage.

To **Buenos Aires** with **Rápido Argentina**
(T800-333 1970), 25 hrs, US$142, otherwise
connect in Bariloche. To **Bariloche** (via
El Bolsón, 2½ hrs), 4-5 hrs, US$19-24, with
**Andesmar, Rápido Argentina** and others.
To **Trelew**, US$44-73, 8-9 hrs overnight, with
**Don Otto**. To **Río Gallegos** (for connections
to El Calafate or Ushuaia), take a bus to Trelew
and change there. To **Trevelin** with **Jacobsen**
(T02945-454676, www.transportejacobsen.
com.ar), Mon-Fri hourly 0600-2300, less
frequent on weekends, US$1. To **Río Pico**,
via Tecka and Gobernador Costa, Mon, Wed
and Fri at 0900, 4½ hrs, with **Jacobsen**. To
**Comodoro Rivadavia**, daily at 1200 and
2100 with **ETAP**.

### Car hire

**Los Alerces**, Sarmiento 763, T02945-456008,
www.losalercesrentacar.com.ar. Good value,
good cars, top service.

### Train

See page 142.

The pretty village of Trevelin, 25 km southwest of Esquel, was once an offshoot of the Welsh colony of Gaiman on the Atlantic coast (see page 174), founded when the Welsh travelled west to find further lands for growing corn. The name means Town (*tre*) of the Mill (*velin*) in Welsh. You can still hear Welsh spoken here, and there is plenty of evidence of Welsh heritage in several good little museums around the town. With a backdrop of snow-capped mountains, the village is an appealing place to rest for a few days, to go fishing and rafting on nearby Río Futuleufu, or to see the beautiful waterfalls at the reserve of Nant-y-fall.

### Sights

Trevelin remains a quiet village of 9123 inhabitants with a strong sense of community, and its history is manifest in several sights. The Welsh chapel (1910), **La Capilla Bethel**, can be visited, with a guided tour to fill you in on a bit of history. A fine old flour mill (1918) houses the **Museo Histórico Regional** ① *Molino Viejo 488, T02945-480545, daily 1100-2000, US$4*, which has fascinating artefacts from the Welsh colony. The **Museo Cartref Taid** ① *El Malacara s/n, ask for directions in the tourist office, T02945-480108, Mon-Fri 1100-2000, Sat-Sun 1400-1830, US$4.25*, is another great place for exploring the Welsh pioneer past. It's the house of John Evans, one of Trevelin's first settlers, and filled with his belongings. There's another extraordinary and touching relic of his life in **La Tumba del Caballo Malacara** ① *200 m from main plaza, guided tours are available, US$4.25*, a private garden containing the grave of his horse, Malacara, who once saved his life.

Eisteddfods are still held here every year in October, and you'll be relieved to hear that Té Galés, that other apparently traditional Welsh ritual, is alive and well in several tea rooms, which offer a ridiculous excess of delicious cakes. Extensive research has established that **Nain Maggie** is, in fact, the town's best. There are good day walks in idyllic scenery around the town; get directions on routes from the tourist office. It's also a good area for horse riding or mountain biking. For more on the history of Welsh emigration to the region, see box, page 172.

### Around Trevelin

For a gentle outing with quite the best insight into the Welsh history in Patagonia, visit the rural flour mill **Molino Nant Fach** ① *Route 259, T02945-15-698058, entry US$4.25*, 22 km southwest towards the Chilean border. This beautiful flour mill was built by Merfyn Evans, descendant of the town's founder, Thomas Dalar Evans, as an exact replica of the first mill built in the town in 1899. Merfyn's fascinating tour (in Spanish, but English booklet available to read) recounts a now familiar tale of the Argentine government's persistent mismanagement of natural resources and industry, through the suppression of the Welsh prize-winning wheat industry. It's a beautiful spot, and Merfyn tells the rather tragic story in a wonderfully entertaining way. Highly recommended.

Before you reach Molino Nant Fach, look out for the **Nant-y-fall Falls** on the same road (Route 259), 17 km southwest of Trevelin, heading to the Chilean border. These are a series of spectacular waterfalls reached by an easy 1½-hour walk along a trail through lovely forest. There's an entry charge of US$4 per person (reductions for children and local residents). Guides will take you to all seven falls.

Route 259 continues to the Chilean border at the spectacularly beautiful Paso Futaleufú. For further details, see box, page 152.

**Fishing** is popular in many local rivers and lakes, most commonly in Río Futuleufú, and Corintos, and Lagos Rosario and Corcovado. The season runs from the end of November to mid-April, and the tourist office (see Tourist information, below) can advise on guides and where to go.

## Listings Trevelin

### Tourist information

**Tourist office**
*Central octagonal plaza, T02945-480120, www.trevelin.gob.ar. Mon-Fri 0800-2200, Sat and Sun 0900-2200.*
The enthusiastic and helpful staff speak English and can provide maps and advice on accommodation and fishing.

### Where to stay

**$$$ Casa de Piedra**
*Almirante Brown 244, T02945-480357, www.casadepiedratrevelin.com.*
Stone and wood cottage in the suburbs. King-size beds, heating and a charming common area, popular.

**$$ Pezzi**
*Sarmiento 351, T02945-480146, see Facebook.*
Charming family house with a beautiful garden, English spoken. Recommended.

**Camping**
Many sites, especially on the road to Futaleufú and Chile; also many *cabañas*; ask for full list at the tourist office, see Tourist information, above.

### Restaurants

**$$ Parrilla Oregón**
*Av San Martín y JM Thomas, T02945-480408.*
Large meals (particularly breakfasts), set menus based on *parrilla* and pastas.

**$ Nain Maggie**
*Perito Moreno 179, T02945-480232, www.nainmaggie.guiapatagonia.net.*
Tea room, offering *té galés* and *torta negra*, expensive but good.

### What to do

**Gales al Sur**, *Patagonia 186, T02945-453379, www.galesalsur.com.ar.* Tours to Chilean border; Los Alerces National Park and Futaleufú dam; *La Trochita.* Recommended for their rafting, trekking, biking, 4WD and horse-riding trips. Friendly and English spoken.

### Transport

**Bus**
To **Esquel**, Jacobsen (T02945-454676, www.transportejacobsen.com.ar), Mon-Fri hourly from 0645 (last at 2345), Sat and Sun less frequent, US$1. To **Paso Futaleufú** (Chilean border) with **Jacobsen**, Jan and Feb daily, Mar-Dec Mon, Wed and Fri.

**emerald waters and ancient forests**

One of the most magnificent and untouched expanses of wilderness in the whole Andes region, this national park was established to protect the stately alerce trees (*Fitzroya cupressoides*). The alerce is among the longest-living tree species in the world, and there are some specimens in the park that are over 4000 years old. They grow deep in the Valdivian rainforest that carpets these mountains a rich velvety green, beside vivid blue Lago Futalaufquen and emerald Lago Verde. There are several good hikes, plus rafting and fishing, in the park, and idyllic lakeside campsites and *hosterías*, making this a great place to spend a few days.

The park is enormous at over 200,000 ha, and it remains the most virgin park in the whole Lake District, since much of it is only accessible on foot. There are four large lakes: navy-blue **Lago Futalaufquen**, with fine fishing; **Lago Menéndez**, which can be crossed by boat to visit the ancient *alerce* trees; the exquisite green **Lago Verde**; and the almost inaccessible **Lago Amutui Quimei**. In order to protect this fragile environment, access by car is possible only to the eastern side of the park, via *ripio* Route 71, which runs between Cholila and Trevelin alongside the eastern side of Lagos Futalaufquen, Verde and Rivadavia. The western side of the park, where rainfall is highest, has areas of Valdivian forest, and can only be accessed by boat or by hiking to Lago Krügger.

## Walks

For all walks, get the *Sendas y Bosques* (Walks and Forests) map and book for El Bolsón, Lago Puelo and Los Alerces. Maps are 1:200,000, laminated and easy to read, and the book is full of great walks, with English summaries and detailed directions in Spanish (www.

# **Essential** Parque Nacional Los Alerces

### Access

There are two main entrances to the park, both off Route 71: one is at the northern end of Lago Rivadavia (south of Cholila), and the other is 12 km south of Lago Futulaufquen. Head from this entrance to the southern tip of the lake, 52 km west of Esquel, to reach the Intendencia (park office) with a **visitor centre** (T02945-471015, www.parquesnacionales.gob.ar, see also www.losalercesparquenacional.blogspot.com). Helpful *guardaparques* give out maps and advise on walks.

Right by the Intendencia, and less than 2 km from Route 71, **Villa Futulaufquen** is a little hamlet with a petrol station, *locutorio*,

food shops and a restaurant, **El Abuelo Monje**. Fishing licences can be obtained at the the Intendencia.

### Entry fees

Park entrance costs US$10.

### Getting around

A daily bus runs along Route 71 in each direction, picking up and dropping off passengers at lakeside campsites and *hosterías*, and also at the petrol station opposite the Intendencia. Ask at the petrol station for bus times, or contact the visitor centre in Villa Futalaufquen, above. See Transport, page 151.

guiasendasybosques.com.ar). The park office Intendencia also has leaflets listing the walks, but these have insufficient detail.

**Cave paintings** There are *pinturas rupestres* to be found just 40 minutes' stroll from the park Intendencia (Km 1). You'll also pass a waterfall and a mirador with panoramic views over Lago Futulaufquen.

**Cascada Arroyo** This is a satisfying and easy four-hour walk south of Villa Futalaufquen to see waterfalls, passing various miradors.

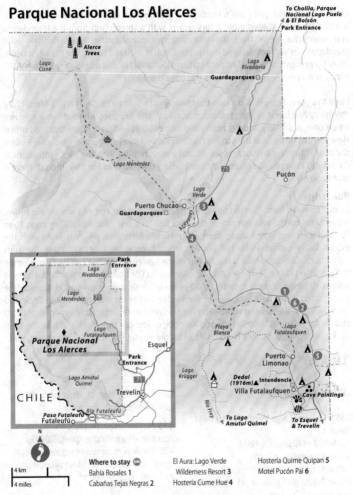

# Parque Nacional Los Alerces

**Where to stay**
Bahía Rosales **1**
Cabañas Tejas Negras **2**

El Aura: Lago Verde
Wilderness Resort **3**
Hostería Cume Hue **4**

Hostería Quime Quipan **5**
Motel Pucón Pai **6**

**Pasarella Lago Verde** Signposted off Route 71 at Km 34.3. The most beautiful walk in the whole park and unmissable, no matter how little time you have, is across the suspension bridge over Río Arrayanes to heavenly Lago Verde. A self-guided trail leads around a peninsula to Puerto Chucao on Lago Menéndez, where boat trips begin (see below). Go in the early evening to see all kinds of birdlife from the beach by Lago Verde, including swifts and swallows darting all around you. While you're in the area, take a quick 20-minute stroll up to **Mirador Lago Verde** for gorgeous views up and down the whole valley. From here you can appreciate the string of lakes, running from Lago Futulaufquen in the south to Lago Rivadavia in the north.

**Cerro Dedal** For a great day hike, there is a longer trek up Cerro Dedal (1916 m). This is a circular walk, at least eight hours return, with a steep climb from the Intendencia and wonderful views over the lake and mountains further west. Register with *guardaparques* and get detailed instructions. You're required to register between 0800-1000. Carry plenty of water. The path up Cerro Dedal was closed due to a fire in early 2016. It may or may not reopen by the time this book is published.

**Lago Krüger** There is also a long but rewarding two- to three-day (12- to 14-hour) hike though *coihue* forest to the southernmost tip of **Lago Krüger**, where there is a *refugio* (open only in January and February) and campsite, as well as a *guardaparque's* office. Here you can take a boat back to Puerto Limonao on Lago Futalaufquen, but check when the boat is running before you set off and always register with the park's Intendencia. From Lago Krüger, you could walk south along the course of Río Frey, though there is no *refugio* here.

### Boat trips

Boat trips leave from Puerto Limonao at the southwestern end of Lago Futalaufquen: follow signs up the western side of the lake, just for a few kilometres. They cross Lago Futalaufquen and travel along the pea-green Río Arrayanes, which is lined with the extraordinary cinnamon-barked *arrayán* trees. Even more spectacular are the trips from Puerto Chucao, which is reached from the suspension bridge crossing Lago Verde, halfway along Route 71. These cross Lago Menéndez (1½ hours) where you land, and walk a short distance to see a majestic 2600-year-old alerce tree, known as 'el abuelo' (the grandfather). From here you walk to the hidden and silent jade-green Lago Cisne and then back past the rushing whitewaters of Río Cisne: an unforgettable experience. Boats also go from Puerto Limonao to Lago Krüger, or you can trek there and take the boat back (see above), but check the boat times before you set off. Boats sail in summer only.

**Listings** Parque Nacional Los Alerces *map page 149.*

### Where to stay

**$$$$ El Aura: Lago Verde Wilderness Resort**
*T011-4813 4340 (Buenos Aires),*
*www.elaurapatagonia.com.*
Exquisite taste in these 3 stone cabins and a guesthouse on the shore of Lago Verde.

Luxury in every respect, attention to detail, eco-friendly. Impressive place.

**$$$ Hostería Quime Quipan**
*East side of Lago Futalaufquen, T02945-425423, www.hosteriaquimequipan.com.ar.*
Comfortable rooms with lake views, dinner included. Recommended.

## $$ Bahía Rosales
*Northeast side of Lago Futalaufquen, T02945-15-403413, www.bahiarosales.com.*
Comfortable *cabaña* for 6 with kitchenette and bath, $ pp in small basic cabin without bath, and camping in open ground, hot showers, restaurant, all recommended. There are also plans to add dome tents.

## $$ Cabañas Tejas Negras
*East side Lago Futalaufquen, T02945-471046, www.tejasnegras.com.*
Really comfortable *cabañas* for 4, also good camp site, and tea room.

## $$ Motel Pucón Pai
*Next to Tejas Negras, T02945-451425.*
Slightly spartan rooms, but good restaurant, recommended for fishing; basic campsite with hot showers.

## Camping
Several campsites at Villa Futalaufquen and on the shores of lakes Futalaufquen, Rivadavia, Verde and Río Arrayanes.

## What to do

Agencies in Esquel or Trevelin run tours including the boat trip across Lago Menéndez to the alerce trees. For short guided trips, ask at the Intendencia in Villa Futalaufquen. Lago Futalaufquen has some of the best fishing in this part of Argentina (the season runs end Nov to mid-Apr); local guides offer fishing trips and boat transport. Ask in the Intendencia or at **Hostería Cume Hue**.

## Transport

### Bus
**Transportes Esquel**, Alvear 1871 (Esquel) T02945-453529, www.transportesesquel. com.ar, runs from Esquel bus terminal daily at 0800 along the east side of Lago Futalaufquen, US$4.50, and ending at **Lago Puelo**, US$11.50.

# South of Esquel

*where wilderness meets emptiness*

The iconic Ruta 40 continues (paved) south from Esquel across very deserted landscapes that give you a taste for the full experience of Patagonia. It's a tricky section for travel by public transport, since there are few settlements or services along this section of road until you reach the small town of Perito Moreno (about 14 hours' drive).

At Tecka, Km 101, Route 62 (paved) branches off east and follows the valley of the Río Chubut to Trelew: another lonely road. (West of Tecka is the Paso Palena border with Chile, see box, page 152.) Ruta 40 continues south to Gobernador Costa, a small service centre for the estancias in this area on the Río Genoa at Km 183. Buses go up and down Ruta 40 to the town of Perito Moreno, and from here you can take a daily service on to El Chaltén or El Calafate; ask in Esquel's bus terminal.

## Río Pico *Colour map 1, C3.*
Río Pico (population 1000) lies in a wide green valley close to the Andes and has become quietly known among trout-fishing circles as a very desirable place to fish. Permits are available from the *municipalidad* in Gobernador Costa. Río Pico is the site of an early 20th-century German settlement and some old houses remain from that period. Nearby are several lakes that are good for fishing and free camping; ask locals for hitching advice.

## BORDER CROSSING
## Argentina–Chile

There are two border crossings south of Esquel, the spectacularly beautiful Paso Futaleufú and Paso Palena. For the Chilean side see box, page 370.

**Paso Futaleufú**
Paso Futaleufú is 70 km southwest of Esquel via Trevelin and is reached by Route 259 (*ripio* from Trevelin). The border is crossed by a bridge over the Río Futaleufú, and formalities should take no longer than an hour. See www.gendarmeria.gov.ar. If entering Chile, change money in Futaleufú (poor rates).
**Argentine immigration and customs** On the Argentine side of the bridge, open 0900-2100.
**Transport** There are regular buses to Paso Futaleufú from Trevelin (see Transport, page 147). From the border, Futaleufú (T+56 65-272 1458) runs a connecting bus service three times a week December-March; two days a week the rest of the year) to Futuleufú and on to Chaitén. From Chaitén there are services to Coyhaique. Cars must have special papers and the registration number etched into all windows: advise your hire company when booking.

**Paso Palena**
Paso Palena, or Río Encuentro, lies 120 km southeast of Esquel and is reached by Route 17 from Trevelin, which runs to Corcovado, 75 km east of Tecka (reached by *ripio* road). From Corcovado it is 26 km west to the border. For the Chilean side, see box, page 370.
**Argentine immigration and customs** At the border, open daily 0900-2100.

The northern shore of Lago Tres, 23 km west of town, is a peaceful and remote place, with a rich birdlife and wild strawberries at the end of January. Some 30 km north of Río Pico lies the huge Lago Vintter, reached by Route 44. There are also smaller lakes good for trout fishing.

### South of Gobernador Costa

At Km 221, Ruta 40 (poor *ripio*) forks southwest through the town of **Alto Río Senguer** from which visits can be made to the relatively unexplored Lago Fontana and Lago La Plata. Provincial Route 20 (paved) heads almost directly south for 81 km, before turning east towards Sarmiento and Comodoro Rivadavia. At La Puerta del Diablo, in the valley of the lower Río Senguer, Route 20 intersects provincial Route 22, which joins with Ruta 40 at the town of Río Mayo (see page 197). This latter route is completely paved and preferable to Ruta 40 for those travelling long distance.

## Listings South of Esquel

### Transport

**Bus**
To **Esquel** via **Gobernador Costa** and **Tecka**, Mon, Wed and Fri at 1400, 4½ hrs, with

**Jacobsen** (T02945-454676, www. transportejacobsen.com.ar).

# Atlantic Coast

Marine life abounds along Patagonia's seemingly endless Atlantic shore. Stop off on your way south at the quaint town of Carmen de Patagones and then head down to Puerto Madryn.

This pleasant seaside town is a great base for exploring the Península Valdés, where sea lions and penguins gather in their thousands, and southern right whales cavort with their young from September to November. Take a walk on the shore and then try the excellent seafood.

Nearby, Trelew has a superb dinosaur museum, while pretty Gaiman keeps the Welsh pioneer heritage alive with a fascinating museum, Eisteddfods and delicious Welsh teas.

Further south you'll find colonies of cormorants at Puerto Deseado and dolphins frolicking in the beautiful bay at Puerto San Julián, while the Parque Nacional Monte León offers accommodation in a wild and splendidly isolated setting.

Leaving the sublime shorelines behind, venture inland to explore the weird lunar landscapes of the *bosques petrificados* – an unforgettably eerie sight.

**Best** for
Petrified forests ▪ Welsh heritage ▪ Wildlife

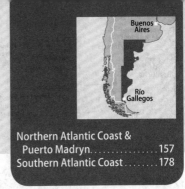

# Footprint
## picks

★ **Península Valdés**, page 167

The greatest concentration of marine life can be found on this peninsula near Puerto Madryn.

★ **Museo Paleontológico Egidio Feruglio**, page 173

Come and learn about the time when dinosaurs ruled South America.

★ **Welsh tea in Gaiman**, pages 174 and 176

Welsh teahouse culture is alive and well in this charming town.

★ **Petrified forest**, page 181

A fascinating geological area where remnants of a volcanic age dot the landscape.

★ **Parque Nacional Monte León**, page 185

Head south to Santa Cruz Province and enjoy more stunning Patagonian coastline.

RÍO NEGRO

CHUBUT

ARGENTINA

SANTA CRUZ

TIERRA DEL FUEGO

CHILE

*Atlantic Ocean*

N

100 km
100 miles

# Northern Atlantic Coast
## & Puerto Madryn

The sight of a mother and baby whale basking in quiet waters just a few metres from your boat is an unforgettably moving sight. Not, perhaps, what you expected to see after travelling for days through the wild, unpopulated, open plains of Patagonia. But the whole Atlantic coast hosts huge colonies of marine life, and there is no region quite as spectacular as Península Valdés. This wide splay of land stretching into the Atlantic from a narrow isthmus enclosing a gulf of protected water attracts an astonishing array of animals which come to breed here each spring, most famously the southern right whales, who can be seen from September to November.

The small breezy town of Puerto Madryn is the best base for exploring the peninsula, though there are estancias on Valdés itself. Just to the south, Trelew is worth a visit for its superb palaeontological museum, and as a base to reach the old Welsh pioneer villages of Gaiman and Dolavon further west. If you're heading south by road, consider stopping off at historic Carmen de Patagones, a quaint Patagonian town. Patagonia's fine estancias start here, with riding and sheep mustering at La Luisa.

These two towns straddle the broad sweep of the Río Negro, about 250 km south of Bahía Blanca, and while neither has any real tourist attractions, you could stop off here on the way south and find warm hospitality and a couple of decent places to stay. The two towns face each other and share a river, but little else.

Capital of Río Negro province, Viedma, on the south bank, was founded as Mercedes de Patagonia in 1779 but was destroyed almost immediately by floods, after which Carmen de Patagones was founded on higher ground on the north bank later that same year. The little town prospered for many years by shipping salt to Buenos Aires. However, in 1827, it was the site of an extraordinary battle and was destroyed. Poor old Viedma was rebuilt, but destroyed again by floods in 1899.

Now, it's a rather dull place, rather less attractive than Patagones, and serves as the administrative centre for the province of Río Negro. Patagones (as it's called by the locals) has more tangible history, with the towers of a handsome church thrusting above charming streets of 19th-century adobe houses near the river, where the tiny ferry takes you across to Viedma, and there's a fabulous little museum.

### Viedma

Viedma (population 60,000) is quite different in character from Carmen de Patagones: it's the provincial administrative centre, rather than the home of farmers and landowners. An attractive *costanera* runs by the river, with large grassy banks shaded by willow trees, and the river water is pleasantly warm in summer and clean, good for swimming. On a calm summer's evening, when groups gather to sip *mate*, the scene resembles Seurat's painting of bathers.

There are two plazas. The cathedral, built by the Salesians (1912), is on the west of Plaza Alsina, with a former convent next door. This was the first chapel built by the Salesians (1887) in the area and is now a cultural centre housing the **Museo del Agua y del Suelo** and the **Museo Cardenal Cagliero**, which has ecclesiastical artefacts. Two blocks east, on Plaza San Martín, is the French-style **Casa de Gobierno** (1926). Most diverting, though, is the **Museo Gardeliano** ① *Rivadavia y Colón (1st floor), Mon-Fri 0930-1230*, a fabulous collection of biographical artefacts of tango singer Carlos Gardel. It also has a space for cultural events.

Along the attractive *costanera*, the **Centro Cultural**, opposite Calle 7 de Marzo, houses a small **Mercado Artesanal** selling beautifully made Mapuche weavings and woodwork.

### Carmen de Patagones

Carmen de Patagones (population 40,000) is the more dynamic of the two towns (which isn't saying much), with a feeling of bustle on the main street on weekday mornings. The town centre, just east of the river, lies around the Plaza 7 de Mayo, and just west is the **Iglesia del Carmen**, built by the Salesians in 1880. Take a stroll down the pretty streets winding down to the river to find many early pioneer buildings along the riverside: the **Torre del Fuerte**, tower of the stone fortress built in 1780 against indigenous attacks; the **Casa de la Tahona**, a disused 18th-century flour mill now housing the **Casa de la Cultura**; and another late-colonial building, **La Carlota**, one block east.

Nearby there's the fascinating **Museo Histórico Regional 'Emma Nozzi'** ① *JJ Biedma 64, T02920-462729, Mon-Fri 1000-1200, 1500-1700, Sat-Sun and bank holidays 1700-1900,* which gives a great insight into early pioneer life. There are Tehuelche arrowheads, stone *boleadoras*, silver gaucho stirrups and great early photos (one of a baptism by Salesians of a 100-year-old Tehuelche man in a field), next to delicate tea cups. There are guided tours too. The **Museo de la Prefectura Naval** ① *Mitre s/n y Costanera, T02920-461742, Mon-Fri 0800-1300, Sat-Sun 1500-1900,* is also worth a look if you're into ships; it's housed in a building dating from 1886 and contains a marine history of the area.

Patagones is linked to Viedma by two bridges and a very small ferry which takes four minutes and leaves every 15 minutes, US$0.40.

## South of Viedma and Carmen de Patagones
This whole stretch of coast is great for shore fishing, with *pejerrey, variada* and even shark among the many other species. Equipment is available in Viedma (see Shopping, below). There's a well-established little fishing resort at **Bahía San Blas**, 100 km east of Patagones, an area renowned for its shark fishing, with plentiful accommodation. For more information, see www.vivesanblas.com.ar.

At **El Cóndor**, 30 km south of Viedma (six buses daily in summer), there is a beautiful beach (also known as La Boca), with the oldest lighthouse in the country, dating from 1887. Facilities include a hotel, restaurants and shops (most facilities have reduced hours or are close entirely after January or February). There's free camping on a beach 2 km south.

**Playa Bonita**, 12 km further southwest is known as a good fishing spot, and offers more good beaches.

Ask the tourist office in Viedma (see Tourist information, below) for their leaflet about the *Lobería Punta Bermeja*, 60 km west of Viedma. This sea lion colony is visited by some 2500 sea lions in summer, which you can see at close range (daily bus in summer; but hitching is easy). There's also an impressive visitor centre (with toilets).

## Listings Viedma and Carmen de Patagones

### Tourist information

#### Viedma

**Municipal tourist office**
*Av Francisco de Viedma 51, T02920-427171, www.viedma.gov.ar. Daily 0900-2100.*
Helpful staff.

**Provincial tourist office**
*Av Caseros 1425, T02920-422150, www.rionegrotur.gob.ar (Spanish only). Mon-Fri 0700-1400, 1800-2000.*

#### Carmen de Patagones

**Tourist office**
*Mitre 84, T02920-464819, www.patagones.gov.ar. Mon-Fri 0800-2000, Sat-Sun 0930-1330 and 1530-1930.*
Helpful and dynamic tourist office.

#### El Cóndor

**Tourist office**
*T02920-497148. Mon-Fri 0900-1900, Sat-Sun 1130-1835.*

### Where to stay

#### Viedma
The best places to stay are in Viedma.

**$$$ Nijar**
*Mitre 490, T02920-422833, www.hotelnijar.com.*
Comfortable, smart, modern, good service.

**$$$ Peumayen**
*Buenos Aires 334, T02920-425222, www.hotelpeumayen.com.ar.*
Old-fashioned friendly place on the plaza.

## $$ Residencial Roca

*Roca 347, T02920-431241.*

A cheap option with comfortable beds, helpful staff, breakfast included.

### Camping

At the sea lion colony, **Trenitos** (T02920-497098), has good facilities.

## Restaurants

### $$ La Balsa

*On the river at Colón and Villarino, T02920-431974.*

By far the best restaurant, inexpensive with a pleasant atmosphere. Delicious seafood accompanied a bottle of superb Río Negro wine, Humberto Canale Merlot, is highly recommended.

## Festivals

### Carmen de Patagones

**Mar Fiesta de 7 de Marzo**, www.maragato. com.ar, when the whole town is packed out for the celebration of the victory at the Battle of Patagones. It's a week of music and handicrafts, fine food, a huge procession, gaucho horse-riding displays and lots of meat on the *asados*. It's great fun but make sure you book accommodation in advance.

## Shopping

### Viedma

**Patagonia Out Doors Life** (25 de Mayo 340), and **Tiburón** (Zatti 250), both stock fishing equipment.

## What to do

### Viedma

**Tour operators**

**Mona Tour**, *San Martín 225, T02920-422933, www.monatour. com.ar.* Sells flights as well as tickets for the train to Bariloche, www. trenpatagonico-sa.com.ar (check first to see if train is in service).

## Transport

### Air

**LADE** (Saavedra 576, T02920-424420, www. lade.com.ar) flies to **Buenos Aires**, **Mar del Plata**, **Bahía Blanca**, **Comodoro Rivadavia** and other Patagonian destinations.

### Viedma

### Bus

The **bus terminal** (Av Pte Perón and Guido, www.terminalpatagonia.com.ar) is 15 blocks from the plaza; a taxi to town costs around US$3.

To **Buenos Aires**, 13 hrs, daily, US$80-100, with **Don Otto** and others. To **Bahía Blanca**, 4 hrs, many daily, US$15-25. To **Puerto Madryn**, 6½ hrs, several daily, US$35-40, with **Don Otto** and others.

### Train

A comfortable sleeper train, which also carries cars, normally goes from Viedma to **Bariloche** overnight. For information on the current state of the service, as well as schedules, T02920-422130, www.trenpatagonico-sa.com.ar.

The undoubted highlight of the whole Atlantic Coast in Patagonia is the splendid array of marine wildlife on Península Valdés, best visited from Puerto Madryn (population 100,000). This seaside town has a grand setting on the wide bay of Golfo Nuevo and is the perfect base for setting off to Valdés to the east, as there are plenty of hotels and reliable tour operators running trips to the peninsula, including boat trips to see the whales. Puerto Madryn itself is a good place to enjoy the sea for a couple of days, with lots of beachfront restaurants selling superb locally caught seafood.

The town is a modern, relaxed and friendly place. It hasn't been ruined by its popularity as a tourist resort with a large workforce occupied by its other main industry: a huge aluminium plant, which you can visit by arrangement through the tourist office (see under Tourist information in Listings, page 163); best during summer.

Puerto Madryn was the site of the first Welsh landing in 1865 and is named after the Welsh home of the colonist, Jones Parry. However, it wasn't officially founded until 1889, when the railway was built connecting the town with Trelew to enable the Welsh living in the Chubut Valley to export their produce.

## Sights
You're most likely to be visiting the town to take a trip to Península Valdés (see page 167), but there are other tourist sights closer to hand. In the town itself, the real pleasure is the sea, and it's a pleasant first day's stroll along the long stretch of beach to **El Indio**, a statue on the road at the southeastern end of the bay, marking the gratitude of the Welsh to the native Tehuelche people whose shared expertise ensured their survival. As the road curves up the cliff here, don't miss the splendid **EcoCentro** ① *Julio Verne 3784, T0280-488 3173, www.ecocentro. org.ar, Wed-Mon 1500-2000 (2100 high season), US$9.50.* This interactive sea life information centre combines an art gallery, café and fabulous reading room with comfy sofas at the top of a turret. The whole place has fantastic views of the bay.

Just a little closer to town, perched on the cliff, is the tiny **Centro de Exposición de Punta Cuevas** ① *daily 1700-2100, www. puntacuevas.org.ar, US$2.50, temporarily closed at the time of writing*, of interest if you're tracing the history of the Welsh in Patagonia. It's little more than a couple of rooms of relics near the caves and basic huts on the cliffs where the settlers first lived,

## Essential Puerto Madryn

### Finding your feet

**El Tehuelche Airport** is 8 km west of the centre and can be reached by taxi, US$10-13. More frequent flights serve Trelew airport (see page 177), some 60 km away, with buses to Puerto Madryn that meet all flights, US$4; the journey takes one hour. The **bus terminal** is on Avenida Dr Avila, entre Necochea e Independencia.

### Getting around

The city centre is easy to get around on foot, with many restaurants and hotels lined up along the seafront at Avenida Roca, and most shops and tour companies on the streets around 28 de Julio, which runs perpendicular to the sea and past the town's neat little plaza, all contained within four or five blocks.

but enthusiastic guides make the visit worthwhile. A more conventional museum, with displays on local flora and fauna, is the **Museo de Ciencias Naturales y Oceanográfico** ⓘ *Domecq García y J Menéndez, T02965-445 1139, Mon-Fri 1000-1800, Sat 1500-1900, US$0.75,* which is informative and worth a visit.

### Around Puerto Madryn

During the right season, you can spot whales at the long beach of **Playa El Doradillo**, 16 km northeast of town, along the *ripio* road closest to the coast. There are also sea lions at the **Punta Loma Reserve** ⓘ *daily 0800-2000, US$7.50, child US$3.75,*

**Tip...**

A great bike ride is from the town to the Punta Loma Reserve along the coastal road; allow 1½ hours to get there. The road to the north of town is another good ride to do.

## Puerto Madryn

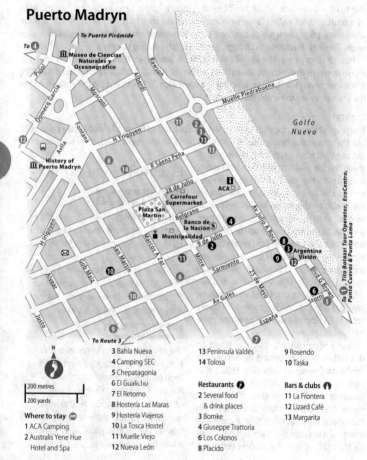

| 200 metres |
| 200 yards |

**Where to stay** 🛌
1 ACA Camping
2 Australis Yene Hue
  Hotel and Spa
3 Bahía Nueva
4 Camping SEC
5 Chepatagonia
6 El Gualicho
7 El Retorno
8 Hostería Las Maras
9 Hostería Viajeros
10 La Tosca Hostel
11 Muelle Viejo
12 Nueva León
13 Península Valdés
14 Tolosa

**Restaurants** 🍴
2 Several food
  & drink places
3 Bomke
4 Giuseppe Trattoria
6 Los Colonos
8 Placido
9 Rosendo
10 Taska

**Bars & clubs** 🍷
11 La Frontera
12 Lizard Café
13 Margarita

*many companies offer tours*, 15 km southeast of Puerto Madryn and best visited at low tide in December and January. Access is via the coastal road from town.

Puerto Madryn is Patagonia's **diving** capital, with dives to see wildlife and many offshore wrecked ships, together with all kinds of courses from beginners' dives to the week-long PADI course on offer from tour operators, such as **Puerto Madryn Buceo**. You can also hire mountain bikes and windsurfing boards here, from many places along the beachfront. For more information, see What to do, page 165.

## Listings Puerto Madryn *map page 162.*

### Tourist information

**Tourist information centre**
*Av Roca 223, just off 28 de Julio, T0280-445 3504, www.madryn.travel. Mar-Nov daily 0700-2100, Dec-Feb daily 0800-2100.*
Efficient and friendly office on the seafront, next to the shopping complex; there's another branch at the **bus station** (daily 0800-2100). The staff are extremely well organized and speak English. They have leaflets on Península Valdés and accommodation, and can advise on tours.

### Where to stay

Accommodation is generally of a high standard, but can be pricey. This is one of several tourist centres in Argentina where higher rates apply for foreigners than Argentines for hotel rooms and some entrance fees; it's hopeless to argue. Book ahead in summer and during whale-watching season.

**$$$$ Australis Yene Hue Hotel and Spa**
*Roca 33, T0280-445 2937, www.hotelesaustralis.com.ar.*
Luxury hotel on the beachfront with a small spa, modern rooms, and a good buffet breakfast. Ask for a room with a view.

**$$$$-$$$ Península Valdés**
*Av Roca 155, T0280-447 1292, www.hotel peninsula.com.ar.*
Luxurious seafront hotel with great views. Spa, sauna, gym.

**$$$ Bahía Nueva**
*Av Roca 67, T0280-445 1677, www.bahianueva.com.ar.*
One of the best seafront hotels, quite small but comfortable rooms, professional staff, cheaper in low season.

**$$$ Hostería Las Maras**
*Marcos A Zar 64, T0280-445 3215, http://lasmarashotel.com.ar.*
Appealing modern place, offering well-decorated rooms with large beds, cheaper with fan. Parking.

**$$$ Tolosa**
*Roque Sáenz Peña 253, T0280-447 1850, www.hoteltolosa.com.ar.*
Extremely comfortable, modern place, with great breakfasts. Disabled access.

**$$ Hostería Viajeros**
*Gob Maíz 545, T0280-445 6457, www.hostelviajeros.com.ar.*
Rooms for 2, 3 and 4 people, big kitchen/dining room, lawn, parking, new superior rooms on 2nd floor (**$$$**), helpful, family-run.

**$$ Muelle Viejo**
*H Yrigoyen 38, T0280-447 1284, www.muelleviejo.com.*
Ask for the comfortable modernized rooms in this funny old place. Rooms for 4 are excellent value.

**$$ Nueva León**
*D Garcia 365, T0280-447 4125, www.nuevaleon.com.ar.*
Good-value bungalows for up to 6 people located 2 blocks from the beach. Each *cabaña* comes equipped with cable TV.

#### $ pp Chepatagonia
*Alfonsina Storni 16, T0280-445 5783,*
*www.chepatagonia hostel.com.ar.*
Good view of the beach (and whales in
season), helpful owners, mixed and single
dorms, doubles with shared bath ($$),
lockers, bicycle hire and many other services.
A good choice.

#### $ pp El Gualicho
*Marcos A Zar 480, T0280-445 4163,*
*www.elgualicho.com.ar.*
Decent budget option, some double rooms
($$), HI discounts, enthusiastic owner,
English-speaking staff, heating, free pick
up from bus terminal, *parrilla*, garden, bikes
for hire, runs tours, parking, pool table.
Recommended.

#### $ El Retorno
*Bartomolmé Mitre 798, T0280-445 6044,*
*www.elretornohostel.com.ar.*
3 blocks from beach, hot water, lockers, cosy
common area, free bus terminal pick-up.
Double rooms available ($$). Also rents
apartments with sea view ($$$).

#### $ pp La Tosca Hostel
*Sarmiento 437, T0280-445 6133,*
*www.latoscahostel.com.*
This hostel was renovated in 2015 to add
lovely new doubles, triples and quadruples
($$). Each has a private bath and is equipped
with all mod cons. There are also dorms with
bathrooms. Free pick up from bus station.
Organizes tours and provides advice about the
area. The kitchen with *parrilla* is open 24 hrs;
a stay includes a big breakfast. Welcoming,
helpful vibe. Highly recommended.

### Camping

#### ACA
*Blv Brown 3869, 1 km south of town centre
(at Punta Cuevas), T0280-488 3485, www.
acamadryn.com.ar. Open year-round.*
Hot showers, café, shop, also duplexes
for 4-6, no kitchen facilities, shady trees,
close to the sea. US$10 per night; cheaper
rates Apr-Nov.

#### Camping SEC
*Río Mayo 800, 5 km from the town centre,
T0280-447 3015.*
Basic campsite from US$6 per night.

### Restaurants

One of the unmissable pleasures of
Puerto Madryn is its great seafood. While
you're here, try at least one plate of *arroz
con mariscos* (rice with a whole selection
of squid, prawns, mussels and clams).
Most restaurants are mid-range and
charge around the same price, but differ
widely in quality. The block of 9 de Julio
between 25 de Mayo and Mitre has an
interesting mix of food and drink places,
including a wine bar, a craft beer pub and
several restaurants.

#### $$$ Placido
*Av Roca 506, T0280-445 5991,*
*www.placido.com.ar.*
On the beach, great location and service,
but food can be hit and miss. Seafood and
vegetarian options, also cheaper pasta dishes.

#### $$$ Taska
*9 de Julio 461, T0280-447 4003.*
Excellent food with a Basque influence;
book ahead. Highly recommended.

#### $$ Giuseppe Trattoria
*25 de Mayo 388, T0280-456 891.*
With its red-checked tablecloths and cosy
family vibe, this pizza and pasta restaurant is
quite popular with locals. The large portions
certainly don't hurt.

#### $$ Los Colonos
*Av Roca y A Storni, T0280-445 8486.*
Quirky, cosy restaurant built into the wooden
hull of a boat, plenty of maritime heritage,
*parrilla*, seafood and pasta.

#### $ Rosendo
*Av Roca 549, 1st floor, T0280-445 0062.*
*Open lunchtime and evenings in high
season, from 1700 in low season.*
Snack bar/café overlooking the main street.
Excellent home-made *empanadas*, snacks,

cocktails and wines. Reading and games room. Recommended.

## Cafés

### Bomke
*Av Roca 540, T0280-447 4094, www.bomke.com.ar. Open late.*
Popular ice cream place with outdoor seating at the back. Excellent ice creams. Recommended.

## Bars and clubs

### La Frontera
*9 de Julio 254, T0280-472-2232, see Facebook. Closes at 0500 Thu-Sat.*
Popular with locals, this nightclub only really gets busy in the small hours.

### Lizard Café
*Av Roca y Av Galés, near the seafront, T0280-472 2232.*
Lively funky place with friendly people. Good for generous pizzas or late-night drinks.

### Margarita
*RS Peña 15, T0280-447 2659, see Facebook.*
Late-night bar for drinks and live music, serves expensive but tasty food.

## Shopping

You'll find clothes, T-shirts, high-quality Patagonian handicrafts and leather goods, and artesanal *alfajores* and cakes for sale on 28 de Julio and Av Roca. For fishing tackle, guns and camping gear, try **Nayfer** (25 de Mayo 366). For diving gear, there's **Pino Sub** (Yrigoyen 200, www.pinosub.com).
**Cardon**, *Shopping El Portal de Madryn, Av JA Roca and 28 de Julio.* Recommended for regional goods and leather bags.
**Portal de Madryn**, *28 de Julio and Av Roca, www.portaldemadryn.com.* The indoor shopping centre has all the smart clothes shops, a café on the ground floor, and a kids' games area with a fast-food place, **Mostaza**, on the top floor (not cheap).

## What to do

### Diving
Puerto Madryn is a diving centre, with several shipwrecked boats in the Golfo Nuevo. A first dive ('bautismo') for beginners costs about US$70 pp.
**Aquatours**, *Av Roca 550, T0280-445 1954, www.aquatours.com.ar.* A variety of options, including PADI courses, good value.
**Lobo Larsen**, *Roca 885, loc 2 (also Blv Brown 860), T0280-447 0277, www.lobolarsen.com.* Friendly company that specializes in diving with the sea lion colony at Punta Lomas. Wide variety of courses offered.
**Scuba Duba**, *Blv Brown 893, T0280-445 2699, www.scubaduba.com.ar.* Professional and good fun, diving with sea lions at Punta Loma, pick up from hotel, offer a hot drink and warm clothes after the dive, good equipment, instructor Javier A Crespi is very responsible.

### Horse riding
**Carlo Bonomi**, *T0280-432 2541, www. cb.fofuente.org.* Equestrian trainer rents horses for US$20 an hour.
**Huellas y Costas**, *Blv Brown 1900, T0280-447 0143, www.huellasycostas.com.* Also whale watching.

### Mountain bike hire
**El Gualicho**, *Marcos A Zar 480, T0280-445 4163.* From US$10.

### Tour operators
Many agencies do similar 7- and 9-hr tours to the Península Valdés, about US$50-60 pp, plus the entrance to the Peninsula. They include the interpretation centre, Puerto Pirámides (the boat trip is US$70 extra), Punta Delgada and Caleta Valdés. Most tour companies stay about 1 hr on location. Shop around to find out how long you'll spend at each place, how big the group is and whether your guide speaks English. On all tours take binoculars. Tours do not run after heavy rain in the low season. Tours to

see the penguins at Punta Tombo and the Welsh villages are better from Trelew (see page 177). Many of the agencies below now also have offices at the bus terminal (Dr Avila 350); all are recommended for Península Valdés:

**Alora Viaggio**, *Av Roca 27, T0280-445 5106, www.aloraviaggio.com.* Helpful company, also has an office in Buenos Aires (T011-4827 1591, daily 0800-1300).

**Argentina Visión**, *Av Roca 536, T0280-445 5888, www.argentinavision.com.* Also 4WD adventure trips and estancia accommodation, English and French spoken.

**Chaltén Travel**, *Av Roca 115, T0280-445 4906, www.chaltentravel.com.* Runs a tourist bus service to Perito Moreno on Ruta 40, for connections north to Bariloche and south to El Chaltén and El Calafate.

**Cuyun Có**, *Av Roca 165, T0280-445 1845, www.cuyunco.com.ar.* Offers a friendly, personal service and a huge range of conventional and more imaginative tours: guided walks with local experts, 4WD expeditions, and can arrange estancia accommodation. Bilingual guides.

**Tito Botazzi**, *Blv Brown y Martín Fierro, T0280-447 4110, www.titobottazzi.com,* and at Puerto Pirámides (T0280-449 5050). Particularly recommended for its small groups and well-informed bilingual guides; very popular for whale watching.

## Transport

### Air
There are daily flights to **Buenos Aires** in high season from the town's airport (T0280-445 6774). Also limited **LADE** (Roca 119, T0280-445 1256) flights to **Buenos Aires**,

Bahía Blanca, Viedma, **Trelew**, **Comodoro Rivadavia** and other Patagonian airports. More frequent flights from Bariloche, Buenos Aires, Ushuaia and El Calafate serve Trelew airport (see page 177), with buses to Puerto Madryn that meet all flights.

### Bus
The bus terminal (T0280-445 1789) has a café, toilets, *locutorio* and a small but helpful tourist office.

To **Buenos Aires**, 18-19 hrs, several companies, US$150. To **Bahía Blanca**, 9½ hrs with **Don Otto** and **Andes Mar**, US$80. To **Comodoro Rivadavia**, 6 hrs, US$45 with **Don Otto** and **Andes Mar**. To **Río Gallegos**, 18 hrs; US$130, with **Andes Mar**. To **Trelew**, 1 hr, every hour, US$5 with **28 de Julio/Mar y Valle**. To **Puerto Pirámides**, Mar y Valle, Mon-Fri 0630, 0945, 1600, returns 0815, 1300, 1800 (1 departure Sat-Sun at 0945) US$7 each way, 1½ hrs.

### Car hire
This is expensive, US$100 per day, and note large excess for turning the car over. Drive slowly on unpaved *ripio* (gravel) roads; it's best to hire 4WD. There are many agencies on Av Roca, including **Dubrovnik**, Av Roca 19, T0280-445 0030, www.rentacardubrovnik. com. Reliable company with offices in El Calafate and Bariloche. **Wild Skies**, Morgan 2274, p 1, Depto 6 B Sur, T0280-15-467 6233, www.wildskies.com.ar. Efficient service, English spoken. Recommended.

### Taxi
Taxis can be found outside the bus terminal, T0280-445 2966/447 4177, and on the main plaza.

Whatever time of year you visit Península Valdés you'll find a wonderful array of marine life, birds and a profusion of Patagonian wildlife such as guanacos, rheas, Patagonian hares and armadillos. But in spring (September-November), this treeless splay of land is host to a quite spectacular numbers of whales, penguins and seals, who come to breed in the sheltered waters south of the narrow Ameghino isthmus and on beaches at the foot of the peninsula's chalky cliffs.

The land is almost flat, though greener than much of Patagonia, and at the heart of the peninsula are large salt flats, one of which, **Salina Grande**, is 42 m below sea level. The peninsula is privately owned – many of its estancias offering comfortable and wonderfully remote places to stay in the middle of the wild beauty – but it is also a nature reserve and was declared a World Heritage Site by UNESCO in 1999. The beach along the entire coast is out of bounds and this is strictly enforced.

The main tourist centre on the peninsula is **Puerto Pirámides**, on the southern side, which has a few good hotels and hostels, places to camp and a handful of restaurants.

## Essential Península Valdés

### Access

Península Valdés can most easily be visited by taking one of the many well-organized full-day tours from Puerto Madryn (see Tour operators, page 165). These usually include a whale-watching boat trip, which departs from Puerto Pirámides (see below), together with a stop or two on the eastern coastline to see sea lions, penguins and other wildlife at close hand. Minibus travel, the boat trip and transfers to your hotel are included, but not lunch or entrance to the peninsula.

### Getting around

You can hire a car relatively inexpensively for a group of four, and then take a boat trip to see the whales (June to December) from Puerto Pirámides. Note that distances are long on the peninsula, and roads beyond Puerto Pirámides are *ripio*, so take your time – hire companies charge a heavy excess if you damage the car.

A cheaper option is the daily bus to Puerto Pirámides with **Mar y Valle**, leaving

Puerto Madryn's terminal daily at 0630, 0945 and 1600, and returning at 0815, 0945 and 1800, 1½ hours, US$5.50 each way (on Saturday and Sunday there is only one daily bus to Península Valdés, leaving at 0945). This would only allow you to see the whales though, since there is no public transport to other areas of the peninsula. To explore the peninsula in more detail and gain closer contact with nature, a stay one of the peninsula's estancias is recommended.

### When to go

Much of Península Valdés' wildlife can be enjoyed throughout the year, with sea lions, elephant seals, dolphins and many species of bird permanently resident. The bull elephant seals can be seen fighting for females from September to early November, and killer whales can sometimes be sighted off the coast at this time too, staying until April. Penguins can be seen from September to March, and the stars of the show, the southern right whales, come to these waters to breed in spring (September to November).

**Around the Peninsula** *The following are the main marine wildlife colonies.*

The entrance to the reserve is about 45 km northeast of Puerto Madryn, in the **interpretation centre** ① *administration T0280-447 0197, www.peninsulavaldes.org.ar, daily 0800-2100 (2000 in low season), US$21.75 for foreigners, children US$11,* where you buy the ticket for visiting all the sites on the peninsula. Twenty kilometres beyond, on the isthmus, there's an interesting **interpretation centre** with stuffed examples of the local fauna, many fossils and a wonderful whale skeleton, which makes a great complement to seeing the real thing gracefully soaring through the water. Ask for the informative bilingual leaflet on southern right whales.

**Isla de los Pájaros**, is in the Golfo San José, 5 km from the interpretation centre. Its seabirds can be viewed through fixed telescopes (at 400 m distance), since only recognized ornithologists can get permission to visit the island itself. Between September and April you can spot wading birds, herons, cormorants and terns.

**Caleta Valdés**, 45 km south of Punta Norte in the middle of the eastern shore, has huge colonies of elephant seals which can be seen at close quarters. In the breeding season, from September to October, you'll see the rather unappealing blubbery masses of bull seals hauling themselves up the beach to make advances to one of the many females in their harem. During the first half of August the bull seals arrive to claim their territory, and can be seen at low tide engaging in bloody battles over the females. At **Punta Cantor**, just south of here, you'll find a good café and clean toilets. There are also three marked walks, ranging from 45 minutes to two hours. **Estancia La Elvira** is a short distance inland from here, and is clearly signposted.

**Punta Delgada**, at the southeastern end of the peninsula, 110 km from the entrance, is where elephant seals and sea lions can be seen from the high cliffs in such large numbers that they seem to stretch out like a velvety bronze tide line on the beautiful beach below. It's mesmerizing to watch as the young frolic in the shallow water and the bulls lever themselves around the females. There's a hotel nearby, **Faro Punta Delgada** (see Where to stay, below), which is a good base for exploring this beautiful area further.

**Punta Norte**, at the northern end of the peninsula, 97 km from the entrance, is not often visited by tour companies, but it has colonies of elephant seals and sea lions. Killer whales (orca) have also been seen here, feeding on sea lion pups at low tide in March and April. **Estancia San Lorenzo** is nearby.

★ **Estancias**

There are several estancias on the peninsula which allow you to really appreciate the space and natural beauty of the land, and give you much more access to some of the most remote places, with great wildlife to observe. Ask the tourist office for advice. Day trips to the estancias can also be arranged, which might include wildlife trips, an *asado* and perhaps horse riding. For further details, see Where to stay, below.

**Whale watching from Puerto Pirámides** *Colour map 4, B2.*

Puerto Pirámides (population 429), 107 km east of Puerto Madryn, is the departure point for whale-watching boat trips, which leave from its broad sandy beach. Every year, between June and December, 400 to 500 southern right whales migrate to the Golfo Nuevo to mate and give birth. It is without doubt one of the best places in the world to watch these beautiful animals, since in many

**Tip...**
If you're prone to sea sickness, think twice before setting off on a whale-watching trip on a windy day.

cases the whales come within just a few metres of the coast. From Puerto Pirámides, boat trips take you gently close to basking whales; if you're lucky, you may find yourself next to a mother and baby. Sailings are controlled by the Prefectura (Naval Police), according to weather and sea conditions.

On land, a 3-km track (beware of the incoming tide), or a 15-km *ripio* road go to a *mirador* at Punta Pardelas where you can see the whales. The prevailing currents may throw smelly carcasses of the young whales that didn't make it onto the beach. Camping is allowed, but there are no services or drinking water.

## Listings Península Valdés

### Tourist information

In addition to the tourist office below, information is also available from the tourist office in Puerto Madryn (see page 163) and from the interpretation centre on the peninsula (see above).

#### Puerto Pirámides

**Tourist office**
*1ra Bajada al Mar, near the beach, T0280-449 5048, www.puertopiramides.gov.ar.*
Offers useful information for hikes and driving tours.

### Where to stay

The following are all in Puerto Pirámides; hotels are packed out in Jan and Feb.

**$$$$-$$$ Las Restingas**
*1ra Bajada al Mar, T0280-449 5101, www.lasrestingas.com.*
Exclusive, 8 rooms with sea views, very comfortable, with sophisticated regional restaurant. Good deals available in low season.

**$$$ ACA Motel**
*Julio A Roca s/n, T0280-449 5004, www.motelacapiramides.com.*
Welcoming, handy for the beach, with good seafood restaurant (you might spot whales from its terrace). There is also an ACA service station (open daily) with a good café and shop.

**$$$ Cabañas en el Mar**
*Av de las Ballenas y 1ra Bajada al Mar, T0280-449 5044, www.piramides.net.*

Comfortable, well-equipped 2-6 bed *cabañas* with sea view.

**$$$ Del Nómade**
*Av de las Ballenas s/n, T0280-449 5044, www.ecohosteria.com.ar.*
Eco lodge using solar power and water recycling, buffet breakfast, heating, café, specializes in wildlife watching, nature and underwater photography, kayaking, scuba diving, adventure sports, courses offered. Discounts via their website.

**$$$ The Paradise**
*2da Bajada al Mar, T0280-449 5030, www.hosteriaparadise.com.ar.*
Large comfortable rooms, suites with jacuzzis, fine seafood restaurant.

**$$ La Nube del Angel**
*2da Bajada al Mar, T0280-449 5070, www.lanubedelangel.com.ar.*
*Open all year.*
Lovely owners, small *cabañas* for 2-6 people, quiet, 5 mins' walk from the beach.

### Camping

Municipal campsite by the black-sand beach, T0280-154202760. Hot showers in evening, good, get there early to secure a place, US$6 per night. Do not camp on the beach: people have been swept away by the incoming tide.

### Estancias

For more estancias in Patagonia, see www.interpatagonia.com/estancias.

#### $$$$ El Pedral
*Punta Ninfas, T0280-154572551,*
*www.elpedral.com.ar.*
By a pebble beach, with lots of wildlife-watching opportunities, farm activities, horse riding, zodiac trips (extra), guesthouse with en suite rooms, restaurant and bar, swimming pool.

#### $$$$ Faro Punta Delgada
*Punta Delgada, T0280-445 8444,*
*www.puntadelgada.com.*
Next to a lighthouse, amazing setting, half and full board, excellent food, very helpful. Recommended; book in advance, no credit cards.

#### $$$ La Elvira
*Caleta Valdés, near Punta Cantor, T0280-445 8444 (contact Gonzalo Hernández),*
*www.laelvira.com.ar.*
Traditional Patagonian dishes and comfortable accommodation (B&B, half and full board available).

#### $$$ San Lorenzo
*On RP3, 20 km southwest of Punta Norte, T0280-445 8444 (contact through Argentina Visión in Puerto Madryn, see Tour operators, page 165).*
Great for day trips to a beautiful stretch of coast to see penguins, fossils, birdwatching and horse treks.

### Restaurants

There are many restaurants on the main street in Puerto Pirámides and reasonably priced ones at Punta Norte, Punta Cantor and the Faro in Punta Delgada. These recommendations are on the beach:

#### $$$ Las Restingas
*1ra Bajada on the beach, Puerto Pirámides, T0280-4495101, www.lasrestingas.com.*
Perfect for a romantic dinner, sea views and tranquillity. An imaginative menu combines quality local produce with a touch of sophistication.

#### $$ Quimey Quipan
*1ra Bajada opposite Las Restingas, Puerto Pirámides, T0280-445 8609.*
By the beach and next to **Tito Bottazzi**, this family-run place specializes in delicious seafood with rice and has a cheap set menu. It's always open for lunch, ring to reserve for dinner. Recommended.

#### $$ The Paradise
*Av de las Bellenas y 2da Bajada, T0280-4495030, www.hosteriatheparadise.com.ar.*
Just off the beach, good atmosphere and great seafood. Also offers lamb and a few vegetarian choices.

#### $ Towanda
*1ra Bajada al Mar s/n, Puerto Pirámides, T0280-422 1460.*
Quirky café and snack bar with outside seating overlooking the main street and beach. Friendly staff, recommended.

### What to do

**Tour operators**
**Hydrosport**, *1ra Bajada al Mar, Puerto Pirámides, T0280-449 5065, www.hydrosport. com.ar.* Rents scuba equipment and boats, and organizes land and sea wildlife tours to see whales and dolphins.
**Whales Argentina**, *1ra Bajada al Mar, T0280-449 5015, www.whalesargentina.com.ar.* Recommended for whale watching.

**outlaw hideouts and Welsh teahouses**

The Río Chubut is one of the most important rivers in Patagonia, flowing a massive 820 km from the eastern foothills of the Andes into the Atlantic at Bahía Engaño. It's thanks to the Río Chubut that the Welsh pioneers came to this part of the world in 1865, and their irrigation of the arid land around it enabled them to survive and prosper. You can trace their history west along the valley from the pleasant airy town of Trelew to the quiet little village of Gaiman, which has a wonderful museum and cafés serving traditional Welsh afternoon tea. Further west, past little brick chapels sitting amidst lush green fields, is the quieter settlement of Dolavon.

If you're keen to investigate further into the past, there's a marvellous museum full of dinosaurs in Trelew and some ancient fossils in the Parque Palaeontológico Bryn-Gwyn near Gaiman. From Trelew you could also visit South America's largest single colony of Magellanic penguins on the coast at Punta Tombo.

### Trelew *Colour map 4, C1.*

Some 70 km south of Puerto Madryn, Trelew (population 110,000) is the largest town in the Chubut Valley. Founded in 1884, it was named in honour of Lewis Jones, an early

**Trelew**

N
100 metres
100 yards

**Where to stay**
1 Galicia
2 Libertador
3 Rayentray
4 Rivadavia

5 Touring Club

**Restaurants**
2 Café de mi Ciudad
3 Café Verdi

5 La Bodeguita
6 La Casona
7 Miguel Angel

# BACKGROUND

## Welsh Patagonia

Among the tales of early pioneers to Argentina, the story of Welsh emigration, in search of religious freedom, is one of the most impressive. The first 165 settlers arrived in Patagonia in July 1865. Landing on the bay where Puerto Madryn now stands, they went south in search of drinking water to the valley of the Chubut river, where they found cultivatable land and settled.

The settlement was partly inspired by Michael D Jones, a non-conformist minister whose aim was to create a 'little Wales beyond Wales', far from the intruding influence of the English restrictions on Welsh religious beliefs. He provided much of the early finance and took particular care to gather people with useful skills, such as farmers and craftsmen, recruiting settlers through the Welsh language press and through the chapels. Between 1865 and 1915, the colony was reinforced by another 3000 settlers from Wales. The early years brought persistent drought, and the Welsh only survived through creating a network of irrigation channels. Early settlers were allocated 100 ha of land and when, by 1885, all irrigable land had been allocated, the settlement expanded westwards along the valley to the town of Trevelin in the foothills of the Andes.

The Welsh colony was tremendously successful, partly due to the creation of its own cooperative society, which sold their excellent produce and bought necessities in Buenos Aires. Early settlers were organized into chapel-based communities of 200 to 300 people, which were largely self-governing and organized social and cultural activities. The colony thrived after 1880, producing wheat from the arid Chubut Valley which won prizes all over the world. However, the depression of the 1930s drove wheat prices down, and poor management by the Argentine government resulted in the downfall of the Welsh wheat business. Many of the Welsh stayed, however; most of the owners of Gaiman's extraordinary Welsh tea rooms are descendants of the original settlers. The Welsh language is kept alive in both Gaiman and Trevelin, and Gaiman's festival of the arts – Eisteddfod – is held every October.

settler, and the Welsh colonization is still evident in a few remaining chapels in the town's modern centre. It's a cheerful place with a quietly busy street life, certainly more appealing than the industrial town of Rawson, 20 km east on the coast. Trelew has a splendid paleontological museum, a great tourist office and a couple of fabulous cafés.

**Sights** There's the lovely shady **Plaza Independencia** in the town centre, packed with mature trees, and hosting a small **handicraft market** ⓘ *every Sat 0900-1800*. Nearby is the **Capilla Tabernacle**, on Belgrano between San Martín and 25 de Mayo, a red-brick Welsh chapel dating from 1889. Heading east, rather more impressive is the **Salon San David** ⓘ *Mon-Fri 0900-1300, extended hours during Sep-Oct*, a Welsh meeting hall first used for the Eisteddfod of 1913. It has a mini-museum of objects donated by descendants of the Welsh settlers and also organizes Welsh language and dance classes. On the road to Rawson, 3 km south, you'll find one of the oldest standing Welsh chapels, **Capilla Moriah**. Built in 1880, it has a simple interior and a cemetery with the graves of many original settlers, including the first white woman born in the Welsh colony.

Back in Trelew itself, not the oldest but quite the most wonderful building is the 1920s **Hotel Touring Club** ① *Fontana 240, www.touringpatagonia.com.ar*. This was the town's grandest hotel in its heyday. Politicians and travellers met in its glorious high-ceilinged mirrored bar, which is now full of old photographs and relics. You can eat lunch here and there's simple accommodation available. Butch Cassidy once called this hotel home when he was on the run from representatives of the Pinkerton detective agency. Ask the friendly owner, Luis, if you can see the elegant 1920s meeting room at the back. Wanted posters of Butch himself adorn the walls.

The town's best museum – and indeed one of the finest in Argentina – is the ★ **Museo Paleontológico Egidio Feruglio** ① *Fontana 140, T0280-442 0012, www.mef.org.ar, Sep-Mar daily 0900-1900, Apr-Aug Mon-Fri 1000-1800, Sat-Sun 1000-1900, US$7.50, full disabled access, guides for the blind*. Imaginatively designed and beautifully presented, the museum traces the origins of life through the geological ages, displaying dynamically poised dinosaur skeletons, with plentiful information in Spanish. Tours are free and are available in English, German and Italian. There's also a reasonably cheap café and a shop. It's highly recommended and great for kids. For details of the **Geoparque Bryn Gwyn** near Gaiman, see below.

The **Museo Regional Pueblo de Luis** ① *Fontana and Lewis Jones 9100, T0280-442 4062, Mon-Fri 0800-2000, US$2.50*, is appropriately housed in the old railway station, built in 1889, since it was Lewis Jones who founded the town and started the railways that exported Welsh produce so successfully. It has interesting displays on indigenous societies, on failed Spanish attempts at settlement, and on Welsh colonization.

Next to the tourist office is the **Museo Municipal de Artes Visuales (MMAV)** ① *Mitre 350, T0280-443 3774, Mon-Fri 0800-1900, Sat-Sun 1400-1900, US$1*, located in an attractive wooden building. Recommended.

## South of Trelew

There is a lovely rock and sand beach at **Playa Isla Escondida**, 55 km south of Trelew along unpaved Ruta 1, which is a possible route to Punta Tombo. It's a favourite spot for sports fishermen, and you can see sea elephants, sea lions and birds here. There's secluded camping but no facilities. The main destination to the south, however, is the **Reserva Natural Punta Tombo** ① *www. puntatombo.com, daily 0800-1800 in high season, US$14, children US$7*, which is the largest breeding ground for Magellanic penguins in Patagonia and the largest single penguin colony on the South American continent. The nature reserve is best visited from September to March,

> **Tip...**
> Visit the Reserva Natural Punta Tombo in the afternoon when it's quieter because noisy colonies of tourists dominate the place in the morning.

when huge numbers of Magellanic penguins come here to breed. Chicks can be seen from mid-November and they waddle to the water in January or February. It's fascinating to see these creatures up close and you'll see guanacos, hares and rheas on the way.

To reach the reserve follow Ruta 1 for 100 km south towards Camarones; this is a *ripio* road best attempted in a high clearance vehicle. Alternatively, take paved Ruta 3 south and then turn onto Ruta Provincial 75 until it reaches Ruta 1, a total distance of 122 km. Tours from Trelew and Puerto Madryn cost US$70, allow 45 minutes at the site and usually include a stop at Gaiman.

## Gaiman Colour map 4, C1.

The quaint village of Gaiman lies west of Trelew, in the floodplain of the Río Chubut, and was made beautifully green and fertile thanks to careful irrigation of these lands by Welsh settlers. After travelling for a few days (or even hours) on the arid Patagonian steppe, it will strike you as a lush green oasis, testimony to the tireless hard work of those hardy Welsh emigrants. Gaiman is the first village you come to on Route 25, which heads west past Dolavon before continuing through attractive scenery to Esquel (see page 142) and the other Welsh colony of Trevelin in the Andes (see page 146). On the way, you'll find old Welsh chapels tucked away amongst the poplars in this green valley.

Gaiman is a pretty little place with old brick houses, which retains the Welsh pioneer feel despite the constant influx of tourists It has several tea rooms, many of them run by descendants of the original pioneers, serving delicious Welsh teas and cakes. Before you fill up on those, gain an insight into the spartan lives of those idealistic pioneers by visiting the **old railway station** (1909), which now houses the wonderful, tiny **Museo Histórico Regional Galés** ⓘ *Sarmiento and 28 de Julio, T0280-154569372, daily 1500-1900, US$1.* This has an impressive collection of Welsh artefacts, objects and photographs that serve as an evocative and moving testimony to extraordinary lives in harsh conditions. It is a great resource if you're looking for books on the subject or trying to trace your emigrant relatives.

Many other older buildings remain, among them the low stone first house, **Primera Casa** (1874) ⓘ *corner of main street, Av Tello y Evans, daily 1100-1800, US$1.* Other notable buildings include the old hotel (1899), at Tello and 9 de Julio; and the Ty Nain tea room (1890), on the Plaza at Yrigoyen 283. Cross the bridge to the south side of the river, and then take the first right to find two old chapels: pretty Capilla Bethel (1913) and the Capilla Vieja.

Some 8 km south of town there are fossil beds dating back 40 million years at the **Geoparque Bryn Gwyn** ⓘ *T0280-442 0012, www.mef.org.ar, Tue-Sun 1000-1600, US$3, US$1.50 children, taxi from Gaiman US$5.* This is a mind-boggling expanse of time brought to life by a good guided tour. It takes two hours to do the circuit, with fossils to see, as well as a visitor centre where you can try some fieldwork in palaeontology.

## Dolavon Colour map 4, C1.

Founded in 1919, Dolavon (population 2500) is the most westerly Welsh settlement in the valley and not quite as inviting as Gaiman, though its quiet streets are rather atmospheric, and on a short stroll you can find a few buildings reminiscent of the Welsh past. The main street, Avenida Roca, runs parallel to the irrigation canal built by the settlers, where willow trees now trail into the swiftly flowing water; there's a Welsh chapel, **Capilla Carmel**, at its quieter end. The old **flour mill** ⓘ *Maipú and Roca, Tue-Sun 1100-1600, US$2,* dates from 1927 and can be visited. There's **Autoservicio Belgrano** at the far end of San Martín for food supplies, but there is only one tea room, **El Molienda** ⓘ *Maipú 61, T0280-449 2290, www.molinoharinerodedolavon.com, US$7.50,* and nowhere really to stay apart from the municipal campsite two blocks north of the river which is free and has good facilities.

If you're in your own transport, it's worth driving from Dolavon back towards Gaiman via the neat squared fields in this beautiful irrigated valley, where you'll see more Welsh chapels tucked away among poplar trees and silver birches. Follow the main road that leads south through Dolavon, and then turn left and take the next right, signposted to Iglesia Anglicana. The **San David Chapel** (1917) is a beautifully preserved brick construction, with an elegant bell tower and sturdy oak-studded door, in a quiet spot surrounded by birches. Further on you'll cross the raised irrigation canals the Welsh built, next to small orchards of apple trees and tidy fields bordered by *álamo* trees.

## West of Dolavon

West from Dolavon, paved Ruta 25 runs to the upper Chubut Valley, passing near the **Florentino Ameghino** dam, 120 km west of Trelew, which is a leafy spot for a picnic. The road from Ameghino to Tecka (on the junction with Ruta 40 south of Trevelín) is one of the most beautiful routes across Patagonia to the Andes, with lots of wildlife to see. It goes through Las Plumas (mind the bridge if driving), reaching Los Altares at Km 321, which has an ACA motel ($$) with restaurant and bar, a basic campsite 400 m behind the service station, fuel and some shops. Beyond, Route 25 continues via Paso de Indios.

## Listings Trelew and the Chubut Valley map page 171.

### Tourist information

#### Trelew
Useful websites include www.trelew turismo.wordpress.com (in Spanish only) and www.trelewpatagonia.gov.ar.

**Tourist office**
*Mitre 387, on the main plaza, T0280-442 0139. Mon-Fri 0800-2000, Sat-Sun 0900-2100.*
Very helpful office. There's another office at bus station (same opening times) and at the airport when flights arrive. They'll give you an excellent map, directing you to the town's older buildings.

#### Gaiman

**Tourist office**
*Av Belgrano 574, on the main plaza, T0280-449 1571, www.gaiman.gov.ar. Daily 0900-1900, Sun 1100-1800 (shorter hours in low season).*

### Where to stay

#### Trelew

**$$$$-$$$ La Casona del Río**
*Chacra 105, Capitán Murga, T0280-443 8343, www.lacasonadelrio.com.ar.*
5 km from town, pick-up arranged, attractive, family-run B&B with heating, TV, meals available, bicycles, massage, laundry, tennis and bowls, English and French spoken. Higher prices Feb-Jul.

**$$$ Galicia**
*9 de Julio 214, T0280-443 3802, www.hotelgalicia.com.ar.*
Central, grand entrance, comfortable rooms, excellent value. Recommended.

**$$$ Libertador**
*Rivadavia 31, T0280-442 0220, www.hotellibertadortw.com.ar.*
Modern hotel, highly recommended for service and comfortable bedrooms.

**$$$ Rayentray**
*Belgrano 397, cnr San Martín, T0280-443 4702, www.cadena rayentray.com.ar.*
Large, modern, comfortable rooms, professional staff, pool, Wi-Fi.

**$$ Rivadavia**
*Rivadavia 55, T0280-443 4472.*
Simple, comfortable rooms, breakfast extra.

**$$ Touring Club**
*Fontana 240, Peatonal Luis Gazín, T0280-443 3997, www.touringpatagonia.com.ar.*
Gorgeous 1920s bar, faded elegance, simple rooms, great value, breakfast included. Open from breakfast until 1230 at night for sandwiches and drinks. Wi-Fi in rooms and bar. Butch Cassidy himself endorsed the place.

#### Camping

**Camping Sero**
*Playa Unión, 25 km from Trelew, T0280-449 6982.*
Located in the quaint seaside village of Playa Unión, this campsite offers lodging from US$7.50 per night.

## Gaiman

**$$$$-$$$ Posada Los Mimbres**
*Chacra 211, 6 km west of Gaiman, T0280-449 1299, www.posadalosmimbres.com.ar. Cheaper Apr-Aug.*
Rooms in the old farmhouse or in modern building, good food, very relaxing.

**$$$-$$ Ty Gwyn**
*9 de Julio 111, T0280-449 1009, tygwyn@tygwyn.com.ar.*
Neat, comfortable, above the tea rooms, excellent value.

**$$ Hostería Ty'r Haul**
*Sarmiento 121, T0280-449 1880.*
Historic building, rooms are comfortable and well lit. Recommended.

**$$ Plas y Coed**
*Yrigoyen 320, T02965-449 1133, www.plasycoed.com.ar.*
Ana Rees' delightful tea shop has double and twin rooms in an annex next door. Highly recommended.

### Camping

**Camping de los Bomberos** is the municipal site.

### Trelew

**$$ La Bodeguita**
*Belgrano 374, T0280-443 7777.*
Delicious pasta and pizzas. Reasonable wine list. Recommended.

**$$ La Casona**
*Pasaje Jujuy and Lewis Jones, near Plaza Centenario, T0280-443-4026, www.lacasona trelew.blogspot.com.*
Patagonian lamb, *parrilla*, good lunchtime venue.

**$$ Miguel Angel**
*Fontana 246, next door to Touring Club (see Where to stay, above), in Peatonal Luis Gazín, Av Fontana.*
Good standard fare of meat and pasta dishes.

## Cafés

### Café de mi Ciudad
*Belgrano 394.*
Smart café serving great coffee; read the papers here. Also has Wi-Fi.

### Café Verdi
*Attached to Teatro Verdi, Bulevú, San Martín 412, T0280-443 6601, see Facebook.*
Cosy café featuring an array of healthy dishes including sandwiches, salads and fresh juices. Mouth-watering bakery. Great for vegetarians.

## Gaiman
### Welsh teas

You're unlikely to be able to resist the Welsh teas for which Gaiman has become famous, though quite how the tradition sprung up remains a mystery. It's hard to imagine the residents' abstemious ancestors tucking into vast plates filled with 7 kinds of cake and scones at one sitting. Tea is served from 1400-1900; all the tea rooms charge US$15-20 and include the most well-known of the 'Welsh' cakes, *torta negra* – a delicious dense fruit cake.

### Casa de Té Gaiman
*Av Yrigoyen 738, T0280-449 1633, amaliaj51@hotmail.com.*
One of the few remaining tea houses in Gaiman still run by the original Welsh descendants.

### Plas Y Coed
*See Where to stay, above.*
The best, and oldest; owner Ana Rees learned how to cook at the feet of Marta Rees, her grandmother and one of the best cooks in Gaiman.

### Ty Gwyn
*9 de Julio 111, T0280-449 1009, tygwyn@ tygwyn.com.ar. Opens 1400.*
Large tea room, more modern than some, welcoming; generous teas.

## Festivals

**Gaiman**
Sep  Eisteddfod (Welsh Festival of Arts).

## Shopping

**Trelew**
The main shopping area is around San Martín and from the plaza to Belgrano. Though Trelew can't compare with Puerto Madryn for souvenirs, it has a good little handicrafts market on the plaza. There is a **Norte** supermarket, Rivadavia y 9 de Julio.

## What to do

**Trelew**
**Tour operators**
Agencies run tours to Punta Tombo, Chubut Valley (half- and full-day). Tours to Península Valdés are best done from Puerto Madryn.
**Explore Patagonia**, *Roca 94, T0280-443 7860, www.explore-patagonia.com.ar.*
A competing operator offering similar tour packages to **Nieve Mar**. Also has an office in Puerto Madryn.
**Nieve Mar**, *Italia 20, T0280-443 4114, www. nievemartours.com.ar.* Trips to Punta Tombo and Valdés, bilingual guides (reserve ahead), organized and efficient. Has a branch in Puerto Madryn (Av Roca 493).

## Transport

**Trelew**
**Air**
The airport is 5 km north of centre. A taxi costs US$7 and local buses to/from Puerto Madryn will stop at the airport entrance if asked.

**Aerolíneas Argentinas** (Rivadavia 548, T0810-222 86527) has flights to/from **Buenos Aires**, **Bariloche**, **El Calafate** and **Ushuaia**. **LADE** (Italia 170, T0280-443 5740) flies to Patagonian airports.

**Bus**
**Local**  **28 de Julio/Mar y Valle** go frequently to **Gaiman**, 30-45 mins, US$1; to **Dolavon** 1 hr, US$3.50; to **Puerto Madryn** (via **Trelew airport**), 1 hr, US$3; to **Puerto Pirámides**, 2½ hrs, US$7, daily.

**Long distance**  The bus terminal is on the east side of Plaza Centenario at Urquiza y Lewis Jones, T0280-442 0121. To **Buenos Aires**, daily, 19-20 hrs, US$100-140, several companies; to **Comodoro Rivadavia**, 5 hrs, US$30-37, many departures; to **Río Gallegos**, 17 hrs; US$90-105 (with connections to **El Calafate**, **Puerto Natales**, **Punta Arenas**), many companies. To **Esquel**, 9-10 hrs, US$45-50, **Don Otto**.

**Car hire**
Car hire desks at the airport are staffed only at flight arrival times and cars are taken quickly. All have offices in town: **AVIS**, airport, T0280-15425997; **Fiorasi**, Urquiza 310, T0280-443 5344; **Hertz**, at the airport, T0280-442 4421.

**Gaiman**
**Bus**
To **Trelew** every 30 mins, US$1, **Don Otto**.

**Dolavon**
**Bus**
To **Trelew**, several a day, 1 hr, US$1.50, with **28 de Julio**.

# Southern
## Atlantic Coast

Quieter, and much less visited by tourists than Puerto Madryn and Península Valdés, the southern stretch of the Atlantic coastline from Camarones to Río Gallegos is extremely rich in marine life of all kinds. There are several wonderful reserves protecting a wide variety of species of bird and mammal, and a few good bases for exploring them at the coastal towns of Camarones, Puerto Deseado and Puerto San Julián, with decent services and accommodation. If you have your own transport, you could head out to the only national park on the coast, Monte León, where you can walk the shore for miles and stay in a remote but comfortable *hostería*. And on the last spit of land before Tierra del Fuego, there's ancient history to explore near the coast at Cabo Vírgenes.

There are two cities in this huge region, of which the most appealing is the southernmost town on the Argentine mainland, Río Gallegos. It's a small, pleasant place, with fair accommodation and tours offered to penguin colonies, though there's little else to draw you here unless you're changing buses. The other city, Comodoro Rivadavia, is probably best avoided, unless you're keen to see the petroleum museum.

Aside from coastal attractions, this region also has the country's finest petrified forest, the Monumento Natural Bosques Petrificados.

### Camarones and around *Colour map 4, C1.*

Camarones (population 2000) is a quiet fishing port on Bahía Camarones, south of Trelew, whose main industry is harvesting seaweed. This is also prime sheep-rearing land, and Camarones wool is world-renowned for its quality. Aside from the salmon festival in early or mid-February, the only real attraction is a penguin colony, which you can walk to from the town.

There's another well-known penguin colony with lots more species of marine life, 35 km southeast at **Reserva Natural Cabo Dos Bahías** ① *open daily, free; there are buses to the reserve from Trelew, see page 171.* This is a small reserve at the southern end of the bay, reached by a dirt road. It protects a large colony of some 100,000 penguins, which you can see close up; there are also seals and sea lions all year round, and whales from March to November; killer whales might be spotted from October to April. On land there are rheas, guanacos and maras.

### Bahía Bustamante

Some 90 km south of Camarones along the coast is Bahía Bustamante, a settlement of seaweed harvesters and sheep ranchers on Golfo San Jorge (180 km north of Comodoro Rivadavia). Its main attractions are the coastal and steppe landscapes of the surrounding Patagonia Austral Marine national park, which offers exceptional opportunities to see birds (including 100,000 penguins), marine and land mammals.

### Comodoro Rivadavia and around *Colour map 2, B5.*

Situated at the end of the Bioceanic Corridor, a fast road to Chile, Comodoro is the hub for terrestrial transport and a bus nexus from all areas of Patagonia. You're most likely to end up here if you need to change buses, and there's little to make you want to stay (certainly not the high prices). With a population of 350,000, Comodoro Rivadavia is the largest city in the province of Chubut.

It was established primarily as a sheep-exporting port, and early settlers included Boer immigrants fleeing British rule in southern Africa. The city began to flourish suddenly when oil was discovered here in 1907, bringing in many international companies. However, since the petrol industry was privatized by President Menem in the 1990s, there's been consequent unemployment and now the town has a slightly sad, rather unkempt feel.

**Around Comodoro Rivadavia** There's a good view of the city from **Cerro Chenque**, 212 m high, a dun-coloured hill, unattractively adorned with radar masts, whose cliffs give the town its drab backdrop. It's interesting to take a taxi up there, if you don't feel like the walk, to see the first pioneers' homes, now dilapidated, but with panoramic views of the bay.

If you're really stuck for something to do, you could also visit the **Museo Nacional del Petróleo** ① *San Lorenzo 250, 3 km north of the centre, T0297-455 9558, Mon-Fri 0900-1700, Sat-Sun 1500-1800, US$4,* for a good history of local oil exploitation.

There's a good beach at the resort of **Rada Tilly**, 8 km south, where you can walk along the beach at low tide to see sea lions. Expreso Rada Tilly runs buses every 30 minutes, US$1; they're packed in summer.

You could use Comodoro Rivadavia as a base for exploring a petrified forest, the **Bosque Petrificado José Ormachea**, but the little town of **Sarmiento**, some 140 km west, is far more pleasant. For information on getting to Sarmiento, see Transport, below.

## Tourist information

### Comodoro Rivadavia

**Tourist office**
*Dr Scocco and Abasolo, T0297-444 0664,*
*www.comodoroturismo.gob.ar.*
Very helpful and English is spoken.
There's another office at the bus terminal;
see Transport, below.

### Where to stay

#### Camarones

For other lodgings see www.argentina
turismo.com.ar/camarones.

**$$$-$$ Complejo Indalo Inn**
*Sarmiento and Roca, T0297-496 3004,*
*www.indaloinn.com.ar.*
Simple but clean, doubles and singles with
en suite. Good food, and the owner runs trips
to the penguin colony. Recommended.

**$$$-$$ El Faro**
*Brown s/n, T0297-414 5510,*
*www.elfaro-patagonia.com.ar.*
2-person private rooms with sea views.
Also rents beachside houses for up to
5 people. Cash only. Under the same
ownership as **Bahía Bustamante**.

#### Bahía Bustamante

**Bahía Bustamante**
*T011-4156 7788/T0297-480 1000, www.*
*bahiabustamante.com. Closed Apr-Sep.*
An award-winning resort offering full-board
and self-catering accommodation, plus
hiking, cycling, riding and kayaking; guides
are on hand. Electricity 1900 to 2400. If you
don't have your own transport, you can
phone or email in advance to be picked up
from the ACA station in Garayalde, or there
are regular buses from Trelew.

### Comodoro Rivadavia

**$$$ Lucania Palazzo**
*Moreno 676, T0297-449 9300,*
*www.lucania-palazzo.com.*
Most luxurious business hotel, superb rooms,
sea views, good value, huge American
breakfast, sauna and gym included.
Recommended.

**$$ Azul**
*Sarmiento 724, T0297-446 7539,*
*info@hotelazul.com.ar.*
Breakfast extra, quiet old place with lovely
bright rooms, kind, great views from the
*confitería.*

**$$ Hospedaje Cari Hue**
*Belgrano 563, T0297-447 2946, see Facebook.*
Sweet rooms, with separate bathrooms,
indifferent owner, breakfast extra. Probably
the cheapest place to stay that's halfway safe.

### Camping

**Camping Municipal**
*Rada Tilly, T445 2689, www.radatilly.com.ar.*
*Open in high season only.*
Reached by **Expreso Rada Tilly** bus from
town. Hot showers.

**San Carlos**
*37 km north on R3, T0297-486 3122.*
Covers 20 ha, open all year.

## Restaurants

### Comodoro Rivadavia

**$$ Cayo Coco**
*Rivadavia 102, T0297-4097 3033.*
Bistro with excellent pizzas, good service.
Also Cayo Coco del Mar, Av Costanera 1051.

**$$ Maldito Peperoni**
*Sarmiento 581, T0297-446 9683.*
Cheerful, modern, pastas.

## Transport

### Camarones

**Bus**

To **Trelew**, Mon, Wed, Fri at 0800, 2½ hrs, US$17, with **Transportes El Ñandu SRL**.

### Comodoro Rivadavia

**Air**

The **airport** is 13 km north of town and bus No 6 leaves hourly for the bus terminal, 45 mins, US$0.50. A taxi from the airport costs US$17.

**Aerolíneas Argentinas** (Rivadavia 156, T0810-222 86527) and **LAN** (www.lan.com) have regular flights to **Buenos Aires** and **Bariloche** (Aerolíneas Argentinas also flies to **Esquel**). **LADE** (Rivadavia 360, T0297-447 0585) flies to all Patagonian destinations.

**Bus**

The bus terminal (Pellegrini 730, T0297-446 7305) is convenient for the town centre. It has a luggage store, a good *confitería* upstairs and toilets. There's a tourist information office (open Mon-Fri from 0800 to 2000, Sat 0900-2000, Sun 1000-2000). In summer buses usually arrive full, so book ahead.

To **Buenos Aires**, several daily, 24-28 hrs, US$135-155. To **Bariloche**, 14½ hrs, US$57-77, with **Don Otto** (T0297-447 0450), **Marga** and **Andesmar** (T0297-446 8894). To **Esquel** (paved road), 9 hrs direct with **EETAP**, T0297-447 4841, and **Don Otto**, US$45-50. To **Río Gallegos**, daily, several companies 10-12 hrs, US$60-70. To **Puerto Madryn**, US$33-40. To **Trelew**, daily, 5 hrs, US$28-35, several companies including **Don Otto**. To **Caleta Olivia**, 1 hr, US$5-8. To **Sarmiento**, 4 daily, 2½ hrs, US$11. To **Puerto Deseado**, Sportman, 2 a day, US$25.

**Car rental**

**Avis**, Moreno 725 (in the Hotel Austral lobby), T0297-4464828; **Patagonia Sur Car**, Rawson 1190, T0297-446 6768.

## South of Comodoro Rivadavia

*towards Tierra del Fuego*

### Caleta Olivia *Colour map 2, B5.*

Caleta Olivia (population 51,733) lies on the Bahía San Jorge, 74 km south of Comodoro Rivadavia. Founded in 1901, it became the centre for exporting wool from the estancias of Santa Cruz. It boomed with the discovery of oil in 1944 but has suffered since the petroleum industry was privatized in the 1990s and is now a rather sad place with high unemployment and a reputation for petty crime. However, there's a lovely 70-km stretch of pebbly beach, popular with locals for bathing, and lots of fishing nearby.

At **Pico Truncado**, some 50 km southwest, there's the gas field that feeds the pipeline to Buenos Aires. There's a daily bus service from Caleta Oliva, and Pico Truncado has a few simple hotels, a campsite, and **tourist information** ⓘ *T0297-499 2202*.

### ★ Monumento Natural Bosques Petrificados

*256 km west of Puerto Deseado; access is via Route 49 which branches off the R3 at Km 2063, 86 km south of Fitz Roy. Daily 1000-2000, donations welcome.*

Extending over 10,000 ha in a bizarre, wind-wracked lunar landscape surrounding the **Laguna Grande**, this park contains much older petrified trees than the forests further north around Sarmiento. The trunks, mainly of giant araucaria trees, are up to 35 m long and 150 cm in diameter. They were

**Tip...**

Bring your own food and drink as there are no facilities, services or water sources in the park.

petrified in the Jurassic period 140 million years ago by intense volcanic activity in the Andes cordillera which blew ash over the entire area. It was the silicates in this volcanic ash that petrified the trunks of fallen trees and created these strange jasper-like hulks, which were only revealed when other organic matter around them eroded. The place is more eerie than beautiful, but it does exert a strange fascination, especially when you consider that the fossils of marine animals that you see on the site are a mere 40 million years old, belonging to a sea that covered the land long after the trees had turned to stone. There is a small visitor centre and museum, and a well-documented 1-km trail that takes you past the most impressive specimens. You may be very tempted to take away your own personal souvenir: don't.

The only way to visit the park, unless you have your own transport, is with a tour: try **Los Vikingos** based in Puerto Deseado. For further information, see What to do, page 184.

## Listings South of Comodoro Rivadavia

### Tourist information

#### Caleta Olivia

**Tourist office**
*San Martín y Güemes, T0297-485 0988, turismocaletaolivia on Facebook.*
The municipal website is www.caletaolivia. gov.ar.

### Where to stay

#### Caleta Olivia

**$$$ Patagonia Hotel**
*Av Eva Perón 1873, T0297-483 0517, www.patagoniahotelco.com.ar.*
Welcoming, slightly dated hotel with clean bright rooms and views of the ocean.

**$$ pp Hotel Robert**
*San Martín 2152, T0297-485 1452, www.hotelrobert.com.ar.*
Comfortable option. All rooms have bathroom, and breakfast is included.

**$ Grand Hotel**
*Mosconi and Chubut, T0297-485 1393.*
Reasonably comfortable rooms.

### Camping

**Camping Gerald**
*Route 3, 5 km south of Caleta Oliva, T0297 485 0613.*
Also *cabañas*.

### Monumento Natural Bosques Petrificados

There is no accommodation in the area, apart from camping at **Estancia La Paloma** (on Ruta 49, 25 km away, T0297-444 3503). Note that camping is not allowed in the park.

### Transport

#### Caleta Olivia
**Bus**

To **Río Gallegos**, with **Andesmar**, **Sportman** and others, US$54-71, 9½ hrs. Many buses to/ from **Comodoro Rivadavia**, 1 hr, US$5-8, and 2 daily to **Puerto Deseado**, 2½-3 hrs, US$18, with **Sportman**. To **Perito Moreno** 5-6 hrs, US$24, 3 a day **Sportman** and **Marga**; to **Los Antiguos** 3-5 hrs US$29, 3 a day.

**a hotbed of wildlife activity on an estuary**

Puerto Deseado (population 20,000) is a pleasant fishing port on the estuary of the Río Deseado, which drains, curiously, into Lago Buenos Aires in the west. It's a stunning stretch of coastline, rich in wildlife: the estuary encompasses a wonderful reserve, and there are more reserves within reach, protecting sea lions and penguins. In fact, Puerto Deseado offers an abundance of marine life in much the same vein as Puerty Madryn, but at a fraction of the cost of visiting that tourist hotspot.

The **Museo Regional Mario Brozoski** ① *Belgrano (9050) and Colón, see Facebook, Mon-Fri 0900-1600, Sat-Sun 1500-1800*, has remains of an 18th-century ship that sank off the coast here in 1770, as well as some evocative photos. Outside the former railway station, a rather fine old building in vaguely English medieval style, is the **Vagón Histórico** ① *San Martín and Almirate Brown, www.deseado.gov.ar*, an 1898 carriage now used as the tourist office.

## Reserva Natural Ría Deseado
The submerged estuary (*ría*) of the Río Deseado, 42 km long, is an important nature reserve and a stunning area to visit. The crumbling chalky cliffs in mauve and ochre are splattered with *guano* (droppings) from many varieties of seabird. There's a colony of Magellanic penguins and five species of cormorant, including the unique red-legged cormorant, most appealing with their smart dinner-jacketed appearance. These birds nest from October to April on four islands offshore. The reserve is also a breeding ground for Commerson's dolphins, beautiful creatures that frolic playfully around your boat. Excellent tours run from the pier in Puerto Deseado; they last about two hours and are best in early morning or late evening (see Tour operators, below).

## Other reserves round Puerto Deseado
There are several other nature reserves within easy reach if you have transport, and all offer good places to walk. North of Puerto Deseado, some 90 km on the northern shore of the peninsula, is **Cabo Blanco**, the site of the largest fur seal colony in Patagonia. It's another magnificent area, a rocky peninsula bursting out from flat lands, with one of the oldest lighthouses on the coast perched on top and thousands of seals on the rocks below. The breeding season is December to January.

A little further west, you should also visit Cañadón de Duraznillo and Monte Loayza, which combine to form the **Reserva Natural Provincial Monte Loayza** ① *www. monteloayza.com.ar*. Cañadón de Duraznillo is an area of Patagonian steppe, while Monte Loayza is a strip of coastal and marine habitat. Here you'll see lots of guanacos, *ñandues*, foxes and birds, as well as the largest seal colony in the province on spectacular unspoilt beaches.

The visitor centre is at Estancia La Madrugada, which is 83 km from Puerto Deseado; the reserve is 18 km further west, towards Jaramillo. Visits are limited to groups of 10 or less from November to March and must be accompanied by a specialist guide; if you arrive without a guide you will only be allowed in to the visitor centre.

South of Puerto Deseado are two more reserves: **Isla Pingüino**, an offshore island with a colony of Magellanic penguins, as well as cormorants and steamer ducks, and the **Reserva Natural Bahía Laura**, an uninhabited bay where black-necked cormorants, ducks and other seabirds can be found in abundance. Isla Pingüino can be reached by boat, and Bahía Laura by *ripio* and dirt roads. For further information, see What to do, below.

The **Gruta de Lourdes**, 24 km west, is a cave which attracts pilgrims to see the Virgen de Lourdes. Further south along the same road is the **Cañadón del Puerto**, a mirador offering fine views over the estuary.

## Listings Puerto Deseado and around

### Where to stay

**Puerto Deseado**

**$$ Isla Chaffers**
*San Martín y Mariano Moreno,*
*T0297-487 2246, administracion@*
*hotelislachaffers.com.ar.*
Modern, central.

**$$ Los Acantilados**
*Pueyrredón y España, T0297-487 2167,*
*reservas.losacantilados@gmail.com.*
Beautifully located, good breakfast.
Travellers report some rooms run down
and dingy.

**Camping**
**Camping Cañadón de Giménez** (4 km
away on R281, T0297-487 2135); **Camping
Municipal** (Av Lotufo, on the seafront).
Lovely locations but the sites are a bit
run down.

### Restaurants

**Puerto Deseado**

**$$ Puerto Cristal**
*España 1698, T0297-487 0387.*
Panoramic views of the port, a great place for
Patagonian lamb, *parrilla* and seafood.

### What to do

**Puerto Deseado**
**Darwin Expediciones**, *España 2551, T0297-15-
624 7554, www.darwin-expeditions.com.* Boat
trips to Ría Deseado reserve and tours to the
Monumento Natural Bosques Petrificados.
**Los Vikingos**, *Prefectura Naval s/n, T0297-
15-624 5141/0297-487 0020, www.losvikingos.
com.ar.* Boat trips to Ría Deseado reserve and
Reserva Provincial Isla Pingüino, bilingual
guides, customized tours.

### Transport

**Puerto Deseado**
**Bus**
To **Caleta Olivia**, daily, US$17, with **Sportman**.

## Puerto San Julián and further south  Colour map 2, C5.

*an oasis between remote outposts*

### Puerto San Julián

The quiet port town of Puerto San Julián (population 6200), lying on a peninsula
overlooking the Bahía San Julián 268 km south of Fitz Roy, is the best place for breaking
the 834-km run from Comodoro Rivadavia to Río Gallegos. It has a fascinating history,
although little of it is in evidence today.

The first Mass in Argentina was held
here in 1520 after the Portuguese explorer
Magellan had executed a member of his
mutinous crew. Then, in 1578, Francis
Drake also put in here to behead Thomas
Doughty, after amiably dining with him. In
1780, Antonio Viedma attempted to found

**Tip...**
The best time to visit the Reserva Natural
San Julián is in December to see dolphins
and cormorants, though there's plenty to
see from December to April.

a colony here, but it failed due to scurvy. (You can visit the ruins of the site at **Florida Blanca**, 10 km west.) The current town was founded in 1901 as a port to serve the sheep estancias of this part of Santa Cruz.

The small **Museo Regional** at Rivadavia and Vieytes houses the amazingly well-preserved dinosaur footprint found in the town. There's plenty of wildlife to be seen in the area, especially in the coastal **Reserva Natural San Julián**, which is very accessible; ask about the superb tours at the **tourist office** (see Tourist information, below) and in the bus station. The reserve, on the shores of Bahía San Julián, includes the islands **Banco Cormorán** and **Banco Justicia**, thought to be the site of the 16th-century executions; there is a colony of Magellanic penguins and nesting areas for several species of cormorant and other birds. You're also very likely to spot Commerson's dolphins. It's a lovely location and the concentration of marine life is stunning.

There are 30 km of spectacular coastline north of San Julián, including **Cabo Curiosa**, 15 km north, which has fine beaches; it's a popular bathing place for the whole of the region. It's also worth visiting Estancia La María, 150 km west, which has one of the main archaeological sites in Patagonia: a huge canyon with 87 caves full of paintings including human hands and guanacos, 4000-12,000 years old. The estancia offers transport and accommodation (see Where to stay, below).

## Piedrabuena *Colour map 2, C4.*

Known officially as Comandante Luis Piedrabuena, the quiet town of Piedrabuena (population 6405) is named after the famous Argentine explorer and sailor, Piedra Buena, who built his home on Isla Pavón, an island in the river Santa Cruz, in 1859. On this small mound in the deep emerald green fast-flowing river you can visit the **Casa Histórica Luis Piedra Buena**, a reconstruction of the original building where he carried on a peaceful trade with local indigenous groups. However, the island has become most popular as a weekend resort for those fishing steelhead trout and it's a world-renowned fishing spot.

Piedrabuena is a good base for exploring the Parque Nacional Monte León, which protects 40 km of coastline and steppe, 30 km south.

## ★ Parque Nacional Monte León and around

The only national park on Argentina's long Atlantic coastline, Monte León is a beautiful stretch of steppe and shore, south of Piedrabuena. It includes 40 km of coastline, with many caves and little bays, as well as the tiny island Monte León, an important breeding area for cormorants and terns. In addition, there's the world's fourth largest colony of penguins and several colonies of sea lions. It was acquired for the Argentine nation by deceased North American billionaire Douglas Tompkins (whose foundation also owns Parque Pumalín in Chile, and **Rincón del Socorro** in Los Esteros

# ON THE ROAD

## National parks and nature reserves

**Parque Nacional Los Glaciares** is the most famous park in Patagonia. At the northern end the main centre is El Chaltén for trekking around **Mount Fitz Roy** and at the southern end are the glaciers, reached from El Calafate. Both have *guardaparques* offices where staff speak English and other languages, hand out maps and can advise on where to walk and camp. See www.parquesnacionales.gov.ar (in Spanish) for more information.

**Parque Nacional Perito Moreno** is also spectacular, and well worth the considerable effort involved in reaching its remote lakes and mountains. Access is via the Ruta 40, but there is almost no infrastructure whatsoever and little information for visitors. The best way to see the park is to stay at an estancia, such as **La Maipú**, and ride horses into the park.

Marine life abounds on the Atlantic Coast in Península Valdés, reached by organized tour or hire car from Puerto Madryn. Although it's not a national park, this is a well-organized area for visits, with several estancias on the peninsula where you can stay in great comfort. Further south, **Parque Nacional Monte León** is reached by Ruta 3, you'll need your own transport, but there is a comfortable *hostería*. There are many other colonies of penguins and other sea life reserves along the Atlantic Coast. Unless you have your own transport it's best to take an organized tour to reach these, as services are few at the sites themselves.

del Iberá), and was looked after by the organization **Vida Silvestre**, before being made a national park in 2004.

It's not easy to access the park, but your efforts to get here will be rewarded by wonderful walks along wide isolated beaches with their extraordinary rock formations, and cliffs dotted with vast caverns, fabulous at low tide. The park also protects an important habitat of seashore steppe, which is home to pumas and wolves as well as guanacos and choiques. The old house at the heart of the park has been converted into a *hostería*; staying here is by far the best way to enjoy the surroundings in comfort (see Where to stay, below). Plans for the national park include improving access and turning the old shearing shed into a visitor centre.

## Tourist information

### Puerto San Julián

Tourist office
*Av San Martín entre Rivadavia y M Moreno,
T02962-452009, www.sanjulian.gov.ar.*

### Piedrabuena

Tourist office
*Av G Ibáñez 157 (bus station),
T02962-1557 3065.*

## Where to stay

### Puerto San Julián

**$$$ Bahía**
*San Martín 1075, T02962-453144,
www.hotelbahiasanjulian.com.ar.*
Modern, comfortable, good value.
Recommended.

**$$ Municipal Costanera**
*25 de Mayo y Urquiza, T02962-452300,
www.costanerahotel.com.*
Attractive, well-run place with good-value
rooms, but no restaurant.

### Estancias

**$$$ Estancia La María**
*150 km northwest of Puerto San Julián;
office in San Julián, Saavedra 1163,
T02962-452328, see Facebook.*
Offers transport, lodging, meals and trips
to cave paintings that are less visited than
Cueva de las Manos (see page 197).

### Camping

Good **municipal campsite** (Magallanes 650,
T02962-454506). Repeatedly recommended,
all facilities.

## Parque Nacional Monte León

**$$$$ Hostería Estancia Monte León**
*R3, Km 2399, T011-15-6155 1220 (Buenos
Aires), www.monteleon-patagonia.com.
Nov-Apr.*
4 tasteful rooms, all decorated with Douglas
Tompkins' considerable style. There's a
good library, living room and even a small
museum. Fishing is good here, too. It's a
fantastic place to stay.

## Restaurants

### Puerto San Julián

**$$ La Rural**
*Ameghino 811.*
Good, but not before 2100.

## Festivals

### Piedrabuena

**Mar National trout festival.**

## What to do

### Puerto San Julián
**Excursiones Pinocho**, *Av Costanera between
San Martín and Mitre, T02962-454600, www.
pinochoexcursiones.com.ar.* Excellent Zodiac
boat trips, lasting 90 mins, into Reserva
Natural San Julián.

## Transport

### Puerto San Julián
**Bus**
Many companies to both **Comodoro
Rivadavia**, US$30-40, and **Río Gallegos**,
6 hrs, US$21-29.

The capital of Santa Cruz province, Río Gallegos (pronounced rio ga-shay-gos, population 120,000) lies on the estuary of the Gallegos river, which is famous for its excellent brown trout fishing. It's a pleasant, airy town, founded in 1885 as a centre for the trade in wool and sheepskins, and is by far the most appealing of the main centres on Patagonia's southern Atlantic Coast (which isn't saying a great deal). It has always been a major transport hub, but receives fewer visitors since the airport opened at El Calafate. However, if you come here to change buses, you could visit the penguin reserve at Cabo Vírgenes some 130 km south, or Monte León National Park 210 km north. The town itself has a couple of museums and a few smart shops and restaurants.

## Sights

The tidy, leafy Plaza San Martín, two blocks south of the main street, Avenida Roca, has an interesting collection of trees, many planted by the early pioneers, and a diminutive corrugated-iron **cathedral**, with a wood-panelled ceiling in the chancel and stained-glass windows.

The best of the town's museums is the small **Museo de los Pioneros** ① *Elcano y Alberdi, T02966-437763, daily 1000-1700, free.* Set in a house built in England and shipped here in 1890, there are interesting photographs and artefacts telling the story of the first Scottish settlers, who came here in 1884 from the Falklands/Malvinas Islands enticed by government grants of land. There's an interesting tour given by the English-speaking owner, a descendent of the Scottish pioneers, and great photos of those first sheep-farming settlers. There's work by local artists at **Museo de Arte Eduardo Minichelli** ① *Maipú 13, T02966-436323 Mon 0800-1500, Tue-Fri 0800-1900, Sat-Sun 1500-1900.* **Museo Regional Provincial Padre Jesús Molina** ① *El Cano and Alberdi, T02966-423290, Mon-Fri 1100-1900, Sat-Sun 1100-1800,* has some dull rocks and fossils and a couple of dusty dinosaur skeletons. **Museo Malvinas Argentinas** ① *Pasteur 72, T02966-437618 Mon-Fri 1100-1600, Sat-Sun 1000-1700,* is quite stimulating. It aims to inform visitors why the Malvinas are Argentine.

**Around Río Gallegos Laguna Azul**, 62 km south near the Monte Aymond border crossing, is nothing more than a perfect royal-blue lagoon in the crater of an extinct volcano, but it does have a certain atmosphere, set in an arid lunar landscape, and it's a good place for a walk. Take a tour, or get off the bus along Route 3, which stops on the main road.

**Reserva Provincial Cabo Vírgenes** ① *134 km south of Río Gallegos via Ruta 3 and Ruta 1 (ripio), 3½ hrs, free entry; tours with tour operators US$60,* is a nature reserve protecting the second largest colony of Magellanic penguins in Patagonia. There's an informative self-guided walk to see their nests amongst the *calafate* and fragrant *mata verde* bushes. It's good to visit from November to January, when chicks are born and there are nests under every bush: fascinating for anyone and wonderful for children. You can climb the **Cabo Vírgenes lighthouse** (owned by the Argentine Navy) for wonderful views. There's a *confitería* close by for snacks and souvenirs. Both the reserve and the lighthouse are usually included in tours from Río Gallegos or you could stay at **Estancia Monte Dinero** (see Where to stay, below) 13 km north of Cabo Vírgenes, which is a wonderful base for visiting the reserve. It is a working sheep farm, where the English-speaking Fenton family offers accommodation, food and trips (US$60 for a day visit); all excellent.

South of Cabo Vírgenes are the ruins of **Nombre de Jesús**, one of the two settlements founded by Pedro Sarmiento de Gamboa in 1584 and where, tragically, all its settlers died.

## Listings Río Gallegos *map below.*

### Tourist information

**Carretón Municipal**
*Kirchner y San Martín. High season only, Mon-Fri 1100-1800, Sat-Sun 0900-2100.*

An information caravan with helpful staff who speak English; they have a list of estancias and will phone round hotels for you.

## Río Gallegos

**Where to stay** ●
2 Comercio
3 Covadonga
5 Oviedo
6 París
7 Punta Arenas
8 Santa Cruz
9 Sehuen

**Restaurants** ●
1 Buffalo Grill House
2 El Chino
3 El Club Británico &
   Café Central
4 La Casa del Sushi

**Municipal tourist office**
*Av Beccar 126, T02966-436920,*
*www.turismo.mrg.gov.ar.*
There's also a small information desk at the
**bus terminal** (T02966-442159, Mon-Fri 0700-
2000, Sat-Sun 0800-1300 and 1500-2000).

**Provincial tourist office**
*Av Pres Kirchner 863, T02966-437412,*
*www.santacruzpatagonia.gob.ar.*
*Mon-Fri 0800-1600.*

## Where to stay

Most hotels are situated within a few
blocks of the main street, Av Roca, running
northwest to southeast. Do not confuse the
street Comodoro Rivadavia with (nearby)
Bernardino Rivadavia.

**$$$ Santa Cruz**
*Kirchner 701, T02966-420601,*
*www.hotelsantacruzrgl.com.ar.*
Good value, spacious rooms with good beds,
full buffet breakfast. Recommended.

**$$$ Sehuen**
*Rawson 160, T02966-425683,*
*www.hotelsehuen.com.*
Good, cosy, helpful.

**$$ Comercio**
*Kirchner 1302, T02966-420209,*
*www.hotelcomercio.com.ar.*
Good value, including breakfast, attractive
design, comfortable, cheap *confitería*.

**$$ Covadonga**
*Kirchner 1244, T02966-420190,*
*www.hotel-alonso.com.ar.*
Small rooms, attractive old building,
breakfast extra. Same owners as the
**Hotel Alonso** at Corrientes 33.

**$$ París**
*Kirchner 1040, T02966-420111,*
*www.hotelparisrg.com.ar.*
Simple rooms, shared bath, good value.

**$$ Punta Arenas**
*F Sphur 55, T02966-427743,*
*www.hotelpuntaarenas.com.*

Rooms with shared bath cheaper. Smart,
rooms in new wing cost more. **Something
Café** attached.

**$ Oviedo**
*Libertad 746, T02966-420118,*
*www.hoteloviedo.com.ar.*
A cheaper budget option, breakfast extra,
laundry facilities, café, parking.

## Around Río Gallegos
**Estancias**

**$$$$ Monte Dinero**
*120 km south of Río Gallegos,*
*near Cabo Vírgenes, T02966-428922,*
*www.montedinero.com.ar.*
Comfortable accommodation on a working
sheep farm. The house is lined with wood
rescued from ships wrecked off the coast,
and the food is delicious and home-grown.
Highly recommended.

## Camping

**Club Pescazaike**
*Paraje Guer Aike, Ruta 3, 30 km west,*
*T02966-423442, info@pescazaike.com.ar.*
Also *quincho* and restaurant.

## Restaurants

**$$ Buffalo Grill House**
*Lista 198, T02966-439 511.*
Popular chowdown spot. Somehow
manages to mix North American,
Mexican and Argentine cuisine.

**$$ El Club Británico**
*Kirchner 935, T02966-432668.*
Good value, excellent steaks.

**$$ La Casa del Sushi**
*Libertad 398, T02966-15 590604,*
*www.lacasadelsushi.com.*
Sushi and Chilean sandwiches.

**$ El Chino**
*9 de Julio 27.*
Varied *tenedor libre*.

### Cafés

Café Central
*Kirchner 923.*
Smart and popular.

## What to do

### Fishing
The southern fishing zone includes rivers
Gallegos, Grande, Fuego, Ewan, San Pablo
and Lago Fagnano, near Ushuaia. It is famous
for runs of sea trout. Ask the tourist office for
fishing guides and information on permits.

### Tour operators
**Maca Tobiano Turismo**, *Av San Martín 1093,
T02966-422466, macatobiano@macatobiano.
com.* Air tickets and tours to Pingüinero
Cabo Vírgenes and to Estancia Monte León,
as well as tickets to El Calafate and Ushuaia.
Recommended.

## Transport

### Air
**Aerolíneas Argentinas** (San Martín 545,
T0810-222 86527) have regular flights to/
from **Buenos Aires**, **Ushuaia** and **Río
Grande** direct. **LADE** (Fagnano 53, T02966-
422316, closed in low season) flies to many
Patagonian destinations between **Buenos
Aires** and **Ushuaia**, including **El Calafate**
and **Comodoro Rivadavia**, but not daily.
Book as far in advance as possible.

### Bus
The **terminal** (T02966-442159) is small
and crowded; there's no left luggage, but
many transport companies will store bags
by the hour. There is a *confitería*, toilets and
some kiosks. For all long-distance trips, turn
up with ticket 30 mins before departure.
Take your passport when buying ticket; for

buses to Chile some companies give out
immigration and customs forms.
　To **El Calafate**, 4-5 hrs, US$28, with **Marga**,
**Sportman** and **Taqsa** (T02966-442194, and
at airport, www.taqsa.com.ar). To **Comodoro
Rivadavia**, with **Andesmar**, **Don Otto/
Transportadora Patagónica**, **Sportman** and
others, 10-12 hrs, US$49-63. To **Bariloche**,
with **Marga**, daily, 24 hrs, US$130, change in
Comodoro Rivadavia.
　To **Buenos Aires**, 36 hrs, several daily
with **Andesmar**, US$200-240. To **Río Grande**
US$43, 9 hrs, with **Marga** and **Tecni Austral**;
also to **Ushuaia**, US$55.
　**To Chile**: Puerto Natales, with **Pacheco**
(T02966-442765, www.busespacheco.com)
and **Bus Sur** (T02966-457047, www.bus-
sur.cl), 4-5 weekly, 4½ hrs, US$121. To
**Punta Arenas**, with **Ghisoni** (T02966-
457047, www.busesbarria.cl), 5 a week
leaving at 1200, 5½ hrs, US$21.

### Car
**To Chile**  Make sure your car papers
are in order: go first to tourist office for
necessary documents, then to the customs
office at the port, at the end of San Martín,
very uncomplicated.
　**Avis** at the airport. **Cristina**, Libertad 123,
T02966-425709. **Localiza**, Sarmiento 245,
T02966-436717. Essential to book rental in
advance in season.

### Taxi
Hiring a taxi for group trips may be the
same price as a tour bus. Taxi ranks are
plentiful; rates are controlled, *remises* are
slightly cheaper. *Remise* meters show metres
travelled, refer to card for price; taxi meters
show cost in pesos. Also consider hiring a car
with driver from **Todo Transfer Patagonia**
(www.interpatagonia.com/tododtransfer/).

# Ruta 40 to the glaciers

the remote heart of Patagonia

The southernmost part of Argentina's iconic road, the Ruta 40 runs alongside the Andes, with access to peaks, glaciers and two national parks – the perfect terrain for your wildest adventure.

There's fewer than one person per square kilometre in this part of the world and you'll drive for hours without seeing a soul. Head south to the mysterious Cueva de las Manos, where thousands of handprints were painted by prehistoric people, or west to the Perito Moreno national park, a virgin landscape, where jagged peaks are reflected in limpid lakes and condors wheel overhead. For a little civilization in the wilderness, stay at an estancia where you can experience the timeless life on the land and feast on Patagonian lamb, or visit tranquil Los Antiguos on the shores of Lago Buenos Aires.

At the northern end of Parque Nacional Los Glaciares, El Chaltén is the base for trekking around the magnificent peaks of Mount Fitz Roy, where you can hike for days, climb glaciers and even get access to the Southern Ice Field. Further south, El Calafate is the gateway to the spectacular Perito Moreno glacier. Walk with crampons on the sculpted surface, or watch with wonder as great walls of ice cleave with a mighty roar into the milky lake below. Best of all, take a boat to Estancia Cristina to see Upsala glacier from above and to reflect on its awesome beauty and power.

**Best** for
Cave paintings ▪ Glaciers ▪ Hiking

192▪

# Footprint
## picks

★ **Travelling along Ruta 40**, page 195

Lose yourself on Ruta 40, where the highways stretches endlessly out to the horizon, and there's nothing but the steppe and wind to keep you company.

★ **Cueva de las Manos**, page 197

Handprint paintings on these cave walls date back some 13,000 years.

★ **Staying at a Patagonian estancia**, page 210

Live, if only briefly, the rugged life of a gaucho on the windswept plains of Patagonia.

★ **Perito Moreno and Upsala glaciers**, pages 215 and 216

Seeing these majestic walls of ice calve into the turquoise waters below is a natural phenomenon not to be missed.

★ **Trekking around Cerro Fitz Roy**, page 217

Some of the best trekking in the world is found amid the twin granite peaks of Fitz Roy.

Footprint
picks

1 **Travelling along Ruta 40**, page 195

2 **Cueva de las Manos**, page 197

3 **Staying at a Patagonian estancia**, page 210

4 **Perito Moreno and Upsala glaciers**, pages 215 and 216

5 **Trekking around Cerro Fitz Roy**, page 217

# Ruta 40

★ The Ruta 40 – known in Argentina simply as *'La Cuarenta'* – is one of the wildest and least travelled roads on the planet. It runs the whole length of Argentina, from La Quiaca on the border with Bolivia in the north, all the way down to El Chaltén and Río Gallegos in the south. Ernesto 'Che' Guevara travelled along much of it on his famous motorcycle jaunts and his experience helped form his revolutionary spirit. You can get a flavour of the toughest parts by travelling this stretch through Patagonia.

In the 14 hours it takes to go from Los Antiguos to El Chaltén, you're likely to see no more than a few cars; you'll also spot condors wheeling high above the Andes, the occasional Patagonian fox, and not much else apart from the clouds, whipped into amazing shapes by the ubiquitous winds.

# Essential Ruta 40

## Access

There are several logical places to start your journey along the Ruta 40 through Patagonia. Travelling from the Atlantic Coast, you can reach Río Mayo from Comodoro Rivadavia, with regular buses along the Route 26. There are also daily buses from Esquel, at the southernmost end of the Lake District. Those travelling south along the Carretera Austral in Chile can take the ferry across Lago General Carrera/Lago Buenos Aires, from south of Coyhaique to Chile Chico, and cross the border into Argentina at Los Antiguos before continuing the journey south along the Ruta 40.

## Getting around

Travelling along the Ruta 40 is quite an experience, and unless you're taking the bus, it's one that requires careful planning. Travelling south, the road is paved as far as Perito Moreno, and then is good *ripio*, improving greatly after Las Horquetas. From Río Mayo to El Calafate, the wide stony *ripio* track of the Ruta 40 zigzags its way across windswept desolate land. Every few hundred kilometres or so, there will be a small, improbable signpost to an estancia, somewhere off the road unseen; many are just ordinary sheep farms and do not accept paying guests.

For travel information on the Ruta 40, see www.rutanacional40.com (in Spanish with good maps).

**Bus** The most efficient way to travel this stretch is by making use of the bus services offered by two companies. **Chaltén Travel** (www.chaltentravel.com) runs a service every other day in each direction between Bariloche and El Calafate, via Los Antiguos and El Chaltén. This service operates from November to Semana Santa. Alternatively a year-round no-frills service is run by **Taqsa** (www.taqsa.com.ar), departing daily in summer and twice a week for the rest of the year between El Calafate and Bariloche.

**Car/motorbike/bike** Hiring a car in one town and dropping it off in another is possible and allows great flexibility. But it can be expensive and is only fun if you're not travelling alone. Make sure you know exactly where the next petrol station is, as they can easily be 300 km apart, carry spare fuel and allow more time than you think to reach your destination before nightfall. There are only a few service stations for fuel along the whole stretch and few places offering accommodation (see below). It's not advisable to travel faster than 60 kph on *ripio* roads. Take warm clothes, liquids and a blanket, in case you become stranded at night. If cycling, note that food and water stops are scarce, the wind is fierce, and there is no shade whatsoever. Hitching along this road is virtually impossible and isn't recommended, as you could be stranded for days.

## Accommodation

Be warned that there are few decent places to stay along this entire route. The best bases for accommodation after Esquel in the north are the pretty little town of Los Antiguos, near the border with Chile, and Perito Moreno. After that, there are only remote rural estancias and some very bleak one-horse towns until you reach the tourist haven of El Chaltén. Take a tent if you're on a bike. To get to the estancias, you'll need to have booked in advance and to have your own transport. Various companies organize tours along the route, with estancia stays and travel included.

## When to go

The best time to go is between October and April. Outside these months travel is still possible, but accommodation and transport is harder to find, and the winter is deadly cold.

## Río Mayo *Colour map 2, A4.*

Set in beautifully bleak landscape by the meandering Mayo river, the rural little town of Río Mayo (population 3800) has little of tourist interest, but it's an important junction at the intersection of routes 40 and 26, so you're likely to find yourself here to change buses or pick up fuel. In January, it is the site for an extraordinary display of dexterity at the **Fiesta Nacional de la Esquila** (national sheep-shearing competition); see Festivals, page 201.

From Río Mayo, Ruta 26 runs west 140 km to the Chilean border at Coyhaique Alto (see box, page 198). South of Río Mayo Ruta 40 is unpaved as far as Perito Moreno (124 km, high-clearance advised).

## Perito Moreno *Colour map 2, B3.*

Not to be confused with the famous glacier of the same name near El Calafate, nor with Parque Nacional Perito Moreno (see page 203), this Perito Moreno is a spruce little town of 10,000 inhabitants, 25 km west of Lago Buenos Aires. The town has no sights as such, apart from the pleasure of watching a rural community go about its business. It's the nearest but not the most attractive base for exploring the mysterious cave paintings at the Cueva de las Manos to the south.

## Around Perito Moreno

Southwest of the town is **Parque Laguna**, where you can see varied birdlife, including flamingos and black-necked swans, and go fishing. You could also walk to the crater of **Volcán Cerro**, from a path 12 km outside Perito Moreno; ask at the tourist office (see Tourist information, below) for directions.

## ★ Cueva de las Manos *Colour map 2, B4.*

*Access is via a 28-km road which branches east off Ruta 40, 88 km south of Perito Moreno; another 46-km access road, branches off Ruta 40 at Km 124, 3 km north of Bazjo Caracoles. The road can be difficult after rain. Compulsory guided tours with rangers Nov-Apr 0900-1900, May-Oct 1000-1800, US$9, under-12s free.*

Situated 47 km northeast of Bajo Caracoles, the stunning canyon of the **Río Pinturas** contains outstanding examples of handprints and cave paintings, estimated to be between 9500 and 13,000 years old. It is one of the major cultural and archaeological sites in South America, declared a World Heritage Site by UNESCO in 1999, and definitely one of the highlights of any trip to Patagonia.

In the cave's four galleries are over 800 paintings by the Toldense peoples of human hands, all but 31 of which are of left hands, as well as images of guanacos and rheas, and various geometrical designs. The red, orange, black, white and green pigments were derived from earth and calafate berries, and fixed with a varnish of guanaco fat and urine. They are mysterious and rather beautiful, albeit indecipherable. The canyon itself is also worth seeing: 270 m deep and 480 m wide, it has strata of vivid red and green rocks that are especially beautiful in the early morning or evening light. *Guardaparques* living at the site give helpful information and a tour. See Transport, page 201.

**Tip...**
Come to Cueva de las Manos in the morning in summer to beat the crowds.

## BORDER CROSSING
### Argentina–Chile

**Paso Huemules**

From Río Mayo, there are two roads crossing the border into Chile to take you to Coyhaique, the main town for visiting the southern part of the Carretera Austral. The more southerly of the two, via Paso Huemules, has better roads and is the crossing used by buses between Comodoro Rivadavia and Coyhaique. It is reached by a road that branches off Ruta 40 some 31 km south of Río Mayo and runs west 105 km via Lago Blanco (small petrol station), where there is an estancia community, 30 km from the border. There's no hotel here but the police are friendly and may permit camping at the police post. The border is open 0800-2200 in summer, 0900-2000 in winter. For the Chilean side, see box, page 379. See www.gendarmeria.gov.ar.

**Coyhaique Alto**

This border crossing is reached by a 133-km road (87 km *ripio*, then dirt) that branches off Ruta 40 about 7 km north of Río Mayo. For the Chilean side see box, page 379.

**Los Antiguos**

The main reason to enter Chile here is either to explore the beautiful southern shore of Lago General Carrera, or to take the ferry over the lake north to Puerto Ibáñez which has minibus connections on to Coyhaique.

**Transport** Four bus companies cross the border by the bridge to the village of Chile Chico, 8 km west, US$4, 45 minutes. For the Chilean side, see box, page 389.

**Paso Roballos**

From Bajo Caracoles Route 41 (unpaved) goes 99 km northwest to the Paso Roballos border with Chile. For the Chilean side see box, page 389.

**Los Antiguos and border with Chile** *Colour map 2, B3.*

Though there are two crossings to Chile west of Perito Moreno, the easiest and most commonly used is via the pretty little village of Los Antiguos (population 7000), which lies just 2 km east of the border. The town lies on the southern shore of Lago Buenos Aires, the second largest lake in South America, extending into Chile as Lago General Carrera, where the landscape is very beautiful and unspoilt. The Río Baker, which flows from the lake, is world-renowned for excellent trout fishing. For further information on crossing the border here, see box, above.

Los Antiguos is a sleepy little place, but it has a pleasant atmosphere, thanks largely to its warm microclimate, and it's a much better place to stay than Chile Chico or Perito Moreno. Modern hotels have been built, and there are countless services, including restaurants, internet cafés and a newish bus terminal on Avenida Tehuelches with a large café/restaurant and free Wi-Fi. Minibuses from Chile arrive at this terminal. It is a good place to stay for two days or longer and to stock up on basics before continuing the journey. The **Parque Municipal** at the east end of the town is a pleasant place to walk, along the bank of the river, with birdlife to look at, and two blocks down, there's a superb campsite. This is a rich fruit-growing area and there are 12 local *chacras* (small farms) worth visiting. You can walk to one of them, **Don Neno**, from the main street, where there are strawberries growing and jam for sale. You'd have to drive, or take a taxi, though, to the idyllic **Chacra el Paraíso**, where the charming owners make delicious jams and chutney.

## Tourist information

### Río Mayo

Tourist office
*Av Argentino s/n, T02903-420058,
www.turismoriomayo.gob.ar.
Daily 0800-1200 and 1500-1800.*

### Perito Moreno

Tourist office
*Av San Martín 2005, http://peritomoreno.
tur.ar. Daily 0700-1200.*
The friendly staff can advise on tours to the cave and estancias.

### Los Antiguos

Tourist office
*Buenos Aires 59, T02963-491261, www.
losantiguous.tur.ar. Dec-Easter daily 0800-
2400, Easter-Nov daily 0800-2000.*
New modern office.

## Where to stay

### Río Mayo

**$$$$ Estancia Don José**
*3 km west of Río Mayo, T02903-420015 or
T0297-15-624 9155, www.turismoguenguel.
com.ar.*
Excellent estancia, with superb food, 2 rooms and 1 cabin. The family business involves sustainable production of guanaco fibre.

**$$ Hotel Aka-Ta**
*San Martín 640, T02903-420054,
hotelacata@gmail.com.*
One of a couple hotels in town that could pass for a chalet in Normandy. Cosy, well-furnished rooms, friendly owners, great vibe. Restaurant open in high season.

**$$-$ El Viejo Covadonga**
*San Martín 573, T02903-420020,
elviejocovadonga@hotmail.com.*
The other chalet-style lodging, this option has a beautiful, expansive reception area. Run for years by 2 helpful and friendly sisters, all rooms have hot water and Wi-Fi. Recommended.

**$$-$ San Martín**
*San Martín s/n, T02903-420066.*
Decent hotel noteworthy mostly for its good restaurant.

### Camping

There is a free campsite on the northern outskirts, near the river.

**Camping Río Mayo**
*On the west side of town.*

### Perito Moreno and around

**$$$-$$ Americano**
*San Martín 1327, T02963-432074,
www.hotelamericanoweb.com.ar.*
19 pleasant rooms, some superior, decent restaurant.

**$$ Belgrano**
*San Martín 1001, T02963-432019.*
This hotel is often booked by Ruta 40 long-distance bus companies, basic, not always clean, 1 key fits all rooms, helpful owner, breakfast extra, excellent restaurant.

**$$ Hotel El Austral**
*San Martín 1381, T02963-432605,
hotelaustral@speedy.com.ar.*
Similar to others on the main street, but clean.

**$ Hospedaje Las Formoseñas**
*O'Higgins 943, T02963-432123.*

The only true budget hostel in town. Bunks with thin mattresses from US$10 per night. Still, the owner is friendly and you stand to save hundreds of pesos by lodging here than at other hotels.

**$ Hotel Santa Cruz**
*Belgrano 1530, T02963-432133.*
Simple rooms.

## Camping

Municipal site at Paseo Roca y Mariano Moreno, near Laguna de los Cisnes, T02963-432130.

Also 2 *cabaña* places near the river on Ruta 43: **Cabañas Las Moras** (T02963-15 400 7549), and **Turístico Río Fénix** (T02963-432458).

## Estancias

**$$$ Hostería Cueva de Las Manos**
*20 km from the cave at Estancia Los Toldos, 60 km south, 7 km off the road to Perito Moreno, T02963-432207 or T0297-15-623 8811 (mobile), www.cuevadelasmanos.net.*
*1 Nov-5 Apr, closed Christmas and New Year.*
Private rooms and dorms, runs tours to the caves, horse riding, meals extra and expensive.

**$$ Estancia Turística Casa de Piedra**
*80 km south of Perito Moreno on Ruta 40, in Perito Moreno ask for Sr Sabella, Av Perón 941, T02963-432199.*
Price is for rooms, camping, hot showers, home-made bread, use of kitchen, trips to Cueva de las Manos and volcanoes by car or horse.

### Los Antiguos

**$$$ Antigua Patagonia**
*Ruta 43, T02963-491055, www. antiguapatagonia.com.ar.*
Luxurious rooms with beautiful views, excellent restaurant. Tours to Cueva de las Manos and nearby Monte Zevallos.

**$$$-$ Mora**
*Av Costanera 1064, T02963-15-540 2444, www.hotelmorapatagonia.com.*
Rooms range from dorms to 1st class with private bath. Parking, lake views.

**$$ Sol de Mayo**
*Av 11 de Julio 1300, T02963-491232, chacrasoldemayo@hotmail.com.*
Basic rooms with shared bath, kitchen, central, also has cabins for rent.

**$ pp Albergue Padilla**
*San Martín 44 (just off main street), T02963-491140.*
Comfortable dorms, doubles ($$); *quincho* and garden. Also camping. El Chaltén travel tickets.

## Camping

**Camping Municipal**
*2 km from centre on Ruta Provincial 43, T02963-491265.*
An outstanding site, with hot showers, US$4 pp, also has cabins for 4 (no linen).

## Restaurants

### Perito Moreno

The restaurant in **Hotel Americano** is highly recommended.

**El Viejo Bar**
*San Martín 991, T02963-432538.*
Good *parrilla* that also rents rooms.

### Los Antiguos

There are several other places in town.

**Viva El Viento**
*11 de Julio 477, T02963-491109, www.vivaelviento.com.*
*Daily 0900-2100 in high season.*
Dutch-owned, great vibe, food and coffee, also has Wi-Fi, lots of information about the area. Live music Tue. Recommended.

## Festivals

### Río Mayo

**3rd weekend in Jan Fiesta Nacional de la Esquila** (national sheep-shearing competition), where teams of 5-6 *esquiladores*, who travel around Patagonia from farm to farm in shearing season, compete to shear as many sheep as possible: a good shearer might get through 10 in an hour.

### Los Antiguos

**Early Jan Fiesta Nacional de la Cereza,** a popular cherry festival that attracts national *folclore* stars.

## What to do

### Perito Moreno
**Tour operators**

**Las Loicas,** *Transporte Lago Posadas, T02963-490272, www.lasloicas.com.* Offers an all-day tour with the option of collecting passengers from Bajo Caracoles. Also does the Circuito Grande Comarca Noroeste, one of the highlights of Santa Cruz, taking in some of the province's scenery.

**Zoyen Turismo,** *San Martín near Saavedra, T02963-432207, T0297-15 623 8811, www.zoyen turismo.com.ar.* The friendly staff can help with R40 connections and estancia visits.

### Los Antiguos
**Tour operators**

**Chelenco Turs,** *11 de Julio 548, T02963-491198, www.chelencoturs.com.ar.* Can arrange trips to the Cueva de las Manos, Monte Zeballos, Lago Posadas and Capilla Mármol in Chile.

## Transport

### Río Mayo
**Bus**

To **Sarmiento** once a day (1900) with **Etap,** US$11, 2 hrs. To **Perito Moreno,** 3 weekly (2100) with **Etap,** US$11.

### Perito Moreno
**Air**

The airport is 7 km east of town and the only way to get there is by taxi.

**Bus**

The bus terminal (T02963-432177) is on the edge of town next to the EG3 service station. It is open only when buses arrive or depart.

Many long-distance buses with **Transporte Ruca** (transporte.ruca@ yahoo.com.ar): **Bariloche** 850 km, US$100; **El Chaltén** 530 km, US$92; **El Calafate** 620 km, US$123; **Esquel** 500 km, US$70; **Cueva de Los Manos** US$23. It is nearly impossible to hitchhike between Perito Moreno and El Calafate as there's hardly any traffic and few services. To **Los Antiguos** border crossing, 2 buses daily in summer, 1 hr, US$7, with **Sportman, T02963-432177.** To **El Chaltén** and **El Calafate, Chaltén Travel** (www.chaltentravel.com) at 0700. **Chaltén Travel** also runs a tourist service to **Puerto Madryn** at 0630 every other day from **Hotel Belgrano.**

**Car**

Several mechanics on C Rivadavia and Av San Martín, good for repairs.

**Taxi**

**Parada El Turista,** Av San Martín y Rivadavia, T02963-432592.

### Los Antiguos
**Bus**

To **Comodoro Rivadavia,** with **ETAP** (at the terminal, T0297-491078) and **Sportman** (at the terminal, T0297-442983) daily, US$34; to **Caleta Olivia** with **Taqsa** (at the terminal T02966-15-419615), **Andesmar** (at the terminal, T0297-15 623 4882) and **Sportman,** daily US$30. **Chaltén Travel** (open only in high season, www.chaltentravel.com) runs to **El Chaltén** (10 hrs) and **El Calafate** (12 hrs), via Perito Moreno, every other (even) day at 0800; also north to **Bariloche,** every even day, mid-Nov to mid-Apr.

After hours of spectacular emptiness, even tiny Bajo Caracoles (population 100) is a relief. It's nothing more than a few houses with an expensive grocery store and very expensive fuel. From Bajo Caracoles Route 41 (unpaved) goes 99 km northwest to the Paso Roballos border with Chile (see box, page 198), passing Lago Ghio and Lago Columna. Route 39, meanwhile, heads southwest from Bajo Caracoles, reaching Lago Posadas and Lago Pueyrredón after 72 km. These two beautiful lakes with contrasting blue and turquoise waters are separated by a narrow isthmus. Guanacos and rheas can be seen and there are sites of archaeological interest.

## South to Tres Lagos
South of Bajo Caracoles Ruta 40 crosses the Pampa del Asador and then, near Las Horquetas, Km 371, swings southeast to follow the Río Chico. Some 92 km south of Bajo Caracoles is the turn-off west to Lago Belgrano and Parque Nacional Perito Moreno (see below). From the Parque Moreno junction to Tres Lagos, Ruta 40 improves considerably. About 23 km east of the turn-off, along Route 521 is **Tamel Aike**, Km 393, where there is a police station and water but little else.

At Km 464, Route 25 branches off to Puerto **San Julián** via **Gobernador Gregores**, 72 km southeast, where there is fuel and a good mechanic. (This is the only place with fuel before Tres Lagos, so carry extra if you want to avoid the 72-km detour.) The Ruta 40, meanwhile, continues southwest towards Tres Lagos. At Km 531, a road heads west to Lago Cardiel, a very saline lake with no outlet and good salmon fishing.

**Tres Lagos**, at Km 645, is a solitary village with a minimarket, restaurant and fuel at the junction with Route 288. A road also turns off northwest here to Lago San Martín, which straddles the Chilean border (the Chilean part is Lago O'Higgins). From Tres Lagos, Ruta 40 deteriorates rapidly and remains very rugged until after the turn-off to the Fitz Roy sector of Parque Nacional Los Glaciares (see page 217). Twenty-one kilometres beyond this turn-off is the bridge over Río La Leona, where delightful **Hotel La Leona** serves good cakes.

## Listings Bajo Caracoles and south to Tres Lagos

### Where to stay

**Bajo Caracoles and south to Tres Lagos**

**$$ Hotel Bajo Caracoles**
*Bajo Caracloes, T02963-490100.*
Old-fashioned but hospitable, meals.

**Estancias**

**$$$ pp La Angostura**
*55 km from Gobernador Gregores, T02962-491501, www.estancialaangostura.com.ar.*

Offers horse riding, trekking and fishing. Recommended.

**Camping**
The campsite is in the middle of Bajo Caracoles. Rooms ($ pp) are also available. A simple and welcoming place, also runs trips to Cueva de las Manos, 10 km by vehicle then 1½-2 hrs' walk, and to nearby volcanoes by car or horse. Ask for **Señor Sabella** (Av Perón 941, Perito Moreno, T02963-432199).

Situated southwest of Bajo Caracoles on the Chilean border, this is one of the wildest and most remote parks in Argentina. It encompasses a large, interconnected system of lakes, lying between glaciated peaks of astonishing beauty, and has good trekking and abundant wildlife. However, since much of the park is dedicated to scientific study, it's largely inaccessible.

### Around the park

**Lago Belgrano**, in the park's centre, is the biggest in the chain of lakes; its vivid turquoise waters contrast with the surrounding mountains which are streaked with a mass of differing colours, and you might find ammonite fossils on its shores. Just outside the park, but towering over it to the north, is **Cerro San Lorenzo** (3706 m), the highest peak in southern Patagonia. Between the lakes are other peaks, permanently snow-covered, the highest of which is Cerro Herros (2770 m). The vivid hues of Sierra Colorada run across the northeast of the park: the erosion of these coloured rocks has given the lakes their differing colours. At the foot of Cerro Casa de Piedra is a network of caves containing cave paintings, accessible only with a guide. Wildlife in the park includes guanacos, foxes and one of the most important surviving populations of the rare huemul deer. Birds include flamingos, ñandus, steamer ducks, grebes, black-necked swans, Patagonian woodpeckers, eagles and condors. The lakes and rivers are unusual for Argentina in that only native species of fish are found here.

## Essential Parque Nacional Perito Moreno

### Access

Access to the park is via the park entrance, a turn-off the paved Ruta 40, 100 km south of Bajo Caracoles, onto 90 km of unpaved road (see above). There is no public transport into the park. Much of the park is closed to visitors. The most accessible part is around Lago Belgrano, 12 km from the entrance. What is accessible is open 0900-2100, free.

### Park information

The **park office**, 9 de Julio 610, T02962-491477, www.parquesnacionales.gov.ar or www.turismoruta40.com.ar/pnperitomoreno.html, is 220 km away in Gobernador Gregores; get information here before reaching the park itself. The *guardaparques* office is 10 km beyond the park entrance (see Access, below) and has maps and leaflets on walks and wildlife.

It's essential to get detailed maps here and to ask advice about hikes and paths.

### What to take

Make sure you carry all fuel you need because there is nowhere to buy it inside the park, unless you're staying at one of the estancias. Cyclists should bring water, as there is no source along the 90-km branch road. Bring an all-season sleeping bag and plenty of warm clothing.

### When to go

The best time to visit is in summer (December to February). The access road may be blocked by snow at other times.

### Accommodation

There is an estancia inside the park boundaries: **Estancia La Oriental**. There are also several good sites for camping (free). For more information, see Where to stay, below.

## BACKGROUND

## Exploring Argentina

Francisco 'Perito' Moreno was one of Argentina's most prolific explorers. He played a leading role in defending Argentine rights in Patagonia and was pivotal in creating Argentina's first national park. Born in Buenos Aires in 1852, by the age of 14 he had created his first collection of specimens, which would go on to form the basis of the famous La Plata History Museum. When he was 20 he embarked on a series of expeditions for the Argentine Scientific Society. By 1876 he had reached Lake Nahuel Huapi in the Lake District. On the same trip, he 'discovered' El Chaltén in the south and named Cerro Fitz Roy. His second expedition was, however, decidedly more dangerous as he was captured by an unfriendly Tehuelche tribe and taken prisoner, before managing to escape. After several more expeditions, namely to claim Patagonian land for Argentina, he was given the name 'Perito' (expert) in 1902. For his exploring efforts the government gave him land in the Lake District, which he subsequently donated in order to create the country's first national park, Parque Nacional Nahuel Huapi. Ironically, Perito Moreno never set eyes on the famed Perito Moreno Glacier; it was simply named after him because he had extensively explored the surrounding lakes and mountains.

### Hiking

Several good hikes are possible from here. There are also longer walks of up to five days. Ask the *guardaparques* for details, and see the website. You should always inform *guardaparques* before setting out on a hike.

**Lago Belgrano** ⓘ *1-2 hrs.* Follow the Senda Natural Península Belgrano to the peninsula of the lake, 8 km, where there are fine views of Cerro Herros and an experience of transition landscape from steppe to forest. **Lago Burmeister** ⓘ *Via Cerro Casa de Piedra, 16 km.* The trail follows the northern shore and offers nice views of the lake. There is free camping (no fires permitted). It is hard to find the official trail in parts, but if in doubt, follow the shore. **Cerro León** ⓘ *4 hrs.* Start at Estancia La Oriental. This walk has fabulous panoramic views over the park and offers the chance to see condors in flight.

## Listings Parque Nacional Perito Moreno

### Where to stay

**$$$ Estancia La Oriental**
*T02962-407197, laorientalpatagonia@
yahoo.com.ar. Nov-Mar. Full board.*

Splendid setting, with comfortable rooms, horse riding, trekking.

# Parque Nacional
## Los Glaciares

Of all Argentina's impressive landscapes, the sight of these immense glaciers stretching out infinitely before you may stay with you longest. This is the second largest national park in Argentina, extending along the Chilean border for over 170 km, almost half of it covered by the 370-km-long Southern Ice Cap. From it, 13 major glaciers descend into two great lakes: Lago Argentino and Lago Viedma. At the southern end, the spectacular glaciers can be visited from El Calafate. At the northern end, reached from El Chaltén, there is superb trekking around the dramatic Fitz Roy massif and ice climbing on glaciers. The central section, between Lago Argentino and Lago Viedma, is composed of the ice cap on the western side. East of the ice fields, there's plentiful southern beech forest, but further east still, the land flattens to the typical wind-blasted Patagonian steppe, with sparse vegetation.

Birdlife is surprisingly prolific, and you'll spot the scarlet-headed Magellanic woodpecker, black-necked swans, and perhaps even the torrent duck, diving for food in the streams and rivers. Guanacos, grey foxes, skunks and rheas can be seen on the steppe, while the rare huemul inhabits the forest. The entire national park is a UNESCO World Heritage Site.

# Essential Parque Nacional Los Glaciares

## Access

Access to the park is very straightforward at both El Calafate and El Chaltén, although all transport gets heavily booked in the summer months of January and February. There are direct flights to El Calafate from Buenos Aires and Ushuaia, as well as charter flights from Puerto Natales in Chile. There are regular bus services into the park from El Calafate, as well as many tourist excursions, combining bus access with boat trips, walking and even ice trekking on Glaciar Perito Moreno. From El Chaltén you can hike directly into the park, with a well-established network of trails leading to summits, lakes and glaciers around Mount Fitz Roy, with many campsites. There are several buses daily to El Chaltén from El Calafate.

## Park information

There is a **park office**, Av del Libertador 1302, T02901-491005, www.losglaciares.com, Monday-Friday 0800-1600, in El Calafate. The **El Chaltén park office**, T02962-493004, same opening hours, is across the bridge at the entrance to town. Both hand out helpful trekking maps of the area, with paths and campsites marked, distances and walking times. Note that the hotel, restaurant and transport situation in this region changes greatly between high and low season. For more information, see www.losglaciares.com.

## Opening hours

The park is open daily 0800-2100 January-February, 0800-2000 March to Easter, 0800-1600 Easter to 31 July, 0800-1800 August-30 October, 0800-1900 in November, 0800-2000 in December.

## Entry fees

US$21.75, payable at the gates of the park, 50 km west of El Calafate.

## When to go

Although this part of Patagonia is generally cold, there is a milder microclimate around Lago Viedma and Lago Argentino, which means that summers can be reasonably pleasant, with average summer temperatures between 5°C and 22°C, though strong winds blow constantly at the foot of the Cordillera. Precipitation on the Hielo Sur, up to 5000 mm annually, falls mainly as snow. In the forested area, rainfall is heavier and falls mainly between March and late May. In winter, the whole area is inhospitably cold, and most tourist facilities are closed, although El Calafate and the Perito Moreno Glaciar are open all year round. The best time to visit is between November and April, avoiding January and early February, when Argentines take their holidays, campsites are crowded and accommodation is hard to find.

# Parque Nacional Los Glaciares

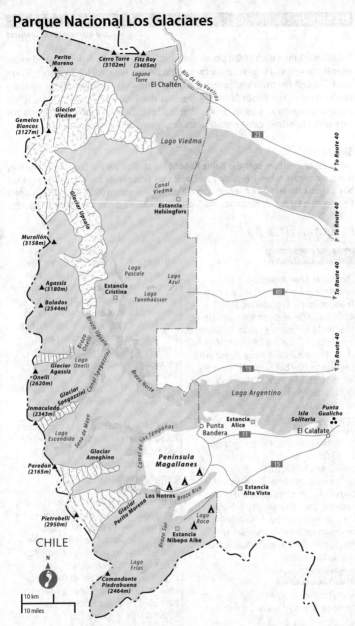

Perito Moreno

Cerro Torre (3102m)

Fitz Roy (3405m)

Laguna Torre

El Chaltén

Río de las Vueltas

Glaciar Viedma

Gemelos Blancos (3127m)

Lago Viedma

23

To Route 40

Glaciar Upsala

Canal Viedma

Estancia Helsingfors

To Route 40

Murallón (3158m)

To Route 40

Lago Pascale

Lago Azul

Agassiz (3180m)

Estancia Cristina

Lago Tannhäusser

69

To Route 40

Bolados (2544m)

Brazo Onelli

Lago Onelli

Glaciar Agassiz

Onelli (2620m)

Brazo Upsala

Canal Spegazzini

Glaciar Spegazzini

Brazo Norte

19

To Route 40

Lago Argentino

Inmaculado (2343m)

Seno de Mayo

Lago Escondido

Isla Solitaria

Punta Gualicho

Glaciar Ameghino

Estancia Alice

Paredon (2165m)

Punta Bandera

11

El Calafate

Canal de Los Témpanos

Península Magallanes

15

Los Notros

Brazo Rico

Estancia Alta Vista

Pietrobelli (2950m)

Glaciar Perito Moreno

Lago Roca

CHILE

N

Brazo Sur

Estancia Nibepo Aike

Lago Frías

10 km

10 miles

Comandante Piedrabuena (2464m)

El Calafate (population 8000) sits on the south shore of Lago Argentino and exists almost entirely as a tourist centre for visiting Parque Nacional los Glaciares, 50 km west. Though the town was founded in 1927, it grew very slowly until the opening of the road to the Perito Moreno Glacier in the 1960s, since which time it has expanded rapidly as a tourist town. Almost all of El Calafate's inhabitants, as is the case with El Chaltén, came from Buenos Aires or other large provincial capitals.

### Sights

Just west of the town centre is **Bahía Redonda**, a shallow part of Lago Argentino that freezes in winter, when ice-skating and skiing are possible. At the eastern edge of the bay, **Laguna Nímez** ① *high season daily 0900-2000, low season 0900-1800, US$7,* is a bird reserve where there are flamingos, black-necked swans and ducks; the 2.5-km self-guided

## Essential El Calafate

### Finding your feet

The airport, **Lago Argentino**, is 23 km east of town. A minibus service run by **Transpatagonia Expeditions**, T02902-494355, runs between the town and airport, US$7 (US$8.50 from the airport) for an open return. A taxi (T02902-491850/491745) costs US$18. Buses from Río Gallegos arrive in the town centre. The **bus terminal** is centrally located on Julio A Roca 1004, up a steep flight of steps from the main street, Avenida del Libertador.

### Orientation

El Calafate's shops, restaurants and tour operators can mostly be found along its main street, Avenida del Libertador, running east to west, with hotels lying within two blocks north and south and smaller *hosterías* scattered through the residential areas sprawling up the hill and north of centre, across the river. There are many estancias on the way to the national park, and also campsites.

### Getting around

A small municipal public transport system carries people from one end of the city to the other, which is useful if you are staying at some of the hotels on the edge of town. Bus travel and tour trips to the Perito Moreno glaciers are well organized, although they can be more difficult to arrange out of season. The cheapest method is with a regular bus service (US$32 return), but tours can be informative and some include a boat trip.

### Money

El Calafate can be expensive. At the moment in El Calafate many ATMS do not accept newer bank cards with smart chips. Only two ATMs in El Calafate accept them: **Banco Patagonia** on Avenida del Libertador 1355 and in the airport. There are no *casas de cambio*, but some hotels may change money.

### When to go

It's best to come in March or April if you can. The town is empty and quiet all winter, when it can be extremely cold, and most tourist services close down. If you can brave the weather, however, you can visit the Perito Moreno Glacier all year round.

Bear in mind that it's essential to book ahead in January and February, when the hotels, hostels and *cabañas* can't quite accommodate the hordes.

trail with multilingual leaflets is recommended for an hour's stroll either early morning or late afternoon. To get there from the **Intendencia del Parque** ⓘ *Av del Libertador 1302,* follow Calle Bustillo up the road to cross the bridge. Keep heading north across a pleasant new residential area: the *laguna* is signposted.

On the way back, you can stop by the **Centro de Interpretación Histórica** ⓘ *Av Brown and Bonarelli, T02902-492799, US$7; half price for children,* a small well-run centre housing an educational exhibition created by an anthropologist and a historian with pictures and bilingual texts about the region. There's also a relaxing café and library. The **Glaciarium** ⓘ *6 km from town on R11, www.glaciarium.com, daily 0900-2000, US$16, free for under-5s, free bus from provincial tourist office hourly,* is a modern museum dedicated to Patagonian ice and glaciers. It has an **ice bar** ⓘ *daily 1130-1700, US$13, under 16s US$9.50, cash only, entry is for 25 mins, includes drink,* café and shop.

## Around El Calafate

From El Calafate you can visit Glaciar Perito Moreno by bus and boat, and even go trekking on its surface. Alternatively, travel by boat along the western arms of Lago Argentino, between

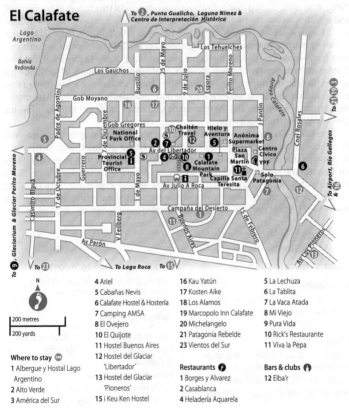

**El Calafate**

**Where to stay** 🛏
1 Albergue y Hostal Lago Argentino
2 Alto Verde
3 América del Sur
4 Ariel
5 Cabañas Nevis
6 Calafate Hostel & Hostería
7 Camping AMSA
8 El Ovejero
9 El Quijote
10 El Quijote
11 Hostel Buenos Aires
12 Hostel del Glaciar 'Libertador'
13 Hostel del Glaciar 'Pioneros'
15 i Keu Ken Hostel
16 Kau Yatún
17 Kosten Aike
18 Los Alamos
19 Marcopolo Inn Calafate
20 Michelangelo
21 Patagonia Rebelde
23 Vientos del Sur

5 La Lechuza
6 La Tablita
7 La Vaca Atada
8 Mi Viejo
9 Pura Vida
10 Rick's Restaurante
11 Viva la Pepa

**Restaurants** 🍴
1 Borges y Alvarez
2 Casablanca
4 Heladería Aquarela

**Bars & clubs** 🍸
12 Elba'r

stately floating icebergs, to see the glaciers of Spegazzini and Upsala. Best of all, take the long-day excursion by boat to **Estancia Cristina**, which gives you the chance to trek or ride horses up to a spectacular viewpoint above the Upsala glacier. All these trips are breathtakingly beautiful and an unforgettable part of your visit to Patagonia. For details, see page 213. However, El Calafate has a number of other attractions, worth considering if you're here for a few days, including some good places for trekking, horse riding and exploring by 4WD.

At **Punta Gualicho** (or Walichu) on the shores of Lago Argentino, 7 km east of town, there are cave paintings. Though they're rather badly deteriorated, a visit is worthwhile. Some tour operators run trips to the top of nearby hills for views of the southern end of the Andes, **Bahía Redonda** and Isla Solitaria on Lago Argentino. An easy five-hour walk (or horse ride with **Cabalgata en Patagonia**, T02902-493 278) is possible to the top of Cerro Calafate for panoramic views too; ask for directions at the **Hostel del Glaciar Pioneros**. Trekking, 4WD or horse-riding trips to the top of Cerro Frías (1030 m) for fantastic views of Mount Fitz Roy, Paine and Lago Argentino are organized by **Cerro Frías** ⓘ *Libertador 1857, T02902-492808, www.cerrofrias.com*, for around US$63 per person, including lunch (US$41 without lunch).

★ Several estancias are within reach, offering a day on a working farm, a lunch of Patagonian lamb, cooked *asado al palo* (speared on a metal structure over an open fire), and activities such as trekking, birdwatching and horse riding. **Estancia Alice** ⓘ *T02902-497503, www.elgalpondelglaciar.com.ar*, also known as 'El Galpón del Glaciar', 21 km west, is a lovely house with views of Lago Argentino. It offers 'El Día de Campo', including tea with home-made cakes, walks through a bird sanctuary where 43 species of bird have been identified, displays of sheep shearing, *asado* and music shows, all for US$64 per person (including transfer to and from hotels); English spoken. See also Where to stay, below. At **Estancia Quien Sabe**, near the airport, strawberries and walnuts are grown, and you can see beehives and sheep shearing, and eat an *asado* lunch; contact **Turismo Leutz**, www.leutzturismo.com.ar.

**Lago Roca**, 40 km southwest of El Calafate, is set in beautiful open landscape, with hills above offering panoramic views, perfect for lots of activities, such as trout and salmon fishing, climbing, walking. There are estancias here too, such as the beautifully set **Estancia Nibepo Aike** ⓘ *on Brazo Sur of Lago Argentino in the national park, 55 km southwest (book at Av Libertador 1215 p 1A, T02902-492797; Buenos Aires T011-5272 0341, www.nibepoaike.com.ar)*, where you can watch typical farm activities, such as the branding of cattle in summer. There is good camping in a wooded area and a restaurant.

## Listings El Calafate *map page 209.*

### Tourist information

**El Calafate**
For more information on El Calafate, see www.losglaciares.com and www.todocalafate.com.

**Tourist office**
*In the bus station, T02902-491476, www. elcalafate.tur.ar, and at Bajada Palma 44, T02902-491090, and another in the Amphitheatre del Bosque at Libertador 1400,*

*T02902-496 497. Daily 0800-2000.*
Friendly staff have folders of helpful information that you can browse.

### Where to stay

Prepare to pay more for accommodation here than elsewhere in Argentina. El Calafate is very popular in Jan-Feb, so book all transport and accommodation in advance. Many hotels are open only from Sep/Oct to Apr/May.

#### $$$$ El Quijote
*Gob Gregores 1191, T02902-491017,*
*www.quijotehotel.com.ar.*
A very good hotel, spacious, well designed
with traditional touches, tasteful rooms with
TV, restaurant, stylish lobby bar, English and
Italian spoken.

#### $$$$ Kau Yatún
*Estancia 25 de Mayo (10 blocks from the centre,*
*east of Arroyo Calafate), T02902-491059,*
*www.kauyatun.com. Closed in low season.*
Renovated main house of a former estancia,
well-kept grounds, 2 excellent restaurants,
half board or all-inclusive packages that
include trips in the national park.

#### $$$$ Kosten Aike
*Gob Moyano 1243, T02902-492424, www.*
*kostenaike.com.ar. Open year-round.*
Relaxed yet stylish, elegant spacious rooms
(some superior), jacuzzi, gym, excellent
restaurant, **Ariskaiken** (open to non-
residents), cosy bar, garden, English spoken.
Recommended.

#### $$$$ Los Alamos
*Guatti 1135, T02902-491144, www.posada*
*losalamos.com. Cheaper in low season.*
Very comfortable, charming rooms, good
service, lovely gardens, good bar and without
doubt the best restaurant in town, **La Posta**.

#### $$$ Alto Verde
*Zupic 138, T02902-491326, www.welcome*
*argentina.com/altoverde. $$ in low season.*
Top quality, spotless, spacious, helpful, also
with apartments for 4.

#### $$$ Cabañas Nevis
*Av del Libertador 1696, T02902-493180,*
*www.cabanasnevis.com.ar.*
Owner Mr Patterson offers good cabins for 5
and 8 (price quoted is for 5), some with lake
view, great value.

#### $$$ Michelangelo
*Espora y Gob Moyano, T02902-491045,*
*www.michelangelocalafate.com.*
Lovely, quiet, welcoming, restaurant.
Recommended.

#### $$$ Patagonia Rebelde
*José Haro 442, T02902-494495*
*(in Buenos Aires T015-5890 1276),*
*www.patagoniarebelde.com.*
Charming building in traditional Patagonian
style, like an old inn with rustic decor, good
comfort with well-heated bedrooms and
comfy sitting rooms.

#### $$$ Vientos del Sur
*up the hill at Río Santa Cruz 2317, T02902-*
*493563, www.vientosdelsur.com.*
Very hospitable, calm, comfortable, good
views, kind family attention.

#### $$$-$$ Ariel
*Av Libertador 1693, T493131,*
*www.hotelariel.com.ar.*
Modern, functional, well maintained.
Breakfast included.

#### $$ Hostel Buenos Aires
*Buenos Aires 296, 200 m from terminal,*
*T02902-491147.*
Quiet, kind owner, helpful, comfortable with
doubles, cheaper without bath, good hot
showers, laundry service, luggage store,
bikes for hire.

#### $$-$ pp Albergue y Hostal Lago
#### Argentino
*Campaña del Desierto 1050-61*
*(near bus terminal), T02902-491423,*
*www.lagoargentinohostel.com.ar.*
**$** pp shared dorms, too few showers when
full, pleasant atmosphere, good flats,
*cabañas* and **$$** doubles on a neat garden
and also in building on opposite side of road.

#### $$-$ pp Calafate Hostel & Hostería
*Gob Moyano 1226, T02902-492450,*
*www.calafatehostels.com.*
A huge log cabin with good rooms: dorms
with or without bath, breakfast extra,
**$$** doubles with bath and breakfast. Book
a month ahead for Jan-Feb, HI discounts,
travel agency, **Always Glacier** and restaurant
**Isabel** on premises.

### $$-$ pp Marcopolo Inn Calafate
*Los Lagos 82, T02902-493899,*
*www.marcopoloinncalafate.com.*
Part of Hostelling International. $ pp in
dorms. Laundry facilities, various activities
and tours on offer.

### $ pp América del Sur
*Puerto Deseado 153, T02902-493525,*
*www.americahostel.com.ar.*
Panoramic views from this comfortable,
relaxed hostel, welcoming, well-heated
rooms (dorms for 4, $$ doubles with views,
1 room adapted for wheelchair users), chill-
out area, fireplace. Warmly recommended,
but can be noisy.

### $ pp Hostel del Glaciar 'Libertador'
*Av del Libertador 587 (next to the bridge),*
*T02902-492492, www.glaciar.com. Sep-Apr.*
Smaller and pricier than **Pioneros**, rooms are
good and well-heated, all with private bath
and safe boxes ($$$-$$ doubles), breakfast
included for private rooms. Laundry service.
Owners run **Patagonia Backpackers** (see
What to do, below). Low energy usage;
owners are environmentally minded.

### $ pp Hostel del Glaciar 'Pioneros'
*Los Pioneros 255, T02902-491243,*
*www.glaciar.com. 1 Nov 1-end of Feb.*
Accommodation for all budgets: standard
$$ doubles (also for 3 and 4) with bath and
safe boxes, superior $$$, shared dorms up to
4 beds, US$17 pp. Many languages spoken,
lots of bathrooms, breakfast is separate, only
for guests in private rooms, laundry service,
Wi-Fi. Arranges tours to glaciers, as well
**NaviMag** boat trips in Chile. Very popular,
so book well in advance.

### $ pp i Keu Ken Hostel
*FM Pontoriero 171, T02902-495482,*
*www.patagoniaikeuken.com.ar.*
On a hill, very helpful, flexible staff,
hot water, heating, luggage store, good.

### Camping
**Ferretería Chuar** (Los Pioneros 539,
T02902-491513) sells camping gas.

### AMSA
*Olavarría 65 (50 m off the main road, turning
south at the fire station), T02902-492247.
Open in summer.*
Hot water, US$7 pp.

### El Ovejero
*José Pantín 64, near the river, T02902-493422,
www.campingelovejero.com.ar.*
Also has dorm ($$)

## Restaurants

### $$ La Lechuza
*Av del Libertador 1301, see Facebook.*
Good-quality pizzas, pasta, salad and meat
dishes. Excellent wine list. Has another
branch up the road at No 935.

### $$ La Tablita
*Cnel Rosales 28 (near the bridge),
www.la-tablita.com.ar.*
Typical *parrilla*, serving generous portions
and quality beef. Recommended.

### $$ La Vaca Atada
*Av del Libertador 1176.*
Good home-made pastas and more
elaborate and expensive dishes based
on salmon and king crab.

### $$ Mi Viejo
*Av del Libertador 1111. Closed Tue.*
Popular *parrilla*.

### $$ Pura Vida
*Av Libertador 1876, near C 17, see Facebook.
Open 1930-2330 only, closed Wed.*
Comfortable sofas, home-made Argentine
food, vegetarian options, lovely atmosphere,
lake view (reserve table). Recommended.

### $$ Rick's Restaurante
*Av del Libertador 1091.*
Lively *parrilla* with a good atmosphere.

### $$ Viva la Pepa
*Emilio Amado 833, see Facebook.
Mon-Sat 1200-2100.*
A mainly vegetarian café with great sandwiches
and crêpes. Wi-Fi, craft beers. Child-friendly.

## Cafés

### Borges y Alvarez
*Av del Libertador 1015, 1st floor, Galería de los Gnomos, T02902-491 464. Daily till 0200.*
Cosy, wooden café-bar with huge windows looking out over the shopping street below. Affordable, with delicious lunch and dinner options, as well as live music and books for sale. Excellent place to hang out. Recommended.

### Casablanca
*25 de Mayo y Av del Libertador.*
Jolly place for omelettes, burgers, vegetarian, 30 varieties of pizza.

### Heladería Aquarela
*Av del Libertador 1197.*
The best ice cream – try the *calafate*. Also home-made chocolates and local produce.

## Bars and clubs

### Elba'r
*9 de Julio 57, T02902-493594, see Facebook.*
Just off the main street, this café/bar serves hard-to-find waffles and juices, as well as home-made beer and sandwiches.

## Festivals

**14 Feb   Lago Argentino Day**. Live music, dancing and *asados*.
**10 Nov   Día de la Tradición**. Displays of horsemanship and *asados*.

## Shopping

There are plenty of touristy shops along the main street, Av del Libertador.
**Estancia El Tranquilo**, *Av del Libertador 935, www.eltranquilo.com.ar.* Recommended for home-made local produce, especially Patagonian fruit teas, sweets and liqueurs.

## What to do

Most agencies charge the same rates for similar trips: minibus tours to the Perito Moreno glacier (park entry not included),
US$31; mini-trekking tours (transport plus a 2½-hr walk on the glacier), US$105. Note that in winter boat trips can be limited or cancelled due to bad weather.

**Calafate Mountain Park**, *Av del Libertador 1037, T02902-491446, www.calafate mountainpark.com.* Trips in 4WDs to panoramic views, 3-6 hrs. Summer and winter experiences including kayaking, quad biking, skiing and more.
**Chaltén Travel**, *Av del Libertador 1174, T02902-492212, also Av Güemes 7, T493092, El Chaltén, www.chaltentravel.com.* Huge range of tours (it has a monopoly on some): glaciers, estancias, trekking and bus to El Chaltén. English spoken. Also sells tickets along the Ruta 40 to Perito Moreno, Los Antiguos and Bariloche (see Transport, below).
**Hielo y Aventura**, *Av del Libertador 935, T02902-492205, www.hieloyaventura.com.* Mini-trekking includes walk through forests and 2½-hr trek on Moreno glacier (crampons included); Big Ice full-day tour includes a 4-hr trek on the glacier. Also half-day boat excursion to Brazo Sur for a view of stunning glaciers, including Moreno. Recommended.
**Lago San Martín**, *Av del Libertad 1215, p 1 A, T02902-492858, www.lagosanmartin.com.* Operates with **Estancias Turísticas de Santa Cruz**, specializing in arranging estancia visits, helpful.
**Mar Patag**, *Libertador 1319 loc. 7, T02902-492118, www.crucerosmarpatag.com.* Exclusive 2-day boat tour to Upsala, Spegazzini and Moreno glaciers, with full board. Also does a shorter full-day cruise with gourmet lunch included.
**Mundo Austral**, *Libertador 1080 piso 1, T02902-492365, www.mundoaustral.com.ar.* For all bus travel and cheaper trips to the glaciers, helpful bilingual guides.
**Patagonia Backpackers**, *at Hosteles del Glaciar, T02902-492492, www.patagonia-backpackers.com.* Alternative Glacier tour takes a more scenic route and is the only one that treks off the tourist trail on the south side of the glacier, entertaining, informative,

includes walking, park entrance not included, US$52. Recommended constantly.
**Solo Patagonia**, *Av del Libertador 867, T02902-491155, www.solopatagonia.com*. This company runs 2 7-hr trips taking in Upsala, Onelli and Spegazzini glaciers, US$92.

## Transport

### Air
The airport (T02902-491220) has daily flights to/from **Buenos Aires**. There are many more flights in summer to **Bariloche**, **Ushuaia** and **Trelew**. **LADE** (J Mermoz 160, T02902-491262) flies to **Ushuaia**, **Comodoro Rivadavia**, **Río Gallegos** and other Patagonian airports). Note that a boarding fee of US$20.50, not included in the airline ticket price, has to be paid at El Calafate.

### Bus
Buses from Río Gallegos (where you can connect with buses to Ushuaia) arrive in the centre of town. The bus terminal (T02902-491476) is open daily 0800-2000, A terminal fee of US$0.35 is always included in the bus ticket price. Some bus companies will store luggage for a fee.

To **Perito Moreno** glacier, with **Taqsa**, US$32 return. Many agencies in El Calafate also run minibus tours (see What to do, above). Out of season trips to the glacier may be difficult to arrange.

To **Puerto Madryn** with **Red Patagonia** (T02902-494250) 2 per day at 0300 and 1330, US$112; to **Río Gallegos** daily, 4-5 hrs, US$28-33, with **Taqsa** (T02902-491843). To **El Chaltén** daily with **Taqsa**, US$30, **Chaltén Travel** (T02902-492212, at 0800, 1300, 1800) and **Cal-Tur** (T02902-491368, www.caltur. com.ar, who run many other services and tours), 3 hrs, US$30. To **Bariloche**, via **Los Antiguos** and **Perito Moreno**, 36 hrs, with

**Chaltén Travel**, departs mid-Nov to Apr 2000 on odd-numbered days from El Chaltén with an overnight stop in Perito Moreno (it's cheaper to book your own accommodation); also **Cal-Tur** and **Taqsa** to **Bariloche** via **Los Antiguos** (Ruta 3 every day in high season; Ruta 40 frequency depends on demand). To **Ushuaia**, take a bus to Río Gallegos for connections US$83.

To **Puerto Natales** (Chile, for Torres del Paine), daily in summer with **Cootra** (T02902-491444), via **Río Turbio**, 8½ hrs US$32, daily at 0830, or with **Turismo Zaahj** (T02902-491631), 3 a week, fewer off-season, 5 hrs, US$32 (advance booking recommended, take your passport when booking, tedious customs check at border). **Note** Argentine pesos cannot be exchanged in Torres del Paine.

### Bike hire
**Patagonia Shop**, Av del Libertador 995, also at 9 de Julio 29.

### Car hire
Average price around US$65 per day for small car with insurance but usually only 200 km are free. **Avis**, Av del Libertador 1078, T02902-492 877, www.avis.com.ar, **Localiza**, Av del Libertador 687, T02902-491398, www.localiza.com.ar, or **Nunatak**, Gregores 1075, T02902-491 987, www. nunatakrentacar.com. All vehicles have a permit for crossing to Chile included in the fee, but cars are in poor condition.

### Taxi
Taxis charge about US$90 for 4 passengers round trip to Perito Moreno glacier including wait of 3-4 hrs. Reliable providers include **El Tehuelche**, T02902-491850, **La Terminal** T02902-490 933, and **Calafate** T02902-492 005. There is a small taxi stand outside the bus terminal.

## ★ Glaciar Perito Moreno

The sight of this expanse of ice, like a frozen sea, its waves sculpted by wind and time into beautiful turquoise folds and crevices, is unforgettable. You'll watch in awed silence, until suddenly a mighty roar announces the fall of another hunk of ice into the milky turquoise water below. Glaciar Moreno is one of the few accessible glaciers in the world that you can see visibly advancing. Some 30 km long, it reaches the water at a narrow point in one of the fjords, **Brazo Rico**, opposite Península Magallanes. At this point the glacier is 5 km across and 60 m high. It occasionally advances across Brazo Rico, blocking the fjord, but, in recent decades, as the water pressure builds up behind it, the ice has broken, reopening the channel and sending giant icebergs (*témpanos*) rushing down the appropriately named **Canal de los Témpanos**. This happened in 1988, 2004, 2006, 2008, 2013 and March 2016. Walking on the ice itself is a wonderful way to experience the glacier: what appear from a distance to be vertical fish scales, turn out to be huge peaks; climb their steep curves and look down into mysterious chasms below, lit by refracted bluish light.

## Essential Glaciar Perito Moreno

### Access

There are various ways to approach the glacier. Tour companies in El Calafate offer all of these or some in combination. The regular bus service and all excursions not involving boat trips will take you straight to the car park that is situated 77 km west of El Calafate (around 30 km beyond the gates of the park). From here you begin the descent along a series of extensive wooden walkways (*pasarelas*) to see the glacier slightly from above, and then, as you get lower, directly head-on. There are several wide viewing areas, where crowds wait expectantly in summer, cameras poised, for another hunk of ice to fall with a mighty roar from the vertical blue walls at the glacier's front into the milky turquoise lake below. There is a large and fairly inexpensive café at the site with clean bathrooms.

You could also approach the glacier on a boat trip from two different piers.

To survey the glacier from the south (and for trekking on the glacier), boats leave from Bajo de las Sombras pier (7 km east of the glacier). To approach from the north, boats leave regularly from Perito Moreno pier (1 km north of the glacier, where there is a restaurant). This latter service is offered as an extra (US$17.50 pp) when you book your standard trip to the glacier or it can be booked directly at the pier.

To get closer still, there are guided treks on the ice itself, known as Big Ice and Mini-trekking, which allow you to walk along the crevices and frozen wave crests in crampons (provided). The latter is not technically demanding and is possible for anyone with a reasonable level of fitness. The glacier is approached by a lovely walk through lenga forest, and there's a place to eat your lunch outside, with wonderful views; but bring your own food and drink. See What to do, page 213.

## ★ Glaciar Upsala

The fjords at the northwestern end of Lago Argentino are fed by four other glaciers. The largest is the Upsala Glacier, named after the Swedish university that commissioned the first survey of this area in 1908. It's a stunning expanse of untouched beauty, three times the area of the Perito Moreno Glacier and the longest glacier flowing off the Southern Patagonian icefield. However, Upsala is suffering tremendously from the effects of global warming. Unusually, it ends in two separate frontages, each about 4 km wide and 60 m high, although only one frontage can be seen on the lake excursion by motorboat from Punta Bandera on Lago Argentino, 50 km west of Calafate. The trip also goes to other, much smaller, glaciers: **Spegazzini**, which has a frontage 1.5 km wide and 130 m high, and **Agassiz** and **Onelli** glaciers, both of which feed into **Lago Onelli**. This is a quiet and very beautiful lake, full of icebergs of every size and sculpted shape, surrounded by beech forests on one side and ice-covered mountains on the other.

The best way to see Upsala Glacier is to visit the remote **Estancia Cristina** ⓘ *see Where to stay, below*, which lies in a lonely spot on the northern shores of Lago Argentina, not far from the glacier. It's beautiful, utterly wild and yet is an unbeatably comfortable base for exploring the region. Accommodation is available, or you can come on a full-day visit offering various trips, including hiking tours lasting 2½-5 hours, as well as horse riding or driving in sturdy 4WD vehicles to a vantage point high above the lake. You'll walk through incredible ancient landscapes, alongside massive rocks polished smooth by the path of glaciers, to see Upsala Glacier from above. This is an overwhelmingly beautiful sight, stretching apparently endlessly away from you, with the deep, still Prussian-blue lake below, and rocks the colour of fire all around. Boat trips and day visits to **Estancia Cristina** are run by the estancia itself; see the website for details.

## Listings Lago Argentino

### Where to stay

**$$$$ Estancia Cristina**
*Office at 9 de Julio 69, El Calafate, T02902-491133 (T011-4218 2333 ext 106/107 in Buenos Aires), www.estanciacristina.com.*

On the northern tip of Lago Argentina, this estancia offers unrivalled access to the Upsala glacier and its surroundings. 20 comfortable rooms available in 5 lodges. Boat transfers from El Calafate are included. See also Glaciar Upsala, above.

*one of the most magnificent mountains in the world*

The soaring granite towers of Mount Fitz Roy rise up from the smooth baize of the flat steppe, more like a ziggurat than a mountain, surrounded by a consort of jagged snow-clad spires, with a stack of spun-cotton clouds hanging constantly above them. Cerro Fitz Roy (3405 m) towers above the nearby peaks, its polished granite sides too steep for snow to settle. Its Tehuelche name was El Chaltén ('smoking mountain' or 'volcano'), perhaps because at sunrise the pink towers are briefly lit up bright red for a few seconds, the *amanecer de fuego* ('sunrise of fire').

Perito Moreno named the peak after the captain of the *Beagle*, who saw it from afar in 1833, and it was first climbed by a French expedition in 1952. It stands in the northern section of Parque Nacional Los Glaciares, at the western end of Lago Viedma, 230 km north of El Calafate. Around it are other high peaks, lakes and glaciers that make marvellous trekking country, every bit as satisfying as Torres del Paine across the border.

### El Chaltén *Colour map 2, C2.*

The small modern town of El Chaltén (population 1000) is set in a wonderful position at the foot of Cerro Fitz Roy and at the mouth of the valley of the Río de las Vueltas. The village was founded very recently, in 1985, in order to settle the area and pre-empt Chilean territorial claims. However, it has grown very rapidly, along with its popularity as a centre for trekking and climbing in summer, and for cross-country skiing in winter. It can be an expensive and not particularly attractive place, especially when the harsh wind blows. But its visitors create a cheerful atmosphere, there are some great bars, and from

## Esssential Cerro Fitz Roy

### Access

The base for walking and climbing around Fitz Roy is the tiny town of El Chaltén. The quickest way to reach the town is by flying to El Calafate's airport, 220 km away. There are frequent bus connections from El Calafate (four hours), and regular bus services in summer from Ruta 40 in the north, useful if you've come from the Lake District in either Argentina or Chile.

### Walking

Most paths are very clear and well worn, but a map is essential, even on short walks. The **park information centre** provides helpful maps of treks, but the best are published by *Zagier and Urruty*, www.patagoniashop.net, regularly updated and available in various scales (1:50,000; 1:250,000; 1:350,000), US$10-13. They

are sold in shops in El Calafate and El Chaltén. Do not stray from the paths. Always wear sunscreen (factor 30 at least) and be prepared for bad weather. See Lago del Desierto, page 213, for minibus services from El Chaltén.

### When to go

Walking here is only really viable from mid-October to April, with the best months usually March to early April when the weather is generally stable and not very cold, and the autumn colours of the beech forest are stunning. Midsummer (December and January) and spring (September to October) are generally very windy. In December and January the campsites can be full to bursting, with many walkers on the paths. Outside of these months most accommodation and many services close.

its concrete and tin dwellings you can walk directly into breathtaking landscapes. There is a small chapel, the **Capilla Tomás Egger**, named after an Austrian climber killed on Fitz Roy and built entirely from materials brought from Austria.

There are two ATMs in town – one in the bus station and the other a block away at Banco de la Nación (Monday-Friday 0800-1300). Many ATMS do not accept newer bank cards with smart chips. Luckily credit cards are accepted in all major hotels and most

# The Fitz Roy area

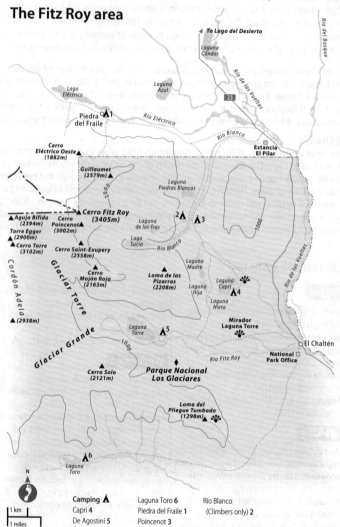

Camping ▲
Capri 4
De Agostini 5

Laguna Toro 6
Piedra del Fraile 1
Poincenot 3

Río Blanco
(Climbers only) 2

# El Chaltén

**Where to stay** 🛏

Albergue
  Patagonia **1**
Albergue Rancho
  Grande **15**
Camping
  del Lago **11**
Cóndor de
  los Andes **3**
Estancia La Quinta **12**
Hospedaje
  La Base **16**
Hostería El Puma **5**
Los Cerros **10**
Lunajuim **7**
Nothofagus **9**
Senderos **17**

**Restaurants** 🍴

Ahonikenk Chaltén **3**
B&B Burger Joint **7**
Domo Blanco **2**
Estepa **9**
Fuegia **6**
Josh Aike **1**
Pangea **4**
Patagonicus **5**

**Bars & clubs** 🍸

La Cervecería
  Artesanal
  El Chaltén **8**

*N*

Not to scale

restaurants. Accommodation is available
and ranges from camping and hostels to
not-quite-luxurious *hosterías* and some
top hotels, all overpriced in high season.
Food is expensive too, though there is an
increasing amount of choice.

## Trekking

The main attraction here is the trekking
around the Fitz Roy or Torre cordons.
Always ask at your accommodation, at the
tourist office or with the *guardaparques*
for up-to-date information on trails and
weather conditions.

**Laguna Torre** For a dramatic approach to
Cerro Torre, take the path to Laguna Torre
(three hours each way). After 1½ hours
you'll come to Mirador Laguna Torre, with
views of Cerro Torre and Cerro Fitz Roy, and
after another 1¼ hours, to **Camping De
Agostini**; see Where to stay, below.

**Laguna de los Tres** For closer views of
Cerro Fitz Roy, take the path to Laguna
de los Tres (four hours each way). Walk up
to **Camping Capri** (just under two hours),
with great views of Fitz Roy, then another
hour to **Camping Poincenot**. Just beyond
it is **Camping Río Blanco** (only for
climbers, previous registration at park
office required). From Río Blanco you
can walk another hour, though it's very
steep, to Laguna de los Tres where you'll
get a spectacular view (although not if
it's cloudy). In bad weather, you're better
off walking an hour to Piedras Blancas
(four hours total from El Chaltén). You can
connect the two walks (to Laguna Torre and
Laguna de los Tres) by taking a transverse
path (two hours) from a point northwest
of Laguna Capri to east of **Camping De**

> **Tip...**
> The best day walks are Laguna Capri and
> Mirador Laguna Torre, both of which
> have great views.

Agostini (see Where to stay, below), passing two lakes, Laguna Madre and then Laguna Hija; but note that this alternative can take more than one day.

**Loma del Pliegue Tumbado** A recommended day walk is to the Loma del Pliegue Tumbado viewpoint (four hours each way) where you can see both *cordones* and Lago Viedma. There's a marked path from the *guardería* with excellent panoramic views, best in clear weather. The onward trek to **Laguna Toro**, a glacial lake on the route across the ice cap (seven hours each way) is for more experienced trekkers.

**Piedra del Fraile** The trek up Río Blanco to Piedra del Fraile (seven hours each way) is beautiful. It starts at Campamento Río Blanco running north along the Río Blanco and west along the Río Eléctrico via Piedra del Fraile (four hours) to Lago Eléctrico. Piedra del Fraile can be reached more easily from the road to Lago del Desierto in about two hours. At Piedra del Fraile, just outside the park, there are *cabañas* ($$) per person, hot showers) and a campsite ($$$); see Where to stay, below. From here a path leads south, up Cerro Eléctrico Oeste (1882 m) towards the north face of Fitz Roy (two hours); it's tough going but offers spectacular views. You should take a guide for this last bit.

## Climbing
Base camp for Fitz Roy (3405 m) is Campamento Río Blanco. Other peaks include Cerro Torre (3102 m), Torre Egger (2900 m), Cerro Solo (2121 m), Poincenot (3002 m), Guillaumet (2579 m), Saint-Exupery (2558 m), Aguja Bífida (2394 m) and Cordón Adela (2938 m): most of these are for very experienced climbers. The best time to climb is generally mid-February to late March; November and December are very windy; January is fair; winter (May to July) is extremely cold, but the weather is unpredictable and it all depends on the specific route being climbed. Permits for climbing are available at the national park information office in El Chaltén. Guides are also available in El Chaltén, see What to do, page 223. **Fitz Roy Expediciones**, www.fitzroyexpediciones.com.ar, are recommended.

## Lago Viedma
Lago Viedma to the south of El Chaltén can be explored by boat. The trips usually pass Glaciar Viedma, with the possibility of ice trekking too. Contact **Fitz Roy Expediciones** (see What to do, page 223) for circuits that connect Lago Viedma and Lago San Martín.

## Lago del Desierto and around
There is stunning virgin landscape to explore around **Lago del Desierto**, 37 km (one hour) north of El Chaltén. The long skinny lake is fjord-like and surrounded by forests. It's reached by unpaved Route 23, which leads north along the Río de las Vueltas. After about 30 minutes' drive, there is a one-hour hike along a marked path to Chorillo del Salto, a small but pristine waterfall. Route 23 continues via **Laguna Cóndor**, where flamingos can be seen, to Lago del Desierto. A short walk to a mirador at the end of the road gives fine views. There is a campsite at the southern end of the lake (sometimes no food, although there is a kiosk that sells drinks, beer and *choripán*), and a path runs along the east side of the lake to its northern tip (4½ hours), where there is a *refugio*. From here a trail leads west along the valley of the Río Diablo to Laguna Diablo.

   **Estancia El Pilar** is the best place to stay on the way to Lago del Desierto; it's in a stunning position and has views of Fitz Roy. Use it as an excellent base for trekking up Río Blanco or Río Eléctrico, with a multi-activity adventure circuit. In summer **Transporte Las Lengas** in El Chaltén (www.transportelaslengas.com; see also page 224) runs a minibus twice daily to Lago del Desierto (US$30), stopping at **El Pilar** (US$13), and three times a day to Río Eléctrico (US$8.50). Highly recommended. There are also excursions with **Chaltén Travel** daily in summer to connect with boats across the lake (see What to do, page 223).

From December to April, it is possible to travel on foot, horseback and boat from Lago del Desierto to **Villa O'Higgins** in Chile, the southernmost town on the Carretera Austral. Take the Las Lengas minibus to Lago del Desierto, then either take a boat (45 minutes, US$32) to the northern end, or walk up the eastern shore (4½ hours). From there you can trek or go on horseback (with a guide, US$45 per horse), 5 km to the border. Hans Silva in Villa O'Higgins (T+56-67-243 1821) offers horses and a 4WD service from the Chilean border to Puerto Candelario Mancilla (14 km, US$22, US$15 for luggage only, reserve in advance) on Lago O'Higgins. Spend the night at Candelario Mancilla (Tito and Ricardo have lodging as well as 4WD and horses) and then, the next day, take a boat to Bahía Bahamóndez (three hours, US$66.50), followed by a bus to Villa O'Higgins, 7 km, US$3.75. For further information on dates, tours and boat availability, see www.villaohiggins.com. Note that the border is closed from May to November.

## Listings Cerro Fitz Roy and around *maps pages 218 and 219.*

## Tourist information

### El Chaltén
There is also an excellent private website with accommodation listed, www.elchalten.com.

### National park office
*Across the bridge, right at the entrance to the town, T02962-493004, www.parquesnacionales.gov.ar.*
Visitors are met by the friendly *guardaparques* (some speak English), who have advice on trekking and climbing.

### Tourist office
*In the bus station, T02962-493370. Daily 0800-2200 high season.*
Helpful and efficient, with plenty of maps on offer. The staff hand out trekking maps of the area that show paths, campsites, distances and walking times. There's another tourist office at the bus station.

## Where to stay

### Cerro Fitz Roy area
**Camping**
A gas/alcohol stove is essential for camping as open fires are prohibited in the national park. Take plenty of warm clothes and a good sleeping bag. It is possible to rent equipment in El Chaltén; ask at the park office or Rancho Grande. There are campsites at Poincenot, Capri, Laguna Toro and Laguna Torre (Camping De Agostini, see below). None has services, but there are very basic public bathrooms. All river water is drinkable, so do not wash within 70 m of rivers. Pack up all rubbish and take it back to town.

### Camping De Agostini
*Next to Laguna Torre.*
With fantastic views of the Cordón Torre.

### Camping Los Troncos/Piedra del Fraile
*On Río Eléctrico beyond the park boundary.*
It is privately owned and has facilities.

### El Chaltén
In high season places are full: you must book ahead. Most places close in low season.

### $$$$ Hostería El Puma
*Lionel Terray 212, T02962-493095, www.hosteriaelpuma.com.ar.*
A little apart, splendid views, lounge with log fire, tasteful stylish furnishings, comfortable, transfers and big American breakfast included. Recommended.

**\$\$\$\$ Los Cerros**
*Av San Martín 260, T02962-493182,*
*www.loscerrosdelchalten.com.*
Stylish and sophisticated, in a stunning
setting with mountain views, sauna,
whirlpool and massage. Half-board and all-
inclusive packages with trips available.

**\$\$\$\$ Senderos**
*Perito Moreno 35, T02962-493336,*
*www.senderoshosteria.com.ar.*
4 types of room and suite in a new, wood-
framed structure, comfortable, warm, can
arrange tours, excellent restaurant.

**\$\$\$ Estancia La Quinta**
*On R23, 2 km south of El Chaltén, T02962-*
*493012, www.estancialaquinta.com.ar.*
*Oct-Apr.*
A spacious pioneer house with renovated
rooms surrounded by beautiful gardens, very
comfortable, has Wi-Fi. A superb breakfast
is included and the restaurant is also open
for lunch and dinner. Transfer to and from
El Chaltén bus terminals is included.

**\$\$\$ Lunajuim**
*Trevisán 45, T02962-493047,*
*www.lunajuim.com.*
Stylish yet relaxed, comfortable (duvets
on the beds), lounge with wood fire.
Recommended.

**\$\$\$ Nothofagus**
*Hensen y Riquelme, T02962-493087, www.*
*nothofagusbb.com.ar. Oct and Apr (\$\$).*
Cosy bed and breakfast, simple rooms,
cheaper without bath and in low season,
good value. Recommended.

**\$\$ Hospedaje La Base**
*C 10 N 16, T02962-493031, see Facebook.*
Good rooms for 2, 3 and 4, tiny kitchen,
self-service breakfast, great video lounge.
Recommended.

**\$ pp Albergue Patagonia**
*Av San Martín 493, T02962-493019, www.*
*patagoniahostel.com.ar. Closed Jun-Sep.*
HI-affiliated, cheaper for members, small and
cosy with rooms for 2 with own bath (\$\$)

or for 2 (\$\$), 4, 5 or 6 with shared bath, also
has cabins, video room, bike hire, laundry,
luggage store and lockers, restaurant, very
welcoming. Helpful information on Chaltén,
also run trips to Lago del Desierto.

**\$ pp Albergue Rancho Grande**
*San Martín 724, T02962-493005,*
*www.ranchograndehostel.com.*
In a great position at the end of town with
good open views and attractive restaurant
and lounge, rooms for 4, with shared
bath, breakfast extra. Also \$\$ doubles,
breakfast extra. Helpful, English spoken.
Recommended. Reservations in Calafate at
**Hostel/Chaltén Travel**.

**\$ pp Cóndor de los Andes**
*Av Río de las Vueltas y Halvorsen, T02962-*
*493101, www.condordelosandes.com.*
Nice little rooms for up to 6 with bath, sheets
included, breakfast extra, also doubles with
bath (\$\$\$-\$\$), laundry service, library, quiet,
HI affiliated.

## Camping

**Camping del Lago**
*Lago del Desierto 135, T02962-493245.*
Centrally located with hot showers.
Several others.

---

### Lago Viedma

**\$\$\$\$ Estancia Helsingfors**
*73 km northwest of La Leona, on Lago*
*Viedma, T011-5277 0195 (Buenos Aires),*
*reservations T02966-675753,*
*www.helsingfors.com.ar. Nov-Apr.*
Fabulous place in a splendid position on
Lago Viedma, stylish rooms, welcoming
lounge, delicious food (full board), and
excursions directly to glaciers and to Laguna
Azul, by horse or trekking, plus boat trips.

---

### Lago del Desierto and around

**\$\$\$ Aguas Arriba Lodge**
*RP23, Km 130, T011-4152 5697,*
*www.aguasarribalodge.com.*

Comfortable wooden lodge on the eastern shore, reached only by boat, 15 mins, or by a 2- to 3-hr walk with guide (luggage goes by boat). Great views and trekking opportunities.

### $$$ El Pilar
*RP23, Km 17, T02962-493002,*
*www.hosteriaelpilar.com.ar.*
Country house in a spectacular setting at the meeting of Ríos Blanco and de las Vueltas, with clear views of Fitz Roy. A chance to sample the simple life with access to the less-visited northern part of the park. Simple comfortable rooms, great food, breakfast and return transfers included.

## Restaurants

### El Chaltén

### $$ Estepa
*Cerro Solo y Antonio Rojo,*
*www.esteparestobar.com.*
Small, intimate place with good, varied meals, friendly staff.

### $$ Fuegia
*San Martín 342. Dinner only.*
Pastas, trout, meat and vegetarian dishes.

### $$ Josh Aike
*Lago de Desierto 105.*
Excellent *chocolatería*, home-made food, beautiful building. Recommended.

### $$ Pangea
*Lago del Desierto 330 y San Martín.*
*Lunch and dinner, drinks and coffee.*
Tranquil atmosphere, with good music and a varied menu. Recommended.

### $$ Patagonicus
*Güemes y Madsen. Midday to midnight.*
Lovely warm place with salads, *pastas caseras* and fabulous pizzas for 2, US$3-8. Recommended.

### $$-$ Ahonikenk Chaltén
*Av Martín M de Güemes 23,*
*T02962-493070.*
Restaurant and pizzeria, good home-made pasta.

### $$-$ B&B Burger Joint
*San Martín between C 6 and Terray.*
Great burgers, microbrews and pub grub.

### $ Domo Blanco
*San Martín 164.*
Delicious ice cream.

## Bars and clubs

### El Chaltén

### La Cervecería Artesanal El Chaltén
*San Martín 564, T02962-493109.*
Brews its own excellent beer, also local dishes and pizzas, coffee and cakes, English spoken. Recommended.

### Laguna de Los Tres
*Trevisán 45, see Facebook.*
Newer bar, live music, craft beer, sandwiches and pizzas. Free salsa classes on Thu.

## Shopping

### El Chaltén
Several outdoor shops. Also supermarkets, although these are all expensive, with little fresh food available. Fuel is available next to the bridge.

## What to do

### El Chaltén
**Casa De Guías**, *Av San Martín s/n,*
*T02962-493118, www.casadeguias.com.ar.*
Experienced climbers who lead groups to nearby peaks, to the Campo de Hielo Continental and on easier treks.
**Chaltén Travel**, *Av Güemes 7, T02962-493092,*
*www.chaltentravel.com.* Huge range of tours (see under El Calafate, page 213).
**El Relincho**, *San Martín s/n, T02962-493007,*
*www.elrelinchopatagonia.com.ar.* For trekking on horseback with guides, also trekking, accommodation and rural activities.
**Fitz Roy Expediciones**, *San Martín 56,*
*T02962-493178, www.fitzroyexpediciones.*
*com.ar.* Organizes trekking and adventure trips including on the Campo de Hielo Continental, ice-climbing schools, and

fabulous longer trips. Climbers must be fit, but no technical experience required; equipment provided. Email with plenty of notice to reserve. Also has an eco-camp with 8 wilderness cabins. Highly recommended.

**Patagonia Aventura**, *San Martín 56, T02962-493110, www.patagonia-aventura.com.* Has various ice trekking and other tours to Lago and Glaciar Viedma, also to Lago del Desierto.

**Transporte Las Lengas**, *Viedma 95, T02962-493023; also at the bus station, T02962-493227, www.transportelaslengas.com.* Transfers from El Calafate airport, plus minibuses to Lago del Desierto and Río Eléctrico.

## Transport

### El Chaltén
### Bus
A tax of US$1.15 is charged at the terminal. In summer, buses fill quickly, so book ahead; there are fewer services off season. Daily buses to **El Calafate**, 3 hrs (most also stop at El Calafate airport), with **Taqsa** (T02962-493 130), US$30, **Chaltén Travel** (T02962-493092), **Los Glaciares** and **Cal-Tur** (T02962-493150). **Chaltén Travel** also go to **Los Antiguos** (1000) in high season daily at 2000 and **Bariloche** (2020), mid-Nov to Apr on odd-numbered days at 2000. To **Piedrabuena** on Ruta 3 (connect in El Calafate and Río Gallegos) with **Taqsa**, 3 daily in high seasons (1050), **Transporte Las Lengas** (T02962 493 023, www. transportelaslengas.com.ar) has a service to **El Calafate airport** 6 times a day in high season, 3 hrs, US$28, reserve in advance.

### Taxi
Taxi/rent Oxalis, T02962-493343.

# El Calafate to Chile

#### on the road to Torres del Paine

If travelling from El Calafate to Torres del Paine in Chile by car or bike, you can take the paved combination of Route 11, Route 40 and Route 5 to La Esperanza (165 km), where there's fuel, a campsite and a large but expensive *confitería* (accommodation $$ with bath). From La Esperanza, paved Route 7 heads west along the valley of the Río Coyle. A shorter but rougher route (closed in winter), missing Esperanza, goes via El Cerrito and joins Route 7 at Estancia Tapi Aike. Route 7 continues to the border, crossing at Cancha Carrera (see box, opposite) and then meets the good *ripio* road between Torres del Paine and Puerto Natales (63 km). For bus services along this route, see Transport, below.

## Río Turbio *Colour map 3, A3.*
Located near the border, 250 km south of El Calafate, Río Turbio (population 8814) is a charmless place you're most likely to visit en route to or from Torres del Paine in Chile. For information on crossing the border near Río Turbio, see box, opposite.

Río Turbio has a cargo railway connecting it with Punta Loyola, and visitors can see Mina 1, where the first mine was opened, but the site of Argentina's largest coalfield hasn't really recovered from the depression that hit the industry in the 1990s. There's a small ski centre nearby, **Valdelén**, which has six pistes and is ideal for beginners; there is also scope for cross-country skiing between early June and late September.

## BORDER CROSSING

### Argentina–Chile

All crossings may have different hours in winter; see www.gendarmeria.gov.ar.
For the crossing from Lago del Desierto to Villa O'Higgins (on foot, on horseback or by bike only), see page 221.

**Paso Río Don Guillermo/Cancha Carrera**
The Paso Río Don Guillermo or Cancha Carrera, 129 km west of La Esperanza and 48 km north of Río Turbio is open all year, and is the most convenient crossing to reach Parque Nacional Torres del Paine in Chile. The fast and friendly **Argentine customs and immigration** (daily 0900-2300) are at Cancha Carrera, 2 km east of the border. For the Chilean side see box, page 425.

**Paso Mina Uno/Dorotea**
Paso Mina Uno/Dorotea is 5 km south of Río Turbio and is open all year, daily 0900-2300. For the Chilean side see box, page 425.

**Paso Casas Viejas/Laurita**
Paso Casas Viejas is 33 km south of Río Turbio via 28 de Noviembre and is open all year, daily 0900-0100. For the Chilean side see box, page 425.

## Listings El Calafate to Chile

### Tourist information

**Río Turbio**
Tourist office
*Plazoleta Agustín del Castillo,
T02902-421950. Also see www.
welcomeargentina.com/rioturbio.*

### Where to stay

**Río Turbio**
Hotels here are almost always full.

**$$ Nazó**
*Gob Moyano 464, T02902-421800,
www.hotelnazo.com.ar.*
Modern building, rooms for 2-4,
laundry service, restaurant and bar.

**$ Hostería Capipe**
*Paraje Julia Dufour, 9 km from town,
T02902-482935, see Facebook.*
Simple, with restaurant.

### Transport

**Río Turbio**
**Bus**
To **Puerto Natales**, daily at 1530, 2 hrs,
US$8, hourly with **Buses Pacheco** (www.
busespacheco.com) and other companies.
To **El Calafate** via **La Esperanza**, with **Taqsa**,
4 hrs, US$17-20. To **Río Gallegos**, 5 hrs,
US$28, with **Taqsa/Marga** (T02902-421422).

# Santiago

one of Latin America's unheralded capital cities

No one can deny that the Chilean capital has an impressive setting, in a hollow surrounded by mountains, with peaks over 5000 m visible on clear days. They are most dramatic just after rainfall in winter, when the smog clears and the new snows glisten.

If you are flying into Chile, you will probably arrive in Santiago. It's a vibrant, progressive city. With its many parks, interesting museums, glittering high-rises and boutiques, it bursts with possibilities.

As far as entertainment goes, there are popular music scenes in everything from techno and progressive rock to Bohemian hangouts and most of the bits in between. Certainly, those who spend an extended period of time in Santiago soon realize there's near limitless possibilities for fun and adventure.

**Best** for
Museums ▪ Nightlife ▪ Restaurants

Santiago

# Footprint
## picks

★ **Museo Chileno de Arte Precolombino**, page 229

The largest collection of pre-Columbian artefacts in the country.

★ **Mercado Central**, page 229

Sample the freshest produce, as well as the most delicious seafood, in all of Santiago.

★ **Museo de la Solidaridad Salvador Allende**, page 233

View 20th-century art by national and international artists, including work by Picasso and Miró.

★ **Cerro San Cristóbal**, page 235

Hike up to the statue of the Virgin and enjoy panoramic views of the magnificent cityscape.

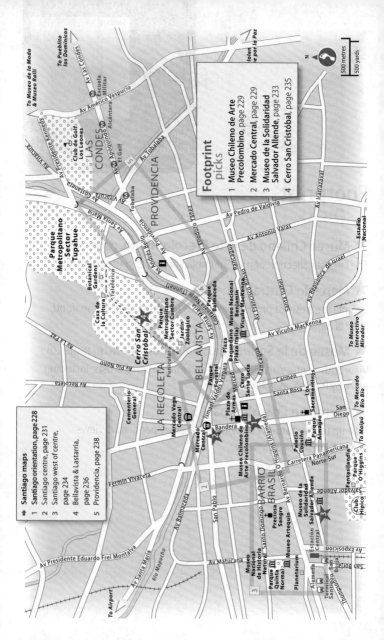

Footprint picks

1 Museo Chileno de Arte Precolombino, page 229
2 Mercado Central, page 229
3 Museo de la Solidaridad Salvador Allende, page 233
4 Cerro San Cristóbal, page 235

Santiago maps

1 Santiago orientation, page 228
2 Santiago centre, page 231
3 Santiago west of centre, page 234
4 Bellavista & Lastarria, page 236
5 Providencia, page 238

500 metres
500 yards

N

from a bustling financial centre to colonial plazas to bohemian enclaves

## Santiago centre

**Around the Plaza de Armas** On the eastern and southern sides of the Plaza de Armas there are arcades with shops; on the northern side is the post office and the Municipalidad; and on the western side the Cathedral and the archbishop's palace. The **Cathedral**, much rebuilt, contains a recumbent statue in wood of San Francisco Javier, and the chandelier, which lit the first meetings of Congress after independence. In the Palacio de la Real Audiencia is the **Museo Histórico Nacional** ① *TT2-2411 7000, www.museohistoriconacional.cl, Tue-Sun 1000-1800, free, signs in Spanish,* covering the period from the Conquest until 1925.

Just west of the Plaza is the ★ **Museo Chileno de Arte Precolombino** ① *in the former Real Aduana, Bandera 361, T2-2928 1500, www.precolombino.cl, Tue-Sun 1000-1800, US$6.50, free 1st Sun of the month, children free, displays in English, guided tours arranged by contacting reservas@museoprecolombiano.cl.* Its collection of objects from the pre-Columbian cultures of Central America and the Andean region is highly recommended for the quality of the objects and their presentation.

At Calle Merced 864 is the **Casa Colorada** (1769), home of the Governor in colonial days and then of Mateo de Toro, first president of Chile. It is now the **Museo de Santiago** ① *T2-2633 0723, Tue-Fri 1000-1800, Sat 1000-1700, Sun and holidays 1100-1400, US$1, students free, only part of the museum is open due to an ongoing renovation project.* It covers the history of Santiago from the Conquest to modern times, with excellent displays and models, some signs in English, guided tours. Paseo Ahumada, a pedestrianized street lined with cafés, runs south to the Alameda four blocks away, crossing Huérfanos.

**North of the Plaza de Armas** Four blocks north of the Plaza de Armas is the interesting ★ **Mercado Central** ① *21 de Mayo y San Pablo,* the best place in Santiago for seafood. The building faces the **Parque Venezuela,** on which is the Cal y Canto metro station and, at its western end, the **Centro Cultural Estación Mapocho** ① *www.estacionmapocho.cl, open only for exhibitions,* in the old Mapocho station.

Immediately south of the Mapocho and east of the Mercado Central is the **Parque Forestal,** through which you can reach Plaza Italia. In the park, the **Museo Nacional de Bellas Artes** ① *www.mnba.cl (Spanish only), Tue-Sun 1000-1900, US$1, students and seniors US$0.50, free Sun, café,* is in an extraordinary example of neoclassical architecture. It has a large display of Chilean and foreign painting and sculpture; contemporary art exhibitions are held several times a year. In the west wing is the **Museo de Arte Contemporáneo** ① *www.mac.uchile.cl.*

**Plaza Italia, Lastarria and around** From the **Plaza Italia,** where there is a statue of Gen Baquedano and the Tomb of the Unknown Soldier, the Alameda runs through the heart of the city for over 3 km. It is 100 m wide and ornamented with gardens and statuary: the most notable are the equestrian statues of Generals O'Higgins and San Martín; the statue of the Chilean historian Benjamín Vicuña MacKenna who, as mayor of Santiago, beautified Cerro Santa Lucía (see below); and the great monument in honour of the battle of Concepción in 1879.

**Tip...**
Almost all museums are closed on Monday and on 1 November.

# Essential Santiago

## Finding your feet

International and domestic flights arrive at the **Aeropuerto Merino Benítez**, 26 km northwest of the city at Pudahuel, off Ruta 68, the motorway to Viña del Mar and Valparaíso. There are frequent bus services between the international and domestic terminals and the city centre, as well as minibuses and taxis.

The four main bus terminals are near the railway station on Avenida Libertador Bernardo O'Higgins. The terminals are all convenient for the metro. There is a fifth bus terminal at Metro Pajarito, handy for connections to the airport (see above). See also Transport, page 246.

## Getting around

The metro (www.metrosantiago.cl) is modern, fast, quiet, and very full at peak times. City buses are operated under the **Transantiago** (www.transantiago.cl), system, which is designed to reduce congestion and pollution, but has not entirely succeeded. There are also *colectivos* (collective taxis) on fixed routes to the suburbs. Taxis are abundant, but Radio Taxis, called in advance, tend to be safer. See also Transport, page 246.

## Orientation

The centre of the old city lies between the Mapocho and the Avenida O'Higgins, which is usually known as the Alameda. This is the main east–west avenue through the city and is within easy reach of Line 1 of the metro. From the Plaza Baquedano (usually called Plaza Italia), in the east of the city's central area, the Mapocho flows to the northwest and the Alameda runs to the southwest. From Plaza Italia the Calle Merced runs due west to the Plaza de Armas, the heart of the city, five blocks south of the Mapocho. An urban motorway runs the length of Santiago from east to west under the course of the Río Mapocho.

## Safety

Like all large cities, Santiago has problems of theft. Pickpockets and bag-snatchers, who are often well-dressed, operate especially on the metro and around the Plaza de Armas. Avoid the *poblaciones* (shanty towns), notably Pudahuel and parts of the north (such as Conchalí), especially if you are travelling alone or have only recently arrived.

## Money

Avoid street money changers (particularly common on Ahumada, Bandera, Moneda and Agustinas): they pull any number of tricks, or will usually ask you to accompany them to somewhere obscure. The passing of forged notes and muggings are reported.

## Weather Santiago

| | | | | | |
|---|---|---|---|---|---|
| **January** | **February** | **March** | **April** | **May** | **June** |
| 29°C | 28°C | 26°C | 22°C | 17°C | 14°C |
| 12°C | 11°C | 9°C | 7°C | 5°C | 3°C |
| 0mm | 0mm | 0mm | 10mm | 50mm | 70mm |
| **July** | **August** | **September** | **October** | **November** | **December** |
| 13°C | 16°C | 18°C | 21°C | 25°C | 27°C |
| 2°C | 3°C | 5°C | 7°C | 8°C | 10°C |
| 70mm | 50mm | 20mm | 10mm | 0mm | 0mm |

Between Plaza Italia, the Parque Forestal and the Alameda is the **Lastarria** neighbourhood (Universidad Católica Metro). Calle José Victorino Lastarria itself has a number of popular, smart restaurants, while the **Plaza Mulato Gil de Castro** ① *C Lastarria 307*, has a mural by Roberto Matta and the **Museo Arqueológico de Santiago** and the **Museo de Artes Visuales** ① *T2-2664 9337, www.mavi.cl, Tue-Sun 1030-1830, US$1.50 for both, free on Sun*. The former exhibits Chilean archaeology, anthropology and pre-Columbian art, and the latter, modern art.

**West along the Alameda** Heading west from here the Alameda skirts, on the right, **Cerro Santa Lucía**, and on the left, the Catholic University. **Cerro Santa Lucía** ① *closes*

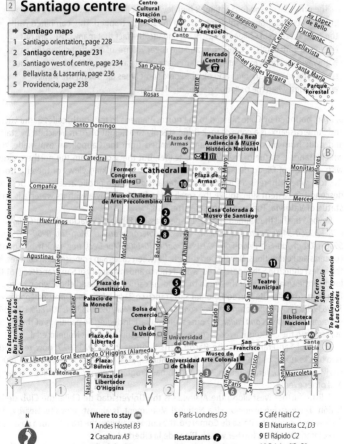

2 **Santiago centre**

➡ **Santiago maps**
1 Santiago orientation, page 228
2 **Santiago centre, page 231**
3 Santiago west of centre, page 234
4 Bellavista & Lastarria, page 236
5 Providencia, page 238

**N**

| 200 metres |
| 200 yards |

**Where to stay** 🛏
1 Andes Hostel *B3*
2 Casaltura *A3*
3 Fundador *D2*
4 Galerías *D3*
5 París *D3*
6 París-Londres *D3*

**Restaurants** 🍴
2 Bar Nacional No 2 *C2*
3 Café Caribe *C2*
4 Café Colonia *C3*
5 Café Haití *C2*
8 El Naturista *C2, D3*
9 El Rápido *C2*
10 Faisán d'Or *B2*
11 Lung Fung *C3*

## Smog trap

While Santiago's smog is not too bad in spring, summer and autumn, those who arrive here during winter could be in for an unpleasant shock. It might not take more than half an hour for your throat to begin to itch and your eyes to water due to one of Santiago's biggest problems – pollution. When Pedro de Valdivia founded the city in 1541, between the coastal mountains and the Andes, it must have seemed like a perfect site; he could never have imagined that the city would one day engulf the whole valley, and that the mountains would become a serious problem.

The principal reason for Santiago's high levels of pollution is that it lies in a bowl, encircled by mountains, which means that the smog is trapped. This, combined with the centralization of Chilean industry in Santiago, the fact that many buses are not equipped with catalytic converters and the sheer volume of cars that choke the city's highways, conspires to create a problem that cannot easily be resolved. It is a serious issue: asthma rates are high and older people sometimes die during the winter *emergencias*, when the pollution gets particularly bad.

---

*at 2100,* bounded by Calle Merced to the north, Alameda to the south, calles Santa Lucía and Subercaseaux, is a cone of rock rising steeply to a height of 70 m (reached by stairs and a lift from the Alameda). It can be climbed from the Caupolicán esplanade, on which stands a statue of that Mapuche leader, but the ascent from the northern side, with a statue of Diego de Almagro, is easier. There are striking views of the city from the top, where there is a fortress, the **Batería Hidalgo** (no public access). It is best to descend the eastern side, to see the small **Plaza Pedro Valdivia** with its waterfalls and **statue of Valdivia**. The area is not safe after dark.

Beyond the hill the Alameda passes the neoclassical **Biblioteca Nacional** ⓘ *Av O'Higgins 651, T2-2360 5400, Santa Lucía metro, www.bibliotecanacional.cl, Mon-Thu 0900-1800, Fri 0900-1700 in Jan-Feb (Mon-Fri 0900-1900, Sat 0910-1400 Mar-Dec), free,* which has good concerts and exhibitions. Beyond, on the left, between calles San Francisco and Londres, is the oldest church in Santiago: the red-walled church and monastery of **San Francisco** (1618). Inside is the small statue of the Virgin that Valdivia carried on his saddlebow when he rode from Peru to Chile. The **Museo Colonial San Francisco** ⓘ *by Iglesia San Francisco, Londres 4, T2-2639 8737, www.museosanfrancisco.com, daily (except Mon) 0930-1330, 1500-1800, US$1.50, discounts for students and children,* houses religious art, including 54 paintings of the life of St Francis; in the cloisters is a room containing poet Gabriela Mistral's Nobel medal.

South of San Francisco is the **Barrio París-Londres**, built 1923-1929, now restored. Two blocks north of the Alameda is **Teatro Municipal** ⓘ *C Agustinas 794, T2-2463 1000, www.municipal.cl,* renovated in 2014, which has programmes of opera, ballet, concerts and other events.

A little further west along the Alameda is the **Universidad de Chile**; the **Club de la Unión** ⓘ *www.clubdelaunion.cl,* a National Monument, is almost opposite. Nearby, on Calle Nueva York is the **Bolsa de Comercio**; the public may view the trading but a passport is required. One block further west is **Plaza de la Libertad**.

North of the plaza, hemmed in by the skyscrapers of the Centro Cívico, the **Presidential Palace** is housed in the **Palacio de la Moneda** (1805) ⓘ *T2-2690 4000, visitas@presidencia.cl* for reservations, Mon-Fri for guided tours of the palace, for access to courtyards Mon-Fri 1000-1800, ceremonial changing of the guard every other day, 1000, containing historic relics, paintings and sculpture, and the elaborate 'Salón Rojo' used for official receptions. Although the Moneda was damaged by air attacks during the military coup of 11 September 1973, it has been fully restored. The large **Centro Cultural Palacio La Moneda** ① T2-2355 6500, www.ccplm.cl, daily 0900-2100, US$7 for foreigners, US$3.50 for foreign students, houses temporary exhibitions as well as an arts cinema and an interesting gallery of Chilean handicrafts.

## West of the centre
**South of the Alameda** Five blocks south of the Alameda is the **Palacio Cousiño** ① C Dieciocho 438, www.palaciocousino.cl, Metro Toesca, closed due to earthquake damage, but you can tour the grounds. This large mansion in French rococo style has a superb Italian marble staircase and other opulent items. A little further west and four blocks south of the Alameda is the ★ **Museo de la Solidaridad Salvador Allende** ① Av República 475, T2-2689 8761, www.mssa.cl, Tue-Sun 1000-1800 (until 1900 Dec-Jan), US$1.50, Sun free, which houses a highly regarded collection of 20th-century works donated by Chilean and other artists (Picasso, Miró, Matta and many more) who sympathized with the Allende government, plus some personal items of the president himself. The contents were hidden during the Pinochet years.

**Parque O'Higgins** ① 10 blocks south of Alameda; take Metro Line 2 to Parque O'Higgins station, bus from Parque Baquedano via Av MacKenna and Av Matta. It has a small lake, tennis courts, swimming pool (open from 5 December), an open-air stage, a club, the racecourse of the **Club Hípico** and an amusement park, **Fantasilandia** ① www.fantasilandia.cl, daily in summer, winter weekends only 1200-2000, US$18 US$10 children and seniors, unlimited rides. There are also about 20 basic restaurants, craft shops, and two small museums: **Acuario Municipal** ① Parque O'Higgins, T2-2556 5680, daily 1000-1900, small charge (around US$0.25); and **Museo de Insectos y Caracoles** ① Local 12, daily 1000-1900, small charge, with a collection of insects and shellfish.

**Barrio Brasil to Parque Quinta Normal** **Barrio Brasil**, with **Plaza Brasil** at its heart and the **Basílica del Salvador** two blocks from the plaza, is one of the earliest parts of the city. It has some fine old buildings, especially around Calle Concha y Toro, but now it's a more bohemian, student-centric area with lots of places to stay as well as numerous bars, clubs, cafés and lively restaurants (Metro República). The next barrio west, Yungay, is in much the same vein, with many once elegant buildings, a leafy plaza and, today, a lot of street art. Visit the historic **Peluquería Francesa** ① Compañía y Libertad, www.boulevardlavaud.cl, which houses a barber's shop dating from 1868, as well as a restaurant, deli and antiques.

The Alameda, meanwhile, continues west to the **Planetarium** ① Alameda 3349, T2-2718 2900, www.planetariochile.cl, US$6.50, discount for students. Opposite it on the southern side is the railway station (**Estación Central** or **Alameda**). On Avenida Matucana, running north from here, is the popular Parque Quinta Normal (at Avenida D Portales; you can walk from Brasil through Yungay to the park). It was founded as a botanical garden in 1830 and now contains several museums. **Museo Ferroviario** ① www.corpdicyt.cl, Tue-Fri 1000-1750, Sat and Sun 1100-1750 (until 1850 in summer), US$1.15, contains the former presidential stagecoach and steam engines built between 1884 and 1953, including a rare Kitson-Meyer. The **Museo Nacional de Historia Natural** ① www.mnhn.cl, Tue-Sat 1000-1730, Sun 1100-1730, was founded in 1830 and is one of Latin America's oldest museums.

Housed in a neoclassical building, it has exhibitions on zoology, botany, mineralogy, anthropology and ethnography.

Near the park is **Museo Artequín** ① *Av Portales 3530, T2-2681 8656, www.artequin.cl, Tue-Fri 0900-1700, Sat-Sun 1100-1800, closed Feb, US$2*. Housed in the Chilean pavilion built for the 1889 Paris International Exhibition, it contains prints of famous paintings and activities and explanations of the techniques of the great masters.

Some 200 m from the Quinta Normal metro station is the public library, the **Biblioteca de Santiago** ① *www.bibliotecasantiago.cl*, in front of which is **Centro Cultural Matucana 100** ① *www.m100.cl*, with several exhibition halls and a theatre. Across Avenida Matucana from Quinta Normal metro station is the **Museo de la de los Derechos Humanos** ① *Av Matucana 501, T2-2597 9600, www.museodelamemoria.cl, Tue-Sun 1000-1800, free until 1200, US$1 after, audio guide for non-Spanish speakers*, a huge block covered in oxidized copper mesh suspended above an open space. On three floors it concentrates on

### ③ Santiago west of centre

**Where to stay** 🛏
2 Conde de Ansúrez
3 Happy House Hostel
4 Hostal de Sammy
6 La Casa Roja

7 Moai Hostel
8 The Princesa Insolente
9 Res Mery
10 Tur Hotel Express

**Restaurants** 🍴
1 Club Santiago
2 Confitería Torres
3 El Hoyo
4 Fuente Mardoqueo

the events and aftermath of 11 September 1973, with videos, testimonies, documents and other items. It also has information on human rights struggles worldwide and temporary exhibits, a gift shop and café.

## Bellavista and Cerro San Cristóbal

The **Bellavista district**, on the north bank of the Mapocho from Plaza Italia at the foot of Cerro San Cristóbal, is one of the main eating and nightlife districts in the old city. On its streets are restaurants and cafés, theatres, galleries and craft shops (most selling lapis lazuli on Calle Bellavista itself). You can cross the Mapocho by bridges from Baquedano or Salvador metro stations, or by a pedestrian bridge between the two, which is adorned with hundreds of lovers' eternity padlocks.

**La Chascona** ① *F Márquez de la Plata 0192, Bellavista, T2-2777 8741, www.fundacion neruda.org, Tue-Sun 1000-1800, Jan-Feb 1000-1900 US$8.75 with audio tour*, was the house that the poet Pablo Neruda built for Matilde Urrutia, with whom he lived from 1955. It was wrecked during the 1973 coup, but Matilde restored it and lived there till her death in 1985.

Northwest of Bellavista, in the barrio of Recoleta, is the **Cementerio General** ① *www.cementeriogeneral.cl, to get there take any Recoleta bus from C Miraflores, or arrive at the Cementario General metro terminal*. This cemetery contains the mausoleums of most of the great figures in Chilean history and the arts, including Violeta Parra, Víctor Jara and Salvador Allende. There is also an impressive monument to the victims, known as the '*desaparecidos*' (disappeared) of the 1973-1990 military government.

The sharp, conical hill of ★ **Cerro San Cristóbal**, to the northeast of the city, forms the **Parque Metropolitano** ① *www.parquemet.cl, daily 0900-2000, the main entrance is at Plaza Caupolicán at the northern end of C Pío Nono in Bellavista (US$4.50 to go up in taxi)*, from where there is a **funicular** ① *Tue-Sun 1000-2000, Mon 1300-2000, US$3 return (US$3.80 on weekends)*; on the way up only you can get out at the zoo (*Tue-Sun 1000-1800, in summer 1000-1700 in winter, US$4.50 adults, discounts for children*) half way up, runs to near the summit.

Further east is an entrance from Pedro de Valdivia Norte, from where a *teleférico* used to run (no longer). Taxi-*colectivos* run to the summit and, in summer, to the

5 Las Vacas Gordas
6 Los Buenos Muchachos
7 Los Chinos Ricos
8 Majestic
9 Ostras Azócar

swimming pools; to get to Tupahue on foot from Pedro de Valdivia metro station is about 1 km. Vehicles have to pay to enter. It is the largest and most interesting of the city's parks. Souvenirs and snacks are sold at the top of the funicular. On the summit (300 m) stands a colossal statue of the Virgin, which is floodlit at night; beside it is the astronomical observatory of the Catholic University which can be visited on application to the observatory's director. Further east in the **Tupahue** sector there are terraces, gardens and paths; nearby is the **Casa de la Cultura Anahuac** which has art exhibitions and free concerts at midday on Sunday. There are two good swimming **pools** at Tupahue and Antilén. East of Tupahue are the **Botanical Gardens** ① *daily 0900-2000 in summer (0900-1900), guided tours available*, with a collection of Chilean native plants.

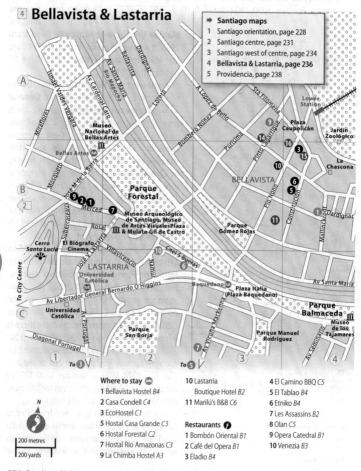

## 4 Bellavista & Lastarria

➡ **Santiago maps**
1 Santiago orientation, page 228
2 Santiago centre, page 231
3 Santiago west of centre, page 234
4 **Bellavista & Lastarria, page 236**
5 Providencia, page 238

**Where to stay** 🛏
1 Bellavista Hostel *B4*
2 Casa Condell *C4*
3 EcoHostel *C1*
4 EcoHostel *C1*
5 Hostal Casa Grande *C3*
6 Hostal Forestal *C2*
7 Hostal Río Amazonas *C3*
9 La Chimba Hostel *A3*
10 Lastarria
   Boutique Hotel *B2*
11 Marilú's B&B *C6*

**Restaurants** 🍴
1 Bombón Oriental *B1*
2 Café del Opera *B1*
3 Eladio *B4*
4 El Camino BBQ *C5*
5 El Tablao *B4*
6 Etniko *B4*
7 Les Assassins *B2*
8 Olan *C5*
9 Opera Catedral *B1*
10 Venezia *B3*

200 metres
200 yards

## East of the centre: Providencia and Las Condes

East of Plaza Italia, the main east–west axis of the city becomes **Avenida Providencia**, residential areas in the eastern and upper areas of the city. Just beyond the centre it skirts **Parque Balmaceda** (Parque Gran Bretaña), perhaps the most beautiful in Santiago. The park is home to the **Museo de los Tajamares** ① *Av Providencia 222 (closed in 2016)*, an exhibition of the 17th- and 18th-century walls and subsequent canalization developed to protect the city from flooding.

> **Tip...**
> In the El Bosque Norte area in Las Condes are lots of good, mid-range and expensive restaurants.

Providencia is a modern area of shops, offices, bars and restaurants around Pedro de Valdivia and Los Leones metro stations. At Metro Tobalaba Avenida Providencia becomes **Avenida Apoquindo**.

Northeast is the residential **Las Condes** and two worthwhile museums. **Museo Ralli** ① *Sotomayor 4110, Vitacura, T2-2206 4224, www.museoralli.cl, Tue-Sun 1030-1700, Jan weekends only, closed Feb, free*, has an excellent collection of works by modern European and Latin American artists, including Dali, Chagall, Bacon and Miró. **Museo de la Moda** ① *Vitacura 4562, Metro Escuela Militar, T2-2219 3623, www.museodelamoda.cl, closed for remodelling in 2016, El Garage café Mon-Fri 0900-1900*, is a fashion museum.

## South of the city

Southeast of the centre, in La Florida district, is the excellent **Museo Interactivo Mirador** (MIM) ① *Punta Arenas 6711, Mirador Metro (Line 5), T2-2828 8000, www.mim.cl, Tue-Sun 0930-1830, US\$5.50, discounts for children and senior citizens*, a fun, interactive science and technology museum, perfect for a family outing. There is also an **aquarium** in the grounds.

A memorial to the troubled Pinochet era is in the southeastern suburb of Peñalolén, the **Parque por la Paz** ① *Av Arrieta 8401, www.villagrimaldi.cl; from Tobalaba Metro take any bus marked Peñalolén heading south down Tobalaba, get off at Tobalaba y José Arrieta and catch a bus, or walk 15-20 mins, up Arrieta towards the mountains.* It stands on the site of **Villa Grimaldi**,

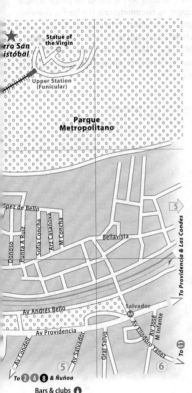

**Bars & clubs** 🎵
11 Patio Bellavista with
   Backstage Life,
   La Casa en el Aire
   & many more *B4*
14 Jammin' Club *A3*
15 La Bodeguita de Julio *B4*
16 La Otra Puerta *B3*

the most notorious torture centre. Audio guides are available in English (leave your passport at reception). The Irish missionary Sheila Cassidy documented the abuses that she underwent when imprisoned without trial in this place. The walls are daubed with human rights graffiti and the park makes for a moving and unusual introduction to the conflict that has eaten away at the heart of Chilean society for over 30 years.

The suburb of Maipú, 10 km southwest of Santiago, is a 45-minute bus ride from the Alameda, also reached from Plaza de Maipú metro station (Línea 5). Here, a monument marks the site of the Battle of the Maipú, 5 April 1818, which resulted in the final defeat of the Spanish royalist forces in mainland Chile. Nearby is the monolithic **National Votive Temple of Maipú** ① *Tue-Sun 1000-1800*. This is a fine example of modern architecture and stained glass (best viewed from the inside). It is located on the site of an earlier temple, built in 1818 on the orders of Bernardo O'Higgins to commemorate the battle. The walls of the old construction stand in the forecourt, having fallen into ruin due to successive earthquakes. Pope John Paul II gave a mass here on his visit to Chile in 1987. The **Museo del Carmen** ① *T2-2531 7967, Tue-Fri 1000-1400, 1500-1800 (last entrance at 1730), www.museodelcarmen.cl, US$0.75*, is part of the same building and contains carriages, furniture, clothing and other items from colonial times and later.

**5 Providencia**

| Where to stay | 4 Grand Hyatt Santiago | Restaurants |
|---|---|---|
| 1 Apart Hotel Santa Magdalena | 5 Orly | 1 A Pinch of Pancho |
| 2 Atton | 6 Sheraton Santiago | 2 Baco |
| 3 Chilhotel | 7 Vilafranca Petit Hotel | 4 Coppelia |
| | | 5 El Árbol |

300 metres
300 yards

## Tourist information

**Municipal Tourist Board**
*North side of Plaza de Armas, T2-2713 6744.*
*Mon-Fri 0900-1800, Sat-Sun 1000-1600.*
Also at Terminal Santiago (Tue-Fri, 0700-2200, Sat, Mon 0900-2000, Sun 0900-1900) and at Cerro Santa Lucía, T2-2386 7186, www.ciudad.cl (Mon-Thu 0900-1800, Fri 1000-1700). Offers free walking tours most days of the week.

**Servicio Nacional de Turismo Sernatur**
*Av Providencia 1550, between metro Manuel Montt and metro Pedro de Valdivia, T2-2731 8310, info@sernatur.cl. Mon-Fri*
*0900-1900, Sat 0900-1400 in summer (until 1800 in winter).*
Maps, brochures. Good noticeboard and free Wi-Fi. Information office also at the airport, daily 0900-1900, T2-2601 8320.

## Where to stay

Accommodation in Santiago is generally about 20% more expensive than elsewhere in the country. Check if breakfast is included in the price quoted. Most 3-, 4- and 5-star hotels do not charge the 19% tax to foreigners who pay in US$ cash. Hostels have double rooms with private or shared bath, **$$**, and dorms for US$12-18pp, **$**.

If you are staying for weeks or months rather than days, serviced apartments are available. Staying with a family is also an economical and interesting option. For private rentals, see the classified ads in *El Mercurio (http://impresa.elmercurio.com)* – where flats, homes and family *pensiones* are listed by district – or in www.elRastro.cl, or try the noticeboard at the tourist office. Rates for 2-bed furnished apartments in a reasonable neighbourhood start at around US$375 per month. A month's rent and a month's deposit are normally required. Some offer daily and weekly lets. Estate agents handle apartments.

### Santiago centre

**$$$$-$$$ Fundador**
*Paseo Serrano 34, T2-2387 1200, www.hotelfundador.cl.*
Helpful, charming, stylish, good location, pool, spa, bar, restaurant.

**$$$$-$$$ Galerías**
*San Antonio 65, T2-2470 7400, www.hotelgalerias.cl.*
Excellent, large rooms, generous breakfast, good location, welcoming.

**$$$-$$ París-Londres**
*Londres 54, T2-2638 2215, www.londres.cl.*

6 El Huerto
7 Oriental

1920s mansion with original features in perfect location near San Francisco church, pleasant common rooms, laundry service, usually full, advance bookings in high season.

### $$$-$ Andes Hostel
*Monjitas 506, T2-2632 9990,*
*www.andeshostel.com.*
In Bellas Artes neighbourhood, dorms, rooms or apartments, bar downstairs with pool table, barbecue nights on roof terrace, well run.

### $$$-$ Casaltura
*San Antonio 811, T2-2633 5076,*
*www.casaltura.com.*
'Boutique hostel', up a long wooden staircase in a renovated house, roof terrace, comfortable and convenient, private rooms and dorms, attentive staff.

### $$ París
*París 813, T2-2664 0921,*
*www.hotelparis813.com.*
Great location, good meeting place, 3 standards of room, breakfast extra, Wi-Fi available in some parts. Phone in advance in summer.

## Plaza Italia, Lastarria and around

### $$$$ Lastarria Boutique Hotel
*Cnel Santiago Bueras 188, T2-2840 3700,*
*www.lastarriahotel.com.*
In a converted 1927 building, beautifully decorated, spacious rooms, with personalized service. Lounge for breakfast and light meals, cocktails and wines, garden, swimming pool.

### $$$ Hostal Río Amazonas
*Plaza Italia, Vicuña Mackenna 47, T2-2635 1631, www.hostalrioamazonas.cl.*
In a restored mansion, good value, helpful, lots of information, parking.

### $$$-$$ Hostal Casa Grande
*Vicuña MacKenna 90, T2-2222 7347,*
*Baquedano metro, www.hostalcasagrande.cl.*
Labyrinthine, old high-ceilinged building, colourful, pleasant patio garden, quiet.

### $$ EcoHostel
*Gral Jofré 349B, T2-2222 6833,*
*www.ecohostel.cl.*
Popular with groups, comfortable beds, well run, smoking patio, tours arranged.

### $$-$ Hostal Forestal
*Cnel Santiago Bueras 120, T2-2638 1347,*
*www.hostalforestal.cl.*
On a quiet side street near the Plaza Italia. Comfy lounge with big screen TV, barbecue area, pool table, information, English spoken.

## West of the centre

### $$$ Conde de Ansúrez
*Av República 25, T2-2696 0807,*
*República metro, www.ansurez.cl.*
Convenient for airport bus, central station and bus terminals, helpful, safe.

### $$$ Tur Hotel Express
*O'Higgins 3750, p 3, in the Turbus Terminal, T2-2685 0100, www.turbus.cl (found under the 'turismo' heading).*
Comfortable business standard. Useful if you need to take an early flight as buses leave for the airport from here. There is an Ibis hotel here, too.

### $$ Residencial Mery
*Pasaje República 36, off 0-100 block of República, T2-2699 4982,*
*www.residencialmery.cl.*
Big green art deco building down an alley, most rooms without bath, all with single beds, quiet, breakfast extra.

### $$-$ Happy House Hostel
*Moneda 1829, Barrio Brasil, T2-2688 4849,*
*www.happyhousehostel.cl.*
In a restored mansion with all mod cons. One of the best hostels in the city, spacious kitchen and common areas, pool table, bar, spa, free tea and real coffee all day, book exchange, English and French spoken, lots of information.

### $$-$ Hostal de Sammy
*Toesca 2335, T2-2689 8772,*
*www.hostaldesammy.com.*

Good-value US-run hostel with decent common areas, table tennis, pool table, big-screen TV with lots of films. Good info, helpful.

## $$-$ La Casa Roja
*Agustinas 2113, Barrio Brasil, T2-2695 0600, www.lacasaroja.cl.*
Huge, renovated mansion, dorms and private rooms, no breakfast, pool party on Sat, guests can be chef for the night, live music, 2 bars, cricket net, lots of activities and tours, Spanish classes, lively. Shares services with **The Princesa Insolente**, below.

## $$-$ Moai Hostel
*Toesca 2335, T2-2689 0977, www.moaiviajerohostel.cl.*
Airport transfer, book exchange, film library, Spanish classes arranged, gay-friendly, popular. 5 blocks from República metro.

## $ The Princesa Insolente
*Moneda 2350, T2-2671 6551, www.princesainsolentehostel.cl.*
4, 6, 8, 11-bed dorms and 3 private rooms ($$) and 2 apartments across the street ($$$), organic café, mountain bike rental, travel information, maps, activities almost every night, great courtyard and bar, and a good meeting place. Breakfast is only included in private rooms. It might have the most comfortable dorm beds in the entire country. Also has hostels in Pichilemu and Pucón. Highly recommended.

## Bellavista and Cerro San Cristóbal

## $$-$ Bellavista Hostel
*Dardignac 0184, T2-2899 7145, www.bellavista.hostel.com.*
European-style, sheets provided but make your own bed, good fun hostel in the heart of this lively area. Guests over 35 not allowed in dorms, only private rooms.

## $$-$ pp La Chimba Hostel
*Ernesto Pinto Lagarrigue 262, Bellavista, T2-2732 9184, www.lachimba.com.*
Popular backpacker hostel near the action. Clean, good facilities: multiple kitchens, TVs, barbecue area, pool table, great showers, etc, with many dorms and expansive doubles and triples. Friendly staff and super-fast Wi-Fi. Over 35s not allowed in dorms. Recommended for exuberant youth.

## East of the centre

## $$ Marilú's Bed and Breakfast
*Rafael Cañas 246 piso 1, T2-2235 5302, www.bedandbreakfast.cl.*
Comfortable, quiet, convenient, some rooms with shared bath with 1 other room, good beds, English and French spoken, secure, very helpful and welcoming, lots of information. Recommended.

## $$-$ Casa Condell
*Condell 114, T2-2209 2343, Salvador metro.*
Pleasant old house, central, quiet, nice roof terrace, free local phone calls, English spoken, good but baths shared between rooms can be a problem. Breakfast included.

## Providencia and Las Condes
For longer-stay accommodation, contact **Santa Magdalena Apartments** (Helvecia 240 L3, Las Condes, T2-2374 6875, www.santamagdalena.cl), which has well-serviced apartments.

## $$$$ Grand Hyatt Santiago
*Av Kennedy 4601, Las Condes, T2-2950 1234, www.santiago.grand.hyatt.com.*
Superb, beautifully decorated, large outdoor pool, gym, 3 restaurants.

## $$$$ Sheraton Santiago
*Santa María 1742, T2-2233 5000, www.sheraton.cl.*
One of the best, good restaurant, good buffet lunch with international offerings, and all facilities.

## $$$$-$$$ Atton
*Alonso de Córdova 5199, Las Condes, T2-2422 7900, www.atton.cl.*
Comfortable, very helpful, full disabled access. Has multiple other branches.

### $$$ Orly
*Pedro de Valdivia 027, Metro Pedro de Valdivia, T2-2630 3000, www.orlyhotel.com.*
Small, comfortable, convenient, **Cafetto** café attached with good-value meals.

### $$$ Vilafranca Petit Hotel
*Pérez Valenzuela 1650, T2-2235 1413, www.vilafranca.cl.*
Metro Manuel Montt. High-end B&B, small but impeccable rooms, quiet, cosy, pleasant garden, English spoken.

### $$$-$$ Chilhotel
*Cirujano Guzmán 103, T2-2264 0643, www.chilhotel.cl.*
Metro Manuel Montt. Small, comfortable, family-run, airport transfer.

## Restaurants

For good seafood restaurants go to the Mercado Central (by Cal y Canto Metro, lunches only, including Donde Augusto, www.dondeaugusto.cl, El Galeón, www.elgaleon.cl, and others; www.mercadocentral.cl), or the Vega Central market (www.lavegacentral.com) on the opposite bank of the Mapocho, or Av Cumming and C Reyes in Barrio Brasil. It is difficult to eat cheaply in the evening apart from fast food, so if you're on a tight budget, make the lunchtime *almuerzo* your main meal.

### Santiago centre

#### $$$-$$ Los Adobes del Argomedo
*Argomedo 411 y Lira, 10 blocks south of the Alameda, T2-2222 2104, www.losadobesdeargomedo.cl.*
Long-established traditional restaurant. Good Chilean food, floor show (Tue-Sat) includes *cueca* dancing, salsa and folk.

#### $$$-$$ Lung Fung
*Agustinas 715 (downstairs), www.lungfung.cl.*
Delicious oriental food, the oldest Chinese restaurant in Santiago.

#### $$ Faisán d'Or
*Plaza de Armas.*
Good *pastel de choclo*, pleasant place to watch the world go by.

#### $ Bar Nacional No 2
*Bandera 317.*
Popular, local specialities, big portions; also at **Huérfanos 1151** (No 1) and at **Matías Cousiño** (No 3, www.barnacional3.cl).

#### $ El Naturista
*Moneda 846 and Huérfanos 1046, www.elnaturista.cl. Closes 2100 during the week.*
Excellent vegetarian, "healthy portions", wide-ranging menu, as well as juices, beer and wine.

### $ El Rápido
*Bandera 347, next to Bar Nacional No 2.*
Specializes in *empanadas* and *completos.*
Good food.

## Cafés

### Café Caribe and Café Haití
*Both on Paseo Ahumada and elsewhere in*
*centre and Providencia, www.cafecaribe.cl*
*and www.cafehaiti.cl.*
Good coffee, institutions for the Santiago
business community.

### Café Colonia
*Mac Iver 133 and 161, www.cafecolonia.cl.*
Splendid variety of cakes, pastries and pies,
fashionable and pricey.

---

### Plaza Italia, Lastarria and around
On C Lastarria are many smart eateries,
several in the precinct at Lastarria 70: also
**Sur Patagónico**, **Don Victorino**, **El Bocanaris**
(www.bocanariz.cl), **El Observatorio** and
**Zabo** (www.zabo.cl). **El Biógrafo** (www.
elbiografo.cl) cinema also has a café with
excruciatingly slow service.

### $$$ Les Assassins
*Merced 297, T2-2638 4280, see Facebook.*
Good French cuisine in small, family-run
bistro, with decent wine list; good-value
set lunches.

### $$$-$$ El Camino BBQ
*Italia 1034, T2-2986 0765,*
*www.elcaminobbq.com.*
The owner spent time in Texas learning
the finer points of American barbecue.
The effort is seen and felt in the top-notch
ribs and brisket as well as the general
ambience, which features communal
patio dining and giant beers.

### $$-$ Bombón Oriental
*Merced 353, Lastarria, T2-2639 1069.*
Serves Middle Eastern food, Turkish
coffee, Arabic snacks and sweets.

## West of the centre

### $$$-$$ Las Vacas Gordas
*Cienfuegos 280, Barrio Brasil, T2-2697 1066,*
*see Facebook.*
Good-value grilled steaks, nice wine
selection. Very popular, so book in advance.

### $$$-$$ Majestic
*Santo Domingo 1526, T2-2694 9400,*
*www.majestic.cl.*
In hotel of same name ($$$, www.hotel
majestic.cl). Excellent Indian restaurant,
with a good range of vegetarian dishes.

### $$ Club Santiago
*Erasmo Escala 2120, www.clubsantiago.cl.*
*Open until 0300 on weekends, happy hour*
*1700-2200.*
Historic restaurant/bar in Concha y Toro
district, lunches, snacks, cocktails.

### $$ El Hoyo
*San Vicente 375, T2-2689 0339. Closed Sun.*
Celebrated 100-year-old *chichería* serving
hearty Chilean fare.

### $$ Fuente Mardoqueo
*Libertad 551, www.fuentemardoqueo.cl.*
*Daily 1200-2300.*
Simply sandwiches, with a limited choice
of fillings, and beer, a wide range, popular.

### $$ Los Buenos Muchachos
*Cumming 1031, T2-2566 4660,*
*www.losbuenosmuchachos.cl.*
'Cavernous hall seating over 400 serving
plentiful traditional Chilean food, traditional
Chilean dance shows at night. Very popular.

### $$ Los Chinos Ricos
*Brasil 373, www.loschinosricos.com. Open*
*until 2300 during the week (0100 Fri-Sat).*
Good Chinese, popular with families on
Sun lunchtime.

### $$ Ostras Azócar
*Gral Bulnes 37, www.ostrasazocar.cl.*
Good prices for oysters. Other seafood
places in same street.

## $ Confitería Torres
*Alameda 1570, www.confiteriatorres.cl.*
Traditional bar/restaurant, good ambience, live music Fri-Sat.

---

## Bellavista and Cerro San Cristóbal
Bellavista is full of restaurants, cafés and bars, particularly C Dardignac and Patio Bellavista, the block between Dardignac, Pío Nono, Bellavista and Constitución.

### $$$-$$ Etniko
*Constitución 172, Bellavista, T2-2732 0119, www.etniko.cl.*
Fusion restaurant with oriental influences and seafood, also tapas bar/*cevichería* and dance floor under transparent roof for night sky, live DJs at weekends.

### $$$-$$ Opera Catedral
*Jose Miguel de la Barra 407, T2-2664 3038, www.operacatedral.cl. Bellas Artes metro.*
Very good, if expensive, French restaurant on the ground floor. Upstairs is a minimalist pub-restaurant, usually packed at night, serving fusion food at reasonable prices.

### $$ Eladio
*Pío Nono 251, www.eladio.cl.*
Good steaks, Argentine cuisine, excellent value. Also has locations in Providencia and Plaza Vespucio.

### $$ El Tablao
*Constitución 110, T2-2737 8648, see Facebook.*
Traditional Spanish restaurant. The food is reasonable but the main attraction is the live flamenco show on Fri-Sat nights.

### $$ Venezia
*Pío Nono, corner of López de Bello.*
Huge servings of traditional Chilean home-cooked fare (allegedly one of Neruda's favourite haunts), good value.

### $$-$ Olan
*Condell 200, www.restaurantolan.com.*
Excellent value, tasty Peruvian food in unpretentious surroundings.

## Cafés

### Café del Opera
*Merced 391.*
For breakfasts, sandwiches, salads, ice creams and breads.

## Providencia

### $$$-$$ A Pinch of Pancho
*Gral del Canto 45, T2-2235 1700.*
Very good fish and seafood on a wide-ranging menu.

### $$$-$$ Baco
*Nueva de Lyon 113, T2-231 4444. Metro Los Leones.*
Sophisticated French restaurant, good food, extensive wine list with many quality wines available by the glass.

### $$$-$$ Oriental
*Holanda 1927, www.restaurantoriental.cl.*
Excellent Chinese, one of the best in Santiago. Also at Av Ossa 1881.

### $$ El Huerto
*Orrego Luco 054, T2-2233 2690, www.elhuerto.cl. Daily.*
Vegetarian, varied menu, very good.

### $$-$ El Arbol
*Huelén 74, T2-2235 0822.*
Vegetarian and vegan café. Cheese used in vegan dishes is made from coconut oil. Also cocktails and snacks.

## Cafés
For snacks and ice cream there are several good places on Av Providencia including **Coppellia**, No 2111 (www.coppelia.cl) and **Bravissimo**, No 1406 (www.bravissimo.cl). There are lots of cafés and some restaurants in the passageways at Metro Los Leones and in the streets nearby, including **Café di Roma**, **The Coffee Factory**, **Sebastián** (Fuenzalida 26 www.heladeriasebastian.cl), and **Tavelli** (Fuenzalida 36, www.tavelli.cl).

## Las Condes

This area has many first-class restaurants, including grills, serving Chilean (often with music), French and Chinese cuisine. They tend to be more expensive than central restaurants. Many are located on El Bosque Norte, near Tobalaba metro stop.

### $$$-$$ Miguel Torres
*Isidora Goyenechea 2874, T2-2245 7332, www.migueltorres.cl.*
Tapas bar owned by the well-known Spanish winery.

### $$$-$$ Puerto Marisko
*Isidora Goyenechea 2918, T2-2233 2096, www.restaurantmariscos.cl.*
Renowned for seafood but also serves pasta and meat dishes, over 20 years of experience.

## Bars and clubs

For all entertainments, nightclubs, cinemas, theatres, restaurants, concerts, El Mercurio Online website has all listings and a good search feature, www.emol.com. Listings in weekend newspapers, particularly *El Mercurio* and *La Tercera*. For an organized night out, contact Santiago Pub Crawl, T9-8299 4086, www.facebook.com/pubcrawlsantiagochile, US$15, every Fri and Sat.

### Santiago centre

**La Piojera**
*Aillavilú 1030, T2-2698 1682, www.lapiojera.cl. Metro Cal y Canto.*
A Santiago institution long held to be the birthplace of the famous *terremoto* cocktail (although local *taxistas* dispute this claim). This is a seedy dive bar in a seedy area, appropriate only for those looking to have a rollicking good time. It's got a nice mix of locals and backpackers, plus a menu of hearty Chilean fare like *pernil* (leg of pork) to help line the stomach. Take a taxi when leaving.

### West of the centre

There are a number of bars and restaurants dotted around the Plaza Brasil and on Av Brasil and Av Cumming, popular with Chilean students (Metro República).

### Bellavista

Bellavista has a good selection of varied restaurants, bars and clubs (Metro Baquedano).

**Backstage Life**
*Patio Bellavista.*
Good-quality live jazz and blues.

**Jammin' Club**
*Antonia López de Bello 49, www.facebook.com/pages/Jamming-Club.*
Reggae.

**La Bodeguita de Julio**
*Constitución 256, see Facebook.*
Cuban staff and Cuban cocktails, excellent live music and dancing possible, very popular, excellent value.

**La Casa en el Aire**
*Patio Bellavista, www.lacasaenelaire.cl.*
Pleasant atmosphere, live music.

**La Otra Puerta**
*Pío Nono 348, www.laotrapuerta.cl.*
Lively salsoteca with live music.

### East of the centre

The 1st couple of blocks of Román Díaz (between metros Salvador and Manuel Montt) have a collection of bars and eateries, eg **Kleine Kneipe** (No 21, also in Ñuñoa, www.kleinekneipe.cl), and **Santo Remedio** (No 152, www.santoremedio.cl). In Providencia, Av Suecia and Av Gral Holley are popular and largely pedestrianized. From Av Providencia, Condell leads to the middle-class suburb of Ñuñoa, 18 blocks, passing various small bars and restaurants on the way, eg at junctions with Rancagua and Santa Isabel, or take metro to Irrarrázaval. Plaza Ñuñoa itself has a number of good bars. There are also many smart places in Las Condes.

**Ilé Habana**
*Bucarest 95, www.ilehabana.cl.*
Bar with salsa music, often live, and a good dance floor.

## What to do

### Language schools

**Bellavista**, *C del Arzobispado 0605, Providencia, T2-2732 3443, www.escuela bellavista.cl*. Group and individual classes, lodging with families, free activities.

**Escuela de Idiomas Violeta Parra**, *Triana 853, Providencia, T2-2236 4241, www.tandem santiago.cl*. Courses aimed at budget travellers, information programme on social issues, arranges accommodation and visits to local organizations and national parks.

**Instituto Norteamericano Santiago**, *Moneda 1467, T2-2677 7155, www.norteamericano.cl*. Institute run through the US embassy with many branches. One of the best options.

**Isabel Correa**, *T9-6360 3533, internationalenglish2000@yahoo.com*. Highly recommended. Teaches Spanish, French and English. Also does translations in 3 languages and offers walking tours/lessons in the city.

### Skiing and climbing

**Club Alemán Andino**, *El Arrayán 2735, T2-2232 4338, www.dav.cl*. Mon-Fri until 1900.

**Club Andino de Chile**, *Av Lib O'Higgins 108, clubandino@skilagunillas.cl*.

**Federación de Andinismo de Chile**, *Almte Simpson 77, T2-2222 0888, www.feach.cl*. Daily (frequently closed Jan/Feb). Has the addresses of all the mountaineering clubs in the country and runs a mountaineering school.

### Tour operators

A number of agencies offer walking tours of the city. Many agencies advertise in the **Sernatur** tourist office (see Tourist information, page 239).

**Adventure tours** **Altue**, *Coyancura 2270, Of 801, Providencia, T2-2333 1390, www.altue. com*. For wilderness trips including tour of Patagonia.

**Azimut 360**, *Gral Salvo 159, Providencia, T2-2235 3085, www.azimut360.com*. Adventure and ecotourism including mountaineering.

**Cascada Expediciones**, *Don Carlos 3227C, Las Condes, T2-2923 5950, www.cascada.travel*. Activity tours in remote areas.

**Chile Excepción**, *T2-2951 5476, www.chile-excepcion.com*. French/Argentine agency offering tailor-made, upper-end tours, fly-drives, themed trips and other services.

**Chile Off Track**, *T9 9783 5904, www.chile offtrack.com*. Customized and tailor-made tours around Santiago and in Patagonia, 6 languages spoken, features include horse riding, mountain excursions, wine tours, visits to hot springs.

**Travel Art**, *Europa 2081, T2-2437 5660, www.chile-reise.com*. Biking, hiking and multi-active tours throughout Chile. German-run.

**Upscape**, *T2-2244 2750, www.upscapetravel. com*. US-run, offering adventure day tours, wine tours, city tours, skiing and Patagonia.

**City tours** **La Bicicleta Verde**, *Loreto 6 esq Santa María, T2-2570 9338, www. labicicletaverde.com*. Sightseeing tours around the capital and of vineyards by bike. Also rents bicycles.

**Spicy Chile**, *www.spicychile.cl*. 3 walking tours of the city, Mon-Sat, pay by tip, good reputation.

**Tours4Tips**, *T2-2570 8986, www.tours4tips. com*. 2 daily walking tours, pay by tip, also in Valparaíso, popular.

**Turistik**, *T2-2820 1000, www.turistik.cl*. Hop-on, hop-off bus tours of the city, US$29, also offers tours outside the city and tour, dinner and show.

## Transport

### Air

International and domestic flights leave from **Arturo Merino Benítez Airport** at Pudahuel, 26 km northwest of Santiago, T2-2690 1752, www.nuevopudahel.cl. The terminal has most facilities, including Afex *cambio*, ATMs, tourist offices that will book accommodation and a fast food plaza. Left luggage costs US$9 per bag per day.

Frequent bus services between the international and domestic terminals and the city centre are operated by 2 companies: **TurBus** (T2-2822 7500, www.turbus.cl, to/from Terminal Alameda (metro Universidad de Santiago, Line 1), every 30 mins 0615-2300, US$2.50) and **Centropuerto** (T2-2601 9883, www.centropuerto.cl to/from metro Los Héroes, every 15 mins 0640-2330, US$2.25). En route the buses stop at Pajaritos metro station (from 0500), **Estación Central Terminal Santiago** and most other regular bus stops. From the airport you could take Tur-Bus to Pajaritos, US$2.50, and take the metro from there.

Minibus services between the airport and hotels or other addresses in the city are operated by several companies with offices in the airport. These include **Delfos** (T2-2913 8800, www.transferdelfos.cl) and **Transvip** (T2-2677 3000, www.transvip.cl). They charge US$10-12 for a shared vehicle or US$30-40 for exclusive use, depending on the zone. Otherwise, transfers to the airport should be booked a day ahead.

Many hotels also run a transfer service. **Taxi** drivers offer rides to the city outside Arrivals, but the official taxi service (T2-2601 9880, www.taxioficial.cl) is more reliable, if a little more expensive: US$20 to Pajaritos or **Quinta Normal**, US$25 to the centre, US$30-35 to **Providencia**, up to US$35 to Las Condes.

For flight information, see Practicalities, page 477.

## Bus
**Local** The city is divided into 10 zones lettered A to J. Within each zone, buses (known as *micros*) are the same colour as that given to the zone (eg white for zone A: central Santiago). Zones are linked by trunk lines, run by white *micros* with a green stripe. The system integrates with the metro. Buses display the number and direction of the route within the system. Payment is by prepaid *Bip* card only. A card costs US$2.25, to which you add however much you want to pay in advance. They are most conveniently bought at metro stations. For a day or so it's probably not worth investing in

a *Bip* card (just use the metro), but for a few days it's good value. Long-term visitors can buy personalized cards, to prevent theft, etc.

*Colectivo* routes are displayed with route numbers. Fares vary, depending on the length of the journey, but are usually between US$1.50-2.50 (higher fares at night).

**Long distance** There are frequent, and good, interurban buses to all parts of Chile. Take a look at the buses before buying the tickets (there are big differences in quality among bus companies); ask about the onboard services, many companies offer drinks for sale, or free, and luxury buses have meals, videos, headphones. Reclining seats are standard and there are also *salón-cama* sleeper buses. Fares are given in the text. On Fri evening, when night departures are getting ready to go, the terminals can be chaotic. There are 5 bus terminals:

**1. Terminal Alameda**, which has a modern extension called Mall Parque Estación with good left luggage (0600-0000) US$2.50-4.50 per day), ATMs and internet, O'Higgins 3712, Metro Universidad de Santiago, T2-2776 2424. All **Pullman-Bus** and **Tur-Bus** services go from here, they serve almost every destination in Chile, good quality but prices a little higher than others. **Tur-Bus** also has booking offices at Universidad de Chile and Tobalaba metro stations, at Cal y Canto, at Av Apoquindo 6421, T2-2212 6435, and in the Parque Arauco and Alto Las Condes malls for those beginning their journeys in Las Condes.

**2. Terminal Santiago**, O'Higgins 3850, 1 block west of Terminal Alameda, T2-2376 1750, www.terminaldebusessantiago.cl, Metro Universidad de Santiago. Services to all parts of southern Chile, including a service to **Punta Arenas** (48 hrs). Also international departures. Has a Redbanc ATM.

**3. Terminal San Borja**, O'Higgins y San Borja, 1 block west of Estación Central, Metro Estación Central, T2-2776 0645. Departures to the Central Valley area and **northern Chile**.

**4**. **Terminal Los Héroes**, on Tucapel Jiménez, just north of the Alameda, Metro Los Héroes, T2-2420 0099. A smaller terminal with booking offices of companies, to the north, the south and Lake District and some international services including Buenos Aires and Bariloche.

**5**. **Metro Pajaritos** (Metro Línea 1), to the central coast.

**International buses** Most services leave from **Terminal Santiago**, though there are also departures from **Terminal Los Héroes**. There are frequent bus and minibus services from **Terminal Santiago** through the Cristo Redentor tunnel to **Mendoza** in Argentina, 6-7 hrs, US$35-47, many companies, departures start around 0745, with a last departure around 2200, touts approach you in Terminal Santiago. Minibuses have a shorter waiting time at customs. Many of these services continue to **Buenos Aires**, 24 hrs, and many companies in Terminal Santiago have connections to other Argentine cities. For destinations like **Bariloche** or **Neuquén**, it is better make connections in Temuco or Osorno.

**Car hire**
Prices vary a lot so shop around first. Tax of 19% is charged, usually included in price quoted. If possible book a car in advance. Information boards full of flyers from companies at airport and tourist office. A credit card is usually asked for when renting a vehicle. Many companies will not hire a car to holders of a driver's licence from a left-hand drive country unless they have an international licence.

Remember that in the capital driving is restricted according to licence plate numbers; look for notices in the street and newspapers. Main international agencies and others are available at the airport. **Automóvil Club de Chile**, www.automovil club.cl, car rental from head office, discount for members and members of associated motoring organizations. **Alameda**,

Av Bernardo O'Higgins 4709, T2-2779 0609, www.alamedarentacar.cl, San Alberto Hurtado metro, Line 1, also in the airport, good value. **Rosselot**, call centre T600 582 9988, www.rosselot.cl. Reputable Chilean firm with national coverage. **Verschae**, T600 5000 700, www.verschae.com. Good value, branches throughout country.

**Ferry and cruise operators**
**Navimag**, Naviera Magallanes SA, www. navimag.com. For services from **Puerto Montt** to **Puerto Chacabuco**, **Puerto Natales** and **Laguna San Rafael**. Reserve online. **M/n Skorpios**, Augusto Leguía Norte 118, Las Condes, T2-2477 1900, www.skorpios.cl. For luxury cruises out of **Puerto Montt** to **Laguna San Rafael** and adventure trips from Puerto Natales to Puerto Edén and the Campo Hielo del Sur.

**Metro**
See www.metrosantiago.cl. **Line 1** runs west–east between San Pablo and Los Dominicos, under the Alameda, linking the bus and train stations, the centre, Providencia and beyond; **Line 2** runs north–south from Vespucio Norte to La Cisterna; **Line 4** runs from Tobalaba on Line 1 south to Plaza de Puente Alto, with a branch (4a) from V Mackenna to La Cisterna; **Line 5** runs north, east and southeast from Plaza de Maipú via Baquedano to Vicente Valdés on Line 4.

The 1st train is at 0600 (Mon-Fri), 0630 on Sat and 0800 (Sun and holidays), the last about 2300 (2330 on Fri-Sat, 2230 on Sun). Fares vary according to time of journey; there are 3 charging periods: the peak rate is US$1.25, the general rate US$1.10 and there is a cheaper rate at unsociable hours, US$1. The simplest solution is to buy a **tarjeta Bip** (see Local buses, above), the charge card from which the appropriate fare is deducted.

**Taxi**
Taxis (black with yellow roofs) are abundant and fairly cheap: minimum charge of US$0.40, plus US$0.20 per 200 m. In every type of taxi

always double check the fare (see www.taximetro.cl). Drivers are permitted to charge more at night, but in the daytime check that the meter is set to day rates. At bus terminals, drivers will charge more – best to walk a block and flag down a cruising taxi.

Avoid taxis with more than 1 person in them especially at night. Various Radio Taxi services operate (eg **Radio Taxis Andes Pacífico**, T2-2912 6000, www.andespacifico.cl); rates are above those of city taxis but they should be more reliable.

# Chilean Lake District

snow-capped volcanoes, glacial lakes and raging rivers

Extending from the Río Biobío south to the city of Puerto Montt, the Lake District is one of the most popular destinations for both Chilean and overseas visitors.

Much of this region has been turned into national parks, and the mixture of forests, lakes and snow-capped volcanoes is sure to leave an indelible mark on the mind of any traveller.

The main cities are Temuco, Valdivia, Osorno and Puerto Montt. The cities of Temuco and Puerto Montt are the most popular; Temuco for excursions into the Mapuche communities towards the coast and Puerto Montt as the starting point for longer voyages south to Puerto Natales, Puerto Chacabuco and the San Rafael glacier, as well as east across the lakes and mountains to the Argentine resort of Bariloche.

The real gems, however, lie further east where a string of lakes stretches down the western side of the Andes. The major resorts include Pucón on Lago Villarrica and Puerto Varas on Lago Llanquihue.

Between Temuco and the Pacific coast is the indigenous heartland of Chile, home to the largest Mapuche communities. Here you will find *rucas* (traditional thatched houses) and communities still fiercely proud of their traditions, the last remnants of a forgotten country that the first *conquistadores* might have found.

**Best** for
Boating ▪ Cycling ▪ Fishing ▪ Trekking

# Footprint
## picks

★ **Temuco's Feria Pinto**,
page 254

Prepare to have your senses assaulted by stall after stall of fresh produce
and regional handicrafts.

★ **Parque Nacional Conguillío**, page 263

Discover some of the finest trekking north of Torres del Paine.

★ **Adventure tourism around Pucón**, page 270

Ski, snowboard, kayak, hydrospeed, or take a hike up to the mouth of
an active volcano.

★ **Lago Llanquihue**, page 306

Coastal hamlets, scenic drives, idyllic farmhouses and fresh-baked pies
are a just few reasons to visit this lake.

★ **The journey from Puerto Montt to Bariloche in
Argentina**, page 323

This three-lake crossing is filled with the most beautiful scenery of the
Lake District.

**Footprint**
**picks**

1 **Temuco's Feria Pinto**, page 254
2 **Parque Nacional Conguillio**, page 263
3 **Adventure tourism around Pucón**, page 270
4 **Lago Llanquihue**, page 306
5 **The journey from Puerto Montt to Bariloche in Argentina**, page 323

# Temuco
## & around

At first sight, Temuco may appear a drab, forbidding place. However, in reality it is a lively industrial and university town. For visitors, it is perhaps most interesting as a contrast to the more European cities in other parts of Chile. Temuco is proud of its Mapuche heritage, and it is this that gives it a distinctive character, especially around the *feria* (outdoor market).

North and east of the city are five national parks and reserves, and several hot springs, while to the west, in the valley of the Río Imperial, are the market towns of Nueva Imperial and Carahue and, on the coast, the resort of Puerto Saavedra.

The city is centred on the Plaza Aníbal Pinto, around which are the main public buildings including the cathedral and the Municipalidad; the original cathedral was destroyed by the 1960 earthquake, when most of the old wooden buildings in the city were also burnt down. On the plaza itself is a monument to La Araucanía featuring figures from local history. Nearby are fountains and a small Sala de Exposiciones, which stages exhibitions.

More compelling, though, is the ★ **Feria Pinto**, the huge produce market at Lautaro y Aníbal Pinto, always crammed with people (many of them Mapuche), who have come from the countryside to sell their produce (see page 258).

## Essential Temuco

### Finding your feet

**Manquehue Airport** is 6 km southwest of city. There is no public bus into the city but a transfer service is run by **Transfer Temuco**, T45-233 4033, www.transfer temuco.cl, US$7.50, book 24 hours in advance; it also goes to hotels in Villarrica and Pucón in season, US$14.50. Taxis charge US$20-25 from airport to the centre.

The long-distance terminal (Rodoviária) is north of city at Pérez Rosales y Caupolicán, and is served by city bus Nos 2, 7 or 10; *colectivo*, or taxi US$4.50. **JAC**, Balmaceda y Aldunate, T45-246 5463, www.jac.cl, has its own efficient terminal seven blocks north of the Plaza, which also serves neighbouring towns. **NarBus** and **Igi-Llaima** are opposite. See Transport, page 258.

### Getting around

Temuco is a large city. *Colectivos* and buses serve the outlying barrios. However, the centre is relatively compact, and few places are more than a 30-minute walk away.

### When to go

For a weather chart for Temuco, see page 17.

West of the centre, the **Museo de la Araucanía** ⓘ *Alemania 84, www.museo regionalaraucania.cl, Tue-Fri 0930-1730, Sat 1100-1700, Sun 1100-1400, free, take bus No 1 from the centre*, houses a well-arranged collection devoted to the history and traditions of the Mapuche nation; there's also a section on German settlement.

A couple of kilometres northeast of the centre is the **Museo Nacional Ferroviario Pablo Neruda** ⓘ *Barros Arana 565, T45-297 3940, www.museoferroviariotemuco.cl, Tue-Fri 0900-1800, Sat-Sun 1000-1800 in summer (1000-1700 in winter), US$1.50, take micro No 1 Variante, 9 Directo, 4b, taxi from centre US$4.50, the national railway museuem*. Exhibits include over 20 engines and carriages (including the former presidential carriage) dating from 1908 to 1953. The grounds contain rusting hulks and machinery, while the annex houses temporary exhibitions.

On the northern edge of the city is the **Monumento Natural Cerro Ñielol** ⓘ *T45-229 8222, daily 08300-2045, US$3*, offering views of the city and surrounding countryside. It is a good spot for a picnic. There is an excellent **visitor centre** run by CONAF and a fine collection of native plants in their natural environment, including the copihue rojo, the national flower. A tree marks the spot where peace was finally made with the Mapuche. Note that the hill has a one-way system for drivers (entry by Prat, exit by Lynch).

# BACKGROUND
## Lake District

After the Mapuche rebellion of 1598, Spanish settlement south of the Río Biobío was limited to Valdivia, although the Spanish had a right of way north from Valdivia along the coast to Concepción. At independence the only other Spanish settlement in this region was Osorno, refounded in 1796. The Chilean government did not attempt to extend its control into the Lake District until the 1840s. In 1845, all land south of the Río Rahue was declared the property of the state and destined for settlement and, in 1850, Vicente Pérez Rosales was sent to Valdivia to distribute lands to arriving European colonists.

The southern Lake District was settled from the 1850s onwards, mainly by German immigrants (see box, page 308). Further north, Chilean troops began occupying lands south of the Biobío after 1862, but the destruction of Mapuche independence did not occur until the early 1880s when Chilean forces led by Cornelio Saavedra founded a series of forts in the area including Temuco (1881), Nueva Imperial (1882), Freire (1883) and Villarrica (1883). A treaty ending Mapuche independence was signed in Temuco in 1881.

White settlement in the area was further encouraged by the arrival of the railway, which reached Temuco in 1893, reducing the journey time from Santiago to 36 hours; the line was later extended to Osorno (1902) and Puerto Montt (1912). In the 1930s the area became popular as a destination for rich Santiaguinos and foreign fishermen.

Today, agriculture is the most important sector of the local economy and the main industries are connected to the region's produce. Proof of Chile's position as a timber producer of international standing is provided by wood-chip piles and cellulose plants dotted along the coast. Fishing is particularly important in the south of the region, where farmed salmon regularly appears on restaurant menus.

Tourism is a mainstay in summer (from mid-December to mid-March), when Chileans flock to the Lake District resorts, prices are high, and it is best to book well in advance, particularly for transport. Out of season, however, many facilities are closed.

## Listings Temuco *map page 256.*

### Tourist information

See also see www.temucochile.com.

**CONAF**
*Bilbao 931, p2, T45-229 8100,
temuco.oirs@conaf.cl.*
For information on national parks.

**Sernap**
*Vicuña Mackenna 51, T45-223 8390.*
For fishing permits.

**Sernatur**
*Bulnes 590, T45-240 6214, infoaraucania@
sernatur.cl. Mon-Fri 0900-1800, Sat 1000-1400.*

Has good leaflets in English. There is also a tourist information kiosk in the municipal market, T45-297 3116, and Plaza Aníbal Pinto, T45-297 3628, daily in summer 0900-1900.

### Where to stay

Accommodation in private houses, **$**, can be arranged by the tourist office.

**$$$ Aitué**
*A Varas 1048, T45-221 2512,
www.hotelaitue.cl.*
Business standard, central, bar, English spoken, comfortable.

### \$\$\$ Bayern
*Prat 146, T45-227 6000, www.hotelbayern.cl.*
Standard 3-star. Small rooms, helpful staff,
buffet breakfast, *cafetería*/restaurant, parking.

### \$\$\$ Frontera
*Bulnes 733-726, T45-220 0400,*
*www.hotelfrontera.cl.*
Good business standard
and comfortable rooms.

### \$\$\$ Holiday Inn Express
*Av R Ortega 01800, T45-222 3300,*
*www.holidayinnexpress.cl.*
A member of the Chileanized version
of this chain, good value, gym, pool,
out of town but convenient for the bus
terminal, worth considering if driving.

### \$\$ Hostal Montt
*M Montt 637, T45-298 2488.*
Comfortable if overpriced, some rooms
with bath, parking, gym.

**$$ La Casa de Juanita**
*Carrera 735, T45-221 3203,*
*www.lacasadejuanita.co.cl.*
Private or shared bath, quiet, good
bathrooms, parking, lots of information.

**$$-$ Cabañas Pehuen Temuco**
*Recreo 209, off Av Alemania, T45-240 9804,*
*www.pehuentemuco.cl.*
Small rooms, helpful, nice atmosphere.
Also has a good-value *cabaña* sleeping 4.

**$$-$ Casa Blanca**
*Montt 1306 y Zenteno, T45-227 2677,*
*hostalcasablancatemuco@gmail.com.*
Slightly run down, but good value for rooms
with bath.

**$$-$ Hospedaje Mateluna**
*Blanco 730, T45-273 0669.*
Lovely multi-story home run by a friendly
husband and wife. Central location, comfy
beds. Good value.

**$$-$ Tante Silvia**
*Pinto Puelma 259, T45-248 4442.*
Rooms or dorms, meals available,
for students and groups.

## Restaurants

Many good restaurants around
Av Alemania and Mall Mirage, about
10 blocks west of centre. For a cheap
lunch, make for the Mercado Municipal
on Aldunate y Portales, or the rural bus
terminal, where there are countless
restaurants serving very cheap set meals.

**$$ La Caleta**
*Mercado Municipal, Aldunate y Portales,*
*T45-221 3002.*
One of the better choices in the covered
market serving fish and seafood.

**$$ La Parrilla de Miguel**
*Montt 1095, T45-227 5182.*
Good for meat, large portions, and wine;
one of the better restaurants.

**$$ Otto**
*Alemania 360.*
Popular place serving sandwiches.

**$ Los Tenedores**
*San Martín 827.*
Good-value lunch.

### Cafés

**Marriet**
*Prat 451, loc 9, www.marriet.cl.*
Excellent coffee.

## Bars and clubs

**Vikingo**
*Alemenia 160, see Facebook.*
Bar with a fun vibe, popular with locals,
live music and karaoke. Good for beer.

**XS disco**
*In Casino Dreams (www.clubxs.cl,*
*see also Entertainment, below).*
Large disco, popular, also location in Valdivia.

## Entertainment

### Music
**Dreams**, *Av Alemania 945, www.mundo*
*dreams.com.* Casino and hotel which hosts
concerts by local and international artists.

## Shopping

If you're heading to the Parque Nacional
Conguillio, buy supplies in Temuco, Curacautín
or Melipeuco, where they are much cheaper
than in the shop in the national park.

### Crafts
Best choice is in the **indoor municipal
market** (Aldunate y Portales, and in the
Agrupación de Mujeres Artesanas, Claro
Solar 1005 y Aldunate, T45-7790 3676,
wanglenzomo@gmail.com, Mon-Fri 1000-
1800), which sells many items, including
textiles made by a Mapuche weavers'
cooperative, all with traditional designs. It also
offers design classes for traditional dresses.

**Fundación Chol-Chol**, *Sector Rengalil, Camino Temuco–Nueva Imperial Km 16, T45-261 4007, www.es.cholchol.org.* This non-profit organization sells traditional Mapuche textiles, naturally dyed and hand woven by local women. Book in advance to sample some traditional, freshly made Mapuche fare.

## Market

**Feria Pinto**, *Lautaro y Aníbal Pinto. Daily.* This is one of the most fascinating markets in Chile, with people bringing excellent fruit and vegetables from the surrounding countryside, including spices, fish, grains, cheese and honey. Sells dried fruit (useful for climbing/trekking). Also many cheap bars and restaurants nearby.

## What to do

Most companies in Temuco offer tours to the **Parque Nacional Conguillio**, 1 day, US$90 (minimum 2 people) and to **Puerto Saavedra** and **Villarrica volcano**, US$120 (minimum 2 people), but unless you are in a hurry it is better and cheaper to book a tour closer to the destination. Some also offer skiing and snowboarding trips.
**Anay Tour**, *Estébanez 580, T9-8448 8633, www.anaytour.com.* Wide range of tours in the Araucania region, including Lago Budi and Conguillio and Nahuelbuta national parks.

## Transport

Temuco is the transport hub for the Lake District, and its municipal bus station serves much of the region, as well as the communities towards the coast.

### Air

**Sky** and **LAN** have flights from **Manquehue Airport**, to **Santiago**, **Concepción**, **Osorno** (LAN only), **Puerto Montt** and **Balmaceda**. For transport from the airport, see box, page 254.

### Bus

**Local** Buses to neighbouring towns leave from **Terminal Rural**, Pinto y Balmaceda, or from bus company offices nearby. To **Coñaripe**, US$5.50, 3 hrs, and **Lican Ray**, US$4.50, 2 hrs with **JAC**. To **Panguipulli**, with **Pangui Sur**, 3 hrs, US$4.50. **JAC** also runs to **Loncoche**, US$2.50, **Los Lagos**, US$6.50, **Mehuin** in summer only. To **Curacautín** via Lautaro, with **Erbuc**, US$2, 3 daily, 2½ hrs. To **Lonquimay**, with **Erbuc**, 5 daily, 3½ hrs, US$4.50. To **Contulmo**, US$5.50, and **Cañete**, US$6.50, with **Igi Llaima**.

**Long distance** The long-distance terminal (Rodoviária) is north of city at Pérez Rosales y Caupolicán. **JAC**, **NarBus** and **Igi-Llaima** services depart from Balmaceda y Aldunate, 7 blocks north of the Plaza. To **Santiago**, many overnight, 8-9 hrs, US$31-52. To **Concepción**, with **Bío Bío**, **Tur Bus**, others US$18, 4 hrs. To **Chillán**, 3½ hrs, US$13. **Cruz del Sur** run 10 buses a day to **Castro**, US$17, many daily to **Puerto Montt** US$11, 5-6 hrs. To **Valdivia**, with **JAC**, **Narbus/Igi Llaima**, Tur Bus several daily, US$7, 2½ hrs. To **Osorno**, US$7.50, 4¼ hrs. To **Villarrica** and **Pucón**, with **JAC**, many between 0705 and 2045, 1½ hrs, and 2 hrs, US$6.

**To Argentina** El Valle and **Caraza** have buses to **Zapala** and **Neuquén**, US$29, via Paso Pino Hachado. To reach **Bariloche**, change in Osorno, or **Andes Mar** has direct routes at 0730 on Thu and Sat US$40-50.

### Car hire

**Ace**, Encalada 838 (also in airport), T877-822 3872. **Automóvil Club de Chile**, San Martín 278, T45-291 0521. **Avis**, San Martin 755, T45-245 6280 (also in airport).

### Train

There are sporadic train connections to/from **Santiago** from the railway station, Av Barros Arana 791, T45-223 3416, US$35. Check times at www.trencentral.cl.

## Chol Chol

To get a flavour of the life of the Mapuche, it is well worth making a trip to this dusty, friendly country town in the heart of Mapuche country. Daily buses, laden with corn, vegetables, charcoal and animals as well as locals make the 30-km journey by paved road from Temuco across rolling countryside, with views of five volcanoes on a clear day. You will see people travelling by ox cart on the tracks nearby, as well as a few traditional round *rucas* (thatched houses). There are also several cheap bars in the town, and a small museum dedicated to Mapuche culture.

## Puerto Saavedra and around

From Temuco a paved road follows the Río Imperial 35 km west to the market town of **Nueva Imperial**, where cattle auctions are held on Mondays and Tuesdays. From here the road continues to **Carahue**, the site of the Spanish colonial city of Imperial that was destroyed by the Mapuche. It has accommodation, a market, supermarkets and shops.

The road continues to **Puerto Saavedra**, which lies behind a sandspit south of the mouth of the Río Imperial. Founded in 1897, the town was destroyed in 1960 by a *maremoto* (or tidal wave; see box, page 297). Fortunately the local population was warned of the disaster by the sight of water draining from the bay, and so few people were killed. However, the impact of the *maremoto* on folktales cannot be overestimated. A local man commented to one of the authors of this book, "We thought it was the end of the world, so we spent two months drunk on the hills until the water receded". One of Chile's most famous films, *La Frontera*, was filmed here.

After the *maremoto*, the centre of the town moved inland and its former site at **Maule**, 2 km south, became a fishing port. Just beyond Maule is a track to the incredibly narrow sandspit created by the *maremoto*. It stretches several kilometres north to the mouth of the Río Imperial, where there's a beautiful beach and uninterrupted views of the ocean. The third distinct area of Puerto Saavedra is the resort of **Boca Budi**, 4 km south, where there's an enormous beach.

From Puerto Saavedra a track leads north 3 km to a free ferry crossing over the Río Imperial to **Nehuentue**, on the north bank (there is an alternative, easier but less interesting crossing via a another bridge further upstream). From here launches may be chartered up the Río Moncul to the pleasant town of **Trovolhue**, four hours. Alternatively, there is a half-paved, half-*ripio* road north to the town of **Tirúa**, 70 km away.

## Lago Budi

The only inland saltwater lake in Chile, Lago Budi lies south of Puerto Saavedra and is visited by over 130 species of water bird, including black-necked swans. Although the lake is marked on maps as having an outlet to the sea, this is dried up for most of the year, when there is a continuous track along the expanses of sandy beach from Puerto Saavedra south to Porma and Toltén. This was the old right of way for the Spanish between Concepción and Valdivia before their final defeat of the Mapuche; wild and remote, it passes many isolated Mapuche communities.

On the east shore of Lago Budi, 40 km by road south of Carahue, is **Puerto Domínguez**, a picturesque little town famous for its fishing. On the west shore is **Isla Huapi** (also spelt Guapi), a peninsula with a Mapuche settlement of *rucas* and fine views of the lake and the Pacific. This is one of the poorest spots in Chile, but is ideal for camping. It can be reached by *balsa* (ferry) either from 10 km south of Puerto Saavedra or from Puerto Domínguez.

# BACKGROUND

## The Mapuche

The largest indigenous group in southern South America, the Mapuche take their name from the words for 'land' (*mapu*) and 'people' (*che*). They were known as Araucanians by the Spanish.

Never subdued by the Incas, the Mapuche successfully resisted Spanish attempts at conquest. At the time of the great Mapuche uprising of 1598 they numbered some 500,000, concentrated in the area between the Río Biobío and the Reloncaví estuary. After 1598, two centuries of intermittent war were punctuated by 18 peace treaties. The 1641 Treaty of Quilín recognized Mapuche autonomy south of the Río Biobío.

Although tools and equipment were privately owned, the Mapuche held land in common, abandoning it when it was exhausted by repeated use. This relatively nomadic lifestyle helps explain their ability to resist the Spanish. Learning from their enemies how to handle horses in battle, they became formidable guerrilla fighters. They pioneered the use of horses by two men, one of whom handled the animal, while the other was armed with bow and arrows. Horses also enabled the Mapuche to extend their territory to the eastern side of the Andes and the Argentine *pampas*.

The conquest of the Mapuche was made possible by the building of railways and the invention of new weapons, especially the breach-loading rifle (which had a similarly disquieting effect in Africa and Asia). The settlement of border disputes between Chile and Argentina enabled Argentine troops to occupy border crossings, while the Chileans subjugated the Mapuche.

Under the 1881 treaty, the Mapuche received 500,000 ha from the government, while 500,000 ha were kept for Chile. The Mapuche were confined to reservations, most of which were situated near large estates for which they provided a labour force. By the 1930s, the surviving Mapuche, living in more than 3000 separate reservations, had become steadily more impoverished and dependent on the government.

The agrarian reforms of the 1960s provided little real benefit to the Mapuche since they encouraged private landholding – indeed some communal lands were sold off at this time – and the military government made continued encroachments on Mapuche communities, which remain among the poorest in Chile.

It is estimated that the Mapuche now occupy only about 1.5% of the lands they inhabited at the time of the Spanish conquest, mainly in communities south of the Biobío and in reserves in the Argentine *cordillera* around Lago Nahuel Huapi.

## Where to stay

**Puerto Saavedra**

**$$$ Hotel Boca Budi**
*Boca Budi, T45-267 6416, www.bocabudi.cl.*
With bath and breakfast. Sea views, heating,
room service, heated swimming pool.
Tours offered. Mid-price restaurant.

**$$ Cabañas Miramar**
*Miramar 4, Puerto Saavedra, T45-263 4290,*
*www.miramarchile.com.*
Fully equipped *cabañas* for 2-8 people,
with picnic and barbecue areas.

**$ Hospedaje Santa Rita**
*Las Dunas 1511, T45-263 4171.*
Lovely, knowledgeable host, home-cooked
food served.

## Restaurants

**Puerto Saavedra**
For places to eat see Where to stay, above.

## Transport

**Puerto Saavedra**
To **Temuco** (Terminal Rural), with **Narbus**,
hourly, 3 hrs, US$2.75.

**Lago Budi**
There are buses from **Puerto Domínguez**
to Temuco, 3 hrs. The **Carlos Schalchli** ferry
leaves Puerto Domínguez for **Isla Huapi** daily
(except Thu) leaving at 0830 and 1600 and
returning at 0930 and 1700, free, 30 mins.

## North and east of Temuco  *Colour map 1, A3.*

**towards the Argentine border**

### Curacautín and around

Some 30 km north of Temuco a paved road branches off the Pan-American Highway
and runs east to the Argentine border at Pino Hachado (see box, page 264), passing
through Curacautín.

A small town situated on the Río Cautín, Curacautín lies 84 km northeast of Temuco and
56 km southeast of Victoria by good paved roads. Deprived by new, stricter deforestation
laws of its traditional timber industry, Curacautín has rebranded itself as a centre for
tourism; it is a useful base for visiting the nearby national parks and hot springs, including
the indoor **Termas de Manzanar** ① *17 km east of Curacautín, www.termasdemanzanar.cl,*
*open all year daily 1000-2000, US$17 for the swimming pool, discounts for children; reached*
*by bus from Temuco and Victoria.* The building dates from 1954.

On the way, at Km 6, the road passes a turn-off to **Laguna Blanca** (25 km north, take
fishing gear) and the **Salto del Indio** ① *Km 13 (Km 71 from Victoria), US$1.50,* a 30-m-high
waterfall, where there are *cabañas* ($$$-$$). Some 3 km beyond Manzanar is the **Salto de
la Princesa**, a 50-m waterfall, with camping and a *hostería*.

### Termas Malleco and Parque Nacional Tolhuaca

The beautiful pine-surrounded **Termas Malleco (formerly Tolhuaca)** ① *www.termas
malleco.cl, open all year, US$17 (US$25 with lunch), taxi from Curacautín US$40-50,* are 35 km
to the north of Curacautín by *ripio* road, or 57 km by unpaved road from just north of
Victoria; a high-clearance 4WD is essential out of season.

Just 2 km further north is the **Parque Nacional Tolhuaca** ① *Dec-Apr, taxi from
Curacautín US$35-40,* which covers 6374 ha of the valley of the Río Malleco at altitudes of
850 to 1830 m and includes the waterfalls of Malleco and Culebra, and two lakes, Laguna

## BORDER CROSSINGS
## Chile Lake District–Argentina

1 From Curacautín and Lonquimay to Zapala via Paso Pino Hachado, or Paso de Icalma (see box, page 264).

2 From Pucón and Curarrehue to Junín de los Andes via Paso Mamuil Malal, also known as the Paso Tromen (see box, page 280).

3 From Lago Pirehueico to San Martín de los Andes via Paso Hua Hum (see box, page 288).

4 From Paso Samoré (formerly Puyehue) to Bariloche (see box, page 302).

5 The lakes route, from Puerto Varas via Ensenada, Petrohué and Lago Todos los Santos to Bariloche (see box, page 323).

Malleco and Laguna Verde. There's superb scenery and good views of the volcanoes from Cerro Amarillo. Park administration is near Laguna Malleco and there is a campsite nearby. Unfortunately, much of the park, together with the neighbouring **Reserva Nacional Malleco**, was damaged by forest fires in 2002, and will take several decades fully to recover, although some half-day trails are open.

### Volcán Lonquimay and around

Situated northeast of Curacautín is **Lonquimay Volcano** (2865 m), which began erupting on Christmas day 1988; the resulting crater was named 'Navidad'. The 31,305-ha Reserva Nacional Nalcas Malalcahuello lies on the slopes of the volcano and is much less crowded than the nearby Parque Nacional Conguillio.

Useful information about the park is available from the CONAF office on the main road in Malalcahuello (east of Curacautín) and from **La Suizandina** (see Where to stay, below), which is also a good base for treks and for the ascent of the volcano. Several marked trails (varying from one hour to two days) leave from the CONAF office. From Malalcahuello it is a one-day hike to the Sierra Nevada (see below), or a two-day hike to Conguillio national park; less experienced climbers should hire a guide.

**Corrolco ski resort** ⓘ *T2-2206 0741, www.corralco.com, season Jun-Oct*, on the southeast side of Volcán Lonquimay, is a high-end resort with six lifts servicing 26 runs that are suitable for beginner, intermediate and advanced skill levels.

**Centro de Ski Los Arenales** ⓘ *access from Lonquimay town, T45-289 1071, www.arenalespark.cl, season Jun-Sep*, is at Las Raíces Pass on the road from Malalcahuello to Lonquimay town. It is a pleasant, small resort with a nice restaurant and four lifts that go up to 2500 m with great views.

In winter the pass is usually snowed out, and the road from Malalcahuello to Lonquimay town is diverted via the **Túnel Las Raíces** ⓘ *toll US$0.60*. This former railway tunnel was, until recently, the longest in South America at 4.8 km. It is in poor condition, unlit and with constant filtration. If travelling by bicycle it is wiser to hitch through the tunnel in a pickup than cycling through yourself.

Access to climb Lonquimay is either from Malalcahuello, 15 km south, or from from the ski resort from where it is a one-hour walk to the municipal *refugio* at the base of the mountain. Walk towards the ski lift and from there head to the spur on the left. Allow four hours for the ascent, one hour for the descent. Crampons and ice-axe are necessary in winter, but in summer it is a relatively simple climb.

*www.parquenacionalconguillio.cl. Entry US$9 in high season. Visitor centre at the park administration by Lago Conguillio, Dec-Mar daily 0900-2300. CONAF runs free slide lectures and short guided walks during the summer, covering flora and fauna, Volcán Llaima and other subjects.*

Situated 80 km east of Temuco and covering 60,833 ha, the park is one of the most popular in Chile though it is deserted outside January and February and at weekends. In the centre is the **Llaima Volcano** (3125 m), which is still active and can be climbed. There are two craters: the western crater was blown out in 1994 and began erupting again in 1996. The volcano came to life again on New Year's Day 2008 and the effects are visible in the massive lava-flow to the north. The last eruption was in 2009. There are two large lakes, Laguna Verde and Lago Conguillio, and two smaller ones, Laguna Arco Iris and Laguna Captrén. North of Lago Conguillio rise the snow-covered peaks of extinct volcano **Sierra Nevada**, which reaches 2554 m.

Much of the park is covered in forests of southern beech but it is also the best place in Chile to see native **araucaria forest**, which used to cover extensive areas of land in this

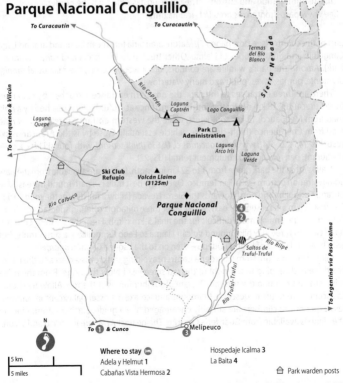

# Parque Nacional Conguillio

*To Curacautín* ▼     *To Curacautín* ▼

Sierra Nevada

Termas del Río Blanco

Río Captrén

Laguna Quepe

*To Cherquenco & Vilcún* ◀

Laguna Captrén

Lago Conguillio

Park Administration

Laguna Arco Iris

Laguna Verde

**Ski Club Refugio**

▲ Volcán Llaima (3125m)

Río Calbuco

*Parque Nacional Conguillio*

Saltos de Truful-Truful

Río Rilpe

Río Truful-Truful

*To Argentina via Paso Icalma* ▶

N

5 km
5 miles

*To* ① *& Cunco*     ○ Melipeuco ③

**Where to stay** 🛏
Adela y Helmut **1**
Cabañas Vista Hermosa **2**

Hospedaje Icalma **3**
La Baita **4**

🏠 Park warden posts

## BORDER CROSSING
### Chile–Argentina

**Paso Pino Hachado**

A paved road runs southeast from Lonquimay to the border at Paso Pino Hachado (1864 m). Temuco lies 145 km southwest of Lonquimay. For the Argentine side, including details of immigration and customs, see box, page 78. Buses from Temuco to Zapala and Neuquén use this crossing.

**Chilean immigration and customs** Liucura, 24 km west of the border. Very thorough searches and two- to three-hour delays reported. See www.pasosfronterizos.gov.cl/cf_pinohachado.html.

**Paso de Icalma**

Paso de Icalma (1303 m) lies 53 km east of Melipeuco via an unpaved road. This border is used as an alternative crossing when other crossings at higher altitude are closed due to snow. For the Argentine side, including details of immigration and customs, see box, page 78.

**Chilean immigration and customs** The police post is 3 km from the border. See www.pasosfronterizos.gov.cl/cf_icalma.html.

---

part of the country (see box, page 77). Mature araucaria forest can be found around Lago Conguillío and on the slopes of Llaima. Other trees include cypress and *canelo* (winter's bark). Among the park's wildlife are condors, black woodpeckers, the marsupial *monito del monte*, pumas, foxes, pudu and many waterfowl.

There are three entrances to the park: the **northern entrance** is reached by *ripio* road from Curacautín, 28 km north; the **southern entrance** at Truful-Truful is reached by a *ripio* road from Melipeuco, 13 km southwest, while the **western entrance** is reached by *ripio* road from Cherquenco (high-clearance vehicle essential). Close by is the **Araucarias ski resort** ⓘ *T45-227 4141, www.skiaraucarias.cl, US$36 (high season)*, with four ski lifts, a café, restaurant, bar, *refugio* and equipment rental (US$22).

**Trails** within the park range from 1 to 22 km in length. Details are available from the park administration or from CONAF in Temuco. One of the best trails is a path round the east side of Lago Conguillío and north towards the Sierra Nevada (allow a full day for the round-trip). The first 10 km are reasonably easy, with two or three miradors offering spectacular views. After this it gets much more difficult for the final 5-km climb. From the western entrance it is a two- to three-day hike around Volcán Llaima to Lago Conguillío – a dusty route, but with beautiful views of Laguna Quepe – then on to the Laguna Captrén *guardería*.

Climb **Llaima** south from **Guardería Captrén**, avoiding the crevassed area to the left of the ridge and keeping to the right of the red scree just below the ridge. From the ridge it is a straight climb to the summit. Beware of sulphur fumes at the top. Allow five hours to ascend, two hours to descend. Crampons and ice-axe are essential except in summer; less experienced climbers are strongly encouraged hire a guide. Further information on the climb is available from **Guardería Captrén**. The nearest ATMs are in Cunco and Vicún.

## Where to stay

### Curacautín and around

**$$ Hostal Las Espigas**
*Prat 710, T45-288 1138,*
*rivaseugenia@hotmail.com.*
Good rooms, dinner available on request.

**$$ Plaza**
*Yungay 157 (main plaza), T45-288 1256,*
*www.rotondadelcautin.cl.*
With **La Cabaña** restaurant, pricey. Also has
**Hostería La Rotunda del Cautín** (Termas de
Manzanar, T45-288 1569). Rooms and good
mid-range restaurant.

**$ Turismo**
*Tarapacá 140, T45-288 1116,*
*www.hotelturismocuracautin.cl.*
Good food, hot shower, comfortable,
good value if old-fashioned.

### Termas de Manzanar

**$$$$-$$$ Termas de Manzanar**
*T45-288 1200, www.termasdemanzanar.cl.*
Overpriced rooms, also has suites with
thermal jacuzzi.

**$$$-$ Andenrose**
*Carretera Internacional Km 68.5, 5 km west*
*of Manzanar, Curacautín, T9-9869 1700,*
*www.andenrose.com.*
Cosy rooms, cabins and camping, restaurant
serving international and Bavarian food,
bike, horse, kayak rental, jeep tours arranged,
German/Chilean-run.

**$ Hostería Abarzúa**
*Km 18, T45-287 0011.*
Simple, cheaper rooms without bath, full
board available (good food), also campsite.

### Termas Malleco and Parque Nacional Tolhuaca

**$$$$-$$ Termas Malleco**
*Km 33, T45-232 4800, www.termasmalleco.cl.*

With breakfast or full board, including use
of baths and horse riding, very good; jacuzzi
and massage. Camping, good facilities and
unlimited use of pools.

### Volcán Lonquimay and around

**$$$-$ La Suizandina**
*3 km before Malalcahuello village, Km 83*
*Carretera Internacional a Argentina (Erbuc*
*bus from Temuco 2½ hrs), T45-2197 3725*
*or T9-9884 9541, www.suizandina.com.*
Hostel offering a range of rooms, in main
house, guesthouse, dorm, cabin or camping.
Large Swiss breakfast with home-baked
bread, half board available, credit cards
accepted, laundry, book exchange, bike and
ski rental, horse riding, hot springs, travel
and trekking information, German and
English spoken. "Like being in Switzerland".

**$$ La Casita de Nahuelcura**
*Balmaceda 320, Malalcahuello, T9-7432 1192,*
*www.hosteriamalalcahuello.cl.*
*Hostería*, lodge and *cabañas*.

### Parque Nacional Conguillio

There are other *hostales* and restaurants
in Melipeuco.

**$$$ La Baita**
*In the park, 3 km south of Laguna Verde, Km 18,*
*T45-258 1073, www.labaitaconguillio.cl.*
*Cabañas* with electricity, hot water, kitchen
and wood stoves, charming, lots of
information, Italian/Chilean-owned.

**$$$-$$ Cabañas Vista Hermosa**
*10 km from the southern entrance, T9-9444*
*1630, www.vistahermosaconguillio.cl.*
Clean but spartan wooden cabins, each
with a wood stove and fantastic views to
the volcano. Solar powered; electricity in
afternoon only. Run by a horse-riding guide
(former champion rider). Good food.

## $$ Adela y Helmut

*Faja 16000, Km 5 Norte, Cunco, T9-8258 2230, www.adelayhelmut.com.*

Guesthouse and restaurant on a Mapuche/German-owned farm, English spoken, room for families and for backpackers in 6-bed dorm, breakfast and dinner available, kitchens, hot showers, solar heating, mountain bike rental, good reports. They run year-round tours to Conguillio National Park, visiting lakes, waterfalls, with hikes adapted to physical ability. They can also arrange fly-fishing packages. The guesthouse is 16 km from Cunco on the way to Melipeuco; website has directions and you can phone for a pick-up from the bus stop; **Nar-Bus**, **Cruzmar** and **InterSur** buses from Santiago and Temuco pass the Faja and will drop passengers. Alternatively, a pick-up from Temuco costs US$42 for up to 4 people.

## $ Hospedaje Icalma

*Aguirre Cerda 729, Melipeuco, T9-9280 8210, www.melipeucohospedaje.cl.*

Spacious, basic rooms.

### Camping

**Cabañas y Camping La Caseta y El Hoyón**

*Administered by SENDAS, T562-2882 1632, www.parquenacionalconguillio.cl.*

## Restaurants

For places to eat in Curacautín and the national parks, see Where to stay, above.

## What to do

### Curacautín and around

**Turismo Tolhuaca**, *Calama 230, T45-288 1211, www.termasdetolhuaca.cl.* Agency for

accommodation, restaurants and riding in the area.

## Transport

### Curacautín and around

**Bus** Terminal on the main road, by the plaza. Buses to/from **Temuco**, **Los Angeles** and **Santiago**.

### Volcán Lonquimay and around

**Buses Bío Bío**, www.busesbiobio.cl, has daily services from Temuco via Lautaro and Curacautín to **Malalcahuello**, 3 hrs, US$5.75, and **Lonquimay** town, 3½ hrs (or 4 hrs via Victoria), US$6.50.

### Parque Nacional Tolhuaca

There are bus services from Victoria to **San Gregorio** (19 km from park entrance).

### Parque Nacional Conguillio

Private transport or taking a tour are the best ways to see the area. For touring, hire a 4WD vehicle in Temuco (essential in wet weather). See also **Adela y Helmut**, under Where to stay, above.

To the **northern entrance**, poor *ripio* road: **taxi** from Curacautín to Laguna Captrén, US$40-50 one way. To **Melipeuco** (paved road, stops at Hospedaje Icalma), buses every hour from 0800-1800 from Balmaceda bus terminal, **Temuco** (or flag down at Mackenna y Varas), 2½ hrs, US$2.75, and once a day to **Icalma** when no snow on road. From May to end Dec the only access is via Melipeuco. Transport can be arranged from Melipeuco into the park (ask in grocery stores and *hospedajes*, US$40-50 one way). To **Cunco**, every 20 mins from same terminal. To the **western entrance**: daily **buses** from Temuco to **Cherquenco**, from where there is no public transport to the park.

# Lago Villarrica
## & around

Wooded Lago Villarrica, 21 km long and about 7 km wide, is one of the star lakes in the region, with the active and snow-capped Villarrica Volcano (2840 m) to the southeast. Villarrica and Pucón, resorts at the lake's southwest and southeast corners, are among the more expensive in the region, but are definitely worth a visit.

## Villarrica  *Colour map 1, A3.*

*a holiday getaway at the foot of Volcán Villarrica*

Pleasantly set at the extreme southwest corner of the lake, Villarrica (population 70,000) can be reached by a paved road southeast from Freire, 24 km south of Temuco on the Pan-American Highway, or from Loncoche, 54 km south of Freire, also paved. Less significant as a tourist resort than nearby Pucón, it is a little cheaper.

Founded in 1552, the town was besieged by the Mapuche in the uprising of 1599: after three years the surviving Spanish settlers, 11 men and 13 women, surrendered. The town was refounded in 1882; the **Museo Leandro Penchulef** ⓘ *O'Higgins 501, T45-241 1667, Dec-Jan Mon-Fri 1000-1900, winter 1000-1800, free*, in the striking Universidad Católica, focuses on this event.

There is a small museum, **Museo Histórico** ⓘ *Pedro de Valdivia 1050 y Zegers, T45-241 5706, Mon-Fri 0900-1300 and 1500-1830, Sat 1000-1300 and 1500-1800*, containing a collection of Mapuche artefacts. Next to it is the **Muestra Cultural Mapuche** ⓘ *Open 1000-1100 in summer, 1000-1800 in winter*, featuring a Mapuche *ruca* and stalls selling good quality handicrafts in summer.

There are good views of the volcano from the *costanera*; for a different perspective over the lake, go south along Aviador Acevedo and then Poniente Ríos towards the Hostería de la Colina. Just south of town (500 m along Avenida Matta), there is a large working farm, **Fundo Huifquenco** ⓘ *T45-241 5040*, with trails, horse riding, carriage rides and meals (book in advance).

## Listings Villarrica *map below.*

### Tourist information

**Tourist office**
*Valdivia 1070, T45-220 6619. Daily 0800-2300 in summer, 1000-1800 off season.*
Friendly office with information and maps.

### Where to stay

Lodging in private homes in our **$$-$** range can be found on Muñoz blocks 400 and 500, Koerner 300 and O'Higgins 700 and 800. More upmarket accommodation is on the lakefront.

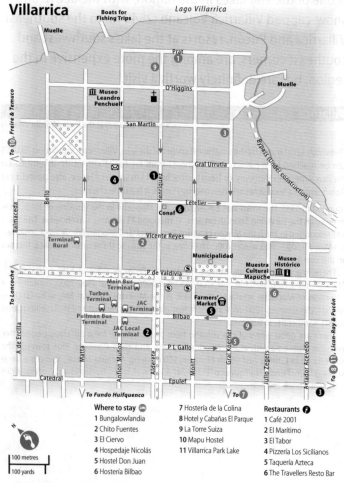

# Villarrica

**Lago Villarrica**

**Where to stay** 🛏
1 Bungalowlandia
2 Chito Fuentes
3 El Ciervo
4 Hospedaje Nicolás
5 Hostel Don Juan
6 Hostería Bilbao
7 Hostería de la Colina
8 Hotel y Cabañas El Parque
9 La Torre Suiza
10 Mapu Hostel
11 Villarrica Park Lake

**Restaurants** 🍴
1 Café 2001
2 El Marítimo
3 El Tabor
4 Pizzería Los Sicilianos
5 Taquería Azteca
6 The Travellers Resto Bar

#### $$$$ Villarrica Park Lake
*Km 13 on the road to Pucón, T44-890 9220,*
*www.hotelvillarricaparklake.redhotelera.cl.*
5-star, all rooms with balconies overlooking
the lake, spa with pools, sauna, solarium,
fishing trips.

#### $$$ El Ciervo
*Koerner 241, T45-241 1215,*
*www.hotelelciervo.cl.*
Comfortable rooms, pleasant grounds,
German-style breakfasts, German and
some English spoken, pool, terrace.

#### $$$ Hostería de la Colina
*Las Colinas 115, overlooking town, T45-*
*241 1503, www.hosteriadelacolina.com.*
Large gardens, good restaurant (the owners
make their own fresh ice cream), fine views,
very attentive service. Fishing, horse riding
and dog sledding can be organized from the
*hostería* as well.

#### $$$ Hotel y Cabañas El Parque
*Camino Villarica, Km 2.5, T45-241 1120,*
*www.hotelelparque.cl.*
Lakeside with beach, tennis courts, good
restaurant set meals.

#### $$$ Parque Natural Dos Ríos
*13 km west of Villarrica, Putue Alto s/n,*
*Casilla 535, T9-9419 8064, www.dosrios.de.*
B&B rooms or self-catering cabins. Tranquil
40-ha nature park on the banks of the Río
Toltén (white-sand beach), birdwatching,
child-friendly, German and English spoken.

#### $$ Bungalowlandia
*Prat 749, T45-241 1635,*
*www.bungalowlandia.cl.*
*Cabañas*, dining room, good facilities, pool.

#### $$ Hostal Don Juan
*Korner 770, T9-94432070,*
*contacto@hostaldonjuan.cl.*
Reputable option close to the centre.
23 rooms on sprawling property with
lush gardens, *parrilla*, expansive dining
room. Spotless. Also triples ($$$). Breakfast
optional. The best option at this price.
Recommended.

#### $$ Hostería Bilbao
*Henríquez 43, T45-241 1186,*
*www.interpatagonia.com/bilbao.*
Small rooms, pretty patio, good restaurant.

#### $$ La Torre Suiza
*Bilbao 969, T45-241 1213, www.torresuiza.com.*
Rooms and dorms, camping, cycle rental,
book exchange, lots of info, reserve in
advance. German and English spoken.

#### $$-$ Hospedaje Nicolás
*Anfion Muñoz 477, T45-241 2637,*
*pincheiranicolas@hotmail.com.*
Simple rooms with bath. Good value,
but thin walls.

#### $ Chito Fuentes
*Vicente Reyes 665, T45-241 1595.*
Basic rooms above a restaurant.

#### $ Mapu Hostal
*Urrutia 302, T45-241 2098,*
*w3.mapuhostal.com.*
Legitimate *hostal* option at the entrance
to Villarica. Dorms for 8, 6 and 4 and
doubles ($$). Laundry service, breakfast
included, Wi-Fi.

### Restaurants

For eating options in the national parks and
lakes east of Pucón, see Where to stay, above.

#### $$$ El Tabor
*S Epulef 1187, T45-241 1901.*
Fish and seafood specialities,
excellent but pricey.

#### $$ The Travellers Resto Bar
*Letelier 753, T45-241 3617, see Facebook.*
Varied menu including vegetarian and
Asian food, bar, English spoken.

#### $$-$ La Taquería Azteca
*Bilbao 581, T45-241 0272, see Facebook.*
Does this central *taquería* disprove the rule
that Mexican food in South America rarely
rises above average? No. Still, the Tex-Mex
tastes good, the vibe is fun, and the cocktails
are strong. Recommended if you are not a
strict *comida mexicana* originalist.

**$$-$ Pizzería Los Sicilianos**
*Munoz 415, T45 260 9189.*
Owner Fabrizzio tosses pies, flirts with women and sings along to Calabreze music, all while delivering the most authentically Italian pizzas in the city.

**$ El Marítimo**
*Alderete 769, T45-241 9755, see Facebook.*
Generally first-rate, unpretentious, serving traditional fish and seafood.

### Cafés

**Café 2001**
*Henríquez 379, T45-241 1470,*
*www.cafebar2001.cl.*
Best coffee in town. Also good cakes and friendly service at a reasonable price. No Wi-Fi. For ice cream, try the stall next door.

### Festivals

Jan/Feb Villarrica has the **Feria Costumbrista**, with many cultural and sporting events and the official rodeo. See www.villarrica.org and www.visitvillarrica.org.

### What to do

**Claudio Rodríguez**, *T7-794 1228.* Private guide, offers river and fly-fishing trips, speaks English.
**Novena Región**, *Parque Ecológico 3 Esteros, 20 km from Villarrica towards Panguipulli, T9-8901 4518, info@auroraaustral.com,* *see Facebook.* Mushing and husky trekking on the winter snow and in summer with Siberian huskies. Unique in Chile.
**Ríos Family**, *T45-241 2408.* Birdwatching and fishing trips.
**Villarica Extremo**, *Valdivia 910, T45-241 0900, www.villaricaextremo.com.* Good excursions featuring the usual suspects like volcano tours, rafting, thermal pools and paintball.

### Transport

**Bus** Terminal at Pedro de Valdivia y Muñoz. **JAC** terminal at Bilbao 610, T45-246 7777, and opposite for Pucón and Lican-Ray. **Terminal Rural** for other local services at Matta y Vicente Reyes. To **Santiago**, 10 hrs, US$30-50, several companies. To **Pucón**, with **Vipu-Ray** (main terminal) and **JAC**, in summer every 15 mins, 40 mins' journey, US$1.25; same companies to **Lican-Ray**, US$1.25. To **Valdivia, JAC**, US$6.50, multiple daily, 2½ hrs. To **Coñaripe** (US$1.75) and **Liquiñe** 5 a day, 2 on Sun US$4.25. To **Temuco, JAC**, US$2.15. To **Loncoche** (Ruta 5 junction for hitching), US$1.50. To **Panguipulli**, go via Lican-Ray US$2.25, occasional direct buses.

**To Argentina** Buses from Valdivia to **San Martín de los Andes** pass through **Villarrica**, US$18.50, **Buses Igi Llaima**, T45-241 2733, book in advance. Note that if the Mamuil Malal pass is blocked by snow buses go via Panguipulli instead of Villarrica and Pucón.

---

★ **Pucón** *Colour map 1, A3.*

**where Chileans and Argentines come to play**

On the southeastern corner of the lake, 26 km east of Villarrica, Pucón is one of the most popular destinations in the Lake District, famous above all as a centre for visiting the 2840 m Villarrica Volcano, which dominates the view to the south. Built across the neck of a peninsula, the town has two black-sand beaches, which are popular for swimming and watersports.

Within easy reach of town is an active climbable volcano where you can also ski in winter, plus rivers for whitewater rafting and fly-fishing, canopy tours in native forests, quadbike excursions, lakes, parasailing, and waterfalls, two national parks and a private nature sanctuary as well as 14 thermal springs. Other activities include winter sports and zip-lining (see What to do, page 275). This makes Pucón an excellent base for visiting the northern Lake District.

**Tip...**
Although there are a few banks with ATMs and several *casas de cambio*, the *cambio* rates are universally poor; it's much better to change money in Temuco.

### Sights

The Pucón of today is very different from the town of 30 years ago, when it was a small, pleasant, quiet village with some seasonal Chilean tourism, but no foreign backpackers. It is now a thriving tourist centre, full of Chileans in summer and gringos in the autumn. But Pucón is still small enough that you can traverse it in a short time.

Pucón

**Where to stay**
1 Antumalal *C1*
2 Cabañas Rucamalal *B3*
3 Donde Germán *C3*
4 El Refugio *C2*
5 Hospedaje Irma *C16*
6 Hospedaje Victor *C2*
7 Hostal Backpackers *C2*
8 Hostal Gerónimo *B3*
9 Hostería iécole! & restaurant *B3*
10 Interlaken *C1*
11 La Bicicleta *B2*
12 La Poza 9 *C1*
13 La Tetera 29 *B2*

**Restaurants**
1 Abuela Goye *B2*
2 Arabian *B2*
3 Café de la P *B1*
4 Café Lounge Brasil *C3*
5 Cassis *B2*
6 La Maga *B2*
7 Mora Sushi Bar *B2*
8 Puerto Pucón *B2*
9 Rap Hamburguesa *B3*
10 Senzo *B2*

Every other house in the town centre seems to offer accommodation, while the main drag is awash with tour operators, bars, restaurants, boutiques and *artesanía*. The commercial centre lies between **Avenida O'Higgins**, the main thoroughfare, and the **Gran Hotel Pucón**. Private land (ask for permission at the entrance) leads west from the centre of town to **La Península**, where there are fine views of the lake and volcano, as well as a golf course. There is also a pleasant walk, along the **Costanera Otto Gudenschwager**, starting at the northern end of Calle Ansorena (beside Gran Hotel Pucón) and following the lakeside north.

**Boat trips** ① *5 a day in summer, 4 in winter, 1 hr, US$7*, on the lake leave from the landing stage at La Poza at the western end of O'Higgins. Walk a couple of kilometres north along the beach from here to the mouth of the Río Trancura for views of volcanoes. Or take a **boat** ① *summer only, US$57 for up to 8 people*, to the mouth of the river from near the Gran Hotel.

To cross the Río Pucón, head east out of Pucón along the main road, then turn north on an unmade road leading to a bridge. There are pleasant walks from here along the north shore of the lake to the Mapuche settlement of **Quelhue** and the beach at **Río Plata**, or northeast towards **Caburga** (the round trip makes a perfect day's outing by mountain bike). You can also strike up into the hills through farms and agricultural land, with views of three volcanoes and the lake (if possible, ask permission to cross first).

From the road to the Villarrica Volcano, a *ripio* road branches off for 5 km to some privately managed **Cuevas Volcánicas** (volcanic caves) ① *US$26, small discount for students and children*, surrounded by a small attractive park with tunnels and a museum, as well as paths through the forest. Although entry to the site is expensive, it's recommended as a bad weather option. Snowmobile tours are also offered at US$35 for 30 minutes.

## Listings Pucón *map page 271*.

### Tourist information

There are private operators displaying 'Tourist Information' signs.

#### Chamber of Tourism
*At the entrance to Pucón from Villarrica, Brasil 315, T45-244 1671, www.pucon turismo.cl. Open 0900-1000 in summer, 1100-1800 in winter.*

#### Municipal tourist office
*Municipalidad, O'Higgins 483, T45-229 3001, ofturismo@municipalidadpucon.cl. Daily 0830-2100 in summer, 0830-1900 in winter.*
Provides information, maps and sells fishing licences Mon-Fri.

#### Parque Nacional Villarica park administration
*Lincoyán 336, T45-244 3781, parque.villarrica@conaf.cl.*
Leaflets and information on the national park.

### Where to stay

In summer (Dec-Feb) rooms may be hard to find. There are plenty of alternatives (usually cheaper) in Villarrica. Prices below are Jan-Feb. Off-season rates are 20-40% lower and often negotiable. Many families offer rooms, look for the signs or ask in bars. Touts offer rooms to new arrivals; check that they are not way out of town.

#### $$$$ Antumalal
*2 km west of Pucón, T45-244 1011, www.antumalal.com.*
Small, luxury, picturesque chalet-type boutique hotel, magnificent views of the lake (breakfast and lunch on terrace), 5 ha of gardens, with meals, open year round, indoor pool, hot tub, sauna, spa, jacuzzis and private beaches. All rooms have a fireplace, heating and lake views. Car hire.

**$$$$ Interlaken**
*Caupolicán 720, T45-244 2709,*
*www.hotelinterlaken.cl.*
Chalets with full facilities, water skiing,
pool, no restaurant.

**$$$ Cabañas Rucamalal**
*O'Higgins 770, T45-244 2297,*
*www.rucamalal.cl.*
Lovely cabins (with satellite TV) in a pretty
garden, spacious, well equipped and
decorated, various sizes, pool.

**$$$-$$ Hostal Gerónimo**
*Alderete 665, T45-244 3762,*
*www.geronimo.cl. Open all year.*
Quiet, smart, multilingual staff, bar, restaurant.

**$$$-$$ Hostería ¡école!**
*General Urrutia 592, T45-244 1675,*
*www.ecole.cl.*
Rooms and dorms, shop, vegetarian
and fish restaurant, forest treks
(departure for Lahuén Foundation's

Cani Forest Sanctuary), rafting and
biking, information, language classes
and massage.

**$$ Donde Germán**
*Las Rosas 590, T45-244 2444,*
*www.dondegerman.cl.*
Single, double or triple rooms with
private or shared bath. Fun, organizes
tours, book in advance.

**$$ El Refugio**
*Palguín 540, T45-244 1596,*
*www.hostalelrefugio.cl.*
Dorm or double room, shared bath, small,
convenient, cosy, Dutch/Chilean-owned.
Trips sold, but shop around.

**$$ Hostal Backpackers**
*Palguín 695, T45-244 1417,*
*www.backpackerspucon.com.*
With or without bath, quiet, next to
JAC buses, lots of activities, **Navimag**
reservations, tourist info.

## $$ La Tetera
*Urrutia 580, T45-246 4126, www.tetera.cl.*
6 rooms, some with bath, English spoken, book swap, information centre, good Spanish classes, car rental, book in advance. Nearby bar music is audible on weekends.

## $$-$ Hospedaje Irma
*Lincoyán 545, T45-244 2226, http://hirma.cl.*
Private or shared bath, tourist information, bicycle hire.

## $$-$ Hospedaje Víctor
*Palguín 705, T45-244 3525,*
*www.hostalvictor.cl.*
Rooms sleep 2-4 with private or shared bath, laundry. A decent choice.

## $$-$ La Bicicleta
*Palguín 361, T45-244 4679.*
Cosy budget hostel offering excursions and bike tours. Owner José can help with all the details.

## $ pp Etnico Hostel and Adventures
*Colo Colo 36, T9-8527 5940,*
*www.etnico.hostel.com.*
Owner is a mountain guide. Double rooms and mixed dorms, car and bike parking, lots of activities and keen on recycling.

## Camping
There are many camping and cabin establishments. Those close to Pucón include **La Poza** (Costanera Geis 769, T45-244 4982, campinglapoza@hotmail.com, see Facebook), with hot showers and a good kitchen. Several sites en route to volcano, including: **L'Etoile** (Km 2, T45-244 2188, www.letoilepucon.com), in attractive forest (US$7 per night).

## Restaurants

There are many upscale and mid range restaurants on Fresia between O'Higgins and Valdivia. See Where to stay, above, for other options.

## $$$ Puerto Pucón
*Fresia 246, T45-244 1592.*

One of Pucón's older restaurants, Spanish, stylish.

## $$$-$$ La Maga
*Alderete 276 y Fresia, T45-244 4277,*
*www.lamagapucon.cl.*
Uruguayan *parrillada* serving excellent steak. So good that several imitations have opened up nearby to take the overspill.

## $$$-$$ Senzo
*Fresia 284, T45-244 9005, see Facebook.*
Fresh pasta and risotto prepared by a Swiss chef.

## $$ Arabian
*Fresia 354-B, T45-244 3469.*
Arab specialities, including stuffed vine leaves, falafel, etc.

## $$ ¡école!
*In a hostería of the same name,*
*see Where to stay, above.*
Good vegetarian restaurant.

## $$ Mora Sushi
*Fresia 236, T45-244 4857,*
*www.morasushibar.cl.*
Decent sushi and a solid happy hour featuring great *mojitos*. A nice change of pace from steaks and fried fish.

## $ Rap Hamburguesa
*O'Higgins 625. Open late.*
Freshly made hamburgers, chips and Chilean fast food.

## Cafés

### Abuela Goye
*Fresia y Urrutia, T9-8760 1580,*
*www.abuelagoye.com.*
Argentine chain specializing in artisanal chocolates, ice cream and gourmet coffee. Also has a menu featuring pizzas, sandwiches and *tablas*. Plays good music and is great for people-watching.

### Café de la P
*O'Higgins y Lincoyán, T45-244 3577,*
*www.cafedelap.cl.*
Real coffee. Also location at the airport.

## Café Lounge Brasil
*Colo Colo 485, T45-244 4035,*
*www.cafeloungebrasil.com.*
Gourmet cafeteria which also has
a 'boutique' hostel. Meals include
vegetarian options, Jamaican coffee.

## Cassis
*Fresia 223, T45-244 9088,*
*www.chocolatescassis.com.*
Chocolates, ice creams, pancakes
and snacks as well as coffee.

### Bars and clubs

At weekends in summer, there are discos
2-3 km east of town, near the airport,
like Kamikaze. Sala Murano is a popular
option near Río Trancura. There are several
bars on O'Higgins.

### Festivals

**10 Jan** Pucón is home to an annual
**international triathlon competition**,
www.ironmanpucon.com, as well as
mountain bike races and other events.

### Shopping

**Camping equipment** is available from
**Eltit supermarket** (O'Higgins y Fresia), and
from **Outdoors & Travel** (Lincoyán 36), which
also sells outdoor clothing, equipment and
maps. There is a **handicrafts market**
just south of O'Higgins on Ansorena; local
specialities are painted wooden flowers.

### What to do

#### Canopy zip-lining
Several agencies can arrange this activity
(sliding from platform to platform among
the treetops along a metal cord). The best
(and most safety conscious) is **Bosque
Aventura** (Arauca 611 y O'Higgins, T9-
9325 4795, www.canopypucon.cl).

#### Climbing
**Sierra Nevada**, *O'Higgins 524-A, T9-5733 5037,*
*see Facebook*. Offers tours to Volcán Villarrica
for all skill levels.

#### Fishing
Pucón and Villarrica are celebrated as
centres for fishing on Lake Villarrica and
in the beautiful Lincura, Trancura and
Toltén rivers. Local tourist office will supply
details on licenses and open seasons, etc.
2 fishing specialists are **Mario's Fishing
Zone** (O'Higgins 580, T9-9760 7280, www.
flyfishingpucon.com), expensive but good,
and **Off Limits** (O'Higgins 560, T9-9949 2481,
www.offlimits.cl), English and Italian spoken.

#### Horse riding
**Centro de Turismo Ecuestre Huepilmalal**,
*Camino a Termas de Huife, Km 25, T9-9643
2673, www.huepilmalal.cl.*
**Rancho de Caballos**, *see Where to stay,
page 281*. Average hire costs about US$28
half day, US$72 full day (transfer from
Pucón extra).

#### Mountain biking
Bike hire from US$14 per day for cross-
country excursions with guide. Available
from several travel agencies on O'Higgins.

#### Tour operators
Tour operators arrange trips to thermal baths,
trekking to volcanoes, whitewater rafting,
etc. For falls, lakes and *termas* it's cheaper
for groups to flag down a taxi and bargain.
There are many agencies, so shop around:
prices vary at times, as do quality of guides
and equipment. In high season, when lots of
groups go together, individual attention may
be lacking.
**Aguaventura**, *Palguín 336, T45-244 4246,
www.aguaventura.com*. French-run, in
summer kayaking and rafting specialities,
in winter 'snowshop' for ski and snowboard
rental, volcano climbing, trekking.
**Elementos**, *Pasaje Las Rosas 640, T45-244
1750, www.elementos-chile.com*. Provider

covering the entire country and specializing in sustainable tourism. Has its own **EcoHostel**. Good option for volcano treks.
**Mountain Life Adventure**, *T9-7472 3665, mountainlifeadventure@hotmail.*com. Villarrica hike plus treks and climbs up other volcanoes in the region, Chilean/Swiss-owned (ask here about new location of the owners' **Hostel One Way**).
**Politur**, *O'Higgins 635, T45-244 1373, www.politur.com.* Well-established and responsible, good for volcano trek and rafting; a little pricier than others.
**Travel Aid**, *Ansorena 425, loc 4, T45-244 4040, www.travelaid.cl.* Helpful general travel agency, sells trekking maps, guidebooks, lots of information, agents for **Navimag** and other boat trips, English and German spoken.
**Volcán Villarrica**, *O' Higgins 555, T45-244 1577, volcan.villarica@hotmail.com.* Specializes in group excursions to Volcán Villarrica as well as a number of other activities, including rafting, canyoning and paintball. English spoken, good equipment.

### Watersports
Waterskiing, sailing, rowing boats and windsurfing at Playa Grande beach by **Gran Hotel** and at **La Poza beach** at the end of O'Higgins (this is more expensive than Playa Grande and not recommended).

### Whitewater rafting and kayaking
Very popular on the Río Trancura: Trancura Bajo (Grade III), US$22; Trancura Alto (Grades III and IV), US$29. Many agencies offer trips, including **Rafting Kayak Chile** (O'Higgins 524, T9-8452 1693, www.rafting kayakchile.com); see also **Pucón Kayak**

**Hostel** (10 km from town on road to Caburga, T9-4247 2676, www.puconkayakhostel.co).

## Transport

**Air** The airport is 2 km east of Pucón on the Caburga road. Check with airlines for summer flights from **Santiago** via Temuco. There are usually very few.

**Bus** There is no municipal terminal: each company has its own terminal: **JAC**, Uruguay y Palguín; **Tur-Bus**, O'Higgins 910, east of town; **Igi Llaima** and **Cóndor**, Colo Colo y O'Higgins. **JAC** to **Villarrica** (very frequent, US$1.25) and **Valdivia** (US$6.75, 3 hrs). **Tur-Bus** direct to **Valdivia**, **Osorno** (US$12), and **Puerto Montt**, US$14, 6 daily. To **Santiago**, 10 hrs, US$44-70, many companies, early morning and late evening. There are many buses to **Temuco**. Buses **Caburgua** run minibuses to many local destinations, including: **Parque Nacional Huerquehue**, 4 daily (3 in winter), 1½ hrs, US$2.85; **Caburga**, every 20 mins, US$1.15; **Los Pozones**, US$2.15 daily, passing by the termas and Reserva Forestal Cani on the way. There are several minibuses daily to **Curarrehue**, US$1.75, and buses weekly to **Puesco**, US$3.

**To Argentina** Buses from Valdivia to **San Martín** pass through Pucón.

**Car hire** Hire prices start at US$30 per day; **Hertz**, Alderete 324, T45-244 1664; **Kilómetro Libre**, Alderete 480, T45-244 4399, www.rentacarkilometrolibre.com; **Pucón Rent A Car**, Valdivia 636, T45-244 3052, www.puconrentacar.cl.

**Taxi** Taxis are available for out-of-town trips.

Within easy reach of Villarrica and Pucón are two more lakes, two national parks and several hot springs. Busy with Chilean tourists in summer, these singular natural attractions are a must-visit for those in the area.

## Parque Nacional Villarrica

*T45-244 3781. Entry fee US$4.25. For the Villarrica Volcano sector there is an ascent fee of US$150 pp, which includes 2 guides, ski and ice equipment and bags; food is not included. The trip takes 1 day to the summit.*

This park, which covers 61,000 ha, stretches from Pucón to the Argentine border near Puesco. There are three sectors: Villarrica Volcano sector (see above for entry fee information); Quetrupillán Volcano sector (see page 279), and the Puesco sector, which includes the slopes of the Lanín Volcano on the Argentine border. Each sector has its own entrance and ranger station.

The **Villarrica Volcano**, 2840 m high lies 8 km south of Pucón. Access to this sector is in theory restricted only to groups with a guide and to individuals who can show proof of membership of a mountaineering club in their own country (contact the **park administration** office in Pucón; see Tourist information, page 272).

There is no public transport, although several agencies offer trips. Entry is refused if the weather is poor. This is due to the fact that Volcán Villarica has an earned reputation as one of the most active volcanoes in South America. It reaffirmed this status in March 2015 when it erupted in a dizzying display of light and ash, lenticular clouds circling it like flying saucers. Good boots, crampons and ice picks are essential; these can be rented from tour operators for US$14, but will generally be included in the price of a tour. You should also take sunglasses, sun block, plenty of water and chocolate or some other snack; equipment is checked at the park entrance. See What to do, page 281.

It is a three- to four-hour trek to the summit, but you can skip the first part of the ascent by taking the **ski lift** ① *US$7.55, additional lift in winter US$3.75*. In summer this is recommended as it saves 400 m climbing scree. If the conditions are right, at the summit you can look down into the crater at the bubbling molten lava below, but beware of the sulphur fumes; take a cloth mask moistened with lemon juice. On exceptionally clear days you will be able to see six or more other volcanoes. If there is enough snow, groups may carry ski and snowboard equipment for the descent; otherwise just slide down the many toboggan chutes.

The **Pucón ski resort** ① *T45-244 1901, www.skipucon.cl*, owned by the Gran Hotel Pucón, is on the eastern slopes of the volcano, reached by a track, 35 minutes. The ski season is July to September, occasionally longer. Information on snow and ski lifts (and, perhaps, transport) is available from the tourist office (see Tourist office, page 272) or Gran Hotel Pucón. The centre offers equipment rental, ski instruction, first aid, restaurant and bar as well as wonderful views from the terrace. The centre is good for beginners; more advanced skiers can try the steeper areas.

## Lagos Caburga and Colico

Lago Caburga (spelt locally Caburgua) is a glassy, tranquil lake in an untamed setting 25 km northeast of Pucón. It is unusual for its beautiful white-sand beach (other beaches in the area have black volcanic sand), and is supposedly the warmest lake in the Lake District.

The western and much of the eastern shores are inaccessible to vehicles, but the village of **Caburga**, at the southern end of the lake, is reached by turning off the main road to Argentina, 8 km east of Pucón. If walking or cycling, there is a very pleasant alternative route: turn left 3 km east of Pucón, cross the Puente Quelhue, then turn right and follow the track for 18 km through beautiful scenery.

Just off the road from Pucón, at Km 15, are the **Ojos de Caburga** ① *US$1; ask the bus driver to let you off, or go by mountain bike from Pucón via the Puente Quelhue,* beautiful pools fed from underground, particularly attractive after rain. The northern tip of the lake can be reached by a road from Cunco, which runs east along the northern shore of **Lago Colico**. This is one of the less accessible lakes and lies north of Lago Villarrica in a remote setting.

## Parque Nacional Huerquehue

*Daily 0800-1900 but often closed after heavy snowfall, US$7. To get there: take the Caburga road from Pucón; 3 km before Caburga turn right along a ripio road to Paillaco, from where another road leads 7 km to the park administration, free parking 1.5 km along the track. Buses Caburga has services from Pucón.*

Located a short distance east of Lago Caburga, Parque Nacional Huerquehue covers 12,500 ha at altitudes rising to 1952 m at Cerro San Sebastián in the **Nevados del Caburga**. It also encompasses about 20 lakes, some of them very small, and many araucaria trees. The entrance and administration is on the western edge, near

> **Tip...**
> Not being particularly taxing, the walking trails in Parque Nacional Huerquehue are a good warm-up for the Volcán Villarrica hike.

**Lago Tinquilco**, the largest lake in the park. From the entrance there is a well-signed track north up a steep hill to **Lago Chico**, where the track divides left to **Lago Verde** and right to **Lago Toro**. Both paths eventually meet up, making a circuit. The lakes are surrounded by trees and are very beautiful. At **Lago Huerquehue**, a further 20 km of trails begin. An adequate map may or may not be provided at the entrance. The warden is generally very helpful. People in the park rent horses and boats, but you should take your own food.

## Termas de Quimey-co, de Huife and los Pozones

South of Parque Nacional Huerquehue and reached via turning off the Pucón–Caburga road are three sets of thermal baths. The most expensive and ostentatious are the **Termas de Huife** ① *Km 33, T45-244 1222, www.termashuife.cl, US$23 in high season (Dec-Mar),* where entry includes the use of one modern, pleasant pool. Closer to Pucón are the recently refitted **Termas de Quimey-co** ① *Km 29, T9-8775 2113, www.termasquimeyco.com, US$20 in high season,* while further on are the **Termas los Pozones** ① *Km 35, US$11.50 per day, US$15 at night (2000-2400),* which have six natural rock pools but little infrastructure and are very popular with travellers, especially at night. The road here is rough.

## Reserva Forestal Cañi

*Park entry US$6, www.santuariocani.cl. There is a self-guided trail, plus transport. For tours with English-speaking guide, contact the reserve or the Cañi Guides Program, www.ecole.cl.*

Situated south of Parque Nacional Huerquehue and accessed from the road to the Termas de Huife, this is a private nature reserve covering 500 ha, owned by the non-profit **Fundación Lahuén**. It is a three- to four-hour trek to its highest peak, **El Mirador**. The first

# BACKGROUND

## Lake District geography

The region between the cities of Temuco and Puerto Montt can claim bragging rights as one of the most spectacular lake regions in the world. There are 12 great lakes, and dozens of smaller ones, as well as imposing waterfalls and snow-capped volcanoes. This landscape has been created by two main geological processes: glaciation and volcanic activity. The main mountain peaks are volcanic: the highest are Lanín (3747 m) and Tronador (3460 m), both on the Argentine border. The most active volcanoes include Llaima and Villarrica, which erupted 22 and 10 times respectively in the 20th century. Not to be outdone, the Calbuco volcano erupted for the first time in 40 years in 2015, resulting in a majestic display of lightning, smoke and lava.

Seven main river systems drain the Lake District, from north to south the ríos Imperial, Toltén, Valdivia, Bueno, Maullín, Petrohué and Puelo. The Río Bueno drains Lago Ranco and is joined by the ríos Pilmaiquén and Rahue, thus receiving also the waters of Lagos Puyehue and Rupanco: it carries the third largest water volume of any Chilean river. In most of the rivers there is excellent fishing.

Rain falls all the year round, most heavily further south, but decreases as you go inland: some 2500 mm of rain fall on the coast compared to 1350 mm inland. There is enough rainfall to maintain heavy forests, mostly of southern beech and native species, though there are increasingly large areas of eucalyptus and other introduced varieties to cater for the booming timber industry.

part of the trek to a basic *refugio* at the park entrance is straightforward, along a wide path winding upwards through ancient native forests of coigue and lenga, with occasional views back to Lagos Villarrica and Caburga. Inside the reserve there are 12 small lakes, snow-covered for much of the year. Between these lakes are dotted millennial araucaria trees. From here it is a steep climb to **El Mirador** (1550 m) from where there are panoramic views over neighbouring parts of Argentina and Chile, including four volcanoes: **Lanín**, **Villarrica**, **Quetrupillán** and **Llaima**. As the reserve is above the snowline for much of the year, independent visits are normally restricted to summer, although guided visits are possible off season. See also What to do, page 281.

### Towards Argentina

From Pucón a road runs southeast along the southern bank of the valley of the Río Trancura to **Curarrehue** and the Argentine border, providing access en route to thermal springs and a number of hikeable *saltos* (waterfalls).

At Km 18, a *ripio* road heads south 10 km to the **Termas de Palguín** ⓘ *T45-244 1968, US$14.50*, and a series of spectacular waterfalls. A hidden 200-m path leads to **Salto Palguín** (which can be seen from the road), and beyond that is the impressive **Salto China**, where there's a restaurant and camping. **Saltos del Puma** and **del León** are 800 m from the Termas. From Pucón take a Vipo Ray bus to Curarrehue from the bus terminal, tell the driver to let you off at the entrance (10 km from Termas). The first bus leaves Pucón at 0730 and the last bus from junction to Pucón leaves at 2030, so you may have to hitch back. A taxi is around US$40.

From the springs, a rough dirt road runs south to Coñaripe, with access to the Volcán Quetrupillán section of the **Parque Nacional Villarrica**. If you're driving, a high-clearance

## BORDER CROSSING
### Chile–Argentina

**Paso Mamuil Malal**

Paso Muil Malal (also known as Paso Tromen) is 76 km southeast of Pucón; see also box, page 93. The road continues south through Parque Nacional Lanín in Argentina to Junín de los Andes, San Martín de los Andes and Bariloche.

4WD vehicle is necessary to reach the national park, and the road is often impassable in winter; but travelling on horseback is best. The treks in this sector are not physically demanding. Palguín is also the starting point for a three-day hike to Puesco, with vistas over the Villarrica and Lanín volcanoes. Further along the road, on the other side of the park are the **Termas Geométricas** (see page 283). Because of the poor state of the road, access is easier from Coñaripe.

Back on the Curarrehue road, at Km 23, a turning leads north to the indoor and outdoor pools at **Termas de San Luis** ① T45-241 2880, www.termasdesanluis.cl, US$22, and **Termas Trancura** ① T45-244 1189, www.termastrancura.com, US$13 or US$20 including transport from Pucón, from where it is 30 minutes' walk to **Lago del León**. At Km 35 another turning leads north for 15 km to the **Termas de Panqui** ① www.panqui.cl, US$28, where there are three pools beautifully situated in the mountains as well as accommodation ($$$).

Beyond the small town of Curarrehue, 36 km east of Pucón, where there is a small but interesting Mapuche museum, the road continues unpaved, climbing south past Puesco to Lago Quellelhue, a beautiful area for trekking, tranquil and with well-marked trails.

Six kilometres southeast is the border at **Paso Mamuil Malal** (also known as Paso Tromen), see box, above. The closest village to the border is **Puesco**, where there is free CONAF camping with no facilities. A bus from Pucón to Puesco takes two hours, US$34.

To the south of the pass rises the graceful cone of **Volcán Lanín** (3747 m), one of the world's most beautiful mountains. Currently dormant, Lanín is geologically one of the youngest volcanoes in the Andes and is climbed from the Argentine side. See also box, page 88.

**Tip...**

This is probably the easiest area to see araucaria forest close-up from the comfort of a car.

## Listings East of Lago Villarrica

### Where to stay

**Lagos Caburga and Colico**

**$$$ Landhaus San Sebastián**
Camino Pucón a Caburga, Pucón 2222,
T9-9443 1786, www.landhaus.cl.
With bath and breakfast, good meals,
laundry facilities, English and German
spoken, Spanish classes, good base for
nearby walks.

**Parque Nacional Huerquehue**

**$$$-$$ Puerto Parque Tinquilco**
Parque Huerquehue, Km 37, T9-8538 7716,
www.parquehuerquehue.cl.
Hotel, cabins, camping and motorhome
parking, restaurant, kayaks, boats for hire.

**$$ Refugio Tinquilco**
2 km from park entrance, where the
forest trail leads to lakes Verde and Toro,

*T2-2278 9831, T9-9539 2728,*
*www.tinquilco.cl.*
Range of cabins, bunk beds or doubles, cheapest without sheets, bring sleeping bag, private or shared bath, meals available, heating, 24-hr electricity, sauna.

## Camping

### $$-$ Camping Olga
*T45-244 1938, www.campingolga.com.*
Camping in the park, 2 km from park entrance, with hot water.

## Termas de Quimey-Co, de Huife and los Pozones

### $$$$ Hostería Termas de Huife
*Termas de Huife, T45-244 1222,*
*www.termashuife.cl.*
The most upmarket of the spa hotels.

### $$$ Hotel Termas de Quimey-Co
*Termas de Quimey-Co, T9-8775 2113,*
*www.termasquimeyco.com.*
Also a campsite and 2 cabins.

## Towards Argentina

### $$ Kila Leufu/Ruka Rayen
*23 km east on road to Curarrehue,*
*T9-9876 4576, www.kilaleufu.cl.*
2 adjacent guesthouses run by the same Austrian/Mapuche owners. Kila Leufu offers rooms on the Martínez family farm, contact Irma or Margot at Ruka Rayen in advance, home-grown food, boat tours. Ruka Rayen is on the banks of the Río Palguín, 15 mins' walk from the main road (regular buses to Pucón). Some rooms with bath, English-speaking hosts (Margot's parents own Kila Leufu), mountain bike hire. Both serve meals,

offer horse riding, trekking information and camping. The perfect choice if you want to avoid the hustle and bustle of Pucón.

### $$ Rancho de Caballos
*Palguín Aito Km 32, T9-8346 1764 (limited signal), www.rancho-de-caballos.com.*
Restaurant with vegetarian dishes; also *cabañas* and camping, self-guided trails, horse-riding trips ½-6 days, English and German spoken.

## What to do

### Parque Nacional Villarrica
Tours from Pucón cost US$150, including park entry, guide, transport to park entrance and hire of equipment (no reduction for those with their own equipment). Bargain for group rates. Travel agencies will not start out if the weather is bad and some travellers have experienced difficulties in obtaining a refund: establish in advance what terms apply in the event of cancellation and be prepared to wait a few days. For information on independent guides, all with equipment, ask for recommendations at the tourist office.

### Towards Argentina
**Escape**, *in Curarrehue, T9-9678 5380, www.patagonia-escape.com.* Owned by John 'LJ' Groth, specializing in SUP, private kayak guiding trips and rafting on some beautiful sections of the Río Trancura and around. Safe, responsible, environmentally aware and different.

### Reserva Forestal Cañi
**Hostería ¡école!**, *General Urrutia 592, T45-244 1675, www.ecole.cl.* See Where to stay, page 273, offers good tours.

# The Seven Lakes

These lakes, situated south of Lago Villarrica, form a beautiful necklace of water, surrounded by thick woods and with views of distant snows giving a picture-postcard backdrop. Six of the lakes lie in Chile, with the seventh, Lago Lácar, in Argentina. After the final peace settlement of 1882 the area around these lakes was reserved for Mapuche settlements. Lago Riñihue is most easily reached from Valdivia and Los Lagos and is dealt with in a later section (see page 297). Most of the lakes have black-sand beaches, although in spring, as the water level rises, these can all but disappear.

## Lago Calafquén  *Colour map 1, A3.*

**lake resorts perfect for watersports**

The most northerly of the seven lakes, Lago Calafquén is a popular tourist destination for Chileans, readily accessible by a paved road from Villarrica, along which there are fine views of the Volcán Villarrica. Wooded and dotted with small islands, the lake is reputedly one of the warmest in the region and makes for a refreshing swim. A mostly paved road runs around the lake.

### Lican-Ray

Situated 30 km south of Villarrica on a peninsula on the north shore, Lican-Ray is the major resort on the lake and is named after a legendary Mapuche woman. There are two beaches, one on each side of the peninsula. Kayaks can be hired for around US$5 per hour, and there are catamaran trips (US$4.75) and water bicycles (US$5.75 for three people). Although crowded in season, Lican-Ray can feel like a ghost town by the end of March, when most facilities have closed. Some 6 km to the east is the river of lava formed when Volcán Villarrica erupted in 1971.

### Coñaripe

Lying 21 km southeast of Lican-Ray at the eastern end of Lago Calafquén, Coñaripe is another popular Chilean tourist spot. At first sight the village is dusty and nondescript, but its setting, with a 3-km black-sand beach surrounded by mountains, is beautiful. Most services are on the Calle Principal.

From Coñaripe a road (mostly *ripio*) around the lake's southern shore leads to **Lago Panguipulli**, see page 285, 38 km west, and offers superb views over Volcán Villarrica, which can be climbed from here. Another dirt road heads northeast through the Parque Nacional Villarrica to Pucón, see page 270; the first few kilometres are good *ripio*. There are several thermal springs here.

**Termas Vergara**, 14 km northeast of Coñaripe by a steep *ripio* road which continues to Palguín, has nice open-air pools. **Termas Geométricas** ⓘ *3 km beyond Termas Vergara, T22-795 1606, www.termasgeometricas.cl, US$34 from 1200-2000 (cheaper in mornings)*, has 17 pools, geometrically shaped and linked by wooden walkways. There is a small café. After the Termas Geométricas the road worsens and is suitable for high-clearance 4WD only.

## Southeast of Coñaripe

From Coñaripe a road runs southeast over the steep Cuesta Los Añiques offering views of **Lago Pellaifa**, a tiny lake with rocky surroundings covered with vegetation and a small beach. **Termas de Coñaripe** ⓘ *Km 15, 2 km from the lakeshore, T45-232 4800, www.termasconaripe.cl, US$24*, has six pools, accommodation, restaurant, cycles and horses for hire. Transport can be organized from Coñaripe.

Further south are the **Termas Río Liquiñe** ⓘ *Km 32, T9-81973546, termasrioliquine@gmail.com, see also Facebook, US$11.50*, with eight thermal springs and accommodation (but little other infrastructure), surrounded by a small native forest.

About 8 km north of Liquiñe is a road going southwest for 20 km along the southeast shore of **Lago Neltume** to meet the Choshuenco–Puerto Fuy road.

**The Seven Lakes**

## Listings Lago Calafquén *map page 283.*

## Tourist information

### Lican-Ray

**Tourist office**
*On the plaza, T63-815 2245. Daily 0900-1600 in summer, Mon-Fri in winter.*

### Coñaripe

**Tourist office**
*On the plaza, T63-231 7378. Daily 0900-1100 in summer, 0900-1800 in winter.*
Can arrange trips to local thermal springs.

## Where to stay

### Lican-Ray

**$$ Cabañas Los Nietos**
*Manquel 125, Playa Chica, T9-5639 3585, www.losnietos.cl.*
Self-catering cabins.

**$ Residencial Temuco**
*G Mistral 517, T45-243 1130.*
Shared bath, with breakfast, good.

### Camping

**Las Gaviotas**
*Km 5 Camino Lican-Ray, T9-9030 1153, www.campinglasgaviotas.cl.*
Beach camping with many amenities, such as hot showers, mini market and volleyball area.

### Coñaripe

**$$-$ Hospedaje Chumay**
*Las Tepas 201, on plaza, T9-9744 8835, www.turismochumay.cl.*
With restaurant, tours (see What to do, below), some English spoken, good.

### Camping

Sites on beach charge US$28, but if you walk 500 m from town you can camp on the beach for free; there are cold municipal showers on the beach, US$0.25. There is another

site with *cabañas* on **Isla Llancahue** in the Río Llancahue, 5 km east, T9-9562 0437.

### Southeast of Coñaripe

**$$$$ Termas de Coñaripe**
*T45-232 4800, www.termasconaripe.cl.*
Excellent hotel with 4 pools, good restaurant, spa with a variety of treatments, cycles and horses for hire. Full board available.

**$$$ Termas de Liquiñe**
*T9-8197 3546.*
Full board, cabins, restaurant, hot pool, small native forest.

**$$ Hospedaje Catemu**
*Camino Internacional, T63-197 1629, neldatrafipan@yahoo.es.*
Known as much for its restaurant as its cosy, wood-panelled cabins, this option can arrange trips to the Termas.

## Restaurants

### Lican-Ray

**$$ Cábala**
*Urrutia 201.*
Nice central location; good pizzas and pastas.

**$$-$ The Ñaños**
*Urrutia 105.*
Good café and restaurant, reasonable prices, helpful owner. Service can be patchy.

### Coñaripe

For eating options, see Where to stay, above.

## What to do

### Coñaripe

**Hospedaje Chumay**, *see Where to stay, above*. Organizes hikes to Villarica volcano and trips to various thermal springs.
**Rucapillán Expediciones**, *Martínez de Rosas 519, T63-231 8220, www.rucapillan.cl.*
Rafting in the rivers Fuy, Enco and San Pedro as well as volcano treks.

## Transport

### Lican-Ray

**Bus** Buses leave from offices around plaza. To **Villarrica**, 1 hr, US$1.50; direct buses to **Santiago** US$38-66, 11 hrs, and **Temuco** US$4.25 with **JAC** frequent in summer. To **Panguipull** every hour until 1930, US$1.45; to **Coñaripe** US$1.75.

### Coñaripe

**Bus** To **Panguipulli**, 5 a day, US$1.50 and regular services to **Villarrica** with **JAC** and **Buses Coñaripe**, US$2.75. Nightly bus direct to **Santiago**, Tur-Bus and **JAC**, 11½ hrs, US$46-72. To **Temuco** US$5.75; to **Lican-Ray** US$1.25.

## Lago Panguipulli  *Colour map 1, A3.*

**trips on the largest of Chile's seven lakes**

Covering 116 sq km, Lago Panguipulli, the largest of the seven lakes, is reached either by paved road from Lanco or Los Lagos on the Pan-American Highway or by *ripio* roads from Lago Calafquén. A road leads along the beautiful northern shore, which is wooded with sandy beaches and cliffs, but most of the lake's southern shore is inaccessible by road.

### Panguipulli

The site of a Mapuche settlement, Panguipulli, meaning 'hill of pumas', is situated on a hillside at the northwest corner of the lake. It grew as a railway terminal and a port for vessels carrying timber from the lakesides, and is now the largest town in the area.

On Plaza Prat is the **Iglesia San Sebastián**, built in Swiss style with twin towers by the Swiss Padre Bernabé; its belltower contains three bells from Germany. From Plaza Prat the main commercial street, Martínez de Rozas, runs down to the lakeshore. In summer, catamaran trips are offered on the lake (US$4.25 for one hour) and excursions can be made to Lagos Calafquén, Neltume, Pirehueico and to the northern tip of Lago Riñihue, see page 297.

The road east to Coñaripe, on Lago Calafquén, offers superb views of the lake and of Volcán Villarrica.

### Choshuenco and around

Choshuenco lies 45 km east of Panguipulli on the Río Llanquihue, at the eastern tip of the lake and can only be reached by road from Panguipulli or Puerto Fuy. To the south is the Reserva Nacional Mocho Choshuenco (7536 ha), which includes two volcanoes: Choshuenco (2415 m) and Mocho (2422 m). On the slopes of Choshuenco the **Club Andino de Valdivia** runs a small ski resort and three *refugios*. (The resort is reached by a turning from the road that goes south from Choshuenco to Enco at the east end of Lago Riñihue, see page 297.)

From Choshuenco a road leads east to **Neltume** and **Lago Pirehueico**, via the impressive waterfalls of **Huilo Huilo**. The falls are a three-hour walk from Choshuenco, or take the Puerto Fuy bus and get off at the Nothofagus Hotel (see Where to stay, opposite), from where it is a five-minute walk to the falls. The Reserva Biológica Huilo Huilo is privately owned, with lots of outdoor activities and a variety of lodgings in the trees; see www.huilohilo.com/en.

## Tourist information

### Panguipulli
See also also www.municipalidad
panguipulli.cl.

**Tourist office**
*By the Plaza, T63-231 0436, www.sietelagos.cl.
Daily 0830-2100 Dec-Feb, otherwise Mon-Fri
0830-1800.*

## Where to stay

### Panguipulli
See www.sietelagos.cl for a full list of lodgings.

**$$ La Casita del Centro**
*J M Carerra 674, T9-6495 5040.*
B&B, refurbished, safe, with restaurant
and parking.

**$ pp Hostal Orillas del Lago**
*M de Rosas 265, T63-231 1710 (or T63-231 2499
if no reply; friends have key).*
From plaza walk towards lake, last house on
left, 8 blocks from terminal. Backpacker place
with good views.

### Camping

**El Bosque**
*P Sigifredo 241, T63-231 1489.*
Small, good, but not suitable for vehicle
camping, hot water. Also 3 sites at Chauquén,
6 km southeast on lakeside.

### Choshuenco and around

**$$$$ Nothofagus Hotel**
*Carretera Internacional Km 55 (to arrive,
take a bus from Panguiplli to Puerto Fuy and
tell the driver to let you off at Huilo Huilo),
T2-2887 3535, www.huilohuilo.com.*
Probably the most famous hotel in the
country, the Nothofagus has 7 sites dotted
over its 100,000 ha. The main hotel is built
like a treehouse, with wooden walkways
spiralling 5 floors up the trunk. There are

also lodges, refuges and *cabañas*. Buffet
meals, a welcome drink and entry to the
Sendero Huilo Huilo, home to wild boars
and huemules are all included. Rafting,
skiing, zip-lining and many more activities
are available. Outdoor/indoor swimming
area, hydromassage therapy rooms and
craft brewery.

**$$$ Hostería Ruca Pillán**
*San Martín 85, T63-231 8220,
www.rucapillan.cl.*
Family-run hotel rooms and cabins
overlooking the lake, restaurant, English
spoken, tours.

**$$$-$$ Cabañas Peumayén**
*Los Cipreses 27, 6 km from Puerto Fuy, T9-
9438 8191, www.turismopeumayen.cl.*
Fully equipped *cabañas*, Wi-Fi, satellite
TV, laundry service, breakfast included. A
5-min drive from the Saltos del Huilo Huilo.

**$$ Cabañas Choshuenco**
*Bernabé 391, T9 5672 9390,
www.choshuencochile.cl.*
Cabañas, fully equipped, self-contained,
for 6-8 people.

## Restaurants

### Panguipulli
There are several cheap restaurants in
O'Higgins 700 block.

**$$-$ El Chapulín**
*M de Rosas 639, see Facebook.*
Good food and value.

**$$-$ Gardylafquen**
*M de Rosas 722.*
Typical Chilean fare. Popular with locals
and tourists.

**$ El Pollo Cototo**
*On the plaza opposite the church,
T9-9587 2782, see Facebook.*
Fast food specializing in chicken.

### Choshuenco and around

For eating options, see Where to stay, above.

## Festivals

**Panguipulli**
2nd half of Feb **La Semana de Rosas**,
with dancing and sports competitions.

## What to do

**Panguipulli**
**Fishing**
The following fishing trips on Lago
Panguipulli are recommended: Puntilla
Los Cipreses at the mouth of the Río
Huanehue, 11 km east of Panguipulli,
30 mins by boat; the mouth of the Río
Niltre, on east side of lake. Licences available
online only at www.sernapesca.cl, US$11.

### Rafting
Good rafting opportunities on the Río Fuy,
Grade IV-V; Río San Pedro, varying grades,
and on the Río Llanquihue near Choshuenco.

## Transport

**Panguipulli**
**Bus** Terminal at Gabriela Mistral y
Portales. To **Santiago** daily, US$40-75.
To **Valdivia** (every 30 mins), several
companies, 2 hrs, US$4.75. To **Temuco**
frequent, **Regional Sur**, US$4.50, 3 hrs.
To **Puerto Montt**, US$11.50. To **Choshuenco**,
US$2.50, **Neltume**, US$3, and **Puerto Fuy**,
US$3.50, 5 daily, fewer on weekends 3 hrs.
To **Coñaripe** (with connections for Lican-Ray
US$1.50 and Villarrica), 5 daily, 1 off season,
1½ hrs, US$1.75.

**untouched nature and the crossing to Argentina**

East of Choshuenco, Lago Pirehueico is a 36-km-long, narrow and deep glacial lake
surrounded by virgin lingue forest. It is beautiful and largely unspoilt, although
there are plans to build a huge tourist complex in Puerto Pirehueico.

There are two ports on the lake: **Puerto Fuy** at the northern end and **Puerto Pirehueico**
at the southern end. The ports are linked by a ferry service (see Transport, below), a
beautiful crossing that is comparable to the more famous lakes crossing from Puerto
Montt to Bariloche (see box, page 323), but at a fraction of the price. They can also be
reached by the road that runs east from Neltume to the Argentine border crossing at
Paso Hua Hum (see box, page 288).

The road south from Puerto Fuy, however, is privately owned and closed to traffic. This
is a shame because it is a beautiful route passing around Volcán Choshuenco and through
rainforest to Río Pillanleufú, Puerto Llolles on Lago Maihue and Puerto Llifén on Lago Ranco.

### Listings Lago Pirehueico

#### Where to stay

Camping is possible on the beach but take
your own food.

**$$ Hospedaje y Cabañas Don Aníbal**
*Puerto Fuy, T9-8725 0827,*
*www.cabañaspuertofuy.cl.*
Hot water, good food in restaurant.

**$ pp Restaurant San Giovanni**
*Puerto Fuy, T63-2197 1562.*
Family atmosphere, good rooms.

#### Transport

**Bus** Puerto Fuy to **Panguipulli** every
hour Mon-Sat 0700-1900, 3 hrs, US$3. Buses
between Puerto Pirehueico and **San Martín**

## BORDER CROSSING
### Chile–Argentina

**Paso Hua Hum**

Paso Hua Hum (659 m) lies 11 km southeast of Puerto Pirehueico. The border is an alternative to the route via Paso Mamuil Malal (Tromen), see page 280. On the Argentine side, the *ripio* road continues along the north shore of Lago Lacar to San Martín de los Andes ; see box, page 95. There are buses from Puerto Pirehueico to San Martín. See www.pasosfronterizos.gov.cl/cf_huahum.html.

de los Andes (Argentina) are run by **Ko Ko** in San Martín, T+54 (0)2972-427422, and connect with the ferry service across the lake.

**Ferry** The **Hua Hum** (www.barcaza huahum.com) sails from **Puerto Fuy** to **Puerto Pirehueico** at 0800, 1300, 1800 (Jan-Feb), 1300 (rest of year), returns 2 hrs later, foot passengers US$1.30, cars US$25, motorbikes US$7.50; to take vehicles reserve in advance on T63-4277 3450, or see **Somarco**'s website, www.barcazas.cl.

# Valdivia
## & around

Surrounded by wooded hills, Valdivia is one of the crown jewels of southern Chile and a good place to rest after arduous treks in the mountains. In the summer tourist season the city comes to life with activities and events, while off season this is a unrelentingly green city with a thriving café culture.

With a high student population (its total population is 150,000) it is also one of the best cities for meeting young Chileans, who will be at the pulse of anything in the way of nightlife in the city.

Valdivia lies nearly 839 km south of Santiago at the confluence of two rivers, the Calle Calle and Cruces, which form the Río Valdivia. To the northwest of the city is a large island, Isla Teja, where the Universidad Austral de Chile is situated. West, along the coast, are a series of important Spanish colonial forts, while to the north are two nature reserves with native forests and a wide range of birdlife. Inland there are two lakes off the beaten tourist path.

## Sights

The city is centred on the tree-lined **Plaza de la República**. In the cathedral, the **Museo de la Catedral de Valdivia** ⓘ *Independencia 514, Mon-Sat 1000-1300, free (donation)*, covers four centuries of Christian history. Three blocks east is the **Muelle Fluvial**, the dock for boat trips down the river. From the Muelle Fluvial there is a pleasant walk north along the *costanera* (Avenida Prat) and under the bridge to Isla Teja and on round the bend in the river (as far as the bus terminal).

On the western bank of the river, **Isla Teja** has a botanical garden and arboretum with trees from all over the world. West of the botanical gardens is the **Parque Saval** ⓘ *daily 1000-1800 in winter, daylight hours in summer, US$0.75*. Covering 30 ha it has areas of native forest as well as a small lake, the Lago de los Lotos. There are beautiful flowers in spring. It often hosts events like Rodeos, and a Mapuche market and craft market in summer.

Also on the island are two museums. The **Museo Histórico y Antropológico** ⓘ *Av Los Laureles s/n, T63-221 2872, www.museosregiondelosrios.com, Mar-Dec Tue-Sun 1000-1300, 1400-1800, Jan and Feb daily 1000-2000, US$2.15, discounts for children and seniors*, is beautifully situated in the former mansion of Carlos Anwandter, a leading German immigrant. Run by the university, it contains sections on archaeology, ethnography and German colonization. Next door, in the former Anwandter brewery, is the **Museo de Arte Moderno Contemporáneo** ⓘ *T63-222 1968, www.macvaldivia.cl, Tue-Sun 1000-1300,*

| | |
|---|---|
| **Where to stay** 🛌 | |
| 1 Airesbuenos Central | |
| 2 Camping Isla Teja | |
| 3 Camping Orilla Verde | |
| 4 Encanto del Río | |
| 5 Hospedaje Arlene | |
| 6 Hostal Ana María | |
| 7 Hostal Anwandter | |
| 8 Hostal Casagrande | |
| 9 Hostal Torreón | |
| 10 Hostal Totem | |
| 11 Hostal Cabañas Internacional | |
| 12 Melillanca | |
| 13 Puerta del Sur | |

**Restaurants** 🍴
2 Café Das Hauss
3 Café Moro
4 Cervecería Kunstmann
6 Entrelagos
7 La Baguette
8 La Calesa
10 Mi Pueblito
11 Sello de Raza

## ON THE ROAD

## Lord Cochrane

Lord Thomas Alexander Cochrane (1775-1860) was born into a Scottish aristocratic family and began his career in the British navy during the Napoleonic Wars. He was elected to Parliament in 1806 as MP for Honiton and in 1807 as MP for Westminster.

Cochrane had never been on good terms with his naval superiors, and when he used his position in the House of Commons to accuse the naval commander, Lord Gambier, of incompetence, he precipitated his own downfall. Cochrane spent the next three years exposing corruption and abuses in the navy. His links with a financial scandal in 1814 provided his enemies with an opportunity for revenge: he was dismissed from the navy, expelled from Parliament and imprisoned for 12 months.

Cochrane was recruited for the Chilean armed forces by an agent in London and quickly became friendly with Chile's independence leader Bernardo O'Higgins. He was put in command of the new republic's 'navy', a few ill-equipped vessels that relied on foreign adventurers for experienced sailors, and with this fleet harassed the Spanish-held ports along the Chilean coast. His audacious storming of the fortresses of Corral, San Carlos and Amargos led to the capture of the key Spanish base of Valdivia.

Later that year Cochrane transported Peruvian liberation troops, led by José de San Martín, along the Pacific coast to invade Peru, but his relations with San Martín were poor and he became very critical of the Peruvian's cautious strategy.

In 1823 the new government of Brazil appointed Cochrane to head its navy in the struggle for independence from Portugal. Once again leading boats manned largely by foreigners, Cochrane drove the colonial fleet from Bahia. In 1825 he fell out with the Brazilian government and returned to Britain. He was reinstated in the British navy in 1832, and spent much of the rest of his life promoting in the use of steam power in shipping.

*1400-1800 in winter, 1000-2000 in summer, times change according to exhibitions, US$2.15, free for students and children.* Boat trips can be made around Isla Teja, offering views of birds and seals.

**Kunstmann Brewery** ⓘ *just out of town on the Niebla road, T63-222 2570, www. cerveza-kunstmann.cl*, offers tours of the working brewery and its beer museum; it also has a good restaurant.

Every Sunday during January and February there is a special **steam train service** ⓘ *T9-91004726, leaves at 1130 returns from Antilhue at 1600, US$11 return, advance booking essential*, from the train station on Equador to **Antilhue**, 20 km to the east. The train is met by locals selling all sorts of culinary specialities. The engine dates from 1913. Special additional trips are often made on public holidays; check departure times before travelling.

Like many Chilean cities, the centre is relatively compact, and few places are beyond walking distance, even those across the river on the Isla Teja.

# BACKGROUND

## Valdivia

Valdivia was one of the most important centres of Spanish colonial control over Chile. Founded in 1552 by Pedro de Valdivia, it was abandoned as a result of the Mapuche insurrection of 1599 and was briefly occupied by Dutch pirates. In 1645 it was refounded as a walled city and the only Spanish mainland settlement south of the Río Biobío. The Spanish continued to fortify the area around Valdivia throughout the 1600s, developing the most comprehensive system of defence in the South Pacific against the British and Dutch navies. Seventeen forts were built in total. They were reinforced after 1760, but proved of little avail during the Wars of Independence, when the Chilean naval squadron under Lord Cochrane seized control of the forts in two days. From independence until the 1880s Valdivia was an outpost of Chilean rule, reached only by sea or by a coastal route through Mapuche territory. In 2007 it became capital of the newly created Región XIV, Los Ríos.

## Listings Valdivia map page 290.

### Tourist information

**CONAF office**
*Los Castaños 100, T65-224 5200.*
For information on national parks.

**Municipal tourist office**
*Upstairs in the bus terminal and other locations. Daily 0800-2200.*

**Tourist office**
*Av Prat (Costanera) at the north side of the Feria Fluvial, T63-223 9060, www.descubre losrios.cl. Mon-Fri 0900-1800, Sat-Sun 1000-1600 in winter, 0900-2100 in summer.*
Good maps of the region and local rivers, a list of hotel prices and examples of local crafts with artisans' addresses.

### Where to stay

Accommodation is often scarce during Semana Valdiviana. In summer, rooms are widely available in private homes, usually **$$**, or **$** for singles.

**$$$$-$$$ Puerta del Sur**
*Los Lingües 950, Isla Teja, T63-222 4500, www.hotelpuertadelsur.com.*
5-star, with all facilities and extensive grounds.

**$$$ Encanto del Río**
*Prat 415, T63-222 5740, www.hotelencantodelrio.cl.*
Small, comfortable, rooms on the middle floor have balconies and river views, disabled access, heating.

**$$$ Melillanca**
*Alemania 675, T63-221 2509, www.hotelmelillanca.cl.*
4-star, decent business standard, with restaurant, sauna.

**$$ Hostal Torreón**
*P Rosales 783, T63-221 3069, mrprelle@gmail.com.*
Old German-style villa, nice atmosphere, rooms on top floor are airy, parking.

**$$ Hostal Totem**
*Anwandter 425, T63-229 2849, www.turismototem.cl.*
Simple rooms, French and basic English spoken, tours arranged, credit cards accepted.

**$$ Hostal y Cabañas Internacional**
*García Reyes 660, T63-221 2015, www.hostalinternacional.cl.*
Self-catering cabins sleep 5, hostel rooms and dorms with private or shared bath,

helpful, English and German spoken, book exchange, trips to the ocean and rainforest.

### $$-$ Airesbuenos Central
*García Reyes 550, T63-222 2202, www.airesbuenos.cl.*
Eco-conscious hostel. Private rooms and dorms, private or shared bath, garden with friendly duck named Gardel, yoga space, tours, many languages spoken by volunteers, HI affiliated.

### Around the bus terminal

### $$ Hostal Ana María
*José Martí 11, 3 mins from terminal, T63-222 2468, anamsandovalf@hotmail.com.*
Good value, also *cabañas*.

### $$ Hostal Anwandter
*Anwandter 601 and García Reyes 249, T63-221 8587, www.hostalanwandter.cl.*
Rooms sleep 1-4, private or shared bathroom, meals available, usual hostel facilities.

### $$ Hostal Casagrande
*Anwandter 880, T63-220 2035, www.hotelcasagrande.cl.*
Heated but small rooms, some gloomy, in attractive house, convenient, great views from breakfast room.

### $ Hospedaje Arlene
*Picarte 1397, T9-7984 5597, arlene_ola@hotmail.com.*
The old charming tumbledown mansion was lost to a fire in 2015. But the owners moved their operation and still offer the same hospitality and welcoming family vibe in an expansive house, albeit far from the main plaza. Still, it's a great budget option during the high season. Doubles and singles, Wi-Fi, use of kitchen, free weekly laundry service, some English spoken. Recommended.

### Camping

### Camping Isla Teja
*T63-222 5855, www.islateja.com/camping.*
25 sites on Isla Teja. Also *cabañas*.

### Camping Orilla Verde
*Pasaje Eusebio Lillo 23, T63-243 3902, www.campingvaldivia.jimdo.com.*
Camping on the river for around US$7.50 per night. Services include Wi-Fi and kayak rental.

## Restaurants

### $$$-$$ Sello de Raza
*Las Encinas 171, Isla Teja, T63-222 6262.*
Steakhouse and traditional Chilean food in a warm atmosphere.

### $$ Cervecería Kunstmann
*Ruta T350, No 950, T63-229 2969, www. cerveza-kunstmann.cl. Open from 1200 for visits; take the orange No 20 bus to Niebla.*
On road to Niebla. German/Chilean food, brewery with 14 types of beer, beautiful interior, museum.

### $$ La Calesa
*O'Higgins 160, T63-222 5467, www.lacalesa.cl.*
Elegant, intimate, Peruvian and international cuisine. Good pisco sours.

### Cafés

### Café Das Hauss
*O'Higgins 394, T63-221 3878, see Facebook.*
A Valdivia institution. Good tea, cakes and *crudos*.

### Café Moro
*Independencia y Libertad, T63-223 9084, see Facebook.*
Airy café with a mezzanine art gallery. Good for breakfast, good-value lunches, popular bar at night.

### Entrelagos
*Pérez Rosales 622, T63-221 2047, www.entrelagos.cl/valdivia.*
Ice cream and chocolates.

### La Baguette
*Yungay 518, T63-221 2345.*
*Panadería* with French-style cakes, brown bread.

### Mi Pueblito
*San Carlos 190, T63-224 5050,*
*www.mipueblito.cl.*
Wholemeal bread and vegetarian snacks
to take away.

## Bars and clubs

Barrio Esmeralda is the place to be any
night of the week. There are many bars,
pubs and restaurants, all with a young,
bohemian vibe. Also summer festivals in
the area.

### Bunker
*Av Los Robles 1345, Isla Teja.*
Lively student bar/pub, various artisanal beers.

### La Bomba
*Caupolicán.*
Pleasant old Valdivian bar, serves *empanadas*
and other dishes.

### La Ultima Frontera
*Pérez Rosales 787 (in Centro Cultural 787).*
Fills up with alternative 20- and
30-something crowd. Cheap artisanal beer
as well as a large variety of sandwiches
(including falafel) and filling soups. Friendly
but slow service and very smoky.

### Santo Pecado
*Yungay 745.*
Refined but laid-back bar also serving a
variety of sandwiches and exotic dishes.

## Entertainment

There's a cinema in the Mall on Calle Arauco.

**Cine Club UACH**, *on the university campus
on Isla Teja, www.2013.cineclubuach.cl.*
Shows films on weekdays (not in summer).

## Festivals

**Last week of Jan** Cerveceria Kuntsmann
holds a **Bierfest** in Saval Park, live music,
activities (games, horse riding), food and
artisanal beer.
**Dec to end of Feb** Semana Valdiviana,
with a series of sporting and cultural

activities such a as a triathlon, theatre and
music, culminates in **Noche Valdiviana**
on the last Sat of Feb with a procession of
elaborately decorated boats that sail past
the Muelle Fluvial.
**Oct** A well-regarded film festival, **Festival
de Cine de Valdivia**. Oktoberfest, also in
Saval Park, has live music from oompah
bands. Lots of leiderhosen and beer.

## Shopping

**Feria Fluvial** is a colourful riverside market
selling livestock, fish, etc. The separate
**municipal market** building opposite has
been restored and is occupied mainly by
*artesanía* stalls. On the riverside of the
market building there are several fish
restaurants serving cheap, tasty food
in a nice atmosphere.

## What to do

### Boat trips
Kiosks along the Muelle Fluvial offer trips
to **Corral**, **Niebla** and elsewhere. Boats will
only leave with a minimum of 10 passengers,
so organize your trip in advance during the
off-season. A full list of operators is available
from the tourist information office.
**Bahia II**, *Costanera s/n, in a kiosk next to the
Feria Fluvial, T63-234 8727.* Offers a range of
trips. Highly recommended.

### Sea kayaking
**Pueblito Expediciones**, *San Carlos 188, T63-
224 5055, www.pueblitoexpediciones.cl.* Offer
classes and trips in the waters around Valdivia.

## Transport

**Air** 6 flights per week to/from **Santiago** with
**Sky**. There are daily flights to **Concepción**.

**Bus** Valdivia is quite sizeable: *colectivos* and
buses serve the outlying barrios.
There is a well-organized bus terminal at
Muñoz y Prat, by the river. To **Niebla**, bus
No 20 from outside bus station or along
calles Anwandter and Carampangue, regular

service 0630-1130, 30 mins, US$0.85 (bus continues to **Los Molinos**). To **Futrono**, US$3.50; also to **Llifén** via Futrono US$3.50, with **Cordillera Sur**, daily. Frequent services to **Riñihue** via Paillaco and Los Lagos with **Buses Runisur**, US$3.50.

To **Santiago**, several companies, 10 hrs, most services overnight, US$30-80. To **Osorno**, every 30 mins, 2 hrs, several companies, US$5.50. To **Panguipulli**, **Empresa Pirehueico**, about every 30 mins, US$4.75. Many daily to **Puerto Montt**, US$7.75, 3 hrs. To **Puerto Varas**, 3 hrs, US$8. To **Frutillar**, US$7.50, 2½ hrs. To **Villarrica**,

with **JAC**, 2½ hrs, US$6.50, continuing to **Pucón**, US$6.75, 3 hrs. To **Bariloche (Argentina)** via Osorno, 7 hrs, **Andesmar/San Martín**, US$28.

**Ferry** The tourist boats to **Isla Mancera** and **Corral** offer a guided 5-hr tour (US$29-46, most with meals) from the Muelle Fluvial, Valdivia, or the Marqués de Mancera (behind the tourist office on Av Prat).

**Niebla**
Somarco vehicle ferry to **Corral**, every 20 mins, US$1.50.

## Along the Río Valdivia to the coast    Colour map 1, A2.

picturesque coastal towns and fresh seafood

The various rivers around Valdivia are navigable: rent a motor boat to explore the Ríos Futa and Tornagaleanes south of town around the Isla del Rey, or visit the interesting and isolated villages at the mouth of the Río Valdivia by road or river boat. The two main centres are Niebla on the north bank and Corral opposite on the south bank, site of two of the most important 17th-century Spanish forts (see below). There is a frequent boat service between the two towns.

Midstream between Niebla and Corral is **Isla Mancera**, a small island dominated by the Castillo de San Pedro de Alcántara, the earliest of the Spanish forts. Inside is a small church and convent. The island is a pleasant place to stop over on the boat trips, but it can get crowded when an excursion boat arrives.

### Niebla and around
Some 18 km west of Valdivia, **Niebla** is a resort with seafood restaurants and accommodation. To the west on a promontory is the **Fuerte de la Pura y Limpia Concepción de Monfort de Lemus** with a **museum** ⓘ *Tue-Sun 1000-1900*, on Chilean naval history, a **tourist information kiosk** ⓘ *daily 1000-2100*, and a telephone office. Around Niebla the north bank is dotted with campsites and *cabañas*.

About 6 km further round the coast is **Los Molinos**, a seaside resort set among steep wooded hills with lots of seaside restaurants. The road continues, rising and falling along the coast, with fine views of beaches deserted outside summer. The paved road runs out about 6 km north of Los Molinos but a *ripio* road continues past Curiñanco as far as the Parque Oncol.

### Corral and around
**Corral** lies 62 km west of Valdivia by road and is the main port serving the city. It is much quieter and more pleasant than Niebla, and its fort, **Castillo de San Sebastián** ⓘ *daily 0830-2000 in summer, 0830-1900 in winter US$2.15 summer, US$1.50 off season*, has a dilapidated, interesting atmosphere. It was built in 1645 as one of the main fortifications on the estuary, and during the 17th century its 3-m-thick walls were defended by a

battery of 21 guns. Inside is a museum (same hours), and in summer (15 December to 15 March) there are re-enactments in period costume of the 1820 storming of the Spanish fort by the Chilean Republican forces (daily 1615, 1730, 1815).

Further north near the mouth of the river are pleasant beaches and the remains of two other Spanish colonial forts, the **Castillo San Luis de Alba de Amargos** and the **Castillo de San Carlos**. The coastal walks west and south of Corral, along very isolated and forested roads above the ocean, are splendid and very rarely visited. The friendly tourist office on the pier can provide some trekking information.

## Listings Along the Río Valdivia to the coast

### Where to stay

#### Niebla

**$$$ El Castillo**
*Antonio Duce 750, T63-228 2061,*
*www.hotelycabanaselcastillo.com.*
Typical Germanic 1920s mansion, lots of character. Rooms and apartments, parking, playground and pool.

**$$ Cabañas Fischer**
*Del Castillo 1115, T63-228 2007,*
*www.cabanasfischer.cl.*
Cabins and 2 campsites. Worth bargaining out of season.

### Restaurants

#### Niebla

**$$-$ Entre Costa**
*Ducce 806, T63-228 2678.*

Popular corner restaurant serving Chilean specialities and seafood.

**$$-$ Ona**
*Ducce 875, T63-220 3969.*
New, modern restaurant with a great view and good-value food. Specializes in seafood and ceviches.

### Festivals

#### Niebla

**Feb Feria Costumbrista**, with lots of good food including *pullmay*, *asado* and *paila marina*.

### Transport

#### Niebla

**Somarco** vehicle ferry to **Corral**, every 20 mins, US$1.50.

## North of Valdivia Colour map 1, A2.

**treks through lush Valdivian rainforest**

Some 27 km to the northwest is the Parque Oncol (T800-370222, www.parque oncol.cl, US$4.25, camping US$13.50 for up to five people). The park runs a tour bus service to/from the park in Jan and Feb, US$22. It consists of 754 ha of native Valdivian forest with several easy trails and lookouts with fine views, canopy zip-lines (US$21.50, Sat-Sun 1100-1800), a picnic area, a good café and campsite.

Stretching from the outskirts of the city along the Río Cruces for 30 km north is the **Santuario de la Naturaleza Carlos Anwandter**, which was flooded as a result of the 1960 *maremoto* (tidal wave) and now attracts many bird species. Boat trips are available from Valdivia aboard the **Isla del Río** ① *Embarcaciones Bahía, on the riverfront near the fish market, T9-9316 5728, www.embarcacionesbahia.cl, daily 1600-1945, US$21.50 per person.*

## ON THE ROAD

## The 1960 earthquake

Southern Chile is highly susceptible to earthquakes: severe quakes struck the area in 1575, 1737, 1786 and 1837, but the tremor that struck around midday on 22 May 1960 caused the most extensive damage throughout southern Chile and was accompanied by the eruption of four volcanoes and a *maremoto* (tidal wave) that was felt in New Zealand and Japan.

Around Valdivia the land dropped by 3 m, creating new *lagunas* along the Río Cruces to the north of the city. The *maremoto* destroyed all the fishing villages and ports between Puerto Saavedra in the north and Chiloé in the south.

Further along the Río Cruces, 42 km north of Valdivia, lies the small town of **San José de la Mariquina**. From the town an unpaved road leads west along the north side of the river to the **Fuerte de San Luis de Alba de Cruces** (22 km), a colonial fortification built in 1647 and largely rebuilt according to the original plans.

West of San José, **Mehuín** is a small, friendly resort and fishing port with a long beach. The fishermen here are usually willing to take people out to see the nearby sealion and penguin colonies, and with a little luck dolphins can also be spotted. A cliff-top *ripio* road, with fantastic views north and south along the coastline, leads 6 km north to **Queule**, which has a good beach, but which is dangerous for bathing at high tide because of undercurrents. (Bathing is safer in the river near the ferry.)

From Queule, a pretty road leads north again to **Toltén**; numerous small ferry crossings provide access to isolated Mapuche communities and there are wonderful beaches along the coast.

## East of Valdivia   Colour map 1, B3.

idyllic farms and villages along Lago Ranco

The route east from Valdivia to the lakes passes through what is, perhaps, the least interesting part of the Lake District, consisting largely of wheatfields and dairy farms. Some 93 km east of Valdivia, beyond Antilhue and Los Lagos, is Lago Riñihue, the southernmost of the Seven Lakes. Riñihue, a beautiful but small and isolated village at its western end, is worth visiting but the road around the southern edge of the lake from Riñihue to Enco is poor and there is no road around the northern edge of the lake.

### Lago Ranco

South of Lago Riñihue is Lago Ranco, one of the largest lakes, covering 41,000 ha, and also one of the most accessible as it has a road, poor in many places, around its edge. The road is characterized by lots of mud and animals. However, it is worth taking the opportunity to escape the gringo trail and witness an older lifestyle while admiring the beautiful lake, starred with islands, and the sun setting on the distant volcanoes. There is excellent fishing on the southern shore; several hotels organize fishing expeditions.

From the Pan-American Highway the north side of the lake can be reached either from Los Lagos or from a better road 18 km further south. These two roads join and meet the road around the lake some 5 km west of **Futrono**. This is the main town on the northern shore and has a daily (except Friday) boat service (leaves at 1030 and 1800, more on weekends, US$1.50) to **Huapi**, the island in the middle of the lake.

From Futrono the road (paved at this point) curves round the north of the lake to **Llifén**, Km 22, a picturesque place on the eastern shore. From Llifén, it is possible visit **Lago Maihue**, 33 km further east, the south end of which is surrounded by native forests. From Llifén the road around Lago Ranco continues via the Salto de Nilahue (Km 14) to **Riñinahue**, Km 23, at the southeast corner, with access to beaches.

Further west is **Lago Ranco**, Km 47, an ugly little town on the south shore, which has a museum with exhibits on Mapuche culture. Paved roads lead from here to Río Bueno and the Pan-American Highway. On the western shore is **Puerto Nuevo**, where there are watersports and fishing on the Río Bueno. Further north, 10 km west of Futrono, is **Coique**, where there are more good beaches.

## Listings East of Valdivia

### Where to stay

Some of the houses around Lago Ranco are available to let in summer.

**$$$$ Hostería Huinca Quinay**
*3 km east of Riñihue, Lago Riñihue,*
*T9-642 1252, www.cabanasrinihue.cl.*
4-star *cabañas* for 5-6 people with restaurant and lots of facilities.

**$$$ Hostería Chollinco**
*3 km out of Llifén, on the road towards Lago*
*Maihue in the Lago Ranco area, T63-197 1979,*
*www.hosteria chollinco.cl.*
Remote country lodge with swimming pool, trekking, horse riding, fishing, hunting and other activities.

**$$$ Hotel Puerto Nuevo**
*Puerto Nuevo, Lago Ranco, T9-8888 7313,*
*www.hotelpuertonuevo.cl.*
Leisure complex in large grounds by the lake, with restaurant.

**$$$ Riñimapu**
*Northwest edge of Lago Riñihue,*
*T9-6300 1463, www.rinimapu.cl.*
Comfortable rooms and suites with views over the lake, gardens, excellent food.

**$$ Hospedaje Futronhue**
*Balmaceda 90, Futrono, T63-248 1265.*
Good breakfast.

### Camping

There are campsites all around Lago Ranco as well as several on Lago Maihue, though many are open in summer only and prices are high.

**Bahía Coique**
*9 km west of Futrono, T63-248 1264 ext 408,*
*www.bahiacoique.cl.*
Autocamping Nov-Mar (between US$30-40 per night depending on the month) and cabins.

**Bahía Las Rosas**
*1 km east of Futrono T9-7451 3238,*
*see Facebook.*
US$22 per site for 2 people, more for larger groups.

**Camping Lago Ranco**
US$5 per pitch.

**Maqueo**
*Eastern shore of Lago Maihue,* **$** *per site.*

**Nalcahue**
*1 km west of Futrono, T63-248 1663.*
**$** *per site.*

# Osorno
## & around

Situated at the confluence of the Rahue and Damas rivers, 921 km south of Santiago, Osorno was founded in 1553 before being abandoned in 1604 and refounded by Ambrosio O'Higgins and Juan MacKenna O'Reilly in 1796. It later became one of the centres of German immigration; their descendants are still of great importance in the area. Although Osorno is an important transport hub and a reasonable base for visiting the southern lakes, it is a drab, overcrowded, uninspiring city, and won't be earning UNESCO honours anytime soon.

It's likely to be a place you will just pass through. Passengers heading overland to Bariloche, Neuquén, Coyhaique or Punta Arenas will pass through here before making for the Samoré (formerly Puyehue) Pass into Argentina; travellers from Santiago may well change buses here.

### Osorno *Colour map 1, B2.*

On the large **Plaza de Armas** stands the modern, concrete and glass cathedral, with many arches and a tower that is itself an open, latticed arch with a cross superimposed.

West of the centre on a bend overlooking the river is the **Fuerte María Luisa**, built in 1793 and restored in 1977; only the river front walls and end turrets are still standing.

East of the main plaza along Calle MacKenna are a number of late 19th-century wooden mansions built by German immigrants, now preserved as national monuments.

Two blocks south of the Plaza is the **Museo Histórico Municipal** ① *Matta 809, entrance in Casa de Cultura, Mon-Thu 0930-1730, Fri 0930-1700, Sat 1400-1800, free*, which has displays on natural history, Mapuche culture, the refounding of the city and German colonization.

Three blocks southwest of the plaza, in the former train station is the **Museo Interactivo de Osorno (MIO)** ① *Portales 901, T64-221 2997, www.municipalidadosorno.cl, in high season Mon-Thu 0900-1300, 1430-1800, Fri 0900-1300, 1430-1730, Sat-Sun 1430-1900, closes 30 mins-1 hr earlier in low season, closed on Sun*, an interactive science museum designed for both children and adults.

> **Tip...**
> Most of the places visitors are likely to visit are within easy walking distance in Osorno.

#### North and west of Osorno

**Río Bueno**, 30 km north, is celebrated for its scenery and fishing. The Spanish colonial fort, dating from 1777, is situated high above the river and offers fine views. Just over 20 km further west on the Río Bueno is **Trumao**, a port with a river launch service to La Barra on the coast. There are beaches at **Maicolpue**, 60 km west of Osorno, and **Pucatrihue**, which are worth a visit in the summer.

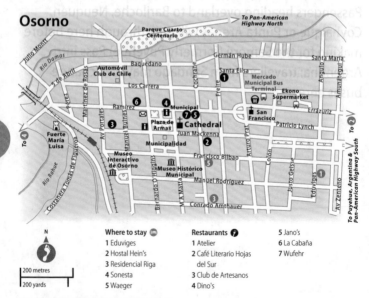

**Osorno**

| Where to stay 🛏 | Restaurants 🍴 | |
|---|---|---|
| 1 Eduviges | 1 Atelier | 5 Jano's |
| 2 Hostal Hein's | 2 Café Literario Hojas del Sur | 6 La Cabaña |
| 3 Residencial Riga | 3 Club de Artesanos | 7 Wufehr |
| 4 Sonesta | 4 Dino's | |
| 5 Waeger | | |

Further north is the **Monumento Natural Alerce Costero**, a park covering 2307 ha of the coastal mountain range and protecting an area of alerce forest (though a fire in 1975 destroyed some of the forest). Access is by a road which runs northwest for 52 km from La Unión. There is a CONAF *guardería* and *refugio* at the entrance, from which a 3-km trail leads to a 3500-year-old alerce tree.

## East of Osorno

From Osorno Route 215 runs east to the Argentine border at the Samoré (formerly Puyehue) Pass via the south shore of Lago Puyehue, Anticura and the Parque Nacional Puyehue (see border box, page 302). **Auto Museo Moncopulli** ① *Route 215, 25 km east of Osorno, T64-210744, www.moncopulli.cl, daily 1000-2000, daily 1000-2200 (1000-1800 in winter) US$6.50 (children 8 years and under US$3.25), bus towards Entre Lagos,* is the best motor museum in Chile. Exhibits include a Studebaker collection from 1852 to 1966. There is also a 1950s-style cafeteria.

## Lago Puyehue and the Parque Nacional Puyehue

Surrounded by relatively flat countryside, 47 km east of Osorno, **Lago Puyehue** extends over 15,700 ha. The southern shore is much more developed than the northern shore, which is accessible only by unpaved road from **Entre Lagos** at the western end. On the eastern side of the lake are the **Termas de Puyehue** ① *www.puyehue.cl, day passes (1000-1900) or night passes (1800-0100) from US$88.*

Stretching east from Lago Puyehue to the Argentine border, Parque Nacional Puyehue covers 107,000 ha, much of it in the valley of the Río Golgol. On the eastern side are several lakes, including Lago Constancia and Lago Gris. There are two volcanic peaks: **Volcán Puyehue** (2240 m) in the north (access via a private track, US$10) and **Volcán Casablanca**

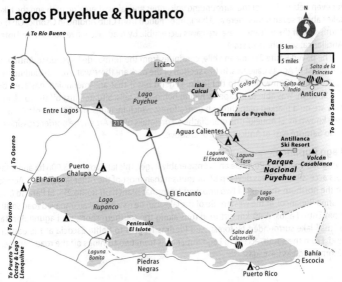

## Lagos Puyehue & Rupanco

**Paso Samoré (formerly Puyehue)**
The Chilean border post is 4 km east of Anticura at Pajaritos (www.pasosfronterizos. gov.cl/cf_cardenalsamore.html). From here it s a further 22 km east to the border at Paso Samoré, although this route is liable to closure after snow. For the Argentine side, including details of customs and immigration, see page 107. If cycling, bear in mind that there are no supplies between Entre Lagos and La Angostura (Argentina).

(also called Antillanca, 1900 m). Leaflets on walks and attractions are available from the park administration at Aguas Calientes and from the ranger station at Anticura.

On the edge of the park, 4 km south of the Termas de Puyehue, **Aguas Calientes** ⓘ *www.termasaguascalientes.cl, daily 0830-1900, day passes US$38-43*, has indoor and very hot open-air thermal pools in a thickly forested valley beside the **Río Chanlefú**, with camping, cabins, massages and other therapies.

From Aguas Calientes the road continues 18 km southeast past three small lakes and through forests to the small ski resort of **Antillanca** (see What to do, page 305) on the slopes of Volcán Casablanca. In winter a one-way traffic system may operate on the last 8 km. There is no public transport between Aguas Calientes and Antillanca, but it is not a hard walk. This is a particularly beautiful section, especially at sunrise, with views over Lago Puyehue to the north and Lagos Rupanco and Llanquihue to the south, as well as the snow-clad peaks of Calbuco, Osorno, Puntiagudo, Puyehue and Tronador forming a semicircle. The tree-line on Casablanca is one of the few in the world made up of deciduous trees (*nothofagus* or southern beech). From Antillanca it is possible to climb Casablanca for even better views of the surrounding volcanoes and lakes; there's no path and the hike takes about seven hours there and back; information from **Club Andino** in Osorno. On the south side of the volcano there are caves (accessible by road, allow five hours from **Hotel Antillanca**; see Where to stay).

The paved Route 215, meanwhile, continues from the Termas de Puyehue to **Anticura**, northeast of Aguas Calientes. In this section of the park are three waterfalls, including the spectacular 40-m wide **Salto del Indio**. Legend has it that an Amerindian, enslaved by the Spanish, was able to escape by hiding behind the falls. Situated just off the road, the falls are on a marked path through dense forest which includes an 800-year-old Coigüe tree known as 'El Abuelo' (the grandfather). For details of the Argentine border crossing of **Paso Samoré** east of Anticura, see box, above.

## Lago Rupanco
Lying south of Lago Puyehue and considerably larger, this lake covers 23,000 ha and is far less accessible and less developed for tourism than most of the other larger lakes. Access to the northern shore is via two unpaved roads that branch off Route 215. **El Paraíso** (aka Marina Rupanco), at the western tip of the lake, can be reached by an unpaved road south from Entre Lagos. A 40-km dirt road runs along the southern shore, via **Laguna Bonita**, a small lake surrounded by forest, and **Piedras Negras** to **Bahía Escocia** at the eastern end. From the south, access to Lago Rupanco is from two turnings off the road between Osorno and Las Cascadas.

## Tourist information

### Osorno

**CONAF office**
*Rosas 430, T64-222 1304.*
For information on national parks.

**Municipal tourist office**
*In the bus terminal, Mercado Municipal,
and in a kiosk on the Plaza de Armas,
www.municipalidadosorno.cl.
Both open Dec-Feb 0900-1900.*

**Sernatur**
*Plaza de Armas, O'Higgins 667, piso 1, T64-223
7575. Mon-Thu 0830-1700, Fri 0830-1630.*

## Where to stay

### Osorno

There are plenty of cheap options near
the bus terminal, none of them ideal.

**$$$ Sonesta**
*Ejército 395 Rahue, T64-255 5000,
www.sonesta.com.*
First-class hotel overlooking river, all
amenities, **El Olivillo** restaurant, attached
to Plaza de los Lagos mall and casino.

**$$$ Waeger**
*Cochrane 816, T64-223 3721,
www.hotelwaeger.cl.*
4-star, restaurant, comfortable but room
sizes vary greatly.

**$$$-$$ Eduviges**
*Eduviges 856, T64-223 5023,
www.hoteleduviges.cl.*
Spacious, quiet, attractive, gardens,
also *cabañas*.

**$$ Residencial Riga**
*Amthauer 1058, T64-223 2945,
resiriga@surnet.cl.*
Pleasant, good value, quiet area,
parking, heavily booked in season.

**$ Hostal Hein's**
*Errázuriz 1757, T64-223 4116.*
Private or shared bath, old-fashioned,
spacious, family atmosphere.

### North and west of Osorno

**$$$-$$ Hostería Miller**
*Maicolpue, 60 km west of Osorno,
T64-255 0277, www.hosteriamiller.com.*
On the beach, clean, with good service,
also a recommended campsite.

### Lago Puyehue and the Parque Nacional

**$$$$ Hotel Termas de Puyehue**
*At the Termas de Puyehue, T64-233 1400,
www.puyehue.cl.*
All inclusive: meals, drinks, use of thermal
pools and all activities (spa extra), well
maintained, in beautiful scenery, heavily
booked Jan-Feb, cheaper May to mid-Dec.

**$$$-$$ Hotel Antillanca**
*Antillanca, T2-261 2070,
http://vive.antillanca.cl.*
Full board. Located at the foot of Volcán
Casablanca and offering skiing and
snowboarding in the winter, outdoor sports
in summer: hiking, caving, climbing and
rappelling. Pool.

**$$ Hospedaje Millaray**
*Ramírez 333, Entre Lagos, T9-9761 6625.*
A very good place to stay.

**$$ Hostal y Cabañas Miraflores**
*Ramírez 480, Entre Lagos, T64-237 1275,
www.hostal-miraflores.cl.*
Pleasant rooms and cabins.

### Camping

There is a basic *refugio* (US$15) at Volcán
Puyehue. Check whether it is open with
the park administrator (T64-197 4572,
carlos.hernandez@conaf.cl).

**Camping Los Copihues**
*Km 58, on south shore of Lake Puyehue, T9-9344 8830, www.campingloscopihues.cl.*
Restaurant, spa, camping (US$12) and *cabañas*.

**Camping Los Derrumbes**
*1 km from Aguas Calientes.*
No electricity.

**Camping No Me Olvides**
*Ruta 215, Km 56, on south shore of Lake Puyehue, T9-7452 3327, www.nomeolvides.cl.*
Tent site and *cabañas*.

## Lago Rupanco
There is no accommodation on the northern shore of the lake.

**$$$ Puntiagudo Lodge**
*Bahía Escocia, T9-9643 4247, www.puntiagudolodge.com.*
With breakfast, very comfortable, good restaurant, fly-fishing, horse riding, boat excursions. Advance bookings only.

**$$ Hostería Club de Pesca y Caza**
*Sector Islote, 7 km east of Piedras Negras, T64-223 2056.*
Basic *refugio* with breakfast and bath.

**Camping**
There are several campsites on the southern shore, including at Puerto Rico.

**Desague del Rupanco**
*Just south of El Paraíso.*
No facilities.

**Puerto Chalupa**
*On northern shore, T64-223 2680.*
($) per site.

### Restaurants

For other eating options in the area, see Where to stay, above.

#### Osorno
There are good cheap restaurants in the municipal market.

**$$$ Atelier**
*Freire 468.*
Fresh pasta and other Italian delights, good.

**$$ Dino's**
*Ramírez 898, on the plaza.*
Restaurant upstairs, bar/cafeteria downstairs, good.

**$$ Wufehr**
*Ramírez 959 loc 2, T64-222 6999.*
Local raw meat specialities and sandwiches. Popular with locals. Also **Rincón de Wufehr**, Manuel Rodríguez 1015.

**$$-$ Club de Artesanos**
*MacKenna 634.*
Decent and hearty traditional Chilean fare.

**$ Café Literario Hojas del Sur**
*MacKenna 1011 y Cochrane.*
More like a living room than a café, cosy, Wi-Fi.

**$ Jano's**
*Ramírez 977, T64-221 1828.*
Bakery with fresh juices and lunch/dinner options. Many vegetarian options as well. Another location in the shopping mall.

**$ La Cabaña**
*Ramírez 774, T64-227 2479.*
Wide variety of cheap lunches ranging from Chinese to home-cooked Chilean. Excellent value.

#### Lago Puyehue and the Parque Nacional

**$$$-$$ Jardín del Turista**
*Ruta 215, Km 46, Entre Lagos, T64-437 1214, www.interpatagonia.com/jardindelturista.*
Very good, also has *cabañas* and suites.

### Shopping

#### Osorno
There is a modern shopping mall on C Freire 542.
**Alta Artesanía**, *MacKenna 1069*. Excellent handicrafts, not cheap.
**Climent**, *Angulo 603*. Fishing tackle.
**Ekono**, *Colón y Errázuriz*. Supermarket.

**The Lodge**, *Los Carrera 1291, local 5.*
Fishing tackle.
**Multilibros**, *Cochrane 653.* Has a small
selection of English titles.

## What to do

### Osorno
**Club Andino**, *O'Higgins 1073, T64-223 2297.*
Information and advice on climbing and
skiing in the area.

### Lago Puyehue and the Parque Nacional
### Skiing
**Hotel Antillanca**, *see Where to stay, above.*
Attached to one of Chile's smaller ski resorts;
17 pistes are served by 3 lifts, ski instruction
and first-aid available. Piste preparation is
unreliable. Skiing is not difficult but quality
depends on the weather: rain is common.
See www.skiantillanca.cl for information on
the state of the pistes.

### Lago Rupanco
### Fishing
Lago Rupanco is very popular for fishing.
**Bahía Escocia Fly Fishing** offers excursions
from the **Puntiagudo Lodge** (see Where to
stay, above). Advance booking required.

## Transport

### Osorno
Taxis or *colectivos* may be useful for
longer trips.

**Air** LAN, 1 flight daily to **Santiago**.

**Bus** The main bus terminal is 4 blocks
from the Plaza de Armas at Errázuriz 1400.
A bus to the city centre costs US$0.60. The
terminal has left luggage facilities, open
0730-2230, US$1.50.

Expreso Lago Puyehue and Buses Barria
leave from the Mercado Municipal terminal
to **Entre Lagos**, every hour in summer, 1st at
0640, last at 2100 reduced service off-season,
1 hr, US$2. Some of these buses continue
to **Aguas Calientes** (off-season according
to demand), 2 hrs, US$5 but do not stop at
Lago Puyehue (unless you want to get off
at **Hotel Termas de Puyehue** and clamber
down). Daily service with **Empresa Ruta 5**
to **Lago Ranco**.

To **Santiago**, frequent, US$30-50, 11 hrs.
To **Concepción**, US$24. To **Temuco**, US$8.
To **Pucón**, US$13, and **Villarrica**, frequent,
US$11. To **Frutillar** (US$1.25), **Llanquihue**
(US$2.50), **Puerto Varas** (US$1.50) and
**Puerto Montt** (US$2.50), services every
30 mins. To **Puerto Octay**, US$2, every
30 mins. To **Bariloche** (Argentina), **Andes
Mar**, **Don Otto** and others, US$25.

### North and west of Osorno
River launches run 0830-2130 between
**Trumao** on the Río Bueno, 22 km west
of Osorno, to **La Barra** on the coast
(US$2, 20 mins).

# Lago
## Llanquihue

⭐ The second largest lake in Chile and the third largest natural lake in South America, Lago Llanquihue is one of the highlights of the Lake District. Three snow-capped volcanoes can be seen across the vast expanse of water: the perfect cone of Osorno (2680 m), the shattered cone of Calbuco (2015 m), which erupted for the first time in over 40 years in April 2015, and the spike of Puntiagudo (2480 m). When the air is clear, you can also spot the distant Tronador (3460 m). On a cloudless night with a full moon, the snows reflect like a mirror in the lake and the peace and stillness seem unrivalled anywhere on the continent.

## Essential Lago Llanquihue

### Access

Access from the south is from nearby Puerto Montt, while there are direct transport links with Santiago along the Pan-American Highway. The northern tip of the lake is also easily reached from Osorno. The largest towns, Puerto Varas, Llanquihue and Frutillar are all on the western shore, linked by the Pan-American Highway.

### Getting around

Although there are roads around the rest of the lake, the eastern shore is difficult to visit without transport, and beyond Las Cascadas, the road is narrow with lots of blind corners, necessitating speeds of 20-30 kph at best in places (see below). Beware of lorries that ply the route servicing the salmon farms. There is no public transport between Las Cascadas and Ensenada and hitching is very difficult.

### Puerto Octay

Puerto Octay, an idyllic place partly due to its lack of tourists, is a sleepy town at the northern tip of the lake, 56 km southeast of Osorno, set amid rolling hills, hedgerows and German-style farmhouses with views over Volcán Osorno.

Founded by German settlers in 1852, the town enjoyed a boom period in the late 19th century when it was the northern port for steamships on the lake: a few buildings survive from that period, notably the church, Iglesia San Agustin, and the enormous German-style former convent. Since the arrival of railways and the building of roads, the town has declined. Much less busy than Frutillar or Puerto Varas, Puerto Octay offers an escape for those seeking peace and quiet. Rowing boats and pedalos can be hired for trips on the lake.

**Museo El Colono** ① *Independencia 591, T64-239 1523, www.museoelcolono.jimdo.com, daily 1000-1300, 1500-1900, US$1.50*, has displays on German colonization. Another part of the museum, housing agricultural implements and machinery for making *chicha*, is just outside town on the road towards **Centinela**. This peninsula, about 3 km south (taxi US$3 one way) along an unpaved road, has accommodation, camping, a launch dock, bathing beaches and watersports. It is a very popular spot in good weather, especially for picnics, with fine views of the Osorno, Calbuco and Puntiagudo volcanoes.

# Lago Llanquihue

## ON THE ROAD

## German colonization in the Lake District

The most important area of German agricultural colonization in Chile was around Lago Llanquihue. The Chilean government declared the area as destined for colonization in 1845 and, to encourage settlement, gave each adult male 75 *cuadras* of land, an extra 12 *cuadras* for each son, a milking cow, 500 planks of timber, nails, a yoke of oxen, a year's free medical assistance and Chilean citizenship on request.

The first groups of German colonists arrived in the area in 1852: one group settled around Maitén and Puerto Octay, another helped found Puerto Montt. The lives of these early settlers were hard and the risks great, yet within 10 years the settlers had cleared much of the forest round the lake and soon they were setting up small industries. In 1880, when the offer to colonists ended, unsettled land was auctioned in lots of 400-800 ha. By then the lake was ringed by a belt of smallholdings and farms. The legacy of this settlement can be seen in the German-looking farmhouses around Puerto Octay and in many of the older buildings in Frutillar and Puerto Varas.

Valdivia was another centre for German colonization. A small number of German and Swiss colonists settled in the city, exerting a strong influence on the architecture, agricultural methods, education, social life and customs of the area. They established most of the industries that made Valdivia an important manufacturing centre until the 1950s. According to an 1884 survey of Valdivia, all breweries, leatherworks, brickworks, mills, bakeries, and machine shops belonged to families with German surnames.

Little of the architectural heritage of this period survived the 1960 earthquake, but the city's German heritage can still be seen in some of its best cafés and restaurants and in the names of its streets.

### Puerto Octay to Volcán Osorno

The eastern lakeside, with Volcán Osorno on your left, is very beautiful. From Puerto Octay two roads run towards Ensenada, one *ripio* along the shore, and one paved. (They join up after 20 km.) At Km 10 along the lakeside route is **Playa Maitén**, a lovely beach, often deserted, with a marvellous view of Volcán Osorno. Continue for another 24 km past **Puerto Fonck**, which has fine 19th-century German-style mansions, and you'll reach **Las Cascadas**, surrounded by picturesque agricultural land, old houses and German cemeteries. To reach the waterfalls that give the village its name turn east at the school along a *ripio* road to a car park, continue along a footpath over two or three log bridges over a stream before arriving at an impressive jungle-like 40-m-high natural cauldron, with the falls in the middle. The round trip takes about 1½ hours.

### Volcán Osorno

The most lasting image of Lago Llanquihue is the near-perfect cone of Volcán Osorno, situated north of Ensenada on the eastern edge of the lake. Although the peak is on the edge of the Parque Nacional Pérez Rosales (see page 319), it is climbed from the western side, which lies outside the park. Access is via two roads that branch off the Ensenada–Puerto Octay road along the eastern edge of Lago Llanquihue. The northern one is at Puerto Klocker, 20 km southeast of Puerto Octay and only suitable for 4WDs, while the main entrance is 2 km north of Ensenada along a good paved road.

Guided ascents of the volcano (organized by agencies in Puerto Varas) set out from the *refugio* at **La Burbuja** where there is a small ski centre in winter and pleasant short walks in summer to a couple of craters and with great views of the lake and across to Puerto Montt. From here it is six hours to the summit. The volcano can also be climbed from the north at La Picada (the *refugio* here burnt down some years ago); this route is easier and may be attempted without a guide, although only experienced climbers should try to climb right to the top as ice-climbing equipment is essential, and there are many craters hidden below thin crusts of ice.

## Ensenada

Despite its lack of a recognizable centre, Ensenada is beautifully situated at the southeast corner of Lago Llanquihue, almost beneath the snows of Volcán Osorno. A good half-day trip from Ensenada itself is to **Laguna Verde**, about 30 minutes from **Hotel Ensenada**, along a beautiful circular trail behind the lake (take first fork to the right behind the information board), and then down the road to a secluded campsite at Puerto Oscuro on Lago Llanquihue.

In April 2015, **Volcán Calbuco** erupted for the first time in over 40 years. While the spectacle itself was breathtaking, thousands of nearby residents had to be evacuated, and much of Ensenada was covered in ash, turning the town into what many referred to as a "grey desert." While many did lose their homes, the city survived. Still, clean-up and rebuilding was going on during 2016 and is likely to continue for some time.

## Listings Puerto Octay to Ensenada

### Where to stay

Wild camping and barbecues are forbidden on the lakeshore.

#### Puerto Octay

**$$$-$$ Zapato Amarillo**
*Km 55, 35 mins' walk north of town,*
*T64-221 0787, www.zapatoamarillo.cl.*
$ pp in dorms. Book in advance in high season, private or shared bath, home-made bread, meals, German/English spoken, mountain bikes, sailboats, tours, house has a grass roof.

**$$ Hostería La Baja**
*Centinela, T9-8218 6897,*
*www.hosterialabaja.cl.*
Beautifully situated at the neck of the peninsula. Good value.

#### Camping

**Camping El Molino**
*Beside lake, T64-239 1375, see Facebook.*
East of Puerto Octay.

#### Puerto Octay to Volcán Osorno

Several farms on the road around the north and east side of the lake offer accommodation; look for signs.

#### Camping

Camping is possible at the **Centro de Recreación**, **Camping Molina** (see Facebook), on the *costanera* by the lake Las Cascadas, T2-2863 2010, and at Playa Maitén.

**$ Camping Doña Irma**
*1 km south of Las Cascadas, T64-239 6227.*
Beach camping (**$$**), hot water.

#### Volcán Osorno

There are 2 *refugios* ($ pp), both of them south of the summit and reached from the southern access road: **La Burbuja**, the former ski-club centre, 14 km north of Ensenada at 1250 m, and **Refugio Teski Ski Club** (T9-6238 3799, www.teski.cl), just below the snowline, with café. **CONAF** runs a good campsite at Puerto Oscuro, beneath the road to the volcano.

## Ensenada

### $$$$ Hotel Ensenada
*Km 45, T65-221 2028, www.hotelensenada.cl.*
Olde-worlde, half-board, good food, great
view of the lake and Osorno Volcano,
mountain bikes and tennis for guests.

### $$$ Cabañas Brisas del Lago
*Km 42, T65-221 2012, www.brisasdellago.cl.*
Chalets for up to 6 and rooms for up to 3 on
beach, good restaurant nearby, supermarket
next door.

### $$ Hospedaje Ensenada
*Km 43, T65-221 2050, www.
hospedajensenada.cl.*
Typical old house, rooms sleep 1-4,
private or shared bath, beach, parking.

## Camping

### Montaña
*Central Ensenada, T9-7306 3545.*
Fully equipped, attractive beach sites,
also a good local restaurant (**$**). Also at
Playa Larga, 1 km further east, and at
Puerto Oscuro, 2 km north.

### Trauco
*4 km west, T65-223 6262, see Facebook.*
Large site with shops, fully equipped.

## Restaurants

### Puerto Octay

### $$ El Rancho del Espantapájaros
*6 km south on the road to Frutillar,
T65-233 0049, www.espantapajaros.cl.*
In a converted barn with wonderful
views over the lake, serves spit-roasted
meat. All-you-can-eat, with salad bar
and drinks included.

### $$ Fogón de Anita
*1 km out of town, T65-239 1276,
www.fogondeanita.blogspot.co.uk.*
Mid-priced grill. Also German cakes
and pastries.

### $ Restaurante Baviera
*Germán Wulf 582, T65-239 1460, see Facebook.*
Cheap and good, salmon and *cazuelas*.

### Ensenada
Most eating places close off season.
There are a few pricey shops. Take your
own provisions.

### $$$ Latitude 42
*Yan Kee Way Resort, T65-221 2030.*
Expensive, excellent and varied cuisine,
very good-quality wine list. Lake views.

### $$$-$$ Don Salmon
*Km 42, T65-220 2108, contacto@donsalmon.cl.*
Expansive restaurant with a magnificent view
of the lake. Specializes in everything salmon.
Lunchtime buffet of fish, *mariscos* and
ceviches. Also *parrilla* (grill) serving barbecue
*picanha* (steak).

### $$ Bombón Oriental
*T9-9506 5694, restorantbombonoriental@
gmail.com.*
Large roadside establishment serving *comida
árabe* of dubious authenticity. Also offers
*cabañas* (**$$$**).

## Shopping

### Puerto Octay
Supermarket on Wulf across from the San
Agustín church.

### Ensenada
There are several shops selling basic supplies.
Most places are closed off season, other
than a few pricey shops, so take your own
provisions. **Kiosko** (Av Fénix, Km 40, 140) and
**Minimarket Anulen** (next to Don Salmón)
are good for supplies.

## What to do

Most tours operate in season only (Sep-May).

### Volcán Osorno
Weather permitting, agencies in Puerto Varas
organize climbing expeditions with

a local guide, transport from Puerto Montt or Puerto Varas, food and equipment, payment in advance (minimum group 2, maximum 6 with 3 guides). Weather conditions are checked the day before. A full refund is given if the trip is cancelled, and a 50% refund is available if the trip is abandoned due to weather before the real climbing begins. Those climbing from La Burbuja must register with the park administrator at La Burbuja, and show they have suitable equipment. Those climbing from the north (La Picada) are not subject to any checks.

Also based at La Burbuja is a small skiing centre, with 11 pistes and 5 ski lifts, usually open Jun-Sep. Ski ticket US$37, equipment rental US$28, ski school US$50 per hr. See www.volcanoosorno.com for conditions; also offers trekking and other mountain excursions in summer.

### Ensenada
**Southern Chile Expeditions**, T65-212 3030, *www.southernchilexp.com*. Expensive fly-fishing tours.

## Transport

### Puerto Octay
**Bus** Terminal Puerto Octay (T64-239 1189, daily 0620-2130) is located on Calle Esperanza 433.

To **Osorno** every 20-30 mins, US$2, last bus at 2015. To **Frutillar** (2 hrs, US$1.50, last bus at 2000), **Puerto Varas** (2 hrs) and **Puerto Montt** (US$2.25, last bus at 1800) with **Thaebus**. Around the east shore to **Las Cascadas** (34 km), Mon-Fri 0800 and 1700, returns next day 0830, 1700, US$2.

### Ensenada
Frequent minibuses run to/from **Puerto Varas** in summer. Buses from Puerto Montt via Puerto Varas to **Cochamó** also stop here. Hitching from Puerto Varas is difficult.

---

# The western shore   Colour map 1, B2.

**weekend retreats and German sweets**

## Frutillar
Lying about halfway along the western side of the lake, Frutillar is in fact two towns: **Frutillar Alto**, just off the main highway, and **Frutillar Bajo**, beautifully situated on the lakeside, 4 km away. The latter, with its postcard panoramas of Osorno and Tronador volcanoes, might just claim the title of most attractive town on the lake. It's also the most expensive. The town's atmosphere is very German and you can't throw a rock without hitting a *kuchen* (strudel) bakery.

In the square are an open-air chess board and the **Club Alemán** restaurant. On the lakeside, **Teatro del Lago** ① *www.teatrodellago.cl*, hosts a highly regarded classical music festival, the **Semanas Musicales** (see Festivals, below) from late January to early February.

Away from the waterfront, the appealing **Museo Colonial Alemán** ① *Vicente Pérez Rosales s/n, T65-242 1142, www.museosaustral.cl, daily 0900-1930 in high season, daily 0900-1730 and 1400-1800, US$3.50,* is set in spacious gardens, with a watermill, replicas of two German colonial houses with furnishings and utensils of the period. It also has a *campanario*, a circular barn with agricultural machinery and carriages inside.

At the northern end of the town is the **Reserva Forestal Edmundo Winckler**, run by the Universidad de Chile and extending over 33 ha, with a guided trail through native woods. Named after one of the early German settlers, it includes a very good collection of native flora as well as plants introduced from Europe.

## Llanquihue

Some 20 km south of Frutillar, Llanquihue lies at the source of the Río Maullín, which drains the lake. The site of a large dairy processing factory, this is the least touristy town on the lake, and makes a cheaper alternative to Puerto Varas and Frutillar. It has uncrowded beaches. Just north of town is the **Colonos** brewery, which has a restaurant and can be visited.

## Listings The western shore

### Tourist information

#### Frutillar

**Tourist office**
*On the Costanera, Philippi 754, T65-246 7450, infoturismo@munifrutillar.cl, www.munifrutillar.cl and www.frutillar.com. Daily 0900-2000 in high season, otherwise Mon-Fri 0900-1800.*
Helpful staff.

### Where to stay

Wild camping and barbecues are forbidden on the lakeshore.

#### Frutillar

During the annual music festival accommodation should be booked well in advance; alternatively stay in Frutillar Alto or Puerto Varas. In most cases on Av Philippi you are paying a premium for the view. If you are staying here, try and ensure your room has one. There are several cheap *hospedajes* along Carlos Richter (the main street) in Frutillar Alto.

**$$$$ Ayacara**
*Av Philippi 1215, Frutillar Bajo, T65-242 1550, www.hotelayacara.cl.*
Beautiful rooms with a lake view, welcoming, have a pisco sour in the library in the evening.

**$$$$-$$$ Salzburg**
*Camino Playa Maqui, north of Frutillar Bajo, T65-242 1589, www.salzburg.cl.*
Excellent, spa, sauna, restaurant, mountain bikes, arranges tours and fishing.

**$$$ Hotel Am See**
*Av Philippi 539, Frutillar Bajo, T65-242 1539, www.hotelamsee.patagoniadechile.cl.*
Good breakfast, café has German specialities.

**$$$ Lagune Club**
*3 km north of Frutillar Bajo, T65-233 0033, www.laguneclub.com.*
In an old country house in 16 ha of land, private beach, fishing trips, free pickup from terminal. Disabled-visitor friendly, discounts for the over-65s. Also *cabañas*. Good value in dollars.

**$$$ Winkler**
*Av Philippi 1155, Frutillar Bajo, T65-242 1388, hosteriawinkler@gmail.com.*
Much cheaper ($) in low season. Also sells cakes from the garage, **Kuchen Laden**.

**$$$-$$ Casa Ko'**
*Camino Playa Maqui s/n, km 1.5, T9-8210 8306, www.casako.com.*
Traditional house, helpful owners, lovely surroundings and views, good meals. Plenty of outdoor activities.

**$$ Hospedaje Tía Clarita**
*Pérez Rosales 658, Frutillar Bajo, T65-242 1806, canfrut@live.com.*
Kitchen facilities, very welcoming, good value.

**$$ Hostería Trayen**
*Av Philippi 963, Frutillar Bajo, T65-242 1346, tttrayen33@hotmail.com.*
Nice rooms with bath.

### Camping

**La Gruta**
*2 km from Fritillar Bajo on 21 de Mayo s/n, T9-7696 1237, see Facebook.*
Most services.

**Playa Maqui**
*6 km north of Frutillar Bajo, T9-7175 1377, see Facebook.*
Fancy, expensive.

## Llanquihue

**$$ Cabañas El Cisne (or Turismo
El Cisne)**
*Av Manuel Montt 89, T65-243222,
www.turismoelcisne.cl.*
*Hospedaje* and *cabañas*.

## Camping

**Baumbach**
*1 km north of Llanquihue, T65-224 2643.*
On lakeside, meals available.

**Playa Werner**
*2 km north of Llanquihue, T65-224 2114.*
On lakeside.

## Restaurants

### Frutillar

**$$ Andes**
*Philippi 1057, Frutillar Bajo.*
Good set menus and à la carte.

**$$ Trattoria**
*Philippi 1000, downstairs from the theatre,
see Facebook.*
Italian chef Alessando Guarneri brings
an eclectic mix of dishes from across his
homeland, like home-made pastas and
pizzas. Recommended.

### Cafés

Many German-style cafés and tea rooms on
C Philippi (the lakefront) in Frutillar Bajo.

**Duendes del Lago**
*Philippe and O'Higgins, T9-8583 9040,
see Facebook.*
Bustling corner café with an extensive
menu of coffees, hot chocolate, salads,
sandwiches and delicious *kuchens* galore.
Fun decor; gnomes (*duendes*).

### Frutillar Alto

**Di Parma**
*Carlos Richter at Winkler T9-89286146,
see Facebook.*
Specializes in strudel. The strawberry one
comes highly recommended. A cheaper
option than cafés in Frutillar Bajo.

**Frutillar Bajo**

To Reserva
Forestal Edmundo
Winckler

To 3 6 7,
Playa Maqui &
Puerto Octay
(Ripio)

Caupolicán

To Frutillar Alto &
Pan-American Highway

S Junginger

18 de Septiembre

Carlos Richter

Av Philippi

Museo
Colonial
Alemán

Prat

1

Av Alemania

Balmacada

San Martín

Municipalidad

O'Higgins

J Montt

5

Las Piedras

A Varas

1    2

Lago
Llanquihue

Pier

Teatro
del Lago

Pérez Rosales

M Rodríguez

8

P. Aguirre

2

21 de Mayo

Lautaro

N

200 metres
200 yards

To Llanquihue

**Where to stay**
1 Am See
2 Ayacara
3 Casa Ko'
4 Hospedaje Tía Clarita
5 Hostería Trayen
6 Lagune Club
7 Salzburg
8 Winkler

**Restaurants**
1 Andes
2 Trattoria

## Bars and clubs

### Frutillar

**O'clock**
*Pérez Rosales 690.*
Many microbrews on offer; great for a pitcher
or a pint.

## Festivals

### Frutillar

27 Jan-5 Feb **Semanas Musicales**, a highly
regarded classical music festival, held in
the town; tickets must be booked well
in advance from the Municipalidad,
T65-242 1261, www.munifrutillar.cl.

### Llanquihue

Late Jan A German-style **beer festival**
(www.bierfestchile.cl) with oom-pah music
is held here.

## Shopping

### Frutillar

Services and shops are generally much
better in Frutillar Alto than in Frutillar Bajo.

## Transport

### Frutillar

**Bus** Most buses use the small bus terminal
at Alessandri y Richter in Frutillar Alto. To
**Puerto Varas** (US$1.50) and **Puerto Montt**
(US$2), frequent, with **Thaebus**. To **Osorno**,
with **Cruz del Sur**, 1½ hrs, US$2. To **Puerto
Octay**, **Thaebus**, 6 a day, US$1.50.

---

# Puerto Varas and around  *Colour map 1, B2.*

the star of Chile's lake towns

Situated on the southwestern corner of the lake, Puerto Varas, with a population of
41,255, is the commercial and tourist centre of Lago Llanquihue. It also serves as a
residential centre for Puerto Montt, 20 km to the south. The self-styled "city of the
roses" has in the past been voted the best place to live in Chile.

In the 19th century, Puerto Chico (on the eastern outskirts) was the southern port for
shipping on the lake. With the arrival of the railway the settlement moved to its current
location and is now a resort, popular with Chilean as well as foreign tourists; in February
especially, the town clogs up with oversized jeeps from Santiago. Despite the numbers of
visitors, though, it has a friendly, intimate feel, and is one of the best bases for exploring
the southern Lake District, near centres for trekking, rafting, canyoning and fly-fishing.

### Puerto Varas

Puerto Varas is small and easily navigable on foot. **Parque Philippi**, on top of a hill, is a
pleasant place to visit, although the views are a bit restricted by trees and the metal cross
at the top is unattractive. To reach the summit walk up to **Hotel Cabañas del Lago** on
Klenner, cross the railway and the gate is on the right.

The centre lies at the foot of the hill, but the town stretches east along the lake to **Puerto
Chico**, where there are hotels and restaurants. The imposing **Catholic church** was built by
German Jesuits in 1918 in baroque style as a copy of the church in the Black Forest. North and
east of the former **Gran Hotel Puerto Varas** (1934) are a number of German-style mansions.

### Around Puerto Varas

Puerto Varas is a good base for trips around the lake. A paved road runs along the south
shore to Ensenada on the southwestern corner of the lake. Two of the best beaches are
**Playa Hermosa**, Km 7, and **Playa Niklitschek**, Km 8, where an entry fee is charged (US$9

high season; US$10.50 weekends). At Km 16, narrow channels overhung with vegetation lead south from Lago Llanquihue to the little lake of **La Poza**. There are boat trips (US$3.50) to the beautiful **Isla Loreley**, an island on the lake, and a channel leads from La Poza to yet another lake, the **Laguna Encantada**. At Km 21 there is a watermill and a restaurant run by **Club Alemán**.

Just past the village of Nueva Braunau, 9 km west of Puerto Varas, is the remarkable **Museo Antonio Felmer** ① *T9-9449 8130, pedrofelmera@gmail.com, summer daily 1100-2000, low season, 1100-1300, 1500-1800, US$3.50,* a huge private collection of machinery, tools and household items used by the first Austrian immigrants to the area, some with English descriptions. On quiet days staff may give demonstrations of the more ingenious objects.

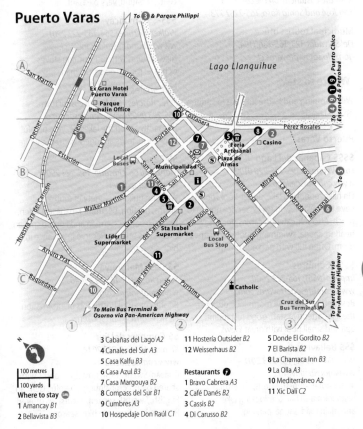

**Puerto Varas**

*To ⓷ & Parque Philippi*

*Lago Llanquihue*

*To ④ ⑨ ⑲ Puerto Chico*

*To ④ ⑨ ⑲ Ensenada & Petrohué*

San Martín

Turismo

Ex Gran Hotel Puerto Varas

Parque Pumalín Office

Av Costanera ⑩

Portales

Local Buses

San Bernardo

San Pedro

⑦ ⑦ ⑤
Feria Artesanal ☐ **Casino**
Plaza de Armas

Pérez Rosales ⑧

**Municipalidad** ⑫ ⑪ ④

San José

del Salvador

Granada

Walker Martínez ①

②
Sta Isabel Supermarket

Ñoño Nono San Francisco

Santa Rosa

Mirador

Rosario

La Quebrada

Manzano

*To ⑤*

**Lider Supermarket**

San Javier

San Luis

Purísima

Imperial

Local Bus Stop

**Catholic** ⛪

*To Puerto Montt via Pan-American Highway*

Arturo Prat

Baquedano

Huerta Sra del Carmen

Bechler

Klenner

La Paz

Estación

*To Main Bus Terminal & Osorno via Pan-American Highway*

Cruz del Sur Bus Terminal 🚌

100 metres
100 yards

**Where to stay** 🛏
1 Amancay *B1*
2 Bellavista *B3*
3 Cabañas del Lago *A2*
4 Canales del Sur *A3*
5 Casa Kalfu *B3*
6 Casa Azul *B3*
7 Casa Margouya *B2*
8 Compass del Sur *B1*
9 Cumbres *A3*
10 Hospedaje Don Raúl *C1*
11 Hostería Outsider *B2*
12 Weisserhaus *B2*

**Restaurants** 🍴
1 Bravo Cabrera *A3*
2 Café Danés *B2*
3 Cassis *B2*
4 Di Carusso *B2*
5 Donde El Gordito *B2*
7 El Barista *B2*
8 La Chamaca Inn *B3*
9 La Olla *A3*
10 Mediterráneo *A2*
11 Xic Dalí *C2*

## Tourist information

Many places close in off season. The information office on the pier belongs to the chamber of tourism and does not give wholly impartial advice. See www.ptovaras.cl.

Information is also available on the **Parque Pumalín** (Klenner 299, T65-225 0079, www.pumalinpark.cl), see page 365.

**Informatur office**
*Near the Costanera, on the corner of San José and Santa Rosa, T65-2237 773.*

**Municipal tourist office**
*Del Salvador 320, T65-236 1194, gonzalo.soto@ptovaras.cl.*

## Where to stay

Wild camping and barbecues are forbidden on the lakeshore.

### Puerto Varas

**$$$$ Cabañas del Lago**
*Luis Welmann 195, T65-220 0100, www.cabanasdellago.cl.*
On hill overlooking lake, upper-floor rooms have the best view in town. Service not up to much. Also self-catering cabins sleeping 5, heating, sauna, swimming pools and games room. Often full with package groups.

**$$$$ Cumbres**
*Imperial 0561, T65-222 2000, www.cumbrespuertovaras.com.*
Best hotel in town. All rooms look out over the lake, attentive staff, good restaurant. Spa and small pool with great views.

**$$$ Bellavista**
*Pérez Rosales 60, T65-223 2011, www.hotelbellavista.cl.*
4-star hotel, king-size beds; cheerful, restaurant and bar, overlooking lake and main road, sauna, parking.

**$$$ Casa Kalfu**
*Tronador 1134, T65-275 1261, www.casakalfu.cl.*
Characterful blue wooden building remodelled in traditional style. Helpful owners, English spoken, good value.

**$$$ Weisserhaus**
*San Pedro 252, T65-234 6479, www.weisserhaus.cl.*
Central, cosy, family-run, German-style breakfast, good facilities, very helpful, central heating, very pleasant.

**$$$-$$ Amancay**
*Walker Martínez 564, T65-223 2201, www.cabanahostalamancay.cl.*
Nice *cabañas* with log-burning stoves or hostel rooms, good, German spoken.

**$$ Canales del Sur**
*Pérez Rosales 1631A, 1km east of town, T65-223 0909, www.canalesdelsur.cl.*
Pleasantly set on the lakeside. Very helpful, family-run, tours arranged, garden, car hire.

**$$ Casa Azul**
*Manzanal 66 y Rosario, T65-223 2904, www.casaazul.net.*
Wooden building, variety of rooms and dorms, heating, beautiful Japanese garden, book exchange, German and English spoken, excursions offered. Reserve in advance in high season.

**$$ Casa Margouya**
*Santa Rosa 318, T65-223 7640, www.margouya.com.*
Bright, colourful hostel, lots of information, French-run, English spoken.

**$$ Compass del Sur**
*Klenner 467, T65-223 2044, www.compassdelsur.cl.*
Chilean/Swedish-run hostel, all rooms with shared bath, comfy lounge, helpful, German, English, Swedish spoken, excursions offered. Reserve in advance in high season.

## $$ Hostería Outsider
*San Bernardo 318, T65-223 1056,*
*www.turout.com.*
Rooms sleep 1-3, private bath,
comfortable, heating, helpful,
restaurant, travel agency, English and
German spoken, book in advance.

### $$-$ Hospedaje Don Raúl
*Salvador 928, T65-231 0897.*
Shared rooms and bath, hostel facilities,
spotless, helpful, camping.

## Camping
Wild camping and use of barbecues is not
allowed on the lakeshore.

### Casa Tronador
*Tronador y Manzanal,*
*campingtronador@gmail.com.*
Expensive but central.

### Playa Hermosa
*Km 7, T65-233 8283, www.*
*campingplayahermosa.com.*
Fancy (negotiate in low season),
take own supplies.

### Playa Niklitschek
*Km 8, T9-8257 0698, www.playanik.cl.*
Full facilities.

## Restaurants

### Puerto Varas

#### $$$-$$ Mediterráneo
*Santa Rosa 068, T65-223 7268, see Facebook.*
On the lakefront, international and local food,
interesting varied menu, often full.

#### $$$-$$ Xic Dalí
*Purísima 690, T65-223 4424.*
Intimate Catalan bistro. Inventive menu,
top-quality preparation and service, good
wine list.

#### $$ Bravo Cabrera
*Pérez Rosales 1071, 1 km east of centre,*
*T65-223 3441, www.bravocabrera.cl.*
Popular bar/restaurant opposite the lake, big
portions, good value, varied menu, lively bar.

### $$ Di Carusso
*San Bernardo 318.*
Italian trattoria, good fresh pasta dishes on Fri.

### $$ Donde El Gordito
*San Bernardo 560, T65-223 3425,*
*downstairs in market.*
Good range of meat dishes, no set menu.

### $$ La Chamaca Inn
*Del Salvador y San Bernard, T65-223 2876.*
Good choice for traditional Chilean seafood.
Larger than life owner.

### $$ La Olla
*Ruta 225, 4 km east of town towards*
*Ensenada, T65-223 4605.*
Good, popular for seafood, fish and meat,
traditional Chilean cuisine.

**$** There are a couple of little snack bars along
the coast on Santa Rosa at the foot of Cerro
Philippi, serving, amongst other things, tasty
vegetarian burgers.

## Cafés

### Café Danés
*Del Salvador 441.*
Coffee and cakes.

### Cassis
*San Juan 430 y San José,*
*www.chocolatescassis.com.*
Cakes, generous ice creams and brownies.

### El Barista
*Walker Martínez 211A, T65-223 3130,*
*www.elbarista.cl.*
Probably the best place for a coffee.
Good-value set lunches and bar.

## Bars and clubs

### Puerto Varas

#### Club Orquídea
*San Pedro 537, T65-223 3024,*
*www.cluborquidea.cl.*
Popular club with tables dotted around
several small rooms and alcoves.
Occasional live music, huge pizzas.

## Shopping

### Puerto Varas

**Líder**, *Gramado 565*. Supermarket with a good selection, reasonably priced.
**Mamusia**, *San José 316*. Chocolates.
**Santa Isabel**, *Salvador 451*. Supermarket.

## What to do

### Puerto Varas
### Horse riding

See **Cochamó Aventura**, page 324, for details of horse-riding trips in the area.

### Kayaking

**Al Sur**, *Aconcagua e Imperial*, T65-223 2300, *www.alsurexpeditions.com*. Sea kayak, rafting and trekking tours, good camping equipment, English spoken, official tour operators to Parque Pumalín.
**Inside Nature Expeditions**, *T9-7872 7672, lactorisfernandeziana@hotmail.com*. Based out of Puerto Varas, owner Carlos gives private 4WD tours throughout the Lake District. Rafting and kayaking are also available.
**Ko'kayak**, *San Pedro 311 and Ruta 225, Km 40, T65-223 3004, www.kokayak.cl*. Kayaking and rafting trips, good equipment and after-trip lunch, French/Chilean-run.
**Miralejos**, *Independencia 50, T65-223 4892, www.miralejos.cl*. Kayaking in northern Patagonia, also trekking, horse riding and mountaineering. Associated is **Trekking Cochamó** (same address, www. trekkingcochamo.cl), which concentrates on adventure sports in Cochamó. Both are part of the **www.secretpatagonia.cl** group of operators who specialize in the area.
**Yak Expediciones**, *owner Juan Federico Zuazo (Juanfe), T9-8332 0574, www.yak expediciones.cl*. Experienced and safe kayaking trips on lakes and sea, in the fjords of Pumalín, enthusiastic and excellent, small groups, also runs courses.

## Zip-lining

Zip-lining (*canopy*), is offered by several operators.
**Canopy Pro**, *Santa Rosa 132, T65-223 5120, www.canopypro.com*. Offers canopy tours in different areas.

## Transport

### Puerto Varas

A taxi from Puerto Montt airport costs US$30-40. Minibuses from the airport are cheaper but will often stop in Puerto Montt first. Only local minibus services enter the town centre.

**Bus** The bus terminal is on the southwestern outskirts. **Pullman** and **ETM** are the only long-distance bus companies to have terminals in the town centre (Diego Portales). Other companies have ticket offices dotted around the centre but buses leave from the outskirts of town (**Turbus**, **Jac** and **Cóndor** from Del Salvador 1093; **Cruz del Sur** from San Fransisco at García Moreno).
To **Santiago**, US$28-42, several companies, 12 hrs. To **Osorno** hourly, US$2.75, 1 hr. To **Valdivia** US$5.50, 3 hrs.
Minibuses to the following destinations leave from San Bernardo y Walker Martínez: **Puerto Montt**, **Thaebus**, **Suyai**, **Puerto Varas Express** and **Full Express** every 5 mins, last bus at 2200, US$1, 30 mins. Every 15 mins to **Frutillar** (US$1, 30 mins). To **Ensenada**, every 45 mins, last bus at 2000.

**Ferry** Cruce Andino, www.cruceandino. com, operates the bus and ferry crossing from Puerto Varas 0800 to **Bariloche** (Argentina), US$280 one way (high-season price; US$230 low season), return 50% of the fare. From 1 May to 30 Aug this trip is done over 2 days with an overnight stay in Peulla at **Hotel Peulla** or **Hotel Natura**. You may break the journey at any point and continue the next day (see box, page 323).

# Parque Nacional
## Vicente Pérez Rosales & around

Established in 1926, this is the oldest national park
in Chile, stretching east from Lago Llanquihue to the
Argentine border. The park is covered in woodland and
contains a large lake, Lago Todos los Santos, plus three
major volcanic peaks: Osorno, Puntiagudo and Tronador.
Several other peaks are visible, notably Casablanca to
the north and Calbuco to the south. Near the lake are
the Saltos de Petrohué, impressive waterfalls on the
Río Petrohué. After visiting the falls, lakes and rivers
in the park, it's easy to convince yourself you've seen
every shade of green and blue in the visible spectrum.
A memorable journey by road and water takes you through
the park from Puerto Varas to Bariloche in Argentina.
South of the park is the beautiful Seno de Reloncaví.

# Essential Parque Nacional Vicente Pérez Rosales

## Access

In season, take one of the minibuses (every 30 minutes) from Puerto Montt and Puerto Varas via Ensenada to Petrohué. They generally allow you to break your journey at the waterfalls at no extra cost. It is impossible to reach the national park by public transport out of season: there are buses only as far as Ensenada, little traffic for hitching and none of the ferries take vehicles.

## Entry fees

Entrance to the park is US$2.50.

## Tip...

Covering up as much as possible with light-coloured clothes in December and January may help to reduce bites by horseflies which infest the park at this time.

## Opening hours

The park is open 0900-1800 (1730 in winter).

## Getting around

A combination of walking and hitching rides in locals' boats is the best way to explore the park. In wet weather many treks in the park are impossible and the road to Puerto Montt can be blocked.

## Information

CONAF has an office in Petrohué (0830-1300 and 1400-1830) with a visitor centre and a small museum (1030-1330 and 1530-1900). There is also a *guardaparque* office in Puella. No maps of treks are available in the park; buy them from a tour operator in Puerto Varas (see page 318).

## Lago Todos los Santos  Colour map 1, B3.

### an emerald green lake surrounded by a deeply wooded shoreline

The most beautiful of all the lakes in southern Chile (except for Lago General Carrera, which is split with Argentina), Lago Todos los Santos is a long, irregularly shaped sheet of water, punctuated by several small islands that rise from its surface. Beyond the hilly shores to the east are several graceful snow-capped mountains, with the mighty Tronador in the distance. To the north is the sharp point of Cerro Puntiagudo, and at the northeastern end Cerro Techado rises cliff-like out of the water.

The lake is fed by several rivers, including the Río Peulla to the east, the ríos Techado and Negro to the north, and the Río Blanco to the south. At its western end the lake is drained by the Río Petrohué. The lake is warm and sheltered from the winds, and is a popular location for watersports, swimming and for trout and salmon fishing. There are no roads round the lake, but private launches can be hired for trips around the lake.

### Petrohué and around

At the western end of the lake, 16 km northwest of Ensenada, Petrohué is a good base for walking tours with several trails around the foot of Volcán Osorno, or to the miradors that look over it, such as Cerro Picada. Near the Ensenada–Petrohué road, 6 km west of Petrohué, is the impressive **Salto de Petrohué** ① US$2.85, which was formed by a relatively recent lava flow of hard volcanic rock. Near the falls are a snack bar and two short trails, the **Sendero de los Enamorados** and the **Sendero Carileufú**.

In Petrohué, boats can be hired to visit Cayetué on the lake's southern shore (see below) or the **Termas de Callao** – actually two large Alerce tubs in a cabin – north of the lake. The boat will drop you at the uninhabited El Rincón (arrange for it to wait or collect you later), from where it's a 3½-hour walk to the baths through forest beside the Río Sin Nombre. The path twice crosses the river by rickety hanging bridges. Just before the baths is a house, doubling as a comfortable *refugio*, where you collect the keys and pay. From the termas there is a two-day trail northwards to Lago Rupanco.

### Peulla and around

Peulla, at the eastern end of the lake, is a good starting point for hikes in the mountains. The **Cascadas Los Novios**, signposted above the **Hotel Peulla**, are a steep walk away, but are stunning once you reach them. There is also a good walk to **Laguna Margarita**, which takes four hours.

### Cayutué and around

On the south shore of Lago Todos Los Santos is the little village of Cayutué, reached by hiring a boat from Petrohué (US$14 per person, minimum three people). From Cayutué (no camping on the beach but there are private sites) it is a three-hour walk to **Laguna Cayutué**, a jewel set between mountains and surrounded by forest, where you can camp and swim. From the lake it is a five-hour hike south to Ralún on the Reloncaví Estuary (see below): the last half of this route is along a *ripio* road built for extracting timber and is part of the old route used by missionaries in the colonial period to travel between Nahuel Huapi in Argentina and the island of Chiloé.

## Listings Lago Todos los Santos

### Where to stay

**$$$$ Hotel Petrohué**
*Ruta 225, Km 64, Petrohué, T65-221 2025, www.petrohue.com.*
Excellent views, half-board available, also has cabins, cosy, restaurant, log fires, sauna and heated pool; hiking, fishing and other activities.

**$$$$ Natura Patagonia**
*Peulla, T65-297 2289, www.hotelnatura.cl.*
Rooms and suites, disabled facilities, lots of activities offered, restaurant.

**$$$ Hotel Peulla**
*Peulla, T65-297 2288, www.hotelpeulla.cl.*
Half board. Beautiful setting by the lake and mountains, restaurant and bar, cold in winter, often full of tour groups (older partner of **Natura**).

### Camping

Camping wild and picnicking in the national park is forbidden. There's a basic site with no services and cold showers at Petrohué beside the lake; locals around the site sell fresh bread (local fishermen will ferry you across). There's also a good campsite 1½ hrs' walk east of Peulla, but you'll need to take your own food. A small shop in Peulla sells basic goods, including fruit and veg. The CONAF office can help find cheap accommodation.

### Restaurants

See Where to stay, above, for hotel restaurants. There is a small shop in the ferry building in Petrohué, with basic supplies and some of the houses sell fresh bread, but if you're camping it's best to take your own food.

**Boat** The **Cruce Andino** service (see page 318) is the only regular sailing between Petrohué and Peulla, although local fishermen may make the trip across the lake for a group.

**Bus** Minibuses run every 30 mins in summer between **Petrohué** and Puerto Montt via Puerto Varas (US$3, 1¼ hrs), much less frequent off season. Last bus to **Ensenada** (US$2.25) at 1800.

## Seno de Reloncaví  *Colour map 1, B3.*

**a quiet and beautiful estuary with sea lions and dolphins**

The Seno de Reloncaví, situated east of Puerto Montt and south of the Parque Nacional Pérez Rosales, is the northernmost of Chile's glacial inlets. It is often shrouded in mist and softly falling rain, which only adds to the mystique, and recommended for its wildlife, and for its peaceful atmosphere. It is relatively easily reached by a road that runs along the wooded lower Petrohué Valley south from Ensenada and then follows the eastern shore of the estuary for almost 100 km to join the Carretera Austral.

### Ralún and around

A small village situated at the northern end of the estuary, Ralún is 31 km southeast from Ensenada by a poorly paved road. There is a village shop and post office, and on the outskirts are **thermal baths** ① *reached by boat across the Río Petrohué, US$3.75 per person, see Facebook*. From Ralún you can either travel along the eastern shore of the estuary to Cochamó (see below) or take the road that branches off and follows the western side of the estuary south, 36 km to Lago Chapo and the Parque Nacional Alerce Andino (see page 361).

### Cochamó and the Gaucho Trail

Some 17 km south of Ralún along a poor *ripio* road is the pretty village of Cochamó (www.cochamo.com). It's situated in a striking setting, on the east shore of the estuary with the volcano behind, and has a small, frequently deserted waterfront, where benches allow you to sit and admire the view. Cochamó's fine wooden church dates from 1900 and is similar to those on Chiloé. It has a clock with wooden hands and an unusual black statue of Christ.

The Gaucho Trail east from Cochamó to **Paso León** on the Argentine border was used in the colonial period by the indigenous population and Jesuit priests, and later by *gauchos*. Four kilometres south of the village a road branches inland for about 3 km, following the course of the Cochamó valley. At the end of the road is the head of the trail up the valley to La Junta (five hours), described as Chile's Yosemite for its imposing granite peaks and now becoming a popular centre for many outdoor activities in and around the alerce forests (trekking, climbing, kayaking, riding, birdwatching and fishing). Beyond La Junta the trail runs along the north side of Lago Vidal, passing waterfalls and the oldest surviving alerce trees in Chile at El Arco. The route takes three to four days by horse or five to six days on foot, depending on conditions and is best travelled between December and March. From the border crossing at Paso León it is a three-hour walk to the main road towards Bariloche.

# BORDER CROSSING
## Chile–Argentina

★ **Three Lakes Crossing**

Cruce Andino (www.cruceandino.com) has the monopoly on this crossing, although tickets are sold by various operators. The mid-2016 season price was US$280 one way, 50% on return ticket; check the website before booking as prices alter with the season.

The journey starts by bus via Puerto Varas, Ensenada and the Petrohué falls (20-minute stop) to Petrohué, where you board the catamaran service (1¾ hours) across Lago Todos Los Santos to Peulla. During the summer there is a two-hour stop in Peulla for lunch (not included) and for **Chilean customs**. This is followed by an hour-long bus ride through the **Paso Pérez Rosales** (www.gendarmeria.gob.ar/pasos-chile/perez-rosales.html) to **Argentine customs** in Puerto Frías. Then it's a 20-minute boat trip across Lago Frías to Puerto Alegre, and a short bus journey (15 minutes) to Puerto Blest. A catamaran departs from Puerto Blest for the beautiful one-hour trip along Lago Nahuel Huapi to Puerto Panuelo (Llao Llao), from where there is a 30-minute bus journey to Bariloche. (The bus drops passengers at hotels, camping sites or in the town centre.) For the route from Argentina, see box, page 124.

## Puelo and beyond

Further south, on the south bank of the Río Puelo (crossed by a bridge), is **Puelo**, a very peaceful place with some expensive fly-fishing lodges nearby. Here the road forks. One branch (very rough) continues to Puelche (see page 362) on the Carretera Austral, while the other heads southeast, past Lago Tagua Tagua (ferry 0900, 1300, return 1200, 1630, with an additional ferry leaving at 0730 and returning at 0815, US$1.50 one way, US$10.50 for vehicles) to the peaceful village of Llanada Grande, nestled in the Andes, with basic accommodation. The road continues to the village of Primer Corral.

An alternative route to Argentina starts with a 45-minute walk to Lago Azul from the road between Llanada Grande and Primer Corral. A 25-minute boat trip across Lago Azul is followed a 45-minute hike through pristine forest to Lago Las Rocas, where another 25-minute boat ride ends at the Carabineros de Chile post on Lago Inferior. Go through immigration then navigate Lagos Inferior and Puelo as far as the pier on Lago Puelo.

## Listings Seno de Reloncaví

### Where to stay

**Ralún**

Lodging is available with families.

**Cochamó**

For details of *cabañas*, campsites and eateries, see www.cochamo.com.

**$$$ Cochamó Aventura Riverside Lodge**
*4 km south of Cochamó in Valle Rio Cochamó, T9-9289 4314, www.campoaventura.cl.*
Full board available (great breakfast), local food and very fresh milk from their own cow. Also have the **Mountain Lodge** further up the valley at La Junta. For details of their multi-day riding and trekking tours, see What to do, below.

### $$$-$ Refugio Cochamó
*La Junta, Cochamó valley,*
*www.cochamo.com. Oct-Apr.*
The perfect base for outdoor activities in
the Cochamó valley, only accessible on foot
(4-6 hrs) or horseback. Private rooms have
bed linen, bring sleeping bag for dorm beds.

### $$ Hostal Cochamó
*Av Aeródromo s/n, T9-6135 2163,*
*www.hostalcochamo.com.*
Private rooms and shared dorms, price pp,
local meals available, activities arranged as
well as transport.

### $$ Hostal Maura
*JJ Molina 12, T9-9334 9213,*
*www.experienciapatagonia.cl.*
Beautiful location overlooking the estuary,
rooms with shared bath, meals served,
kayaks, horse riding, good information,
sauna and hot tub (at extra cost).

### $$-$ Edicar
*Prat y Sgto Aldea, T9-7445 9230,*
*on seafront by the dock/ramp.*
With breakfast, hot shower, good value.

#### Puelo and beyond
Basic lodging is available with families.

### $$$ Posada Martín Pescador
*Lago Totoral, 2 km from Llanada*
*Grande on road to Primer Corral,*
*www.posadamartinpescador.cl.*
Rooms with bath and hot water, plus meals,
barbecues, horse riding, trekking, fishing,
canoeing and rafting.

## Restaurants

Eateries in Cochamó include **Donde Payi**,
opposite the church, and Reloncaví, on
the road down to the waterfront. On the
seafront there is a cheap fish/seafood
restaurant, which also hires out canoes.

## What to do

Fly-fishing guides in Puelo generally charge
around US$30 per hr, boat included.

**Cabalgatas Cochamó**, *Cra Principal,*
*Cochamó, T9-7764 5289, www.cabalgatas*
*cochamo.wix.com/chile.* On a farm by the
water, riding trips from 1 to 8 days, also
boat trips, climbing and fishing.
**Cochamó Aventura**, *T9-9289 4318, www.*
*campoaventura.cl.* Specializes in tailor-made
horse-riding and trekking tours between the
Reloncaví estuary and the Argentine border
including accommodation at their 2 lodges
(see Where to stay, above).

## Transport

**Boat** In summer boats sail up the estuary
from **Angelmó**. The **Sernatur** office in
Puerto Montt, see page 327, has details of
scheduled trips.

**Bus** **Trans har** (T65-225 4187) and **Buses
Río Puelo** (T9-9123 0838) run buses
from Puerto Montt, via Puerto Varas and
Ensenada, to **Ralún** (US$3), **Cochamó**
(2½ hrs, US$3.75) and **Puelo**, US$6, 3 a day
Mon-Sat, 2 on Sun, US$4. Minibus services
from Puerto Montt airport cost between
US$12 and US$140-200 depending on size
of vehicle (see www.cochamo.com).

# Puerto Montt
## & around

The capital of Región X (Los Lagos), Puerto Montt lies on the northern shore of the Seno de Reloncaví, 1016 km south of Santiago. It is a busy, modern and often windy city, flourishing with the salmon-farming boom, and this fish can be found in almost every restaurant in town. As the fastest growing city in Chile, it sometimes seems as if it is buckling under the pressure, with infrastructure struggling to keep up with population growth. It was founded in 1853, as part of the German colonization of the area, on the site of a Mapuche community known as Melipulli, meaning four hills. Good views over the city and bay are offered from outside the Intendencia Regional on Avenida X Región. There is a wide range of accommodation, but most people will prefer to stay in Puerto Varas, more picturesque and only 20 minutes away by bus.

## Sights

The **Plaza de Armas** lies at the foot of steep hills, one block north of Avenida Diego Portales, which runs east-west parallel to the shore. Near the plaza, the **Casa del Arte Diego Rivera** ⓘ *Varas y Quillota, T65-226 1836, www.corporacion culturalpuertomontt.cl*, has a theatre and holds regular exhibitions. Two blocks west of the square, on Calle Gallardo, is the **Iglesia de los Jesuitas**, dating from 1872, which has a fine blue-domed ceiling; behind it on a hill is the **campanario** (clock tower).

Further west, near the bus terminal, is the **Museo Regional Juan Pablo II** ⓘ *Diego Portales 997, Mon-Fri 1000-1300, 1430-1800, free (but there's been talk of charging in the future)*, documenting local history. It has a fine collection of historic photos of the city and memorabilia of Pope John Paul II's visit in 1988. Next to the museum is a small park with an old crane and a couple of rusting steam engines. The **Casa Pauly** ⓘ *Rancagua 210, T65-248 2611, Mon-Fri 1000-1700*, is one of the city's historic mansions, now in a poor state, which holds temporary exhibitions. The little fishing port of **Angelmó**, 2 km west along Avenida Diego Portales, has become a tourist centre, thanks to its dozens of seafood restaurants and handicraft shops (reached by Costanera bus along Portales and by *colectivos* Nos 2, 3, 4, 22, 33 from the centre, US$0.80). Launches depart from Angelmó (US$0.65 each way), for the wooded **Isla Tenglo** offshore. It's a favourite place for picnics, with views from the summit. The island is famous for its *curanto*, a meat and fish stew, served by restaurants in summer. Boat trips round the island from Angelmó last for 30 minutes and cost US$4.25. A longer boat trip (two hours) will take you to **Isla Huar** in the Seno de Reloncaví (US$43 for up to 10 people, T9-9698 4394, www.taximar.cl). If you are lucky you can stay at the island's church, but it may be best to camp.

## Essential Puerto Montt

### Finding your feet

**El Tepual Airport** is 13 km northwest of town. **Andes Tur** buses (T65-229 0100, www.etm.cl, US$3.50) run between the terminal and the city centre. Andes Tur also has a minibus service to/from hotels, US$8 per person, or US$10 per person (US$9 per person) for two people to Puerto Varas. A taxi to the town centre costs US$14, or around US$21-28 to Puerto Varas.

The bus terminal (www.terminalpm.cl) is on the seafront at Portales y Lota with rural buses leaving from one side and long-distance buses from the other.

### Getting around

Puerto Montt is quite a large city, with many *colectivos* and buses serving the barrios on the hill above the town. The central area is down by the port, though, and everything here is within walking distance.

### Useful addresses

**Argentine consulate**, Pedro Montt 160, p 6, T65-228 2878, www.cpmon. cancilleria.gov.ar. Quick visa service.

### Tip...

Get your cash in Puerto Montt, because the only other Visa ATMs before Coyhaique are in La Junta and Chaitén. Make sure you obtain Argentine pesos before leaving Chile.

## Tourist information

See also www.puertomonttchile.cl.

### CONAF
*Ochogavía 458, T65-248 400,*
*loslagos.oirs@conaf.cl.*
Information on national parks.

### Sernatur
*Just southwest of the Plaza de Armas,*
*Antonio Varas 415 y San Martín, T65-*
*222 3016, turismopuertomontt@gmail.com.*
*High season daily 0900-2100; low season*
*Mon-Fri 0830-1300, 1500-1730.*
For information and town maps. There are
also information desks at the airport and
the bus station (daily 0830-1600).

## Where to stay

Accommodation is often much cheaper
off season. Check with the tourist office.

### $$$$ Club Presidente
*Av Portales 664, T65-22 480 3000,*
*www.presidente.cl.*
4-star, very comfortable, rooms, suites,
some with sea view. Often full Mon-Fri
with business travellers.

### $$$ Holiday Inn Express
*Mall Paseo Costanera, T65-256 6000,*
*www.holidayinn.cl.*
Good business standard. Spacious rooms
with desks and great views, some with
balcony. Slightly pokey bathrooms but the
best in its category.

### $$$ Puerto Sur
*Huasco 143, T65-235 1212,*
*www.hotelpuertosur.cl.*
Small business-oriented hotel in a quiet
part of town. 4 floors, no lifts or views but
otherwise good value, parking.

### $$$ Tren del Sur
*Santa Teresa 643, T65-234 3939,*
*www.trendelsur.cl.*

'Boutique' *hostal* with pleasant public areas,
objects recycled from the old railway, some
rooms without windows, café, heating,
helpful English-speaking owner.

### $$ Hostal Pacífico
*J J Mira 1088, T65-225 6229,*
*www.hostalpacifico.cl.*
Comfortable, some rooms a bit cramped.
Parking, transfers.

### $$ Vista al Mar
*Vivar 1337, T65-225 5625,*
*www.hospedajevistaalmar.cl.*
Impeccable small guesthouse, good
breakfast, peaceful, great view from the
double en suite.

### $$-$ Casa Perla
*Trigal 312, T65-226 2104, www.casaperla.com.*
French, English spoken, helpful, use of kitchen,
pleasant garden, good meeting place.

### $$-$ Hospedaje Corina
*Los Guidos 329, T65 227 3948,*
*www.hospedajecorina.cl.*
Pleasant doubles and triple in a charming
house, breakfast included. Located near
**Casa Perla**.

### Camping

**Camping Los Alamos**
*Chinquihue Km 15, T65-226 4666,*
*www.complejolosalamos.com.*
Also has *cabañas*. Others on this road.

## Restaurants

In Angelmó, there are several dozen small
seafood restaurants in the old fishing port,
past the fish market; these are very popular.
Open until late in Jan-Feb. Local specialities
include *picoroco al vapor*, a giant barnacle
whose flesh looks and tastes like crab and
smoked oysters, and *curanto*, meat and fish
stew. There are other seafood restaurants in
Chinquihue, west of Angelmó.

### $$$ Club Alemán
*Varas 264, T65-229 7000,*
*www.elclubaleman.cl.*
Old fashioned, good food and wine.

### $$$ Club de Yates
*Juna Soler s/n, Costanera, east of*
*centre, T65-228 2810, www.clubdeyates.*
*wix.com/bannercdy.*
Excellent seafood, fine views from a pier.

### $$$-$$ Cotele
*Juan Soler 1661, www.cotele.cl, Pelluco,*
*4 km east, T65-227 8000. Closed Sun.*
Only serves beef, but serves it as well
as anywhere in southern Chile.
Reservations advised.

### $$ Café Haussman
*San Martín 185, T65-229 3390,*
*www.cafehaussmann.cl.*
German cakes, beer and *crudos* (steak tartare).

### $$-$ Dresden
*Varas 500, T65-225 0000, see Facebook.*
Corner café in in the centre with an extensive
menu of breakfast, lunch and dinner options.
Great coffee and fast Wi-Fi.

### $ Café Central
*Rancagua 117.*
Spartan decor, generous portions of
sandwiches and *pichangas*, a savoury
salad snack. Giant TV screen.

## Shopping

Woollen goods and Mapuche-designed rugs
can be bought at roadside stalls in Angelmó
and on Portales opposite the bus terminal.
Prices much the same as on Chiloé, but
quality often lower. There is a **supermarket**
opposite the bus terminal, open 0830-2100
daily, and in the **Paseo del Mar** shopping
mall, Talca y A Varas. **Paseo Costanera** is

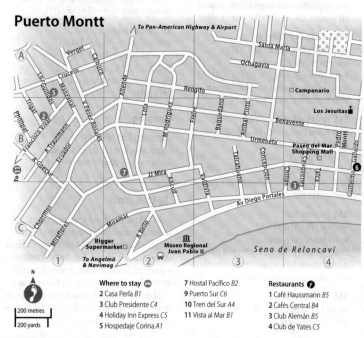

## Puerto Montt

To Pan-American Highway & Airport

Santa María
Ochagavia
Vergel
Cabuco
Crucero
Los Guimos
Manzanal
Allende
Yerez Rosales
Rengifo
Campanario
Los Jesuitas
Pilmal
Francisco Vivar
A Trautmann
Ecuador
Loto
M Rodriguez
Freire
Baquedano
Benavente
Urmeneta
Paseo del Mar Shopping Mall
Pedro Montt
A Goecke
Talcahuano
Concepción
Chillan
Cruguenes
Tara
Guillermo Gallardo
Chorrillos
JJ Mira
Ancud
Valdivia
Miramar
A Pelio
Av Diego Portales
Mitrafios
Bigger Supermarket
Museo Regional Juan Pablo II
Seno de Reloncaví
To Angelmó & Navimag

200 metres
200 yards

**Where to stay** 🛏
2 Casa Perla *B1*
3 Club Presidente *C4*
4 Holiday Inn Express *C5*
5 Hospedaje Corina *A1*
7 Hostal Pacífico *B2*
9 Puerto Sur *C6*
10 Tren del Sur *A4*
11 Vista al Mar *B1*

**Restaurants** 🍴
1 Café Haussmann *B5*
2 Cafés Central *B4*
3 Club Alemán *B5*
4 Club de Yates *C5*

a big mall on the seafront opposite the Sernatur office.

## What to do

### Diving
**Ecosub**, *Panamericana 510, T65-226 3939, www.ecosub.cl.* Scuba-diving excursions.

### Sailing
**Club de Deportes Náuticos Reloncaví**, *Camino a Chinquihue Km 7, T65-225 5022, www.nauticoreloncavi.com.* Marina, sailing lessons.
**Marina del Sur (MDS)**, *Camino a Chinquihue, Km 4.5, T65-225 1958, www.marinadelsur.cl.* All facilities, restaurant, yacht charters, notice board for crew (*tripulante*) requests, specialists in cruising the Patagonian channels.

5 Cotele *C5*
6 Dresden *B4*

## Tour operators
There are many tour operators. Some companies offer 2-day excursions along the Carretera Austral to Hornopirén, including food and accommodation. Most offer 1-day excursions to Chiloé and to Puerto Varas, Isla Loreley, Laguna Verde and the Petrohué falls: both are much cheaper from bus company kiosks inside the bus terminal.

## Transport

**Air** The airport (T65-229 4161, www. aeropuertoeltepual.cl) has ATMs, a **Sernatur** tourist information desk (daily 0900-1700) and car hire desks. **LAN** and **Sky** have several flights daily to **Santiago**, **Balmaceda** (for Coyhaique) and **Punta Arenas**. Flights to **Chaitén** (or nearby **Santa Bárbara**) leave from the Aerodromo la Paloma on the outskirts of town. Charters, sightseeing trips and air taxi services can be arranged with **Aerocord**, La Paloma aerodrome, T65-226 2300, www.aerocord.cl; **Aerotaxis del Sur**, A Varas 70, T9-9583 8374, www. aerotaxisdelsur.cl; **Cielo Mar Austral**, Quillota 245 loc 1, T65-226 4010, www. cielomaraustral.cl. For Transport from the airport, see box, page 326.

**Boat** Ferries and catamarans serve **Chaitén**, **Puerto Cisnes** and **Puerto Chacabuco**; there's also a weekly service south to **Puerto Natales** with **NaviMag**. See also Sea routes south of Puerto Montt, below.

**Bus** Puerto Montt is the departure point for bus services north to Santiago, and all the intermediate cities, and south to Punta Arenas. The bus terminal has telephones, restaurants, ATMs, a *casa de cambio* and left luggage service (0700-2245, US$2 per item, US$3.15 for big bags, for 24 hrs). There is an official taxi rank on level 1.

To **Puerto Varas**, US$1.15, every 15 mins, with **Expreso Puerto Varas** and **Thaebus**. **Buses JM** several daily (with transfers to **Ensenada**, **Puerto Octay**, **Llanquihue**, etc.). To **Cochamó**, US$3.75, 2½ hrs. To

**Hornopirén**, 5 hrs, US$5.50, with **Kémel** (which also runs daily to **Chaitén**, US$10). To **Osorno** US$2, 2 hrs. To **Valdivia**, US$7.50, 3½ hrs. To **Pucón**, US$14, 6 hrs. To **Temuco**, US$11-50. To **Concepción**, US$22. To **Valparaíso**, 14 hrs, US$40 (same to Viña del Mar). To **Santiago**, 12 hrs, US$35-50, several companies including **Tur-Bus**.

To **Bariloche (Argentina)**, daily services via Osorno and the Samoré pass are run by **Vía Bariloche** and others, 7 hrs. US$26; out of season, services are reduced. Buy tickets for international buses from the bus terminal; book well in advance in Jan and Feb. Ask for a seat on the right-hand side for the best views. To **Punta Arenas** (through Argentina via Bariloche), with **Cruz del Sur**, 3 a week

(1100), 32-38 hrs, US$57. Take US$ cash for Argentina expenses en route and take plenty of food for this "nightmare" trip; book well in advance in Jan-Feb and check if you need a multiple-entry Chilean visa; also book any return journey before setting out. For services to **Chiloé**, see page 337.

**Car hire** **Autovald**, Sector Cardenal, Pasaje San Andrés 50, T65-221 5366, www.auto vald.cl. Cheap rates. **Full-Car**, O'Higgins 525, T65-223 3055, www.full-car.cl. **Hunter**, T65-225 1524 or T9-9920 6888; office in Puerto Varas, San José 130, T65-223 7950, www. interpatagonia.com/hunter/. Good service. **Salfa Sur**, Pilpilco 800, also at airport, T600-600 4004, or T65-229 0201, www.salfasur.cl. Good value, several regional offices.

## Around Puerto Montt   *Colour map 1, B2.*

*alerce forest and sea voyages south of Puerto Montt*

### West of Puerto Montt
**Parque Provincial Lahuen Nadi** ⓘ *T65-248 6101 or T65-248 6400, US$2*, lies along a *ripio* road signed 'Lagunillas', which branches north off the main road, 5 km before the airport. There is a pleasant, short and easy (30-minute) trail through mixed native forest. This is perhaps the most easily accessible place in Chile to see alerce forests, although they are nowhere near as old or impressive as in other parts. Note that it is easy to get lost on the way back to the main road from the park.

The old coast road west from Puerto Montt is very beautiful. **Chinquihue** (the name means 'place of skunks'), beyond Angelmó, has many seafood restaurants, oysters being a speciality. Also located here is the **Estadio Regional de Chinquihue**, where Puerto Montt's local football team plays.

Further south is **Calbuco**, the scenic centre of the fishing industry. It is situated on an island linked to the mainland by a causeway and can be visited direct by boat or by road. West of here is the Río Maullín, which drains Lago Llanquihue, and has some attractive waterfalls and good salmon fishing. At its mouth is the little fishing village of **Maullín**, founded in 1602. On the coast to the southeast is **Carelmapu**, with an excellent beach and *cabañas* at windswept Playa Brava, about 3 km away.

### Sea routes south of Puerto Montt
Puerto Montt is the departure point for several popular trips along the coast of southern Chile. All sailings are from Angelmó; timetables should be checked carefully in advance as schedules change frequently. See Transport, page 332.

**To Puerto Natales** One of the classic journeys in Chile is the 1460-km voyage between Puerto Montt and the southern port of Puerto Natales, made by Navimag ferries. It is quicker and cheaper to fly or even to go by bus via Argentina, but the voyage by boat is a trip for the ages, provided the weather breaks your way.

The route south from Puerto Montt crosses the Seno de Reloncaví and the Golfo de Ancud between the mainland and the large island of Chiloé, then continues south through the Canal Moraleda and the Canal Errázuriz, which separate the mainland from the outlying islands. It then heads west through the Canal Chacabuco to Bahía Anna Pink and across the infamous Golfo de Peñas (Gulf of Sorrows), 12 to 17 hours, where seasickness pills come in more than handy; if you haven't brought any, you can buy them on board – you'll be advised when to take them!

After this stretch of open sea you reach a series of channels – Canal Messier, Angostura Inglesa, Fiordo del Indio and Canal Kirke – which provide one of the narrowest routes for large shipping in the world. There are spectacular views of the wooded fjords, weather permitting, particularly at sunrise and sunset, and a sense of tranquility pervades everything except the ship, which is filled with travellers having a raucous good time.

The only regular stop on this route is at the fishing village of **Puerto Edén** on Isla Wellington, one hour south of the Angostura Inglesa. It has some shops (scant provisions), one off-licence, one café, and a *hospedaje* for up to 20 people (open intermittently). The population of 180 includes five *carabineros* and a few remaining native Alacaluf people. Puerto Edén is the drop-off point for exploring **Isla Wellington**, which is largely untouched, with stunning mountains. If you do stop here, take all food; maps (not very accurate) are available in Santiago.

These ferries also carry freight (including live animals); they aren't cruise liners. Standards of service and comfort vary, depending on the number of passengers, weather conditions and the particular vessel running the service. On-board entertainment consists of a book exchange, bingo, film screenings and bilingual talks on fauna, botany, glaciation and history. Food is good and plentiful and includes vegetarian options at lunch and dinner. Passengers tend to take their own alcohol and extra food.

**To Puerto Chacabuco** Navimag also runs a twice-weekly ferry service between Puerto Montt and **Puerto Chacabuco**, 80 km west of Coyhaique. This beautiful voyage passes forested cliffs, so close it seems you can reach out and touch them, and offers glimpses of distant snows. However, taking this route south means that travellers miss out on the attractions of much of the Carretera Austral. From Puerto Chacabuco there are further services to visit **Laguna San Rafael**; see box, page 375, for more information.

**To Laguna San Rafael** The luxury ship m/n *Skorpios 2* cruises for six days and five nights from Puerto Montt to San Rafael, via Chiloé and Puerto Aguirre. Generally service is excellent, the food superb, and, at the glacier, you can chip ice off the face for your whisky. After the visit to San Rafael the ship visits **Quitralco Fjord**, where there are thermal pools and boat trips on the fjord, and **Chiloé**.

## Where to stay

### West of Puerto Montt

**$$ Hotel Colonial**
*Goycolea 16, Calbuco, T65-246 1546,*
*www.hotelcolonialdecalbuco.cl.*
One of several decent hotels.

## Restaurants

### West of Puerto Montt

**$$ Kiel**
*Chinquihué, T65-225 5010, www.kiel.cl.*
Good meat and seafood dishes.

## Transport

### Sea routes south of Puerto Montt
**Navimag** (Naviera Magallanes SA), Terminal
Transbordadores, Angelmó 1735, T65-243
2360 or T2-2869 9900, www.navimag.com,
sails to **Puerto Natales** throughout the
year leaving Puerto Montt usually on Mon
(check in 0900-1300, board 1700, depart
2000), arriving Thu. The return from Puerto
Natales is on Fri (check-in Fri 0900-1830,
board 2100 (day prior to departure), depart
0600 Sat), arriving in Puerto Montt Tue
morning (though dinner is not included).
Always confirm times and booking well
in advance. In winter especially days and
vessels may change. The fare, including
meals, ranges from US$350 pp for a bunk in
a shared cabin on the *Amadeo* in low season,
to US$2100 for 2 people in AAA double
cabin. 1st class is recommended, but hardly

luxurious. Check the website for discounts
and special offers. Mid-size cars are carried
for US$450 (SUVs for US$475), motorcycles
for US$137. Tickets can be booked by credit
card through many travel agencies, in
**Navimag** offices throughout the country, or
direct from www.navimag.com. Book well
in advance for departures between mid-Dec
and mid-Mar. It is well worth going to the
port on the day of departure if you have no
ticket. Departures are frequently delayed by
weather conditions.

**Navimag**'s ferry sails twice a week (Wed
and Sun) to **Puerto Chacabuco** (80 km
west of Coyhaique). The cruise to Puerto
Chacabuco lasts about 24 hrs. Cabins sleep
4 or 6 (private bath, window, bed linen and
towel) with a berth costing US67-155 in high
season. Cars, motorcycles and bicycles are
also carried. There is a canteen; long queues
if the boat is full. Meals are included, but
extra food is expensive so take your own.

**Skorpios Cruises**, Augusto Leguía
Norte 118, Santiago, T2-2477 1900, www.
skorpios.cl, sail from Puerto Montt to **Laguna
San Rafael**, via Chiloé and Puerto Aguirre.
The fare varies according to season, type
of cabin and number of occupants: double
cabin from US$2000 pp in high season.

**Naviera Austral**, Angelmó 1673, T65-
227 0430, www.navieraustral.cl, runs to
**Chaitén**, via Ayacara, as well as Hornopirén–
Ayacara, but check with the company for
schedules. It also has services Chacabuco–
Quellón and Chaitén–Quellón and, in Jan-
Feb only, Chaitén–Castro on Chiloé.

# Chiloé

The lush archipelago of Chiloé is one of the most mythical areas of Chile. Its one main island, La Isla Grande de Chiloé, has numerous islets and rolling hills, covered in patchwork fields and thick forest, which provide a lasting sense of rural calm.

You are almost always within sight of the sea, with dolphins playing in the bay and, on a clear day, there are views across to the twisting spire of Volcán Corcovado on the mainland.

Just under half the population of 170,000 live in the two main towns, Ancud and Castro, and there are also many fishing villages. The Cordillera de la Costa runs at low altitudes along the Pacific side of the island. South of Castro a gap in the range is filled by two connected lakes: Lago Huillinco and Lago Cucao. The sparsely populated western and southern parts of the island are densely forested; elsewhere hillsides are covered with wheat fields and dark green plots of potatoes and the roads are lined with wild flowers in summer. East of the main island are several groups of smaller islands, where the way of life is even more peaceful.

Chiloé is famous for its legends and rich mythology; here witches are said to fly around at night. Chiloé is equally well known for its wooden churches, some dating back to the late colonial period.

**Best** for
Island hopping ▪ Kayaking ▪ Penguin spotting

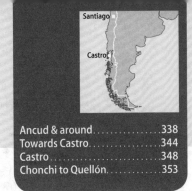

# Footprint
## picks

★ **Penguins at Puñihuil**, page 340

Waddling feathered friends reign supreme in islets near Ancud.

★ **Curanto**, page 343

This southern Chilean comfort food consists of meat, shellfish and potatoes, and is best when cooked in the ground.

★ **The church at Tenaún**, page 345

Chiloé is known for its churches, and this national monument is as impressive as they come.

★ **Quinchao and Lemuy**, pages 346 and 353

Hedgerow fields and wooden Jesuit churches transport you back in time.

★ **The beach at Cucao**, page 354

This seemingly endless beach is the doorstep to the Parque Nacional Chiloé.

★ **Parque Nacional Chiloé**, page 354

Fox, deer and over 110 species of bird are abundant in this lush rainforest.

Puerto Montt
Pelluco
7
Isla Maitén
Lenca
Seno de Reloncaví
Maullín
Astillero
Carelmapú
Pargua
Calbuco
Contao
Faro Corona
Chacao
2
Caulín
Golfo de Ancud
Mar Brava
Ancud
Puñihuil
Pumillahue
Río Anhuay
Linao
Vilcún
Belbén
Chepu
Degán
Quemchi
Isla Caucahue
Pacific Ocean
Isla Butachauques
Isla Metalqui
6
Península Huequi
Parque Nacional Chiloé
Dalcahue
Tenaún
3
Isla Mechuque
Ayacara
Abtao
Curaco de Velez
Achao
4
Isla Quinchao
Anay
6
Castro
Aldachildo
Isla Apiao
Isla Chulín
Cucao
Ichuac
Puqueldón
Lago Cucao
Chonchi
Lago Huillinco
4
Isla Lemuy
Isla Cahulinec
Isla Talcán
5
Detif
Huillinco
Lago Natri
Caleta Santa Bárbara
Chaitén
Lago Tepuhueico
Queilén
Chiloé
Isla Tranquil
Lago Chaiguata
Yaldad
Quellón
Quellón Viejo
Punta de Lapa
Volcán Corvovado (2290m)
Golfo Corcovado
To Puerto Chacabuco ▼

N

10 km
10 miles

# Essential Chiloé

## Access

**Air** An airport outside Castro opened in late 2012, with **LAN** flights from Santiago, via Puerto Montt.

**Bus** It is possible to travel direct to Chiloe from many cities, including Santiago, Osorno, Valdivia, Temuco and Los Angeles. Buses from Puerto Montt to the ferry terminal in Pargua are frequent (US$4, one hour); most continue via the ferry to Ancud (3½ to four hours) and Castro. Transport to the island is dominated by **Cruz del Sur**, Panamericano 500, at end of Avenida Salvador Allende, Puerto Montt, T65-243 6410, www.busescruzdelsur.cl, who also own **Trans Chiloé** and have their own ferries. **Cruz del Sur** run frequent services from Puerto Montt to Ancud (US$5.50) and Castro (US$8), plus six services a day to Chonchi (US$9) and Quellón (US$10.50); their fares are highest but they are faster than other operators because their buses have priority over cars on **Cruz del Sur** ferries. The main independent long-distance bus operator to the island is **Queilén Bus** (cheaper but less regular). Construction started on a bridge to the island across the Chacao channel in 2015; it is scheduled to be finished 2019.

**Ferry** There are regular ferry crossings from about 0630 to 0000 daily (30 minutes) between Pargua, 55 km southwest of Puerto Montt on the mainland, and Chacao on Chiloé, operated by several companies including **Transmarchilay** and **Cruz del Sur**; all ferries carry buses, private vehicles (cars US$17.50 one way, motorcycles US$11, bicycles US$3) and foot passengers (US$0.90). Sea lions, penguins, birds and occasionally dolphins can be seen in the straits of Pargua. There are also ferry services to the island from Chaitén on the Carretera Austral, mostly in summer.

## Getting around

Provincial bus services are crowded, slow and often wet, but provide a good picture of life in rural Chiloé. Mountain bikes and horses are ideal for travelling slowly through remote parts of the archipelago.

## When to go

The appalling climate of Chiloé is almost as legendary as the witches that are said to live there. The west coast has particularly vile conditions – it can rain here for three weeks at a time – while the sheltered east coast and offshore islands are only a little drier. Some of the best weather is in early December and late March.

The main benefits of the climate are culinary: the Humboldt Current and the sheltered east coast ensure a wide variety of fresh shellfish is available all year.

## Weather Ancud

| January | February | March | April | May | June |
|---|---|---|---|---|---|
| 18°C 11°C 109mm | 19°C 11°C 103mm | 17°C 10°C 139mm | 14°C 9°C 202mm | 12°C 8°C 326mm | 11°C 7°C 344mm |

| July | August | September | October | November | December |
|---|---|---|---|---|---|
| 10°C 5°C 335mm | 11°C 6°C 292mm | 12°C 6°C 212mm | 13°C 7°C 153mm | 15°C 8°C 121mm | 17°C 10°C 121mm |

Situated on the northern coast of Chiloé, 34 km west of the Straits of Chacao, Ancud lies on a great bay, the Golfo de Quetalmahue. It is a little humdrum compared to some of the other towns on the island but is nevertheless the best centre for visiting the villages of northern Chiloé. There is a friendly small-town feel; everyone knows each other and everything happens in its own time.

Tourism is slowly reviving Ancud's fortunes following the disaster of the *maremoto* (tidal wave) in 1960. Within striking distance are white-sand beaches, Spanish colonial forts and an important colony of Magellanic and Humboldt penguins.

### Ancud

By the Plaza de Armas is the **Museo Regional** ⓘ *Libertad 370, T65-262 2413, www. museoancud.cl, Mar-Dec Tue-Fri 1000-1730, Sat-Sun 1015-1330, Jan-Feb Tue-Fri 1000-1930, Sat-Sun 1015-1530, free*, with an interesting collection on the early history of Chiloé. It also displays a replica of a traditional Chilote thatched wooden house and of the small sailing ship, *Ancud*, which claimed the Straits of Chacao for Chile, pipping the French to the post by a day. In the patio is a skeleton of a blue whale. Beside it is the Centro Cultural, with details of events and handicrafts outside.

The modern cathedral stands on the plaza, built anew after the 1960 tsunami. Two kilometres east is a mirador offering good views of the island and across to the mainland, even to the Andes on a clear day.

## Essential Ancud

### Finding your feet

There are two long-distance bus terminals: the Terminal Municipal, on the outskirts of town, 1.5 km east of the centre, at Avenida Prat y Marcos Vera. Bus No 1 or Pudeto *colectivos* run from here to the centre. The much more convenient Cruz del Sur terminal is at Los Carrera 850. The Terminal Rural for local services is on Colo Colo, up a ramp behind the Unimarc supermarket. Timetables are posted on the door to the admin office and toilet.

### Getting around

Ancud is big enough for you to want to take the occasional *colectivo*; there are many of these, with their destinations signed on the roof (US$0.60, US$1 after 2100). Rural buses serve nearby beaches and villages.

The small fishing harbour at Cochrane y Prat is worth a visit, especially towards the end of the morning when the catch is landed. The port is overlooked by the **Fuerte San Antonio** ⓘ *Mon-Fri 0800-2100, Sat and Sun 0900-2000, free*, the fort where the Spanish surrendered Chiloé to Chilean troops in 1826. It has a few cannon and a surrounding wall. Close to it are the unspectacular ruins of the Polvorín del Fuerte. A lovely 1-km walk north of the fort is a secluded beach, **Arena Gruesa**, where public concerts are held in summer. Heading in the other direction, along the coast road to the west, you can see concrete pillars, remnants of the old railway, destroyed by the 1960 earthquake.

The **Faro Corona** lighthouse lies 34 km west of Ancud along a beach, which, although unsuitable for swimming (because it has absolutely freezing water and dangerous currents), offers good views with interesting birdlife and dolphins. The best time of day to see birds is early

# BACKGROUND
## Chiloé

The original Chilotes (inhabitants of Chiloé) were the Chonos tribe, who were pushed south by the Huilliches, invading from the north. The first Spanish sighting of the islands was by Francisco de Ulloa in 1553 and, in 1567, Martín Ruiz de Gamboa took possession of the islands on behalf of Spain. The small settler population divided the indigenous population and their lands between them, but the Huilliche uprising after 1598 drove the Spanish out of the mainland south of the Río Biobío, isolating the 200 Spanish settlers on Chiloé. Following a violent earthquake in 1646, the Spanish population asked the viceroy in Lima for permission to leave, but this was refused. Much of Chiloé's distinctive character derives from 200 years of separation from mainstream Spanish colonial development.

The islanders were the last supporters of the Spanish Crown in South America. When the Chilean patriot leaders rebelled, the Spanish governor fled to the island and, in despair, offered it to Britain. George Canning, the British foreign secretary, turned the offer down; Chiloé finally surrendered to the patriots in 1826. Visiting less than a decade later, Charles Darwin still clearly distinguished Chiloé from the rest of Chile, saying that here the Andes were not nearly "so elevated as in Chile".

Throughout the 19th and the first part of the 20th century, Ancud was the capital of Chiloé. All that changed with the earthquake and *maremoto* (tidal wave) of 1960. This drastically altered the landscape in Ancud, bringing petrified trees to the surface and causing forests to submerge. The whole of the lower town was destroyed, except for the cathedral, which was badly damaged and then blown up rather than renovated; until then, this had been the second largest cathedral in South America. The capital was moved back to its former site at Castro, which is the only place in Chiloé that really feels urban today. The *maremoto*, and the rivalry between Ancud and Castro that it spawned, have never entirely been forgotten.

The relatively high birth rate and the shortage of employment in Chiloé have led to regular emigration, with Chilotes settling across Chile; they were prominent as shepherds in late 19th-century Patagonia and as sailors and fishermen along the coast. However, with the recent growth in the salmon farming industry, a major source of employment, more Chilotes are choosing to stay. Also see www.chiloe.cl.

morning or late afternoon/evening. The duty officer may give a tour. There isn't much there, so take something to eat and drink. To the south is **Fuerte Ahuí**, an old fort with good views of Ancud.

## Chacao and around

Most people travelling to Chiloé will arrive in **Chacao** on the north coast. The town has a small, attractive plaza; and there's a pretty church and old wooden houses in Chacao Viejo, east of the port. Black-necked swans arrive here in summer from their winter habitat in Paraguay and Brazil. The *Panamericana* heads west from here to Ancud, while a coastal road branches south, towards Quemchi. Turn north off the *Panamericana* along the coast to reach **Caulín**; the road is only passable at low tide. There are good beaches here; in Caulín you can see many black-necked swans in summer and flamingos in autumn.

## Pumillahue

Pumillahue is 27 km southwest of Ancud, on the Pacific coast. About 10 km before is **Mar Brava**, a vast, deserted curved beach, wonderful for horse riding.

About 3 km away from Pumillahue at ★ **Puñihuil**, there is colony of both Humboldt and Magellanic penguins as well as sea otters, sea lions and a wide range of marine birdlife, situated on an island facing the beach. Local fishermen

> **Tip...**
> The best time to see penguins at Puñihuil is in the early morning or evening.

will provide a guided tour in Spanish, often with exaggerated hand gestures to make up for the lack of informed commentary. The penguins are there from October to late March. For an account of penguin-watching at Puñihuil, read Ben Richards' *The Mermaid and the Drunks* (Weidenfeld, 2003). To get there, catch one of the two or three buses that leave daily from Ancud, take a tour (US$22 per person, twice a day, 3½ hours including short boat trip; several agencies run trips), hire a taxi, or hitch.

# Ancud

| | Where to stay | Hospedaje Austral 7 | Restaurants |
|---|---|---|---|
| | 13 Lunas 3 | Hostal Altos de Bellavista 2 | El Cangrejo 3 |
| | Ancud 12 | Hostal Lluhay 14 | El Embrujo 1 |
| | Balai 1 | Hostal Vista al Mar 13 | El Pingüinito 4 |
| 100 metres | Don Lucas 11 | Mundo Nuevo 17 | La Pincoya 8 |
| 100 yards | Galeón Azul 4 | | La Ñaña 5 |

South of Pumillahue a poor road continues south some 5 km to Duhatao. From here it is a wild coastal walk of seven hours to Chepu (see below). The route is difficult to follow so take extra food and a tent and wear light-coloured clothes in summer to protect against *tábanos* (horseflies).

## Chepu and around

Twenty-six kilometres south of Ancud, a dirt road heads west from the Pan-American Highway to the coast at Chepu, famed for its river and sea fishing. It is a base for exploring the drowned forest and the waterways of the Río Chepu and its tributaries (a result of the 1960 *maremoto*). There is a wide range of birdlife here and excellent opportunities for kayaking, boat trips and horse riding. There's a bus to Chepu on Monday, Wednesday and Friday at 0630 and 1600, US$2.25; a taxi costs US$30-35.

Chepu is also the entrance to the northern sector of the **Parque Nacional Chiloé** (see page 354). From here, it is a 1½-hour walk to Playa Aulén, which has superb forested dunes and an extinct volcano. At **Río Anguay** (also known as Puerto Anguay), there is a campsite and *refugio*.

**Boat trips** can be organized in Río Anguay to **Laguna Coluco**, one hour up the Río Butalcura (a tributary of the Río Chepu). Two-day trips, navigating the ríos Grande, Carihueco and Butalcura, usually start further inland and finish at Río Anguay. These can be arranged in Ancud (see page 344), or contact Javier Silva, at Puente Anhuay, T9-9527 8719, turismo_riochepu@hotmail.com.

The Mirador de Chepu information centre gives views of the wetlands and has information about the flora, fauna and tourist options. It also has a café, kayaks for hire and accommodation in cabins or dorms.

---

**Listings** Ancud and around *map page 340.*

## Tourist information

### CONAF
*Errázuriz 317, Mon-Wed 0900-1250 and 1430-1730, Fri 0900-1250 and 1430-1630.*

### Fundación Amigos de las Iglesias de Chiloé
*Errázuriz 227, T262 1046. Open daily.*
Suggested donation US$1. In a precinct off the street, this place has an exhibition of various churches and styles of construction, as well as a shop.

### Sernatur
*Libertad 665, on the plaza, T65-262 2800, infochiloe@sernatur.cl. Mon-Thu 0830-1730, Fri 0830-16300.*
Ask here about the Agro Turismo programme, staying with farming families. There is another tourist office in the Feria Municipal.

## Where to stay

### Ancud

**$$$ Don Lucas**
*Salvador Allende (Costanera) 906, T65-262 0950, www.hoteldonlucas.cl.*
Nice rooms, some with sea view, disabled access, restaurant. A good choice.

**$$$ Galeón Azul**
*Libertad 751, T65-262 2567, www.hotelgaleonazul.cl.*
Small heated rooms, rather basic for the price but excellent views. Bright restaurant.

**$$$ Hotel Ancud**
*San Antonio 30, T65-262 2340, www.panamericanahoteles.cl.*
Nice views of the bay, attractive, very comfortable, helpful, restaurant, tours offered, English spoken.

## $$ Balai
*Pudeto 169, T65-262 2541, www.hotelbalai.cl.*
With heating, parking, restaurant, interesting
local paintings, models and artefacts on
display. Tours arranged.

## $$ Hostal Lluhay
*Cochrane 458, T65-262 2656,*
*www.hostal-lluhay.cl.*
Attentive, sea views, heating, meals,
nice lounge, kayak and bicycle rental,
tours with Ancud Mágico.

## $$ Hostal Vista al Mar
*Salvador Allende (Costanera) 918,*
*T65-262 2617, www.vistaalmar.cl.*
Close to Cruz del Sur buses, cabins for 2-5,
also private rooms with or without bath.
Views over the bay, safe, heating, parking.

## $$-$ 13 Lunas
*Los Carrera 855, T65-262 2106,*
*www.13lunas.cl.*
Opposite Cruz del Sur bus terminal, single-
sex and mixed dorms, private rooms,
wheelchair accessible, very helpful, *asados*
and ping pong in the basement, parking,
great penguin tour and other activities.

## $$-$ Mundo Nuevo
*Salvador Allende (Costanera) 748, T65-*
*262 8383, www.backpackerschile.com.*
Comfortable hostel, dorms, rooms with and
without bath, one room has a boat bed,
great views over the bay, lots of info, heating,
good showers, car and bicycle hire, English
and German spoken.

## $ pp Hospedaje Austral
*A Pinto 1318, T65-262 4847,*
*www.ancudchiloechile.com.*
Cosy wooden house, near long-distance
bus station, with small breakfast, lots of
bathrooms, double room ($$), family of
Mirta Ruiz, very welcoming and caring,
lots of information.

## $ pp Hostal Altos de Bellavista
*Bellavista 449, T65- 262 2384,*
*cecilia2791@gmail.com.*

Rooms for 1-5, with or without bath, family
atmosphere, long stay available, tatty outside
but welcoming inside. Several other places to
stay on Bellavista.

## Camping

### Hostal y Cabañas Arena Gruesa
*Av Costanera Norte 290, T65-262 3428,*
*www.hotelarenagruesa.cl.*
US$9-10 for campsite, also mobile homes,
with light, water and services, also cabins
for 2-10 and hotel.

---

### East of Ancud

## $$$-$$ Caulín Lodge
*Caulín, T9-9236 2667, www.caulinlodge.cl.*
Native Chilote trees grow in the
garden, *cabañas* and a sauna
available. Decent restaurant.
Horse riding and other trips offered.

---

### Chepu and around

## $$$-$ Mirador de Chepu
*Chepu Adventures, T9-9227 4517,*
*www.chepu.cl.*
Cabins or dorms; no children under 14.

## $$ Armando Pérez and Sonia Díaz
*T9-9899 8914, www.agroturismochepu.cl,*
*offer agrotourism stays.*
Make cheese, tend cattle and sheep, and
go for good walks in the Chepu area. To
get there from Ancud, travel 26 km south
on Route 5, turn right (east) for 5 km to
Coipomó, there turn left, and after 3.5 km
turn right. The farm is on the left after 2 km.

---

Restaurants

### Ancud
As well as abundant shellfish due to the
presence of the Humboldt Current, Chiloé
also has indigenous elephant garlic, which is
used to make a very tasty garlic sauce, as well
as several dozen endemic varieties of potato.
   Above the handicrafts in the Mercado
Municipal are 2 restaurants, **Los Artesanos**

## ★ Curanto

Particularly associated with Puerto Montt and Chiloé, *curanto* is a very filling fish, meat and seafood stew, which is delicious despite the rather odd combination of ingredients. Though of pre-Hispanic origins, it has developed by adding new ingredients according to new influences. In its original pre-Conquest form, a selection of fish was wrapped in leaves and baked over hot stones in a hole; some specialists wonder if this way of cooking may have come from the Pacific islands, where pit baking is still practised.

With the arrival of the Spanish, the dish was modified to include pork, chicken and white wine. Today, it is often cooked in a large pan and advertised as *pullmay* or *curanto en olla*, to distinguish it from the pit-baked form.

(loc 71), and **Rincón Sureño** (loc 53), both serving *comida típica*. Walking up Dieciocho towards the Feria Municipal there are many eating places behind the Mercado, including **La Ñaña**, which is cheap and good. All serve much the same local fare. In an alley from Dieciocho to Prat is a row of even cheaper lunch spots, including **El Pingüinito**, decent lunches, but more basic than others. In the Feria Municipal there are 4 restaurants upstairs, all much the same with lunch specials at US$4-7.

### $$ La Pincoya
*Prat 61, near the dock entrance, T65-262 2511.*
Good seafood, service and views.

### $$ Quetalmahue
*12 km west of Ancud on the road to Faro Corona and Fuerte Ahui, T9-9033 3930, www.restaurantequetalmahue.es.tl.*
The best place for traditional *curantos al hoyo* (cooked in the ground, daily in summer). For more on *curanto* see box, above.

### $ El Cangrejo
*Dieciocho 171.*
Has a good reputation for its seafood.

### $ El Embrujo
*Maipú 650.*
Café serving teas, coffees, sandwiches, cakes, beers and *tragos*.

### East of Ancud

### $$$-$$ Ostras Caulín
*Caulín, T9-9643 7005, www.ostrascaulin.cl.*
Excellent, very fresh oysters served in any number of ways.

### Pumillahue
There are restaurants at Puñihuil, all with similar menus and prices. The best of these is probably **Bahía Puñihuil** (T9-9655 6780, punihuil@gmail.com), who also offer trips to see the penguins.

## Bars and clubs

### Ancud

### Lumière
*Ramírez 278.*
The place to be seen for the younger crowd. Also serves good food.

### Retro's Pub
*Ramírez 317, T65-262 6410.*
Appealing ambience, food (including vegetarian fare and Tex-Mex) and good cocktails.

## Shopping

### Ancud
**Mercado Municipal** is on Libertad between Dieciocho and Prat. The **Feria Municipal** (or Rural) is at Pedro Montt y Prat, selling

local produce, fish and handicrafts on the 2nd floor. It also has a tourist office. Opposite is a huge **Unimarc** supermarket.

## What to do

### Ancud

**Aki Turismo**, *patio de Mercado Municipal*, *T65-262 0868, www.akiturismochiloe.cl*. Good-value trips to the penguin colony and other tours.

**Austral Adventures**, *Salvador Allende (Costanera) 904, T65-262 5977, www.austral-adventures.com*. Bespoke small-group tours of the archipelago and northern Patagonia (including Parque Pumalín) on land and sea. Good English-speaking guides, lots of interesting choices; director Britt Lewis.

**Mistyk's**, *Los Carrera 823, T9-9644 3767, www.turismomistyks.com*. For local tours and diving.

**Viajes Nativa**, *in Cruz del Sur bus terminal, T65-262 2303, www.viajesnativa.cl or www.*

*chiloetour.com, T65-254 6390*. Tours to the penguin colony.

### Chepu and around

This area offers great opportunities for horse riding, with long beaches that are perfect for a windswept gallop. Ask around for independent guides who offer riding, fishing and kayaking. See also **Mirador de Chepu/ Chepu Adventures** (www.chepu.cl).

## Transport

### Ancud

**Bus** To **Castro**, US$2.25, frequent (see below), 1½ hrs. To **Puerto Montt**, US$6, frequent services, see box, page 337. There are buses every 30 mins to **Quellón**. Cruz del Sur have several buses daily to **Valdivia**, **Temuco** and **Santiago**. To **Quemchi**, most via Degán, 2 hrs, US$2; to **Dalcahue** US$2.25. Cruz del Sur terminal, T65-262 2249.

---

## Towards Castro  *Colour map 1, B2.*

*making your way across the island*

There are two alternative routes from Ancud to Castro: direct along the Pan-American Highway, crossing rolling hills, forest and agricultural land, or the more leisurely route via the east coast. This is a dramatic journey on roads that plunge up and down forested hills.

The road is paved to Huillinco, a few kilometres before Linao, then is *ripio* to Quemchi. The route passes through small farming and fishing communities and offers a real insight into rural life in Chiloé. The two main towns along the coastal route, Quemchi and Dalcahue, can also be reached by paved roads branching off the Pan-American Highway.

### Quemchi and around

South of Chacao is the small village of **Hueihue**, where fresh oysters can be bought. Further south, before Quemchi, is a small lake with model sailing boats, which are made in the town. Quemchi itself is a quiet place with long beaches, overlooking a bay speckled with wooded islands.

Every summer cultural events are held. Kayaks are offered in January and February from Restaurante Barloventos (barloventos.quemchi@gmail.com). A short walk up the road north towards **Linao** leads to high ground from where there are views to the temperate rainforest on the mainland. Some 4 km from Quemchi is **Isla Aucar**, once linked by bridge (now ruined), where black-necked swans can be seen.

The road from Quemchi to Dalcahue (50 km) passes many places that are the essence of Chiloé. The road rises up and down steep forested hills, rich with flowers, past salmon

# BACKGROUND
## Chilote folklore

Chiloé's distinctive history and its maritime traditions are reflected in the strength of its unique folklore. There is widespread belief in witches, who are said to meet at caves near Quicaví (between Dalcahue and Quemchi), see below. Legend has it that Chiloé's dead are rowed along the reaches of Lago Huillinco and Lago Cucao in a white ship, out into the Pacific. For further information about the myths associated with the islands, read *Casos de Brujos de Chiloé* by Umiliana Cárdenas Saldivia (1989, Editorial Universitaria) and *Chiloé, Manual del Pensamiento Mágico y Creencia Popular* by Renato Cárdenas and Catherine Hall (1989, El Kultrún).

Visitors to Chiloé should beware of these four unlikely mythological hazards.

**El Trauco** A small, ugly and smelly man who wears a little round hat made of bamboo and clothing of the same material; he usually carries a small stone hatchet, with which he is reputed to be able to fell any tree in three strokes. He spends much of his time haunting the forests, sitting on fallen tree trunks and weaving his clothes.

El Trauco specializes in seducing virgins and is – conveniently – held to be responsible for unwanted pregnancies. He uses his magic powers to give them erotic dreams while they are asleep; they wake and go to look for him in the forest and are seduced by his eyes. Despite his ugliness, he is irresistible and the girl throws herself on the ground. You should be careful not to disturb the Trauco while he is thus occupied: those who do so are immediately deformed beyond recognition and sentenced to die within 12 months.

**La Fiura** A small ugly woman who lives in the forests near Hualdes, where she is reputed to bathe in the streams and waterfalls, combing her hair with a crystal comb. Known as the indefatigable lover of bachelors, she attracts her victims by wearing colourful clothes. As the man approaches he is put to sleep by her foul breath. After La Fiura has satisfied her desire, the unfortunate man goes insane. Refusing her advances is no escape either: those who do so, whether animals or men, become so deformed that they are unrecognizable.

**La Sirena** and **El Caleuche** A dangerous double act for those travelling by sea. La Sirena is a mermaid who lies alluringly on rocks and entices sailors to their deaths. Once shipwrecked, sailors are whisked into the bowels of *El Caleuche*, the ghost ship that is said to patrol the channels of the archipelago. Both the Chilean navy and merchant ships have reported sightings of the *Caleuche*. One of the authors of this book has also met several people on Chiloé who claim to have seen the ghost ship; but a word of warning was sounded by an old cynic in Castro: "I knew a fisherman who used to walk along the beach shouting 'I've seen La Sirena'. All the other fishermen fled, and then he stole their fish."

farms and views of distant bays. Some 20 km from Quemchi is a turn-off to **Quicaví**, legendary as the home to the witches of Chiloé; see box, above. A few kilometres further brings you to the beautiful village of ★ **Tenaún**, whose church with three towers, dating from 1837, is a UNESCO World Heritage Site.

## ON THE ROAD

## Jesuits in Chiloé

The Jesuits arrived in Chiloé in 1608 and the first Jesuit residence was established four years later. Although in Chiloé they introduced few of the missions for which they became famous in Paraguay, at their expulsion in 1767 there were 79 churches on the island.

The key to the Jesuits' influence lay in their use of *fiscales*: indigenous people who were trained to teach Christian doctrine and to ensure that everyone observed religious duties. One *fiscal* was appointed for every 50 inhabitants. On 17 September each year, two missionaries set sail from Castro in small boats, taking with them statues of saints and essential supplies. They spent the next eight months sailing around the islands of Chiloé, visiting all the parishes in a set order. In each parish they would spend three days officiating at weddings and baptisms, hearing confessions and reviewing the work of the *fiscales*.

Most of the old churches for which Chiloé is famous date from after the expulsion of the Jesuits, but some writers claim that their influence can still be seen, for example in the enthusiasm for education on the island, which has long boasted one of the highest literacy rates in the world. Many villages in Chiloé still have *fiscales* who are, according to tradition, responsible for keeping the church keys.

Offshore is Isla Mechuque in the **Chauques Archipelago**. This is a group of 16 islands east of Dalchahuen that are interconnected by sandbars which are accessible at low tide. **Mechuque** has two small museums of island life and there are *palafito* houses in the town, plus beautiful views of the mainland in good weather. Boats go from Tenaún (45 minutes), Quicaví and Dalchahue (not daily), but the easiest way to get there is on a tour from Castro, with **Turismo Pehuén** or **Turismo Mi Tierra** (see What to do, page 352).

Beyond Tenaún, you will pass numerous small communities with churches and views to the coast before you reach Dalchahue.

### Dalcahue and around

Some 74 km south of Ancud via the Pan-American Highway, Dalcahue is more easily reached from Castro, 30 km further south. The wooden church on the main plaza dates from the 19th century (under repair in 2014). There is a large *artesanía* market on the waterside, near which are several restaurants. A good-quality market is held near the handicraft market on Sunday mornings. There is a tourist kiosk in season and various hotels. Between Dalcahue and Castro is the **Rilán Peninsula**, with several traditional villages but also a growing number of upmarket hotels, golf and agrotourism.

### ★ Quinchao

The island of Quinchao (population 3500) is a 10-minute ferry journey from Dalcahue. Passing the pretty village of Curaco de Velez (handicrafts sold on the plaza in summer), you reach the main settlement, **Achao**, 25 km southeast of Dalcahue. This is a large fishing village serving the smaller islands offshore, with a boarding school attended by pupils from outlying districts. Its wooden church, built in 1730, is the oldest surviving church in Chiloé. In 1784 a fire destroyed much of the town, but the church was saved by a change in the wind direction. It is a fine example of Chilote Jesuit architecture (see box, page 350) and contains a small **museum** ⓘ *US$0.75*.

A beautiful road leads 9 km south of Achao to the small village of **Quinchao** in a secluded bay at the foot of a hill; an important religious festival is held in the fine church here on 8 December (see Festivals, below). For more information, see www.islaquinchao.cl.

With patience and persistence, boats can be found to take you from Achao to outlying islands, where facilities are basic and shops non-existent but lodging can be found with families; ask around. It is recommended to go with a local friend, if possible.

## Listings Towards Castro

### Tourist information

#### Quemchi and around

**Tourist office**
*In the plaza, Quemchi, www.muniquemchi.cl.*
*Summer only 0830-1300.*
Small office.

#### Quinchao

**Tourist office**
*Serrano y Progreso, Achao. Dec-Mar only.*
Small seasonal office.

### Where to stay

#### Quemchi and around

**$$ Hospedaje y Cabañas Costanera**
*D Bahamonde 141, Quemchi, T65-269 1230,*
*www.chiloe.cl/hospedajecostanera.*
*Cabañas* for up to 5 people, as well as bed and breakfast in rooms with shared bath.

Other basic places to stay include
**Camping La Casona** (T9-9909 9015).

#### Quemchi to Dalcahue

**$ Hospedaje**
*Rural María Humilde, Isla Mechuque,*
*T9-9012 6233, http://turismoislamechuque.*
*blogspot.co.uk.*

#### Dalcahue and around

**$ Residencial Playa**
*Rodríguez 9.*
Price per person. Basic.

**$ Residencial San Martín**
*San Martín 1.*
Price per person. Basic, clean, also meals.

#### Quinchao

**$$ Hostería La Nave**
*Prat y Aldea, Achao, T65-266 1219.*
Breakfast provided, cheaper rooms without bath, restaurant with fine views over bay.

**$ Hospedaje Achao**
*Serrano 061, Achao, T9-8291 9829.*
Without bath, good, clean.

**$ Hospedaje São Paulo**
*Serrano 54, Achao, T65-266 1245.*
Basic, hot water.

#### Camping

**Camping Garciá**
*Aquiles Descouvieres s/n, T65-266 1401.*

### Restaurants

#### Quemchi to Dalcahue

**$ Fogón La Pincoya**
*Isla de Mechuque, T9-6287 7400.*
For traditional meals and handicrafts.

#### Dalcahue and around

There are numerous small restaurants along the harbour and around the market in Dalcahue, serving excellent and cheap seafood. Note that if you ask for *té*, you will be served a mug of white wine.

**$ Restaurant La Dalca**
*Freire 502, Dalcahue.*
Good cheap food. Recommended.

### Quinchao

**$ Hostería La Nave**
*Quinchao, see Where to stay, above.*

## Festivals

### Quinchao

**8 Dec** People come from all over Chiloé for **Día de la Virgen** and watch as a huge model of the Virgin is carried with great reverence to the church.

## Shopping

### Dalcahue

Dalcahue's weekly market is held on Sun. It has quality goods, but bargaining is practically impossible, and in recent years it has become somewhat overrun with tourists. It's good for *curantos*, though; see box, page 343.

## What to do

### Dalcahue and around

**Altue Active Travel**, *3 km south of Dalcahue, office for reservations in Santiago at Encomenderos 83, piso 2.* **Las Condes**, *T2-333 1390, www.altue.com.* Sea kayaking and other activities.

## Transport

### Dalcahue and around

**Bus** To **Castro**, frequent services, US$1; daily bus to **Puerto Montt**, via Ancud.

**Ferry** To **Quinchao**, 10 mins, frequent, in summer it runs till 0100, cars US$3, free for pedestrians.

### Quinchao

Ferry to **Dalcahue**, 10 mins, frequent, in summer it runs till 0100, cars US$3, free for pedestrians. San Cristóbal buses to **Ancud** and Castro (multiple daily, fewer on weekends, US$2).

---

## Castro  *Colour map 1, C2.*

**bustling town life in the island's capital**

The capital of Chiloé, with a population of around 44,000, lies 88 km south of Ancud on a fjord on the east coast. Founded in 1567, it is a small, friendly town, full of bars and seafood restaurants. It is far livelier and more commercial than other towns and is the major tourist centre on the island. The centre is on a promontory, from which there is a steep drop to the port.

# Essential Castro

## Finding your feet

Castro is Chiloé's transport hub. There are two bus terminals: the crowded Terminal Municipal, San Martín 667, from which all buses and micros from island and long-distance destinations arrive; and Cruz del Sur terminal, San Martín 486, T65-263 5152. **Trans Chiloé**'s office is in Terminal Municipal.

## Getting around

There are some *colectivos* and public buses serving the barrios high above the town near the *media luna*, but it is unlikely that you will need to use these. It is only a 30-minute walk up there in any case.

## Sights

On the Plaza de Armas is the large wooden **cathedral**, unmissable in bright lilac and yellow, designed by the Italian architect, Eduardo Provosoli, and dating from 1906. It contains models of other churches on the islands.

One block south is the **Museo Municipal** ① *C Esmeralda, T65-263 5967, Mon-Fri 0900-1300 and 1500-1900,* with displays on the history, handicrafts and mythology of Chiloé, as well as photos of the effects of the 1960 earthquake.

Further south, on the waterfront, is the **Feria de Artesanía**, where local woollen articles, such as hats, sweaters, gloves, can be bought. Behind it are four traditional *palafito* restaurants, built on stilts above the water. More traditional *palafitos* can be seen on the northern side of town and by the bridge over the Río Gamboa (Calle Riquelme, with a number of *hostales*, cafés and handicraft shops).

There are good views of the city from **Mirador La Virgen** on Millantuy hill above the cemetery. **Museo de Arte Moderno** ① *T65-263 5454, www.mamchiloe.cl, daily 1000-1900,*

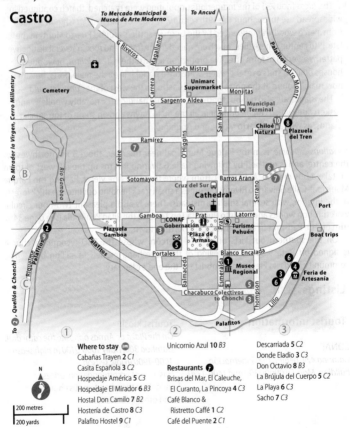

**Castro**

To Mercado Municipal & Museo de Arte Moderno
To Ancud
To Mirador la Virgen, Cerro Millantuy
To ② , Quellón & Chonchi

Río Gamboa
Palafitos
Riquelme
Cemetery

Riveros
Magallanes
Los Carrera
Gabriela Mistral
Unimarc Supermarket
Sargento Aldea
Monjitas
San Martín
Municipal Terminal
Chiloé Natural
Plazuela del Tren
Palafitos Pedro Montt

Ramírez
Freire
O'Higgins

Sotomayor
Barros Arana
Cruz del Sur
Cathedral
Serrano
Port

Gamboa
CONAF
Gobernación
Plazuela Gamboa
Plaza de Armas
Prat
Latorre
Turismo Pehuén
Boat trips

Palafitos
Portales
Balmaceda
Blanco Encalada

Chacabuco
Esmeralda
Museo Regional
Thompson
Lillo
Feria de Artesanía

Colectivos to Chonchi

Palafitos

**N**

200 metres
200 yards

### Where to stay

Cabañas Trayen **2** *C1*
Casita Española **3** *C2*
Hospedaje América **5** *C3*
Hospedaje El Mirador **6** *B3*
Hostal Don Camilo **7** *B2*
Hostería de Castro **8** *C3*
Palafito Hostel **9** *C1*
Unicornio Azul **10** *B3*

### Restaurants

Brisas del Mar, El Caleuche,
El Curanto, La Pincoya **4** *C3*
Café Blanco &
Ristretto Caffé **1** *C2*
Café del Puente **2** *C1*
Descarriada **5** *C2*
Donde Eladio **3** *C3*
Don Octavio **8** *B3*
La Brújula del Cuerpo **5** *C2*
La Playa **6** *C3*
Sacho **7** *C3*

## BACKGROUND
## Art and architecture in Chiloé

The availability of wood and the lack of metals on the islands have left their mark on Chilote architecture. Some of the earliest churches were built entirely of wood, using pegs instead of nails. These churches often displayed German influence as a result of the missionary work of Bavarian Jesuits. Four notable features were the *esplanada* or porch that ran the length of the front of the church, the not quite semi-circular arches, the central position of the tower directly above the door and the fact that they have three levels representing the Holy Trinity. Few of the oldest churches have survived, but there are still over 150 on the islands and even small villages almost invariably have churches with pretty cemeteries; in 2001, UNESCO declared them World Heritage Sites. Examples include churches in Tenaún and Nercón.

The *rucas* (houses) of the indigenous population were thatched; thatch continued in widespread use throughout the 19th century. The use of thin *tejuelas* (shingles) made from alerce wood was influenced by the German settlers around Puerto Montt in the late 19th century; these tiles, which are nailed to the frame and roof in several distinctive patterns, overlap to form effective protection against the rain. *Palafitos*, or wooden houses built on stilts over the water, were once popular in all the main ports, but are now mainly found at the northern end of Castro, to the west of the *Panamericana*.

The islands are also famous for their traditional handicrafts, notably woollens and basketware, which can be bought in all the main towns and on some of the smaller islands, as well as in Puerto Montt and Angelmó.

*donations welcome*, is in the Parque Municipal near the river, about 3 km northwest of the centre, and is reached by following Calle Galvarino Riveros up the hill west of town (or take a bus marked 'Al Parque'), from where there are fine views. Passing the Parque Municipal, Calle Galvarino Riveros becomes a small track heading out into the thick forests of the interior, with several small farmsteads. There is also a pleasant two-hour circular walk through woods and fields to **Puntilla Ten Ten** and the Rilán Peninsula (see page 346); turn off the Pan-American Highway 2 km north of town.

On the southern outskirts of town is **Nercón**, whose UNESCO-recognized church is signed off Ruta 5. From the ceiling of the nave hang models of sailing boats. The community holds its Fiesta Costumbrista at the end of January.

**Listings** Castro *map page 349.*

### Tourist information

**CONAF**
*Gamboa 424, behind the Gobernación building. Mon-Fri 0900-1300 and 1400-1730.*

Tourist kiosk
*On the Plaza de Armas opposite the cathedral, Gamboa 300. Daily 1000-2100 in high season; 1000-1900 in low season.*
Has a list of accommodation, prices, models of the area's famous churches, and other information.

## Where to stay

**$$$$-$$$ Cabañas Trayen**
*Nercón, 5 km south of Castro, T65-263 3633,*
*www.trayenchiloe.cl.*
Lovely views, cabins for 4 to 6.

**$$$$-$$$ Hostería de Castro**
*Chacabuco 202, T65-263 2301,*
*www.hosteriadecastro.cl.*
The newer section is spacious and
comfortable, with wonderful views and nice
suites. Spa, pool. Good restaurant and bar.

**$$$ Unicornio Azul**
*Pedro Montt 228, T65-263 2359,*
*www.hotelunicornioazul.cl.*
Striking pink and blue building climbing the
hillside from the waterfront, good views over
bay, comfortable, restaurant.

**$$$-$$ Palafito Hostel**
*Riquelme 1210, T9-9229 0576.*
In a restored traditional *palafito* building on
stilts over the water, downhill from centre
and across bridge. Helpful staff, good
breakfast, tours arranged. (On same street
are places with similar names: **Palafito
Azul** (No 1242, www.palafitoazul.cl), and
**Palafito 1326** (No 1326, www.palafito1326.cl).

**$$ Casita Española**
*Los Carrera 359, T65-263 5186,*
*www.hosteriadecastro.cl.*
Heating, parking, good, in same
group as **Hostería de Castro**.

**$$ Hostal Don Camilo**
*Ramírez 566, T65-263 2180,*
*hostaldoncamilo@gmail.com.*
Pleasant accommodation in functional
rooms with all services, good value
restaurant, secure parking.

**$$-$ Hospedaje El Mirador**
*Barros Arana 127, T65-263 3795,*
*www.hostalelmiradorcastro.cl.*
Private or shared bath, rooms a bit small,
cosy, relaxing, kitchen (shared with family).

**$ pp Hospedaje América**
*Chacabuco 215, T65-263 4364,*
*hosameri@telsur.cl.*
Good location, family welcome, shared bath,
comfortable. They offer an evening meal
service: you buy, they cook, everyone shares.

### Camping

Several sites on road to Chonchi, including
**Llicaldad** (6 km south of Castro, T9-9100
1361, apachecocornejo@gmail.com), also
has *cabañas*.

**Camping Pudú**
*Ruta 5, 10 km north of Castro.*
Cabins, showers with hot water, sites
with light, water, kids' games.

## Restaurants

Breakfast before 0900 is difficult to find.
There are several eating places and bars
on the south side of the Plaza, on Portales
and Balmaceda. By the market many places
offer set lunch, usually fish dishes. In the
market, try *milcaos*, fried potato cakes with
meat stuffing. Also *licor de oro* like Galliano.

**$$$-$ Donde Eladio**
*Lillo 97.*
Meat and seafood specialities on offer.

**$$$-$ La Playa**
*Lillo 41, www.playachiloe.cl.*
Good seafood, also meat dishes.

**$$ Don Octavio**
*Pedro Montt 261.*
Good food and nice views over bay,
specializes in seafood.

**$$ Palafito restaurants**
*Near the Feria de Artesanía on the waterfront.*
Offer good food and good value: **Brisas del
Mar**, **El Caleuche** (see Facebook), **El Curanto**
and **La Pincoya**.

**$$-$ Descarriada**
*Esmeralda y Blanco Encalada,*
*corner of the Plaza.*

Good local dishes, meat and fish, nice atmosphere, also desserts, tea and coffee, ice cream cart outside.

### $$-$ Sacho
*Thompson 213. Tue-Sat 1205-1530 and 2000-2330, Sun 1205-1530.*
Good sea views and food.

## Cafés

### Café Blanco
*Blanco 268.*
Busy little place for coffee, teas, juices, sandwiches, cakes, *piscos*, beers and wine. Similar, at No 264, is Ristretto Caffé.

### Café del Puente
*Riquelme 1180-B, T65-263 4878. Tue-Sun 0900-2100.*
Smart café over the water serving breakfast, lunches, afternoon tea (30 varieties of tea), coffee, sandwiches, cakes, juices and ice cream.

### La Brújula del Cuerpo
*O'Higgins 302, Plaza de Armas, see Facebook.*
Fast food, grill, snacks, drinks and coffee.

## Bars and clubs

### Kaweshkar Lounge
*Blanco Encalada 31.*
Minimalist bar with wide range of cocktails and occasional live music. Also serves food.

## Festivals

**Late Jan/Early Feb Muestra custumbrista de Chiloé**, when the Chilote community celebrates its culture.

## Shopping

**Feria de Artesanía** (Lillo on the wharf), sells good-value woollens. The **Mercado Municipal** is up the hill on Yumbel, for fish and veg. **Unimarc supermarket** (O'Higgins y Aldea), bakes good bread.

## What to do

**Chiloé Natural**, *P Montt next to Unicornio Azul, T65-6319 7388, www.chiloenatural.org.* Lots of activities, trips to islands and boat trips.
**Mar y Magia**, *cabin on the dockside or at Chacabuco 202, T9-7139 5499, www.marymagia.cl.* Fjord trips by boat, US$9 pp, longer trips in summer.
**Turismo Mi Tierra**, *San Martín 473-A, T9-7793 4685, www.turismomitierra.cl.* Trips to Isla Mechuque, including a meal of *curanto al hoyo* and a visit to waterfalls at Tocoihue on the main island.
**Turismo Pehuén**, *Chacabuco 498, T65-263 5254, www.turismopehuen.cl.* **Naviera Austral** agency, kayak and boat trips, trips to national park, penguin colony, around the island and car hire.

## Transport

**Bus** Frequent services to **Ancud**, **Quellón** (hourly), **Chonchi** and **Puerto Montt** by Cruz del Sur, **Queilén Bus** and others. **Cruz del Sur** goes as far as **Santiago**, US$36.75, and all cities in between, including **Valdivia** and **Temuco**. Isla de Chiloé and Ojeda both run to **Cucao**, almost hourly in summer, 2-3 a day in winter, 1½ hrs, US$2.15, To **Dalcahue** every 30 mins, US$1.15. To **Achao** (Quinchao) via Dalcahue and Curaco de Vélez, see above. To **Puqueldón** on the island of Lemuy, **Gallardo**, **Llamaca**, multiple daily Mon-Fri, fewer Sat-Sun, US$3. To **Quemchi**, daily with **Queilén Bus**, 1½ hrs, US$2. To **Queilén**, **Queilén Bus** and others, US$2.50.

**Ferry** Although most passenger ferries leave from Quellón, Castro is sometimes used as a port services to Chaitén and Puerto Montt. **Naviera Austral**, Chacabuco 492, T65-263 5254, www.navieraustral.cl, has occasional services to **Chaitén** when Quellón's port is out of action.

The Pan-American Highway continues south to Quellón, the southernmost port in Chiloé, with paved side roads leading east to Chonchi and west to Cucao. From Chonchi, a partially paved road continues southeast to Queilén. Winding across forested hills, this is probably the most attractive route on the island; numerous tracks branch off to deserted beaches where you can walk for hours and hear nothing but the splashing of dolphins in the bay. The ferry to Lemuy sails from a port just south of Chonchi on this road.

### Chonchi
A picturesque fishing village 23 km south of Castro, Chonchi is a good base for exploring the island. Known as the *Ciudad de los Tres Pisos* (city built on three levels), it was, until the opening of the Panama Canal in 1907, a stopping point for sailing ships. In the years that followed, it was the cypress capital of Chile: big fortunes were made in the timber industry and grand wooden mansions were built in the town. In the 1950s, Chonchi boomed as a free port but, in the 1970s, it lost that status to Punta Arenas. Its harbour is now a supply point for salmon farms almost as far south as Coyhaique.

On the main plaza is the wooden **church** ① *Mon-Sat 0900-2000, Sun 1000-2000*, built in 1754 and remodelled in neoclassical style in 1859 and 1897. The nave roof is painted blue and dotted with stars. Its impressive tower was blown off in a storm in 2002 and has been rebuilt.

From the plaza, **Calle Centenario** drops steeply to the harbour, lined with several attractive but sadly neglected wooden mansions. The small **Museo de Tradiciones Chonchinas** ① *Centenario 116, T65-267 2802, US$1, Mon-Fri 0930-1330 and 1430-1800, Sat 0930-1330,* is housed in a former residence, and laid out to give an idea of domestic life in the first decade of the 20th century, when Chonchi was the most important port in Chiloé. It shows videos on the churches of Chiloé.

Fishing boats bring in the early morning catch, which is carried straight into the new **market** on the seafront.

The tiny **Museo del Acordeón of Sergio Colivor Barria** ① *Andrade 183 next to Restaurant La Quila, daily 1100-1900,* has some 50 instruments on display. There is another, undecorated 18th-century **church** ① *Tue-Sun 1000-1330 and 1430-1830,* at Vilupulli, 5 km north (sign on Ruta 5, *ripio* road). The woman who has a tiny handicraft stall behind the church, Sra Teresa Velásquez (T9-9395 5635) holds the key.

### ★ Lemuy
*Ferry departs 4 km south of Chonchi at Huicha on the road to Queilén every 10 mins 0700-0100, cars US$3, foot passengers free (micro from Castro).*

In the bay opposite Chonchi lies the island of **Lemuy**. It covers 97 sq km and offers many good walks along quiet unpaved tracks through undulating pastures and woodland. From the ferry dock, a road runs east across the island, passing a fine 19th-century wooden church at **Ichuac** before reaching **Puqueldón**. This is the main settlement on the island and is built on a very steep hill stretching down to the port. There's a post office and a telephone centre here, as well as a small private park, **Parque Yayanes** ① *T9-8861 6462, www.parqueyayanes.cl*, which offers a 30-minute walk across a hanging bridge and through mixed forest, has lodging in cabins and serves traditional food.

From Puqueldón, the road continues a further 16 km on a ridge high above the sea, passing small hamlets, with views of the water and the patchwork of fields. There are old churches at **Aldachildo**, 9 km east of Puqueldón, and at **Detif**, in the extreme south of the island.

## Queilén

Some 46 km southeast of Chonchi, Queilén is a pretty fishing village on a long finger-shaped peninsula. On the north side is a sandy beach, which curves round the head of the peninsula, while on the south side is the old wooden pier, which doubles as the port. There are fine views across the straits to Tanqui Island and the mainland, as well as the **Museo Refugio de Navegantes** ⓘ *Pres Alessandri s/n, T65-236 7149, Jan and Feb 1100-2000*. Also here are places to stay and several restaurants (see Restaurants, page 356).

## West of Chonchi

West of Chonchi at Km 12 is **Huillinco**, a charming village on Lago Huillinco, with *cabañas* and cafés. Beyond here the narrow and sinuous paved road continues west to ★ **Cucao**, one of the few settlements on the west coast of Chiloé. The immense 20-km-long beach is battered by thundering Pacific surf and dangerous undercurrents, making it one of the most dramatic places along the whole coast of Chile.

Cucao is divided by a creek. The landward side is beside the lake and has the small church, a helpful tourist information desk (www.turismocucao.cl) and a couple of traditional restaurants, plus places to stay. Cross the bridge to the newer sector, with *hostales*, eating places, adventure sports agencies (horse riding, trekking, kayaks, SUP) and the road to the national park (see below). Beyond the park entrance the rough road continues to Canquín, with a bridge shaped like a boat. Over the bridge, on the left, is a track through private property to the beach (US$1.50 to park car). It's about 30 minutes' walk from Cucao bridge to Canquín bridge.

## ★ Parque Nacional Chiloé

*T65-297 0724, parque.chiloe@conaf.cl, daily 0900-1700, US$2.25.*

The park, divided into three sections, covers extensive areas of the wild and uninhabited western side of the island, much of it filled by temperate rainforest. Wildlife includes the Chilote fox and pudu deer. There are over 110 species of bird resident here, including cormorants, gulls, penguins and flightless steamer ducks.

The northern sector, covering 7800 ha, is reached by a path which runs south from Chepu (see page 341). The second section is a small island, Metalqui, off the coast of the northern sector. The southern sector (35,207 ha) is entered 1 km north of Cucao, where there is an **administration centre**, small museum, restaurant Fogón, *cabañas* ($$$ for five to six people) and camping ($ per person). The centre provides maps of the park, but they are not very accurate and should not be used to locate *refugios* within the park. From the administration centre six short trails ranging from 108 m to 1700 m run along the lakeside and through dunes to the beach.

A path with great views runs 3 km north from the administration centre to **Laguna Huelde** and then north for a further 12 km to **Cole Cole**. Once you reach **Río Anay**, 9 km beyond Cole Cole, you can wade or swim across the river to reach a beautiful, secluded beach from where you can enjoy the sight of dolphins playing in the huge breakers. The journey can also be made on horseback; allow nine hours for the round trip. Take lots of water and your own food.

There are several other walks in the national park, but signposts are limited so ask at the administration centre or at horse-riding agencies about trips further into the park. *Tábanos* (horse flies) are bad in summer, so wear light-coloured clothing.

## Quellón and around

The southernmost port in Chiloé, located 92 km south of Castro, Quellón has suffered its fair share of misfortunes in recent years. In 2002, the arrival of the lethal *marea roja* microorganism caused the collapse of the shellfish industry, provoking demonstrations from fishermen and dockers who destroyed part of the pier. There is not much to interest the traveller here. Note that the street numbering system in Quellón is unfathomable.

**Museo Municipal Amador Cárdenas** ① *Gómez García s/n, T65-268 3543, Mon-Fri 0830-1300, 1430-1745*, has an odd collection of antique typewriters and sewing machines. There are pleasant beaches nearby: **Viejo**, 4 km west, where there is an old wooden church; **Punta de Lapa**, 7 km west, and **Yaldad**, 9 km west along a pretty road over the hills.

Boat trips go to Isla Cailín in summer from the pier, US$30 for a full day (www.turismochiloe.cl). A trip can also be made to **Chaiguao**, 11 km east, where there is a small Sunday morning market. The Golfo de Corcovado, between southern Chiloé and the mainland is visited by blue whales from December to April.

The far south of the island has been bought by a private foundation and has been turned into a nature sanctuary known as the **Parque Tantauco** ① *information from Ruta 5 Sur 1826, Club Aero Gamboa, Castro, T65-263 3805, www.parquetantauco.cl, US$5, children US$0.75.* Covering some 120,000 ha of native woodland, wetlands, lagoons and rivers, it is home to a range of endangered wildlife. There are two campsites (no electricity) ($$), a *casa de huéspedes* ($$$, breakfast included) and a *refugio* ($). Kayaks are available for rent. There are 120 km of trails from three hours to five days. Access is by road or by plane from Quellón to **Inio** (US$300) with **Air Club**, next to the park administration office. Reservations can be made online through Parque Tantauco.

## Listings Chonchi to Quellón

### Tourist information

#### Chonchi

**Tourist information kiosk**
*At the crossroads 1 block uphill from the main plaza, T65-267 1522. Summer only, daily 0830-1230 and 1330-1700.*

#### Quellón

**Tourist office**
Vargas y García. Often closed, even in summer.
Another source of information is the **Municipalidad** (www.muniquellon.cl).

### Where to stay

#### Chonchi and around

**$$$ Cabañas Treng Treng**
*José Pinto Pérez 420, T65-267 2532, www.trengtreng.cl.*
Impeccable fully furnished cabins sleeping 2-7. Splendid views, some English spoken.

**$$ Hostal Emarley**
*Irarrázabal 191, T65-267 1202.*
Near market, cheaper rooms with shared bath.

**$$ Hostal La Tortuga**
*Pedro Montt 241, T9-9098 2925, www.hostallatortuga.com.*
In a historic house on the main plaza, comfortable rooms, cafeteria, laundry.

## $$ Huildín
*Centenario 102, T65-267 1388,*
*www.hotelhuildin.com.*
Old-fashioned, decent rooms with good
beds but windows are onto interior passages,
also *cabañas*, garden with superb views.

### West of Chonchi
Most lodgings and restaurants in Cucao are
open Jan-Mar, but you can camp all year.

## $$$-$$ Hostal Palafito Cucao
*300 m from national park entrance,*
*T65-297 1164, www.hostelpalafitocucao.cl.*
*Open all year.*
Built from native timber and with large
windows for great views of Lake Cucao.
Transfers and excursions arranged. Private
rooms and a 6-bed dorm, comfortable, good
breakfast and kitchen, meals available.

## $$ La Paloma
*Behind the church on lakeshore.*
*Open all year.*
*Cabañas* and camping ($).

### Camping
There are campsites, some with restaurants
and shops, on the road to the national park,
others on the road east of Cucao. There are
minimarkets on the little street behind Jostel
and another before the tourist office.

### Quellón

## $$ El Chico Leo
*P Montt 325, T65-268 1567.*
Private or shared bath, heating,
games room, restaurant.

There are several other places to stay
including *cabañas* and campsites:
see www.turismochiloe.cl.

## Restaurants

### Chonchi and around
There are a few places to eat on
Av Irrarrázabal. Most places close on Sun,
even in summer. **Supermercado Economar**

(Irrarrázabal 49), far end of Costanera
from Mercado, has a café. Next door is
**Chocolatería Pastelería Alejandra**.

## $$-$ Tres Pisos
*Pedro Andrade 296 y Esmeralda,*
*near the market.*
Serves good food.

## $ Café Sueños de la Pincoya
*PJ Andrade 135. All day Sun, until 2100*
*Mon-Fri and until 0100 Sat-Sun.*
For sweet *empanadas*, cakes, teas and coffee.

### Quellén
There are several restaurants here.

## Restaurant Melinka
*Alessandri 126, www.restaurantmelinka.*
*blogspot.cl.*
Good food.

### West of Chonchi
In Huillinco try **Café de Lago**, on the
lakeshore by Camping Huillinco, for teas,
coffees, cakes, sandwiches (Jan to mid-Mar
daily and weekends to Semana Santa); or
**Los Coihues**, above Huillinco, for more
substantial fare.

## $$-$ Las Luminarias
*Cucao, T9-8289 6981.*
Sells excellent *empanadas de machas*
(*machas* are local shellfish). It also has
accommodation ($) with breakfast and hot
shower. There are several other restaurants
and cafés in Cucao across the bridge
on the road towards the national park,
among them **El Fogón de Cucao** (also has
accommodation), **Las Terrazas de Cucao**
(with shop and campsite, see Facebook),
**Maervi** and others.

### Quellón

## $$ Tierra del Fuego
*P Montt 445, T65-268 2079.*
For fish, seafood and other local dishes.
In a hotel of the same name.

**$ Fogón Onde Agüero**
*La Paz 307, T65-268 3653.*
Good cheap traditional food.
Popular at lunchtime.

## Festivals

**Chonchi and around**
2nd week of Feb **La Semana Chonchina**
is the anniversary festival.

## Shopping

**Chonchi and around**
Handicrafts (woollens, jams, liqueurs)
are sold at the **Feria Artesanal**, on the
waterfront and from the *parroquia*,
next to the church (open Oct-Mar only).

**Quellón**
Handicrafts can be bought from the **Feria
Artesanal** on Ladrilleros y Gómez García.

## What to do

**West of Chonchi**
Many houses in Cucao rent horses. It usually
costs US$80-100 for 2 people per day for the
round trip on horseback to Río Anay. Bear
in mind that the horses will be of varied
temperament, and that if you hire a guide,
you pay for his horse too.

## Transport

**Chonchi and around**
Buses and taxis to **Castro**, frequent, US$1.25,
from the main plaza. Services to **Quellón**
(US$1.50), **Cucao** and **Queilén** from Castro
and Puerto Montt also call here.

**West of Chonchi**
There are buses to **Cucao** from Castro,
via Chonchi and Huillinco.

**Quellón**
**Bus** To **Castro**, 2 hrs, frequent, **Quellón
Expreso** and **Cruz del Sur** (Pedro Aguirre
Cerda 052, T65-268 1284, US$2.75); also
to **Ancud**, US$6, and **Puerto Montt** US$10.50.

**Ferry Naviera Austral**, Pedro Montt 457,
T65-268 2207, www.navieraustral.cl, runs
ferries from Quellón to **Chaitén** once a week
(more in high season), 5 hrs, seat US$18,
bicycle US$14, motorbike US$23, car US$95.
To **Puerto Chacabuco** (via Melinka, Raúl
Marín Balmaceda, Santo Domingo, Melimoyu,
Puerto Gala on Isla Toto, Puerto Cisnes, Puerto
Gaviota and Puerto Aguirre) twice weekly,
28 hrs, reclining seat US$24, cars US$193. All
services leave from Castro when Quellón's
port is out of commission and schedules
are subject to last-minute changes due to
inclement weather. Check with the company
for current schedules and fares.

# Carretera Austral

Travelling along the Carretera Austral is one of the last great journeys in an untouched wilderness that South America – and indeed the world – has to offer.

It is a largely unpaved *ripio* road stretching almost 1200 km through spectacular ever-changing scenery and with a similar length of branch roads heading either to the fjords or the mountains and Argentine Patagonia beyond. Before the road opened, this part of Chile was largely inaccessible and it remains breathtaking.

The journey will take you past trees growing out of vertical cliffs; impenetrably thick millennial forests; burned pastures dotted with glacial debris; innumerable waterfalls rushing right down to the road's edge, while sparkling glaciers feed turquoise lakes and fast-flowing rivers. The whole area is rich with southern Chile's unique flora.

The only town of any size, Coyhaique, lies in the valley of the Río Simpson. South of Coyhaique is Lago General Carrera, the largest lake in Chile, and the Río Baker, one of the longest rivers in the country, which reaches the sea at Caleta Tortel.

Further south still is Villa O' Higgins and the icefields of the Campo de Hielo Sur, which feed several magnificent glaciers.

**Best** for
Camping ▪ Cycling ▪ Fly-fishing ▪ Rafting

# Footprint
## picks

★ **Mountain biking the Carretera Austral**, page 363

The scenery along this highway's some 1200 km is unmatched anywhere in the world.

★ **Parque Pumalín**, page 365

Numerous trails amid snow-capped peaks, turquoise rivers and glassy lakes.

★ **Rafting near Futaleufú**, page 370

Experience what many professionals call the best river rafting in the world.

★ **Laguna San Rafael**, page 375

Get up close and personal with the San Rafael glacier, and walk the Northern Patagonian Ice Field.

★ **Lago General Carrera**, page 385

The majesty of this lake's marble caves and cerulean blue waters buttress its reputation as the most beautiful in Chile.

★ **Trekking in the Reserva Nacional Lago Jeinimeni**, page 389

Head off into this forested protected area with waterfalls and glaciers where Chile meets Argentina.

## Footprint picks

1 **Mountain biking the Carretera Austral**, page 363
2 **Parque Pumalín**, page 365
3 **Rafting near Futaleufú**, page 370
4 **Laguna San Rafael**, page 375
5 **Lago General Carrera**, page 385
6 **Trekking in the Reserva Nacional Lago Jeinimeni**, page 389

# Puerto Montt
## to Chaitén

This 242-km section of the Carretera Austral is perhaps the most inaccessible and secluded stretch along the entire route, passing through two national parks and the private Parque Pumalín. Beautiful old trees close in on all sides, the rivers and streams sparkle, and on (admittedly rare) clear days, there are beautiful views across the Golfo de Ancud to Chiloé. The 2008 eruption of Volcán Chaitén caused considerable damage around the town of Chaitén, with many homes still submerged in ash even today.

**Travelling from Puerto Montt to Chaitén** *Colour map 1, B2/C2.*
This section of the route includes two ferry crossings at La Arena and Hornopirén. Before setting out, it is imperative to check when the ferries are running (weather conditions can alter itineraries) and, if driving, to make a reservation for your vehicle: do this in Puerto Montt (not Santiago), on the website of **Transportes Austral** ⓘ *www.taustral.cl*, which is a consortium of the three ferry companies that operate the routes, or at the offices of the ferry companies listed in Transport, page 367. Hitching to Chaitén takes several days, and there is a lot of competition for lifts: you must be prepared for a day's wait if you find yourself out of luck. The experience of riding in the back of a pickup, however, will make the hanging around worthwhile. An alternative route to Chaitén is by ferry from Puerto Montt or Castro/Quellón (see pages 332 and 352/357).

## South of Puerto Montt
The Carretera Austral (Ruta 7) heads east out of Puerto Montt through **Pelluco**, where there is a polluted bathing beach with black sand and some good seafood restaurants, and then follows the shore of the beautiful Seno de Reloncaví (Reloncaví Estuary, see page 322).

Between the sound to the south and west and Lago Chapo to the northeast is **Parque Nacional Alerce Andino** ⓘ *entrances 2.5 km from Correntoso (35 km west of Puerto Montt) and 7 km west of Lenca (40 km south of Puerto Montt), T65-248 6115, loslagos.oirs@conaf.cl, US$2.* The park covers 39,255 ha of steep forested valleys rising to 1500 m and containing ancient alerce trees, some over 1000 years old (the oldest are estimated to be 4200 years old). There are also some 50 small lakes and many waterfalls in the park. Wildlife includes pudu, pumas, *vizcachas*, condors and black woodpeckers. **Lago Chapo** (5500 ha) feeds a hydroelectric power station at Canutillar, east of the park. There are ranger posts at Río Chaicas, Lago Chapo, Laguna Sargazo and at the north entrance. These can provide very little information, but a map is available from **CONAF** in Puerto Montt. To get to the north entrance, take a Fierro or Río Pato bus from Puerto Montt to Correntoso (or a **Lago Chapo** bus which passes through Correntoso) – there are several daily except Sunday – then walk. To reach the south entrance, take the bus marked 'La Arena/Chaicas' Puerto Montt towards Lenca, US$1.50. Tell the driver to let you off in **Lenca** at the road leading to the park entrance, then walk (signposted).

Some 45 km south of Puerto Montt (allow one hour), **La Arena** is the site of the first ferry, across the Reloncaví Estuary to **Puelche**. From Puelche there is an unpaved road east to Puelo, from where transport can be found north to Cochamó and Ralún (see page 322).

### Hornopirén and around

Also called Río Negro, Hornopirén lies 54 km south of Puelche at the northern end of a fjord. Although a branch of the Carretera Austral runs round the edge of the fjord to Pichanco, 35 km further south, that route is a dead-end. Instead, to continue south you

# Parque Nacional Alerce Andino

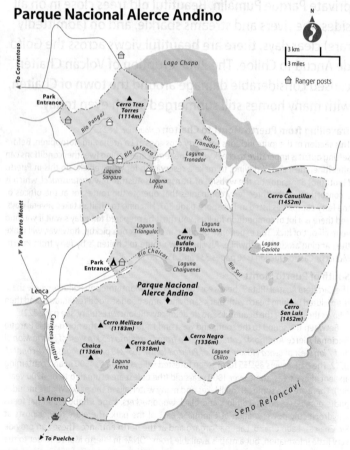

# ★ Travelling along the Carretera Austral

The road can be divided into three sections: **Puerto Montt to Chaitén** (143 km), plus two ferry crossings; **Chaitén to Coyhaique** (445 km); and **Coyhaique to Villa O'Higgins** (559 km), plus one ferry crossing. There is also a main branch that runs along the southern shore of **Lago General Carrera** from Puerto Guadal to Chile Chico, as well as important branches to Futaleufú, Palena, Raúl Marín Balmaceda, Lago Verde, Puerto Cisnes, Puerto Aysén, Bahía Exploradores and Tortel. The Puerto Montt–Chaitén section can only be travelled in summer, when the ferries are operating, but three alternative routes exist year round, either direct by ferry from Puerto Montt to Chaitén, through Chiloé and then by boat to Chaitén, or overland through Argentina via Osorno, Bariloche, Esquel and Futaleufú. The road is paved just south of Chaitén and around Coyhaique, from just north of Villa Amengual to Villa Cerro Castillo and Puerto Ibáñez.

The condition of the road can vary dramatically depending on the time of year and amount of traffic. January and February are the best months to travel, with strong westerly winds but plenty of sunshine too. Some sections can be difficult or even impossible after heavy rain or snowfall, and widening/paving/repair work is constantly being undertaken. If you are **driving**, take a 4WD vehicle and fill up your tank whenever possible. Drivers should carry adequate fuel and spares, especially if intending to detour from the main route, and should protect their windscreens and headlamps. After heavy rain, parts of the Carretera are liable to flood, so check the weather carefully and be prepared to be stuck in one place for a few days while conditions improve.

Many of the **buses** that ply the Carretera Austral are minibuses (and in more than one case, converted transit vans) operated by small companies, and often they are driven by their owners. Services are less reliable than elsewhere in Chile and timetables change frequently. Booking your ticket in advance means that if your bus does not leave, and the company is at fault, they are liable to pay for your accommodation until the bus is ready to depart. Complaints should be directed to SERNAC, in Coyhaique.

**Hitching** is popular in summer, but extremely difficult out of season, particularly south of Cochrane. Watching the cloak of dust thrown up by the wheels from the back of a pickup, while taking in the lakes, forests, mountains and waterfalls, is an unforgettable experience, but be prepared for long delays, carry a tent and plenty of food and allow at least three days from Chaitén to Coyhaique.

The Carretera Austral is highly recommended for **cycling** as long as you have enough time and are reasonably fit. A good mountain bike is essential and a tent is an advantage. Most buses will take bicycles for a small charge.

Be sure to take enough cash. There are Cirrus and MasterCard ATMs in Chaitén, and Visa is being accepted in more and more locales. As well as Puerto Aysén and Cochrane, Coyhaique is another place between Puerto Montt and Villa O'Higgins with Visa ATMs.

have to catch a ferry to Leptepu, travel 10 km by road to Fiordo Largo and then catch another ferry to Caleta Gonzalo. There is excellent fishing in the area and Hornopirén is a base for excursions to the **Hornopirén Volcano** (1572 m) and to **Lago Cabrera**, which lies further north. At the mouth of the fjord is **Isla Llancahué**, a small island with a hotel

# BACKGROUND

## Carretera Austral

The original inhabitants of northern Patagonia were Alacalufes (Kaweshkar or *canoeros*), who were coast dwellers living off the sea, and Tehuelches (Tzónecas, or Patagones), who lived on the pampa hunting guanacos, *ñandúes* (rheas) and huemules (see box, page 380).

The Spanish called the region Trapalanda, but initially explored little more than the coast. This was the last territory to be occupied by the Chilean state after Independence from Spain. In the late 19th century, expeditions up the rivers led by George Charles Musters (1869) and Enrique Simpson Baeza (1870-1872) were followed by a failed attempt to found a settlement at the mouth of the Río Palena in 1884. Fearing that Argentina might seize the territory, the Chilean government appointed Hans Steffen to explore the area. His seven expeditions (1892-1902) were followed by an agreement with Argentina to submit the question of the frontier to arbitration by the British crown.

The Chilean government granted concessions to three large cattle companies in an attempt to occupy the area. Until the 1920s, there were few settlers; early pioneers settled along the coast and brought supplies from Chiloé. Although the first town, Baquedano (modern-day Coyhaique), was founded in 1917, followed by Puerto Aysén in 1924, the first road, between Puerto Aysén and Coyhaique, was not built until 1936. It was not until the 1960s that this region began to be integrated with the rest of the country. Although the road has helped transform the lives of many people in this part of Chile, the motivation behind its construction was mainly geopolitical. Ever since Independence, Chilean military and political leaders have stressed the importance of occupying the southern regions of the Pacific coast and preventing any incursion by Argentina.

Begun in 1976, the central section of the Carretera Austral, from Chaitén to Coyhaique, was opened in 1983. Five years later, the northern section, linking Chaitén with Puerto Montt, and the southern section, between Coyhaique and Cochrane, were officially inaugurated. Since then, the Carretera has been extended south of Cochrane to Puerto Yungay and Villa O'Higgins. Work is continuing, building branch roads (which currently amount to around 1300 km) and widening and paving the most important sections. The road is the work of the army corps of engineers and dotted along the route are memorials to the dozens of young recruits who died during its construction.

Despite recent growth, this remains one of the most sparsely populated areas of Chile, with around 100,000 inhabitants, most of whom live in Coyhaique or in nearby Puerto Aysén. Agriculture is limited by the climate and poverty of the soil, but fishing, forestry and mining are key industries. A project for a huge aluminium plant was abandoned after continued protests. Similarly, plans for damming some of Chile's most spectacular rivers, including the Baker and Futaleufú, were scuttled in 2014.

and thermal springs, good for hiking in the forests amid beautiful scenery. The island is reached from Hornopirén by **boat** ① *US$14.50 one way, minimum 4 passengers, 25 mins.* Look out for dolphins and fur seals on the crossing.

Some 16 km by *ripio* road east of Hornopirén and covering 48,232 ha, **Parque Nacional Hornopirén** includes the **Yates Volcano** (2187 m) as well as the basins of two rivers, the

Blanco and the Negro. The park protects some 9000 ha of alerce forest as well as areas of mixed native forest including lenga and coigue. From the entrance a path leads 8 km east up along the Río Blanco to a basic *refugio*.

## ★ Parque Pumalín and around
*Information from Klenner 299, Puerto Varas, T65-225 0079 (in USA T415-229 9339), www. parquepumalin.cl. Open all year, free.*

Situated on the southern edge of the Fiordo Reñihue, Caleta Gonzalo is the base for visiting Parque Pumalín. Created by the US billionaire Douglas Tompkins and seen by many as one of the most important conservation projects in the world, this private reserve extends over 700,000 ha and is in two sectors: one just south of the Parque Nacional Hornopirén and the other stretching south and east of Caleta Gonzalo to the Argentine border. Much of this section of the park was covered in ash after the 2008 eruption of Volcán Chaitén.

Its purchase aroused controversy, especially in the Chilean armed forces, who saw it as a threat to national sovereignty. Initially Tompkins was frustrated by stonewalling from the Chilean government, but progress has been made and the park now has nature sanctuary status. The death of Tompkins in 2015 revived strongly held opinions and criticisms of the foundation. Whatever visitors may think of the billionaire conservationist and his legacy, Tompkins still remains a polarizing figure to many locals.

Covering large areas of the western Andes, most of the park is occupied by temperate rainforest. The park is intended to protect the lifestyles of its inhabitants as well as the physical environment. Tompkins established a native tree nursery, producing 100,000 saplings of native endangered species, and developed apiculture. There are treks ranging from short trails into the temperate rainforest to hikes lasting for several days (these are very arduous). The trail heads are all on the main road. Three marked trails lead to a waterfall, **Cascadas Escondidas**; to an area of very old alerce trees; and to **Laguna Tronador**. The road through these forests was only built in the 1980s, meaning that, unlike areas to the north and south, endangered trees have been protected from logging (laws protecting alerces, araucaria and other native species were passed in the 1970s). As a result, Parque Pumalín is home to perhaps the most diverse temperate rainforest in the world, and is the only place where alerce forests remain intact just a few metres from the main road. It is a truly humbling experience looking up from the base of a 3000-year-old, 3-m-wide alerce, and this, in itself, is a reason to visit the park. There are weekly buses and hitching is not difficult in season.

The Carretera Austral runs through the park, climbing steeply before reaching two lakes, **Lago Río Negro** and **Lago Río Blanco**. The coast is reached at **Santa Bárbara**, 48 km south, where there is a black sand beach. Towards sunset dolphins often swim right up to the beach. You can join them, although the water is very cold.

## Chaitén
Chaitén lies in a beautiful spot, with a forest-covered hill rising behind it, and a quiet inlet leading out into the Patagonian channels. In many ways Chaitén is a cultural crossroads. Until relatively recently, the town had more contact with Argentina than the central Chilean mainland, while a Chilote influence is clear in the town's architecture. Indeed until the construction of the Carretera this area was known as Chiloé Continental and was governed as part of the island opposite.

In May 2008 Volcán Chaitén, previously thought to be extinct, erupted, spewing a 20-cm layer of ash over the surrounding countryside and causing the Río Blanco to shift its banks. It flooded most of the town of Chaitén, destroying many buildings and covering much of the town with a thick layer of volcanic mud. The government decided to abandon Chaitén, cutting off utilities, moving the seat of provincial government to Futaleufú and starting to rebuild the town 10 km north at Santa Bárbara. Chaitén, however, survived without running water but with generators and fuel, and in 2011 the government reversed former decisions and the town was reestablished in the northern part of Chaitén, at which point water was turned back on.

There are shops, *hospedajes* and *cabañas* and good transport links: ferries to Puerto Montt and Chiloé (see Transport, below), flights and buses. See www.municipalidadchaiten.cl.

There is excellent fishing nearby, especially to the south in the Ríos Yelcho and Futaleufú and in Lagos Espolón and Yelcho.

## Listings Puerto Montt to Chaitén

### Where to stay

#### South of Puerto Montt

There are basic *refugios* at Río Pangal, Laguna Sargazo and Laguna Fría in the Parque Nacional Alerce Andino; no camping is permitted inside the boundaries of the park.

#### $$$$ Alerce Mountain Lodge
*Km 36 Carretera Austral, T65-225 3044, www.mountainlodge.cl.*
In Los Alerces de Lenca private reserve, beside Parque Nacional Alerce Andino, remote lodge, rooms and cabins, all-inclusive 2- to 4-night packages, with hiking, guides speak English, good food.

#### Hornopirén and around

#### $$$$ Hotel Termas de Llancahué
*Isla Llancahué, T9-9642 4857, www.termasdellancahue.cl.*
Full board (excellent food), hot spring at the hotel, boat trips, fishing, kayaking.

#### $$ Hornopirén
*Carrera Pinto 388, T65-221 7256, h.hornopiren@gmail.com.*
Rooms with shared bath, also *cabañas* and restaurant at the water's edge.

#### $$ Hostería Catalina
*Ingenieros Militares s/n, T65-221 7359, www.hosteriacatalina.cl.*
Comfortable rooms and *cabañas*, meals, trips, a good place to stay.

#### Camping
There's a good site on Ingenieros Militares, and more sites south of Hornopirén on the road to Pichanco.

#### Parque Pumalín and around
There is a restaurant, *cabañas* and a campsite in Caleta Gonzalo, as well as a visitor centre (not always open) and demonstrations of agricultural techniques in the region. Camping is available in the park at several well-run sites from US$3.75 per tent.

#### Chaitén
There are many *hospedajes* and hostels in the centre and along the waterfront.

#### $$$-$$ Hotel Schilling
*Corcovado 230, T65-273 1295, hotelschilling@hotmail.com.*
Probably the most upscale hotel in town. Rooms have ocean views.

#### $ El Quijote
*O'Higgins 42, T65-273 1204, relquijotechaiten@live.cl.*
Hostel located right across from the bus station, homely feel, also has restaurant. Dorms from US$11.50 per night.

#### $ Hostería Llanos Corcovado 378
*T65-273 1332.*
Pleasant, family-run B&B on the waterfront. Good breakfast.

## What to do

### Chaitén

**Chaitur**, *O'Higgins 67, T9-7468 5608, www. chaitur.com.* Nicolás La Penna runs this agency making bus, boat, plane and hotel reservations, transfers, tours to Parque Pumalín, Volcán Chaitén, hot springs, glaciers, Santa Bárbara beach, bike rentals, Carretera Austral and photography trips. Still the best place for local information. English and French spoken, helpful, book exchange, internet.

## Transport

### South of Puerto Montt

**Bus** There are buses from Puerto Montt to **Correntoso** and **Lago Chapo**, with **Fierro**, several daily Mon-Sat. There are also minibuses to **Chaicas**, **La Arena**, **Contau** and **Hornopirén**.

**Ferry** From La Arena, 2 roll-on, roll-off ferries cross the Reloncaví Estuary to **Puelche**, every 45 mins daily 0715-2045 (0645-2000 from Puelche), 30 mins, US$14 for a car, US$10.50 for motorcycle, US$4 for bicycle, US$1 for foot passengers. Arrive at least 30 mins early to guarantee a place; buses have priority. See www. taustral.cl, or contact **Naviera Puelche**, Av Italia 2326, Parque San Andrés, Puerto Montt, T65-227 0761, www.naviera puelche.cl, or **Naviera Paredes**, T65-227 6490, www.navieraparedes.cl.

### Hornopirén and around

**Bus** To **Puerto Montt**, **Kémel** (T65-225 3530) has daily services US$5.75.

**Ferry** Hornopirén to **Chaitén** via Leptepu (once daily each way, twice in high season) and Fiordo Largo to **Caleta Gonzalo** (twice daily each way, 4 in high season): check on www.taustral.cl, or with **Naviera Puelche**

(T65-227 0761, www.navierapuelche.cl) for updated schedules. If driving your own car, it is essential to reserve a place: cars US$46, motorbikes US$11.50, bicycles US$7.75, car passengers US$7.75, bus passengers US$3; one fare covers both ferries.

### Chaitén

**Air** Flights leave Mon-Sat at 0930 between Puerto Montt and Santa Bárbara with **Aerocord** (19 passengers), US$72.

**Bus** Terminal at Chaitur, O'Higgins 67. **Kémel** (as above) have a daily bus/ferry service from **Puerto Montt**, 0700, US$16, 10 hrs, return from Chaitén 1200, 12 hrs. To **Coyhaique**, direct with **Becker** Sun, Mon 1130, also **Terraustral** via an overnight stay in La Junta, 12 hrs, Mon, Fri at 1700 and Tue, Thu, Sat at 1200, with connections to **Puyuhuapi** and **Coyhaique** next day at 0500. **Terraustral** direct to Coyhaique Mon and Sat at 0700. Minibuses usually travel full, so can't pick up passengers en route. Buses to **Futaleufú**, twice daily 1200, 1700; change here for buses to the Argentine border, Mon, Fri (also Wed in summer.) And **Palena** twice daily at 1200 and 1700.

**Ferry** The ferry port is about 1 km north of town. Schedules change frequently and ferries are infrequent off season. Check with **Naviera Austral**, Corcovado 466, T65-273 1011, www.navieraaustral.cl or on www. taustral.cl for all future sailings.

To **Chiloé**, **Naviera Austral** operates ferry services to **Quellón** or **Castro** (Jan-Feb only), once a week (Tue), more in summer (Dec-Mar); fares given under Quellón, see page 357.

To **Puerto Montt**, **Naviera Austral**, Mon, Thu, Fri via Ayacara, 10 hrs, passengers US$24, seat US$55-62, car US$131, motorbike US$29, bicycle US$14.

# Chaitén to
# Coyhaique

This section of the Carretera Austral, 422 km long, runs through long stretches of virgin rainforest, passing small villages, the perfectly still waters of Lago Yelcho, and the Parque Nacional Queulat, with its hanging glaciers and cascading waterfalls. Roads branch off east to the Argentine border and west to Puerto Cisnes. Near Coyhaique, the road passes huge tracts of land destroyed by logging, where only tree stumps remain as testament to the depredations of the early colonists.

## Amarillo, Puerto Cárdenas and Lago Yelcho

thermal pools, fishing and hiking

### Amarillo

At Amarillo, 25 km south of Chaitén, there is a turning to the **Termas de Amarillo** ① *5 km east*, consisting of two wooden sheds with a very hot pool inside, and an outdoor swimming pool; it's worth a visit. There is superb salmon fishing in the nearby rivers. From here, it is possible to hike along the old trail to Futaleufú (see page 370). The hike takes four to seven days and is not for the inexperienced; be prepared for wet feet all the way. The trail follows the Río Michinmawida, passing the volcano of the same name, to **Lago Espolón** (see below). A ferry with a sporadic schedule crosses the lake, taking cargo, foot passengers and bicycles to Futaleufú.

### Puerto Cárdenas and Lago Yelcho

Situated 46 km south of Chaitén and surrounded by forest, **Puerto Cárdenas** lies on the northern tip of **Lago Yelcho**, a beautiful glacial lake on the Río Futaleufú, surrounded by hills and with views of the stunning Yelcho glacier. The lake is frequented by anglers for its salmon and trout. Further south at Km 60, a path leads to the **Yelcho glacier**, a two-hour walk each way (there is a viewing station halfway up). There is a campsite here.

# BACKGROUND
## Carretera Austral geography and climate

South of Puerto Montt the sea has broken through the coastal Cordillera and drowned the central valley. The higher parts of the coastal Cordillera form a maze of islands, stretching for over 1000 km and separated from the coast by tortuous fjords and *senos* (inlets). There is no real dry season near the coast, with annual rainfall of over 2000 mm on the offshore islands. Westerly winds are strong and temperatures vary little day to night.

The Andes are much lower in this region than they are further north, and eroded by glacial action; inland they form a high steppe around 1000 m, where the climate is drier, warm in summer and cold during the winter months. To the south of Coyhaique are two areas of highland covered by ice, known as *campos de hielo* (icefields). The Campo de Hielo Norte, over 100 km from north to south and some 50 km from east to west, includes the *ventisqueros* (glaciers) San Rafael, Montt and Steffens. The Campo de Hielo Sur covers a larger area, stretching south from the mouth of the Río Baker towards Puerto Natales.

Five main rivers flow westwards: from north to south these are the Futaleufú or Yelcho, the Palena, the Cisnes, the Simpson or Aysén and the Baker. The three largest lakes in this region, Lagos General Carrera, Cochrane and O'Higgins, are shared with Argentina.

## Listings Amarillo, Puerto Cárdenas and Lago Yelcho

### Where to stay

**Amarillo**

**$ Residencial Marcela**
*Amarillo, T65-248 5053.*
Also *cabañas* and camping.

**Puerto Cárdenas and Lago Yelcho**
There are no shops or restaurants in Puerto Cárdenas, but **Viola** (T9-9884 2946), a bungalow next to the old *carabinero* post, offers half board (**$$**) with excellent food.

**$$$ Cabañas Yelcho en La Patagonia**
*Lago Yelcho, 7 km south of Puerto Cárdenas, T65-257 6005, www.yelcho.cl.*
Cabins and rooms on the lakeshore.
Also expensive campsite and cafeteria.

### What to do

**Puerto Cárdenas and Lago Yelcho**
**Martín Pescador Lodge**, *www.martin pescadorfishing.com.* Offers packages at 3 lodges, on Lago Yelcho, near La Junta and on Lago Verde.

## BORDER CROSSING
### Chile–Argentina

**Paso Futaleufú**

**Chilean immigration** This is on the border, 8 km east of Futaleufú (see www.pasos fronterizos.gov.cl/cf_futaleufu.html). The border is a straightforward crossing. There is nowhere to change money at the border but you can pay the bus fare to Esquel (Argentina) in US dollars. For the Argentine side, see box, page 152.

**Paso Palena**

**Chilean immigration** This is 8 km west of the border and is much quieter than the crossing at Futaleufú. Check conditions locally before crossing at this border. **Trevelin** is 45 km east of Futaleufú, 95 km east of Palena (page 146), but there is a much wider range of services at Esquel, 23 km northeast; see page 142.

### Towards Argentina  *Colour map 1, C3.*

whitewater rafting and dolphins

Southeast of Chaitén the Argentine border is reached in two places, Futaleufú and Palena, along a road that branches off the Carretera Austral at Villa Santa Lucía (Km 81), named after General Pinochet's wife, where there are a handful of houses, a military camp and one small shop; bread is available from a private house. The road to the border is *ripio* of variable standard, passable in a regular car, but best with a good, strong high-clearance vehicle. The scenery is beautiful.

At **Puerto Ramírez**, at the southern end of **Lago Yelcho**, the road divides: the north branch runs along the valley of the Río Futaleufú to Futaleufú, while the southern one continues to Palena. See box, above.

### ★ Futaleufú

Futaleufú has established itself as the centre for the finest whitewater rafting in the southern hemisphere. Every year, hundreds of fanatics travel to spend the southern summer here and there is no shortage of operators offering trips. The river is an incredible deep blue and offers everything from easy Grade II-III sections downstream to the extremely challenging Grade V Cañón del Infierno (Hell Canyon). Although the town is only at 350 m, the spectacular mountain scenery makes you feel as if you were up in the High Andes.

The Río Espolón provides a peaceful backdrop to this pleasant town, with wide streets lined with shrubs and roses and Chilote-style houses. Changing foreign currency is difficult, but US dollars and Argentine pesos are accepted in many places. There's a **Banco del Estado**.

**Lago Espolón**, west of Futaleufú, is reached by a turning 41 km northeast of Puerto Ramírez. It is a beautiful lake and enjoys a warm microclimate, regularly reaching 30°C in the day in summer. The lake is even warm enough for a quick dip, but beware of the currents.

### La Junta and around

From Villa Santa Lucía, the Carretera Austral follows the Río Frío and then the Río Palena to La Junta, a tranquil, nondescript village at the confluence of Río Rosselot and Río Palena, 151 km south of Chaitén. La Junta has a service station for fuel and a minimarket. Some

9 km east is **Lago Rosselot**, surrounded by forest and situated at the heart of a *reserva nacional* (12,725 ha) with a well-equipped campsite and cabins.

From here, the road continues east for 74 km, to the unofficial border crossing at picturesque **Lago Verde** ① *summer only, 0800-2000*, and on to Las Pampas in Argentina. There is also a road leading northwest from La Junta, past some rustic thermal springs (not always open), across the broad expanse of the Río Palena (ferry runs 0830 to 1830) and on to **Puerto Raúl Marín Balmaceda** on the coast, a tranquil fishing village with more than its share of rainfall. Different species of dolphin can be seen, and when it is clear there are wonderful views of Volcán Melimoyu from the beach. Accommodation is available and camping is possible. Raúl Marín forms one apex of the blue whale triangle, and the giant cetacean can sometimes be sighted on the ferry to Quellón in the summer.

## Listings Towards Argentina *map below.*

### Tourist information

#### Futaleufú

**Tourist office**
*On the plaza at O'Higgins 596, T65-272 1241, www.futaleufu.cl. Oct-Apr, daily 0930-2200 (1030-1330 and 1500-1900 low season).*
Also sells fishing licences.

### Futaleufú

**Where to stay** 🛏
Adolfo B&B **1**
Cabañas Río Espolón **2**
Continental **4**

El Barranco **5**
Hostería Río Grande **6**

**Restaurants** 🍴
Futaleufú **1**
Martín Pescador **2**
Sur Andes **3**

### Where to stay

There are several options on the main street in Villa Santa Lucía; none has hot water.

**$ Residencial La Chilenita**
*Pudeto 681, Palena.*
Simple rooms.

#### Futaleufú

**$$$$ El Barranco**
*O'Higgins 172, T65-272 1314, www.elbarrancochile.cl.*
Elegant rustic rooms, luxurious, pool, sauna, good restaurant, and expert fishing guides, horses and bikes for hire.

**$$$ Cabañas Río Espolón**
*Follow Cerda to the end, T65-272 1423.*
Cosy *cabañas* in secluded riverside setting, restaurant overlooking Río Espolón, *parrilla*, bar. Popular with river-rafting groups, book ahead.

**$$$ Hostería Río Grande**
*O'Higgins y Aldea, T65-272 1320, www.pachile.com.*
Also upmarket, spacious attractive rooms, international restaurant, popular with rafting groups.

**$$-$ Adolfo B&B**
*O'Higgins 302, T65-272 1256.*
Best value in this range, comfortable rooms in family home, shared hot showers.

**$ pp Continental**
*Balmaceda 595, T65-272 1543.*
Oldest in town, no breakfast, basic, but clean and welcoming.

## Camping

### Aldea Puerto Espolón
*Sector La Puntilla, 400 m from town, T9-5324 0305, www.aldeapuertoespolon.blogspot.com.*
Teepees, dome tents or your own tent, take sleeping bag, hot showers. Several other sites.

## La Junta and around

### $$$ Espacio y Tiempo
*T67-231 4141, www.espacioytiempo.cl.*
Spacious rooms, warm and cosy atmosphere, restaurant, attractive gardens, fishing expeditions.

### $$ Hostal Casa Museo Copihue
*Varas 611, T67-231 4184.*
Some rooms with bath, good meals.

### $$-$ Hostería Valdera
*Varas s/n, T67-231 4105.*
Private bath, meals served. Excellent value.

## Restaurants

### Futaleufú

### $$ Futaleufú
*Cerda 407, T65-272 1295.*
Serves typical Chilean meat dishes and local foods.

### $$ Martín Pescador
*Balmaceda y Rodríguez, T65-272 1279.*
For fish and meat dishes, rustic.

### $$-$ Sur Andes
*Cerda 308, T65-272 1405.*
Café serving cakes, sweets, light meals and real coffee. Also sells handicrafts.

## Festivals

### Futaleufú
**Late Feb Futa Festival** (see Facebook). Rafting and kayaking races on the river.

## What to do

### Futaleufú
Tour operators arrange whitewater rafting trips, prices starting from US$80 pp. There are good fishing opportunities on Río Futaleufú and Lago Espolón (ask for the Valebote family's motorboat on the lake); local fishing guides can also be found in the village.
**Expediciones Chile**, *Mistral 296, T65-272 1386 (in US T1-208-629 5032), www.exchile.com.*
Whitewater rafting, kayaking, etc. Offers the best multi-day trips, book in advance. Day trips can be booked at office.
**Futaleufú Explore**, *O'Higgins 772, T9-7433 4455, www.futaleufuexplore.com.* A respected rafting company.
**Rancho Las Ruedas**, *Pilota Carmona 337, T9-7735 0989, guide.stallion@gmail.com.*
The best horse riding in the area.

### The Río Cisnes and further south
There's good fishing around Puerto Cisnes; contact **Cabañas Río Cisnes** (see Where to stay, page 376).

## Transport

### Futaleufú
**Bus** To **Chaitén**, 6 days a week, information from **Chaitur** in Chaitén (see page 367). A **Jacobsen** bus (www.transportejacobsen. com.ar) departs from west side of plaza to the Argentine border, 3 times a week Mar-Dec, and Mon-Fri in Jan-Feb, US$2, 30 mins, connecting with services to **Trevelin** and **Esquel**. Buses also run between Futaleufú and **Palena**, US$1.50.

### La Junta and around
**Bus** To **Chaitén**, 4 a week, information from **Chaitur** (see page 367). To **Coyhaique**, with **Daniela** (T9-9512 3500), **Becker** (T9-8554 7774, www.busesbecker.com), and **Aguilas Patagónicas** (T67-252 3730, www.aguilaspatagonicas.cl) 7 hrs, US$18.

### a fjord, thermal springs and a hanging glacier

From La Junta, the Carretera Austral runs south along the western side of Lago Risopatrón, past several waterfalls, to Puyuhuapi (also spelt Puyuguapi), 45 km further south. Located in a beautiful spot at the northern end of the Puyuhuapi fjord, the village is a tranquil stopping place, about halfway between Chaitén and Coyhaique with phone, fuel, shops, but no banks (some hotels may change dollars).

It was founded by four Sudeten German families in 1935, and its economy is based around fishing, ever-increasing tourism and the factory where Puyuhuapi's famous handmade carpets are produced and which can be visited: **Alfombras de Puyuhuapi** ① *T67-232 5131, www.puyuhuapi.com, daily in summer.*

From Puyuhuapi, the road follows the eastern edge of the fjord along one of the most beautiful sections of the Carretera Austral, with views of the **Termas de Puyuhuapi** ① *18 km southwest of Puyuhuapi; day packages including lunch and transfer, US$80.* This resort is on the western edge of the fjord and is accessible only by boat. It has several 40°C springs filling three pools near the beach. The resort can be visited as part of a three- to five-day package with **Patagonia Connection SA/Puyuhuapi Lodge & Spa** (see page 374) and day trips are possible from Puyuhuapi.

More easily accessible are the **Termas del Ventisqero** ① *6 km south of Puyuhuapi by the side of the Carretera overlooking the fjord, T9-7966 6862, www.termasventisquero puyuhuapi.cl, daily 1000-2100 (until 2000 in low season), US$24.50, US$14.50 for children under 10.* A café is open during the day.

## Parque Nacional Queulat
*Administration at the CONAF office in La Junta, T67-221 2225, aysen.oirs@conaf.cl, Dec-Mar daily 0830-2100, rest of year 0830-1830, US$7.50, reductions for Chileans and children.*

Covering 154,093 ha of attractive forest around Puyuhuapi, the **Parque Nacional Queulat** is, supposedly, the former location of the legendary Ciudad de los Césares, a fabulously wealthy mythological city built between two hills made of gold and diamonds and inhabited by immortal beings. According to legend, the city was protected by a shroud of fog and hence was impossible for strangers to discover. The Carretera Austral passes through the park, close to **Lago Risopatrón** north of Puyuhuapi, where boat trips are available. Some 22 km south of Puyuhapi, a road turns off to the main entrance of the park, continuing for 3.5 km past the hut of the *guardaparques* to a campsite and car park.

Three walks begin from here: a short stroll through the woodland to a viewpoint of the spectacular **Ventisquero Colgante** hanging glacier; or cross the river where the path begins to **Laguna Tempanos**, where boats cross the lake in summer. The third trail, 3.25 km, takes 2½ hours to climb to a panoramic viewpoint of the **Ventisquero**, where you can watch the ice fall into huge waterfalls.

The Carretera Austral climbs out of the Queulat valley towards the Portezuelo de Queulat pass through a series of narrow hairpin bends surrounded by an impressive dense jungle-like mass of giant Nalcas. There are fine views of the forest and several glaciers. Near the pass (250 m off the main road) is the **Salto Pedro García** waterfall, with the **Salto del Cóndor** waterfall some 5 km further on. Steep gradients mean that crossing the park is the hardest part of the Carretera for those travelling by bicycle.

## BORDER CROSSING
### Chile–Argentina

**La Tapera**
Chilean immigration is 12 km west of the border. For information on the Argentine side, see www.gendarmeria.gob.ar/pasos-chile/rio-frias.html.

On the Argentine side, the road continues, unmade, through the village of Apeleg to meet up with Route 40, the main north–south road at the foot of the Andes. This stretch of road has few services for fuel or food and there is no public transport.

On the southern side of the pass there is a sign labelled **Bosque Encantado** with a small parking area. A path leads west through a forest of Arayanes, like something out of a fairytale. After crossing a series of small bridges the path runs out at the river. Follow the river bank around to the right to get to a beautiful lagoon with floating icebergs and a hanging glacier. The trek to the lagoon and back should not take more than three hours and is well worth the effort.

### Río Cisnes and further south
Stretching 160 km from the Argentine border to the coast at Puerto Cisnes, the Río Cisnes is recommended for rafting or canoeing, with grand scenery and modest rapids, except for the horrendous drop at Piedra del Gato, about 60 km east of Puerto Cisnes. Good camping is available in the forest.

Possibly the wettest town in Chile, **Puerto Cisnes** is reached by a 33-km winding road that branches west off the Carretera Austral about 59 km south of Puyuhuapi. Once a peaceful fishing port where traditional knitted clothes were made, it is now an important salmon-farming centre. Fuel is available.

Fifteen kilometres further on, at Km 92, south of **Villa Amengual**, a road branches west for 104 km to the **Argentine border** via La Tapera, see box, above.

**Reserva Nacional Lago Las Torres** is 98 km south of Puyuhuapi and covers 16,516 ha. There are no trails, but it includes the wonderful **Lago Las Torres**, which offers good fishing and a small *hospedaje* and campsite. Further south, at Km 125, a road branches east to **El Toqui**, where zinc is mined.

**Villa Mañihuales**, at Km 148, is a small, nondescript town with a Copec petrol station and several basic *residenciales* and restaurants. Most buses stop here for 15 to 30 minutes. Nearby is the **Reserva Forestal Mañihuales**. The reserve covers 1206 ha and encompasses a huemul sanctuary. Fires largely destroyed the forests in the 1940s but reforestation is being studied here.

## Listings Puyuhuapi and around

### Tourist information

**Puyuhuapi**

**Tourist office**
*By the Municipalidad on the main street.*
*Oct-May Mon-Sat 0900-1200 and 1500-1830.*
Decent tourist information.

### Where to stay

**$$$$ Puyuhuapi Lodge and Spa**
*Reservations T2-2225 6489,*
*www.puyuhuapilodge.com.*
Splendidly isolated on a nook in the sea fjord, the hotel owns the outdoor thermal baths

## ★ Laguna San Rafael

Situated west of Lago General Carrera and some 200 km south of Puerto Aysén, Laguna San Rafael is one of the highlights for many travellers to Chile. The **Ventisquero San Rafael**, one of a group of four glaciers that emanate in all directions from Monte San Valentín in the giant **Campo de Hielo Norte**, flows into the Laguna, which, in turn, empties into the sea northwards via the Río Tempano. About 45 km in length and towering 30 m above water level, the deep blue glacier groans and cracks as it calves icebergs, which are carried across the Laguna and out to sea. Around the shores of the lake is thick vegetation and above are snowy mountain peaks.

Laguna San Rafael and the Campo de Hielo Norte are part of the **Parque Nacional Laguna San Rafael**, which extends over 1,740,000 ha, and is a UN World Biosphere Reserve. In the national park are puma, pudu, foxes, dolphins, occasional sea lions and sea otters, and many species of bird. Walking trails are limited (about 10 km in all) but a lookout platform has been constructed, with fine views of the glacier. There is also a small ranger station that provides information, and a pier. The rangers are willing to row you out to the glacier in calm weather, an awesome three-hour adventure, past icebergs and swells created when huge chunks of ice break off the glacier and crash into the Laguna. Sadly, the glacier is disintegrating and is predicted to disappear entirely; some suggest that the wake from tour boats is contributing to the erosion.

The only access is by plane or boat; either provides spectacular views. Official cruises from Puerto Montt are run by Skorpios (see page 424) and Compañía Naviera Puerto Montt; various private yachts for six to 12 passengers can also be chartered. From Puerto Chacabuco, cruises to the Laguna are run throughout the year by Navimag (www.navimag.com), and from September to April by Catamaranes del Sur (www.catamaranesdelsur.cl), see page 384 for company contact details. Local fishing boats from Puerto Chacabuco and Puerto Aysén take about 18-20 hours each way and charge a little less than the tourist boats; ask at the port. Note that these unauthorized boats may have neither adequate facilities nor a licence for the trip. Trips to Laguna San Rafael out of season are very difficult to arrange.

and indoor spa complex. Good packages for riding, fishing, kayaking, trekking, mountain biking, yoga and the thermals included.

### $$$-$$ Casa Ludwig
*Otto Uebel 202, T67-232 5220,*
*www.casaludwig.cl. Oct-Mar;*
*enquire in advance at other times.*
In a beautiful 4-storey house built by first German settlers, wonderful views, a range of rooms, good breakfast, comfortable; charming owner Luisa is knowledgeable about the area, speaks German and English. Cheaper with shared bath.

### $$ Aonikenk
*Hamburgo 16, T67-232 5208,*
*aonikenkturismo@yahoo.com.*
Pleasant heated rooms or *cabañas* (not sound-proofed), good beds, meals, helpful, informative, bike hire.

### $$ Hostería Alemana
*Otto Uebel 450, T67-232 5118,*
*www.hosteriaalemana.cl.*
A large traditional wooden house on the main road by the water, very comfortable, lovely lake views and garden.

## Parque Nacional Queulat

### $$$ El Pangue
*18 km north of Puyuhuapi, Km 240,*
*at end of Lago Risopatrón, T67-252*
*6906, www.elpangue.com.*
Rooms and luxurious *cabañas* for 4 to 7 in
splendid rural setting, fishing, horse riding,
trekking, mountain bikes, pool, sauna, hot
tubs, great views, restful.

### Camping
There's a **CONAF** campsite at
Lago Risopatrón.

## Río Cisnes and further south

### $$$-$$ Cabañas Río Cisnes
*Prat 101, Puerto Cisnes, T67-234 6404.*
Cabins sleep 4 to 8. Owner, Juan Suazo,
offers sea-fishing trips in his boat.

### $$ Hostería El Gaucho
*Holmberg 140, Puerto Cisnes,*
*T67-234 6514.*
With bath and breakfast, dinner available.

Puerto Cisnes also has various *cabañas*
and *residenciales*.

### $ pp Hospedaje El Encanto
*Pasaje Plaza 3, Villa Amengual,*
*T9-9144 8662.*
With restaurant and café, one of several
cheap options in Villa Amengual.

### $$ Café Rossbach
*Costanera.*
Run by the descendants of the original
German settlers, an attractive place by the
water for delicious salmon, tea and *küchen*.

### $$ Lluvia Marina
*Next to Casa Ludwig.*
The best café, also selling handicrafts. Superb
food in relaxed atmosphere, a great place to
just hang out, owner Verónica is very helpful.

### Río Cisnes and further south
There's good fishing around Puerto Cisnes;
contact **Cabañas Río Cisnes** (see Where to
stay, above).

### Puyuhuapi and around
If you are travelling in your own vehicle, ask
at the police station about road conditions
and temporary road closures.

**Bus** A bus timetable is pinned up outside
the tourist office, see under Tourist
information, above. Daily to **Coyhaique**,
US$10, 6 hrs, plus 2 weekly to **Lago Verde**.

### Río Cisnes and further south
**Bus** **Aguilas Patagónicas** run daily
between Puerto Cisnes and **Coyhaique**
(on Sun towards Coyhaique only), US$8-10.

# Coyhaique
## & around

Located 420 km south of Chaitén, Coyhaique (also spelt Coihaique) lies in the broad green valley of the Río Simpson. The city is encircled by a crown of mountains and, for a few hours after it has rained, the mountainsides are covered in a fine layer of frost, a spectacular sight.

Founded in 1929, it is the administrative and commercial centre of Región XI and is the only settlement of any real size on the Carretera Austral, with a population of around 60,000. Despite its stature as a relatively modern municipality, you can still hear the occasional call of chickens in people's gardens and catch sight of bow-legged elderly men making their way slowly about town, a hallmark of a generation who feel more comfortable on horseback than on foot.

A rapidly growing and increasingly lively city, it also provides a good base for day excursions in the area. Rafting down the Río Simpson is a memorable experience, while in the Reserva Nacional Río Simpson, the best protected area in the vicinity, there are picturesque waterfalls and the occasional sighting of the elusive huemul.

# **Essential** Coyhaique

### Finding your feet

There are two airports in the Coyhaique area: **Teniente Vidal**, 5 km southwest of town, handles only smaller aircraft; **Balmaceda**, 56 km southeast of Coyhaique via paved road, 5 km from the Argentine border at Paso Huemules, one hour, is the most direct way into Coyhaique from Santiago or Puerto Montt, with several flights daily. There are buses between Balmaceda and Coyhaique

as well as minibuses; contact **Transfer Valencia**, Lautaro 828, T67-223 3030, www.transfervalencia.cl; US$7.50 per person, buy tickets at the airport baggage carousel. A taxi from Balmaceda to Coyhaique takes one hour and costs US$40. Car rental agencies at the airport are very expensive and closed on Sunday.

There is a **main bus terminal**, Lautaro y Magallanes, T67-223 2067, but most buses leave from their own offices.

Coyhaique

| Where to stay | Restaurants | |
|---|---|---|
| 1 Belisario Jara | 1 Café Oriente | 7 La Casona |
| 3 Cabañas Mirador | 2 Casino de Bomberos | 8 Mamma Gaucho |
| 5 Cabañas San Sebastián | 3 Club Sandwich Patagonia | |
| 6 El Reloj | 4 Donde Ramiro | **Bars & clubs** |
| 7 Hospedaje Simón Bolívar | 5 El Mastique | 9 Pepe le Pub |
| 9 Hostal Las Quintas | 6 Histórico Ricer & | 10 Piel Roja |
| 11 Hostal Salamandras | Café Ricer | |

## BORDER CROSSING
## Chile–Argentina

### Coyhaique Alto
This crossing is 43 km east of Coyhaique. Chilean immigration is 6 km west of the border (http://www.pasosfronterizos.gov.cl/cf_coyhaiquealto.html). It is reached by a *ripio* road that runs east of Coyhaique past the **Monumento Natural Dos Lagunas**, US$3, a small park that encompasses Lagos El Toro and Escondido with black-necked swans among the wildlife that can be seen from the short interpretive trails.

For the Argentine side, see box, page 198.

### Paso Huemules
This crossing is 61 km southeast of Coyhaique (www.pasosfronterizos.gov.cl/cf_balmaceda.html). It is reached by a paved road, Route 245, which runs southeast from Coyhaique, via Balmaceda airport. There is no accommodation at the frontier or at the airport and no public transport between the border and the airport. For the Argentine side, see box, page 198.

## Coyhaique *Colour map 2, A3.*
Although a visit to the tourist office will throw up far more attractions outside Coyhaique than in the town itself, this is a pleasant, friendly place, perfect for relaxing for a couple of days or as a base for day trips.

The town centre is an unusual pentagonal plaza, on which stand the cathedral, the Intendencia and a handicraft market. The plaza was built in 1945, supposedly inspired by the Place de l'Étoile in Paris. Two blocks northeast of the plaza at Baquedano y Ignacio Serrano, there is a monument to El Ovejero (the shepherd). Further north on Baquedano is a display of old military machinery outside the local regimental headquarters. In the Casa de Cultura the **Museo Regional de la Patagonia Central** ⓘ *Lillo 23, T67-221 3175, Mon-Fri 0800-2145, Sat 0900-1300 and 1500-2000*, has sections on history, mineralogy, zoology and archaeology, as well as photos of the construction of the Carretera Austral (no information in English).

Near the city, on the east bank of the Río Simpson, is the **Piedra del Indio**, a rock outcrop which, allegedly, looks like a face in profile. This is best viewed from the Puente Simpson, west bank of the Río Simpson.

### Around Coyhaique
There are two national reserves close to Coyhaique. Five kilometres northwest off the Carretera Austral is **Reserva Nacional Coyhaique** ⓘ *information from CONAF, 0830-1730, US$4.50, camping (US$6.75)*, which covers 2150 ha of forest (mainly introduced species) and has a number of well-marked trails of between 20 minutes and five hours. The walks to Laguna Verde and Laguna Venus are particularly recommended. Follow Baquedano to the end, over the bridge, and past the hut of the *guardaparque* to where all the trails begin.

Around the valley of the Río Simpson west of Coyhaique (take any bus to Puerto Aysén) is the **Reserva Nacional Río Simpson** ⓘ *administration office is 32 km west of Coyhaique, just off the road, campsite opposite turning to Santuario San Sebastián (US$10)*, covering 40,827 ha of steep forested valleys and curiously rounded hills rising to 1878 m. One of these, near the western edge of the park, is known as 'El Cake Inglés'. There are beautiful

## ON THE ROAD

### Native deer

The Andean **huemul** (*Hippocamelus bisulcus*) is a mountain deer native to the Andes of southern Chile and Argentina. Sharing the Chilean national crest with the Andean condor, the huemul (pronounced 'way-mool') is a medium-sized stocky cervid adapted to survival in rugged mountain terrain. Males grow antlers and have distinctive black face masks.

Human pressures have pushed the huemul to the brink of extinction and current numbers are estimated at less than 1500. The huemul has become the focal point of both national and international conservation efforts, carried out primarily by CONAF and the Comité Pro Defensa de la Fauna y Flora de Chile (CODEFF).

Your best chance of seeing the huemul is in one of two reserves managed by CONAF: the Reserva Nacional Río Claro, which lies on the southeastern corner of the larger Reserva Nacional Río Simpson just outside Coyhaique (see page 379), and the Reserva Nacional Tamango, near Cochrane (see page 394). To visit either of these you will need to be accompanied by a warden: ask in Coyhaique or Cochrane to make sure someone is available.

The Carretera Austral area is also one of the best places for trying to spot the equally rare **pudu**. This miniature creature, around 40 cm tall and weighing only 10 kg, is the smallest member of the deer family in the world. Native to southern Argentina and Chile, the pudu is listed in Chile as vulnerable to extinction, largely due to habitat loss, but also because its unique appearance (the males grow two short spiked antlers) has made it a target for poaching for zoos. Reddish-brown in colour, the pudu is ideally adapted to the dense temperate rainforests of Chile and Argentina, scooting along on trails through the undergrowth, leaving behind minuscule cloven tracks.

waterfalls, lovely views of the river and very good fly-fishing here, as well as trekking options. Wildlife includes pudu, pumas and huemul, as well as a variety of birds, ranging from condors to several species of duck. On the southern side of the Reserva, 12 km west of Coyhaique reached by a separate *ripio* road, is the **Cerro Huemules**, where lots of wildlife can be seen including 23 bird species, foxes, wildcats and of course, the huemul. See also box, above.

### Puerto Aysén and around

Puerto Aysén lies at the confluence of the rivers Aysén and Palos. First developed in the 1920s, the town grew as the major port of the region although it has now been replaced by Puerto Chacabuco, 15 km downriver. Few vestiges of the port remain today: boats lie high and dry on the riverbank when the tide is out and the foundations of buildings by the river are now overgrown with fuchsias and buttercups. To see any maritime activity you have to walk a little way out of town to **Puerto Aguas Muertas**, where the fishing boats come in.

The town is linked to the south bank of the Río Aysén by the Puente Presidente Ibáñez, once the longest suspension bridge in Chile. From the far bank a paved road leads to **Puerto Chacabuco**; a regular bus service runs between the two.

A good 10-km walk north along a minor road from Puerto Aysén leads to **Laguna Los Palos**, calm, deserted and surrounded by forested hills. En route is a bridge over a deep, narrow river; it's freezing cold but offers the chance for a bracing swim. **Lago Riesco**, 30 km south of Puerto Aysén, can be reached by an unpaved road that follows the Río Blanco. In season, the *Apulcheu* sails regularly from Puerto Chacabuco to **Termas de Chiconal** ① *US$25, 1 hr, on the northern shore of the Seno Aysén,* offering a good way to see the fjord; take your own food.

## Listings Coyhaique and around *map page 378.*

### Tourist information

#### Coyhaique

**CONAF**
*Ogana 1060, T67-221 2109,
aysen.oirs@conaf.cl. Mon-Fri 0830-1730.*

**Sernatur office**
*Bulnes 35, T67-224 0290, infoaisen@
sernatur.cl. Daily 0900-2100.*
English is spoken at this very helpful tourist office, which has up-to-date bus timetables. There's also an information kiosk on the plaza.

#### Puerto Aysén

**Tourism Cerro Mirador**
*Carrera with O'Higgins, off the plaza.
Daily in summer 0815-1930, in winter
Mon-Thu 0815-1730, Fri 0815-1630.*
Helpful tourist office.

### Where to stay

#### Coyhaique

**$$$$-$$$ El Reloj**
*Baquedano 828, T67-223 1108,
www.elrelojhotel.cl.*
Tasteful, in a former sawmill, with a good restaurant, charming, comfortable wood-panelled rooms, some with wonderful views, nice lounge, the best in town.

**$$$ Belisario Jara**
*Bilbao 662, T67-223 4150, www.belisariojara.cl.*
Most distinctive and delightful, an elegant and welcoming small place.

**$$$ Cabañas Mirador**
*Baquedano 848, T67-223 3191.*
Attractive, well-equipped *cabañas*, also rooms, in lovely gardens with panoramic views of the Reserva Forestal, and Río Coyhaique below.

**$$$ Cabañas San Sebastián**
*Freire 554, T67-223 1762,
www.cabsansebastian.cl.*
Central, very good.

**$$ Hostal Las Quintas**
*Bilbao 1208, T67-223 1173,
nolfapatagonia@hotmail.com.*
Spartan, but clean and very spacious rooms (some in very bizarre design) with bath.

**$$-$ Hospedaje Simón Bolívar**
*Simon Bolívar 616, T9-9761 6918,
www.patagoniain.cl.*
This family-run *hospedaje* is a welcoming change of pace from the party *hostales* in the area. Dorms start at US$15, also doubles. Wi-Fi, breakfast and refreshing rainwater showers.

**$$-$ Hostal Salamandras**
*Sector Los Pinos, 2 km south in
attractive forest, T67-221 1865,
www.hostalsalamandras.com.*
Variety of rooms, dorms cabin and camping, kitchen facilities, trekking and other sports and tours.

Many more *hospedajes* and private houses with rooms; ask the tourist office (see above) for a list.

## Camping

Tourist office on plaza or **Sernatur** in Coyhaique has a full list of all sites in XI Región. There are numerous sites in Coyhaique and on the road between Coyhaique and Puerto Aysén, including **Camping Alborada** (at Km 2, T67-223 8868), with hot showers.

## Puerto Aysén and around

Accommodation is hard to find, most is taken up by fishing companies in both ports. There are several places to eat along Tte Merino and Aldea in Puerto Aysén.

### $$$$ Loberías del Sur
*José Miguel Cra 50, Puerto Chacabuco, T67-235 1112, www.loberiasdelsur.cl.*
5-star hotel, whose restaurant serves the best food in the area (handy for a meal or a drink before boarding the ferry, climb up the steps direct from the port). Same owner as Catamaranes del Sur (see Transport, below), which also has a nearby nature reserve, Parque Aiken del Sur.

### $$$ Patagonia Green
*400 m from bridge (on Pto Chacabuco side), T67-233 6796, www.patagoniagreen.cl.*
Nice rooms or cabins for up to 5, kitchen, heating, gardens, arranges tours to Laguna San Rafael, fishing, mountain biking, riding, trekking, etc, English spoken.

### $$$-$$ Caicahues
*Michimalonco 660, Puerto Aysén, T67-233 6623, hcaicahues@puertoaysen.cl.*
Popular business hotel, with heating, book ahead.

## Restaurants

### Coyhaique

### $$$ Histórico Ricer
*Horn 48 y 40, p 2, T67-223 2920, www.historicoricer.wordpress.com.*
Central, warm and cosy, serving breakfast to dinner, regional specialities, with good vegetarian options and historical exhibits. Also has **Café Ricer** at No 48, serving light food.

### $$ La Casona
*Obispo Vielmo 77, T67-223 8894.*
Justly reputed as best in town, charming family restaurant serves excellent fish – *congrio* especially – but is best known for grilled lamb.

### $$-$ Casino de Bomberos
*Next to the fire station, Gral Parra 365, T67-223 1437.*
For great atmosphere and a filling lunch, but it can be slow when serving groups.

### $$-$ Donde Ramiro
*Freire 319.*
Good set lunches, big-screen TV.

### $$-$ Mamma Gaucha
*Horn 47, T67-221 0721.*
Pizzas and big salads. Also rumoured to have the best locally brewed beer in all of Chile.

### $ Club Sandwich Patagonia
*Moraleda 433.*
24-hr fast food and huge Chilean sandwiches, a local institution.

### $ El Mastique
*Bilbao 141.*
Cheap but good pasta and Chilean food.

## Cafés

### Café Oriente
*Condell 201.*
Serves a good lunch and tasty cakes.

### Puerto Aysén and around
There are many cheap places on Aldea, between Municipal and Dougnac.

### $$ Restaurante La Cascada
*Km 32 between Coyhaique and Puerto Aysén.*
Waterfalls nearby. Recommended for meat and fish.

## Bars and clubs

### Pepe le Pub
*Parra 72, see Facebook.*
Good cocktails and snacks, relaxed,
live music at weekends, karaoke.

### Piel Roja
*Moraleda y Condell, www.pielroja.cl.*
Good music, laid back, open for dancing, pub
other nights, karaoke. Happy hour 1900-2100.

## Festivals

### Puerto Aysén and around
**2nd week of Nov**  Local **festival of folklore**
is held in Puerto Aysén.

## Shopping

### Coyhaique
#### Handicrafts
**Artesanía Manos Azules**, *Riquelme 435.*
Sells fine handicrafts. **Feria de Artesanía**
on the plaza.

## What to do

### Coyhaique
#### Language classes
**Baquedano International Language
School**, *Baquedano 20, T67-223 2520,
www.balasch.cl.* US$600 per week
including lodging and meals, other
programmes are less expensive.

#### Skiing
**El Fraile**, *near Lago Frío, 29 km southeast
of Coyhaique, www.chileanski.com/eng/
el-fraile.* This ski resort has 5 pistes, 2 lifts,
a basic café and equipment hire (season
May-Sep).

#### Tour operators
Many tours operate Sep to Apr, some Dec-
Mar only. The surrounding area is famous for
trout fishing with several estancias offering
luxury accommodation and bilingual guides.
Most tour operators also offer specialist
fishing trips.

**Andes Patagónicos**, *Casilla 241, T67-221
6711, www.ap.cl.* Trips to local lakes, Tortel,
historically based tours and bespoke trips
all year round. Good, but not cheap.
**Aysén Tour**, *Pasaje Río Backer 2646, T67-223
7070, www.aysentour.cl.* Tours along the
Carretera Austral, also car rental.
**Camello Patagón**, *Condell 149, T67-224
4327, www.camellopatagon.cl.* Daily trips to
Cavernas de Marmol in Río Tranquilo, among
others, also car rental and other services.
**Casa del Turismo Rural**, *Odeón Plaza de
Armas, T67-221 4031, www.casaturismorural.cl.*
An association of 40 families, mostly in
the countryside, who offer activities such
as horse riding and fishing. Many do not
have telephones or internet, so make
reservations here.
**Expediciones Coyhaique**, *Portales 195,
T67-223 1783, www.coyhaiqueflyfishing.com.*
Fly-fishing experts.
**Geo Turismo**, *21 de Mayo 398, T67-258 3173,
www.geoturismopatagonia.cl.* Offers a wide
range of tours, English spoken, professional.
**Turismo Prado**, *21 de Mayo 417, T67-223 1271,
www.turismoprado.cl.* Tours of local lakes and
other sights, Laguna San Rafael trips and
historical tours.

## Transport

Within Región XI, Coyhaique is the
transport hub.

### Coyhaique
**Air**  Aerocord (www.aerocord.cl) offers
services in the region from Coyhaique
to various towns, such as **Puerto Montt**,
**Chaitén** and **Puyuhuapi**.
  Balmaceda airport has daily flights to
**Santiago** with **LAN**, mostly via **Puerto
Montt**, and **Sky**, which sometimes makes
several stops. Landing can be dramatic
owing to strong winds. **LAN** also flies to
**Punta Arenas**, twice a week, once via
Puerto Montt and the other via Santiago.

Bus from Balmaceda to **Puerto Aysén** US$8-11. For transport from Balmaceda to Coyhaique see box, page 378.

**Bicycle** Austral Biker, Av Norte Sur 1228, T9-7618 3588, see Facebook. Rental and tours.

**Bus** Full list of buses from the tourist office, see under Tourist information, above. Minibuses (**Alí**, Dussen 283, T67-223 2788, www.busesali.cl; **Suray**, A Prat 265, T67-223 4085) run every 45 mins to **Puerto Aysén**, 1 hr, US$3; change here for **Puerto Chacabuco**, 20 mins, US$0.75. Several minibus companies operate services to **Puerto Ibáñez** on Lago Gral Carrera to connect with the ferry to Chile Chico, pick up 0530-0600 from your hotel, 1½ hrs; book the day before.

Buses on the Carretera Austral vary according to demand, and they are usually full so book early. Bikes can be taken by arrangement. North towards Chaitén: twice a week direct with **Becker** (Parra 335, T67-223 2167, www.busesbecker.com), US$36, otherwise change in La Junta (with an overnight stop in winter). To **Futaleufú**, with **Becker**, 2 a week, US$36. To **Puerto Cisnes**, **Aguilas Patagónicas** (Lautaro 109, T67-221 1288, www.aguilaspatagonicas.cl), US$8-10. South to **Cochrane**, daily in summer with **Don Carlos** (Subteniente Cruz 63, T67-223 1981), Aguilas Patagónicas, or **Acuario 13** (at terminal, T67-252 2143), US$21. All buses stop at **Villa Cerro Castillo** (US$7), **Bahía Murta** (US$12), **Puerto Tranquilo** (US$13) and **Puerto Bertrand** (US$18).

Buses (several weekly) to **Puerto Montt** have to take the route via Argentina, which is long and expensive. There are also 1-2 weekly buses to Comodoro Rivadavia.

**Car hire** If renting a car, a high 4WD vehicle is recommended for the Carretera Austral. There are several rental agencies in town, charging at least US$100 a day, including insurance, for 4WD or pickup. Add another US$50 for paperwork to take a vehicle into Argentina. Buy fuel in Coyhaique.

**Ferry** Ferries (1-2 a week) make the journey from Puerto Montt or Chiloé to Puerto Chacabuco, 77 km west of Coyhaique. **Navimag**, Eusebio Lilo 91, T67-223 3306, www.navimag.com. **Naviera Austral**, Paseo Horn 40, of 101, T67-221 0727, www.navieraustral.cl.

**Taxi** US$6 to Tte Vidal airport. Fares in town US$2. Taxi *colectivos* (shared taxis) congregate at Prat y Bilbao, average fare US$0.75.

## Puerto Aysén

**Bus** Minibuses (**Alí**, Aldea 1143, T67-233 3335, www.busesali.cl; **Suray**, T67-223 8387) run every 45 mins to **Coyhaique**, 1 hr, US$3. To **Puerto Chacabuco**, 20 mins, US$0.75.

**Ferry** For information on shipping, see www.chacabucoport.cl. **Navimag** (Terminal de Transbordadores, Puerto Chacabuco, T67-235 1111, www.navimag.com) sails twice a week from Puerto Chacabuco to **Puerto Montt**, taking about 24 hrs (for details, see page 332). **Catamaranes del Sur** (J M Carrera 50, T67-235 1112, www.loberiasdelsur.cl) have sailings to **Laguna San Rafael** (see page 331). It is best to make reservations in these companies' offices in Puerto Montt, Coyhaique or Santiago. Other shipping offices: **Agemar** (Terminal Aysén, T67-235 1151); **Naviera Austral** (Terminal de Transbordadores, T67-235 1493, www.navieraustral.cl).

# Lago General
## Carrera

★ The section of the Carretera Austral around the north and western sides of Lago General Carrera makes a good case for being the most spectacular stretch of all. Straddling the border with Argentina, this is the largest lake in South America after Lake Titicaca and is believed to be the deepest lake on the continent; soundings in 1997 established its maximum depth as 590 m.

The lake is a beautiful azure blue, surrounded at its Chilean end by predominantly alpine terrain and at the Argentine end by dry pampa.

### Reserva Nacional Cerro Castillo and around *Colour map 2, B3.*

Beyond Coyhaique, the Carretera Austral runs through slightly wilder, more rugged land, with the occasional cow or wild horse feeding by the side of the road. Some 40 km south of Coyhaique, it enters the **Reserva Nacional Cerro Castillo** ① *US$3*, which extends over 179,550 ha. The park is named after the fabulous **Cerro Castillo** (2675 m), which resembles a fairy-tale castle with rock pinnacles jutting out from a covering of snow. It also encompasses Cerro Bandera (2040 m) just west of Balmaceda and several other peaks in the northern wall of the valley of the Río Ibáñez.

## Essential Lago General Carrera

### Getting around

The main towns, Puerto Ibáñez on the north shore and Chile Chico on the south, are connected by a ferry, *La Tehuelche* (two hours, US$4). Overland routes between Coyhaique and Chile Chico are much longer, passing either through Argentina, or along the Carretera Austral, which runs west around the lake (this route is described below). Minibuses run along the Carretera Austral in summer and air taxis link the small towns of the region.

### When to go

The region prides itself on having the best climate in southern Chile, with some 300 days of sunshine a year; much fruit is grown as a result, especially around Chile Chico, where rainfall is very low for this area. In general, the climate here is more similar to Argentine Patagonia than to the rest of the Carretera Austral region.

There is a *guardería* at the northeastern end of the park, 50 m to the left of the main road (as you head south), opposite Laguna Chinguay to the right, with access to walks and a **campsite** ① *T67-221 2225, Nov-Mar, US$7.50 per site; take equipment, there are no refugios*. The picnic ground is open summer 0830-2100, winter to 1830.

The park offers a number of excellent day treks and some of the best self-contained multi-day trekking in Patagonia. A truly spectacular four-day trek goes around the peaks of Cerro Castillo, starting at Las Horquetas Grandes, a bend in the river Río Ibáñez, 8 km south of the park entrance, where any bus driver will let you off. It follows Río La Lima to the gorgeous Laguna Cerro Castillo, then follows animal trails around the peak itself, returning to Villa Cerro Castillo (see below). This is a challenging walk: attempt it only if fit, and ideally, take a guide, as trails are poorly marked (IGM map essential, purchase in advance in Coyhaique). Another equally spectacular five-day trek goes around Lago Monreal; ask in Villa Cerro Castillo for details.

At Km 83 the Carretera Austral crosses the **Portezuelo Ibáñez** (1120 m) and drops through the **Cuesta del Diablo**, a series of bends with fine views over the Río Ibáñez. Beyond the turning to Puerto Ibáñez (see below) the road goes through **Villa Cerro**

**Lago General Carrera**

**Castillo** (Km 8), a quiet village in a spectacular setting beneath the striking, jagged peaks of Cerro Castillo, overlooking the broad valley below. There's a petrol station, public phone, several food shops and a tiny tourist information kiosk by the road side (January and February only), with details of trekking guides and horse rides. The village is a good place to stop for a few days to explore the reserve. There is also a small **local museum** ① *2 km south of Villa Cerro Castillo, Dec-Mar daily 0900-1200.*

A few kilometres further south is the **Monumento Nacional Manos de Cerro Castillo** ① *open all year, US$1.50.* In a shallow cave, a few handprints have been made on the side of vertical rocks high above the Río Ibáñez. There's no clue to their significance, but they're in a beautiful place with panoramic views. This makes a delightful two-hour walk and is signposted clearly from the road.

## Puerto Ibáñez

The principal port on the Chilean section of the lake, Puerto Ibáñez (officially Puerto Ingeniero Ibáñez) is reached by taking a paved branch road, 31 km long, from La Bajada, 97 km south of Coyhaique. You will probably just pass through Puerto Ibáñez to reach the ferry. It is, however, a centre for distinctive pottery, leather production and vegetable growing (you can visit potters and buy salad from greenhouses). Local archaeology includes rock art and the largest Tehuelche cemetery in Patagonia. There are some fine waterfalls, including the **Salto Río Ibáñez**, 6 km north. There is also a road from Puerto Ibáñez to **Perito Moreno** in Argentina. It is poor-quality *ripio*, suitable for 4WD only, and there is no public transport.

## The western shore

Beyond Villa Cerro Castillo, the road climbs out of the valley, passing the emerald-green **Laguna Verde** and the Portezuelo Cofré. It descends to the boggy Manso Valley, with a good campsite at the bridge over the river; watch out for mosquitoes. Some 5 km from the Carretera Austral, at Km 203, is **Bahía Murta**, situated on the northern tip of the central arm of Lago General Carrera. This sleepy, almost forgotten village dates from the 1930s, when it exported timber to Argentina via Chile Chico. Petrol is available from a house with a sign just before Puerto Murta.

Back on the Carretera, the road follows the lake's western shore. At Km 207 from Coyhaique is a small privately owned forest of ancient and gnarled *arrayanes* that is worth a visit. Some 20 km further south is **Río Tranquilo**, where the buses stop for lunch and fuel is available. The lake's surface acts as a mirror, reflecting images of the mountains that surround it and the clouds above. Close to Río Tranquilo is the unusual **Capilla y Catedral de Mármol**, a peninsula made of marble, with fascinating caves that can be visited by **boat** ① *2 hrs, group tours US$12.* Go early in the morning when the lake is calmer and prepare to get wet.

The village also has an unusual cemetery made up of mausolea in the form of miniature Chilote-style houses. A new branch of the Carretera Austral heads northwest from Río Tranquilo to **Puerto Grosse** on the coast at Bahía Exploradores. At Km 52 on this road is a *refugio* from which a well-maintained path leads to a lookout opposite the Exploradores glacier. **Guided hikes** ① *6 hrs including 2-3 hrs on the glacier,* US$75 *per person, crampons provided,* are available. The hike can be treacherous in bad weather. Book though **El Puesto** in Río Tranquilo, www.elpuesto.cl.

## South to Puerto Bertrand

The road continues along the edge of the azure lake, with snow-covered mountains with pointed peaks visible in the distance. At the southwestern tip of Lago General Carrera, at Km 279, is **El Maitén**, from where a road branches off east along the south shore of the lake towards Chile Chico.

South of El Maitén, meanwhile, the Carretera Austral becomes steeper and more winding; in winter this stretch is icy and dangerous. The picturesque, tranquil village of **Puerto Bertrand**, 5 km away, is a good place for fishing and the best base in the region for whitewater rafting and kayaking. Day hikes are possible along decent trails.

Nearby is a sign showing the *Nacimiento del Río Baker*: the place where the turquoise Río Baker begins. This area is home to the most impressive hydrological system in Chile, with its most voluminous river, its biggest lake to the north and a huge icefield to the west.

Beyond Puerto Bertrand, the road climbs up to high moorland, passing the confluence of the Neff and Baker rivers, before winding south along the east bank of the Río Baker. On a sunny day it is hard to imagine more pleasant surroundings. The road is rough but not treacherous and the scenery is splendid all the way to Cochrane. Watch out for cattle and hares on the road (and the occasional huemul) and take blind corners slowly.

## The southern shore of Lago General Carrera

Some 10 km east of El Maitén, **Puerto Guadal** is a friendly, picturesque town that is a centre for fishing. It also has shops, accommodation, restaurants, a post office, petrol and a lovely stretch of lakeside beach. Further east along the shore, just past the nondescript village of **Mallín Grande**, Km 40, the road runs through the **Paso de las Llaves**, a 30-km stretch carved out of the rock face on the edge of the lake. The south side of the lake is much drier than the rest of the Carretera but there are still gorges and waterfalls dotted along the route. The landscape is more open as there is less of an influence from the icefields. The road climbs and drops, narrow and poor in places, offering wonderful views across the lake and the icefields to the west.

At Km 74, a turning runs to **Fachinal**. A further 5 km east is the **Garganta del Diablo**, an impressive narrow gorge of 120 m with a fast-flowing stream below. Further on there is an open-cast mine, which produces gold and other metals.

## Chile Chico and around

Chile Chico (www.chilechico.cl) is a quiet, friendly but dusty town situated on the lakeshore 122 km east of El Maitén, close to the Argentine border (for details of the border crossing, see box, opposite).

The town dates from 1909 when settlers crossed from Argentina and occupied the land, leading to conflict with cattle ranchers who had been given settlement rights by the Chilean government. In the showdown that followed (known as the war of Chile Chico) the ranchers were driven out by the settlers, but it was not until 1931 that the Chilean government finally recognized the town's existence.

Now the centre of a fruit-growing region, it has an annual festival at the end of January and a small **Casa de la Cultura** ① *0800-1300, 1400-1700*. There are fine views from the **Cerro de las Banderas** at the western end of town.

To the south and west of Chile Chico is good walking terrain, through weird rock formations and dry brush scrub. The northern and higher peak of **Cerro Pico del Sur** (2168 m) can be climbed by the agile from Los Cipres (beware dogs in the farmyard). You will need a long summer's day and the 1:50,000 map. Follow the horse trail until it peters out, then navigate by compass or sense of direction until the volcano-like

## BORDER CROSSING
### Chile–Argentina

**Chile Chico**
A road runs 2 km east from Chile Chico (see below) to Chilean immigration,
(www.pasosfronterizos.gov.cl/cf_chilechico.html). For the Argentine side,
see box, page 198. There are daily buses from Chile Chico to Los Antiguos in
summer, taking one hour, US$4.

**Paso Roballos**
Some 17 km north of Cochrane, a road runs east through Villa Chacabuco (see page 395)
and continues east for 78 km to enter Argentina at Paso Roballos. The road continues on
to Bajo Caracoles. There isn't any public transport along this route and, although the
road is passable in summer, it is generally in a poor state and often flooded in spring.
For details of the Argentine side, see box, page 198.

summit appears. After breaching the cliff ramparts, there is some scrambling and a
3-m pitch to the summit, from where you'll enjoy indescribable views of the lake and
the Andes.

About 20 km south of Chile Chico towards Lago Jeinimeni is the **Cueva de las Manos**,
a cave full of Tehuelche paintings, the most famous of which are the *manos azules* (blue
hands). From the road, climb 500 m and cross the Pedregoso stream. The path is difficult,
and partly hidden, so it is recommended to take a guide.

### ★ Reserva Nacional Lago Jeinimeni
*52 km south of Chile Chico, open all year but access may be impossible Apr-Oct due to
high river levels, US$2.85, camping US$14 (up to 10 people); contact the CONAF office for lifts
from Chile Chico.*

This park covers 160,000 ha and includes two lakes, **Lago Jeinimeni** and **Lago Verde**,
which lie surrounded by forests in the narrow valley of the Río Jeinimeni. Impressive
cliffs, waterfalls and small glaciers provide habitat for huemul deer, pumas and condors.
Activities include fishing for salmon and rainbow trout, trekking and rowing. Access is
via an unpaved road, which branches south off the road to the Argentine border at Los
Antiguos and crosses five rivers, four of which have to be forded. At Km 42, there is a small
lake, **Laguna de los Flamencos**, where large numbers of flamingos can be seen. The park
entrance is at Km 53; just beyond is a ranger station, a campsite and fishing area at the
eastern end of Lago Jeinimeni. Take all supplies, including a good map.

## Tourist information

### Puerto Bernard

There is no tourist office, but a tour operator can be reached at T9-8817 7525.

### Chile Chico

**Tourist office**
*O'Higgins S/N, T67-241 1303,*
*infochilechico@sernatur.cl.*
Somewhat helpful but usually closed. An unofficial purple tourist kiosk, on the quay where the ferry arrives, sells bus tickets for Ruta 40 (Argentina) and has some accommodation information.

## Where to stay

### Reserva Nacional Cerro Castillo and around

**$ Cabañas Don Niba**
*Los Pioneros 872, Villa Cerro Castillo,*
*T9-9474 0408, see Facebook.*
Friendly but basic *hospedaje*, good value.

**$ Residencial Villarrica**
*O'Higgins 592, next to Supermercado*
*Villarrica, Villa Cerro Castillo, T9-6656 0173,*
*hospedajevillarrica@gmail.com.*
Welcoming, basic, hot showers and restaurant, owners can arrange trekking guides and horse riding. There are other *residenciales* in town.

### Puerto Ibáñez

**$$ Cabañas Shehen Aike**
*Luis Risopatrón 55, T67-242 3284.*
Swiss/Chilean-owned, large cabins, lots of ideas for trips, bike rental, organizes tours, fine food, welcoming, English spoken, best to phone in advance.

**$ pp Hospedaje Don Francisco**
*San Salvador y Lautaro, T9-8503 3626.*
Very hospitable, lunch or dinner extra, good food round the clock, camping US$7, tents and free bike rental.

**$ Vientos del Sur**
*Bertrán Dixon 282, T9-8972 6519.*
Good place to stay, friendly family, dorms, cheap meals (restaurant open till late); also arranges adventure activities.

### The western shore

**$$$ Hostal El Puesto**
*Pedro Lagos 258, Puerto Río Tranquilo,*
*T9-6207 3794, www.elpuesto.cl.*
No doubt the most comfortable place in Río Tranquilo, with breakfast. Also organizes tours.

**$$$ Hostal Los Pinos**
*Godoy 51, Puerto Río Tranquilo, T67-241 1572,*
*lospinos_hosteriasuite@outlook.com.*
Family-run, well maintained, and café with good mid-price meals.

**$$ Campo Alacaluf**
*Km 44 towards Río Tranquilo-*
*Bahía Exploradores, T67-241 9500,*
*campoalacaluf@yahoo.de.*
Wonderful guesthouse hidden away from civilization. Run by very friendly German family.

**$$ Hostal Carretera Austral**
*1 Sur 373, Río Tranquilo, T67-241 9500.*
Also serves meals (**$$-$**).

**$ Hospedaje/Camping Bellavista**
*Población Esperanza s/n, T9-7619 5125,*
*transportebellavista@hotmail.com.*
Budget option with camping for US$14 per night.

### South to Puerto Bertrand

**$$$$ Hacienda Tres Lagos**
*Carretera Austral Km 274, just west of*
*cruce El Maitén, T2-2333 4122 (Santiago),*
*www.haciendatreslagos.com.*
Small, boutique resort on the lakeshore with bungalows, suites and cabins. Good restaurant, wide range of trips offered, sauna, jacuzzi, good service. English spoken.

**$$$$ Mallín Colorado Ecolodge**
*Carretera Austral Km 273, 2 km west
of El Maitén, T9-7137 6242, www.
mallincolorado.cl. Oct-Apr.*
Comfortable *cabañas* in sweeping gardens,
complete tranquility, charming owners,
packages available, including transfers
from Balmaceda, horse riding, estancia
trip, superb meals.

**$$$ Patagonia Baker Lodge and
Restaurant**
*3 km from Puerto Bertrand, towards the south
side of the lake, T67-241 1903, www.pbl.cl.*
Stylish *cabañas* in woodland, fishing lodge,
birdwatching, fabulous views upriver
towards rapids and the mountains beyond.

**$$$-$$ Cabañas Buena Vista**
*Ventisquero Neff s/n, T9-7881 4999.
All year.*
*Cabañas* with private bath.

**$$ Hostería Puerto Bertrand**
*Puerto Bertrand, T67-241 9900,
casaturismorural.cl.*
With breakfast, other meals available,
also *cabañas*, activities.

---

**The southern shore of Lago General
Carrera**

**$$$ El Mirador Playa Guadal**
*2 km from Puerto Guadal towards
Chile Chico, T9-9234 9130, www.
elmiradordeguadal.com.*
*Cabañas* near beach, trips and activities
with or without guide, walks to nearby
waterfalls, restaurant.

**$$$-$$ Terra Luna Lodge**
*On lakeside, 2 km from Puerto Guadal,
T9-8449 1092, www.terra-luna.cl.*
Welcoming well-run place with lodge,
bungalows and camping huts, also has
restaurant, sauna, cinema, private disco,
climbing wall, many activities offered.

**$$ La Perla del Lago**
*Los Notros, s/n, T9-5722 1356,
tarcila-fica2007@hotmail.com.*

The lovely English-speaking owner
has comfy beds in well-furnished
doubles and triples (also a *cabaña*
$$$). Can offer information about tours.
Laundry service, breakfast included and
great home-cooked meals.

**$ El Gringo**
*Los Lidios 510, on the corner of the plaza,
T9-7394 0396. Open all year.*
Very friendly owner offers 2 private rooms
for a decent price (extra with breakfast).
No Wi-Fi. Also restaurant serving good
pizzas and great juices.

**$ Hospedaje Ventisqueros**
*35 km from Guadal on the road to Coyhaique,
T9-7805 4165, elidadaguirre@hotmail.com.*
Quaint *hospedaje* set on the Río León.
Organizes tours, horse riding and has a
*parrilla*. Breakfast included and the owner
prepares home-made lunches and dinners.
Also camping for US$4.25.

**Camping**

**Camping Cerro Color**
*3 km from Guadal on the road to Cochrane,
T9-5663 1830.*
Owner Filomena offers campsites from
US$7 per night. Also sells marmalade
and vegetables in summer. Good spot
for sheep watching.

**Camping El Parque**
*Km 1 on road to Chile Chico.*

---

**Chile Chico**

**$$ Hostal La Victoria**
*O'Higgins 210 (corner of the plaza),
T67-241 1344, lavictoria@outlook.com.*
Pricey *hostal* option (with privates). But the
rooms are spotless with TVs, breakfast is
included and there is a great kitchen and
communal area with plush sofa. Helpful
owner has maps galore.

**$$ Hotel Austral**
*O'Higgins 501, T67-241 1815.*

Large hotel with doubles and
matrimonial suites.

**$ Hospedaje Jerafita**
*Carrera 150, T9-7627 6497,*
*hospedaje.jerafita@gmail.com.*
No-frills lodging with unkempt rooms.
The walls are so thin you're practically
right there when the couple next door
gets amorous. But it's one of the cheaper
options in town.

### Camping
Free site at **Bahía Jara**. It's 5 km west of
Chile Chico, then turn north for 12 km.

## Restaurants

Most *hosterías* and *residenciales* will serve
meals (see Where to stay, above). The
2 supermarkets on O'Higgins also have
good options for meals.

### Chile Chico

**Cafetería Loly y Elizabeth**
*PA González 25, on plaza.*
Good for coffee as well as delicious cakes.
Offers Middle Eastern food on Wed.

**Restaurant Turístico J&D**
*O'Higgins 455.*
Solid food including lake-caught trout. Same
owner as **Hotel Austral** (see Where to Stay,
above) and the supermarket next door.

## Bars and clubs

### Chile Chico

**Pub Restaurant Taberna**
*O'Higgins 416-B, T9-6901 1314, taberna.*
*restobar@gmail.com. Closes at 0500 Sat-Sun.*
Recommended for a drink. Also extensive
menu featuring pizza.

## Festivals

### South to Puerto Bertrand
**3rd weekend of Feb Semana de Bertrand.**
3 days of drunken revelry.

### Chile Chico
**Last week of Jan** The town hosts the
**Festival Internacional de la Voz.**

## What to do

### The western shore
**El Puesto Expediciones**, *Lagos 258, Río*
*Tranquilo, T9-6207 3794, www.elpuesto.cl.*
Fishing, ice hiking, kayaking and other trips.

### South to Puerto Bertrand
Horse riding, fishing guides and whitewater
rafting on the Río Baker (generally easy with
a few Grade III rapids) can all be arranged
through **Hacienda Tres Lagos**, see Where
to stay, above.
**Patagonia Adventure Expeditions**,
*T9-8182 0608, www.adventurepatagonia.*
*com.* Professional outfit running exclusive
fully supported treks to the Campo
de Hielo Norte and the eastern side of Parque
Nacional Laguna San Rafael. Expensive but
a unique experience. Also rafting on the Río
Baker and general help organizing tours,
treks and expeditions.

### The southern shore
**Turismo Kalem Patagonia**, *cabalgasur@*
*hotmail.com.* Leads trips to nearby fossil fields.

## Transport

### Reserva Nacional Cerro Castillo and
around
There are weekly buses in summer from
Villa Cerro Castillo to both **Coyhaique**
(US$7) and **Cochrane** (see Coyhaique
Transport, page 384).

### Puerto Ibáñez
**Bus** Minibuses and jeeps meet the ferry in
Puerto Ibáñez for connections to **Coyhaique**,
2 hrs US$7.

**Ferry** The ferry, *La Tehuelche*, sails from
**Puerto Ibáñez** to **Chile Chico** 1 a day,
cars for around US$28, US$5 motorcycles,
passengers US$3. The number of foot

passengers is limited to 255. Reserve at least 2 days in advance through **Turismo Ayacara** (www.ayacara.cl) and arrive 30 mins before departure. This is a very cold crossing even in summer: take warm clothing.

## The western shore
All buses from Coyhaique to Cochrane stop at **Bahía Murta** (US$11) and **Puerto Tranquilo** (US$12.50).

## South to Puerto Bertrand
All buses from Coyhaique to Cochrane stop 1 km from **Puerto Bertrand** on the main *carretera* (US$18).

## The southern shore
Buses between Coyhaique and Los Antiguos (Argentina) travel via **Puerto Guadal**: **ECA** (T67-243 1224/252 8577) on Tue and Fri, **Seguel** (T67-243 1214/224 5237) on Wed.

## Chile Chico
**Bus** Minibuses leave Mon, Wed and Fri at 0800 to **Cochrane**, US$18, 5 hrs. In summer, minibuses to **Los Antiguos** (Argentina) multiple daily, US$7, 30 mins-1 hr (purchase from Martín Pescador, O'Higgins 497, T67-2411 033, daily 0800-2000. See above for ferry to **Puerto Ibáñez** and connecting minibus to Coyhaique. Ferry and minibus tickets from **Martín Pescador** and **Miguel Acuña**, Sector Muelle, T9-8900 4590.

# Cochrane &
## further south

Travelling by bus along the final 224-km stretch of the Carretera Austral from Cochrane to Villa O'Higgins can be frustrating, as you will undoubtedly want to stop every 15 minutes to marvel at the views. This is a beautiful trip through thick forest, with vistas of snow-capped mountains and waterfalls.

## Cochrane and around *Colour map 2, B2.*

### a good base for walking and fishing in the nearby countryside

Sitting in a hollow on the northern banks of the Río Cochrane, 343 km south of Coyhaique, Cochrane is a simple place with a pleasant summer climate.

There is a small **museum** ⓘ *San Valentín 555, Mon-Fri 0900-1300 and 1500-1800; in 2016, the museum was closed. Check with the tourist office for new hours,* with displays on local history. On the same street is an odd, *mate*-shaped house. Fuel is available and there is an ATM for MasterCard and Visa.

### Essential Cochrane

#### Access

Cochrane can be reached bus from Coyhaique, or on a poor unpaved road from Chile Chico. The southern tip of the Carretera at Villa O'Higgins is linked in summer by a ferry service to Calendario Mansilla, from where it is a day-long journey to/from El Chaltén in Argentina. Public transport is scarce. Hitching is a possibility in summer (be prepared for long waits), but a pick-up or 4WD vehicle will make getting around much easier. Better still, travel by mountain bike. See Transport, page 399.

Just 4 km northeast of Cochrane is the entrance to the **Reserva Nacional Tamango** ⓘ *Dec-Mar 0830-2100, Apr-Nov 0830-1830, US$4.25, plus guided visits to see the huemules Tue, Thu, Sat, US$14 pp for up to 6 people and boat tours of Lago Cochrane, US$28 for up to 6 people*; ask in the **CONAF** office (see under Tourist information, below) before visiting. The reserve covers 6925 ha of lenga forest and is home to one of the largest colonies of the rare huemul as well as guanaco, foxes and lots of species of bird, including woodpecker and hummingbird. There are marked paths for walks between 45 minutes and five hours, up to **Cerro Tamango** (1722 m) and **Cerro Temanguito** (1485 m). Take water and food, and windproof clothing if climbing the *cerros*. The views from the reserve are superb, over the town, the nearby lakes and to the Campo de Hielo Norte to the west. Tourist facilities, however, are rudimentary and it is inaccessible in the four winter months.

Trips can also be made to **Lago Cochrane**, which straddles the frontier with Argentina (the Argentine section is called **Lago Puerredón**). The lake, which covers over 17,500 ha, offers excellent fishing all year round, and there are boats for hire. Some 17 km north of Cochrane, a road runs east through **Villa Chacabuco** and continues east for 78 km to enter Argentina at Paso Roballos. See also box, page 389.

## Tortel and Puerto Yungay

A branch of the Carretera Austral, beginning 2 km south of Vagabundo and continuing south for 23 km, was completed in early 2003, making the village of Tortel accessible by road. Built on a hill at the mouth of the river 135 km from Cochrane, Tortel has no streets, the village being connected by 7 km of stairs and walkways made of cypress wood. There are a couple of beaches and some plazas built on stilts, roofed for protection from the almost constant drizzle. Its main industries are wood, for trade with Punta Arenas, shellfish, and now tourism.

From Tortel, you can hire a boat to visit two spectacular glaciers: **Ventisquero Jorge Montt**, five hours' round trip by boat, or **Ventisquero Steffens**, north on the edge of the Parque Nacional San Rafael, 2½ hours by boat (US$56 per person for 10 people, includes a snack and a whiskey with glacier ice) and then a three-hour trek on a very wet, but well-signed trail including a river crossing by rowing boat to a viewing point from which the glacier can be seen across the lake. Trips can also be made to the nearby **Isla de los Muertos** (boat for 10 people US$70), where some 100 Chilote workers died in mysterious circumstances early in the 20th century.

The main spine of the Carretera, meanwhile, continues southwards to **Puerto Yungay** (allow 1¼ hours by car from Tortel under normal conditions), a tiny village with a military post and a pretty church. The small **Cafetería Pellegrino** sits next to the ferry dock. This section of the road is hilly and in places very bad; it is not advisable to drive along here at night.

From Puerto Yungay, there is an army-run **ferry crossing** ⓘ *www.barcazas.cl, 3 daily at 1000, 1200 and 1800; return 1 hr later, 45 mins, free,* to Río Bravo, with capacity for four to five cars; check timetables locally off season. If you miss the last boat the *carabineros* will help you find accommodation. Beyond the ferry crossing, the road continues south. After 9 km there is a turn-off marked 'Ventisquero Montt'. Carry on through more spectacular scenery – lakes, moors, dense forest, swamps, rivers and waterfalls, often shrouded in mist – before arriving at the Carretera's final destination, Villa O'Higgins.

The road beyond Río Bravo is very beautiful but very remote, with few people and few vehicles for hitching, and it is often closed by bad weather.

> **Tip...**
> If you're travelling south of Río Bravo take food and fuel, as there are no shops or service stations on the entire route.

## Villa O'Higgins

Villa O'Higgins lies 2 km from the northeastern end of an arm of **Lago O'Higgins**, which straddles the Argentine border (it's known as **Lago San Martín** in Argentina; see box, page 396, for border crossing information). With a population of around 500, the town is friendly with something of a frontier feel.

There is a tiny museum, the **Museo de la Patagonia Padre Antonio Ronchi** ⓘ *Mon-Fri 0900-1230, 1430-1700,* on the plaza. Fuel is available 24 hours from the **Copec** station.

# BORDER CROSSING
## Chile–Argentina

### Villa O'Higgins–El Chaltén

With the opening of this route it is possible to do the Carretera Austral and go on to Argentina's Parque Nacional Los Glaciares and Chile's Torres del Paine without doubling back on yourself. Note that the route is closed from April to October.

From Villa O'Higgins (see page 395), the road continues 7 km south to Bahía Bahamóndez on Lago O'Higgins (minibus/bus US$3.75), from where the boat Quetru leaves for Chilean immigration at Candelario Mancilla. The boat service runs daily from November to April, 2¾ hours, US$66.50. The number of departures varies each year, but there is usually two a week in November, three a week in December, four a week throughout January/February, and three total in March. The last departure leaves 2 April. Exact dates should be checked in advance, and sailings may be cancelled if the weather is bad. Camping and beds are available in Candelario Mancilla at the home of Tito and Ricardo, two brothers who offer 4WD and horses to the Argentine border. Home-cooked meals are available from their mother.

From Candelario Mancilla, it's 1 km to Chilean immigration (daily, 24 hours), 14 km to the border, and a further 5 km to Argentina immigration at Punta Norte on Lago del Desierto. The first part can be done on foot, on horseback, or by 4WD service (US$22 for two to four passengers and luggage, US$15 luggage only). The next 5 km is a demanding hike, or you can take a horse for the whole 19 km (US$45 per horse), with an extra horse to carry bags. The route descends sharply towards Lago de Desierto, with breathtaking panoramas, including of Cerro Fitz Roy. Note, however, that bridges are sometimes washed away; make sure to wear good boots for crossing wetland. A short detour to Laguna Larga (on the left as you walk towards the border) is worth it if you have the energy.

The 40-minute boat crossing of Lago de Desierto aboard the Huemul (embarks daily at 1000 and 1700, US$32) passes glaciers and ice fields. Several minibus companies, including Transporte Las Lengas and JR Turismo, await the boat for the final hour-long journey on a gravel road to El Chaltén (37 km, US$30). There is no food available on the Argentine side of the lake, but immigration officials at Punta Norte are friendly and, if you are cold, may offer you coffee, food and shelter.

The best combination is to take 4WD from Candelario Mancilla to the border and then continue on horseback. This ensures that the trip can be done in a day (depart Villa O'Higgins 0800, arrive El Chaltén 2115). Allow for delays, though, especially if horses aren't available for hire. It's a good option to pay for each portion of the route separately, as there can be a lack of communication from Villa O'Higgins to Candelario Mancilla.

Full details of the crossing and up-to-date itineraries and prices are available from Villa O'Higgins Expeditions (aka Robinson Crusoe), T67-243 1811/1821, www.villaohiggins.com, who also own Robinson Crusoe Deep Patagonia Lodge in town (Carretera Austral, Km 1240, T67-243 1909, www.robinsoncrusoe.com).

On rare sunny days, Villa O'Higgins' pleasant setting can be fully appreciated. Half way up a wooded hill behind the town, a mirador has spectacular views of nearby mountains, lakes and glaciers. There are large numbers of icebergs in Lago O'Higgins, which have split off the glaciers of the Campo de Hielo Sur to the west. A six-hour trek from the town goes through native forest to the **Mosco Glacier**; allow two days for a return trip. Fresh water is plentiful and there is a *refugio* on the way, but the route is difficult after heavy rain. From Villa O'Higgins, the road continues 7 km south to **Bahía Bahamóndez** on the shores of Lago O'Higgins.

## Listings Cochrane and around

## Tourist information

### Cochrane

**CONAF**
*Río Neff 417, T67-252 2164,*
*piero.caviglia@conaf.cl.*
For information on national parks and other protected areas.

**Kiosk**
*On corner of plaza on Dr Steffen, T067-252 2115, www.cochranepatagonia.cl. Summer only Tue-Sun 0900-1400 and 1500-1800.*

### Tortel

**Tourist office**
*At the entrance to the village, 0900-2300 in high season; closed in low season.*
A small office with information on the dozen or so *residenciales* in the village, and a useful map.

### Villa O' Higgins

See also www.villaohiggins.com.

**Tourist information kiosk**
*On the plaza. Mon-Fri 0900-1230 and 1430-1700, shorter hours in winter.*
Can provide trekking guides.

## Where to stay

### Cochrane

In summer it is best to book rooms in advance.

**$$$ Wellmann**
*Las Golondrinas 565, T67-252 2171,*
*hotelwellmann@gmail.com.*
Comfortable, warm, hot water, good meals.

**$$$-$$ Cabañas Rogeri**
*Río Maitén 80, T9-8827 1342,*
*rogeri3@hotmail.cl.*
*Cabañas* with kitchen for 4.

**$$ Residencial Sur Austral**
*Prat 334, T67-252 2150.*
Private or shared bath, hot water and *cabañas* (**$$$**). Swanky.

**$ Hospedaje La Katita**
*Pratt 536, T67-252 2061,*
*gonzalezvasquezanamaria@gmail.com.*
Run by a welcoming older couple, this is the best budget option. Breakfast included; Wi-Fi.

**Camping**
Camping in **Reserva Nacional Tamango** US$5.50 per night.

### Tortel and Puerto Yungay

Prices are cheaper in the low season. There is camping at sector Junquillo at the far end of town.

**$$$ Entre Hielos Lodge**
*Sector centro, Tortel, T9-9599 5730,*
*www.entrehielostortel.cl.*
Upmarket place in town, trips, boat trips.

## $$ Estilo
*Sector Centro, T9 8255 8487.*
Warm and comfortable, good food.
Entertaining, talkative host (Spanish).

### $$-$ Hospedaje Don Adán
*Sector Rincón T9-8135 6931.*
Norma runs a cosy, warm, well-kept
*hospedaje* with shared rooms as well as
private ones. Breakfast optional. Amazing
view of the bay. Wi-Fi. The best option
in Tortel. Recommended. Also runs the
restaurant **Comedor Venus** at the entrance
to the town.

## Villa O'Higgins

### $$$$-$$$ Robinson Crusoe
*Carretera Austral Km 1240, T67-431909,
www.robinsoncrusoe.com.*
Newer hotel that stands out as the
best lodging in town. Wi-Fi; breakfast
included. Has an expedition kiosk next
door that arranges trips to nearby
glaciers and El Chaltén.

### $$-$ El Mosco
*At the northern entrance to the town, T067-
243 1819, patagoniaelmosco@yahoo.es.*
Rooms (14), dorms or camping (US$7.50)
and cabins ($$$). Spanish-run hostel.
English spoken, trekking maps and
information. Breakfast included. Nothing
else competes in terms of infrastructure.

### $$-$ Hostería Patagonia
*Río Paqua 195, in front of the plaza.*
Family-run with private and shared rooms.
Breakfast included; serves home-made lunch
and dinner. A good choice for small groups.

## Camping

### Los Nires
*Located adjacent to the Robinson
Crusoe office.*
Camping for US$6 and a shared *cabaña*
for US$10.50.

## Restaurants

For other eating options,
see Where to stay, above.

## Cochrane

### Ada's
*Merino 374, T9-8399 5889,
adascaferestaurant@gmail.com.*
Fancy family-run restaurant with an
extensive menu featuring grilled meats,
among many other dishes.

## Tortel and Puerto Yungay

### Bella Vista
*Tortel, Costanera s/n, Sector Rincón,
T9-6211 7430.*
Good for salmon, lamb and beef.

## Villa O'Higgins

### $$ Entre Patagones
*At the northern entrance to the town,
T9-6621 5046, www.entrepatagones.cl.*
The only restaurant in town with any
sort of style. Great fish and meat dishes.
A great dining option after a long journey
to the end of the road.

## What to do

### Cochrane
**Jimmy Valdez**, *T9-84252419, lordpatagonia@
gmail.com.* Tours to Glaciar Calluqueo.
Also **Acto Expediciones** (T9-8548 5839,
actoexpediciones@gmail.com).
**Katenke**, *Esmeralda 464, T9-8209 4957.* Offers
scuba and snorkelling in Río Cochrane and
Lago Cochrane.
**Marcelo Soto**, *T9-6699 9081,
sotomarcelo286@gmail.com.* Professional
fly-fishing guide.

### Tortel and Puerto Yungay
Charter boats can easily be arranged in
Tortel to **Ventisquero Jorge Montt** and
**Isla de los Muertos** for up to 8-10 people
The standard of the boats varies; check

first. In theory the harbourmaster will only allow boats out in good weather, however conditions can change very quickly and occasionally boats will have to turn back mid-trip. Make sure you agree beforehand with your guide whether you get any sort of refund if this happens.

## Villa O'Higgins

**Alfonso Díaz**, T9-6621 5046, *www.entre patagones.cl*. Fishing trips on Lagos Ciervo, Cisnes, El Tigre, Colorado and Sector Mayer. Also owns **Entre Patagonias** restaurant. **Hielo Sur**, *www.hielosur.com (contact through Robinson Crusoe, see Where to stay, above)*. Runs a boat to Calendario Mancilla, 2½ hrs, US$65; with a glacier visit 12 hrs, US$108. **Villa O'Higgins Expeditions**, *T67-243 1821, www.villaohiggins.com*. Treks and expeditions, including the route to El Chaltén in Argentina. Also rents bicycles (US$4.50 for 2 hrs or US$13.50 for the day).

### Transport

**Bus** There are buses every day between **Coyhaique** and Cochrane (currently at 0630 and 0800, but check with companies for the most up-to-date timetables), US$20. To **Río Tranquilo**, US$10.50. To **Villa O'Higgins** with **Katalina** (T67-252 2333) Wed, Sat 0800, 6-7 hrs, US$11.25. To **Tortel** with Aldea,

Las Golondrinas 399, T67-252 2448), Tue, Thu, Fri, Sun, 0930, return 1500, US$10. Minibuses (T67-252 2242) run Mon, Wed, Fri to **Chile Chico**, US$18. Other companies include: **Don Carlos** (Prat 334, T67-252 2150); **Aguilas Patagónicas** (Río Maitén at Dr Steffens, T67-252 3730); **Acuario 13** and **Sao Paulo** (Río Baker 349, T67-252 2143). Petrol is available at the **Esso** and **Copec** servicentros.

## Tortel and Puerto Yungay

**Bus** Tortel to **Cochrane** with **Buses Aldea** (see above), daily, US$10. Tortel to **Villa O'Higgins**, Tue, Fri only Sun 1530, 4 hrs, US$21, T9-8180 1962.

## Villa O'Higgins

**Air** Aerocordo offers trips from Villa O'Higgins to **Coyhaique** Mon and Thu at 1100, US$41.

**Boat** For details of the boat service across Lago O'Higgins to **Candelario Mancilla**, see the border box, page 396.

**Bus** Bus Katalina (T67-243 1823), Lago Cisne. If you have a return bus ticket northwards, reconfirm on arrival at Villa O'Higgins. There are 1 or 2 buses weekly to **Cochrane**, with **Katalina** on Mon, Fri 1000, 6-7 hrs, US$20 A local bus run by the owner of **Hostería Patagonia** leaves Mon and Fri at 0800 for **Tortel**, T9-7376 5288.

# Southern
# Patagonia

follow the ice and wind to Torres del Paine

A spectacular land of fragmenting glaciers and teetering icy peaks, southern Patagonia feels like nowhere else on earth.

Although Chileans posted here will often say that they are a 'long way from Chile', this is the country's most popular destination for visitors.

The jewel in the crown is the Parque Nacional Torres del Paine, a natural magnet for travellers from all over the world. The 'towers', three massif-like fingers after which the park is named, point vertically upwards from the Paine, surrounded by glaciers, turquoise-coloured lakes and thick forests of native trees.

Puerto Natales is the base for exploration of Torres del Paine and for boat trips to the glaciers in the Parque Nacional Bernardo O'Higgins. It also provides access to El Calafate and the Parque Nacional Los Glaciares in Argentina.

Further south, Punta Arenas is a European-style city with a lively Chilote community and remnants of earlier English and Croatian influences.

**Best** for
Camping ▪ Glacier walks ▪ Horse riding ▪ Trekking

# Footprint
## picks

★ **Museo Regional Salesiano Maggiorino**, page 406

Let this must-visit regional museum be your introduction to all
things Patagonian.

★ **A cruise to Tierra del Fuego**, page 412

Pamper yourself with a southern cruise replete with excellent scenery,
from Punta Arenas to Ushuaia.

★ **Penguins at Seno Otway**, page 415

Walk alongside thousands of Magellanic penguins and snap photos from
viewing stations.

★ **Visiting glaciers in Bernardo O'Higgins National Park**,
page 426

Take a Zodiac boat up Río Tyndall and visit the majestic Glacier Balmaceda.

★ **Trekking in Parque Nacional Torres del Paine**, page 427

No trekker's appetite is sated until they've completed the 'W' circuit at
this magnificent national park.

Footprint
picks

1 Museo Regional Salesiano Maggiorino, page 406
2 A cruise to Tierra del Fuego, page 412
3 Penguins at Seno Otway, page 415
4 Visiting glaciers in Bernardo O'Higgins National Park, page 426
5 Trekking in Parque Nacional Torres del Paine, page 427

Puerto Yungay
Villa O'Higgins
Lago O'Higgins
Alesna (2480m)
Isla Wellington
Fitz Roy (3405m)  El Chaltén
Helsingfors  Lago Viedma
Cerro Norte  Tres Lagos
Parque Nacional Los Glaciares
Paso Río La Leona
ARGENTINA
Laguna Grande
Lago Argentino
Perito Moreno Glacier
Río Bote
El Calafate
Gendarme Barreto
REGION XII
Parque Nacional Bernardo O'Higgins
El Cerrito
Fuentes del Coyle
La Esperanza
Parque Nacional Torres del Paine
Paso Cerro Castillo
Cerro Castillo
Campo de Hielo Sur
Río Turbio
Paso Dorotea
Ferry to Puerto Montt
Paso Casas Viejas
Puerto Natales
El Zurdo
Morro Chico
Parque Nacional Pali Aike
Villa Tehuelches
Punta Delgada
Punta Espora
Río Verde
Monumento Natural Los Pingüinos
Cerro Sombrero
Cordillera Riesco
Seno Otway
Primavera
Reserva Forestal Magallanes
Punta Arenas
Porvenir
Onaisin
Reserva Forestal Laguna Parillar
Fuerte Bulnes
Camerón
To Puerto Williams

N

30 km
30 miles

# Punta Arenas
## & around

Capital of Región XII, Punta Arenas lies 2140 km due south of Santiago. The city was originally named 'Sandy Point' by the English, but adopted the Hispanic equivalent under Chilean colonization. A centre for natural gas production, sheep farming and the fishing industry as well as an important military base, it is also the home of Polar Austral, one of the most southerly breweries in the world.

Although Punta Arenas has expanded rapidly, it remains a tranquil and pleasant city. The climate and architecture give it a distinctively northern European atmosphere, quite unlike anywhere else in Chile.

Around the attractive Plaza Muñoz Gamero in Punta Arenas (population 160,000) are a number of mansions that once belonged to the great sheep-ranching families of the late 19th century.

A good example is the **Palacio Sara Braun** ① *Mon 1000-1300, Tue-Sat 1000-1300 and 1600-1930, US$1.50,* built between 1894 and 1905 with materials from Europe. The Palacio has several elegantly decorated rooms open to the public and also houses the **Hotel José Nogueira**. In the centre of the plaza is a statue of Magellan with a mermaid and two indigenous Fuegians at his feet. According to local wisdom, those who rub or kiss the big toe of one of the Fuegians will return to Punta Arenas.

Just north of the plaza is the fascinating **Museo Regional de Magallanes** ① *Palacio Braun Menéndez, Magallanes 949, T61-224 2049, www.museodemagallanes.cl, Wed-Mon 1030-1700 (May-Sep closes 1400), free,* the opulent former mansion of Mauricio Braun, built in 1905. A visit is recommended. Part of the museum is set out as a room-by-room regional history; the rest of the house has been left with its original furniture. Guided tours are in Spanish only, but an information sheet written in butchered English is also available. In the basement there is a permanent exhibition dedicated to the indigenous people of southern Patagonia, somewhat ironic considering the leading part the Braun Menéndez family played in their demise.

## Essential Punta Arenas

### Access

Punta Arenas is cut off from the rest of Chile. Puerto Natales, 247 km north, is easily reached on a paved road, with many buses daily, but other than that the only road connections are via the Argentine towns of Comodoro Rivadavia and Río Gallegos, either from Coyhaique on the Carretera Austral (20 hours; buses weekly in summer) or from Puerto Montt via Bariloche (36 hours, daily buses in summer); it is quicker, and often cheaper, therefore to take one of the many daily flights to/from Puerto Montt or Santiago instead.

### Finding your feet

**Carlos Ibáñez del Campo Airport** is 20 km north of town. A minibus service is run by **Transfer Austral**, Av Cólon and Magallanes, T61-224 5811, www.transferaustral.com, US$4. Alternatively, a taxi costs US$11 to the city. Note that in most taxis much of the

luggage space is taken up by natural gas fuel tanks. Buses from Puerto Natales to Punta Arenas will only stop at the airport if they are scheduled to drop passengers there.

### Getting around

Punta Arenas is not a huge city and walking about is a pleasant way of getting to know it. Buses and *colectivos* are plentiful and cheap (around US$0.50; US$0.60 at night and Sundays): a taxi is only really necessary for out-of-town trips. For further details, see Transport, page 413.

### Useful addresses

**Argentine Consulate**, 21 de Mayo 1878, T61-226 0600. Monday-Friday 1000-1500. Visas take 24 hours.

### When to go

For a weather chart of Punta Arenas, see page 18.

# BACKGROUND
## Southern Patagonia

Southern Patagonia was inhabited from the end of the Ice Age, mainly by the Tehuelche people, who roamed from the Atlantic coast to the mountains (see box, page 406). When Magellan sailed through the Straits in 1520, the strategic importance was quickly recognized. The route became less important after 1616 when Dutch sailors discovered a quicker route into the Pacific round Cape Horn.

At Independence, Chile claimed the far southern territories along the Pacific coast but little was done to carry out this claim until 1843 when, concerned at British activities in the area, President Bulnes ordered the preparation of a secret mission. The expedition, on board the vessel *Ancud*, established Fuerte Bulnes; the fort was abandoned in 1848 in favour of a new settlement 56 km north, called Punta Arenas.

The development of sheep farming in Patagonia and on Tierra del Fuego (with the help of arrivals from the nearby Falkland Islands), and the renewed importance of the Magellan Straits with the advent of steam shipping, led to the rapid expansion of Punta Arenas in the late 19th century.

Sheep farming remains vital to the local economy, although wool exports have dropped in recent years. Forestry has become more important, but is controversial, as native forests are used for woodchips to export. This is especially serious on Tierra del Fuego. Although oil production has declined, large quantities of natural gas are now produced and Riesco Island contains Chile's largest reserves of coal. Tourism is growing rapidly, making an increasingly important contribution to the local economy.

### Geography and climate
Chilean southern Patagonia stretches south from the icefields of the Campo de Hielos Sur to the Estrecho de Magallanes (Straits of Magellan), which separate continental South America from Tierra del Fuego. The coastline is heavily indented by fjords; offshore are numerous islands, few of which are inhabited. The remnants of the Andes stretch along the coast, seldom rising above 1500 m, although the Cordillera del Paine has several peaks over 2600 m and Cerro Balmaceda is 2035 m. Most of the western coast is covered by thick rainforest but further east is grassland, stretching into the arid Patagonian plateau across the Argentine border. Together with the Chilean part of Tierra del Fuego, Isla Navarino and Chilean Antarctica, this part of Chile is administered as Región XII (Magallanes); the capital is Punta Arenas. The region covers 17.5% of Chilean territory, but the population is only around 150,000, less than 1% of the Chilean total.

People from Punta Arenas say they often have four seasons in one day. Frequently, however, the only season appears to be winter. Cold winds, often exceeding 100 kph, blow during the summer bringing heavy rain to coastal areas. Further east, the winds are drier; annual rainfall at Punta Dungeness at the east end of the Straits is only 250 mm compared to over 4000 mm on the offshore islands. Coastal temperatures seldom rise above 15°C in summer. In winter, snow covers the whole region, except near the sea, making many roads impassable. There is little wind in the winter months, meaning tourism remains possible for most of the year.

## The original big foots

The original wanderers of the dry Patagonian plateau were one principal indigenous group, the Tehuelches, who inhabited the eastern side of the Andes, as far north as modern-day Bariloche. They were hunter-gatherers, subsisting on guanaco and rheas. In the 18th century, they began to domesticate the wild horses of the region and sailed down the Patagonian rivers to reach the Atlantic coast.

The Tehuelches were very large, almost mythically so. It is said that when the Spanish first arrived in this area, they discovered Tehuelche footprints in the sand, exclaiming '*qué patagón*' ('what a large foot'), hence the name Patagonia.

In the 18th and early 19th centuries, the Tehuelche interacted with European whalers and were patronizingly described as 'semi-civilized'. The granting by the Chilean government of large land concessions in the late 19th century, combined with Argentine President Julio Roca's wars of extermination against Patagonian native peoples in the 1870s, spelled the end for the Tehuelches. They were hunted and persecuted by settlers and only a few survived diseases and the radical change of lifestyle.

Towards the end of the 20th century, a belated sense of moral guilt arose among the colonizers, but it was too late to preserve the Tehuelche way of life. Today, only a few isolated groups remain in Argentine Patagonia.

For details of the indigenous groups further south and in the Patagonian fjords, see box, page 446.

Three blocks east of the plaza, the **Museo Naval y Marítimo** ⓘ *Pedro Montt 981, T61-224 5987, www.museonaval.cl, Tue-Sat, 0930-1230, 1400-1700, US$1.50,* houses an exhibition of local and national maritime history with sections on naval instruments, cartography, meteorology, and shipwrecks. There is a video in Spanish and an information sheet in English.

West of the Plaza Muñoz Gamero on Waldo Seguel are two reminders of British influence in the city: the **British School** and **St James's Anglican Church** next door. Nearby on Calle Fagnano is the **Mirador Cerro de La Cruz** offering a view over the city and the Magellan Straits complete with its various shipwrecks.

Three blocks further west is the **Museo Militar** ⓘ *Zenteno y Balmaceda, T61-222 5240, Tue-Sun, 1000-1200, and 1400-1730, free, closed at the time of writing but due to reopen in 2017,* at the Regimiento Pudeto. Lots of knives guns, flags and other military memorabilia are displayed here plus many items brought from Fuerte Bulnes. There are explanatory notes in excruciating English.

North of the centre along Bulnes is the ★ **Museo Regional Salesiano Maggiorino Borgatello** ⓘ *Colegio Salesiano, Av Bulnes 336, entrance next to church, T61-222 1001, see Facebook, Tue-Sun 1000-1230 and 1500-1730, hours change frequently, US$4,* an excellent introduction to Patagonia and easily the most complete and fascinating regional museum in Chile. It covers the interesting history of the indigenous peoples and their education by the Salesian missions, alongside an array of stuffed birds and gas extraction machinery. The Italian priest, Alberto D'Agostini, who arrived in 1909 and presided over the missions, took wonderful photographs of the region and his 70-minute film can be seen on video (just ask to see it).

Three blocks further on, the **cemetery** ⓘ *Av Bulnes 029, daily 0730-2000 in summer, 0800-1800 in winter US$5*, is one of the most interesting places in the city, with cypress avenues, gravestones in many languages that bear testimony to the cosmopolitan provenance of Patagonian pioneers, and many mausolea and memorials to pioneer

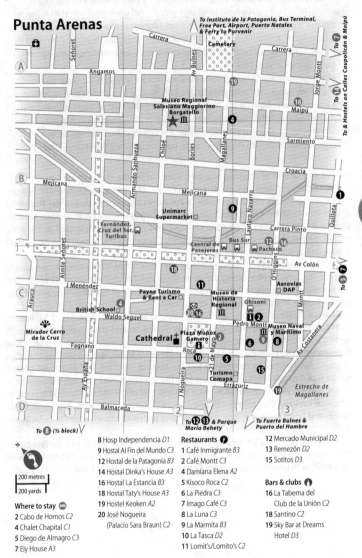

Punta Arenas

**Where to stay** 🛏
2 Cabo de Hornos C2
4 Chalet Chapital C1
5 Diego de Almagro C3
7 Ely House A3

8 Hosp Independencia D1
9 Hostal Al Fin del Mundo C3
12 Hostal de la Patagonia B3
14 Hostal Dinka's House A3
16 Hostal La Estancia B3
18 Hostal Taty's House A3
19 Hostel Keoken A2
20 José Nogueira
   (Palacio Sara Braun) C2

**Restaurants** 🍴
1 Café Inmigrante B3
2 Café Montt C3
4 Damiana Elena A2
6 Kisoco Roca C2
6 La Piedra C3
7 Imago Café C3
8 La Luna C3
9 La Marmita B3
10 La Tasca D2
11 Lomit's/Lomito's C2

12 Mercado Municipal D2
13 Remezón D2
15 Sotitos D3

**Bars & clubs** 🍸
16 La Taberna del
   Club de la Unión C2
18 Santino C2
19 Sky Bar at Dreams
   Hotel D3

# BACKGROUND
## Punta Arenas

After its foundation in 1848, Punta Arenas became a penal colony modelled on Australia. In 1867, it was opened to foreign settlers and given free-port status. From the 1880s, it prospered as a refuelling and provisioning centre for steam ships and whaling vessels. It also became a centre for the new sheep estancias as it afforded the best harbour facilities. The city's importance was reduced overnight by the opening of the Panama Canal in 1914.

Although immigrants from Britain and Croatia were central in the growth of Punta Arenas (their influence can be seen to this day), most of those who came to work in the estancias were from Chiloé; many people in the city have relatives in Chiloé and feel an affinity with the island (the barrios on either side of the upper reaches of Independencia are known as Chilote areas); the Chilotes who returned north took Patagonian customs with them, hence the number of *mate* drinkers on Chiloé.

families and victims of shipping disasters. Look out for the statue of Indicito, the 'little Indian', on the northwest side, which is now an object of reverence, bedecked with flowers.

Further north still, the **Instituto de la Patagonia** houses the **Museo del Recuerdo** ⓘ *Av Bulnes 1890, Km 4 northeast (opposite the university), T61-220 7051, outdoor exhibits, Mon-Sat 0830-1700, US$2.75,* an open-air museum with 3000 artefacts used by the early settlers, pioneer homes and botanical gardens. Opposite is the Zona Franca with a mall and ice rink (see Shopping, page 411).

On 21 de Mayo, south of Independencia, is a small ornate Hindu temple, one of only two in Chile, while further along the same street, on the southern outskirts of the city, the wooded **Parque María Behety** features a scale model of Fuerte Bulnes, popular for Sunday picnics. In winter, there is an ice rink here.

**Reserva Nacional Magallanes** ⓘ *9 km west of town, US$2.50, taxi US$5.50,* known locally as the Parque Japonés, extends over 13,500 ha and rises to 600 m. Although getting there by taxi is the easiest option, it can also be reached on foot or by bike: follow Independencia up the hill and take a right for Río de las Minas, about 3 km from the edge of town; the entrance to the reserve is 2 km beyond. Here you will find a self-guided nature trail through lenga and coigue trees. The road continues through the woods for 14 km passing several picnic sites. From the top end of the road a short path leads to a lookout over the **Garganta del Diablo** (Devil's Throat), a gorge with views over Punta Arenas and Tierra del Fuego. From here a slippery path leads down to the Río de las Minas Valley and then back to Punta Arenas.

Within the reserve, 8 km west of Punta Arenas, Cerro Mirador is one of the few places in the world where you can ski with a sea view. In summer there is a good two-hour walk on the hill, with labelled flora; contact **Club Andino** ⓘ *T61-224 1479, www.clubandino.cl.*

## Tourist information

### CONAF office
*Av Bulnes 0309, p 4, T61-223 8554,*
*magallanes.oirs@conaf.cl.*
For information on national parks
and other protected areas.

### Municipal tourist information
*Opposite Centro Español in the Plaza de*
*Armas, T61-220 0610, www.puntaarenas.cl.*
*High season Mon-Fri 0800-1900, Sat-Sun*
*0900-1700; Mon-Fri 0800-1700.*
Helpful staff. There is also a kiosk in the plaza
with experienced, English-speaking staff and
a good town map with all hotels marked.

### Sernatur
*Lautaro Navarro 999 y Pedro Montt,*
*T61-222 5385, www.patagonia-chile.com.*
*High season Mon-Fri 0830-2000, Sat-Sun*
*1000-1800; in low season Mon-Fri 0830-1800,*
*Sat-Sun 1000-1800.*

## Where to stay

Hotel prices are lower during winter
months (Apr-Sep). A few streets, in
particular Caupolicán and Maipú, some
10-15 mins' walk from the centre have
become are packed with hostels, most
of them with similar facilities and similar
prices (**$$**). These include Ely House, Maipú
Street and Hostal Dinka's House; the
latter is painted bright-red and run by the
indomitable Dinka herself. The area is also
full of car repair places, which can make
it noisy during the day and occasionally
at night. For accommodation in private
houses, usually **$** pp, ask at the tourist
office. There are no campsites in or near
the city, except in certain hostels.

### $$$$-$$$ Cabo de Hornos
*Plaza Muñoz Gamero 1039, T61-271 5000,*
*www.hoteles-australis.com.*

4-star, comfy, bright and spacious rooms,
with good views from 4th floor up.

### $$$$-$$$ Diego de Almagro
*Av Colón 1290, T61-220 8800,*
*www.dahotelespuntaarenas.com.*
Very modern, good international standard,
on waterfront, many rooms with view,
heated pool, sauna, small gym, big bright
rooms, good value.

### $$$$-$$$ José Nogueira
*Plaza de Armas, Bories 967 y P Montt,*
*in former Palacio Sara Braun, T61-*
*271 1000, www.hotelnogueira.com.*
Best in town, stylish rooms, warm
atmosphere, excellent service. Smart
restaurant in the beautiful *loggia*. A few
original rooms now a 'small museum'.

### $$$ Chalet Chapital
*Sanhueza 974, T61-273 0100,*
*www.hotelchaletchapital.cl.*
Small well-run hotel, smallish rooms, helpful
staff, a good choice in this price range.

### $$$ Hostal de la Patagonia
*O'Higgins 730, T61-224 9970,*
*www.ecotourpatagonia.com.*
Rooms with heating, good services, dining
room, 10 mins' walk from centre. Organizes
a variety of tours, including fly-fishing.

### $$ Hostal Al Fin del Mundo
*O'Higgins 1026, T61-271 0185,*
*www.alfindelmundo.hostel.com.*
Rooms and dorms, bright, cosy, shared baths,
central, helpful, pool table, English spoken.

### $$ Hostal La Estancia
*O'Higgins 765, T61-224 9130, www.estancia.cl.*
Simple but comfortable rooms, some with
bath. **$** pp in dorms. English spoken, small
shop attached, music and games room.

### $$ Hostal Taty's House
*Maipu 1070, T61-224 1525,*
*www.hostaltatyshouse.cl.*

Nice rooms with good beds, decent choice in this price bracket, basic English spoken.

## $$ Hostel Keoken
*Magallanes 209, T61-224 4086/6376, www.hostelkeoken.cl.*
Light, wooden, spacious building on 3 floors each with its own entrance up rickety outside staircases. Some rooms with small bath. Good value, some info. Top-floor rooms with shared bathroom have paper thin walls. Recently expanded into an even bigger, rambling place.

## $ Hostal Independencia
*Independencia 374, T61-222 7572, www.hostalindependencia.es.tl.*
Private rooms, dorms (3-4 beds) and camping with use of kitchen and bathroom. Trekking equipment rental, parking, fishing and other tours, lots of information; very knowledgeable owners. Discount without breakfast. Recommended.

## Restaurants

Many eating places close on Sun. There are seasonal bans on *centolla* (king crab) fishing to protect dwindling stocks; out of season *centolla* served in restaurants will probably be frozen. Note that *centolla* is caught illegally by some fishermen using dolphin, porpoise and penguin as live bait. If there is an infestation of red tide (*marea roja*), a disease which is fatal to humans, bivalve shellfish must not be eaten. Mussels should not be picked along the shore because of pollution and the *marea roja*. Sernatur and the Centros de Salud have leaflets.

## $$$ Remezón
*21 de Mayo 1469, T61-224 1029, see Facebook.*
Regional specialities such as krill. Very good, but should be, given the prices.

## $$$-$$ Damiana Elena
*Magallanes 341, T61-222 2818. Mon-Sat from 2000-2400, see Facebook.*

Stylish restaurant serving Mediterranean food with a Patagonian touch, popular with locals, book ahead at weekends.

## $$$-$$ La Tasca
*Plaza Muñoz Gamero 771, in Casa Español.*
Large helpings, limited selection, decent set lunch, views over the plaza.

## $$$-$$ Sotitos
*O'Higgins 1138, T61-224 3565, see Facebook. Daily lunch and dinner, Sun 1200-1500 only.*
An institution, famous for seafood in elegant surroundings, excellent. Book ahead in season. 2nd floor serving local specialities and Italian food.

## $$ La Luna
*O'Higgins 1017, T61-222 8555, www.laluna.cl.*
Fish, shellfish and local specialities, huge pisco sours, popular, reasonable. Quirky decor, friendly staff. Recommended.

## $$ La Marmita
*Plaza Sampaio 678, T61-222 2056, www.marmitamaga.cl. Mon-Sat 1230-1500 and 1830-2330, Sun 1830-2330.*
Regional dishes with international twist, vegetarian options, good sized portions, prettily presented, chatty owner, generally very good.

## $$-$ La Piedra
*Lautaro Navarro 1087, T9-665 1439. Mon-Sat 1200-2300.*
Meat dishes, fish, soups, salads, good burgers and sandwiches, daily lunch specials, housed over 2 floors.

## $ Kiosco Roca
*Roca 875. Mon-Fri 0700-1900, Sat 0800-1300.*
Unassuming sandwich bar, voted the best in Punta Arenas; it's always packed. Also serves breakfast and brunch. Takeaway or there are a few seats available at the counter.

## $ Lomit's/Lomito's
*Menéndez 722.*
A fast-food institution with bar attached, cheap snacks and drinks (local beers are

good), open when the others are closed, good food.

## $ Mercado Municipal
*21 de Mayo 1465. Daily 1000-2000.*
Wide range of *cocinerías* offering cheap *empanadas* and seafood on the upper floor of the municipal market.

## Cafés

### Café Inmigrante
*Quillota 599, esq Mejicana, T61-222 2205, www.inmigrante.cl. Daily afternoons and evenings.*
Hugely popular café run by 3rd generation Croatian expats. Beautifully prepared sandwiches, daily changing cake menu, huge portions, family history on menus. Quirky and popular. Book in advance if possible. Highly recommended.

### Café Montt
*Pedro Montt 976, T61-222 0381, www.cafemontt.cl.*
Coffees, teas, cakes, pastries and snacks, Wi-Fi. Cosy, friendly. Recommended.

### Imago Café
*Costanera y Colón.*
Tiny, laid-back café hidden away in a beachfront bunker overlooking the straits. Live music occasionally.

## Bars and clubs

### La Taberna del Club de la Unión
*In the Sara Braun mansion.*
Atmospheric bar, good for evening drinks.

### Santino
*Colón 657, T61-271 0882, www.santino.cl. Open 1800-0300.*
Also serves pizzas and other snacks, large bar, good service, live music Sat.

### Sky Bar
*O'Higgins 1235.*
Bar with panoramic views on the top floor of the luxury **Dreams** hotel and spa.

## Entertainment

There is a single-screen **cinema** (Mejicana 777, www.cinesalaestrella.cl). The **casino** (www.mundodreams.com), is at O'Higgins 1235, just north of the port.

## Festivals

**Late Jul Carnaval de invierno** The winter solstice is marked by a carnival on 23-24 Jul.

## Shopping

Punta Arenas has free-port facilities: **Zona Franca**, 4 km north of the centre, opposite Museo del Recuerdo (Instituto de la Patagonia), is cheaper than elsewhere. The complex has over 100 shops and is open daily 1000-2100 (www.zonaustral.cl); take bus No 8 or catch *colectivo* 15 or 20; taxi US$5.

### Handicrafts
**Chile Típico**, *Carrera Pinto 1015, T61-222 5827, Mon-Sat 0900-2130, Sun 1000-2000.* Beautiful knitwear and woollen ponchos.
**Mercado Municipal** *(see Restaurants, above).* Excellent handicrafts and souvenirs.

## What to do

### Skiing
**Cerro Mirador** in the Reserva Nacional Magallanes has skiing Jun-Sep, weather and snow permitting. Midway lodge with food, drink and equipment rental. Taxi US$7.

### Tour operators
Most organize trips to Torres del Paine, the *pingüineras* on Isla Magdalena and Otway Sound, and Tierra del Fuego; shop around.
**Adventure Network International**, *T+1-801 266 4876, www.adventure-network.com.*
Antarctic experiences of a lifetime, operating out of Punta Arenas, flying to the interior of the Antarctic Continent. Flights to the South Pole, guided mountain climbing and fully guided skiing expeditions. Camping with emperor penguins in Nov.

## ON THE ROAD

### ★ A cruise at the end of the world

From September to April, Australis have two vessels running cruises between Punta Arenas and Ushuaia, the *Vía Australis* and the *Stella Australis*. *Vía Australis* has capacity for 136 passengers, while *Stella Australis* can accommodate 210. (For the 2017-2018 season, the *Vía Australis* will be replaced by the *Ventus Australis*, similar to *Stella Australis*.) Passengers sail in comfort, treated to fine food and expert service, through the Straits of Magellan and the channels and fjords between Tierra del Fuego and the islands that cling to its southern shore. These were the waters fished by the Yámana and Kawéskar people and surveyed by Robert Fitzroy and his crew.

The cruise takes four nights from Punta Arenas to Ushuaia (three nights the opposite way). Each includes a visit to Cape Horn where, sea conditions permitting, you can land to see the monuments and to sign the visitors' book in the lighthouse, manned by a Chilean naval officer and his family. The landing follows a rigorous procedure: everyone is togged up in waterproofs and lifejackets, and is transferred from ship to Zodiac, before disembarking with the aid of crew standing in the surf. From the shore, 160 wooden steps lead up the cliff to wooden walkways. On a relatively benign day – sunny, with an icy breeze – it's hard to imagine the tragedies of so many mariners lost, to remember the many souls that, according to legend, have become albatrosses, and to accept that this is the last piece of terra firma before Antarctica.

Other shore trips are followed by a whisky or hot chocolate. You need the sustenance, especially after a visit to Piloto and Nena glaciers in the Chico fjord. The blue ice of Piloto calves into the water, while Nena is scarred by rocky debris. All around water pours off the mountains; sleet and rain drive into your face as the Zodiac powers away.

En route from Ushuaia to Punta Arenas (the itinerary varies according to the route and the weather), there are other landings. At Wulaia Bay on Isla Navarino two walks are available, up a hill or along the shore to look for birds and flora. An information centre, in an old radio station, tells the history of the place. It was here that one of Fitzroy's Fuegians, Jemmy Button, who was briefly a celebrity in England in the 1830s, was reportedly present at the massacre of missionaries in 1859. Another visit is to Isla Magdalena, just off Punta Arenas. Here, between November and January, 60,000 pairs of Magellanic penguins breed in burrows.

At all times the ship is accompanied by giant petrels, black-browed albatross and king cormorants. Occasionally, dolphins ride the wake. If it is too cold on deck, you can go onto the bridge and be entertained by the navigator. The bar is open until midnight; stewards and guides are on hand at any hour; and there are lectures and films, visits to the engine room and cookery lessons to fill the hours at sea. Everything runs like clockwork thanks to clear instructions for safety and fine-tuned organization: when the captain says you'll dock at 1100, dock at 1100 you will.

For more information on these cruises, see www.australis.com, and Australis, at Turismo Comapa, Lautaro Navarro 1112, T61-220 0200 (in Santiago: Avenida El Bosque Norte 0440, p 11, T2-2840 0100; in Buenos Aires: T011-5128 4632; in USA: T01-877 678 3772; in Europe: T34-93-497-0484).

**Arka Patagonia**, *Manuel Señoret 1597, T61-224 8167, www.arkapatagonia.com*. All types of tours, whale watching, trekking, Cape Horn.

**Go Patagonia**, *Lautaro Navarro 1013, T61-237 1074, www.gopatagoniachile.com*. Tours to Torres del Paine, Tierra del Fuego and Seno Otway.

**Solo Expediciones**, *Nogueira 1255, T61-271 0219, www.soloexpediciones.com*. Operate their own service to Monumento Natural Los Pingüinos on a small fast boat, also passing by Isla Marta, half-day tour, mornings only.

**Turismo Aventour**, *Soto 2876, T9-7827 9479, www.aventourpatagonia.cl*. Specialize in fishing trips, organize tours to Tierra del Fuego, helpful, English spoken.

**Turismo Comapa**, *Lautaro Navarro 1112, T61-220 0200, www.comapa.com*. Tours to Torres del Paine (responsible, well-informed guides), Tierra del Fuego and to see penguins at Isla Magdalena. Agents for **Australis** cruises (see opposite).

**Turismo Laguna Azul**, *21 de Mayo 1011, T61-222 5200, www.turismolagunaazul.com*. Full-day trips to a colony of king penguins on Tierra del Fuego. Trips run all year round. Also city tours, trips to glaciers and others.

**Turismo Yamana**, *T61-222 2061, www.yamana.cl*. Conventional and deluxe tours, trekking in Torres del Paine, kayaking the fjords of Parque Nacional Alberto de Agostini (Tierra del Fuego), multilingual guides.

**Whale Sound**, *Lautaro Navarro 1191, T9-9887 9814, www.whalesound.com*. Whale-watching trips in the Magellan Straits.

## Transport

Most transport is heavily booked from Christmas to Mar so book in advance.

There is a daily ferry service on the **Melinka** from Punta Arenas and Porvenir on Tierra del Fuego, but buses to Tierra del Fuego use the more northerly ferry crossing at Punta Delgada (many daily) to Puerto Espora.

### Air

To **Santiago**, **LAN** and **Sky**, direct, many daily. To **Porvenir**, **Aerovías DAP** (O'Higgins 891, T61-261 6100, www.aeroviasdap.cl), 3 times daily Mon-Fri (0815, 1230, 1700), 2 on Sat (0815, 1230), 9 passengers, 12 mins. To **Puerto Williams**, daily except Sun, 1¼ hrs (book a week in advance for Porvenir, 2 in advance for Puerto Williams).

To **Ushuaia**, private charter with **DAP**. Take passport when booking tickets to Argentina. To **Falkland Islands/Islas Malvinas**, with **LAN**, once a week on Sun; for information contact **International Tours & Travel Ltd**, PO Box 408, 1 Dean St, Stanley, Falkland Islands, T+500 22041, www.falklandislands.travel, Mon-Fri 0800-1700, Sat 1000-1200, who are the Falkland Islands agents for LAN. They also handle inbound tourist bookings, book FIGAS flights and arrange tours.

### Bus

The bus terminal is at the northern edge of town by the Zona Franca. To book all

tickets visit the **Central de Pasajeros**, Colón y Magallanes, T61-224 5811, also *cambio* and tour operator. At the time of writing, bus companies were maintaining their own offices in the city centre: **Cruz del Sur**, **Fernández**, and **Turibus**, Sanhueza 745, T61-224 2313/222 1429, www.busesfernandez.com; **Pacheco**, Colón 900, T61-224 2174, www.busespacheco.com; **Pullman**, Colón 568, T61-222 3359, www.pullman.cl, tickets for all Chile; **Bus Sur**, Colón 842, T61-222 2938, www.bussur.com; **Ghisoni** and **Tecni Austral** (also tours), Lautaro Navarro 975, T61-261 3420, www.turismoghisoni.com.

To **Puerto Natales**, 3-3½ hrs, **Fernández**, **Bus Sur** and **Pacheco**, up to 8 daily, last departure 2100, US$8.50, look out for special offers and connections to Torres del Paine. Buses may pick up at the airport with advance booking and payment. To **Otway Sound**, with **Fernández** daily 1500, return 1900, US$9.

To **Tierra del Fuego** via Punta Delgada (see Essential Tierra del Fuego, page 439; no buses via Porvenir) **Pacheco**, **Sur**, **Tecni-Austral**, **Pullman** and others (check with companies for schedules); to **Río Grande** Mon-Fri 0900, 8 hrs, US$28, heavily booked; to **Ushuaia**, 12 hrs, US$42-50; some services have to change in Río Grande for Ushuaia, others are direct; book well in advance in Jan-Feb.

To **Río Gallegos** (Argentina), via Route 255, **Pacheco**, Sun, Mon, Tue, Fri; **Barria/Ghisoni** (www.busesbarria.com), Mon, Wed, Thu, Fri, Sat, Sun, **Bus Sur** Mon, Wed, Thu, Fri, Sat; fares US$20, 5-8 hrs, depending on customs: 15 mins on Chilean side, up to 2 hrs on Argentine side (see also box, page 417).

To **Puerto Montt** with **Bus Sur** and **Pullman**, Mon, Wed, Fri, 0800 US$63, 34 hrs, also **Osorno**, US$63, 30 hrs.

## Car hire

Note that you need a hire company's authorization to take a car into Argentina. This takes 24 hrs (not Sat or Sun) and involves mandatory international insurance for US$100, plus notary fees. In addition to the multinationals, there are some local companies: **EMSA**, Kuzma Slavic 706, T61-261 4378, www.emsarentacar.cl; **Payne**, Menéndez 631, T61-224 0852, www.payne.cl, also tours, treks, birdwatching, etc.

## Ferry and cruise services
**To Tierra del Fuego** The ferry dock is 5 km north of Punta Arenas centre, at Tres Puentes. For all ferry services to the island, see box, page 439.

To **Puerto Montt** Contact **Navimag**, Navarro 1225, 1st floor, T61-220 0200, www.navimag.com. For **Australis**, see box, page 412.

To **Antarctica** Most cruise ships leave from Ushuaia, but a few operators are based in Punta Arenas. Try **Adventure Network International** (see above) or **Antarctica XXI**, O'Higgins 1170, T61-261 4100, www.antarcticaxxi.com, for flight/cruise packages. See also Santiago Tour operators, page 246. Otherwise, another possibility is with the Chilean Navy vessels *Galvarino* and *Lautaro* (around US$50, 1 month; enquire at the Tercera Zona Naval, Lautaro 1150, T61-220 5599), which sail regularly (no schedule; see www.armada.cl). Note that the navy does not encourage passengers, so you must approach the captain direct. Present yourself as a professional or student as opposed to a tourist. Spanish is essential.

## Taxi
Ordinary taxis have yellow roofs. *Colectivos* (all black) run on fixed routes and pick up from taxi stands around town, US$0.50 flat fee.

## Reserva Forestal Laguna Parrillar

About 25 km south of Punta Arenas, there is a fork in the road to the right; 21 km further on is the very peaceful Parrillar reserve, covering 18,814 ha and surrounded by snow-capped hills. It has older forest than the Magallanes Reserve and sphagnum bogs, and offers excellent salmon and trout fishing. There is a three-hour walk to the treeline (and others along poorly marked, boggy paths) and fine views from the mirador. There are CONAF-administered campsites and picnic sites. Note that there is no public transport to the reserve and hitching is virtually impossible; a radio taxi will cost about US$55.

## Fuerte Bulnes and further south

Some 56 km south of Punta Arenas, **Fuerte Bulnes** ⓘ *US$17, US$8.50 children*, is a replica of the wooden fort erected in 1843 by the crew of the Chilean vessel *Ancud*. Built in the 1940s and originally designed to house a museum, nearly all the interesting exhibits and artefacts were moved to museums in Punta Arenas and Santiago in 1986 and now only the empty shells of the various buildings remain. Several agencies run half-day tours to here, but hitching is not difficult at weekends or in summer, as there are many holiday camps in the area.

Nearby is **Puerto Hambre**, where there are ruins of the church built by Sarmiento de Gamboa's colonists in 1584 (see box, page 416). The views towards the towering ice mountains near Pico Sarmiento cut an impressive scene; it was of Puerto Hambre that Darwin wrote: "looking due southward … the distant channels between the mountains appeared from their gloominess to lead beyond the confines of this world". Southern dolphins can often be seen in the straits around this point.

At the intersection of the roads to Puerto Hambre and Fuerte Bulnes, 51 km south of Punta Arenas, is a small monolith marking the **Centro Geográfico de Chile**, the midway point between Arica and the South Pole. Bypassing Fuerte Bulnes, the road continues past a memorial to Captain Pringle Stokes, Captain of the *Beagle*, who committed suicide here in 1829, being replaced as captain by Fitz Roy. The road carries on, past San Juan to the lighthouse at San Isidro. The last part of this journey can only be done in summer in a high-clearance vehicle and at low tide, as it involves crossing an estuary at the mouth of the Río San Pedro. Alternatively, leave your vehicle on the north side of the estuary, ford the river (at low tide) and walk 2½ hours to San Isidro. From here, it is a day hike to **Cape Froward**, the southernmost point of the continent of South America, marked by a 24-m-high cross. There is no path, and a guide is essential (this can be arranged by the hostería at San Isidro with advance notice).

Some 70 km west of Cape Froward along the Magellan Straits is *Isla Carlos III*, a popular base for humpback whale watching.

## North of Punta Arenas

Some 70 km north of Punta Arenas, ★ **Seno Otway** ⓘ *Oct to mid-Mar, US$10.50*, is the site of a colony of thousands of Magellanic penguins that can be viewed from walkways and bird hides; rheas, skunks and foxes can also be seen. There are beautiful views across the sound to the mountains to

**Tip...**
It is best to go to Seno Otway early in the day. Try to avoid going at the same time as the large cruise ship tours; it is not much fun having to wait behind 200 people for your turn at the viewing stations.

## ON THE ROAD

## Port Famine (Puerto Hambre)

In 1582, Felipe II of Spain, alarmed by Drake's passage through the Straits of Magellan, decided to establish a Spanish presence on the Straits. A fleet of 15 ships and 4000 men, commanded by Pedro Sarmiento de Gamboa, was despatched in 1584. Before the ships had left the Bay of Biscay, a storm arose and scattered the fleet, sinking seven ships and killing 800 people. Further depleted by disease, the fleet of three remaining ships at length arrived at the Straits, with just 300 men on board. Led by Sarmiento this small force founded two cities: Nombre de Jesús on Punta Dungeness at the eastern entrance to the Straits and Rey Don Felipe near Puerto Hambre.

Disaster struck when their only remaining vessel broke its anchorage in a storm near Nombre de Jesús; the ship, with Sarmiento on board, was blown into the Atlantic, leaving many of Sarmiento's men stranded on land. After vain attempts to re-enter the Straits, Sarmiento set sail for Río de Janeiro where he organized two rescue missions: the first ended in shipwreck, the second in mutiny. Captured by English corsairs, Sarmiento was taken to England where he was imprisoned. On his release by Elizabeth I, he tried to return to Spain via France, but was jailed again. Until his death in 1608, Sarmiento besieged Felipe II with letters urging him to rescue the men stranded in the Straits.

When the English corsair Thomas Cavendish sailed through the Straits in 1587 he found only 18 survivors at Rey Don Felipe. With the English and Spanish at war, only one – Tomé Hernández – would trust Cavendish when he first arrived. A sudden spell of fine weather arose, and Cavendish set sail, leaving the rest of the men to die. He named the place Port Famine as a reminder of their grisly fate.

the north, and it is also becoming a popular area for sea kayaking and other adventure sports. Several agencies offer trips to the colony lasting five hours (US$14 plus entry fees at peak season); if you wish to visit independently, a taxi from Punta Arenas will cost US$80 return or there are daily buses with Fernández. Access to the colony is via a private road where a toll of US$2 per person is charged.

A small island, 30 km northeast, **Isla Magdalena** is the location of the **Monumento Natural Los Pingüinos** ① *US$7, free for children*, a colony of 80,000 pairs of Megallanic penguins, administered by CONAF. Deserted apart from during the breeding season from November to early February, Magdalena is one of a group of three islands visited by Drake (the others are Marta and Isabel), whose men killed 3000 penguins for food. Boat trips to the island are run by **Comapa** and **Solo Expediciones**, while the **Australis** cruise ships also call here (see box, page 412). Take a hat, coat and gloves.

Beyond, Route 255 heads northeast towards the Argentine border (see box, opposite), passing **Kamiri Aike** where a road branches southeast towards Punta Delgada for ferries to Tierra del Fuego (see box, page 439).

There is also a turn-off north along a *ripio* road for 26 km to **Parque Nacional Pali Aike** ① *managed by CONAF, T61-223 8554, magallanes.oirs@conaf.cl, US$1.50; children free*, a fantastic volcanic landscape dotted with small cones and craters. It's one of the oldest archaeological sites in Patagonia, with evidence of aboriginal occupation from 10,000-12,000 years ago. (Pali Aike means 'desolate place of bad spirits' in Tehuelche.) There are five easy, marked trails, all of which can be done in a day. Tour operators offer full-day trips, US$47.

## BORDER CROSSING
### Chile–Argentina

**Integración Austral**

The border is located 30 km north of Kamiri Aike via Route 255 (190 km from Punta Arenas) and is open daily 24 hours in summer and 0900-2300 from 1 April to 3 October. On the Argentine side the road continues as Route 3 for 67 km northeast to Río Gallegos. For bus passengers the border crossing is easy, although you have about a 30-minute wait at each border post as luggage is checked and documents are stamped. Hire cars from Argentina need special documents in order to cross the border. For more information see www.gendarmeria.gob.ar/pasos-chile/integracion-austral.html.

**Listings** Around Punta Arenas

### Where to stay

**Fuerte Bulnes and further south**

**$$$$ Hostería Faro San Isidro**
*75 km south of Punta Arenas, booking office Lautaro Navarro 1163, Punta Arenas, T9-934 93862, www.hosteriafarosanisidro.cl.*

The southernmost lodging on the American continent and within striking distance of Cape Froward. Trips offered.

# Puerto Natales
## & around

From Punta Arenas, a good paved road runs 247 km north to Puerto Natales through forests of southern beech and prime pastureland; this is the best area for cattle- and sheep-raising in Chile. Ñandúes and guanacos can often be seen en route. Puerto Natales lies between Cerro Dorotea (which rises behind the town) and the eastern shore of the Seno Ultima Esperanza (Last Hope Sound), over which there are fine views, weather permitting, to the Península Antonio Varas and the jagged peaks and receding glaciers of the Parque Nacional Bernardo O'Higgins beyond.

Founded in 1911, the town grew as an industrial centre and, until recent years, the town's prosperity was based upon employment in the coal mines of Río Turbio, Argentina. Today, Puerto Natales is the starting point for trips to the magnificent O'Higgins and Torres del Paine national parks, and tourism is one of its most important industries; the town centre has a prosperous if somewhat touristy atmosphere.

# Essential Puerto Natales

## Finding your feet

The **Aerodromo Teniente Julio Gallardo** is 7 km north of town. All buses use the bus terminal 20 minutes outside town at Avenida España 1455. *Colectivos* to/from the centre cost US$0.55 (US$0.65 at night and Sun); taxis charge a flat fee of US$1.75 (US$2 at night and Sun) throughout Puerto Natales.

## Getting around

Puerto Natales itself is small, so taxis are only needed for journeys out of town. For further details, see Transport, page 424.

### Tip...

If driving between Punta Arenas and Puerto Natales, make sure you have enough fuel.

**Puerto Natales**

To ㉑ ㉓ ㉔, Punta Arenas & Parque Nacional Torres del Paine

Seno Ultima Esperanza

Estero Natales

**Pier for Balmaceda Glacier**

**Pier for Puerto Montt**

Plaza de Armas

Museo Municipal

To Bus Terminal & ⑩

To ㉒

Bus Sur

200 metres
200 yards

### Where to stay
1 Aquaterra *C2*
4 Casa Cecilia *B2*
6 Costaustralis *C1*
7 Hosp Casa Lili *B1*
8 Hosp Nancy *C3*
9 Hostal Amerindia *B1*
10 Hostal La Estancia Patagónica *B3*
11 Hostal Sir Francis Drake *A2*
12 Hostel Natales *B1*
13 Indigo Patagonia *B1*
14 Josmar 2 Camping *C2*
15 Keoken *B1*
16 Lili Patagónico's *C3*
17 Martín Gusinde *B2*
20 Patagonia Adventure *B2*
21 Remota *A2*
22 The Singing Lamb *C3*
23 The Singular *A2*
24 Weskar Patagonian Lodge *A2*

### Restaurants
1 Afrigonia *B2*
3 Angelica's *B2*
4 Cormorán de las Rocas *A2*
5 El Asador Patagónico *B2*
6 El Living *B2*
7 La Mesita Grande *B2*
8 La Picada de Carlitos *C3*
9 Parrilla Don Jorge *B2*
10 Patagonia Dulce *B1*
11 Ultima Esperanza *B2*

### Bars & clubs
12 Baguales Brewery *B2*
13 Pampa Restobar *C2*
14 Por que No Te Callas *B2*

**Puerto Natales** *Colour map 3, A2.*

In Puerto Natales (population 19,000) the **Museo Histórico Municipal** ⓘ *Bulnes 285, T61-241 1263, Nov-Apr, Mon-Fri 0800-1900, May-Oct, 0800-1700, Sat-Sun 1000-1300 and 1500-1900, US$2,* houses a small collection of archaeological and native artefacts as well as exhibits on late 19th-century European colonization, with reasonable descriptions in English.

The colourful old steam train in the main square was once used to take workers to the **meat-packing factory** ⓘ *daily 0930-1300 and 1500-1830, US$7, 45 mins,* at **Puerto Bories**, 5 km north of town. It is a pleasant hour-long walk along the shore to Bories with glimpses of the Balmaceda Glacier across the sound. In its heyday the plant was the biggest of its kind in Chile with a capacity for 250,000 sheep. Bankrupted in the early 1990s, much of the plant was dismantled in 1993. Belatedly the plant was given National Monument status and in 2013 it was restored. The remaining buildings and machine rooms can be visited. It's also the site of **The Singular Hotel** (see Where to stay, below).

The slab-like **Cerro Dorotea** dominates the town, with superb views of the whole Seno Ultima Esperanza. It can be reached on foot or by any Río Turbio bus or taxi (recommended, as the hill is further away than it seems). The trail entrance is marked by a sign that reads 'Mirador Cerro Dorotea'. Expect to be charged US$7 in one of the local houses. It is a 1½-hour trek up to the 600-m lookout along a well-marked trail. In theory you can continue along the top of the hill to get better views to the north, but the incredibly strong winds often make this dangerous.

## Listings Puerto Natales *map page 419.*

## Tourist information

### CONAF
*Baquedano 847, T61-241 1438, patricio.salinas@conaf.cl.*
For information on national parks and other protected areas.

### Municipal tourist office
*At the bus station, Av España 1455. Open all year 0600-1200.*

### Sernatur office
*On the waterfront, Av Pedro Montt 19, T61-241 2125, infonatales@sernatur.cl. Oct-Mar Mon-Fri 0830-2000, Sat-Sun 0900-1300 and 1500-1800, Apr-Sep Mon-Fri 0830-1800, Sat 1000-1600.*
Good leaflets in English on Puerto Natales and Torres del Paine, as well as bus and boat information.

## Where to stay

In season cheaper accommodation fills up quickly. Hotels in the countryside are often open only in the summer months. Good deals in upper-range hotels may be available, out of season especially, when prices may be 50% lower.

### $$$$ Costaustralis
*Pedro Montt 262, T61-241 2000, www.hoteles-australis.com.*
Very comfortable, tranquil, lovely views (but not from inland-facing rooms), lift, English spoken, waterfront restaurant **Paine** serves international and local seafood.

### $$$$ Indigo Patagonia
*Ladrilleros 105, T2-2432 6800, www.indigopatagonia.cl.*
Relaxed atmosphere, on the water front, great views, a boutique hotel with rooftop spa, rooms and suites, café/restaurant serves good seafood and vegetarian dishes. Tours organized.

#### $$$$ Remota
*Ruta 9 Norte, Km 1.5, Huerto 279,*
*T61-241 4040, www.remota.cl.*
Modernist design with big windows, lots of trips, activities and treks offered, spa, all-inclusive packages, good food, first-class.

#### $$$$ The Singular
*Km 5 Norte, Puerto Bories, T61-272 2030,*
*www.thesingular.com.*
Luxury hotel in converted warehouses a short distance from the town centre, in a scenic spot overlooking the Ultima Esperanza Sound. Spa, gourmet restaurant and varied trips offered.

#### $$$$-$$$ Martín Gusinde
*Bories 278, T61-271 2100, www.*
*hotelmartingusinde.com.*
Modern 3-star standard, smart, parking, laundry service, excursions organized.

#### $$$$-$$$ Weskar Patagonian Lodge
*Ruta 9, Km 05, T61-241 4168, www.weskar.cl.*
Quiet lodge overlooking the fjord, standard or deluxe rooms with good views, 3-course dinners served, lunch boxes prepared for excursions, many activities offered, helpful.

#### $$$ Aquaterra
*Bulnes 299, T61-241 2239,*
*www.aquaterrapatagonia.com.*
Good restaurant with vegetarian options, 'resto-bar' downstairs, spa, warm and comfortable but not cheap, very helpful staff. Trips and tours.

#### $$$ Hostal Sir Francis Drake
*Phillipi 383, T61-241 1553,*
*www.hostalfrancisdrake.com.*
Calm and welcoming, tastefully decorated, smallish rooms, good views.

#### $$$ Keoken
*Señoret 267, T61-241 3670,*
*www.keokenpatagonia.com.*
Cosy, upmarket B&B, spacious living room, some rooms with views. All rooms have bathroom but not all are en suite, English spoken, helpful staff, tours.

#### $$$-$$ Hostel Natales
*Ladrilleros 209, T61-241 4731,*
*www.hostelnatales.cl.*
Private rooms or dorms in this high-end hostel, comfortable, minibar and lockboxes.

#### $$ Casa Cecilia
*Tomás Rogers 60, T61-241 2698,*
*www.casaceciliahostal.com.*
Welcoming, popular, with small simple rooms, private or shared bath. English, French and German spoken, rents camping and trekking gear, tour agency and information for Torres del Paine.

#### $$ Hospedaje Nancy
*Ramírez 540, T61-241 0022,*
*www.natieslodge.cl.*
Warm and hospitable, information, tours, equipment rental.

#### $$ Lili Patagónico's
*Prat 479, T61-241 4063,*
*www.lilipatagonicos.com.*
$ pp in dorms. Small but pleasant heated rooms, helpful staff. Lots of information, good-quality equipment rented. Tours offered. Indoor climbing wall.

#### $$ Patagonia Adventure
*Tomás Rogers 179, T61-241 1028,*
*www.apatagonia.com.*
Lovely old house, bohemian feel, shared bath, $ pp in dorms, equipment hire, bike and kayak tours and tour arrangements for Torres del Paine.

#### $$-$ Hostel Amerindia
*Arana 135, T61-241 1945,*
*www.hostelamerindia.com.*
Central option near restaurants as well as the plaza. Dorms and private rooms. Breakfast included and served in the popular café, which also serves sundry and artisanal products.

#### $$-$ pp The Singing Lamb
*Arauco 779, T61-241 0958,*
*www.thesinginglamb.com.*
Very hospitable New Zealand-run backpackers, dorm accommodation

only but no bunks. Home-from-home feel. Good information.

## $ Hospedaje Casa Lili
*Bories153, T61-241 4039, lilipatagonia@gmail.com.*
Dorms or private rooms, small, family-run, rents equipment and can arrange tickets to Paine. Free bag storage.

## $ Hostal La Estancia Patagónica
*Juan MacLean 567, T9-9224 8601, hostallaestanciapatagonica@gmail.com.*
Friendly, family-run *hostal* near the bus terminal. Private rooms (**$$**) and 4-bed dorms. Breakfast included. Thin walls, great showers.

## Camping

### Josmar 2
*McLean 367, T61-241 1685, www.josmar.cl.*
Family-run, convenient, hot showers, parking, barbecues, electricity, café, tent site (US$9.50) or shared room (US$9.50).

### Vaiora
*Kruger 233, T61-241 1737, see Facebook.*
Camping and *hospedaje* option in centre. US11, $ per night.

## Restaurants

### $$$ Afrigonia
*Eberhard 343, T61-241 2877.*
An unexpected mixture of Patagonia meets East Africa in this Kenyan/Chilean-owned fusion restaurant, considered by many to be the best, and certainly the most innovative, in town.

### $$$ Angelica's
*Bulnes 501, T61-241 0007.*
Elegant Mediterranean style, well-prepared pricey food with quality ingredients.

### $$$-$$ Cormorán de las Rocas
*Miguel Sánchez 72, T61-261 5131-2, www.cormorandelasrocas.com.*

Patagonian specialities with an innovative twist, wide variety of well-prepared dishes, pisco sours, good service and attention to detail, incomparable views.

### $$$-$$ El Asador Patagónico
*Prat 158 on the Plaza, T61-241 3553, www.elasadorpatagonico.cl.*
Spit-roast lamb, salads, home-made puddings.

### $$$-$$ Parrilla Don Jorge
*Bories 430, on Plaza, T61-241 0999, reservas@parrilladonjorge.cl.*
Also specializes in spit-roast lamb, but serves fish too, good service.

### $$ La Mesita Grande
*Prat 196 on the Plaza, T61-241 1571, www.mesitagrande.cl.*
Fresh pizzas from the wood-burning oven, also pasta and desserts. Poor service but good food. Wildly popular.

### $$ Ultima Esperanza
*Eberhard 354, T61-241 1391, www.restaurantuesperanza.galeon.com.*
One of the town's classic seafood restaurants.

### $$-$ El Living
*Prat 156, Plaza de Armas, www.el-living.com. Mon-Sat in high season.*
Comfy sofas, good tea, magazines in all languages, book exchange, good music, delicious vegetarian food, British-run, popular, Wi-Fi. Recommended.

### $$-$ La Picada de Carlitos
*Esmeralda and Encalada, T61-241 4885, Blanco Encalada y Esmeralda.*
Good, cheap traditional Chilean food, popular with locals at lunchtime, when service can be slow.

### $ Artimaña
*Bories 349, T61-241 4856, see Facebook.*
Newer café/restaurant offering fresh salads, sandwiches, juices and desserts. Bright, intimate surroundings; Wi-Fi.

## Cafés

### Amerindia
*See Hostal Amerindia in Where to stay, above.*
Located in a hostel and recommended for coffee and hot chocolate. Fun vibe; also sells artisan sundry and baked goods.

### Patagonia Dulce
*Barros Arana 233, T61-241 5285.*
*Tue-Sun 1400-2100.*
For the best hot chocolate in town, good coffee and chocolates.

## Bars and clubs

### Baguales Brewery
*Bories 430, on the plaza,*
*www.cervezabaguales.cl.*
Sep-Mar Mon-Sat 1300-0200. Pub with microbrewery attached. Also serves hamburgers and other snacks. Great lunch specials.

### Pampa Resto Bar
*Bulnes 371, T95-32236, see Facebook.*
Fun vibe with live music on Tue nights. Good spot for meeting both travellers and locals. In high season expect to pay premium prices for what is merely decent bar food.

### Por Qué No Te Callas
*Magallanes 247, T61-241 4942.*
Neighbourhood bar with beer, pizza and Chilean favourites like *chorillana* on the menu. Live music various nights.

## Shopping

**Casa Cecilia**, **Lili Patagónico's**, **Sendero Aventura** and **Erratic Rock** (see Where to stay, above, and What to do, below) all hire out camping equipment (deposit required). Always check the equipment and the prices carefully. Camping gas is widely available in hardware stores. There are several supermarkets in town and the town markets are also good.

## What to do

It is better to book tours direct with operators in Puerto Natales than through agents in Punta Arenas or Santiago. There are many agencies along Arturo Prat. Several offer single-day tours to the Perito Moreno glacier in Argentina, US$70-80 for a 14-hr trip, including 2 hrs at the glacier, excluding food or park entry fee; reserve 1 day in advance. You can then leave the tour in Calafate to continue your travels in Argentina.

**Baguales Group**, *Encalada 353, T9-5168 8447, www.bagualesgroup.com.* Specialists in the route from Torres del Paine back to Puerto Natales. Tailor made multi-activity tours that can incorporate zodiacs, horse riding, kayaking and trekking, mostly off the beaten track.

**Blue Green Adventures**, *Galavarino 618, T61-241 1800, www.bluegreenadventures.com.* Adventure tour specialist and travel agent, with trekking, riding, kayaking, fishing and multi-activity options, estancia, whale watching, wine and yoga programmes. Also caters for families.

**Chile Nativo Travel**, *Eberhard 230, T2-2717 5961, T1-800 649 8776 (toll-free in US and Canada), www.chilenativo.travel.* Specializes in 'W' trek, Paine circuit trek, horse riding, multi-sport options and tailor-made tours.

**Comapa**, *Bulnes 541, T61-241 4300, www. comapa.com.* Large regional operator offering decent day tours to Torres del Paine.

**Erratic Rock**, *Baquedano 719 and Zamora 732, T61-241 4317, www.erraticrock.com.* Trekking experts offering interesting expeditions from half a day to 2 weeks. Also hostel (walk-ins only), good-quality equipment hire and daily trekking seminar at 1500.

**Estancia Travel**, *Casa 13-b, Puerto Boris, T61-241 2221, www.estanciatravel.com.* Based at the Estancia Puerto Consuelo, 5 km north of Puerto Natales, offers horse-riding trips from 1 to 12 days around southern Patagonia and Torres del Paine, with accommodation at traditional estancias. Also kayaking trips, British/Chilean-run, bilingual, professional guides, at the top of the price range.

**Kayak in Patagonia**, *Rogers 235, T61-261 3395, www.kayakenpatagonia.com*. Specializes in half-day, full-day and multi-day kayaking trips around Cisne Bay and the Serrano and Gray rivers. Also runs **Hello Patagonia**.

**Punta Alta**, *Blanco Encalada 244, T61-241 0115, www.puntaalta.cl*. Sailings in a fast boat to the Balmaceda glacier and the possibility to continue by zodiac to Pueblito Serrano at the southern edge of Torres del Paine national park (from US$180 one way). You can return to Natales on the same day by minibus along the southern access road, thus avoiding Torres del Paine entry fees. Also offers car hire.

**Sendero Aventura**, *T9-6171 3080, www.senderoaventura.com*. Adventure tours by land rover, bike or kayak.

**Skorpios Cruises**, *Augusto Leguía Norte 118, Santiago, T2-2477 1900 (and the the terminal in Puerto Bories) www.skorpios.cl*. The *Skorpios 3* sails from Puerto Natales to Glaciar Amalia and Fiordo Calvo in the Campo de Hielo Sur, 4 days, fares from US$1400 pp, double cabin. An optional first day includes a visit to Torres del Paine or the Cueva del Milodón. No office in Puerto Natales; book online or through an agency.

**Turismo 21 de Mayo**, *Eberhard 560, T61-614420, www.turismo21demayo.com*. Sailings to the Balmaceda glacier and the possibility to continue by zodiac to Pueblito Serrano at the southern edge of Torres del Paine national park (from US$144 one way from Puerto Natales, includes lunch).

## Transport

**Air** Starting in 2017 **LAN** and **Sky** will operate direct flights to **Santiago** all year. There are also charter services from **Punta Arenas** and onward connections to Argentina with **Aerovías DAP**. Other airlines use Punta Arenas airport, see page 404.

**Bicycle repairs** El Rey de la Bicicleta, Galvarino 544, T61-241 1905. Good, helpful.

**Bus** In summer book ahead. All buses leave from the bus terminal 20 mins outside town at Av España 1455, but tickets can be bought at the individual company offices in town: **Bus Fernández**, E Ramírez 399, T61-241 1111, www.busesfernandez.com; **Pacheco**, only in the terminal, T61-241 4800, www.busespacheco.com; **Bus Sur**, Baquedano 668, T61-241 0784, www.bussur.com; **Zaahj**, Prat 236, T61-241 2260, www.turismozaahj.co.cl. For transport from the bus terminal, see box, page 419.

To **Punta Arenas**, several daily, 3-3½ hrs, US$7-9, with **Fernández**, **Pacheco**, **Bus Sur** and others. In theory buses from Punta Arenas to Puerto Natales will also pick passengers up at Punta Arenas airport (US$8) as long as reservations and payment have been made in advance through **Buses Pacheco** (T61-241 4800); in practice, though, they are often unreliable.

For buses to **Torres del Paine**, see page 435.

**To Argentina** To **Río Gallegos** direct, with **Bus Sur**, 2-3 weekly each, US$28, 4-5 hrs. To **Río Turbio**, hourly with **Cootra**, Pacheco and others, US$8, 2 hrs (depending on customs at Paso Dorotea; change bus at border; see box, opposite). To **El Calafate** daily 0830 and 1800, US$20, with **Cootra** daily, 5 hrs; or with **Zaahj**, daily 0700-1630, 5 hrs; otherwise travel agencies run several times a week depending on demand (see above). To **Ushuaia**, with **Bus Sur**, Oct-Apr Mon, Wed, Fri Sat at 0700, 13 hrs, US$56.

To **Ushuaia** with **Pacheco**, Tue, Thu, Sun direct at 0730, US$55 15 hrs. Note that buses from Argentina invariably arrive late.

**Car hire** Hire agents can arrange permission to drive into **Argentina**; it takes 24 hrs to arrange and extra insurance is required. Try **EMSA**, Arana 118, T61-261 4388, www.emsarentacar.com, or **Punta Alta**, Blanco Encalada 244, T61-241 0115, www.puntaalta.cl.

**Ferry** The town is the terminus of the *Navimag* ship to Puerto Montt. **Navimag**, in the bus terminal, T61-241 1421, www.navimag.com, runs ferries to/from **Puerto Montt**; for details, see page 330.

# BORDER CROSSING
## Chile–Argentina

There are three crossing points east of Puerto Natales. For further information, see www. pasosfronterizos.gov.cl and www.gendarmeria.gov.ar, which gives details of all three crossings in its Santa Cruz section. Information on these sites is generally up to date.

### Paso Casas Viejas/Laurita
This crossing, 16 km east of Puerto Natales, is reached by turning off Route 9 (towards Punta Arenas) at Km 14. For the Argentine side see box, page 225.

### Paso Dorotea/Mina Uno
This crossing is reached by branching off Route 9 (towards Punta Arenas) 9 km east of Puerto Natales and continuing north for a further 11 km. For the Argentine side see box, page 225.

### Paso Río Cerro Castillo/Paso Río Don Guillermo
**Chilean immigration** is 7 km west of the border in the small settlement of Cerro Castillo, which lies 65 km north of Puerto Natales on the road to Torres del Paine. Cerro Castillo is well-equipped with toilets, ATM, tourist information, souvenir shop, several *cafeterías* and *hospedajes*, including $ pp Hospedaje Mate Amargo, Santiago Bueras, s/n, T9-536 1966, which offers rooms for four, Wi-Fi and luggage storage. There's sheep shearing in December, and a rodeo and rural festival in January. For **Argentine immigration** at Cancha Carrera, a few kilometres east of the border, where there are few facilities; see box, page 225. All buses between Puerto Natales and El Calafate go via Cerro Castillo, making it the most convenient route for visiting the Parque Nacional Los Glaciares from Chile. Travelling into Chile, it is possible to stop in Cerro Castillo and transfer to a bus passing from Puerto Natales to Torres del Paine.

## Around Puerto Natales  *Colour map 3, A2.*
### prehistoric relics, windswept landscapes and the best trekking in the world

### Monumento Nacional Cueva Milodón
*25 km north, in high season daily 0800-1900 (0830-1800 in low season), www. cuevadelmilodon.cl. US$5.50 (US$2.75 in low season), getting there: regular bus from Prat 297, T61-241 5891 (Huellas del Milodón), leaves 0900, 1500, returns 1300 and 1900, US$21 (includes guide); taxi US$27 return, 20 mins each way; the taxi driver waits 1 hr.*

This is the end point of Bruce Chatwin's travelogue *In Patagonia*. The cave, a massive 70 m wide, 220 m deep and 30 m high, contains a plastic model of the prehistoric ground sloth whose remains were found there in 1895. The remains are now in London. Evidence has also been found here of occupation by Patagonians some 11,000 years ago. Nearby, a visitor centre has summaries in English. There's also a handicraft shop.

## ★ Parque Nacional Bernardo O'Higgins

*US$7, only accessible by boat from Puerto Natales summer daily 0800, returning 1730 (Sun only in winter), US$100-130, minimum 10 passengers, heavily booked in high season; book through a tour operator, see page 423.*

Often referred to as the **Parque Nacional Monte Balmaceda**, this park covers much of the Campo de Hielo Sur, plus the fjords and offshore islands further west. A three-hour boat trip from Puerto Natales up the Seno de Ultima Esperanza takes you to the southernmost section, passing the Balmaceda Glacier, which drops from the eastern slopes of **Monte Balmaceda** (2035 m). The glacier is retreating; in 1986 its foot was at sea level. The boat docks further north at **Puerto Toro**, from where it is 1-km walk to the base of the Serrano Glacier on the north slope of Monte Balmaceda. On the trip, dolphins, sea lions (in season), black-necked swans, flightless steamer ducks and cormorants can often be seen. Take warm clothes, including a hat and gloves.

There is a route from Puerto Toro on the eastern side of the Río Serrano for 35 km to the Torres del Paine administration office (see page 428); guided tours are available on foot or on horseback. It is also possible to continue to the southern edge of Torres del Paine by boat or zodiac. For further details, see What to do, page 423.

## Listings Around Puerto Natales

### Where to stay

**$$$$ Hostería Monte Balmaceda**
*Parque Nacional Bernardo O'Higgins; contact Turismo 21 de Mayo (see Puerto Natales Tour operators, above).*
Although the park is uninhabited, guest accommodation is available in the southern section by the mouth of the Serrano river.

**$$$$-$$$ Estancia Tres Pasos**
*40 km north of town, T9-9644 5862, www.hotel3pasos.cl.*

Simple and beautiful lodge between Puerto Natales and Torres del Paine. Horse-riding trips offered.

**$$$ Cabañas Kotenk Aike**
*2 km north of town, T61-241 2581, www.kotenkaike.cl.*
Sleeps 4, modern, very comfortable, great location.

**$$$ Hostería Llanuras de Diana**
*Ruta 9, Km 215 (30 km south of Puerto Natales), T61-241 0661.*
Hidden from road, beautifully situated. Recommended.

# Parque Nacional
## Torres del Paine

⭐ Covering 242,242 ha, 145 km northwest of Puerto Natales, this national park is a UNESCO Biosphere Reserve and a trekker's mecca for its diverse wildlife and spectacular surroundings. Taking its name from the Tehuelche word 'Paine', meaning 'blue', the park encompasses stunning scenery, with constantly changing views of peaks, glaciers and icebergs, vividly coloured lakes of turquoise, ultramarine and grey, and quiet green valleys filled with wild flowers. In the centre of the park is one of the most impressive mountain areas on earth, a granite massif from which rise oddly shaped peaks of over 2600 m, known as the 'Torres' (towers) and 'Cuernos' (horns) of Paine.

## Landscape and wildlife   Colour map 3, A2.
### volcanic peaks, expansive ice fields and rugged terrain

There are 15 peaks above 2000 m, of which the highest is Cerro Paine Grande (3050 m). Few places can compare to its steep, forested talus slopes topped by 1000-m vertical shafts of basalt with conical caps; these are the remains of frozen magma in ancient volcanic throats, everything else having been eroded. On the western edge of the park is the enormous Campo de Hielo Sur icefield. Four main *ventisqueros* (glaciers) – Grey, Dickson, Zapata and Tyndall – branch off it, their meltwater forming a complex series of lakes and streams, which lead into fjords extending to the sea. Two other glaciers, Francés and Los Perros, descend on the western side of the central massif.

A microclimate exists that is especially favourable to plants and wildlife. Over 200 species of plant have been identified and, although few trees reach great size, several valleys are thickly forested and little light penetrates. The grassland here is distinct from the monotony of the pampa and dispersed sclerophyll forest. Some 105 species of bird call the park home, including 18 species of waterfowl and 11 birds of prey. Particularly noteworthy

# Essential Parque Nacional Torres del Paine

## Access

The most practical way to get to Torres del Paine is with one of the many bus or tour companies that leave Puerto Natales daily. Hiring a pickup truck is another option. There are two *ripio* roads to the park from Puerto Natales. The old road goes via Cerro Castillo and Lago Sarmiento, entering the park at Laguna Amarga and continuing through the park to the **administration office** on Lago del Toro, 147 km northwest of Puerto Natales (3½ hours); this is the route taken by public buses. The other road, 85 km, links Natales to the south side of the park via the Pueblito Serrano. While it is a more direct route – total journey time to the administration is around 1½ hours – the road is narrow with lots of blind corners and sudden gusts of wind and can be rough in patches. An alternative way to access the park is on a three-hour zodiac trip up the Río Serrano from Parque Nacional Bernardo O'Higgins, see page 426.

There are entrances at Laguna Azul in the northeast, Laguna Amarga and Lago Sarmiento in the east and at the Puente Serrano in the south. See also Transport, page 435.

## Entry fees

Park entrance fees are US$25 (low season US$21) for foreigners, payable in Chilean pesos, euros and dollars; only pesos in low season. You are also required to register and show your passport when entering the park, since rangers (*guardaparques*) keep a check on the whereabouts of all visitors. If you are based outside the park and plan on entering and leaving several times, explain this to the rangers in order to be given a multiple-entry stamp valid for three consecutive days.

## Getting around

The park is well set up for tourism, with frequent bus services from Puerto Natales running through the park to pick up and drop off walkers at various hotels and trailheads and to connect with boat trips (see Transport, page 435). In season there are also boats and minibus connections within the park itself: from Laguna Amarga to **Hotel Las Torres**, US$4, and from the administration centre to **Hostería Lago Grey**, US$14. Other than these routes, getting around the park without your own transport is difficult and expensive. When public services are reduced, travel agencies run buses subject to demand; arrange your return date with the driver and try to coincide with other groups to keep costs down.

## When to go

Do not underestimate the severity of the weather here. The park is open all year round, although snow may prevent access to some areas in the winter. The warmest time is December to March, but this is when the weather is the most unstable: strong winds often blow off the glaciers, and rainfall can be heavy. The park is most crowded in the summer holiday season January to mid-February, less so in December or March. October and November are recommended for wild flowers. Visiting in winter (April to September) is becoming increasingly popular as, although the temperature is low, there can be stable conditions with little wind, allowing well-equipped hikers to do some good walking. However, some treks may be closed and boats may not be running.

## Time required

Allow a week to 10 days to see the park properly.

### Torres tips

Torres del Paine has become increasingly popular, receiving over 100,000 visitors a year and the impact is showing. Try to ensure your visit does not have a negative effect on this unique landscape. See also Equipment, below.

- The summer months (January and February) should be avoided due to overcrowding. Try to visit in late November/early December or mid-April.
- When trekking, keep to the trails.
- Set out early to catch the sunrise, and to arrive early at the next campsite.
- Stay at less popular campsites.

- Most campsites are riddled with field mice so string up all your food in plastic bags, and hang it from a tree.
- Take all your rubbish out of the park, including toilet paper.
- Forest fires are a serious hazard. Open fires are prohibited throughout the park.

are condors, black-necked swans, kelp geese, ibis, flamingos and austral parakeets. The park is also one of the best places on the continent for viewing rheas and guanacos. Apart from the 3500 guanacos, 24 other species of mammal can be seen here, including hare, fox, skunk, huemul and puma (the last two only very rarely).

### Trekking

for the novice as well as the seasoned pro

There are about 250 km of well-marked trails. Visitors must keep to the trails: cross-country trekking is not permitted. Some paths are confusingly marked and it is all too easy to end up on precipices with glaciers or churning rivers waiting below; be particularly careful to follow the path at the Paso John Gardner on El Circuito (see below). In addition to those mentioned below there are also plenty of shorter walks in the park; see www.torresdelpaine.com for details.

#### Equipment

It is essential to be properly equipped against the cold, wind and rain. A strong, streamlined, waterproof tent is essential if doing El Circuito (although you can hire camping equipment for a single night at the *refugios* on the 'W'). Also essential are protective clothing, strong waterproof footwear, hat, sunscreen, compass, good sleeping bag and sleeping mat. In summer also take shorts. Do not rely on availability of food at the *refugios* within the park; the small shops at the *refugios* (see below) and at the **Posada Río Serrano** are expensive and have a limited selection. You are strongly advised to bring all necessary equipment and your own food from Puerto Natales, although all running water within the park is fine to drink. You are not allowed to make open fires in the park, so take a camping stove but only cook in designated areas. A decent map is provided with your park entrance ticket (also available in the CONAF office); other maps (US$4) are obtainable in many places Puerto Natales but most have one or two mistakes. The map produced by **Patagonia Interactiva** has been recommended as more accurate.

## El Circuito

The park's most emblematic trek is a circuit round the Torres and Cuernos del Paine. Although most people start at the *guardería* at **Laguna Amarga**, it is probably best done anticlockwise starting from Lodge Paine Grande at the western edge of Lago Pehoé.

# Parque Nacional Torres del Paine

**Where to stay** 🏠
1 Ecocamp Patagonia
2 Explora
3 Hostería Mirador del Payne
4 Hostería Pehoé
5 Lago Grey
6 Las Torres
7 Patagonia Camp
8 Tierra Patagonia

**Refugios** 🏠
1 Chileno (Fantástico Sur)
2 Dickson Shelter (Vértice)
3 Grey (Vértice)
4 Las Torres (Fantástico Sur)
5 Los Cuernos
  (Fantástico Sur)
6 Mountain Lodge Paine
  Grande (Vértice)

**Campsites with
facilities** ▲
A Chileno
B Dickson
C Grey
D Las Torres
E Los Perros
F Paine Grande
G Serón
H Serrano

**Basic campamentos** ▲
I Británico
J Italiano
K Japonés
M Las Carretas
N Los Guardas
O Paso
P Pingo
Q Torres
R Zapata

Ranger stations
(guarderías) 🏠

## Safety

It is vital to be aware of the unpredictability of the weather (which can change in a few minutes). Rain and snowfall are heavier the further west you go and bad weather sweeps off the Campo de Hielo Sur without warning. The only means of rescue are on horseback or by boat; the nearest helicopter is in Punta Arenas and high winds usually prevent its operation in the park. Four visitors have died since 2013 due to accidents in the park. Report your route to staff and don't be tempted to stray off the marked trails. Mobile phone coverage is erratic. See also When to go, page 428.

Some walkers advise doing the route clockwise so that you climb to Paso John Gardner with the wind behind you. The route normally takes between seven and 10 days. The circuit is often closed in winter because of snow; major rivers are crossed by footbridges, but these are occasionally washed away.

From Laguna Amarga the route is north along the western side of the Río Paine to **Lago Paine**, before turning west to follow the pastures of the valley of the Río Paine to the southern end of **Lago Dickson** (it is possible to add a journey to the *campamento* by the Torres on day one of this route); the *refugio* at Lago Dickson lies in a breathtaking position in front of the icy white lake with mountains beyond. From Lago Dickson the path runs along the wooded valley of the **Río de los Perros**, past the Glaciar de los Perros, before climbing through bogs and up scree to **Paso John Gardner** (1241 m, the highest point on the route), then dropping steeply through forest to follow the Grey Glacier southeast to **Lago Grey**, continuing to **Lago Pehoé** and the administration centre. There are superb views en route, particularly from the top of Paso John Gardner.

The longest stretch is between Refugio Laguna Amarga and Refugio Dickson (30 km, 10 hours in good weather; there is camping on the way at Serón and a food preparation area at Cairon), but the most difficult section is the very steep, slippery slope from Paso John Gardner down to the Campamento Paso; the path is not well signed at the top of the pass, and some hikers have got dangerously lost. Camping gear must be carried, as many of the campsites do not have *refugios*.

### The 'W'

A more popular alternative to El Circuito, this four- to five-day route can be completed without camping equipment as there is accommodation in *refugios* en route. In summer this route is very crowded and far from being the solitary Patagonian experience many people expect. It combines several of the hikes described separately below. From Refugio Laguna Amarga the first stage runs west via **Hostería Las Torres** and up the valley of the **Río Ascensio** via Refugio Chileno to the base of the **Torres del Paine** (see below). From here return to the **Hostería Las Torres** and then walk along the northern shore of **Lago Nordenskjold** via Refugio Los Cuernos to **Campamento Italiano**. From here climb the **Valley of the Río del Francés** (see below) before continuing to **Lodge Paine Grande**. From here you can complete the third part of the 'W' by walking west along the northern shore of **Lago Grey** to Refugio Grey and the Grey Glacier before returning to **Lodge Paine Grande** and the boat back across the lake to the **Guardería Pudeto**.

## To the base of the Torres del Paine

From Refugio Laguna Amarga, this six-hour route follows the road west to Hostería Las Torres (1½ hours), before climbing along the western side of the Río Ascensio via Refugio Chileno (two hours) and Campamento Chileno to Campamento Las Torres (two hours), close to the base of the Torres del Paine (be careful when crossing the suspension bridge over the Río Ascensio near Hostería Las Torres, as the path is poorly marked and you can end up on the wrong side of the ravine). The path alongside the Río Ascensio is well marked, and the Campamento Las Torres is in an attractive wood (no *refugio*). A further 30 minutes or more up the moraine (the last bit involves a hard scramble over rocks at a near-vertical grade) takes you to a lake at the base of the towers themselves; they seem so close that you almost feel you could touch them. To see the Torres lit by sunrise (spectacular but you must have good weather), it's well worth carrying your camping gear up to Campamento Torres and spending the night. One hour beyond Campamento Torres is Campamento Japonés, another good campsite (only for climbers; non-climbers need to arrive with guide).

## Valley of the Río del Francés

From Lodge Paine Grande this route leads north across undulating country along the western edge of Lago Skottberg to Campamento Italiano and then follows the valley of the Río del Francés, which climbs between Cerro Paine Grande and the Ventisquero del Francés (to the west) and the Cuernos del Paine (to the east) to Campamento Británico; the views from the mirador, a half-hour's walk above Campamento Británico, are superb. Allow 2½ hours from Lodge Paine Grande to Campamento Italiano, 2½ hours further to Campamento Británico.

## Treks from Guardería Grey

Guardería Grey, 18 km west by road from the administration centre, is the starting point for a five-hour trek to Lago Pingo, recommended if you want to get away from the crowds, and one of the best routes in the park for birdwatching. It can only be undertaken with a certified private guide (check with CONAF for available guides). To reach the lake from the *guardería*, follow the Río Pingo, via Refugio Pingo and Refugio Zapata (four hours), with views south over Ventisquero Zapata; look out for plenty of wildlife and for icebergs in the lake. Ventisquero Pingo can be seen 3 km away over the lake. Note the bridge over a river here, marked on many maps, has been washed away. The river can be forded when it is low, however, allowing access to the glacier.

Two short signposted walks from Guardería Grey have also been suggested: one is a steep climb up the hill behind the ranger post to Mirador Ferrier, from where there are fine views; the other is via a suspension bridge across the Río Pingo to the peninsula at the southern end of Lago Grey, from where there are good views of the icebergs on the lakes.

## To Laguna Verde

From the administration centre follow the road north 2 km, before taking the path east over the Sierra del Toro and then along the southern side of Laguna Verde to the Guardería Laguna Verde. Allow four hours. This is one of the easiest walks in the park and may be a good first hike.

## To Laguna Azul and Lago Paine

This route runs north from Laguna Amarga to the western tip of Laguna Azul, from where it continues across the sheltered Río Paine valley past Laguna Cebolla to the Refugio Lago Paine at the eastern end of Lago Paine. Allow 8½ hours. Good birdwatching opportunities.

## Tourist information

See also www.parquetorresdelpaine.cl.

### CONAF administration centre
*In the southeast of the park, at the northwest end of Lago del Toro, T61-2360 496, magallanes.oirs@conaf.cl. Summer daily 0800-1900, winter daily 0800-1800.*
Has interesting videos and exhibitions, as well as the latest weather forecast. There are 13 ranger stations (*guarderías*) staffed by rangers, who offer help and advice. The outlying *guarderías* are open Oct-Apr only. Luggage can be stored for US$3 per day. On payment of the park entry fees (proceeds are shared between all Chilean national parks) you will receive a reasonable trail map to take with you (not waterproof). Climbing the peaks requires 2 permits, first from **DIFROL** (can be obtained free online, www.difrol.cl; takes 2 weeks to receive permit), then from **CONAF** in the park itself (take passports, **DIFROL** permit, insurance and route plan). See also www.torresdelpaine.com.

## Where to stay

Accommodation is available on 3 levels: hotels, which are expensive, not to say overpriced (over US$300 for a double room per night); privately run *refugios*, which are generally well equipped and staffed, offering meals and free hot water for tea, soup, etc; and campsites with amenities, and basic *campamentos*. All options fill up quickly in Jan and Feb, so plan your trip and book in advance. Pay in dollars to avoid IVA (VAT). Agencies in Puerto Natales offer accommodation and transfers or car hire.

### $$$$ Ecocamp Patagonia
*reservations T2-2923 5950, www.ecocamp.travel.*
Luxurious, all-inclusive accommodation is provided in geodesic domes, powered by renewable energy. This is the only environmental sustainability-certified hotel in Chile. Offers 4- to 10-day hiking, wildlife-watching and multi-sport trips, meals included. Their partner, **Cascada Expediciones**, page 246, offers eco-friendly tours and custom trips to Torres del Paine and other destinations.

### $$$$ Explora (Hotel Salto Chico Lodge)
*T61-241 1247 (reservations: Av Américo Vespucci Sur 80, p 5, Santiago, T2-2395 2800, www.explora.com).*
The park 's priciest and most exclusive place is nestled into a nook at Salto Chico on edge of Lago Pehoé, superb views. It's all included: pool, gym, horse riding, boat trips, tours. Arrange packages from Punta Arenas.

### $$$$ Hostería Mirador del Payne
*Estancia Lazo, 52 km from Sarmiento entrance, reservations from Fagnano 585, Punta Arenas, T9-9640 2490, miradordelpayne@gmail.com.*
Comfortable, meals extra, riding, hiking, birdwatching. Lovely location on Laguna Verde on east edge of the park, but inconvenient for most of the park. Private transport essential, or hike there from the park.

### $$$$ Hostería Pehoé
*T61-296 1238, 5 km south of Pehoé ranger station, 11 km north of park administration.*
Beautifully situated on an island with spectacular view across Lago Pehoé, restaurant.

### $$$$ Hotel Lago Grey
*Head office Lautaro Navarro 1077, Punta Arenas, T61-2360280, www.turismolagogrey.com.*
Great views over Lago Grey, superior rooms worth the extra, glacier walks.

### $$$$ Hotel Las Torres
*T61-261 7450, www.lastorres.com.*
Comfortable rooms, beautiful lounge with wood fire and great views of the Macizo,

good service, horse riding, transport from Laguna Amarga ranger station, spa, disabled access. Visitor centre and *confitería* open to non-residents.

### $$$$ Patagonia Camp
*Reservations from Eberhard 230, Puerto Natales, T61-241 5149, www.patagonia camp.com.*
Luxury yurts outside the park at Lago Toro, 15 km south of the administration.

### $$$$ Tierra Patagonia
*T2-2207 8861, www.tierrapatagonia.com.*
Excellent, environmentally sensitive luxury hotel with spa, pool and outdoor jacuzzi on the edge of the national park overlooking Lago Sarmiento. Full- and half-day guided trips by minibus, on foot or on horseback. Gourmet dining in panorama restaurant overlooking the lake and mountains. Highly recommended.

## Refugios

2 companies, **Fantástico Sur** and **Vértice Refugios**, between them run the *refugios* in the park, which provide comfortable dormitory or *cabaña* accommodation with hot showers; bring your own sleeping bag, or hire sheets for US$8-10 per night. Prices start from US$45pp bed only and go up to US$200 pp in a *cabaña* with full board. Meals can be bought individually (**$$**) and restaurants are open to non-residents. Kitchen facilities are available in some Vértice Refugios but Fantástico Sur will not let you prepare your own hot food unless you are camping. *Refugios* also have space for camping (**$**) per night (book in advance for Vértice Refugios as they have very few tents available). Most close in winter, although 1 or 2 may stay open, depending on the weather. Advance booking essential in high season.

**Fantástico Sur** Book through agencies in Puerto Natales or direct at Esmeralda 661, Puerto Natales, T61-261 4184, www.fslodges.com.

**Refugio El Chileno**, in the valley of Río Ascencio, at the foot of the Torres.
**Refugio Las Torres** (Torre Central, Torre Norte), 2 *refugios* next to the Hotel Las Torres (see above), good facilities, especially in the newer **Torre Central**.
**Refugio Los Cuernos**, on the northern shore of Lago Nordenskjold. Also has 8 cabins (**$$$$**).

**Vértice Refugios** Book through agencies in Puerto Natales, or direct at Bulnes 100, Puerto Natales, T61-241 2742, www.verticepatagonia.com.
**Mountain Lodges Paine Grande**, on the northwest tip of Lago Pehoé, with kitchen facilities and internet.
**Vértice Grey**, on the northeast shore of Lago Grey.
**Vértice Dickson Shelter**, southern end of Lago Dickson. Basic.

## Camping

Equipment is available to hire in Puerto Natales (see above). The wind tends to rise in the evening so pitch your tent early. Mice can be a problem; do not leave food in packs on the ground. Fires may only be lit at organized campsites, not at *campamentos*. The *guardaparques* expect people to have a stove if camping.

There are 4 sites run by
**Vértice Patagonia**: **Camping Los Perros**, **Paine Grande**, **Dickson** and **Grey** (from US$11 pp).
**Camping Chileno**, **Serón** and **Las Torres** (by the **Refugio Las Torres**) are run by **Fantástico Sur** (US$11), hot showers.

### Lago Pehoé
*www.campingpehoe.com.*
US$14 pp, tent rental US$24 for 2 including sleeping mat, also pre-pitched dome tents, hot showers, shop, restaurant.

### Camping Río Serrano
*Just outside the park's southern entrance.*
On a working estancia, also has horse rides and hikes.

Free camping is permitted in 9 other locations including Torres, Italiano and Paso, Las Carretas (see map, page 430) in the park: these sites are known as *campamentos* and are generally extremely basic.

## What to do

See under Puerto Natales, What to do, page 423 for Tour operators. Before booking a tour, check the details carefully and get them in writing.

## Transport

**Boat** Catamarán Hielos Patagónicos, Los Arrieros 1517, Puerto Natales (also in bus terminal, 2nd floor, T61-241 1133, info@hielospatagonicos.com, runs boats from Guardería Pudeto to **Refugio Paine Grande**, 30 mins, US$20 one way with 1 backpack (US$7 for extra backpacks), US$33 return, leaving Pudeto at 0930, 1200, 1800, returning from Paine Grande 1000, 1230, 1830; reserve in advance. Services are reduced off season with only 1 sailing from Pudeto at at 1200 and Lago Payne Grande at 1230 1 Apr-15 Nov. At all times check in advance that boats are running. There are also boats from **Hotel Lago Grey** (booked through **Hotel Martín Gusinde**) to the face of the glacier, 2-4 times daily, 3½ hrs, US$55 return, and from the hotel via the glacier face to/from Refugio Grey for US$48 one-way.

**Bus** After mid-Mar there is little public transport and trucks are irregular. **Bus Gómez** (in terminal, T61-241 5700), **JB** (Prat 258, T61-241 0242) and **Trans Vía Paine** (in terminal, T61-2411 927) run daily services into the park, leaving **Puerto Natales** in high season between 0630 and 0800, and again at 1430, using the old road, with a 15-min stop at Cerro Castillo (see box, page 425), then

**Laguna Amarga**, 3 hrs to **Guardería Pudeto** and 4 hrs to the administration centre, all charge US$11 one way, US$20 open return (return tickets are not interchangeable between different companies). Buses will stop anywhere en route, but all stop at Laguna Amarga entrance, Salto Grande del Paine and the administration centre. Return buses to Puerto Natales stop at Laguna Amarga from 1430 to 2000. In high season the buses fill quickly. Depending on route, for the return trip to Puerto Natales it's best to catch the bus for the return trip at Laguna Amarga if you are coming from Mirador Los Torres; take a bus at Pudeto if you are coming from Glaciar Grey; or take a bus from administration if you don't have a boat pass. All buses wait at Guardería Pudeto until the boat from **Refugio Paine Grande** arrives.

To **El Calafate** (Argentina) Either return to Puerto Natales for onward connections (see page 418), or take a bus from the park to **Cerro Castillo** (106 km east of the administration centre) then catch a direct service to Calafate. **Zaahj** (in terminal and Prat 236, T61-249 1631) has a very comfortable **Super Pullman** service Cerro Castillo–El Calafate, US$20. Beware that the border crossing can take up to several hours in peak season (see box, page 425).

**Car hire** Hiring a pick-up in Punta Arenas is an economical proposition for a group (up to 9 people): US$400-450 for 4 days. A more economical car can cope with the roads if you go carefully; ask the rental agency's advice. If driving to the park yourself, note that the shorter road from Puerto Natales is narrow with lots of blind corners and sudden gusts of wind and can be rough in patches. In the park, the roads are also narrow and winding with blind corners: use your horn a lot. Always fill up with fuel in Puerto Natales.

# Tierra del Fuego

The island of Tierra del Fuego is the most captivating part of all Patagonia. This is America's last remaining wilderness and an indispensable part of any trip to the south.

At the very foot of the South American continent and separated from the mainland by the intricate waterways of the Straits of Magellan, the island is divided between Argentina and Chile by a north–south line that grants Argentina the Atlantic and southern coasts and gives Chile an expanse of wilderness to the west, where the tail of the Andes sweeps east in the form of the mighty Darwin range.

The Chilean side is largely inaccessible, apart from the small town of Porvenir, though expeditions can be organized from Punta Arenas to take you hiking and trout fishing. On the Argentine side, glaciers and jagged peaks offer a dramatic backdrop to the city of Ushuaia, the island's main centre, set in a serene natural harbour on the Beagle Channel, with views of the Dientes de Navarino mountains on the Chilean island of Navarino opposite.

Sail from Ushuaia along the channel to the pioneer home of Harberton; to Cape Horn; or even to Antarctica. Head into the small but picturesque Parque Nacional Tierra del Fuego for strolls around Bahía Lapataia and for steep climbs with magnificent views out along the channel.

**Best** for
Sailing the Beagle Channel ▪ Skiing ▪ Trekking ▪ Wildlife

# Footprint picks

⭐ **Dientes de Navarino**, page 445

These jagged peaks let you know that you've reached the end of the world.

⭐ **Fishing around Río Grande**, page 451

Trout run the waters and make for some of the best fly-fishing in the region.

⭐ **Museums in Ushuaia**, page 456

Discover the history of Tierra del Fuego's indigenous people in the city's fine museums.

⭐ **Estancia Harberton**, pages 465 and 466

The site where missionary Thomas Bridges all but invented Ushuaia in the 1800s, and which is still a working estancia today.

⭐ **A boat trip on the Beagle Channel**, page 466

Sail the same waters as Darwin, when he was riding the *HMS Beagle* nearly two centuries ago.

⭐ **Parque Nacional Tierra del Fuego**, page 468

A number of good walks are a great way to experience Patagonian forests, and the end of the Andes.

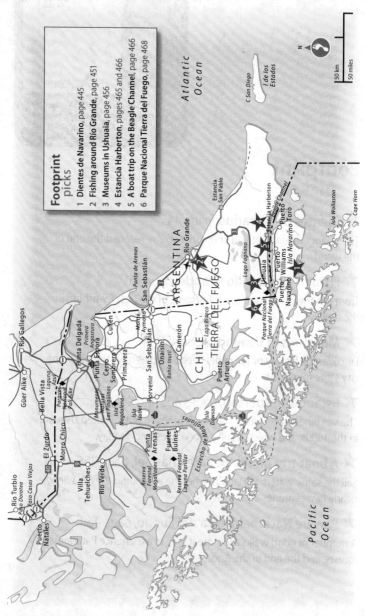

## Footprint picks

1 **Dientes de Navarino**, page 445
2 **Fishing around Río Grande**, page 451
3 **Museums in Ushuaia**, page 456
4 **Estancia Harberton**, pages 465 and 466
5 **A boat trip on the Beagle Channel**, page 466
6 **Parque Nacional Tierra del Fuego**, page 468

Atlantic Ocean

I de los Estados

C San Diego

ARGENTINA

Río Grande

Estancia San Pablo

Estancia Harberton

Puerto Harberton

Ushuaia

Lago Fagnano

Puerto Navarino

Puerto Williams

Isla Navarino

Isla Navarino Toro

Isla Wollaston

Cape Horn

CHILE

TIERRA DEL FUEGO

Lago Blanco

San Sebastián

Punta de Arenas

Cullen

Monte Aymond

Cameron

Onaisin

San Sebastián

Primavera

Cerro Sombrero

Bahía Inútil

Puerto Arturo

Parque Nacional Tierra del Fuego

Porvenir

Isla Dawson

Isla Isabel

Estrecho de Magallanes

Isla Magdalena

Los Pingüinos

Monumento Natural

Parque Nacional Pali Aike

Laguna Azul

Punta Delgada

Primera Angostura

Punta Arenas

Fuerte Bulnes

Reserva Forestal Magallanes

Reserva Forestal Laguna Parillar

Río Verde

Villa Tehuelches

Morro Chico

El Zurdo

Bella Vista

Güer Aike

Río Gallegos

Río Turbio

Puerto Natales

Paso Dorotea

Paso Casas Viejas

Pacific Ocean

N

50 km
50 miles

438·Tierra del Fuego

# **Essential** Tierra del Fuego

Access

**Argentine Tierra del Fuego** is easy to reach with several flights daily from Buenos Aires to Río Grande and Ushuaia, and less frequent flights from El Calafate, and some other towns in Patagonia. Flights are heavily booked in advance in summer (December to February). **Chilean Tierra del Fuego** is only reached by plane from Punta Arenas to Porvenir, daily, and to Puerto Williams on Isla Navarino, Monday to Saturday (but always check for seasonal variations).

There are no road or ferry crossings between the Argentine mainland and Argentine Tierra del Fuego. You have to go through Chilean territory.

From Río Gallegos, Route 3 reaches the Integración Austral border at Monte Aymond, after 67 km, passing Laguna Azul (see box, page 417). The road continues beyond the border as Chilean Route 255, reaching Kamiri Aike after 30 km. Take Route 257 for 16 km east of here to reach the dock at Punta Delgada for the 20-minute Straits of Magellan ferry crossing over the Primera Angostura (First Narrows) to Bahía Azul in Chilean Tierra del Fuego. For more on this crossing, see page 444. From Bahía Azul, the road is paved to Cerro Sombrero, from where *ripio* roads run southeast to Chilean San Sebastián (130-140 km from ferry, depending on the route taken). It's 15 km east, across the border (see box, page 444), to Argentine San Sebastián. From here the road is paved to Río Grande (see below) and Ushuaia.

The second main ferry crossing is Punta Arenas to Porvenir. The ferry dock is 5 km north of Punta Arenas centre, at Tres Puentes. The ferry crosses to Bahía Chilota, 5 km west of Porvenir. From Porvenir a 234-km *ripio* road runs east to Río Grande (six hours, no public transport) via San Sebastián. Note that fruit and meat may not be taken onto the island, nor between Argentina and Chile.

There is also a weekly ferry service on the **Yaghan** (also www.tabsa.cl) from Punta Arenas to Puerto Williams on Isla Navarino. For more details of the Punta Arenas–Porvenir ferry, see page 444 and for Punta Arenas–Puerto Williams ferries, see Transport, page 449.

## Getting around

There are good bus links from Punta Arenas to Río Grande in Argentina, with an option of going via Porvenir, along the decent loop of road on the Chilean side. From Porvenir your options are limited to a *ripio* road around Bahía Inútil to near Lago Blanco, though there's no public transport here. Argentine Tierra del Fuego is much easier to get around, via Route 3 between Río Grande and Ushuaia with several buses a day. A fan of roads spreads out south and west from Río Grande to the estancias on the Argentine side, but these are unpaved and best attempted in a 4WD vehicle. A good *ripio* road leads east of Ushuaia along the south coast, and another goes part of the way along the north coast to Estancia Cabo San Pablo; there is no public transport here either.

**Tip...**
It's essential to book ahead. Accommodation is sparse, and planes and buses fill up quickly from November to March.

# Chilean
## Tierra del Fuego

The Chilean half of Tierra del Fuego is in two sections: the western half of Isla Grande (the main island) and the whole of Isla Navarino, to the south of the main island. Much less developed than the Argentine side of Tierra del Fuego, it has just two small towns where Chile's Fuegians are mostly concentrated: Porvenir on Isla Grande, easily reached by ferry from Punta Arenas; and Puerto Williams on Isla Navarino, which can be reached by a flight from Punta Arenas, a twice-weekly ferry also from Punta Arenas and by boat from Ushuaia.

The northern part of Isla Grande is flat steppe, but the south is dominated by the Darwin range of mountains, which provide a dramatic visual backdrop, even if you can't easily get to them.

Tourism on Chilean territory is limited, but it's possible to organize trekking tours from Punta Arenas, and there are fishing lodges offering magnificent trout fishing, particularly on the Río Grande.

**Weather** Porvenir

| January | February | March | April | May | June |
|---|---|---|---|---|---|
| 13°C | 13°C | 12°C | 9°C | 6°C | 3°C |
| 7°C | 7°C | 5°C | 3°C | 1°C | -1°C |
| 30mm | 20mm | 40mm | 40mm | 40mm | 30mm |

| July | August | September | October | November | December |
|---|---|---|---|---|---|
| 3°C | 5°C | 7°C | 10°C | 11°C | 13°C |
| -1°C | 0°C | 1°C | 3°C | 4°C | 6°C |
| 30mm | 30mm | 20mm | 20mm | 20mm | 30mm |

## Puerto Porvenir

Chilean Tierra del Fuego has a population of around 8000, with 5600 living in the small town of Porvenir, the only town on the Chilean half of the main island. Founded in 1894 during the gold boom, when many people came seeking fortunes from Croatia and Chiloé, Porvenir is a quiet place with a wide open pioneer feel, streets of neat, brightly painted houses of corrugated zinc and quaint, tall-domed trees lining the main avenue.

There is a small museum, the **Museo Fernando Cordero Rusque** ⓘ *Zavattaro 402, on the plaza, T61-258 1800, Mon-Thu 0800-1730, Fri 0900-1600, Sat-Sun 1030-1330 and 1500-1700, US$1*, with archaeological and photographic displays on the Onas, and good displays on natural history and the early gold diggers and sheep farmers. There's little else to do here, but you could stroll around the plaza, with its **Iglesia San Francisco de Sales**, and down to the shoreside promenade, where there's a strange collection of 19th-century farm machinery and a striking wooden monument to the Selk'nam.

## Beyond Porvenir

Beyond Porvenir there is wonderfully wild virgin territory to explore. However, if you want an adventure, your best bet is to arrange a trip through tour operators in Punta Arenas (such as **Go Patagonia**, www.gopatagoniachile.com, or see page 413), since there's still very little infrastructure on

> **Tip...**
> Cabo Boquerón, the headland at the start of Bahía Inútil, has great views on a clear day, as far as Cabo Froward, Isla Dawson and the distant Cordillera Darwin's snow peaks.

the Chilean side of the island. All roads are good *ripio* except a paved section from Bahía Chilota to Porvenir and in Porvenir itself. For tour operators, see page 411.

North of Porvenir, 6 km, is the **Monumento Natural Laguna de los Cisnes**. Access is across private land; the owner will give permission. Another place to see wildfowl, including black-necked swans from December, is **Laguna Santa María**, not far from Porvenir on the road to **Bahía Inútil**, a wonderful windswept bay.

Driving east along the bay you pass Los Canelos, with trees, a rare sight, and then the junction for the Cordón Baquedano, on the **Circuito de Oro**. This is a recommended tour, on which you can see gold panning using the same techniques that have been employed since mining began in 1881; it's a four-hour, 115-km round trip.

## Camerón and further south

About 90 km east of Porvenir, roads head east to San Sebastián and south to Camerón via Onaisin (99 km from Porvenir). Camerón is a large farm settlement and the only other community of any size on the Chilean part of the island. It is 149 km from Porvenir on the opposite shore of Bahía Inútil. This wonderful windswept bay, with views of distant hills and the snow-capped Darwin range all along the southern horizon, was named 'useless' by British engineers making a hydrographic survey here in 1827 because it has no useful port. Nevertheless, as you near Camerón, the road passes secluded canyons and bays, interspersed with a few farms, and the palpable sense of isolation drowns out civilization, leaving nothing but the sound of wind and the wild silence of nature.

Other options are sailing from Porvenir to **Río Cóndor** across Bahía Inútil, south of Camerón, and trekking or riding from Camerón to **Seno Almirantazgo**, a beautiful, wild and treeless place, where mountains sink into blue fjords with icebergs.

## ON THE ROAD
## Shipwrecked in the Magellan Straits

The Estrecho de Magallanes, 534 km long, is a treacherous sea passage linking the Atlantic and the Pacific oceans. The eastern entrance to the straits is between Punta Dúngeness on the Argentine mainland and Cabo del Espíritu Santo on Tierra del Fuego. From here the route heads west and then south, past Punta Arenas and Fuerte Bulnes, before negotiating the channels and islands of southern Chile. The straits have a long history of claiming victims, and the hostile conditions are eloquently conveyed in the words of Sir John Narborough: "horrible like the ruins of a world destroyed by terrific earthquakes".

From the Atlantic, the first navigational problem facing sailors is simply the difficulty of entering the straits against the fierce westerly gales that prevail. Once in the straits the dangers are far from over: many ships have fallen victim to the notorious *Williwaws*, winds with the ferocity of tornados that spring up from nowhere; no less vicious are the *Pamperos*, which blow off the land with enough force to capsize a vessel.

Although in 1520 Magellan succeeded in passing through the straits that bear his name, few others managed to do so in the years that followed; of the 17 ships that attempted the passage in the early 16th century, only one, the *Victoria*, succeeded in reaching the Pacific and returning to Europe. Twelve were lost near the eastern entrance and four returned in failure. The reason these early navigators chose to attempt the dangerous voyage was the lure of a short route between Europe and the spices of the East. Even when it became clear that there was no such short route, the straits still provided a useful means for Europeans to reach the rich Pacific ports of Peru and Chile without disembarking to cross Mexico or Panama overland.

Even with the development of advanced navigation techniques in the 19th century, losses continued: in 1869, the *Santiago*, an iron paddle-steamer built in Glasgow and owned by the Pacific Mail line, went down off Isla Desolación at the western end of the straits with a cargo of gold and silver. While the Panama Canal now provides a shorter route between the Atlantic and Pacific Oceans, the size of modern ships means that the straits are still a busy shipping route. The most common cargo is now oil; casualties still occur but now, of course, with the added risk of environmental disaster from oil spillage.

A large part of the peninsula between Bahía Inútil and Seno Almirantazgo is covered by the **Karukinka nature reserve** ⓘ *search for Karukinka on www.wcs.org*. From Camerón a road runs southeast past an airfield and into the hills, through woods where guanacos hoot and run off into glades, and the banks are covered with red and purple moss. The north shores of **Lago Blanco** can be reached by cutting east through the woods from Sección Río Grande, with superb views of the mountains surrounding the lake and the snows in the south.

Meanwhile, the rough road continues as far south as Estancia Lago Fagnano on Lago Fagnano, four hours from Onaisin. The government is hoping to complete the road to **Yendegaia** on the Beagle Channel with a view to having a summer route, including ferry, to Puerto Navarino. This would traverse the **Parque Nacional Yendegaia**, which was created in 2013 and which adjoins the Parque Nacional Tierra del Fuego in Argentina. They hope to finish the project in 2020. It's essential to organize any trip to this area through a reliable tour operator with solid infrastructure.

## Tourist information

Tourist information is available at the **Museo Fernando Cordero Rusque** (the best option; see above), on notice boards outside the Municipalidad, on the seafront and elsewhere, and from a handicrafts stall in a kiosk on the seafront (opposite **Comercial Tuto**, No 588). See also www.patagonia-chile.com.

## Where to stay

**Puerto Porvenir**

**\$\$\$ Hostería Yendegaia**
*Croacia 702, T61-258 1919.*
Comfortable, family-run inn with good facilities and helpful staff. English-speaking owner runs birdwatching tours and to the king penguins.

**\$\$ Central**
*Phillipi 298, T61-258 0077, opposite Rosas, see below.*
All rooms with bath.

**\$\$ España**
*Croacia 698, T61-258 0540,*
*www.hotelespana.cl.*
Comfortable, well equipped, light and spacious rooms, helpful and friendly. Good restaurant with food all day.

**\$\$ Rosas**
*Phillippi 269, T61-258 0088.*
Heating, restaurant and bar.

**\$ pp Hostal Kawi**
*Pedro Silva 144, T61-258 1570.*
Comfortable, rooms for 3, meals available, offers fly-fishing trips.

**Beyond Porvenir**
If you get stuck in the wilds, note that it is almost always possible to camp or bed down in a barn at an estancia.

**\$\$\$-\$\$ Hostería Tunkelen**
*Arturo Prat Chacón 101, Cerro Sombrero,*
*T61-221 2757, www.hosteriatunkelen.cl.*
3 buildings with rooms of different standards: some with private bathrooms, shared bathrooms or backpacker dorms. Restaurant. Good for groups.

**\$\$-\$ Hostería de la Frontera**
*San Sebastián, T61-269 6004.*
Where some buses stop for meals and cakes, cosy, with bath (the annex is much more basic), good food.

## Restaurants

**Puerto Porvenir**
There are many lobster fishing camps nearby, where fishermen prepare lobster on the spot.

**\$\$ Club Croata**
*Señoret entre Phillippi y Muñoz Gamero,*
*next to the bus stop on the waterfront.*
A lively place with good food.

**\$\$-\$ El Chispa**
*Señoret 202, T61-258 0054.*
Good restaurant for seafood and other Chilean dishes.

## What to do

**Puerto Porvenir**
For adventure tourism and trekking activities contact tour operators in Punta Arenas (see What to do, page 411).

## Transport

For details of how to get to Tierra del Fuego, see box, page 439, and Boat, below.

**Puerto Porvenir**
**Air** To **Punta Arenas** (weather and bookings permitting), with **Aerovías DAP**, Señoret s/n, T61-258 0089, www.aerovias dap.cl. Heavily booked so make sure you have your return reservation confirmed.

## BORDER CROSSING

## Chile–Argentina

### San Sebastián
This is the border between the Chilean and Argentine sides of Tierra del Fuego. Chilean San Sebastián is located 130 km southeast of the ferry dock at Bahía Azul, via Cerro Sombrero. It consists of just a few houses with Hostería La Frontera 500 m from the border. Argentine San Sebastián is 15 km further east, across the border. It has a seven-room ACA hostería (T02961-15-405834) and a service station, open 0700-2300. For further details, see www.gendarmeria.gob.ar/pasos-chile/san-sebastian.html and www.pasosfronterizos.gov.cl/cf_sansebastian.html.

**Boat** For information on getting to Tierra del Fuego by boat, see also box, page 439.

**To Argentina** At **Punta Delgada** is the **Hostería El Faro** where you can get food and drink. There are 3 boats working continuously to cross Bahía Azul, each with a café, lounge and toilets on board. Buses can wait up to 90 mins to board and the boats run every 40 mins 0830-0100, US$21 per vehicle, foot passengers US$2.50. See www.tabsa.cl for more information.

Ferries to **Punta Arenas** operate Tue-Sun taking 2 hrs 20 mins, US$65 per vehicle, motorcycles US$18.50, foot passengers US$10. **Transportadora Austral Broom** (www.tabsa.cl) publishes a timetable a month in advance but this is dependent on tides and subject to change, so check in advance. Reservations are essential, especially in summer.

**Bus** The only public transport on Chilean Tierra del Fuego is Jorge Bastián's minibus **Porvenir–Cerro Sombrero**, T61-234 5406, jorgebastian@hotmail.com, or axelvig20@hotmail.com, which leaves Sombrero at 0830 on Mon, Wed and Fri; returns from Porvenir Municipalidad, 2 hrs, US$3.

## Isla Navarino   *Colour map 3, C5.*

**jagged peaks, exotic animals and ancient archaeological finds**

Situated on the southern shore of the Beagle Channel, Isla Navarino is totally unspoilt and beautiful, offering great geographical diversity, thanks to the Dientes de Navarino range of mountains, with peaks over 1000 m, covered with southern beech forest up to 500 m, and south of that, great plains covered with peat bogs, with many lagoons abundant in flora.

The island was the centre of the indigenous Yaganes (Yámana) culture, and there are 500 archaeological sites, the oldest dated as 3000 years old. Guanacos and condors can be seen inland, as well as large numbers of beavers, which were introduced to the island and have done considerable damage. The flight from Punta Arenas is beautiful, with superb views of Tierra del Fuego, the Cordillera Darwin, the Beagle Channel and the islands stretching south to Cape Horn.

### Puerto Williams
The only settlement of any size on the island is Puerto Williams (population 2500), a Chilean naval base situated about 50 km east of Ushuaia on Argentine seas across the Beagle Channel. Puerto Williams is the southernmost permanently inhabited town in the

# Essential Isla Navarino

Access

**Ushuaia Boating** travels from Ushuaia to Puerto Williams, US$125 each way, which includes a 40-minute crossing in a semi-rigid boat to Puerto Navarino. Then it's a one-hour ride in a combi on a lovely *ripio* road to Williams; make sure you are clear about transport arrangements for your return. **Fernández Campbell** (www.fernandezcampbell.com) has a 1½-hour crossing from Ushuaia, on Friday, Saturday and Sunday at 1000, returning at 1500. Tickets (US$125 for foreigners) are sold at **Naviera RFC** in Puerto Williams and **Zenit Explorer**, Juana Fadul 126, in Ushuaia, T02901-433232.

world; 50 km east-southeast is **Puerto Toro**, the southernmost permanently inhabited settlement on earth. Some maps mistakenly mark a road from Puerto Williams to Puerto Toro, but it officially doesn't exist (although the military travels frequently along the route); access is only by sea.

Due to past border disputes with Argentina, the Chilean navy maintains a heavy presence in Puerto Williams. Outside the naval headquarters, you can see the bow section of the *Yelcho*, the tug chartered by Shackleton to rescue men stranded on Elephant Island.

Your main purpose for visiting the island is likely to be the trekking on the Dientes de Navarino. But you should also take time to explore the indigenous heritage here too. It's beautifully documented in the **Museo Martín Gusinde** ① *Aragay 1, T61-262 1043, www.museomartingusinde.cl, 1 Nov to late Mar Tue-Fri 0930-1300 and 1500-1800, Sat-Sun 1430-1830; 1 Apr-30 Oct Tue-Fri 0930-1300 and 1500-1800, Sat 1430-1830, free,* known as the Museo del Fin del Mundo (End of the World Museum), which is full of information about vanished indigenous tribes, local wildlife and the famous voyages by Charles Darwin and Fitzroy of the *Beagle*. A visit is highly recommended.

One kilometre west of the town is the yacht club (one of Puerto Williams' two nightspots), whose wharf is made from a sunken 1930s Chilean warship. The town has a bank, supermarkets and a hospital.

## Exploring the island

For superb views climb **Cerro Bandera** which is reached by a path from the dam 4 km west of the town (it's a steep, three- to four-hour round trip, take warm clothes). There is excellent trekking around the ★ **Dientes de Navarino** range, the southernmost trail in the world, through impressive mountain landscapes, frozen lagoons and snowy peaks, resulting in superb views over the Beagle Channel. It's a challenging hike, over a distance of 53 km in five days, possible only from December to March, and a good level of fitness is needed. One highlight is hiking to Lago Windhond and searching the guestbook at the entrance to the reserve. Inside you'll find previously unknown routes imparted by former trekkers. Some of these even lead to Windhond Bay, which offers views of Cape Horn.

There is no equipment rental on the island. Ask for information in the tourist office at Puerto Williams, but it's best to go with an organized expedition from Punta Arenas.

Travellers can also visit Omora Ethnobotanical Park, an NGO dedicated to conservation and biological research in the Cape Horn Region. The park offers three different circuit tours between one to two hours each. Entrance is US$50 (with a guide) and can be booked through **Lakutaia Lodge** in Puerto Williams (see Where to Stay, below).

Beyond Cerro Bandera, a road leads 56 km west of Puerto Williams to **Puerto Navarino**, where there is a jetty, the Alcaldía del Mar and four more houses, plus a few horses and

# BACKGROUND
## Tierra del Fuego

Tierra del Fuego has been inhabited by indigenous groups for some 10,000 years. The most populous of these groups, the Onas (also known as the Selk'nam), were hunter-gatherers in the north, living mainly on guanaco. The southeastern corner of the island was inhabited by the Haus or Hausch, also hunter-gatherers. The Yaganes or Yámana lived along the Beagle Channel and were seafaring people surviving on seafood, fish and birds. The fourth group, the Alacalufe, lived in the west of Tierra del Fuego as well as on the Chonos Archipelago, surviving by fishing and hunting seals.

The first Europeans to visit the island came with the Portuguese navigator Fernão Magalhães (Magellan), who, in 1520, sailed through the channel that now bears his name. Magellan named the island 'Land of Fire' when he saw the smoke from many fires lit along the shoreline by local inhabitants. The indigenous population were left undisturbed for three centuries.

Fitzroy and Darwin's scientific visits in 1832 and 1833 recorded some fascinating interaction with the indigenous peoples. Fitzroy and Darwin's visits were a precursor to attempts to convert the indigenous groups to Christianity so that the island could be used by white settlers without fear of attack. Several disastrous missions followed, encountering stiff resistance from the inhabitants.

In 1884, Reverend Thomas Bridges founded a mission at Ushuaia. He was the first European to learn the Yámana language, and he compiled a Yámana-English dictionary. He soon realized that his original task was a destructive one. The purpose of the missionary work had been to facilitate lucrative sheep farming on the island, but the Ona were attracted to the 'white guanacos' on their land and took to hunting sheep, easier than catching the fast-footed guanaco. In response, the colonists offered two sheep for each Ona that was killed (proof was provided by a pair of Ona ears). The indigenous groups were further ravaged by epidemics of European diseases. In a desperate attempt to save the Ona, Salesian missionaries founded three missions in the Straits of Magellan in the early 20th century, but, stripped of their land, the Ona lost the will to live, and the last Ona died in 1999. The Hausch also died out. The last of the Yámana, a woman called Cristina Calderón, presently survives near Puerto Williams. She is 89 years old.

Imprecision in the original colonial land division and the greed of the rush southwards led to border disputes between Argentina and Chile, which have mostly been quelled despite the underlying tension. The initial settlement of the dispute in 1883 was followed by a desire by both governments to populate the area by allocating large expanses of land for sheep farming.

For many years, the main economic activity of the northern part of the island was sheep farming, but Argentine government tax incentives to companies in the 1970s led to the establishment of new industries in Río Grande and Ushuaia and a rapid growth in the population of both cities. Tourism is increasingly important in Ushuaia.

cows. There is little or no traffic on this route and it is very beautiful, with forests of lengas stretching right down to the water's edge. You can also visit **Villa Ukika**, 2 km east of town, the place where the last descendants of the Yámana people live, relocated from their original homes at Caleta Mejillones, which was the last indigenous reservation in the province, inhabited by hundreds of Yámana descendants. At **Mejillones**, 32 km from Puerto Williams, is a graveyard and memorial to the Yámana people.

Just before Estancia Santa Rosa (10 km further on), a path is said to cross the forest, lakes and beaver dams to Wulaia (10 km, one to two days), where the *Beagle* anchored in 1833; however, even the farmer at Wulaia gets lost following this track.

## Cape Horn

It is possible to catch a boat south from Isla Navarino (enquire at the yacht club) to Cape Horn (the most southerly piece of land on earth apart from Antarctica). There is one pebbly beach on the north side of the island; boats anchor in the bay and passengers are taken ashore by motorized dinghy. A stairway climbs the cliff above the beach, up to the building which houses the naval post. A path leads from here to the impressive monument of an albatross overlooking the wild, churning waters of the Drake Passage below. See also box, page 412.

## Listings Isla Navarino

### Tourist information

**Puerto Williams**

Tourist office
*Municipalidad de Cabos de Hornos, corner of Arturo Pratt and Piloto Pardo, T61-262 1018 extension 25, www.ptowilliams.cl/turismo. html. Mon-Thu 0800-1300 and 1430-1700, Fri 0800-1300 and 1400-1600, closed in winter.*
For maps and details on hiking.

### Where to stay

**Puerto Williams**

**$$$$ Lakutaia**
*2 km west of town, T61-261 4108 (Santiago: T9-6226 8448), www.lakutaia.cl.*
A 'base camp' for a range of activities and packages (horse riding, trekking, birdwatching, boating, kayaking, flight tours. Book 48 hrs in advance. 24 double rooms in simple but attractive style, lovely views from spacious public areas, free bike rental, 3 golf 'holes' – most southerly in world!

**$$$-$$ Hostal Beagle**
*Presidente Ibañez 147, T9-7765 9554, contacto.hostalbeagle@gmail.com.*
Pleasant self-service *hostal*. No dorms, but doubles and triples.

**$$ Hostal Akainij**
*Austral 22, T61-262 1173, www.turismoakainij.cl.*
Comfortable rooms, very helpful, excellent, filling meals, basic English spoken, adventure tours and transfers.

**$$ Hostal Cabo de Ornos**
*Maragaño 146, T61-262 1849.*
Decent central option above Plaza O'Higgins. Above the *hostal* is a good restaurant run by the same owners (see Restaurants, below).

**$$ Hostal Coirón**
*Maragaño 168, T61-262 1227.*
Double rooms or dorms, shared and private bath, helpful, good food, relaxed, quite basic, but OK.

**$$ Hostal Miramar**
*Muñoz 155, T61-262 1372, aibanjou@hotmail.com.*

Small, family-run *hostal*, Comfortable living spaces, good food upon request.

## $$ Hostal Pusaki
*Piloto Pardo 222, T61-262 1116,*
*pattypusaki@yahoo.es.*
Double room or dorms, good meals available, owner Patty is helpful and fun.

## $$ Refugio El Padrino
*Costanera 276, T61-262 1136,*
*ceciliamancillao@yahoo.com.ar.*
The vivacious Cecilia Mancilla is great fun. Good food served, and musical instruments are on hand. Also offers camping. Recommended.

## Restaurants

### Puerto Williams
There are several grocery stores; prices are very high because of the remoteness. **Simón & Simón** and **Temuco** are opposite each other on Piloto Pardo, junction Condell. The former seems to be the reference point in town. Most hotels and hostels will offer food.

## $$-$ Resto del Sur
*Maragaño 146, T61-262 1849.*
Located above **Hostal Cabo de Ornos**, this restaurant has more food options than other places, including all-you-can-eat pizza on Fri nights.

## $ Los Dientes de Navarino
*Centro Comercial Sur.*
*Open until 0400 on weekends.*
Colombian owner Yamilla incorporated much of her native flavour into this popular eatery, down to the Caldas rum stocking the shelves and Romeo Santos playing on the TV. Good, hearty fare. Set menu.

## Cafés

### Puerto Luisa
*Costanera 317, T9-9934 0849, see Facebook.*
*Mon-Fri 1200-2000, Sat 0830-1800.*
Owner Valeria welcomes people with espressos, hot chocolate, teas and home-made cakes and pastries.

## What to do

### Puerto Williams
#### Boat trips
**Note** No tour companies in Puerto Williams go to Cape Horn. It's possible to enquire at the yacht club about boat hire, but it all depends on the owner.
**Navarino Travel**, *Centro Comercial (in the Fío Fío souvenir shop), T9-6629 9201, navarinotravel@gmail*.com. Knowledgeable owner Maurice offers boat trips to different destinations around the island, including glaciers.
**Wulaia Expeditions**, *Yelcho 224, T9-9832 6412, wulaiaexpediciones@gmail*.com. Runs all-day boat tours and fishing trips from Puerto Williams to Wulaia Cove. Lunch included. Around US$700 per trip for parties of 2 people; it's better value with parties of 4-6.

### Estancias
**Estancia Santa Rosa**, *Piloto Pardo s/n, T9-8464 2053, fcofilgueira29@gmail*.com. Francisco offers day tours at the oldest estancia on the island. Activities include kayaking in Bahía Santa, horse riding, trekking and a traditional Chilean barbecue. US$100 for the day.

### Tour operators
**Akainij**, *see Where to stay, above.*
**Navarino Beaver**, *T9-9548 7365, barberjorge@ gmail.com.* Hunters Miguel and Jorge run beaver-watching tours (including trips to a tannery), beaver hunting, beaver meat sampling. Pretty much everything beaver.
**Shila**, *O'Higgins 322 (a hut at entrance to Centro Comercial), T(569)-7897 2005, www. turismoshila.cl.* Luis Tiznado González is an adventure expert offering trekking and fishing, plus equipment hire (bikes, tents, sleeping bags, stoves, and more). Lots of trekking information, sells maps.

## Trekking

You must register first with *carabineros* on C Piloto Pardo, near Brito. Tell them when you get back, too.

## Transport

### Puerto Williams

**Air** To **Punta Arenas** with **DAP** (details under Punta Arenas). Book well in advance; there are long waiting lists (be persistent). The flight is beautiful (sit on right from Punta Arenas) with superb views of Tierra del Fuego, the Cordillera Darwin, the Beagle Channel, and the islands stretching south to Cape Horn. Also army flights are available (they are cheaper), but the ticket has to be bought through DAP. The airport is in town.

**Boat** See box, page 439, for details of the **Yaghan** ferry of Broom, www.tabsa.cl. For boat services between Puerto Navarino and Ushuaia, see box, page 445. The *Isla Navarino* to **Punta Arenas** is a 30- to 34-hr trip through beautiful channels. It takes 65 passengers, US$142 for a pullman seat, US$200 for sofa-bed seat.

# Argentine
## Tierra del Fuego

The Argentine half of Tierra del Fuego is much easier to visit than the Chilean half and more rewarding. The northern half of the island is windswept steppe, and its only town, Río Grande, once rich in oil, is now very faded.

But before you head straight for Ushuaia pause to visit two splendid estancias. Viamonte (www.estanciavia monte.com) was built by Lucas Bridges to protect the indigenous Ona people and is an evocative place to stay, while Estancia María Behety (see www.maribety.com.ar) is world famous for its brown trout fishing. The landscape turns to hills as you head south, and there's a lovely silent lake, Lago Fagnano, ideal for a picnic.

Ushuaia is the island's centre, beautifully set on the Beagle Channel, with a backdrop of steep mountains. With a picturesque national park on its doorstep, boat trips up the Beagle Channel to the Bridges' other superb estancia, Harberton, and a ski centre at Cerro Castor, there's plenty to keep you here. Huskies will draw your sledge in winter, and in summer you can walk around Bahía Lapataia and contemplate the serenity of the end of the world.

a town torn between the old and the new

Río Grande (population 100,000) is a sprawling modern coastal town, the centre for a rural sheep-farming community. It's a friendly place which you are most likely to visit in order to change buses. There are a couple of good places to stay, however, and a small museum worth seeing.

Río Grande grew rapidly in the 1970s, with government tax incentives for sheep farming. The new population was stranded when incentives were withdrawn, but revival came with expansion into mobile phone and white goods assembly. This in turn declined when Argentina relaxed import restrictions and currently the town is benefitting from the exploitation of oil and gas in the vicinity.

## Sights
The city's architecture is a chaotic mix of smart nouveau-riche houses and humble wooden and tin constructions. It was founded by Fagnano's Salesian mission in 1893, and you can visit the original building, **La Candelaria** ① *11 km north, T02964-421642, Mon-Sat 1400-1900, US$6.75, getting there: taxi US$8 with wait,* whose museum has displays of natural history and indigenous artefacts, with strawberry plantations, piglets and an aviary. The **Museo Virginia Choquintel** ① *Alberdi 555, T02964-430647, see Facebook, Mon-Fri 1000-1900, Sat 1500-1900,* is recommended for its history of the Selk'nam, the pioneers, missions and oil. Next door is a handicraft shop called **Kren** ('sun' in Selk'nam), which sells good local products.

## ★ Around Río Grande
The **fly-fishing** in this area is becoming world-renowned and it's now possible to stay in several comfortable lodges in Río Grande and at Lago Escondido. This area is rich in brown trout, sea run brook trout and steelheads, weighing 2-14 kg; you could expect to catch an average of eight trout a day in season. Contact specialist fly-fishing tour operators. The season runs from 15 October to 14 April, with the best fishing from January to April.

**Estancia María Behety**, 15 km from town, built by the millionaire José Menéndez, has a vast sheep-shearing shed and is heaven for brown trout fishing. **Estancia Viamonte**, on the coast, 40 km south of town, is a working sheep farm with a fascinating history. Here, Lucas Bridges, son of Tierra del Fuego's first settler, built a home to protect the large tribe of indigenous Onas, who were fast dying out. The estancia is still inhabited by his descendants, who will take you riding and show you life on the farm. There is also a house to rent and superb accommodation, highly recommended.

## Tourist information

### Provincial tourist office
*Av Belgrano 319, T02964-422887, infuerg1@*
*tierradelfuego.org.ar. Mon-Fri 0800-1600.*

### Tourist office
*Rosales 350, T02964-430516, www.tierradel*
*fuego.org.ar. Mon-Fri 0900-2000.*
In the blue-roofed hut on the plaza is this
small but helpful tourist office.

### Where to stay

Book ahead, as there are few decent
choices. Several estancias offer full board
and some, mainly on the northern rivers,
have expensive fishing lodges; others offer
horse riding.

### $$$ Grande Hotel
*Echelaine 251, T02964-436500.*
Modern hotel with standard rooms,
executive suites and lofts, spa services and
a pool fit for a debauched Roman emperor.
Also has a highly regarded restaurant
featuring Argentine and Patagonian dishes.

### $$$ Posada de los Sauces
*Elcano 839, T02964-432895,*
*www.posadadelossauces.com.*
The best by far, with breakfast, beautifully
decorated, comfortable, good restaurant
(trout recommended), cosy bar, very
helpful staff.

### $$$ Villa
*Av San Martín 281, T02964-424998,*
*hotelvilla@live.com.*
Central, modern, restaurant/*confitería*,
parking, discount given for cash.

### Estancias

### $$$$ Estancia María Behety
*16.5 km from Río Grande, T02964-424215*
*reservations at The Fly Shop (www.theflyshop.*
*com), www.maribety.com.ar.*

Established in 1897 on a 40-km stretch
of the river that has become legendary
for brown trout fishing, this estancia has
accommodation for 18 anglers, and good
food. It is one of the country's priciest
fishing lodges, deservedly so. Guides and
equipment included.

### $$$$ pp Estancia Viamonte
*40 km southeast on the coast, T02964-*
*430861, www.estanciaviamonte.com.*
For an authentic experience of Tierra
del Fuego, built in 1902 by pioneer Lucas
Bridges, writer of *Uttermost Part of the Earth*,
to protect the Selk'nam/Ona people, this
working estancia has simple and beautifully
furnished rooms in a spacious cottage.
Price is for full board and all activities:
riding and trekking; cheaper for dinner,
bed and breakfast only. Delicious meals.
Book a week ahead.

### Camping

### Club Náutico Ioshlelk-Oten
*Montilla 1047, T02964-420536, see Facebook.*
Situated 2 km from town on the river.
Clean, cooking facilities, heated building
available in cold weather. YPF petrol station
has hot showers.

### Restaurants

The restaurants in Hotel Villa and
Hotel Grande have good reputations.

### $$ Don Peppone
*Perito Moreno 247, T02964-432066,*
*see Facebook.*
For pizzas, pastas, *empanadas* and
sandwiches. One of the most popular
spots in town.

### Cafés

### El Roca
*Espora 643, ½ block from the plaza,*
*T02964-430693, see Facebook.*

A *confitería* and bar in historic premises (the original cinema), good and popular.

**Tío Willy**
*Alberdi 279.*
Serves *cerveza artesanal* (microbrewery).

## Festivals

Jan **Sheep Shearing Festival**. Definitely worth seeing if you're in the area.
Feb **Rural Exhibition**. Exhibition with handicrafts in 2nd week.
Mar **Shepherd's Day**. An impressive sheep-dog display during the 1st week.
20-22 Jun **Winter solstice**. The longest night. Fireworks and ice-skating contests; this is a very inhospitable time of year.

## Transport

Book ahead in summer as buses and planes fill up fast. Take your passport when buying ticket.

**Air** There is an **airport** (T02964-420699), 4 km west of town. A taxi to the centre costs US$7. To **Buenos Aires**, daily, 3½ hrs direct. LADE flies to **Río Gallegos**.

**Bus** To **Punta Arenas**, Chile, via Punta Delgada, 7-9 hrs, with **Pacheco** (Perito Moreno 647, T02964-421554, Mon-Sat) and **Tecni Austral** (Moyano 516, T02964-432885), US$40. To **Río Gallegos**, with **Tecni Austral**, Mon-Sat 0500, 8 hrs; with **Marga/Taqsa** (Mackinley 545, T02964-434316), daily 0700, US$55, connection to El Calafate and Comodoro Rivadavia. To **Ushuaia**, 3½-4 hrs, with **Montiel** (25 de Mayo 712, T02964-420997) and **Líder** (Perito Moreno 635, T02964-420003, www.lidertdf.com.ar), US$22; both use small buses and have frequent departures; they stop en route at **Tolhuin**, US$15; also with **Marga**.

---

## Río Grande to Ushuaia    Colour map 3, B5/C4.
### a sparsely populated area, with lakes and mountains

From Río Grande, several roads fan out southwest to the heart of the island, though this area is little inhabited. The paved road south, Route 3, continues across wonderfully open land, more forested than the expanses of Patagonian steppe further north and increasingly hilly as you near Ushuaia. After around 160 km, you could turn left along a track to the coast to Cabo San Pablo. There are also other trips to places of interest within reach. Route 3 then climbs up above Lago Fagnano and Tolhuin.

### Tolhuin and around

This is a friendly, small settlement close to the shore of Lago Fagnano, a large expanse of water, right at the heart of Tierra del Fuego. The village has a stretch of beach nearby and is a favourite Sunday afternoon destination for day trippers from Ushuaia. There's a YPF service station just off the main road, but it's worth driving into the village itself for the famous bakery **La Unión** (see Restaurants, page 454), where you can buy delicious bread, *empanadas* and fresh *facturas* (pastries). It's also a good source of information. Handicrafts, including fine leather goods, are available at El Encuentro half a block from the tourist information office (see Tourist information, below). From the village a road leads down to the tranquil lakeshore, where there are a couple of good places to stay.

Further along Route 3, 50 km from Ushuaia, a road to the right swoops down to **Lago Escondido**, a fjord-like lake with steep, deep-green mountains descending into the water. After Lago Escondido, the road crosses the cordillera at Paso Garibaldi. It then descends to the Cerro Castor winter-sports complex and the Tierra Mayor Recreation area (see What to do, page 464). There is a police control just as you enter Ushuaia city limits; passports may be checked.

## Listings Río Grande to Ushuaia

### Tourist information

**Tolhuin and around**

**Tourist office**
*Av de los Shelknam 80, T02901-492125,*
*tolhuinturismo@tierradelfuego.org.ar.*
*Daily 0900-1500.*
Tiny, friendly office with very helpful staff.

### Where to stay

**Tolhuin and around**

**$$$ Cabañas Khami**
*on Lago Fagnano, 8 km from Tolhuin, T02964-*
*15-611243, www.cabaniaskhami.com.ar.*
Well-equipped, rustic cabins, good value
with linen. Price given for 6 people, 3-night
weekend rates available.

**$$ Terrazas del Lago**
*R3, Km 2938, T02964-422710,*
*www.lasterrazasdellago.com.ar.*
A little way from the shore, smart wooden
*cabañas*, well decorated, and also a *confitería*
and *parrilla*.

**Camping**

**Camping Hain del Lago**
*T02964-1560 3606,*
*robertoberbel@hotmail.com.*

Lovely views, fireplaces, hot showers,
and a *quincho* for when it rains.

**Camping Rural La Correntina**
*See Facebook, T02964 15-612518 137,*
*17 km from Tolhuin.*
In woodland, with bathrooms,
and horses for hire.

### Restaurants

**Tolhuin and around**

**La Posada de los Ramírez**
*Av de los Shelknam 411, T02901-492382,*
*see Facebook. Open weekends only,*
*lunch and dinner.*
A cosy restaurant and *rotisería*.

**Panadería La Unión**
*Jeujepen 450, T02901-492202, www.*
*panaderialaunion.com. Daily 0600-2400.*
Deservedly famous bakery.

### What to do

**Tolhuin and around**
**Sendero del Indio**, *T02901-15-476803,*
*see Facebook.* For horse riding.

## Ushuaia   Colour map 3, C4.

### the last town before the edge of the world

The most southerly town in the world, Ushuaia's setting is spectacular. Its brightly coloured houses look like toys against the dramatic backdrop of vast jagged mountains. Opposite are the forbidding peaks of Isla Navarino, and between flows the serene green Beagle Channel. Sailing those waters you can just imagine how it was for Darwin, arriving here in 1832, and for those early settlers, the Bridges, in 1871.

Though the town has expanded in recent years, its population of 55,000 sprawling untidily along the coast, Ushuaia still retains the feel of a pioneer town, isolated and expectant. There are lots of places to stay, which fill up entirely in January, a fine museum and some great fish and crab restaurants.

There is spectacular landscape to be explored in all directions, with good treks in the accessible **Parque Nacional Tierra del Fuego** (see page 468), just to the west of the city, and more adventurous expeditions offered into the wild heart of the island, trekking, climbing or riding. There's splendid cross-country skiing and downhill skiing nearby at **Cerro Castor** ⓘ www.cerrocastor.com.

And to the east, along a beautiful stretch of coastline is the historic estancia of Harberton, which you can reach by a boat trip along the Beagle Channel. Ushuaia is also the starting point for expeditions to Antarctica; for more information, see www.dna.gov.ar. For more about Ushuaia, see www.e-ushuaia.com.

## Essential Ushuaia

### Finding your feet

The airport, **Aeropuerto Internacional Malvinas Argentinas**, T02901-431232, www.aeropuertoushuaia.com, is 4 km from town on a peninsula in the Beagle Channel. A taxi to or from the airport costs US$10-15 (there is no bus). Buses and minibuses from Río Grande arrive at their respective offices around town. See Transport, page 464.

### Getting around

It's easy to walk around the town in a morning, since all its sights are close together. You'll find banks, restaurants, hotels and shops along San Martín, which runs parallel to the shore, a block north of the coast road, Avenida Maipú. Ushuaia is very well organized for tourism, and there are good local buses to the national park and other sights, as well as many boat trips. Urban buses run from west to east across town; most stop along Maipú, US$0.50 (it can be a bit of a wait to catch a bus).

The tourist office provides a list of minibus companies that run daily to nearby attractions; most of these use the bus stop at the junction of Maipú and Fadul (see map).

Boat trips leave from the Muelle Turístico (tourist pier) by a small plaza, 25 de Mayo on the seafront.

### When to go

Ushuaia is at its most beautiful in autumn (March to May), when the dense forests all around are turned a rich red and yellow, and there are many bright days with clear azure skies. Summer (December to February) is best for trekking, when maximum temperatures are around 15°C, but try to avoid January, when the city is swamped with tourists. Late February is much better. The ski season is mid-June to October, when temperatures are around zero, but the wind drops.

### Money

Banks are open 1000-1500 in summer. ATMs are plentiful all along San Martín; using credit cards is easiest (but machines can be empty on Saturdays, Sundays and holidays). **Agencia de Cambio Thaler**, San Martín 209, T02901-421911, Monday-Friday 1000-1500 (extended hours in high season).

### Useful addresses

**Biblioteca Popular Sarmiento**, San Martín 1589, T02901-423103. **Monday-Friday** 1000-2000, www.bpsarmientoush.com.ar. Library with a good range of books about the area. **Chilean Consulate**, Jainén 50, T02901-430909, Monday-Friday 0900-1300 (telephone 0900-1700). **Dirección Nacional de Migraciones**, Fuegia Basket 187, T02901-422334.

## ★ Sights

There are several museums worth visiting if bad weather forces you indoors, and the most fascinating is **Museo del Fin del Mundo** ⓘ *along the seafront at Maipú y Rivadavia, T02901-421863, Mon-Fri 1000-1900, Sat, Sun and bank holidays 1400-2000, US$9, guided tours at 1100, 1400 and 1700, fewer in winter.* Located in the 1912 bank building, it tells the history of the town through a small collection of carefully chosen exhibits on the indigenous groups, missionaries, pioneers and shipwrecks, together with nearly all the birds of Tierra del Fuego (stuffed), and you can get an 'end of the world museum' stamp in your passport. There are helpful and informed staff, and also an extensive reference library. Recommended.

Further east, the old prison, Presidio, at the back of the naval base, houses the **Museo Marítimo** ⓘ *Yaganes y Gobernador Paz, www.museomaritimo.com, daily 0900-2000 (1000-2000 in winter), excellent guided tours in Spanish at 1130, 1630 and 1830 (1130 and 1630 in winter), US$13.50, ticket valid 24 hrs,* with models and artefacts from seafaring days. The cells of most of the five wings of the huge building also house the **Museo Penitenciario**, which details the history of the prison. Guided visits also include a tour of the lighthouse (a life-size replica of the original) that inspired Jules Verne's novel, *Around the World in Eighty Days*. Recommended. Much smaller but also interesting is **Museo Yámana** ⓘ *Rivadavia 56, T02901-422874, museoyamana@gmail.com, see Facebook), daily 1000-2000, US$7.50,* which has interesting scale models showing scenes of everyday life of Yámana people and the geological evolution of the island.

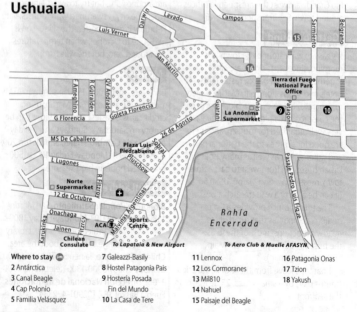

# Ushuaia

**Where to stay**
- 2 Antártica
- 3 Canal Beagle
- 4 Cap Polonio
- 5 Familia Velásquez
- 7 Galeazzi-Basily
- 8 Hostel Patagonia Pais
- 9 Hostería Posada Fin del Mundo
- 10 La Casa de Tere
- 11 Lennox
- 12 Los Cormoranes
- 13 Mil810
- 14 Nahuel
- 15 Paisaje del Beagle
- 16 Patagonia Onas
- 17 Tzion
- 18 Yakush

## BACKGROUND

### Ushuaia

Founded in 1884 after missionary Thomas Bridges had established his mission in these inhospitable lands, Ushuaia attracted many pioneers in search of gold. Keen to populate its new territory, the government set up a penal colony on nearby Staten Island, which moved to the town in 1902, and the town developed rapidly. Immigration was largely Croatian and Spanish, together with those shipwrecked on the shores, but the town remained isolated until planes arrived in 1935. As the prison closed, a naval base opened and in the 1970s there was a further influx, attracted by job opportunities in assemblage plants of electronic equipment that flourished thanks to reduced taxes.

Now the city is capital of Argentina's most southerly province, and though fishing is still a traditional economic activity, Ushuaia has become an important tourist centre, particularly as the departure point for voyages to Antarctica.

The most recently opened museum is the **Galería Temática** ① *San Martín 152, PB, 1er y 2do pisos, T02901-422245, www.historiafueguina.com, Mon-Sat 1100-2000, US$10,* where numerous life-sized displays take you through an informative history of Tierra del Fuego with a useful audioguide in different languages. There is also a themed garden at the back, reached through a huge souvenir shop with good knitwear and other goods.

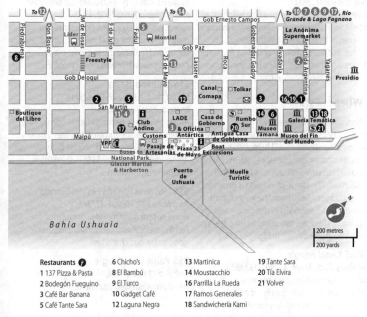

| Restaurants | | |
|---|---|---|
| 1 137 Pizza & Pasta | 6 Chicho's | 13 Martinica | 19 Tante Sara |
| 2 Bodegón Fueguino | 8 El Bambú | 14 Moustacchio | 20 Tía Elvira |
| 3 Café Bar Banana | 9 El Turco | 16 Parrilla La Rueda | 21 Volver |
| 5 Café Tante Sara | 10 Gadget Café | 17 Ramos Generales | |
| | 12 Laguna Negra | 18 Sandwichería Kami | |

## Tourist information

### Oficina Antártica
*At entrance to the port, near the main tourist office at the pier (Muelle Turístico), T02901-430015, antartida@tierradelfuego.org.ar. Mon-Fri 0900-1700.*
Information on Antarctica and a small library with navigational charts.

### Provincial tourist office
*Maipú 505, T02901-423423, info@tierradelfuego.org.ar.*

### Tierra del Fuego tourist office
*San Martín 1395, T02901-421315.*
Can provide a basic map of the park.

### Tourist office
*Prefectura Naval 470, at the Pier (Muelle Turístico), T02901-432000, www.turismo ushuaia.com. Mon-Fri 0800-2100, Sat-Sun 0900-2000.*
One of the best in Argentina. The helpful staff speak several languages. They have a map and a series of leaflets about all the things to see and do, and can provide bus and boat times. Another tourist office is at the airport (T02901-423970, open at flight times only).

## Where to stay

The tourist office (see above) has a comprehensive list of all officially registered accommodation and will help with rooms in private homes, campsites, etc. An excellent choice is to stay with Ushuaia families on a B&B basis. The range of lodging is growing at all budget levels, from the very chic, to *cabañas*, to basic B&Bs in the centre and the suburbs. There are too many to list here. You must book in advance in high season.

### $$$$ Canal Beagle
*Maipú y 25 de Mayo, T02901-432303, www.hotelcanalbeagle.com.ar.*
ACA hotel (discounts for members), Apr-Oct, comfortable and well-attended, with a small

pool, gym, spa, business centre, some rooms with channel views (others overlook the container dock), good restaurant.

### $$$$ Cap Polonio
*San Martín 746, T02901-422140, www.hotelcappolonio.com.ar.*
Smart, central, modern, comfortable, popular restaurant/café **Marcopolo**.

### $$$$ Lennox
*San Martín 776, T02901-436430, www.lennoxhotels.com.*
Boutique hotel on the main street, with breakfast, services include hydromassage, minibar, restaurant and *confitería* on 4th floor. Laundry service.

### $$$$ Mil810
*25 de Mayo 245, T02901-437710, www.hotel1810.com.*
City hotel with 30 standard rooms, 1 with disabled access, no restaurant but breakfast and *confitería* (0700-1000, 1700-2000), all rooms with minibar, safe, quite small but cosy, calm colours, good views, business centre and multiple use room where you can hang out while waiting for flight.

### $$$ Galeazzi-Basily
*G Gob Valdez 323, T02901-423213, www.avesdelsur.com.ar.*
Among the best, beautiful family home, incredible welcome, in pleasant area 5 blocks from centre, 4 rooms with shared bath. Also excellent *cabañas* ($$$) in the garden. Highly recommended.

### $$$ Hostería Posada Fin del Mundo
*Rivadavia 610, T02901-437345, www.posadafindelmundo.com.ar.*
Family atmosphere, comfortable rooms, good value, has character.

### $$$ Paisaje del Beagle
*Gob Paz 1347, T421214, www.paisajedelbeagle.com.ar.*

Family-run, quiet, with a cosy dining area for good breakfast, laundry service. Recommended.

### $$$ Tzion
*Gob Valdez 468, T02901-432290, tzion_byb@hotmail.com.*
B&B with 3 rooms, 1 with bath, high above town, 10 mins' walk from centre, nice family atmosphere, cheaper low season, laundry service, English and French spoken, great views. Highly recommended.

### $$ pp La Casa de Tere
*Rivadavia 620, T02901-422312, www.lacasadetere.com.ar.*
Shared or private bath, use of kitchen facilities, freshly baked bread, open fire, singles, doubles and triples, hot water, helpful owner.

### $$ Nahuel
*25 de Mayo 440, T02901-423068, see Facebook.*
Charming Sra Navarrete has a comfortable B&B with channel views from the upper rooms and the terrace, good value, but noisy street.

### $$-$ Familia Velásquez
*Juana Fadul 361, T02901-421719, losnokis_figueroa@hotmail.com.*
Cosy, welcoming house of a pioneer, with basic rooms, breakfast, cooking and laundry facilities, good.

### $ pp Antárctica
*Antártida Argentina 270, T02901-435774, www.antarcticahostel.com.*
Central, welcoming, spacious chill-out room, excellent 24-hr bar, dorms for 6 and large doubles, breakfast included, game night Thu with good prizes. Recommended.

### $ pp Los Cormoranes
*Kamshén 788 y Alem, T02901-423459, www.loscormoranes.com.*
Large hostel, with good views, cosy rooms with lockers, OK bathrooms, *parrilla*. Doubles ($$) available. They can book tours. HI members can still receive discount.

### $ Patagonia Onas
*Onas 176, T0291-433389, www.patagoniaonas.com.*
Owned by the same husband and wife who run **Patagonia Pais**, see below. This tranquil option is more central, and less of a party hostel. Also has doubles with shared bath ($$). Breakfast is included.

### $ Patagonia Pais
*Alem 152, T0291-431886, www.patagoniapais.com.*
Just above the centre, this welcoming, family-run hostel is a good meeting point. Dorms from US$17, laundry service, *parrilla*, breakfast included, information on tours and trips. Be sure to say hi to Gordita ("little fat one"), the hostel's canine mascot. Highly recommended.

### $ pp Yakush
*Piedrabuena 118 y San Martín, T02901-435807.*
Very well run, central with spacious dorms, also doubles ($$, cheaper without bath), book exchange and library, dining room, steep garden with views. Information centre has details on various tours. Recommended.

## Camping

### La Pista del Andino
*Leandro N Alem 2873, T02901-435890.*
Set in the Club Andino ski premises in a woodland area, it has wonderful views over the channel. Electricity, hot showers, tea room and grocery store, very helpful. Recommended.

## Restaurants

There are lots of restaurants along San Martín and Maipú. Most are open 1200-1500 and again from 1900 at the earliest. Several cafés are open all the time. Ask around for currently available seafood, especially *centolla* (king crab) and *cholga* (giant mussels). It's much cheaper if you prepare your own meal. But note that *centolla* may not be fished Nov-Dec. Beer drinkers should try the handcrafted brews of the Cape Horn brewery: Pilsen, Pale Ale and Stout.

### $$$ Bodegón Fueguino
*San Martín 859, T02901-431972,*
*www.tierradehumos.com/bodegon.*
Snacks, home-made pastas and good roast
lamb with varied sauces in a renovated 1896
*casa de pioneros.*

### $$$ Tía Elvira
*Maipú 349, T02901-424705.*
*Mon-Sat 1200-1500, 1900-2300.*
Excellent seafood.

### $$$ Volver
*Maipú 37, T02901-423907.*
Delicious seafood and fish in atmospheric
1896 house, with ancient newspaper all
over the walls. Recommended.

### $$$-$$ Moustacchio
*San Martín 298, T02901-430548,*
*www.moustacchio.com.ar.*
Long established, good for seafood and meat.

### $$$-$$ Parrilla La Rueda
*San Martín y Rivadavia, T02901-436540.*
Good *tenedor libre* for beef, lamb and great
salads. Recommended for freshness.

### $$ 137 Pizza & Pasta
*San Martín 137, T02901-435005.*
Tasty filling versions of exactly what the
name says, plus excellent *empanadas*,
elegant decor.

### $$ Chicho's
*Rivadavia 72, T02901-423469.*
Bright, cheerful place just off the main street,
friendly staff, kitchen open to view. Fish,
meat and chicken dishes, pastas, wide range
of *entradas.* Also recommended for *centolla.*

### $$ El Turco
*San Martín 1410.*
A very popular place, serving generous
*milanesas*, pastas, pizzas, seafood and meat.
Very tasty *empanadas.*

### $$-$ Martinica
*San Martín 68 (between Antártida Argentina
and Yaganes).*
Cheap, small, busy, sit at the bar facing the
*parrilla* and point to your favourite beef cut.

Takeaway (T02901-432134) and good meals
of the day, also pizzas and *empanadas.*

## Cafés

### Café Bar Banana
*San Martín 273, T02901-424021, see Facebook.*
Quite small, always busy, pool table, offers
good fast food, such as burgers, small pizzas,
puddings, breakfasts and an all-day menu
for **$$**.

### Café Tante Sara
*San Martín 701, opposite the tourist office,
T02901-423912, www.tantesara.com.*
Very good, smart, good coffee, tasty
sandwiches, always busy, open late. Also
has a restaurant and *panadería* at San
Martín 175 called **Tante Sara**, selling breads,
sandwiches, chocolates, *empanadas* and
snacks, coffee, lots of choice.

### El Bambú
*Piedrabuena 276, T02901-437028.*
*Daily 1100-1700.*
One of few purely vegetarian places in town,
takeaway only, home-made food, delicious
and good value.

### Gadget Café
*San Martín 1256, T0800-999 0223,*
*www.gadgettugelateria.com.ar.*
The best ice cream parlour in town, multiple
flavours, friendly. Recommended.

### Laguna Negra
*San Martín 513, T02901-431144,*
*www.lagunanegra.com.ar.*
Mainly a shop selling chocolate and other
fine produce, catering to the cruise ship
passengers, but has a good little café at
the back for hot chocolate and coffee. Also
has a bigger branch at Libertador 1250,
**El Calafate**. Sells postcards and stamps, too.

### Ramos Generales
*Maipú 749, T02901-424317, www.ramos
generalesush.com.ar. Daily 0900-2400
in high season.*
An old warehouse with wooden floors and
a collection of historic objects. Sells breads,

pastries, wines and drinks, also cold cuts, sandwiches, salads, ice cream, Argentine *mate* and coffee. Not cheap but atmospheric.

### Sandwichería Kami
*San Martín 54, T02901-430870. Daily until 2100.*
Friendly, simple sandwich shop, selling rolls, baguettes and *pan de miga*.

## Bars and clubs

### Bar Ideal
*San Martín 393, T02901-437860, www.elbarideal.com.*
Funky corner backpacker bar with a solid drink menu. Also serves food.

### Dublin Bar Irlandés
*9 de Julio 168, T02901-434704. Daily 2100-0400.*
A favourite with locals and tourists.

### Küar
*Av Perito Moreno 2232, east of town, T02901-437396, www.kuaronline.com. Daily for lunch from 1230 and dinner from 1800.*
Great setting by the sea, restaurant, bar and brewery.

## Festivals

**20-22 Jun Winter solstice**. The longest night. Torch-lit procession and fireworks.
**Aug Dog Sled Race**. Held annually.
**Aug Marcha Blanca**. www.marchablanca. com. A ski trek from Lago Escondido to Tierra Mayor valley.
**Oct Classical Music Festival**, www.festivaldeushuaia.com.

## Shopping

Ushuaia's tax-free status doesn't produce as many bargains as you might hope. Lots of souvenir shops on San Martín offer good-quality leather and silver ware. The **Pasaje de Artesanías** (by the Muelle Turístico), sells local arts and crafts.

**Atlántico Sur**, *San Martín 627*. The (not especially cheap) duty free shop.

**Boutique del Libro**, *San Martín 1120, T02901-424750, www.boutiquedellibro.com.ar. Mon-Sat 1000-1300 and 1530-2030.* An excellent selection of books, including several in English and other languages on Tierra del Fuego. CDs and DVDs upstairs.

## What to do

### Boat trips and sea cruises
**Sightseeing trips** All short boat trips leave from the Muelle Turístico. Take your time to choose the size and style of boat you want. Representatives from the offices are polite and helpful. All have a morning and afternoon sailing and include Isla de los Lobos, Isla de los Pájaros and Les Eclaireurs lighthouse, with guides and some form of refreshment. Note that weather conditions may affect sailings, prices can change and that port tax is not included. See also **Rumbo Sur** and **Tolkeyen** under Tour operators, below.
**Canoero**, *T02901-433893, www.catamaran escanoero.com.ar.* Runs 2 catamarans (one can accommodate 138 passengers), 2½- to 3-hr trips to the 3 main sites and Isla Bridges, US$53. They also have a 4½-hr trip almost daily to the Pingüinera on Isla Martillo near Estancia Harberton (Oct-Mar only), boats stay for 1 hr, but you cannot land on Martillo, US$75 (US$112 including Harberton – entry extra). Also longer tours to Estancia Harberton and Lapataia Bay.
**Patagonia Adventure Explorer**, *T02901-15-465842, www.patagoniaadvent.com.ar.* Has a sailing boat (US$60 plus US$1.50 port tax) and motor boats for the standard trip, plus Isla Bridges. Good guides.
**Pira-Tour**, *San Martín 847, T02901-435557, www.piratour.com.ar.* Runs 2 buses a day to Harberton, from where a boat goes to the Pingüinera on Isla Martillo: 20 people allowed to land (maximum 4 groups per day; the only company licensed to do this). US$110 plus US$20 for entrance to Harberton. Also offers various trekking and Beagle Channel tours.
**Tres Marías**, *T02901-436416, www.tres mariasweb.com.* The only company licensed

to visit Isla H, which has archaeological sites, cormorants, other birds and plants. 2 departures 1000 and 1500, 4 hrs. Also has a sailing boat for no more than 10 passengers; specialist guide, café on board. Trip costs US\$70. Highly recommended.

**To Antarctica** From Oct to Mar, Ushuaia is the starting point, or the last stop en route, for cruises to Antarctica. These usually sail for 9 to 21 days along the western shores of the Antarctic peninsula and the South Shetland Islands. Other trips include stops at Falkland/Malvinas archipelago and at South Georgia. Go to the **Oficina Antártica** for advice (see page 458). Agencies sell 'last-minute tickets', but the price is entirely dependent on demand. Coordinator for trips is **Turismo Ushuaia**, Gob Paz 865, T02901-436003, www.ushuaiaturismoevt.com.ar, which operates with IAATO members only. See the website for prices for the upcoming season. Port tax is US\$1.50 per passenger and an exit tax of US\$10 is also charged. **Freestyle Adventure Travel**, Gob Paz 866, T02901-15-609792, www.freestyleadventure travel.com. Organizes 7- to 22-day cruises to Antarctica, particularly good for last-minute deals. Wide variety of itineraries. Cape Horn expeditions also available. **Polar Latitudes**, T(1) 802 698 8479 (US) sales@polar-latitudes.com, www.polar-latitudes.com. Antarctic cruises aboard small expedition vessels, some itineraries take in the Falklands/Malvinas and South Georgia. All-suite accommodation onboard.

**To Chile** You can ask at **Muelle AFASYN** (near the old airport, T02901-437842), about possible crossings with a club member to Puerto Williams, about 4 hrs; from Puerto Williams a ferry goes once a week to Punta Arenas. There may also be foreign sailing boats going to Cabo de Hornos or Antarctica. **Australis**, www.australis.com. Operates 2 luxury cruise ships between Ushuaia and **Punta Arenas**, with a visit to Cape Horn, highly recommended. Full details are given in the box, page 412. Check-in at **Comapa** (see below).

**Fernández Campbell**, www.fernandez campbell.com. Has a 1½-hr crossing to **Puerto Williams**, Fri-Sun 1000, return 1500, US\$125 for foreigners, tickets sold at **Zenit Explorer**, Juana Fadul 126, Ushuaia, T02901-433232, and **Naviera RFC** in Puerto Williams. **Ushuaia Boating**, Gob Paz 233, T02901-436193 (or at the Muelle Turístico). Operates a channel crossing to Puerto Navarino (Isla Navarino) all year round, 30-90 mins depending on weather, and then bus to Puerto Williams, 1 hr, US\$125 one way, not including taxes.

## Fishing

Trout season is Nov to mid-Apr, licenses US\$19 per day (an extra fee is charged for some rivers and lakes). **Asociación de Caza y Pesca**, Maipú 822, T02901-423168, www.cazaypescaushuaia.org. Mon-Fri 1600-2000. Sells all licences and has a list on the door of other places that sell them.

## Hiking and climbing

The winter sports resorts along Ruta 3 (see below) are an excellent base for summer trekking and many arrange trips. **Antartur**, 25 de Mayo 296, T02901-430329, www.antartur.com.ar. Organizes treks, canoeing, mountain biking and 4WD trips to Lagos Escondido and Fagnano. Good winter trips. **Club Andino**, Alem 2873, T02901-440732, www.clubandinoushuaia.com.ar. Mon-Fri 1000-1300 and 1500-2000. Sells maps and trekking guidebooks; sports programmes like skiing, snowboarding, ice hockey and mountain climbing.

## Horse riding

**Centro Hípico**, Ruta 3, Km 3021, T02901-15-569099, www.horseridingtierradelfuego.com. Rides through woods, on Monte Susana, along coast and through river, 2 hrs, US\$48; 4-hr ride with light lunch, US\$96; 7-hr ride with asado, US\$144. Also offers a 10-day expedition on Península Mitre with a stay in an estancia, food included, US$3600. Gentle horses, which are well-cared for; all guides have first-aid training. Very friendly and helpful. All rides include transfer from town and insurance. Hats provided for children; works with disabled children.

## Tour operators

Lots of companies offer imaginative adventure tourism expeditions. All agencies charge the same fees for trips; ask the tourist office for a complete list: Tierra del Fuego National Park, 4½ hrs, US$40 (entry fee US$9.50 extra, valid for 48 hrs); Lagos Escondido and Fagnano, 7 hrs, US$60 without lunch. With 3 or 4 people it might be worth hiring a *remise* taxi.

**All Patagonia**, *Juana Fadul 58, T02901-433622, www.allpatagonia.com*. Trekking, ice climbing, and tours; trips to Cabo de Hornos and Antarctica.

**Canal**, *Roca 136, T02901-435777, www.canalfun.com*. Huge range of activities, trekking, canoeing, riding, 4WD excursions. Recommended.

**Comapa**, *San Martín 409, T02901-430727, www.comapa.tur.ar*. Conventional tours and adventure tourism, bus tickets to Punta Arenas and Puerto Natales, trips to Antarctica, agents for **Australis**. Recommended.

**Compañía de Guías de Patagonia**, *Godoy 193B, T02901-437753, www.companiadeguias. com.ar*. The best agency for walking guides,

expeditions for all levels, rock and ice climbing (training provided), also diving, sailing, riding, 7-day crossing of Tierra del Fuego on foot and conventional tours. Recommended.

**Rumbo Sur**, *San Martín 350, T02901-421139, www.rumbosur.com.ar*. Flights, buses, conventional tours on land and sea, including to Harberton, plus Antarctic expeditions, mid-Nov to mid-Mar, English spoken.

**Tolkar**, *Roca 157, T02901-431412, www.tolkarturismo.com.ar*. Flights, bus tickets to Argentina and Punta Arenas/Puerto Natales, conventional and adventure tourism, canoeing and mountain biking to Lago Fagnano.

**Tolkeyen**, *San Martín 1267, T02901-437073, www.tolkeyenpatagonia.com*. Bus and flight tickets, catamaran trips (50-300 passengers), including to Harberton (Tue, Thu, Sat in summer; itineraries vary in winter, US$101) and Parque Nacional, large company.

**Travel Lab**, *San Martín 1444, T02901-436555, www.travellab.com.ar*. Conventional and unconventional tours, mountain biking, trekking, etc, English and French spoken, helpful.

## Winter sports

Ushuaia is popular as a winter resort with 11 centres for skiing, snowboarding and husky sledging. Cerro Castor is the only centre for Alpine skiing, but the other centres along Ruta 3, 18-36 km east of Ushuaia, offer excellent cross-country skiing and alternative activities in summer.

**Cerro Castor**, *Ruta 3, Km 26, T02901-499301, www.cerrocastor.com*. 31 *pistas* including a vertical drop of 800 m and powder snow. It's an attractive centre with complete equipment rental, also for snowboarding and snowshoeing.

**Llanos del Castor**, *Ruta 3, Km 3033, www. llanosdelcastor.com.ar*. Wide range of activities throughout the year (plus a *refugio* and restaurant), but in winter they focus on dog-sledging expeditions.

**Tierra Mayor**, *20 km from town, T02901-437454*. The largest and most recommended. Lies in a beautiful wide valley between steep-sided mountains. It offers half- and full-day excursions on sledges with huskies, as well as cross-country skiing and snowshoeing. Equipment hire and restaurant.

## Transport

**Air** Book ahead in summer; flights fill up fast. In winter flights are often delayed. Schedules tend to change from season to season.

To **Buenos Aires** (Aeroparque or Ezeiza), daily, 3½ hrs. Frequent flights to **El Calafate**, 1 hr 20 mins, and **Río Gallegos**, 1 hr; also to **Río Grande**, 1 hr, several a week (but check with agents). The **Aeroclub de Ushuaia** flies to **Puerto Williams** and organizes flight tours of Tierra del Fuego from the downtown airport (US$155 pp, 30 mins), www.aeroclubushuaia.com.

**Boat** See What to do, above.

**Local bus** To **Parque Nacional Tierra del Fuego**, in summer buses and minibuses leave hourly from 0900 from the bus stop on Maipú at the bottom of Fadul, including **Transporte Santa Lucía** (www. transportesantalucia.com), 3 a day each, last return 1900, US$21 return. From same bus stop, many *colectivos* go to the **Tren del Fin del Mundo** (0900 and 1400, return 1145 and 1745, US$10.50 return), **Lago Escondido**, **Lago Fagnano** (1000 and 1400 return at 1400 and 1800), US$50 pp, minimum 6 people) and **Glaciar Martial** (1000 and 1200, return 1400 and 1600, US$10.50). For **Harberton**, check the notice boards at Maipú y Fadul. The only regular bus is run by **Pira-Tur**, see What to do, above.

**Long-distance bus** Passport needed when booking international bus tickets. Buses always booked up Nov-Mar; buy your ticket to leave as soon as you arrive. To **Río Grande**, 3½-4 hrs, combis run by **Líder** (Gob Paz 921, T02901-436421, www.lidertdf. com.ar), and **Montiel** (Gob Paz 605, T02901-421366), US$25, also buses en route to Río Gallegos and Punta Arenas. To **Río Gallegos**, with **Tecni Austral**, 0500, and **Marga/Taqsa** (Gob Godoy 41), 0700, 13 hrs, US$55 (book through Tolkar; see Tour operators). To **Punta Arenas**, US$55, with **Tecni Austral**, Mon, Wed, Fri 0500, 11-12 hrs (book through Tolkar); with **Pacheco**, 0700 Mon, Wed, Fri, 12-13 hrs (book through Tolkeyen, see above), with **Bus Sur** (at Comapa) Tue, Thu, Sat, Sun 0800; Bus Sur also goes to **Puerto Natales**, US$67, Tue, Sat 0800.

**Car hire** Most companies charge minimum US$60-70 per day, including insurance and 200 km per day, special promotions available. **Localiza**, Sarmiento 81, T02901-437780, www.localizadietrich.com. Cars can be hired in Ushuaia to be driven through Chile and then left in any Localiza office in Argentina, but you must buy a one-off customs document for US$107 to use as many times as you like to cross borders. Must reserve well in advance and pay a drop-off fee. **Budget**, Godoy 49, T02901-437373.

**Taxi** Cheaper than *remises*, Maipú at Lasserre, T02901-422007, T02901-422400. Taxi stand by the Muelle Turístico. **Remises Carlitos y Bahía Hermosa**, San Martín y Rosas, T02901-422222.

For exhilarating views along the Beagle Channel and to Isla Navarino opposite, visit Cerro Martial, 7 km from town, there is a chairlift (*aerosilla*) up the *cerro*, but it has been out of service since 2014, and now the only option is trekking.

To reach the base, follow Magallanes out of town; allow 1½ hours. Several companies run sporadic minibus services in summer from the corner of Maipú and Fadul, but they are more expensive than taxis. Taxis charge US$7-9 (up to four people) to the base, from where you can walk all the way back. There are several marked trails, ranging from 600 m to 1 km, including to a viewpoint and to Glaciar Martial itself.

There is a splendid **tea shop** ① *0900-2030*, at the Cumbres de Martial *cabañas* at the base, and a basic *refugio* with no electricity up at the *cerro*. Also by the lower platform is the **Canopy** ① *T02901-15-510307, www.canopyushuaia.com.ar, US$35, US$25 for a shorter run, US$32 and US$22 under 12s, daily 1000-1700*, a series of zip-lines and bridges in the trees. All visitors are accompanied by staff; it's safe and good fun. The café at the entrance, Refugio de Montaña, serves hot chocolate, coffee, cakes, pizzas and has a warm stove.

Parque Nacional Tierra del Fuego (see page 468), just outside Ushuaia, is easily accessible by bus and offers superb walks for all levels of fitness. Another way to get to the park is on the **Tren del Fin del Mundo** ① *T02901-431600, www.trendelfindelmundo.com.ar, 3 departures daily, US$36.50 (US$7.50 for children aged 5-15), US$58.50 1st class return, US$75.50 premium and US$720 VIP special (up to 6 people, includes private bath, kitchenette, food, park entrance fees, unlimited drinks, souvenirs), cheaper in winter, plus US$10 park entrance*. This is the world's southernmost steam train, running new locomotives and carriages on track first laid by prisoners to carry wood to Ushuaia. It's a totally touristy experience with commentary in English and Spanish. Sit on the left side on the outbound journey to get the views. See Transport, below, for buses to the train station.

The ★ **Estancia Harberton** ① *T02901-422742, open 1 Oct to mid-Apr daily 0930-1900, except 25 Dec, 1 Jan and Easter, US$13 (see box, page 466)*, 85 km from Ushuaia, is the oldest estancia on the island and is still run by descendants (currently the fifth generation) of the British missionary Thomas Bridges. It's a beautiful place, with the attractive wood-framed house that Thomas built sitting in quiet contemplation on a tranquil bay.

The impressive **Museo Akatushún** ① *phone as above, 1 Oct to mid-Apr daily 0930-1900, except 25 Dec, 1 Jan and Easter, 8 tours a day, entrance fee is included in the estancia admission price*, has skeletons of South American sea mammals, the result of more than 35 years' scientific investigation in Tierra del Fuego, with excellent tours in English.

You can camp for free with permission from the owners, or stay in cottages or one of the original remodelled farm buildings; see Where to stay, below. Access is along a good unpaved road (Route 33, ex 'J') that branches off Route 3, 40 km east of Ushuaia and runs about 45 km through forest and then through the open country around Harberton with marvellous views; it takes about an hour and a half, and there's no petrol outside Ushuaia and Tolhuin. See What to do and Transport, below, for trips to Harberton with Pira-Tur and bus services (irregular). For boat trips to Harberton, see below.

Trips can be made to Lagos Fagnano and Escondido: agencies run seven-hour tours for US$60 per person without lunch; US$140 for nine hours including canoe rides, or check the list of cheaper but rather unreliable minibuses that go there, which is available at the tourist office. Tour agencies offer many good packages, which include trekking, canoeing,

## ON THE ROAD

# Estancia Harberton

In a land of extremes and superlatives, Harberton stands out as special. The oldest estancia in Tierra del Fuego, it was built in 1886 on a narrow peninsula overlooking the Beagle Channel. Its founder, the missionary Thomas Bridges, was granted land by President Roca for his work amongst the indigenous people and for his help in rescuing victims of numerous shipwrecks in the channels.

Harberton is named after the Devonshire village where his wife Mary was born. The English connection is evident in the neat lawns, shrubs and trees between the jetty and the farmhouse. Behind the buildings is a large vegetable garden, a real rarity on the island, and there's noticeably more wildlife here than in the Tierra del Fuego National Park, probably owing to its remoteness.

Still operating as a working farm, mainly with cattle and sheep, Harberton is run by Thomas Goodall, great-grandson of the founder, whose wife Natalie has created an impressive museum of the area's rich marine life with a thriving research centre. Visitors receive a bilingual guided tour of the museum, or of farm buildings and grounds with reconstructions of the Yámana dwellings. Tea or lunch (if you reserve ahead) are served in the tea room overlooking the bay, and you may well be tempted to rent one of the two simple cottages on the shore. There are wonderful walks along the coast, and nowhere in Argentina has quite the feeling of peace you'll find here.

birdwatching and horse riding in landscape accessible only by 4WDs. See the tourist office's list of trips, indicating which companies go where.

## Boat trips

All these trips are highly recommended, but note that the ★ **Beagle Channel** can be very rough. Food and drink on all boats is pricey. Trips can be booked through most agencies, or at the Muelle Turístico where boat companies have their ticket offices; most boats leave from the Muelle Turístico, with a few trips leaving from Muelle AFASYN (next to the old airport). All passengers must pay US$1.40 port tax; this is not included in tickets.

Most popular excursions visit the small islands southeast of Ushuaia in 2½ to three hours, all year round, passing next to the sea lion colony at Isla de los Lobos, Isla de los Pájaros and Les Eclaireurs lighthouse. Alternatively, they add an hour or so for a landing on Bridges Island. Prices vary depending on whether trips are made on big catamarans or on more exclusive sailing boats. A few pricier services include lunch on board; otherwise a light snack or a coffee is served. Summer options add more to the itinerary, with some trips going further east past the Isla Martillo penguin colony and on to Estancia Harberton. Note that Harberton is included only on a few trips, and you should check that your tour actually visits the estancia and not just the bay, as some do. A few trips also go west to the national park in about 5½ hours. See What to do, page 461, for companies and prices.

## Where to stay

### $$$$ Cabañas del Beagle
*Las Aljabas 375, T02901-432785,*
*www.cabanasdel beagle.com.*
3 rustic-style cabins 1.3 km above the
city, kitchen, hydromassage, fireplace,
heating, phone, self-service breakfast,
very comfortable, personal attention.

### $$$$ Cumbres del Martial
*Luis F Martial 3560, 7 km from town, T02901-*
*424779, www.cumbresdelmartial.com.ar.*
At the foot of the *aerosilla* to Glaciar Martial,
4 *cabañas* and 6 rooms, beautifully set in the
woods, charming, very comfortable, cabins
have whirlpool baths. Small spa (massage
extra) with saunas and gym. The tearoom,
with disabled access, is open all year,
restaurant with traditional fondues.

### $$$$ Las Hayas
*Luis Martial 1651 (road to Glaciar Martial),*
*T02901-442000, www.lashayashotel.com.*
4 standards of room, all very good with
TV, jacuzzi, safe, 3 types of view, channel,
mountains or forest. Restaurant and bar.
Everything is included in room price
(including breakfast), except massages
and hairdresser. A fine hotel. Just beyond
and run by the same family company is:

### $$$$ Los Acebos
*Luis F Martial 1911, T02901-442200,*
*www.losacebos.com.ar.*
All rooms with channel view, safe, games
room. Golf days organized. Very comfy,
as expected, but less characterful than
**Las Hayas**.

### $$$$ Los Cauquenes
*At Bahía Cauquen, De La Ermita 3462,*
*T02901-441300, www.loscauquenes.com.*
High-quality 5-star hotel overlooking
Beagle Channel, price varies according
to size and view, spa, very tastefully
decorated, prize-winning restaurant,
regional food on dinner menu, wine
bar with over 100 Argentine wines.

### $$$$ Los Yámanas
*Costa de los Yámanas 2850, western suburbs,*
*T02901-446809, www.hotelyamanas.com.ar.*
All rooms with Channel view, spacious, well-
decorated, hydromassage, fitness centre, spa
outside in wooded grounds, shuttle to town.
Very pleasant.

### $$$$ Tierra de Leyendas
*Tierra de Vientos 2448, T02901-446565,*
*www.tierradeleyendas.com.ar.*
In the western suburbs. 5 very comfortable
rooms with safe, views of the Beagle Channel,
or the mountains at the back, 1 room with
jacuzzi, all others with shower, excellent
restaurant serving regional specialities. No
cable TV, but DVDs, living room with games,
library, deck overlooking Río Pipo's outflow.
Wi-Fi. Only for non-smokers. Recommended
and award-winning.

### $$$ pp Estancia Harberton
*T02901-422742. 1 Oct to mid-Apr.*
Restored buildings on the estancia (see
above), very simple rooms, wonderful views,
heating. Price includes walking tour and
entry to museum; 2 rooms with bath, 1 room
with 2 beds, shared bath, 1 room with bunks,
shared bath. There is also a guest-house
with 2 triple rooms, and a *hostal* (**$$**) with
3 private rooms with shared bathroom.
Kitchenette for tea and coffee. Lunch and
dinner extra. Offers half and full-board
options. No credit cards. See opposite.

Covering 63,000 ha of mountains, lakes, rivers and deep valleys, this small but beautiful park stretches west to the Chilean border and north to Lago Fagnano, though large areas have been closed to tourists to protect the environment. All walks are best early morning or afternoon to avoid the tour buses. You'll see lots of geese, the beautiful torrent duck, Magellanic woodpeckers and austral parakeets.

## Walks

**Senda Costera** ⓘ *8 km, 3 hrs each way.* This lovely easy walk along the shore gives you the essence of the park, its rocky coastline, edged with a rich forest of beech trees and glorious views of the low islands with a backdrop of steep mountains. Start at Bahía Ensenada (where boat trips can be taken around the bay, and where the bus can drop you off). Walk along a well-marked path along the shoreline, and then rejoin the road briefly to cross Río Lapataia (ignoring signs to Lago Acigami to your right). After crossing the broad green river and a second stretch of water (where there's a small camping spot and the *gendarmería*), it's a pleasant stroll inland to the beautifully tranquil **Bahía Lapataia**, an idyllic spot, with views across the sound.

**Senda Hito XXIV** ⓘ *Along Lago Acigami (Roca), 3.5 km, 90 mins one way.* Another easy walk beside this peaceful lake, with lovely pebble beaches, and through dense forest at times, with lots of birdlife. This is especially recommended in the evening. Get off the bus at the junction for Lago Acigami, turn right along the road to the car park (passing the *guardaparque*'s house) and follow the lake side.

# Parque Nacional Tierra del Fuego

# Essential Parque Nacional Tierra del Fuego

## Access

The park entrance is 12 km west of Ushuaia, on the main road west signposted from the town centre, where you'll be given a basic map with marked walks. The **park administration**, San Martín 1395, T02901-421315, tierradelfuego@apn.gov.ar, Monday-Friday 0900-1600, is in Ushuaia.

## Entry fees

US$14.

## Tourist information

Ask at the tourist office for bus details (see also Transport, below) and a map of the park, with walks. There are no legal crossing points from the park to Chile. There's a helpful *guardaparque* (ranger) at Lago Acigami (formerly known as Roca).

## What to take

Wear warm, waterproof clothing: in winter the temperature drops to as low as -12°C, and although it can reach 25°C in summer, evenings can be chilly.

**Cerro Guanaco** ① *4 km, 4 hrs one way.* A challenging hike up through the very steep forest to a mirador at the top of a hill (970 m) with splendid views over Lago Acigami, the Beagle Channel and mountains. The ground is slippery after rain; take care and don't rush. Allow plenty of time to return while it's light, especially in winter. The path branches off Senda Hito XXIV (see above) after crossing Arroyo Guanaco.

## Listings Parque Nacional Tierra del Fuego *map page 468.*

### Where to stay

**Camping Lago Roca**
*T02901-422748, 21 km from Ushuaia, by forested shore of Lago Acigami (Roca), a beautiful site with good facilities, reached by bus Jan-Feb.*
It has a backpackers' *refugio*, toilets, showers, restaurant and *confitería*, expensive small shop; camping equipment for hire.

There are also campsites with facilities at **Río Pipo**, 16 km from Ushuaia, and at **Laguna Verde**, 20 km, near Lapataia, and at **Bahía Ensenada**, with no facilities.

### What to do

For a really rich experience, go with guides who know the territory well and can tell you about the wildlife. Inexpensive trips for all levels are available with the highly recommended **Compañía de Guías de Patagonia** (www.companiadeguias.com.ar).

# Background

# A sprint through
## history

### Early days
50,000 years ago, the first people cross the temporary land bridge between Asia and America at the Bering Straits and begin a long migration southwards, reaching Tierra del Fuego 12,000 years ago. Hunters and foragers, they follow in the path of huge herds of animals such as mammoths, giant sloths, mastodons and wild horses, adapting to fishing along the coasts. The area remains sparsely populated and many Patagonian peoples remain nomadic until the encroachment of European settlers in the 19th century.

### 15th-16th centuries
The Incas expand their empire into central Chile. They are stopped by hostile forest tribes at the Río Maule, near present-day Talca. Due to its topography, Patagonia is not touched by Inca incursions.

### 1516
Juan Díaz de Solís arrives in the Plata estuary. He and his men are killed by the indigenous Guaraníes. Other Europeans follow, including Portuguese explorer Ferdinand Magellan who ventures south into the Pacific via the straits north of Tierra del Fuego. The straits become an important trade route until the building of the Panama Canal in 1914.

### 1541
Following the overthrow of the Incas by a tiny force of Spaniards led by Francisco Pizarro, Pedro de Valdivia is given the task of conquering Chile. He reaches the fertile Mapocho valley and founds Santiago. The settlements of Concepción, Valdivia and Villarica follow.

### 1580s
A group of settlers led by Pedro de Sarmiento seeks to found a colony on the north banks of the Magellan Straits. The colony is a disaster and only two people survive. This is the end of attempts at European settlement in southern Patagonia for centuries.

### 1598
A rebellion by the Mapuche in the Chilean Lake District (see box, page 260) drives the Spanish back to the north of the Río Biobío, leaving isolated groups of settlers in Valdivia and on Chiloé, ensuring that European influence in Patagonia will remain marginal.

### 17th century
In 1616, a Dutch navigator names the southernmost tip of Argentina Cape Horn after his hometown, Hoorn. Meanwhile, the indigenous groups and the Spanish authorities are in a state of permanent war. The Spanish want to enslave the natives into a system of *encomiendas* – a feudal regime that has been successful in Peru. The colonizers have more sophisticated weapons, but the indigenous peoples use guerrilla warfare and fight using spears, bows and arrows. The Spanish are unable to defeat the Mapuche and there is something of a stand-off. During this period a generation of *criollos* (Spaniards born in the colonies) develops and intermarriage takes place resulting in *mestizo* populations. The

indigenous people are gradually weakened due to famine, lack of resistance to diseases such as small pox and the production of alcohol. However, it is not until 1881 that the treaty ending Mapuche Independence from Chile is signed.

## 1808-1816

Napoleon invades Spain and deposes King Ferdinand VII. Argentine independence from Spain is declared on 9 July 1816 by José de San Martín.

## 1827

The royalist citizens of Carmen de Patagones – an outpost at the gateway to Patagonia – are reluctant to accept the *criollo* government and, in 1827, soldiers, gauchos, slaves and pirates are sent to stamp the new government's authority on the region.

## 1829-1834

General Rosas, Juan Manuel de Rosas, a powerful governor of Buenos Aires, brings order, gaining support by seizing lands from indigenous peoples and handing them to friends in the 'Campaign of the Desert' (1833-1834). This is followed by a new era of growth and prosperity, but also increasing authoritarianism as Rosas consolidates power. The indigenous Pampas peoples' independence and way of life is destroyed and the incursion of European forces into Patagonia begins.

## 1843

Alarmed by widespread naval activity in the region, the Chilean navy sends a cutter to the Magellan Strait and erects a fort at Fuerte Bulnes, to claim the straits for Chile – the rest of Patagonia between here and the mainland now falls under Chilean jurisdiction.

## 1845-1880

The Chilean government encourages settlement around Lago Llanquihue, provoking extensive immigration to the area by German colonists. Legacy of this settlement can be seen in the German-looking buildings around Puerto Octay, Frutillar and Puerto Varas.

In 1848, Chile founds Punta Arenas, making Chile's claim of the Strait of Magellan permanent. It becomes a penal colony modelled on Australia, and in 1867 is opened to foreigners and given free port status. The town prospers as a refuelling and provisioning centre for steam ships until the opening of the Panama Canal in 1914.

## 1865

Welsh immigrants arrive in Puerto Madryn on the Atlantic coast and settle inland along the Chubut Valley. Their aim is to free themselves of their English oppressors and to find a haven in which to practise their religion in their own language. They learn from the indigenous Tehuelche people and successfully irrigate the valley for agriculture. In 1889 a railway connects Puerto Madryn with Trelew, enabling the Welsh to export their produce.

## 1879

Expansion in the south becomes more aggressive with increasing confrontation with indigenous populations. Colonel Julio A Roca's 'Conquest of the Wilderness' sends a force against the indigenous peoples of Patagonia, exterminating many of them and herding the rest into settlements. The government pushes the frontier, and the railway, south, paving the way for further European settlement.

## Late 19th century

Large swathes of land are divided up and settlers are allocated 40 ha apiece. Thomas Bridges founds a mission in Tierra del Fuego (see page 446).

## Early 20th century
Rural poverty in both countries leads to urbanization and high unemployment, wealth is concentrated in the hands of the very few. The wool boom encourages the creation of large farms for sheep-raising in Patagonia. Many migrants come from the island of Chiloé to work at farms in Argentine Patagonia and on Chilean Tierra del Fuego.

## 1940s-1950s
Following a military coup in 1943, Juan Perón wins the presidency in 1946 and 1952. An authoritarian and charismatic leader, he institutes stringent reforms against the economic elite and in favour of the workers.

## 1960s-1970s
Chile's politics become increasingly polarized. The Marxist coalition led by Salvador Allende introduces sweeping reforms, such as redistribution of income and the takeover of many private enterprises. The country is plunged into economic chaos.

## 11 September 1973
General Pinochet seizes power in a bloody coup. Allende allegedly commits suicide and thousands of his supporters are murdered. During the dictatorship which follows, an estimated 80,000 are tortured, murdered or exiled; one of the early detention centres is on Isla Dawson in the Magellan Straits.

## 1976-1983
In Chile, the building of the Carretera Austral begins. The new military government in Argentina institutes a reign of terror known as the 'Dirty War'. Any vaguely left-wing thinking, opposition or criticism of the military is met with violent torture and elimination by death squads. Up to 30,000 people 'disappear'. Internal conflict ends with the war against Britain over the disputed Islas Malvinas (Falkland Islands). Democracy returns, when Alfonsín becomes president in 1983.

## 1978
Argentina and Chile nearly go to war over a territorial dispute over three islands – Lennox, Nueva and Picton – in the Beagle Channel. The Pope has to intervene and the islands are awarded to Chile.

## 1973-1990
Pinochet dissolves Congress in Chile, bans leftist parties and suspends all opposition. His economic policies bring prosperity, but a referendum in 1988 sees him rejected. Democracy returns and Christian democrat Patricio Aylwin is elected President in 1990.

## 1990s
In Argentina, Peronist president Carlos Menem institutes major economic reforms, selling off nationalized industries and opening the economy to foreign investment. The country falls heavily into debt. In 1999 President Fernando de la Rua of the UCR centre-left Alliance promises a crackdown on corruption and tough measures to balance Argentina's budget.

## 2001
In December, nationwide demonstrations erupt when access to bank accounts is restricted in the 'corralito'. Argentina is plunged into serious economic and political crisis. Rioting, looting and widespread civil chaos result in the death of 27 people.

## January 2002

Eduardo Duhalde becomes Argentina's fifth president in two weeks. He is forced to devalue the peso in order to borrow money from the International Monetary Fund. The middle class is devastated, many losing their life savings. Widespread poverty becomes a reality, with child malnutrition and unemployment over 20%.

## 2003

Argentine elections threaten to return Menem to power, even though he bankrupted the nation by selling off national industries. Néstor Kirchner wins by a narrow margin, promising to reduce corruption and lessen the burden of government employees. The country recovers some stability. Tourism flourishes – both from foreigners enjoying low prices and Argentines realizing that holidaying in their own country is more magnificent than in Miami, which had become the aspirant norm under Menem.

## 2006

Michelle Bachelet is voted in as Chile's first female president. In December, General Augusto Pinochet dies, aged 91.

## 2007

Néstor Kirchner decides to stand down as president of Argentina and his wife, Cristina Fernández de Kirchner, wins the election to become Argentina's first female head-of-state.

## 2009

Sebastián Piñera and his right-wing Alianza por Chile defeat the Concertación coalition.

## 2010

Piñera's first challenges are to deal with reconstruction after the massive earthquake of February 2010 and the rescue of 33 miners trapped underground near Copiapó for 69 days beginning in August.

## 2011

Student protests over inequality in education begin in Chile. They are to last, on and off, for a further two years. In October, Fernández de Kirchner wins a big majority in presidential elections; her victory was helped greatly by a thriving economy.

## 2013

Cardinal Jorge Bergoglio, former archbishop of Buenos Aires, is elected Pope Francis I in March; he is the first pope from Latin America. In December Michelle Bachelet, at the head of the Nueva Mayoría coalition, is re-elected president of Chile.

## 2015

Mauricio Macri of the Cambiemos party is elected Argentina's first non-Peronist president in 14 years. One of his first moves is to allow the peso to float against other currencies.

## Today

Patagonia remains very much an extremity of both Argentina and Chile. Historically absent from the national boundaries until the 19th century, it still feels very different to the rest of the countries. Some long for the utopia of a united Patagonia, free of the internal wranglings of the power bases of Buenos Aires and Santiago.

# Land & environment

## Glacial landscapes

Patagonia provides some of the best examples of glacial landscapes on earth. One common sign of the region's glacial past is the U-shaped valleys. Perhaps one of the best examples is the Río Simpson between Coyhaique and Puerto Aysén. High above these valleys, sharp mountain ridges can be seen. In some places, the resulting debris or 'moraine' formed a dam, blocking the valley and creating a lake, as in the Lake District at Lagos Calafquén, Panguipulli and Riñihue.

The drowned coastline south of Puerto Montt also owes its origin to glaciation. The ice that once covered the southern Andes was so heavy that it depressed the relatively narrow tip of South America. When the ice melted and the sea level rose, water broke through, leaving the western Andes as islands and creating the Chilean fjords, glaciated valleys carved out by the ice and now drowned.

## Wildlife

The varied geography of Patagonia has created a number of different ecosystems. Chile in particular is an ecological island: fauna that is commonplace in neighbouring countries has not been able to migrate here because of the terrain and the country's isolation has contributed to a range of endemic wildlife.

### Land mammals

Typical of Patagonia, is the **guanaco** – a coffee-coloured, cousin of the llama, with a long neck and small head. Two species of deer found in Patagonia are the **huemul** and the **pudu**. Other land mammals include a small hairless vole called the **tucotuco**, unique to Tierra del Fuego; a type of chinchilla called a **vizcacha** and; and a rodent called a **mara**.

### Marine mammals

Numerous colonies of **seal** (including the elephant seal which can weigh up to three tonnes) and **sea lion** live all along the Patagonian coast and come ashore to mate in December and January. Five species of **dolphin** can be spotted, frequently off the coast of Chiloé. Types of whale include the **southern right whale**, which comes to breed off the coast of Península Valdés and can be spotted from June to December; and the orca/**killer whale**, which arrives to feed on the young seal pups from March to April.

### Birds

The **choique**, known as 'Darwin's rhea', is a large, flightless, ostrich-like bird, which roams the Patagonian steppes. Once hunted for its feathers, it is now farmed for meat and protected in the wild. The **southern flamingo**, most commonly seen around lake shores, it also inhabits coastal areas on the Península Valdés and the Isla de los Pájaros. Birds of prey include the **condor** and various species of **eagle**, **hawk** and **buzzard**. Two regional birds of prey, the **jote** and the **tiuque**, are also common. Half the world's species of **penguin** can be found along the coast of Chile.

# Practicalities

General landscapes

# Getting there

## Air

It is not possible to fly directly to Patagonia from outside Argentina or Chile (apart from a weekly flight to Punta Arenas from the Falklands Islands/Islas Malvinas). Instead you must choose to fly into either Buenos Aires' **Ezeiza International Airport** (EZE; see page 479) or Santiago's **Aeropuerto Arturo Merino Benítez** (SCL; see page 479) and pick up onward transport there. There are several flights a day between Santiago and Buenos Aires. Check-in time for international flights is at least two hours before departure, one hour for domestic flights. Most airlines expect you to check in online. If a flight does not involve e-tickets or online check-in, you should reconfirm bookings in advance.

**Prices and discounts** Fares vary considerably from airline to airline, so it's worth checking with an agency for the best deal for when you want to travel. The cheap-seat allocation will sell out quickly in holiday periods. The busiest seasons for travelling to Argentina and Chile are December to mid-January, Easter and July to mid-September, when you should book as far ahead as possible. There might be special offers available from February to May and September to November. **Open-jaw fares** allow you to arrive at and depart from different airports, which can be useful on multi-country trips, but you should check the details carefully.

**Baggage** Check your baggage allowance as airlines vary widely. The limit is usually between 20 and 32 kg per person for economy class, strictly enforced with high charges for excess baggage. You must check with your airline for its rules. Weight limits for internal flights in Chile are usually 23 kg for economy class, but can be as low as 10 kg on smaller aircraft in Patagonia. For internal flights in Argentina, the baggage limit with **Aerolíneas Argentinas** is 15 kg, and they are extremely inflexible, also charging wildly for excess. This means you will either have to leave some things in your hotel in Buenos Aires, or consider limiting your baggage to 15 kg when you leave home.

**Entry fees and taxes** By law Argentine airport taxes must be included in the price of your air ticket. In 2010 Argentina introduced entry fees for citizens of countries which require Argentines to obtain a visa and pay an entry fee, namely Australia (US$100, valid one year) and Canada (US$100, valid 10 years). The reciprocity fee for US citizens (US$160, valid 10 years) was suspended in March 2016 for an undefined period. The fee is only payable by credit card online before arrival. You must print the receipt and present it to immigration wherever you enter the country. Go to www.migraciones.gov.ar and click on Tasas de Turismo on the home page and then Tasa de Reciprocidad on the following page for instructions. There is also www.ivisa.com/visa-argentina-reciprocity-fee to help you.

Chilean airport **departure tax** is US$30 for international flights, US$11.80 for flights under 500 km; US$4.65 for domestic flights, as well as occasional fuel surcharges, all of which should be included in the price of the ticket. **Reciprocity charges**, valid for the lifetime of the passport, are to be paid in US dollars by nationals of Australia (US$117) and Mexico (US$23).

## Flights from Europe

There are flights to Buenos Aires from London, Amsterdam, Barcelona, Madrid, Frankfurt, Paris, Milan, Rome and Zurich with **Aerolíneas Argentinas** ⓘ *Gatwick House, Peeks Brook Lane, Horley, Surrey, RH6 9ST, T0871-644 4453 or T0800-0969 747, www.aerolineas.com.ar*, LATAM and other European carriers (some examples are listed below, also Air Europa via Madrid). From Britain, only British Airways goes direct to Buenos Aires. With other carriers you will have to change planes in another European city and the whole journey can take up to 24 hours. Alternatively, fly to New York or Miami and get a connecting flight from there.

Flights from the UK to Santiago take 18 to 20 hours, including a change of plane. It is impossible to fly directly to Santiago from London, so connections have to be made on one of the following routes: **Aerolíneas Argentinas** ⓘ *www.aerolineas.com.ar*, via Madrid/Rome and/or Buenos Aires; **Air France** ⓘ *www.airfrance.com*, via Paris; **British Airways**, connecting through LATAM via Madrid and/or in Buenos Aires; **Iberia** ⓘ *www. iberia.com*, via Madrid or Barcelona; **LATAM** ⓘ *www.latam.com*, via Madrid or São Paulo; **Lufthansa** ⓘ *www.lufthansa.com*, via Frankfurt or Munich and São Paulo; or with one of the American carriers via New York, Atlanta, Dallas, Houston or Miami.

## Flights from North America

**Aerolíneas Argentinas** and other South American and North American airlines fly from Miami, New York, Washington, Los Angeles, San Francisco, Atlanta, Dallas and Chicago to Buenos Aires. **American Airlines** ⓘ *www.aa.com*, and LATAM fly direct from Miami (nine hours), New York and Dallas Fort Worth to Santiago. LATAM also has flights to Santiago from Los Angeles (connecting in Lima), while **Delta** ⓘ *www.delta.com*, has a service from Atlanta. Additional flights from Los Angeles, Miami and New York to Santiago are operated by **Copa** ⓘ *www.copaair.com*, via Panama City, and **Avianca** ⓘ *www. avianca.com*, via San Salvador, San José, Bogotá and/or Lima.

**Air Canada** ⓘ *www.aircanada.com*, and LATAM fly from Toronto and Montreal to Buenos Aires; Air Canada also has the only direct flights from Toronto to Santiago. LATAM offers connections with sister airlines from Vancouver to Los Angeles and thence to Santiago, or from Toronto to New York or Miami and on to Santiago. Both American and Delta also have services from Canada to Santiago via the US.

## Flights from Australasia and elsewhere

Santiago is the closest hub for travellers from Australia and New Zealand. **LATAM/United** flies direct to Santiago from Auckland and Sydney (some flights are via Auckland). **Qantas**, www.qantas.com, flies between Sydney and Santiago direct. Flights to Buenos Aires from Sydney with **Aerolíneas Argentinas**, LATAM and Qantas are all via Auckland or Santiago, several times a week. **South African Airways** fly four times a week from Johannesburg to Buenos Aires, via Sao Paulo, and to Santiago via São Paulo.

## Flights from Latin America

**Aerolíneas Argentinas** and other carriers fly between Buenos Aires and all the South American capitals, plus Santa Cruz and Cochabamba (Bolivia) and Guayaquil (Ecuador). Several flights between Buenos Aires, Rio de Janeiro and São Paulo (Brazil) stopover in Porto Alegre, Florianópolis and Curitiba. There are also flights from Belo Horizonte, Salvador, Recife and Fortaleza (Brazil), Havana (Cuba), Mexico City and Cancún (Mexico).

**LATAM** and other carriers have services to Santiago from Buenos Aires (every hour or so), Montevideo (Uruguay), Rio de Janeiro and São Paulo (Brazil), La Paz and Santa

Cruz (Bolivia), Lima (Peru), Guayaquil and Quito (Ecuador), Bogotá (Colombia), Caracas (Venezuela), Mexico City and Cancún (Mexico).

## Airport information

**Ezeiza International Airport** (officially known as Ministro Pistarini) ① *35 km southwest of Buenos Aires, T011-5480 6111, www.aa2000.com.ar,* handles most international flights to Buenos Aires, apart from those from neighbouring countries. Ezeiza has three terminals: 'A', 'B' and 'C'.

Domestic flights from Buenos Aires (as well as some flights to/from neighbouring countries) are handled from Jorge Newbery Airport, known as **Aeroparque** ① *4 km north of the centre of Buenos Aires, T011-5480 6111, www.aa2000.com.ar.* **Manuel Tienda León** ① *Av Madero 1299 y San Martín, T011-4315 5115, www.tiendaleon.com.ar,* runs efficient buses between the two airports, 1½ hours, US$14. They have a desk inside Ezeiza arrivals hall, where you can also book a *remise* taxi to Aeroparque, US$50. See also box, page 38.

**Aeropuerto Arturo Merino Benítez** ① *26 km northwest of Santiago at Pudahuel, help desk T2-2690 1752, www.nuevopudahuel.cl,* handles both international and domestic flights, and is the only airport in Chile with intercontinental connections. It is a modern, safe and efficient terminal. Domestic and international flights leave from different sections of the same terminal. You will go through customs and immigration in international arrivals before transferring to the domestic section of the same terminal. Procedures at customs (*aduana*) are quick and efficient. Outside customs there are kiosks for minibus and taxi companies serving Santiago, as well as car hire companies. See also box, page 230.

# **Getting** around

## Air

If you're short on time, flying is preferable to long bus journeys and can be relatively inexpensive – sometimes cheaper than taking a *salón-cama* bus. Consider buying two single tickets for the same price as a return, flying to one destination and leaving from another, to allow you to explore an area in detail by hired car or bus. Always book well in advance from December to March.

### Air passes
Air passes allow you to pre-book between three to six internal flights at a discount, as long as your international flight is also with that company. However, air passes are no longer the cheapest way of getting around, and can be very restricting since you have to book all dates when you book your international ticket. You'll probably find it easier to book internal flights separately, but check with the airlines directly, in case they have a promotion.

Aerolíneas Argentinas and Austral have a Visite Argentina internal air pass which offers domestic flights at cheaper rates than those bought individually. Details can be found on www.aerolineas.com.ar: go to the 'Cheap flights' menu. LATAM offers a multi-country air pass that includes Argentina; see www.latam.com. LATAM sells a South America Air Pass, which is available only from tour operators that package the air pass with hotels, tours and services. This is only recommended if you are planning on doing several long-distance flights and are willing to pay for a tour package.

### Air services in Argentina
Internal air services are run by Aerolíneas Argentinas (AR) ① *freephone within Argentina* T0810-222 86527, www.aerolineas.com.ar; Austral (part of AR); LATAM ① T0810-999 9526, *within Chile* T600-526 2000, www.latam.com, and the army airline LADE ① *freephone within Argentina* T0810-810 5233, www.lade.com.ar; its flights are booked up ahead of time. Andes ① T0810-777-26337, www.andesonline.com, based in Salta, flies between Buenos Aires and Salta, Jujuy and Puerto Madryn.

From Buenos Aires there are several flights daily to Neuquén, Chapelco (for Junín and San Martín de los Andes, two hours), Bariloche (2½ hours) and Esquel; there are also daily flights from Buenos Aires to Viedma, Puerto Madryn (in high season), Trelew (two hours), Comodoro Rivadavia, Río Gallegos, El Calafate (3¼ hours) and Ushuaia. Within Argentine Patagonia, connecting flights are largely only provided by the army airline LADE on a weekly basis, which can make travel frustrating. LATAM flies to Ushuaia from Argentine destinations as well as from Punta Arenas, Puerto Montt and Santiago in Chile.

All internal flights fill up very quickly, so it's vital that you book in advance in the summer (December to March) and during the winter ski season for Ushuaia (July and August). At other times of the year, flights can be booked with just a few days' notice, though note that flights to Ushuaia are always heavily booked. It's wise to leave some flexibility in your schedule to allow for bad weather, which may delay flights particularly in the south. Meals are rarely served on internal flights, though you'll get a hot drink and a snack. Most provincial airports in Argentina have a tourist information desk, banking facilities and a *confitería* (cafeteria) as well as car hire. There are usually minibus services into the nearest town and taxis are available. Don't lose your baggage ticket; you won't be able to collect your bags without it.

## Air services in Chile

LATAM flies between Santiago and major cities under the banner **Latam Express**. The other main domestic airline is **Sky** ① *T02-2352 5600, www.skyairline.cl*, which operates three weekly flights between Balmaceda (Coyhaique) and Punta Arenas. Destinations in the far south are served by DAP ① *www.dap.cl*, based in Punta Arenas.

Check with airlines for student and other discounts. Note that flight times may be changed without warning; always double check the time of your flight when reconfirming.

The most important routes from Santiago to Patagonian destinations are to Temuco (1½ hours), Valdivia (summer only, 1½ hours), Osorno (2½ hours), Puerto Montt (1¾ hours), Balmaceda (Coyhaique, 2½ hours) and Punta Arenas (4½ hours). **LATAM** also flies from Santiago to Mount Pleasant on the Falkland (Malvinas) Islands via Punta Arenas and Río Gallegos. There are flights from Puerto Montt to Balmaceda or Punta Arenas; from Punta Arenas to Puerto Williams, Ushuaia or Porvenir, and from Puerto Natales to El Calafate (summer only). **LATAM** and **Sky** will have direct services from Santiago to Puerto Natales in summer in 2017.

## Rail

The only long-distance train within Patagonia runs from **Viedma** on the Atlantic coast to **Bariloche** in the Argentine Lake District (www.trenpatagonico-sa.com.ar; see page 68). It is advisable to check in advance if the service is running. Patagonia's best-known train, *La Trochita*, www.latrochita.org.ar, made famous by Paul Theroux as the *Old Patagonian Express*, is a purely tourist affair that departs from Esquel in the southern Lake District for the remote Mapuche station at Nahuel Pan (see page 143). Even more touristy is the *Tren del Fin del Mundo*, www.trendelfindelmundo.com.ar, which travels from Ushuaia to the Tierra del Fuego national park (see page 465).

There are no long-distance passenger train services in Chilean Patagonia.

## Road

Argentina and Chile have very comfortable buses that travel overnight, enabling you to sleep. However, the 24-hour bus ride along Argentine Ruta 40 from Los Antiguos to El Chaltén has fantastic views that you'll want to stay awake for. On long bus journeys, carry small packs of tissues, hand wipes and bottled water, as toilets on buses can be unpleasant. Also take a jumper to combat the fierce air conditioning.

### Buses in Argentina

The country is connected by a network of efficient long-distance buses, which is usually the cheapest way of getting around. They run all year, are safe and comfortable, and travel overnight, which saves time on long journeys. The biggest bus companies are: **Andesmar** ① *T0810-122 1122, www.andesmar.com*; **Chevallier** ① *T011-4000 5255, www.nuevachevallier. com.ar*; **Flecha Bus** ① *T011-4000 5200, www.flechabus.com.ar*; and **Vía Bariloche** ① *T0810-333 7575, www.viabariloche.com.ar*. Book seats a day in advance in January. Regional services to tourist destinations within Patagonia tend to be limited after mid-March.

Bear in mind that *común* buses have lots of stops (*intermedios*), are uncomfortable and not recommended for long journeys. *Semi-cama* buses have slightly reclining seats, meals and a toilet on board. *Coche-cama* buses have fully reclining seats, meals, a toilet, only a few stops and are worth the small extra expense for a good night's sleep.

# BORDER CROSSINGS

## Argentine and Chilean Patagonia

The main routes between Argentine and Chilean Patagonia are by boat and bus between Bariloche and Puerto Varas in the Lake District; by road from El Calafate to Puerto Natales and Torres del Paine or by road; and ferry from El Calafate via Río Gallegos to Tierra del Fuego. There are many other crossings (some little more than a police post), which are detailed throughout the guide. See also www.gendarmeria. gov.ar (in Spanish only; click on the Pasos Fronterizos page) and www.difrol.gob.cl. For some crossings, prior permission must be obtained from the authorities. Note that passes across the Andes may be blocked by snow from April onwards. See also Customs and duty free, page 486, and Visas and immigration, page 497.

- Crossing the border is not a lengthy procedure unless you're on a bus, when each individual is checked. It is your responsibility to ensure that your passport is stamped in and out when you cross borders. Do not lose your tourist card; replacing one can be inconvenient and costly. Immigration and customs officials are generally friendly, helpful and efficient, however, the police at Chilean control posts a little further into the country can be extremely bureaucratic.

- Tourist card holders returning across a land border to Argentina will be given a further 90 days in the country. Visa holders should check regulations with the Chilean/Argentine embassies.

- Fruit, vegetables, meat, flowers and milk products may not be imported into Chile; these will be confiscated at all borders. Searches are thorough.

- If you plan to take a hired car across the border, obtain an authorization form from the hire company; you will be charged about US$100. This is exchanged at the outgoing border control for another form, one part of which is surrendered on each side of the border. If you plan to leave more than once you will need to photocopy the authorization. Make sure the number plate is etched on the car windows and ensure that the hire company gives you the vehicle's ownership papers, which have to be shown at police and military checks. At some crossings, you must pay for the car's tyres to be sprayed with pesticides.

- There are often no exchange facilities at the border so make sure you carry small amounts of both currencies. Remember to change your watch if crossing the border between early March and September/October.

At www.plataforma10.com, www.omnilineas.com.ar and www.xcolectivo.com.ar (all in English) you can check bus prices and times and book tickets throughout the country. Note that if you buy a bus ticket with a credit card online, you must show the receipt and your identity (eg passport) when you collect your ticket. Student discounts of 20% are sometimes available – always ask. Discounts aren't usually available December to March. Make sure your seat number is on your ticket. Luggage is safely stored in a large hold at the back of the bus, and you'll be given a numbered ticket to reclaim it on arrival. *Maleteros* take the bags off the bus, and may expect a small tip – a couple of pesos is fine.

## Buses in Chile

Bus services in Chile are frequent and comfortable. Buses tend to be punctual, arriving and leaving on time. Along the Carretera Austral, however, services are far less reliable, less frequent and usually in minibuses. Services improve again between Punta Arenas and Puerto Natales in the far south. In addition, there are long-distance international services from Santiago to Buenos Aires, from Osorno to Bariloche, from Coyhaique to Comodoro Rivadavia and from Punta Arenas to Río Gallegos and Ushuaia.

When choosing a bus in Chile, remember *clásico/salón-ejecutivo* are comfortable enough for daytime travel but are not ideal for long distances. *Semi-cama* buses have more leg room and fewer stops but are 50% more expensive. *Salón-cama* are similar to a *coche-cama* in Argentina (see above), and *cama premium* have flat beds. *Salón-cama* buses are the most spacious, with dinner available on overnight services. They are 50% more expensive than *semi-cama*. The premium service with fully reclining seats runs between Santiago and the lakes (30% more expensive than *salón-cama*).

Apart from at holiday times, there is little problem getting a seat on a long-distance bus and you only need to reserve ahead in high season. Prices are highest from December to March but competition between bus companies means you may be able to bargain for a lower fare, particularly just before departure; discounts are also often available for return journeys. Students may also get discounts out of season. Most bus companies will carry bicycles, but may ask for payment.

## Car

Hiring a car is an excellent idea if you want to travel independently and explore the more remote areas of Patagonia, although it can be complicated to take a hire car across the border between Argentina and Chile (see box, opposite). The most important routes in Argentine Patagonia are Ruta 40, which runs along the east side of the Andes and faster Ruta 3, which runs down the Atlantic coast. Santiago is linked to the Chilean Lake District by the paved toll road, the **Pan-American Highway** (or **Panamericana**), marked on maps as Ruta 5, which runs all the way from the Peruvian frontier south to Puerto Montt. The **Carretera Austral**, a mostly *ripio* (gravel) road marked on maps as Ruta 7, runs south of Puerto Montt, punctuated by three ferry crossings as far as Villa O'Higgins, from where the southbound boat does not carry cars. There is an excellent paved road between Punta Arenas and Puerto Natales from where there are two *ripio* roads to Torres del Paine. Buy road maps from service stations or the **Automóvil Club Argentino** ⓘ *www.aca.org.ar*, in Argentina, Copec service stations or the **Automóvil Club de Chile** ⓘ *www.automovilclub.cl*.

Generally, main roads are in good condition but on some *ripio* roads, particularly south of Puerto Montt, a high-clearance, 4WD vehicle is required, as road surfaces can degenerate to earth (*tierra*). Most roads in Patagonia are single lane in each direction. There's little traffic and service stations for fuel, toilets, water and food are much further apart than in Europe and the US, so always carry water and spare fuel and keep the tank full. Safety belts are supposed to be worn, if fitted.

**Car hire** The cost of hiring a vehicle is similar in Chile and Argentina, but can be more expensive in Patagonia than in other parts of either country. There are few hire cars available outside the main tourist centres, although small towns may have cheaper deals. Hiring a car from one place and dropping it off somewhere else is possible but will incur extra charges. The multinational companies (**Hertz**, **Avis**) are represented all

## ON THE ROAD
### Road trips

The sheer size and remoteness of Patagonia means that long-distance road trips are an exhilarating way of exploring the region. What's more, the terrain of endless steppes interrupted by rivers, gorges and gullies is also ideal for off-roading. The two most popular road trips in Argentine Patagonia are the **Ruta de los Siete Lagos** (Seven Lakes Route) in the Lake District and the endless **Ruta 40**, a little-used highway running directly south from Bariloche to El Calafate. The Seven Lakes Route is stunning at any time of year. It is a curling, curving road that rings the seven interconnecting lakes of this region, with panoramic views every step of the way. Visit friendly small towns, stay in wonderful luxury hotels or cheaper wooden cabins and sample locally brewed beer, handmade ice creams and delicious jams. Otherwise, if you are looking for something a little more challenging, the desolate plains south of the Lake District hold immense appeal and are best accessed by the lonely Ruta 40 (which actually starts in La Quiaca on the Bolivian border). Take plenty of food and fuel as houses, let alone towns, are sparse. It is a surreal and unique experience.

In Chilean Patagonia, one road trip stands head and shoulders above the rest: the **Carretera Austral**, or southern highway. The main spine, which is largely gravel, winds through 1000 km of dramatic scenery. If the forests of the northern section seem too green to be real, the lakes and rivers further south are an even more extraordinary hue. Driving will give you the liberty to stop and marvel at the landscape whenever it takes your fancy, and if you want a different perspective, hitchhike instead and enjoy its beauty from the back of a pickup, a truly exhilarating experience.

over Patagonia but local companies may be cheaper and usually just as reliable. You must be 25 or over in Argentina and 22 or over in Chile to hire a car; a national driver's licence and a credit card should be sufficient. Vehicles may be rented by the day, the week or the month, with or without unlimited mileage. Rates quoted should include insurance and VAT but always check first. Note that the insurance excess, which you'll have to pay if there's an accident, can be extremely expensive. Check the vehicle carefully with the hire company for scratches and cracks in the windscreen before you set off, so that you won't be blamed for them on your return. Hire companies will take a print of your credit card as their guarantee instead of a deposit but are honourable about not using it for extra charges. Ensure that the hire company gives you the vehicle's ownership papers, which have to be shown at police and military checks. For information on crossing the border with a car, see box, page 482.

**Fuel** Petrol (known as *nafta* in Argentina, *bencina* or *gasolina* in Chile) becomes more expensive in Chile the further south you go, but tends to be cheaper in Argentine Patagonia. Diesel (*gasoil* in Argentina, *diesel* in Chile) is available in both countries and is cheaper than petrol.

### Cycling

Given ample time and reasonable energy, cycling is one of the best ways to explore Patagonia. A mountain bike can be ridden, carried by almost every form of transport from a plane to a canoe, and lifted across your shoulders over short distances. Cyclists can travel at their own pace, explore more remote regions and meet people who are less commonly in contact with tourists.

The challenges for cyclists are the enormous distances, the state of some roads and the lack of places to buy supplies. Wind, too, can be a serious problem when cycling in Patagonia, with gusts of 80 kph around the clock at some times of year. Try to make the best use of the mornings when wind speeds are lowest. Take care to avoid dehydration by drinking regularly, and carry the basic food staples (sugar, salt, dried milk, tea, coffee, porridge oats, raisins, dried soups, etc) and supplement these with local foods wherever possible. There's little traffic on most roads, but make yourself conspicuous by wearing bright clothing and, for protection, wear a helmet. Bring a tool-kit and as many spare parts as you can. Bike shops are few and far between, although there are excellent shops in the Lake District, for example. Try not to leave a fully laden bike on its own and always secure your bike with a lock. Both the Ruta 40 and the Carretera Austral have become long-distance favourites among hardy cyclists, and riding along them can be an amazing experience. But do your research first into road conditions, weather and stopping points. A mountain bike and a tent are essential for these routes, as the road can be rough and there are very few *hosterías* or places to stay.

## Hitchhiking
Hitchhiking is relatively easy and safe (although you should always exercise caution) and often involves an exhilarating ride in the back of a pickup truck. Traffic is sparse in the south, however, and roads in places like Tierra del Fuego rarely see more than a few vehicles per day.

## Taxis, colectivos and remises
Taxis usually have meters and can either be hailed in the street or booked in advance, although they tend to be more expensive when booked from a hotel. Surcharges are applied late at night and at weekends. Agree fares beforehand for long journeys out of city centre or for special trips; also compare prices among several drivers.

Collective taxis (*colectivos* in Chile, *remises* in Argentina) operate on fixed routes (identified by numbers and destinations) and are a good way of getting around cities. They are usually flagged down on the street corner, but make sure you have small notes and coins to pay the driver. In Chile, *colectivos* also operate on some inter-urban routes, leaving from a set point when full; they compete favourably with buses for speed but not for comfort.

## Sea and lake

In the Lake District, ferries can be used as a means of transport, as well as a day out. The Three Lakes Crossing to Chile from Bariloche is a good way of getting to Puerto Varas or Puerto Montt in Chile, but the bus is cheaper. In the south of Chile, maritime transport is very important. Vital routes are, from north to south: Puerto Montt to Chiloé (many daily, but a bridge is to be built); Puerto Montt to Chaitén (several weekly) and Puerto Chacabuco (weekly); Puerto Montt to Puerto Natales (weekly); Castro or Quellón to Chaitén (several weekly in summer, fewer in winter); Quellón to Puerto Chacabuco (once weekly); Punta Arenas to Porvenir (six times weekly); and Punta Arenas to Puerto Williams (twice monthly). Note that routes and timetables change frequently and reservations are essential for the ferries in high summer. Details of all routes are given under the relevant chapters.

# Essentials A-Z

## Accident and emergency

### Argentina
**Ambulance** T107, **Police** T101 and 911 (*31416 from mobile). **Medical** T107. **Fire service** T100. **Tourist police**, Comisaría del Turista, Av Corrientes 436, Buenos Aires, T011-4346 5748 (24 hrs) or T0800-999 5000 (English spoken), turista@policiafederal. gov.ar. Note that you will most likely not get your stolen goods back, but a police report is essential for your insurance claim.

### Chile
**Air rescue** T138; **Ambulance** T131; **Fire brigade** T132, www.bomberos.cl; **Forest fires** T130; **Police** T133; **Police detectives** T134; **Sea rescue** T137.

Policía Internacional, E Ramírez 852, Santiago, T2-2737 1292, Mon-Fri 0800-1400, handle immigration and lost tourist cards.

Contact the relevant emergency service and your embassy (see Embassies and consulates, below). Make sure you obtain police/medical reports required for insurance claims.

## Children

Chileans and Argentines will go out of their way to make children welcome. More expensive hotels provide a babysitting service; children's meals are offered in many restaurants and most have high chairs. Self-catering cabañas may be the best sleeping option for families as they are good value and usually well equipped.

Most tourist attractions charge less for children; on sightseeing tours try to bargain for a family rate. Chilean domestic airlines charge around 66% for children under 12 but long-distance bus fares in Argentina and Chile are calculated per seat, so you'll have to seat small children on your knee to save money. Distances are long; consider flying if possible. Adventure tourism in Patagonia is not really suitable for very young children and the climate is often too cold, wet and windy for them. However, there is plenty for slightly older children to enjoy. Highlights might include the wildlife at Península Valdés and Punta Tumbo; the tourist trains in the Argentine Lake District (Tronchita) and on Tierra del Fuego (Tren del Fin del Mundo), and boat trips on the Seven Lakes.

## Customs and duty free

### Argentina
Visitors coming from countries not bordering Argentina are exempt from taxes on items brought into the country, including new items up to US$300 (US$100 from neighbouring countries), and an additional US$300 if goods are purchased at duty free shops within Argentina. The duty and tax payable amounts to 50% of the item's cost. At the airport, make sure you have the baggage claim tag (usually stuck to your ticket or boarding card), as these are inspected at the exit from the customs inspection area. 2 litres of alcoholic drink, 400 cigarettes and 50 cigars are also allowed in duty-free. For tourists originating from neighbouring countries the quantities allowed are 1 litre of alcoholic drink, 200 cigarettes and 25 cigars.

### Chile
The following may be brought into Chile duty free: 400 cigarettes or 50 cigars or 500 g of tobacco, plus 2500 cc of alcoholic drinks, and all articles for personal use, including vehicles, radios, cameras, personal computers and similar items. Fruit, vegetables, meat, flowers, seeds and milk products may not be imported into Chile; these will be confiscated at all borders, where there are thorough searches. This

applies even to those who have had to travel through Argentina in the far south to get from one part of Chile to another.

## Disabled travellers

Facilities for the disabled in Argentina and Chile are improving but remain inadequate. Airlines are extremely helpful, especially if you let them know your needs in advance, but some long-distance buses are still unable to accommodate wheelchairs, although drivers will help those with some mobility. The **Metrobús** system in Buenos Aires has buses that are wheelchair-friendly and work is underway to make the metro more accessible. Almost the entire Santiago metro system is accessible to disabled users. Elsewhere you won't find ramps or even lowered kerbsides, and pavements tend to be shoddy and broken even in big cities. Many upmarket hotels have been fully adapted for wheelchair use, but tourist sights, particularly in national parks, generally only have limited access for disabled visitors. However, the best museums have ramps or lifts and some may offer special guided tours for the visually or hearing impaired: the superb dinosaur museum in Trelew is setting the standard here. Boat trips to some of the glaciers should also be possible with prior arrangement.

Argentines and Chileans generally go out of their way to help you, making up for any lack of facilities with kindness and generosity. Speaking Spanish is obviously a great help and travelling with a companion is advisable.

**Useful organizations and websites**
**Disability Action Group**, www.disabilityaction.org. Information on independent travel.
**Disability Rights UK**, www.disabilityrightsuk.org.
**Global Access Disabled Network**, www.globalaccessnews.com/index.htm.
**Mobility International USA**, www.miusa.org.

**Society for Accessible Travel and Hospitality**, www.sath.org. Lots of advice on how to travel with specific disabilities.

Other useful sites include **www.gimponthego.com** and **www.makoa.org/travel.htm**.

## Drugs

Using drugs, even soft ones, without medical prescription is illegal and penalties are severe (up to 10 years in prison) even for possession. The planting of drugs on travellers by traffickers or the police is not unknown. If offered drugs on the street, make no response and keep walking. People who roll their own cigarettes are often suspected of carrying drugs and may be subjected to intensive searches.

## Electricity

220 volts AC (and 110 too in some Argentine hotels), 50 cycles. Chile has 2- or 3-round-pin European-style plugs. Argentina has European-style plugs in old buildings and Australian 3-pin flat-type in new buildings. Bring a universal adapter, as these are not readily available.

## Embassies and consulates

For all Argentine and Chilean embassies and consulates abroad and for all foreign embassies and consulates in Argentina and Chile, see http://embassy.goabroad.com.

## Gay and lesbian travellers

Discrimination on the grounds of sexual orientation was banned in Argentina in 1996, and in 2005 it became the first South American country to legalize same-sex marriages. The country is fast becoming one of the most popular gay destinations in the world and there is enough happening in Buenos Aires to keep you busy for a few weeks, with a range of gay-oriented travel agencies to help you plan your stay. However, in the interior of the country and in Chile you may well encounter homophobia and being openly demonstrative in public will certainly raise eyebrows. Overall, Chile and Argentina remain macho cultures; gay men and lesbian women are not encouraged to be open about their sexuality and there are few places where you can go to meet other gay/lesbian friends.

## Useful websites
**www.gaytravel.com** Excellent site with information on gay travel.
**www.globalgayz.com**, **www.iglta.org** (International Gay and Lesbian Travel Association), **www.lghei.org** (Lesbian and Gay Hospitality Exchange International) and **www.passportmagazine.com**.
**www.nexo.org** A useful site for gay information within Argentina (Spanish only).
**www.purpleroofs.com/southamerica/argentina.html** For help in planning your trip.
**www.gaycities.com** A guide to gay life in world cities, including Buenos Aires and Santiago.
**www.thegayguide.com.ar** For travel tips on bars in Buenos Aires.

In Chile, the sites of movements such as **www.acciongay.cl**, **www.mums.cl** (Movimiento por la Diversidad Sexual) and **www.movilh.org** (Movimiento de Integración y Liberación Homosexual).

## Health

See your GP or travel clinic at least 6 weeks before departure for general advice on travel risks and vaccinations. Try phoning a specialist travel clinic if your own doctor is unfamiliar with health conditions in Patagonia. Make sure you have sufficient medical travel insurance, get a dental check, know your own blood group and if you suffer a long-term condition such as diabetes or epilepsy, obtain a Medic Alert bracelet/necklace (**www.medicalert.org.uk**). If you wear glasses, take a copy of your prescription.

## Vaccinations and anti-malarials
Vaccinations for **hepatitis A**, **tetanus**, **typhoid** and, following the 2009 outbreak, **influenza A (H1N1)** are commonly recommended for Argentina and Chile. Sometimes advised are vaccines for **hepatitis B** and **rabies**. The final decision, however, should be based on a consultation with your GP or travel clinic. You should also confirm your primary courses and boosters are up to date.

## Health risks
Temperate regions of South America, such as Patagonia, present far fewer health risks than tropical areas to the north. However, travellers should take precautions against: **diarrhoea/intestinal upset**; **hanta virus** (carried by rodents and causing a flu-like illness); **hepatitis A**; **hypothermia**; **marea roja**; **rabies**; **sexually transmitted diseases**; **sun burn** (a real risk in the far south due to depleted ozone); and **ticks**. **Malaria** is a substantial risk in parts of north and northeastern Argentina but not in Patagonia, where mosquitoes are more of a nuisance than a serious hazard. Sleep off the ground and use a mosquito net and some kind of insecticide.

## If you get sick
Contact your embassy or consulate for a list of doctors and dentists who speak your language, or at least some English. Doctors and health facilities in major cities are also listed below. Good-quality healthcare is available in the larger centres but it can be expensive, especially hospitalization. Make sure you have adequate insurance (see below). Bear in mind that in Chile, hospitals are public facilities, while clinics are private. Those with adequate insurance who find themselves in a medical emergency will want to request a *clínica* instead of a hospital to avoid long waiting times.

## Medical services

### Bariloche
Hospital Zonal, Moreno 601, T0294-442 6119, www.hospitalbariloche.com.ar.

### Buenos Aires
**Urgent medical service**: for free municipal ambulance service to an emergency hospital department (day and night) **Casualty ward**, **Sala de guardia**, T107, or T011-4923 1051/58 (SAME).

**Inoculations**: Hospital Rivadavia, Av Las Heras 2670, T011-4809 2000, Mon-Fri 0700-1200 (bus Nos 10, 37, 59, 60, 62, 92, 93 or 102 from Plaza Constitución), or **Dirección de Sanidad de Fronteras y Terminales de Transporte**, Ing Huergo 690, T011-4343 1190, Mon-Fri 1100-1500, bus No 20 from Retiro, no appointment required (yellow fever only; free injection; take passport). If not provided, buy the vaccines in **Laboratorio Biol**, Uriburu 153, T011-4953 7215, biol.com.ar, or in larger chemists. Many chemists have signs indicating that they give injections. Any hospital with an infectology department will give hepatitis A. **Centros Médicos Stamboulian**, 25 de Mayo 464, T011-4515 3000, Pacheco de Melo 2941, also in Belgrano, Villa Crespo, Villa Urquiza and Flores, www.stamboulian.com.ar. Private health advice for travellers and inoculations centre.

**Public hospitals**: Hospital Argerich, Almte Brown esq Py y Margall 750, T011-4121 0700. **Hospital Juan A Fernández**, Cerviño y Bulnes, T011-4808 2600, www.hospitalfernandez.org. Probably the best free medical attention in the city. **British Hospital**, Perdriel 74, T011-4309 6400, emergencies T011-4309 6633/4 www.hospitalbritanico.org.ar. **German Hospital**, Av Pueyrredón 1640, between Beruti and Juncal, T011-4827 7000, www.hospitalaleman.com.ar. Both have first-aid centres (*centros asistenciales*) as do other main hospitals.

**Dental treatment**: there's an excellent dental treatment centre at **Croid**, Vuelta de Obligado 1551 (Belgrano), T011-4781 9037, www.croid.com.ar. **Dental Argentina**,

Laprida 1621, p 2 B, T011-4828 0821, www.dental-argentina.com.ar.

### Castro
Hospital de Castro, Freire 852, www.hospitalcastro.gov.cl.

### Chile Chico
**Hospital**: Lautaro s/n, T67-241 1334.

### Futaleufú
**Hospital**: Balmaceda y Aldea, T65-272 1231.

### Los Antiguos
Hospital Patagonia, Argentina 68, T02963-491303. **Farmacia Rossi Abatedaga**, Av 11 Julio 231, T02963-491204.

### Puerto Madryn
SEP, Sarmiento 125, T02965-445 4445.

### Puerto Varas
Clínica Puerto Varas, Otto Bader 810, T65-2239100, usually has English-speaking doctors.

### Punta Arenas
Hospital Clínico Magallanes, 'Dr Lautaro Navarro Avaria', Av Los Flamencos 1364, T61-229 3000, www.hospitalclinicomagallanes.cl. Public hospital, for emergency room ask for urgencias. **Clínica Magallanes**, Bulnes 01448, T61-220 7200, www.clinicamagallanes.cl. Private clinic, medical staff the same as in the hospital but fancier surroundings and more expensive.

### San Martín de los Andes
Hospital Ramón Carrillo, San Martín y Coronel Rodhe, T02972-427211.

### Santiago
**Note** If you need to get to a hospital, it is better to take a taxi than wait for an ambulance.

Emergency hospital at Marcoleta 377, T2-2633 2051 (emergency), T2-2770 9500 (general enquiries). **Hospital del Salvador**,

Av Salvador 334 or J M Infante 551, T2-2575 4000 general, open 24 hrs but reception hours are Mon-Fri 0800-1700, Sat, 0800-1300, 1400-1700. **Vacunatoria Internacional**, Marcoleta 350, T2-2235 4534. **Hospital Luis Calvo**, MacKenna, Antonio Varas 360, T2-2575 5800, www.calvomackenna.cl. **Clínica Alemana**, Av Manquehue 1410, p 2, Vitacura, T2-2210 1301, pacienteinternacional@alemana.cl. Mon-Fri 0800-1700. **Clínica Central**, San Isidro 231-243, Santa Lucía metro, T02-2402 4200 (call centre), open 24 hrs, German spoken.

### Tortel
Medical centre near the tourist information office offers emergency care.

### Villa La Angostura
**Hospital Rural Arraiz**, Copello 311 (at Barrio Pinar), T02944-494170.

### Villa O'Higgins
**Medical Centre Posta de Salur Rural** near the plaza.

---

**Useful websites**
**www.bgtha.org** British Global Travel Health Association.
**www.cdc.gov** US government site that gives excellent advice on travel health and details of disease outbreaks.
**www.fco.gov.uk** British Foreign and Commonwealth Office travel site has useful information on each country, people, climate and a list of UK embassies/consulates.
**www.fitfortravel.scot.nhs.uk** A-Z of vaccine/health advice for each country.
**www.nathnac.org** National Travel Health Network and Centre (NaTHNaC).
**www.nhs.uk/nhsengland/Healthcareabroad/pages/Healthcareabroad.aspx** Department of Health advice for travellers.
**www.who.int** World Health Organization.

## Insurance
Always take out comprehensive insurance before you travel, including full medical cover and extra cover for any activities (hiking, rafting, skiing, riding, etc) that you may undertake. Check exactly what's being offered, the maximum cover for each element and also the excess you will have to pay in the case of a claim. Keep details of your policy and the insurance company's telephone number with you at all times and get a police report (*constancia*) for any lost or stolen items.

## Internet
The best way to keep in touch is undoubtedly online. Broadband is widely available in Argentina and Chile, even in remote areas, and most hotels and hostels have Wi-Fi. Dedicated centres/internet cafés are widespread, particularly in towns and tourist centres and most *locutorios* (phone centres, known as *centros de llamadas* in Chile) also have an internet connection.

## Language
*See also Language schools under What to do in Listings of individual towns and cities and also Basic Spanish for travellers, page 499.*
Although English is understood in many major hotels, tour agencies and airline offices (especially in Buenos Aires and Santiago), travellers are advised to learn some Spanish before setting out. Argentines and Chileans are welcoming, and are very likely to strike up conversation on a bus, in a shop or a queue for the cinema. They're also incredibly hospitable (more so away from the capital cities), and may invite you for dinner, to stay or to travel with them, and attempts to speak Spanish will be enormously appreciated. Spanish classes are available at low cost in Chile and Argentina.

If you would like to arrange classes before you arrive as well as your accommodation try one of the following organizations:

**Academia Buenos Aires**, Hipólito Yrigoyen 571, 4th floor, Buenos Aires, T011-4345 5954, www.academiabuenos aires.com. Spanish classes in Buenos Aires, Bariloche and Montevideo.

**Amerispan**, T0800-511 0179, www.amerispan. com. North American company offering Spanish immersion programmes, educational tours, and volunteer and internship positions in Buenos Aires, Córdoba and Mendoza. Also programmes for younger people.

**Contact Chile**, Rafael Cañas 174, Providencia, Santiago, T2-2264 1719, www.contact chile.cl, offers courses throughout the country.

**Expanish**, 25 de Mayo 457, 4th floor, T011-5252 3040, www.expanish.com. A Buenos Aires-based agency that can organize packages including accommodation, trips and classes in Buenos Aires, and Patagonia in Argentina, as well as in Peru, Ecuador and Chile. Highly recommended.

**Spanish Abroad**, T1-888-722 7623, www. spanishabroad.com. Spanish classes in Buenos Aires and Córdoba.

### Argentina

The distinctive pronunciation of Argentine Spanish is Italian-influenced – in Buenos Aires, you might even hear the odd word of *lunfardo*, Italian-orientated slang. It varies from standard Spanish chiefly in the replacement of the '*ll*' and '*y*' sounds by a soft '*j*' sound, as in 'beige'. Grammatically, the big change is that the Spanish '*tú*' is replaced by '*vos*' which is also used almost universally instead of '*usted*', unless you're speaking to someone much older or higher in status. In the conjunction of verbs, the accent is on the last syllable (eg *vos tenés, podés*).

### Chile

Chilean pronunciation, which is very quick and lilting, with final syllables cut off, can present difficulties to the foreigner, even those that speak good standard Spanish. Chileans also have a wide range of unique idioms that even other Latin Americans find difficult to understand. In rural areas of Región IX, travellers may encounter Mapudungún, the Mapuche language.

## Money

### Argentina

*US$1 = AR$15.03, £1 = AR$18.80, €1 = AR$17, AUS$1 = AR$11.50, CL$1 = AR$0.02 (Oct 2016).*
The unit of currency is the Argentine peso (AR$), divided into 100 centavos. Peso notes in circulation are 2, 5, 10, 20, 50 and 100, with 200 and 500-peso bills to be released in 2016, as well as a 1000-peso note to be released in 2017. Coins in circulation are 5, 10, 25 and 50 centavos, 1 peso and 2 pesos. For many years, restrictions on Argentines buying US dollars created a free, or "blue", market rate for dollars (*mercado azul*). On taking office in 2015, President Macri lifted the exchange controls put in place by the previous Kirchner administration. The result was a free-floating peso that all but eliminated the blue market. For the time being the official bank rate is the normal rate of exchange. Still, it's often wiser to change large amounts of money at an exchange house rather than pay the transaction fees for multiple ATM withdrawals. You can also find decent rates by wiring US dollars from a US bank account via www.xoom.com, which allows transfers to its Argentine outlet, **More Argentina** (www.moreargentina. com.ar), for a single fee for up to a US$2000 transfer. **Note** The exchange rate tends to change on a daily basis and inflation is high, so prices fluctuate. Prices given in this edition are calculated at the official exchange rate at the time of research. Always pay the exact amount of a bill as small change is in short supply. Fake notes circulate, mostly AR$100, 20 and 10. Check that the green numbers showing the value of the note (on the left hand top corner) shimmer; that there is a watermark, and that there is a continuous line from the top of the note to the bottom about three-quarters of the way along. US dollar bills are often scanned electronically for forgeries.

## Chile

*US$1 = CL$669, £1 = CL$830, €1 = CL$748,*
*AUS$1 = CL$508, AR$1 = CL$44 (Oct 16).*
The unit is the Chilean peso ($). Peso notes in circulation are 1000, 2000, 5000, 10,000 and 20,000; coins come in denominations of 1, 5, 10, 50, 100 and 500. US dollar bills are also widely accepted.

### Credit, debit and currency cards

In general, the easiest way to get cash while in Patagonia is to use an international credit or debit card at an ATM (*cajero automático*), although it is wise to inform your bank before you use your cards abroad. ATMs can be found in every town or city, but be sure to take enough cash for remoter areas. In Chile ATMs operate under the sign **Redbanc** and are listed on the website, www.redbanc.cl. **Cirrus** (MasterCard), **Maestro** and **Plus** (Visa) are widely accepted in both Argentina and Chile. In Argentina ATMs are usually **Banelco** or **Link**, accepting international cards, but they dispense only pesos, impose withdrawal and daily limits and a charge per transaction (limits change, check on arrival). In Chile daily transactions are limited to up to 200,000 Chilean pesos s per day. Commission and fees are charged for each transaction; check with your card company before leaving home. Note that Argentine ATMs give you your cash and receipt before the card is returned: don't walk away without your card.

Credit cards are accepted for payment only in large hotels, city shops and restaurants and for expensive tours. In shops, ID is usually necessary. Credit card use may incur a commission in smaller establishments in Chile, and places accepting **Visa** and **MasterCard** usually display a 'Redcompra' sticker in the window. In parts of Argentina commission of 10% is often charged. If you lose your credit card, contact **MasterCard**, T0800-627 8372, or **Visa**, T0800-666 0171.

Pre-paid currency cards allow you to preload money from your bank account, fixed at the day's exchange rate. They look like a credit or debit card and are issued by specialist money changing companies, such as **Travelex** and **Caxton FX**. You can top up and check your balance by phone, online and sometimes by text.

### Changing money

Most major towns in both countries have **bureaux de change** (*casas de cambio*). They are often quicker to use than banks but may not have the best rates, so shop around. US dollars (US$) and euro (€) are easier to change than other currencies but will only be accepted if in good condition. Travellers to rural areas of Chile should carry supplies of small denomination notes, as 10,000 and 20,000 peso notes are difficult to change. There is a severe shortage of notes and coins in Argentina and you will find that hardly anyone can break large notes. Use them in supermarkets, restaurants and hotels and take out odd amounts from the bank like $190 pesos instead of $200 pesos. **Traveller's cheques** (TCs) are not very convenient for travel in Patagonia. The exchange rate for TCs is often lower than for cash and the commission can be very high (usually 10% in Argentina).

### Cost of travelling

You can find comfortable accommodation with a private bathroom and breakfast for around US$45-60 for 2 people, while a good dinner in the average restaurant will be around US$12-20 per person. Prices are much cheaper away from the main touristy areas: El Calafate, Ushuaia and Buenos Aires can be particularly pricey. For travellers on a budget, hostels usually cost US$10-20 per person in a shared dorm. Cheap breakfasts can be found in any ordinary café for around US$4-5, and there are cheap set lunches at many restaurants, costing around US$7, US$10 in Buenos Aires. Camping costs vary widely, but expect to pay no more than US$3-6 per tent – usually less. Long-distance bus travel on major routes is very cheap, and it's well worth splashing out an extra 20% for the *coche-cama* service on overnight journeys.

Chile is more expensive than much of South America and southern Chile is even more expensive from 15 Dec to 15 Mar. You can usually find a basic lunch for around US$4-5. City bus fares are around US$1 in Santiago (using the Transantiago system), less in the provinces. Prices for food tend to rise in proportion to the distance from central Chile (being highest in Punta Arenas). A budget of US$45 per person per day will allow for basic lodgings, food and overland transport (not taking into account flights, tours, car hire, etc). With a budget of US$700 a week, you will be able to stay in good hotels, eat in smart restaurants and not skimp on trips.

## Police and the law

The police in Chile and Argentina are usually courteous and will be helpful to tourists. However, always be wary of anyone who claims to be a plain clothes policeman. If you get into trouble, the worst thing that you can do is offer a bribe, as this will be seen as both an insult and an admission of guilt.

Legal penalties for most offences are similar to what you might expect in a Western European or North American country, although the attitude towards possession of soft drugs, such as cannabis, is very strict. If you get into trouble, your first call should be to your consulate, which should be able to put you in touch with a lawyer who speaks English.

There are several types of police operating in Chile: *Carabineros* (green uniforms) handle all tasks except immigration; *Investigaciones* (in civilian dress) are the detectives; *Policía Internacional*, a division of the *Investigaciones*, which handle immigration and customs.

## Public holidays

1 Jan  **New Year's Day** (Argentina and Chile).
Feb/Mar  **Carnival Monday** and **Shrove Tuesday** (Argentina).
Mar/Apr  **Good Friday** (Argentina and Chile).
Mar/Apr  **Holy Saturday** (Chile).

24 Mar  **Memorial Day** (Argentina).
2 Apr  **Day of the Veterans** (Argentina).
1 May  **Labour Day** (Argentina and Chile).
21 May  **Navy Day** (Chile).
25 May  **National Day** commemorating the May Revolution of 1810 (Argentina).
20 Jun  **Flag Day** (Argentina).
29 Jun  **St Peter and St Paul** (Chile).
9 Jul  **Independence Day** (Argentina).
16 Jul  **Virgen del Carmen** (Chile).
15 Aug  **Assumption** (Chile).
17 Aug  **Anniversary of San Martín's death** (Argentina).
18 Sep  **National Day** (Chile).
19 Sep  **Army Day** (Chile).
12 Oct  **Columbus Day** (Argentina and Chile).
31 Oct  **Reformation Day** (Chile).
1 Nov  **All Saints' Day** (Chile).
Late Nov  **Day of Sovereignty** (Argentina).
8 Dec  **Immaculate Conception** (Argentina and Chile).
25 Dec  **Christmas Day** (Argentina and Chile).
26 Dec  **Boxing Day** (Argentina).
31 Dec  **New Year's Eve** (Argentina and Chile).

## Safety

Buenos Aires is much safer than most Latin American cities, but petty crime can be a problem in busy tourist areas in Buenos Aires, especially La Boca and Retiro. Chile is generally a safe country to visit but, like all major cities, Santiago does have crime problems. Travelling in Patagonia itself is very safe indeed. The main threats to your safety are more likely to come from natural hazards and adventure activities than from crime. Don't hike alone in remote areas and always register with *guardaparques* (rangers) before you set off.

### General advice

· Keep valuables out of sight.
· Keep all documents and money secure.
· Split up your main cash supply and hide it in different places.

- Lock your luggage together with a chain/cable at bus or train stations.
- At night, take a taxi between transport terminals and your hotel.
- Use the hotel safe deposit box and keep an inventory of what you have deposited. Notify the police of any losses and get a written report for insurance.
- Look out for tricks used to distract your attention and steal your belongings.
- Don't fight back – it is better to hand over your valuables rather than risk injury.

## Student travellers

If you're in full-time education you are entitled to an **International Student Identity Card (ISIC)**, www.isic.org, which is distributed by student travel offices and travel agencies. The **ISIC** gives you special prices on all forms of transport and access to a variety of other concessions and services. The card can be ordered online or obtained in person (photo and proof of status required). In Argentina it is available from **Almundo** (Florida 835, p 3, oficina 320, T0810-4328 7907, www.almundo.com.ar, Mon-Fri 0900-2000, Sat 0900-1500, with many branches in Buenos Aires and around the country), a helpful youth and student travel organization which runs a student flight booking centre for flights, hotels and travel. They can provide information for all South America, and have a noticeboard for travellers. English and French spoken. In Chile (**www.isic.cl**), it can be obtained from **ISIC** (Hernando de Aguirre 201, of 201, Providencia, Santiago, T2-577 1200).

## Tax

### Airport tax

By law Argentine airport taxes must be included in the price of your air ticket. The same should be true in Chile but it is wise to check. For details of entry fees, see page 477.

### VAT

VAT (IVA) is 21% in Argentina and 19% in Chile. You can claim back the IVA (VAT) on some products bought in the country at the airport when you leave. Ask for the necessary form when you buy the goods.

## Telephone

If calling a number in Patagonia from abroad, dial the country code (either +54 for Argentina or +56 for Chile) and then the area code, leaving out the initial '0', followed by the number. (Note that all telephone numbers in this guide show the full area code as it is dialled within the country. Chile removed the zero on all area and mobile prefixes in 2016.) For international calls from Patagonia, dial 00, the country code and city code.

In both countries, avoid calling from hotels, which charge very inflated prices unless you have a prepaid phone scratch card; these are widely available from *kioskos* in both countries and may be the cheapest way to call abroad. *Locutorios* and *centros de llamadas* (phone centres) are the easiest way to make a call from a landline. They have private booths where you can talk for as long as you like and pay afterwards, the price appearing on a small screen in your booth. They often have internet, photocopying and fax services too. An alternative to *locutorios* in Argentina is to buy a phone card and use it with your mobile. Many *kioskos* and *locutorios* sell mobile phone cards offered by Argentina's largest communications providers, like **Movistar** and **Claro**, for around US$2. Alternatively, **Skype**, www.skype.com, is the cheapest way to keep in touch.

### Mobile phones

International roaming is becoming more common and cost-effective, although buying a local pay-as-you-go phone may be a cheaper option. Major airports and hotels often have rental desks, or can advise on local outlets.

### Argentina

**Country code** +54. **Directory enquiries**
T110. **Mobile phone prefix** (within the
country): area code +15.

### Chile

**Country code**: +56. **Directory enquiries**
T103. **Mobile phone prefix** (within the
country): 9.

## Time

Argentina is 3 hrs behind GMT. Chile is
4 hrs behind early Mar to Sep/Oct and
3 hrs behind mid-Sep/Oct to early Mar.

## Tourist information

**Wanderlust Publications Ltd**, T01753-
620426, www.wanderlust.co.uk. A magazine
for independent-minded travellers.

### Argentina

Tourism authorities in Argentina are generally
well equipped to deal with visitors. You
might have to be patient in some parts of
the country, even when requesting the most
basic information, but the major centres of
Bariloche, San Martín de los Andes, Villa la
Angostura, Puerto Madryn, El Calafate and
Ushuaia all offer good tourist resources. Staff
in these popular tourist areas usually speak
at least some English and opening hours
are long, typically 0800-2000 in summer
although they may close at weekends or
during low season. Provincial websites, with

information on sights and accommodation,
can be accessed via the excellent government
tourist website: **www.turismo.gov.ar**. Also
consult **www.patagonia.com.ar** or **www.
patagonia-argentina.com**.

### Chile

The national secretariat of tourism, **Sernatur**
(www.sernatur.cl), has provincial offices
in Temuco, Osorno, Puerto Montt, Ancud,
Coyhaique, Punta Arenas and Puerto Natales
(addresses are given under the relevant
destination). These can provide town
maps, leaflets and other useful information;
otherwise contact head office in Santiago.
Other towns have municipal tourist offices.
A useful region-specific website is **www.
patagonia-chile.com**.

## Tour operators

### In the UK

See **Latin America Travel Association**
(**LATA**), www.lata.org, for a full list.
**Abercrombie and Kent**, T01242-547760,
www.abercrombiekent.co.uk. Upmarket
tailor-made travel.
**Adventures Abroad**, T1-800-665 3998,
www.adventures-abroad.com. Impressive
company running superb and imaginative
tours for small groups to Patagonia and
Puerto Madryn, the glaciers and Ushuaia.
Great itineraries.
**Audley Travel**, T01993-838 000, www.audley
travel.com. High-quality tailor-made travel,
including the Argentine Lake District and

Patagonia. Good on-the-ground knowledge. Recommended.

**Chimu Adventures**, T020-7403-8265, www. chimuadventures.com. Provide tours, treks, active adventures and accommodation throughout South America and the Antarctic.

**Exodus**, T0203-811 3155, www.exodus. co.uk. Excellent, well-run trekking and climbing tours of Patagonia, including Torres del Paine, cycling in the Lake District, Antarctica and a great tour following in Shackleton's footsteps.

**Explore**, T01252-883509, www. explore. co.uk. Quality small-group trips, especially in Patagonia. Also offers family adventures, or with a focus on culture, wildlife or trekking.

**Journey Latin America**, T020-3131 5274, www.journeylatinamerica.co.uk. Deservedly well regarded, this excellent long-established company runs adventure tours and tailor-made tours to Argentina and other destinations in South America. Also cheap flights and expert advice. Well organized and very professional. Recommended.

**Last Frontiers**, T01296-653000, www.last frontiers.com. Excellent company offering top-quality tailor-made trips, including horse riding in Patagonia. By far the best company for estancia stays. Highly recommended.

**Naturetrek**, T01962-733051, www.nature trek.co.uk. Small group birdwatching tours.

**Select Latin America**, T020-7407 1478, www.selectlatinamerica.co.uk. Specializing in tailor-made and small-group tours with a cultural or natural history emphasis, this is a friendly small company with some good itineraries, including Antarctica and the R40.

**The South America Specialists**, T01525-306555, www.thesouthamericaspecialists. com. A luxury travel company with hotel reviews, photos and HD videos.

**STA Travel**, offices worldwide, www.sta travel.com. Arranges cheap flights, and sells Dragoman's trip which includes Argentina.

**Trailfinders**, T020-7938 3939, www. trailfinders.com. Cheap flights and tours.

## In North America

**Argentina For Less**, T1-817-230 4971, www. argentinaforless.com. Progressive tourism company with a focus solely on Latin America. US-based but with local offices and operations (T020-3002 0571 in the UK).

**International Expeditions**, T1-855 1231 4326, www.internationalexpeditions.com. Travel company specializing in nature tours.

**Mila Tours**, T1-800-367 7378, www. milatours.com. Arranges a wide variety of tours from rafting to photography.

**Mountain Travel Sobek**, T1-888 831 7526, www.mtsobek.com. A specialist offering a range of trekking tours.

**Myths and Mountains**, T1-800-670 6984, www.mythsandmountains.com. Cultural, wildlife and environmental trips.

**South American Explorers**, T1-607 277 0488, T1-800-2740568 (toll-free in USA), www.saexplorers.org. Gives good advice.

**Wilderness Travel**, T1-800-368 2794 (toll free), www.wildernesstravel.com. Organizes trips worldwide, including Patagonia. **Worldwide Horseback Riding Adventures**, toll free T0800-545 0019, www.ridingtours.com. US-based horse-riding company.

### In Australia and New Zealand

**Viva Expeditions**, T09-950 5918 (New Zealand) or 020-3286 6246 (UK), www.vivaexpeditions.com. Small group expeditions and custom tours to Latin America.

## Visas and immigration

Visa and immigration regulations change frequently so always check with the Argentine and Chilean embassies before you travel. Keep photocopies of essential documents and some additional passport-sized photographs, and always have a photocopy of your passport with you.

### Argentina

Visitors from neighbouring countries only need to provide their ID card to enter Argentina. Citizens of the UK, Western Europe, USA, Australia, New Zealand and South Africa (among other countries) require a **passport**, valid for at least 6 months, and a **tourist card**, which is given to you on entry. This allows you to stay for a period of 90 days and can be renewed for another 90 days (US$40), either by leaving the country at a border and immediately re-entering, or by visiting the **National Directorate of Migration**, Antártida Argentina 1365, Buenos Aires, T011-4317 0200, Mon-Fri 0800-1400, or any other delegation of the **Dirección Nacional de Migraciones** (www.migraciones.gov.ar) in person: ask for Prórrogas de Permanencia. No renewals are given after the expiry date.

Other foreign nationals should consult with the Argentine embassy in their home country about visa requirements.

### Chile

Citizens of the UK, Western Europe, USA, Canada, Australia, New Zealand and South Africa require only a passport, valid for at least 6 months, and a **tourist card**, which is handed out at major border crossings and at Chilean airports. This allows visitors to stay for 90 days and must be surrendered on departure from Chile. Other foreign nationals should consult with the Chilean embassy in their home country about visa requirements.

After 90 days the tourist card must either be renewed by leaving and re-entering the country at a land border or extended (US$140) at the **Ministerio del Interior** (*Extranjería*) in Santiago (www.extranjeria.gob.cl) or (preferably) at any local government office (*Gobernación*), where the procedure is slightly less time-consuming.

Remember that it is your responsibility to ensure that your passport is stamped in and out when you cross borders. The absence of entry and exit stamps, or passports stamped with the wrong date of entry, can cause serious difficulties.

## Women travellers

Argentine and Chilean men are generally respectful of a woman travelling alone, although you may hear the traditional *piropo* as you walk past: it's an inoffensive compliment that you can ignore. You can discourage unwanted attention by wearing a wedding ring and, when accepting a social invitation, ask if you can bring a friend, to check the intentions of whoever's inviting you. In other respects, women travellers should follow the general safety tips given on page 493 and avoid walking around after dark or in remote areas alone. Women travelling in Argentina and Chile should be aware that tampons and towels must never be flushed down the toilet, since the water pressure is too low to cope. For more advice, see **www.womens-travel-club.com**.

# Footnotes

## Women travellers

# **Basic** Spanish for travellers

Learning Spanish is a useful part of the preparation for a trip to Latin America and no volumes of dictionaries, phrase books or word lists will provide the same enjoyment as being able to communicate directly with the people of the country you are visiting. It is a good idea to make an effort to grasp the basics before you go. As you travel you will pick up more of the language and the more you know, the more you will benefit from your stay.

## General pronunciation

Whether you have been taught the 'Castilian' pronunciation (*z* and *c* followed by *i* or *e* are pronounced as the *th* in think) or the 'American' pronunciation (they are pronounced as *s*), you will encounter little difficulty in understanding either. Regional accents and usages vary, but the basic language is essentially the same everywhere. See Language, page 491, for details of the distinct pronunciation of Argentine and Chilean Spanish.

### Vowels
*a*    as in English *cat*
*e*    as in English *best*
*i*    as the *ee* in English *feet*
*o*    as in English *shop*
*u*    as the *oo* in English *food*
*ai*   as the *i* in English *ride*
*ei*   as *ey* in English *they*
*oi*   as *oy* in English *toy*

### Consonants
Most consonants can be pronounced more or less as they are in English. The exceptions are:
*g*    before *e* or *i* is the same as *j*
*h*    is always silent (except in *ch* as in *chair*)
*j*    as the *ch* in Scottish *loch*
*ll*   as the *y* in *yellow*
*ñ*    as the *ni* in English *onion*
*rr*   trilled much more than in English
*x*    depending on its location, pronounced *x*, *s*, *sh* or *j*

## Spanish words and phrases

### Greetings, courtesies
hello *hola*
good morning *buenos días*
good afternoon/evening/night
  *buenas tardes/noches*
goodbye *adiós/chao*
pleased to meet you *mucho gusto*
see you later *hasta luego*
how are you? *¿cómo está?/¿cómo estás?*
I'm fine, thanks *estoy muy bien, gracias*
I'm called... *me llamo...*
what is your name? *¿cómo se llama?/*
  *¿cómo te llamas?*
yes/no *sí/no*
please *por favor*

thank you (very much) *(muchas) gracias*
I speak Spanish *hablo español*
I don't speak Spanish *no hablo español*
do you speak English? *¿habla inglés?*
I don't understand *no entiendo/*
  *no comprendo*
please speak slowly *hable despacio por favor*
I am very sorry *lo siento mucho/disculpe*
what do you want? *¿qué quiere?/*
  *¿qué quieres?*
I want *quiero*
I don't want it *no lo quiero*
leave me alone *déjeme en paz/no me moleste*
good/bad *bueno/malo*

## Questions and requests

Have you got a room for two people?
*¿Tiene una habitación para dos personas?*
How do I get to_? *¿Cómo llego a_?*
How much does it cost?
*¿Cuánto cuesta? ¿cuánto es?*
I'd like to make a long-distance phone call
*Quisiera hacer una llamada de larga distancia*
Is service included? *¿Está incluido el servicio?*
Is tax included? *¿Están incluidos los impuestos?*

When does the bus leave (arrive)?
*¿A qué hora sale (llega) el autobús?*
When? *¿cuándo?*
Where is_? *¿dónde está_?*
Where can I buy tickets?
*¿Dónde puedo comprar boletos?*
Where is the nearest petrol station?
*¿Dónde está la gasolinera más cercana?*
Why? *¿por qué?*

## Basics

bank *el banco*
bathroom/toilet *el baño*
bill *la factura/la cuenta*
cash *el efectivo*
cheap *barato/a*
credit card *la tarjeta de crédito*
exchange house *la casa de cambio*
exchange rate *el tipo de cambio*

expensive *caro/a*
market *el mercado*
note/coin *le billete/la moneda*
police (policeman) *la policía (el policía)*
post office *el correo*
public telephone *el teléfono público*
supermarket *el supermercado*
ticket office *la taquilla*

## Getting around

aeroplane *el avión*
airport *el aeropuerto*
arrival/departure *la llegada/salida*
avenue *la avenida*
block *la cuadra*
border *la frontera*
bus station *la terminal de autobuses/ camiones*
bus *el bus/el autobús/el camión*
collective/ fixed-route taxi *el colectivo*
corner *la esquina*
customs *la aduana*
first/second class *primera/segunda clase*
left/right *izquierda/derecha*
ticket *el boleto*
empty/full *vacío/lleno*
highway, main road *la carretera*
immigration *la inmigración*
insurance *el seguro*

insured person *el/la asegurado/a*
to insure yourself against *asegurarse contra*
luggage *el equipaje*
motorway, freeway *el autopista/la carretera*
north, south, east, west *norte, sur, este (oriente), oeste (occidente)*
oil *el aceite*
to park *estacionarse*
passport *el pasaporte*
petrol/gasoline *la gasolina*
puncture *el pinchazo/la ponchadura*
street *la calle*
that way *por allí/por allá*
this way *por aquí/por acá*
tourist card/visa *la tarjeta de turista*
tyre *la llanta*
unleaded *sin plomo*
to walk *caminar/andar*

## Accommodation

air conditioning *el aire acondicionado*
all-inclusive *todo incluido*
bathroom, private *el baño privado*
bed, double/single *la cama matrimonial/ sencilla*
blankets *las cobijas/mantas*

to clean *limpiar*
dining room *el comedor*
guesthouse *la casa de huéspedes*
hotel *el hotel*
noisy *ruidoso*
pillows *las almohadas*

power cut *el apagón/corte*
restaurant *el restaurante*
room/bedroom *el cuarto/la habitación*
sheets *las sábanas*
shower *la ducha/regadera*

soap *el jabón*
toilet *el sanitario/excusado*
toilet paper *el papel higiénico*
towels, clean/dirty *las toallas limpias/sucias*
water, hot/cold *el agua caliente/fría*

## Health

aspirin *la aspirina*
blood *la sangre*
chemist *la farmacia*
condoms *los preservativos, los condones*
contact lenses *los lentes de contacto*
contraceptives *los anticonceptivos*
contraceptive pill *la píldora anti-conceptiva*
diarrhoea *la diarrea*

doctor *el médico*
fever/sweat *la fiebre/el sudor*
pain *el dolor*
head *la cabeza*
period/sanitary towels *la regla/las toallas femeninas*
stomach *el estómago*
altitude sickness *el soroche*

## Family

family *la familia*
friend *el amigo/la amiga*
brother/sister *el hermano/la hermana*
daughter/son *la hija/el hijo*
father/mother *el padre/la madre*

husband/wife *el esposo (marido)/la esposa*
boyfriend/girlfriend *el novio/la novia*
married *casado/a*
single/unmarried *soltero/a*

## Months, days and time

January *enero*
February *febrero*
March *marzo*
April *abril*
May *mayo*
June *junio*
July *julio*
August *agosto*
September *septiembre*
October *octubre*
November *noviembre*
December *diciembre*

Monday *lunes*
Tuesday *martes*
Wednesday *miércoles*

Thursday *jueves*
Friday *viernes*
Saturday *sábado*
Sunday *domingo*

at one o'clock *a la una*
at half past two *a las dos y media*
at a quarter to three *a cuarto para las tres/ a las tres menos quince*
it's one o'clock *es la una*
it's seven o'clock *son las siete*
it's six twenty *son las seis y veinte*
it's five to nine *son las nueve menos cinco*
in ten minutes *en diez minutos*
five hours *cinco horas*
does it take long? *¿tarda mucho?*

## Numbers

one *uno/una*
two *dos*
three *tres*
four *cuatro*
five *cinco*
six *seis*
seven *siete*
eight *ocho*

nine *nueve*
ten *diez*
eleven *once*
twelve *doce*
thirteen *trece*
fourteen *catorce*
fifteen *quince*
sixteen *dieciséis*

seventeen *diecisiete*
eighteen *dieciocho*
nineteen *diecinueve*
twenty *veinte*
twenty-one *veintiuno*
thirty *treinta*
forty *cuarenta*

fifty *cincuenta*
sixty *sesenta*
seventy *setenta*
eighty *ochenta*
ninety *noventa*
hundred *cien/ciento*
thousand *mil*

## Food *See also Menu reader, page 31.*

avocado *la palta*
baked *al horno*
bakery *la panadería*
banana *la banana*
beans *los frijoles/las habichuelas*
beef *la carne de res*
beef steak *el lomo*
boiled rice *el arroz blanco*
bread *el pan*
breakfast *el desayuno*
butter *la manteca*
cake *la torta*
chewing gum *el chicle*
chicken *el pollo*
chilli or green pepper *el ají/pimiento*
clear soup, stock *el caldo*
cooked *cocido*
dining room *el comedor*
egg *el huevo*
fish *el pescado*
fork *el tenedor*
fried *frito*
garlic *el ajo*
goat *el chivo*
grapefruit *la toronja/el pomelo*
grill *la parrilla*
grilled/griddled *a la plancha*
guava *la guayaba*
ham *el jamón*
hamburger *la hamburguesa*
hot, spicy *picante*
ice cream *el helado*
jam *la mermelada*
knife *el cuchillo*

lemon *el limón*
lobster *la langosta*
lunch *el almuerzo/la comida*
meal *la comida*
meat *la carne*
minced meat *la carne picada*
onion *la cebolla*
orange *la naranja*
pepper *el pimiento*
pasty, turnover *la empanada/el pastelito*
pork *el cerdo*
potato *la papa*
prawns *los camarones*
raw *crudo*
restaurant *el restaurante*
salad *la ensalada*
salt *la sal*
sandwich *el bocadillo*
sauce *la salsa*
sausage *la longaniza/el chorizo*
scrambled eggs *los huevos revueltos*
seafood *los mariscos*
soup *la sopa*
spoon *la cuchara*
squash *la calabaza*
squid *los calamares*
supper *la cena*
sweet *dulce*
to eat *comer*
toasted *tostado*
turkey *el pavo*
vegetables *los legumbres/vegetales*
without meat *sin carne*
yam *el camote*

## Drink

beer  *la cerveza*
boiled  *hervido/a*
bottled  *en botella*
camomile tea  *la manzanilla*
canned  *en lata*
coffee  *el café*
coffee, white  *el café con leche*
cold  *frío*
cup  *la taza*
drink  *la bebida*
drunk  *borracho/a*
firewater  *el aguardiente*
fruit milkshake  *el batido/licuado*
glass  *el vaso*
hot  *caliente*

ice/without ice  *el hielo/sin hielo*
juice  *el jugo*
lemonade  *la limonada*
milk  *la leche*
mint  *la menta*
rum  *el ron*
soft drink  *el refresco*
sugar  *el azúcar*
tea  *el té*
to drink  *beber/tomar*
water  *el agua*
water, carbonated  *el agua mineral con gas*
water, still mineral  *el agua mineral sin gas*
wine, red  *el vino tinto*
wine, white  *el vino blanco*

## Key verbs

| **to go** | **ir** |
|---|---|
| I go | *voy* |
| you go (familiar) | *vas* |
| he, she, it goes, you (formal) go | *va* |
| we go | *vamos* |
| they, you (plural) go | *van* |

| **to have** (possess) | **tener** |
|---|---|
| I have | *tengo* |
| you (familiar) have | *tienes* |
| he, she, it, you (formal) have | *tiene* |
| we have | *tenemos* |
| they, you (plural) have | *tienen* |
| there is/are | *hay* |
| there isn't/aren't | *no hay* |

| **to be** | **ser** | **estar** |
|---|---|---|
| I am | soy | estoy |
| you are | eres | estás |
| he, she, it is, you (formal) are | es | está |
| we are | somos | estamos |
| they, you (plural) are | son | están |

(*ser* is used to denote a permanent state, whereas *estar* is used to denote a positional or temporary state)

This section has been assembled on the basis of glossaries compiled by André de Mendonça and David Gilmour, formerly of South American Experience, London, and the Latin American Travel Advisor, No 9, March 1996.

# Index

*Entries in bold refer to maps*

# FOOTPRINT
## Features

## Advertisers' index

# **About** the authors

**Ben Box**

One of the first assignments Ben Box took as a freelance writer in 1980 was subediting work on the *South American Handbook*. The plan then was to write about contemporary Iberian and Latin American affairs, but in no time at all the lands south of the Rio Grande took over, inspiring journeys to all corners of the subcontinent. Ben has contributed to newspapers, magazines and learned tomes, usually on the subject of travel, and became editor of the *South American Handbook* in 1989. He has also been involved in Footprint's Handbooks on *Central America & Mexico*, *Caribbean Islands*, *Brazil*, *Peru*, *Cuzco & the Inca Heartland*, *Bolivia*, *Peru*, *Bolivia and Ecuador* and *Jamaica*. On many of these titles he has collaborated with his wife and Footprint Caribbean expert, Sarah Cameron.

Having a doctorate in Spanish and Portuguese studies from London University, Ben maintains a strong interest in Latin American literature. In the British summer he plays cricket for his local village side and year round he attempts to achieve some level of self-sufficiency in fruit and veg in a rather unruly country garden in Suffolk.

**Chris Wallace**

Chris Wallace has been travelling through, and writing about, Central and South America since 2004. He has lived in Colombia, Argentina, Chile, Brazil and Peru. He has tailored travel and tourism content for entrepreneurs and publishers alike, and, more than 10 years in, feels he's barely scratched the surface of what the South American continent has to offer.

# Acknowledgements

Here are some of the folks in Argentina instrumental in helping me complete this book, and they have my everlasting thanks: Marcos Torres, Danny Feldman, Myrta Rojas, Ana Laura Rodríguez Esquercia, Patricia from Yo Amo el Norte Argentino, Cony and the staff at the BA Stop Hostel, Remy at Posada 21 Oranges, Juan from La Lechuza Hostel and all the helpful people at the tourist offices throughout Argentina.

For Chile, I would like to thank: Marilú Cerdá of Marilú's B&B in Santiago; Juane Vargas of The Princesa Insolente Hostel in Santiago; Gonzalo and Anna of La Chimba Hostel in Santiago; Patricia Rosas and everyone at the Nothofagus Hotel in Huilo Huilo; and of course, all the good work done on previous editions of the Patagonia Handbook by Ben Box.

# Credits

## Footprint credits

**Editor**: Jo Williams
**Production and layout**: Emma Bryers
**Maps**: Kevin Feeney
**Colour section**: Patrick Dawson

**Publisher**: Felicity Laughton
Patrick Dawson
**Marketing**: Kirsty Holmes
**Sales**: Diane McEntee
**Advertising and content partnerships**:
Debbie Wylde

## Photography credits

**Front cover**: sunsinger/Shutterstock.com
**Back cover top**: Eduardo Rivero/
Shutterstock.com
**Back cover bottom**: elbud/Shutterstock.com
**Inside front cover**: Andrea Izzotti

Printed in Spain by GraphyCems

## Publishing information

Footprint Patagonia
5th edition
© Footprint Handbooks Ltd
December 2016

ISBN: 978 1 911082 08 8
CIP DATA: A catalogue record for this book
is available from the British Library

® Footprint Handbooks and the
Footprint mark are a registered
trademark of Footprint Handbooks Ltd

Published by Footprint
5 Riverside Court
Lower Bristol Road
Bath BA2 3DZ, UK
T +44 (0)1225 469141
footprinttravelguides.com

Distributed in the USA by
National Book Network, Inc.

## Colour section

**Page 1**: Christian Schoissingeyer/Shutterstock.com. **Page 2**: Serjio74/Shutterstock.com. **Page 4**: Matyas Rehak/
Shutterstock.com; diegorayaces/Shutterstock.com. **Page 5**: elnavegante/Shutterstock.com; Eduardo Rivero/Shutterstock.
com; Durk Talsma/Shutterstock.com. **Page 6**: Wouter van den Broek/Dreamstime.com; JeremyRichards/Shutterstock.
com; Hugo Brizard - YouGoPhoto/Shutterstock.com. **Page 7**: sunsinger/Shutterstock.com; Christian Handl/SuperStock.
com; Heeb Christian/SuperStock.com; Colin Monteath/SuperStock.com. **Page 9**: Maciej Bledowski/Shuttestock.
com. **Page 10**: Michael Runkel/SuperStock.com. **Page 11**: Matyas Rehak/Shutterstock.com. **Page 12**: Eduardo Rivero/
Shutterstock.com. **Page 13**: iladm/Shutterstock.com; meunierd/Shutterstock.com; Richard Cummins/SuperStock.com. **Page
14**: Galyna Andrushko/Shutterstock.com; sunsinger/Shutterstock.com. **Page 15**: Maciej Bledowsk/Shuttestock.com;
Michal Knitl/Shuttesrtock.com; kavram/Shutterstock.com. **Page 16**: kavram/Shutterstock.com

## Duotones

**Page 34**: DSBfoto/Shutterstock.com. **Page 64**: saiko3p/Shutterstock.com. **Page 154**: rm/Shutterstock.com. **Page 192**:
jorisvo/Shutterstock.com. **Page 226**: Jose Luis Stephens/Shutterstock.com. **Page 250**: Yoann Combronde/Shutterstock.
com. **Page 334**: JeremyRichards/Shutterstock.com. **Page 358**: Jose Arcos Aguila/Shutterstock.com. **Page 400**: Pichugin
Dmitry/Shuterstock.com. **Page 436**: unmillonedeelefantes/Shutterstock.com.

# Footprint Mini Atlas
# **Patagonia**

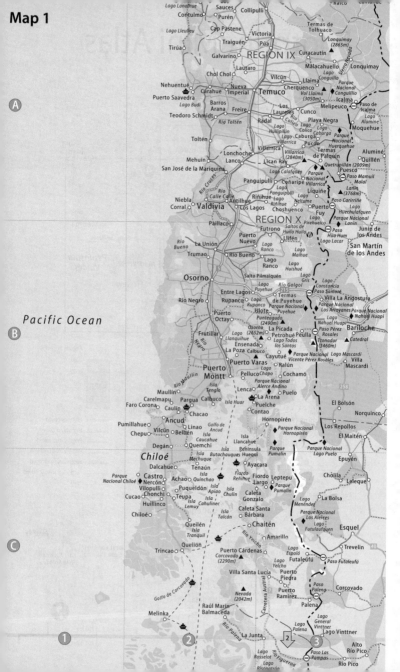

# Map 1

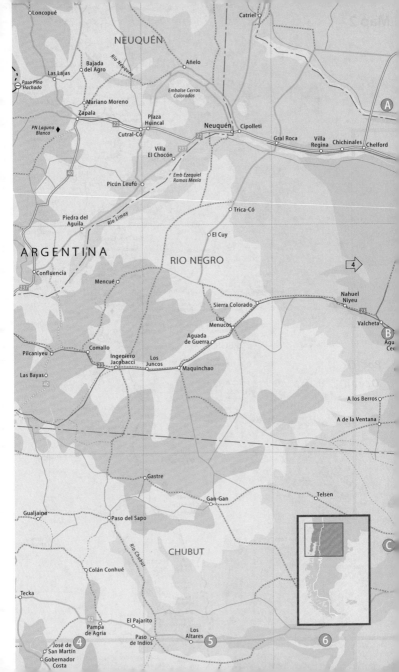

# Map 2

**Pacific Ocean**

Golfo de Peñas

Golfo Trinidad

Isla Guamblin

Archipiélago de los Chonos

Canal Messier

CHILE

REGION XI

Puerto Edén
Isla Wellington

Tortel

Puerto
Yungay

Villa
O'Higgins

Candelario
Mancilla

Lago
O'Higgins

Lago
San Martín

Fitz Roy
(3405m)

Glaciar
Viedma

Estancia
Helsingfors

Cerro Norte
Parque Nacional
Los Glaciares

Glaciar
Upsala

El Chaltén

Lago Viedma

Tres Lagos

Estancia
La Angostura

Lago Cardiel

Lago Strobel

Las Horquetas

Bajo Caracoles

Lago
Salitroso

Lago
Posadas

Lago
Pueyrredón

Estancia La Oriental

Parque Natural Perito Moreno
Herros (2770m)
San Lorenzo (3706m)

Cochrane

Reserva
Nacional
Tamango
Lago
Cochrane

Paso
Roballos

Cevallos
(2743m)

Estancia Telken

Campa de
Hielo Norte

Río Baker

Campo de Hielo
San Valentín

Laguna
San Rafael

Parque Nacional
Laguna
San Rafael

Puerto
Grosse

Puerto Guadal
Lago
Bertrand
Puerto Bertrand

Lago
Bertrand

El Maitén

Río
Chacabuco

Jeinimeni
(2600m)

Reserva Nacional
Lago Jeinimeni

Pico Sur (2190m)

Estancia La
Serena

Perito
Moreno

Chile
Chico

Los Antiguos

Río Tranquilo

Mallín
Grande

Fachinal

Bahía Murta

Lago
General
Carrera

Lago
Buenos Aires

Levicán

Puerto Ibáñez

Villa Cerro Castillo

Cerro
Castillo

Reserva Nacional
Cerro Castillo

Río Ibáñez

Hudson

Lago
Atravesado

El Blanco

Lago
Elizalde

Reserva Nacional
Río Simpson

Reserva Nacional
Lago Las Torres

Coyhaique

Lago
Castor

Lago
Pollux

Coyhaique
Alto

Paso Coyhaique Alto

Paso
Triana

Alto
Río Mayo

Balmaceda
Paso Huemules

Lago
Blanco

Lago Blanco

Río Simpson

Puerto
Aysén

Puerto
Chacabuco

Santa María
del Mar

Fiordo Aysén

Puerto
Aguirre

Puerto Cisnes

Villa
Amengual

Mañihuales

La Tapera

Lago
La Plata

Lago
Fontana

Alto Río Sanguer

Paso Pampa Alta

Termas de
Puyuhuapi

Puyuhuapi

Parque
Nacional
Queulat

Lago
Risopatrón

Lago
Verde

Lago
Rosselot

Río Figueroa

La Junta

Lago
Palena

Río Palena

Lago
General
Vinttner

Lago Vinttner

Alto
Río Pico

Paso Las
Pampas

Río Pico

Paso Río
Frías-Appeleg

Cordillera Austral

Puerto
Bandera

Estancia Alice

Lago Argentino

Río Santa Cruz

Leona

Parque Nacional

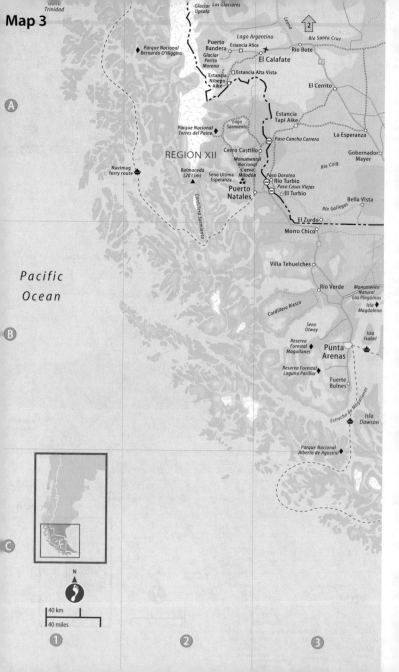

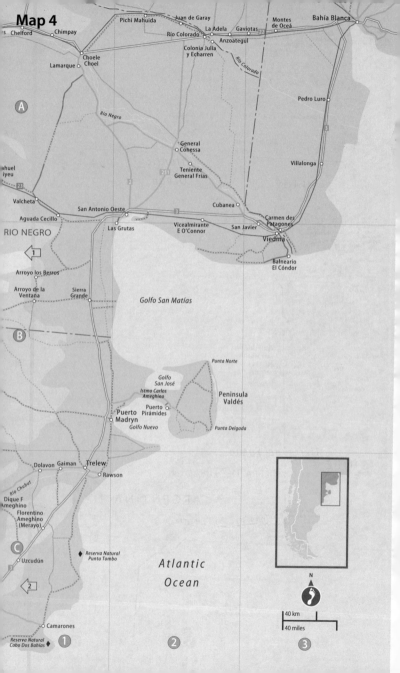

# Map 4